HOW THE LIGHT GETS IN

How the Light Gets In

Ethical Life I

GRAHAM WARD

OXFORD
UNIVERSITY PRESS

OXFORD
UNIVERSITY PRESS

Great Clarendon Street, Oxford, OX2 6DP,
United Kingdom

Oxford University Press is a department of the University of Oxford.
It furthers the University's objective of excellence in research, scholarship,
and education by publishing worldwide. Oxford is a registered trade mark of
Oxford University Press in the UK and in certain other countries

First Edition published in 2016

Impression: 2

Published in the United States of America by Oxford University Press
198 Madison Avenue, New York, NY 10016, United States of America

British Library Cataloguing in Publication Data
Data available

Library of Congress Control Number: 2015951580

ISBN 978–0–19–929765–8

Printed in Great Britain by
CPI Group (UK) Ltd, Croydon, CR0 4YY

For Mary

Preface

Why is it important to present a systematic account of the teachings of the Christian faith? There are various levels on which this question can be answered. Top tier is the theological level and the answer goes something like this: because we were created in such a way that we might seek to understand the order of things; that there is an order to things; and that God has accommodated our creatureliness such that we can know *something* of that order. The truth is the way God knows things. The attempt to grasp the way the articles of the Christian faith relate coherently to each other is a groping towards that divine knowledge of truth in Christ. For Christ is the Godhead's greatest and most gracious accommodation to our creatureliness *and* the revelation of that divine knowledge. Not that we can attain the heights of divine truth: we are creatures. But there is a dignity in creatures continually stretching to understand why they were created and what it means that we were created. The thoughts of God are not our thoughts; the ways of God are not our ways. But to seek to understand those thoughts and ways is to seek to give due thanks and honour for the divine work of which we are a part. To present a systematic account of the teachings of the Christian faith is to offer a vision, certainly from a human, created, and limited perspective, of the ways all things might be understood from the divine perspective. That limited perspective is not just bound by our creatureliness, however. It is bound also by our sinfulness. Theologians are also in the process of sanctification and the damages of sin effect human dispositions, thinking, affections, and behaviour. Christian theologians, in their ongoing submission to Christ, are partaking in the divine pedagogy, redemption, whose *telos* is 'to know even as we are known' (I Cor.13.12). But theology is never pure; it is never innocent; it is never free from the pull of *amor sui* and the seduction of human projections. It is never free from being ideological. It is written by human beings not angels; human beings embedded deep within very human situations, personal and collective. But theology can be made to appear pure, innocent, and free from ideology—in faith's pursuit of the truth. In that lies a danger that cannot be avoided or evaded. But the danger can be discerned and judged, in the self-reflections of the theologian him or herself, and by other theological readers. Nevertheless, at the top tier level, systematic theology in the vision it provides seeks to become a hymn of praise, a doxology that all creation participates in, as faith seeks its broadest and deepest understandings.

There are other levels of answering the question of why theologians seek to present a systematic account of the teachings of the Christian faith. The melodic baseline is love. Love is not an easy word to use in the abstract; I'm not sure it has much conceptual content. But holding together the fact that we are at all, that all things have been created, is a continuous act of gratuitous divine love. A systematic account of the teachings of the Christian faith offers a global understanding of God's love *to us*; God's disposition *towards us*. And what makes any systematic account decidedly Christian is Christ himself; Emmanuel, God *with us*. There is a theology in prepositions—to, with, towards, through, in, for. Divine love plays out a universal intimacy through such prepositions in and through a continuous acceptance, forgiveness, and redemption—the words morph one into another in the act of loving. The operation and power of such love is not at all easy to apprehend when we see what human beings can do to each other in their fear and hatred, their anger and envy. So in the brutality and the brokenness of our condition, the ability not just to hear the melodic baseline of divine love but to allow its rhythms to resonate within us, to attune ourselves to that deep, structural intimacy, lies way outside of human nature as we know it. But Christ is *for us*; God is *for us*. So a systematic account of the Christian faith seeks to make sense of that work of Christ, that healing not just of the individual (my salvation), but the collective bodies of which any individual is a part: the healing of the nations; the restoration of humanity; the restitution of creation.

There are other levels on which that question of why a systematic account of the Christian faith is important. I will mention only one more because the others will emerge as we begin the presentation itself, but this level returns us to one key aspect in the brutality and brokenness of the human condition. Within the Christian faith there are many interpretations. Ours is not a homogenous piety—if indeed there are any homogenous pieties. There are, and always have been, different pieties within the single faith in Christ. Furthermore, there are other pieties outside the Christian faith, religious and non-religious. The non-religious pieties lie somewhat outside the realm of faith—though only 'somewhat': humanism in its ethical form and commitment has historical, affective, and social affiliations with religious pieties. But it is with other practices of the Christian faith and with other religious pieties that a systematic presentation of the Christian faith must primarily engage, because of the damaging and agonistic exclusivism of many of these pieties with respect to each other, because of the competing claims that 'we are the true faith' and 'ours is the true religion'. We cannot expound and examine Christian theology today without hearing the Adhan and the Shofar, the Muslim and the Jewish calls to prayer. These are other monotheistic faiths and traditions. We cannot expound and examine Christian theology today without hearing also Hindu mantras and the turnings of Buddhist prayer wheels. These faiths are part of the larger corporations we belong to and work for, impacting upon ecclesial bodies, included in civic bodies, and a recognizable part of national bodies.

With respect to the internal divisions within the Christian faith, a systematic presentation of Christianity can only strive to be ecumenical. But as an Anglo-Catholic priest serving in an Anglican cathedral I come from somewhere and from some place. Place is multi-layered. It is not just geographical, historical, or cultural. Thankfully, there are other Christian theologians who have and will continue to produce their own systematic accounts of the faith; these accounts do, will, critique, compliment, and modify mine. And that is good; that is a blessing. With respect to other religious faiths, a systematic presentation of Christianity can only strive to be as lucid as possible that there might be greater understanding of what is believed, why, and with what consequences. Only then can what is shared become clear and what is different be respected. There is so much listening between religious faiths and so much living alongside each other still required. But to give an account of what we believe is a beginning. To recognize in that account that the Christian faith occupies a place within a matrix of other global religious pieties is also a beginning. We can go further. We can offer within that systematic account of the Christian faith a theology of religions; and not one that stakes out of some claim that Christianity has the exclusive truth. As I said in the opening paragraph: only God has, because God is, the truth. But we can offer a theology of religions because the Christian faith is practised amid the practices of these other religions, and therefore, unless it renounces its claim of a divine love gratuitously given *for* all humanity *to* all creation, Christianity must already be living out some notions of what it means *for* Christians that there are these other religious devotions. Each religious faith announces a vision of ethical life, of a good that is, can, or should be lived out if only in hopes and aspirations, benchmarked rights and acts of human compassion; a life given in our being created, in there being a creation at all. What theological account can be given of ethical life?

The structure of the systematic account of the Christian faith that follows is closely related to the levels of answers given above as to why such an account is important. In this opening volume, I begin by situating this systematic account of the Christian faith within a tradition of such accounts, in order to develop what I call an 'engaged systematic theology' and show why I believe this approach to theology is necessary. This way of doing systematic theological enquiry gives due attention to our historical, cultural, and social placement—and therefore the locatedness and provisionality of its own enquiry. But it has learnt to do theology this way from the tradition of such enquiry, and in this way bears that tradition forward. This, it seems to me, is a mode of theological enquiry concomitant with the incarnation of God in Christ and the Church as the body of Christ involved in the operations of redemption in and through the materialities of our embodiment and our cultures. 'Involved' is a vague word; it needs to be explained. The whole of this enterprise is concerned with understanding and explaining that involvement.

From an examination of creeds, *summa* and the first dogmatics, I will outline some basic theological coordinates that inform, structure, navigate, and
justify the approach to systematics that follows. I will then outline some basic
orientations that govern the theological reasoning that follow before ending
this first volume with a clarification of the title for all four volumes: ethical life.

Volume II (*Another Kind of Normal: Ethical Life II*) focuses on the foundation: Christ. The basic premise is that with the scandal of the incarnation
and the revelation of God *for us* then soteriology has epistemic and ontological priority. This is the work of Christ with respect to sin and its judgement.
While I provide insights into the nature of revelation throughout this first
volume (in most detail in Chapters 6 and 7), we can only treat revelation fully
with respect to the revelation of God in Jesus Christ. We have no immediate
access to this revelation as such, and our appreciations of it are thick with
interpretations, sin-laden distortions, and wishful thinking. We will have to
examine the difficulties here because the incarnation reveals not only God,
but also what it is to be human, fully human. So the nature of the revelation
of God in Christ, like the nature of Christ Himself, has to be thought through
alongside a theological anthropology and, indeed, a doctrine of creation. We
can only seek a creaturely understanding of God's eternal Triune nature (that
is, what is revealed) on the basis of salvation history.

Volume III (*The Vision of God: Ethical Life III*) treats the Church and its sacramental ministry as an extension of Christology in and through the working
of the Spirit. It examines the work of prayer and liturgy, and both again with
respect to revelation and sanctification. It also examines the Church with
respect to a sociology and politics of institutional life, for the Church (like the
incarnation) lives both within the world and beyond it. Only having treated
Christology, ecclesiology, and pneumatology can we approach the doctrine of
the triune God. A question evidently arises, a question related to the engaged
approach throughout: Why leave the Trinity so late? In the main, it remains
a late examination because of a distinction that I will say much more about
between what the early Church Fathers called *theologia* and *oikonomia*. The
distinction is not radical—otherwise the unity of God is ravaged. Our theologies can only analytically treat the truth of Godhead revealed in Jesus Christ
through reflecting back upon what that means for our understanding of God
in the Hebrew Scriptures. It can also only treat the economic operations of the
Godhead in the Spirit as they manifest themselves in both God's providential actions, the traditions of the church, and our experience as those who are
being saved. Which means that Rahner's dictum that the economic Trinity is
the immanent Trinity and the immanent Trinity is the economic Trinity is
both right and wrong. An aporia needs to be recognized and acknowledged.
There is no identity. Theology can treat the truth available to us because of
the truth's ontic relations to us as created in the image of that God. It cannot
treat directly the nature of the Father, although the Father is fully revealed

in the Son and the Spirit. The Father is not absent from us. The Father is not even distant from us. He is most intimately with us in both Christ, as the Son, and the Spirit. The intimacy of the Father is a deep dazzling darkness in the Son and the Spirit, accommodated to what we are as creatures. The Father is given to us completely, the Godhead is given to us completely, but that which is given is made accessible to us through the Son and Spirit. Volumes II and III both articulate God *for us*. We live the Trinity—it pervades and makes possible the whole of the enquiry. But we can only grasp how fundamental the Trinity is having examined what it does and how it does it. For we live *en Christō* and the 'one [*eis*] God and Father of us all . . . is above all and through all and in all [*epi pantōn kai dia pantōn kai en pansin*]' (Eph.4.6). I will then reflect, at the end of Volume III, upon the doctrine of the Trinity as the culmination of the vision of God.

The final volume (*Communio Sanctorum: A Theology of Religions*) will attempt to begin that conversation I spoke of above, opening a systematic account of the Christian faith to other religious pieties that qualify its claims and contextualize its practices, starting from the heterogeneity of the Christian piety as manifest in world Christianities.

So there's the basic roadmap and several nodal points, but the most important part is making the journey. Faith seeks understanding and understanding is a venture, a praxis, not a solution to a mathematical problem. As such, understanding and faith are both subsumed within the dynamic of seeking. And seeking becomes a way of living.

Acknowledgements

I began thinking through this project seven years ago, on completing *The Politics of Discipleship*. In part, it was to show myself that the various disciplines I had been working across—systematic theology, philosophical theology, historical theology, Biblical Studies, Literary and Cinema Studies, Critical Theory, prominently—really did speak to each other and foster a theology that was both dogmatic and apologetic, responding to the world in which we live. I began with the Christology that is developed in Volume II, but increasingly that made me aware of methodological issues, and also the need to have an overview of the contents of all four volumes. In working through some of the basic questions that shape and determine, and are shaped and determined by, any theological project, I came to an impasse with respect to the nature and work of faith and belief. So I took two years out to research the relationship between faith and belief that grew into a separate study: *Unbelievable: Why We Believe and Why We Don't*. The work resumed again to complete this first volume. The resources available to me an Oxford considerably facilitated that completion—most particularly talking with colleagues with expertises with whom I could chat and consult. They were many, but certainly the work of the historical studies that forms most of Part One of this volume could not have been done without the suggestions offered by Averil Cameron, Mark Edwards, Lydia Schumacher, and Simeon Zahl. My particular thanks to my graduate student Andrew Turnbull for assistance with compiling the index. Any number of senior and postdoc members of Christ Church was invaluable in working through the scientific material on cell biology and theoretical physics that I have drawn upon. Any errors, though, are entirely my own. Finally, I must acknowledge the importance of the graduate students with whom I have worked over these years, the seminars and colloquia that I have led and participated in, attended, and organized by them.

The title for this first volume was inspired by a daring novel by a former colleague at Manchester, M.J. Hyland, though it was my friend and publisher, Tom Perridge, at OUP, who reminded me of another source heard many many years ago now when I was a teenager in Salford—Leonard Cohen's *Anthem*: 'There's a crack in everything, that's how the light gets in.'

Graham Ward

Contents

Part One

An Engaged Systematics

1

Credo

BEING CHURCHED

We enter the Cathedral. It's the mother church of the diocese. The air is cool, the shadows deep and in the silence distant sounds reverberate. *I believe in God.* Who is God or *this* God? What does this appellation signify? What is this God? How did we learn to use words in this way and a name like this? How did we invent the literary genres that disseminated these words, this naming? The word 'God' softly implodes, becoming meaningless in its density, its fragrance. Its meaning opens and closes, vibrates like a vast diaphanous forcefield that enfolds this place with its elevations, tall, curved arches, and attenuated sight-lines. It draws us into its circulations making of this space a heterotopia: a different kind of space.

Heterotopia? Well, this is not the world, enclosed or otherwise, presented to me as I walk around Oxford's shops or its indoor market. I walk differently here. I tread more softly; my pace is slower; and my posture bends or cranes according to what I am seeing and trying to understand. Although I have been here a thousand times I can't domesticate the place; I cannot appropriate it even though it has become familiar. It is a holy space; a space within which I am taught about that name, that God, that who or what or operation circulating among so many of my other more mundane beliefs. Names mean other things in here. I can learn the names but how did I learn that these names named something for me? Were meaningful for me? *Made* sense? And what it is that makes this space holy? How do we learn this holiness? How are we made holy? It's not just the religious symbolism—crosses, an octagonal font, and the vast eagle across whose back is stretched a heavy Bible. It's not just that prayer has been said here for over a millennium. There is some inherent quality to this place, difficult to define, that makes it holy, that generates and requires holy practices that make us holy—liturgies that are set aside from the routines of daily life, performances undertaken in, and expressions of, a belief in *the father almighty, maker of heaven and earth*, services in which there is praise and worship offered, prayer said and blessings given, ministrations received, sacred Scriptures read, the gospel preached, and a healing emanates. This is a place invested with care and value and attentiveness where people have wept and petitioned and fumbled for words and delighted. But what does 'father' mean to someone like me who has not known his father since the age of fourteen, who is himself a father (for better, for worse), who has known many other fathers (for better, for worse) and who has known many other sons and daughters down the years? What does 'father' mean to those who are mothers and sisters and aunts? Those who practise their belief in this *father almighty* themselves become holy, a chosen people, a royal priesthood (1 Peter 2.9). And these practices have been continuing daily here since the earliest Anglo-Saxon foundations were laid for a convent, possibly with royal associations. The present building was constructed as an Augustinian priory in the 'royal' style of Romanesque, from the twelfth century. The space created—the lofty vaulted ceiling, the light falling from clerestory windows on the sandstone pillars, the rich colours in the stained glass and vestments, the scents of ancient incense and waxed candles, the different surfaces of brass and silver, wood, and the different textures of linen and wool, wine and water, the sounds of an organ voluntary or a canticle sung by the choir—invites and offers a reorientation and pedagogy of the senses. An orientation to what? To what is most present and most allusive: the base note of a resonant silence that insists we listen. But what are we listening for in this circumscribed location where time distorts around a saint's remains that have been interred? I have been summoned to attend.

The sight-lines of this heterotopian space and this pedagogy converge on the high altar on which a crucifix stands. *I believe in Jesus Christ.* Who is this Christ? The very plan of the church is cruciform. In a rose window above the altar, facing out into the rising son, is the figure of Jesus Christ as Pantokrator; He through whom and in whom all things were created. And this includes the materials fashioned by human beings from which this place has been constructed and decorated. His is the body broken by the priest; His is the blood filling the chalices; ours is the making of bread and wine. His is the name invoked throughout the liturgical practices; the anchor point for all the ecclesial activity. He is present as God, the almighty one, the Incarnated, the Son of God, God with us and for us; God in our time and histories and attested to in the writing of the Scriptures. *Conceived by the Holy Spirit, born of the Virgin Mary, suffered under Pontius Pilate, was crucified dead and buried. On the third day he rose again.* He is the incarnation, the embodiment of the Father Almighty, the *Son of God.* The church in all its holy, peopled devotions and in all its tactile stone and wooden seating, in all its sound and sights, in all its tastes and smells is His body. He is present in and through the operations of salvation opened by Him and proceeding from Him in and through and as the Spirit.

I believe in the Holy Spirit. What is the Spirit? How did I learn the language of the Spirit speaking; recognize the Spirit's voice—in me, in the world? The one through whom salvation is effected, the one who sanctifies. The one who is also God, though not as Father and not as Son. So as what then? The Spirit fills the breathing, thinking, and acting of the body of Christ, His living body: yesterday in the nuns gathering around the relics of the saint, the canons in the choir stalls, the Protestant reformers, and the Victorian Anglo-Catholics; today in the priests and deacons, the vergers, choir, and sidespeople, those who come to worship, those who come as pilgrims, those who believe, *the holy Catholic church, the communion of the saints.* Those forgiven. Those baptized. Those looking for *the resurrection of the body,* who participating now in the diurnal and universal operations of the living Jesus Christ, anticipate the perfection and consummation of a resurrection life in Him. *The life of the world to come.*

The *credo* is lived; it is not just recited. It has always been lived. In its origins lies the beginnings of theological reflection in a systematic form; that is, the logical structure of the Christian faith in which one dogmatic article relates organically to another. It is only because God is the Father Almighty that there can be a sending and the miraculous (in Volume II I will say 'scandalous') incarnation of the Son. It is only because of the coming of the Son of God that there can be salvation for the whole of creation through the Spirit. It is only because of the Spirit's proceeding that there is a church. An articulation of one Christian dogma will impact on the articulation of all the others: to accept that human beings are capable of saving themselves (and I leave aside for the moment what is it that is understood by 'salvation') is to understand Jesus Christ as an *exemplum.* It is to deny participation in Christ and to deny the Son of God's participation in human nature. The Church becomes an assembly of self-helpers, like a group of weight-watchers, each encouraging another. There are many ways of believing in Christ, but there are some ways of believing that are better. That is: more transformative. That is: opening us up to being transformed in His name.

THE CREEDS

Although there was in the Gospels a Christian story, a story narrated according to the chronological order of God's providential dispensation in several retellings of the Christ-event in *Acts of the Apostles*—there was no system-atic theology until the creeds. Just as the story of Christ's coming, minis-try, and death required the development of a new literary genre called the 'Gospel'—so too systematic theological reflection required the development of a new literary genre: the creed. To understand how systematic theological reflection emerged is to understand what systematic theology is and what it is attempting to do. It enables us to see how the Church learnt its lan-guage, or the grammar by which it could generate its various discourses. Not that systematic theological reflection and its purpose have remained the same since the foundations of the creeds were laid. In fact, as we will see, the establishment of the recognized and catholic creeds of the Church—the Apostles' Creed and the Nicene Creed—took a long, long time to be real-ized. Subsequently, systematic theological reflection changed, as we will also see. This was not simply in accordance with a change in its purpose and self-understanding. Systematic presentations of Christian doctrine changed because their discursive contexts changed. Cultural transformation brought theology into contact with new ideas, new practices, and new epistemo-logical conditions. Again we will be noting some of this. Nevertheless, to see something of how systematic theological reflection was formed and why, and the unity of the Christian faith it sought to give expression to, is also to recognize what has been forgotten about the nature of theology, that theol-ogy might well recover.

To unveil that forgetting and to recover that which was lost as the tradition passed from age to age is certainly one of the purposes of these four volumes. The challenges of those who would shout 'nostalgia' will be dealt with as we proceed. For the moment it is only important to plot how the Church learnt and continues to learn its language, how it systematized what it learnt and generated new literary genres for the transmission of that learning. Learning, as will become increasingly apparent, is at the very core of this project; a ped-agogy lies in the very performance of its discursive practice as it lies also at the very core of a theology's liturgical practice.

The 'Prologue' to Gregory of Nyssa's 'Great Catechetical Oration' is instruc-tive. He is addressing those teaching the faith to candidates seeking admis-sion to the Church, to those he calls the 'presiding ministers [*proestēkosi*] of the mystery of godliness [*mustērou tēs eusebeias*]'. And he tells them that they 'have need of a system [*logos anagkaios*] in their instructions in order that the Church may be replenished by the accession of such as should be saved [*an plēthunoito tē prosthēkē tōn sōdzomenōn ē ekklēsia*].' This frequently cited translation is clumsy, especially the 'replenished by the accession' when the Greek is simply 'the church of those being saved by the assistance' of the *proestēkosi*—those who have a ministerial care 'through the teaching of the word of the Faith [*pistou logou*] being brought home to the hearing of unbelievers [*apistōn*]'.¹ But what is interesting is that they translate '*logos*' (the subject of the sentence) as 'system'. The *anagkaios* is a characteristic of the *logos*. So it is not the 'presiding ministers' who 'have need of', as the translation here suggests. Rather, it is the *logos* that 'constrains' or 'compels' and in that sense is 'necessary'. The catechesis [*katēchēseōs*] in the opening clause of the original Greek text² is a genitive belonging to the compelling nature of the Logos itself.

So what does all this mean? Fundamentally, that the 'system' is not an abstract set of propositions set out by the ministers who preside and to which allegiance is given by those taught. It is, first of all, intrinsic to the word itself as the Logos; the word of faith that teaches. The system is the constraining and necessary logic of the Logos. It is co-relative to both a social and institutional practice (teaching) and an operation (being saved). It is implicated in 'the mystery of godliness' or the hidden working of piety. Its aim is salvation through conversion. And it is a teaching belonging to the 'word of faith', the Logos who is believed in—Christ who is the way, the truth and the life of that faith.

The 'system' is a pedagogy issuing from Christ as the Logos for the divine sanctification of those who accept it. The basis for there being a 'system' at all, for Gregory, is explained in Chapter 1 of the same 'Catechism': God has His Logos. The logic of the system is then the necessary or compelling effect of the Logos abiding in and as the trinitarian God. The logic is Christological through and through and pneumatological in its operation. It is does not stand as an independent set of connected human prescriptions. It is engaged in a dynamic. If the faith taught is the faith 'of the Logos' then the Logos must be revealed in and through the logic of the system. Furthermore, it is from this constraining logic that a 'method of instruction [*tēs didaskalias tropos*]' issues, which Gregory goes on to suggest needs to be adapted to catechumens with different religious backgrounds (Jews, Greeks, Manichees, Gnostics, etc.). The 'system' isn't a system then in the way we have come to use and understand that term. It is flexible and adaptive.

An explication of the nature of that relation between Logos and logic and that manifestation of the Logos in the logic will have to wait until Volume II (although I make some suggestions in the final part of this volume when I talk about *Sittlichkeit* or ethical life, following Hegel).

¹ 'The Great Catechism', trans. William More and Henry Austen Wilson, *Nicene and Post-Nicene Fathers: Gregory of Nyssa: Dogmatic Treatises* vol.5: ed. Philip Schaff and Henry Wace (Peabody, MA: Hendrickson Publishers, 1994), p.473.
² See *Oratio Catechetica* in *Gregorii Nysseni Opera Dogmatica Minora, Pars IV*, ed. Ekkehardus Mühlenberg (Leiden: E.J. Brill, 1996), p.5.

THE EMERGENCE OF THE CREEDS
AS THE EARLIEST FORMS OF SYSTEMATIC
THEOLOGICAL REFLECTION

Gregory of Nyssa's 'Prologue' enables us to recognize that, in their beginnings, creeds were not sets of formal and declaratory propositions. Their origins lie in the internalization of Scriptures read, heard, and inwardly digested in a liturgical setting. In particular: 'Go therefore and teach all nations, baptizing them in the name of the Father, and the Son, and the Holy Spirit' (Matt. 28.19)—where the ergonomics of faith are associated with the activities of mission and teaching, and the liturgy of baptism—and early church writings such as: 'After first explaining all things, baptize in the name of the Father, and of the Son, and of the Holy Spirit, in flowing water' (*Didache* 7.1)—where faith is associated with the same three activities. The origins of the creed lie in acts, not dogmatic prescriptions.[3] They emerged from *rules of faith* that appeared in the second century in the wake of Gnosticism, as they 'resemble creeds quite closely except that their overall structure is not fixed and their wording fluent'.[4] But there were no 'formal pledge[s] of allegiance to a set of doctrinal statements', no declaratory confessions of the faith, before well into the fourth century.[5] So conclusions about the creeds emphasize that the creeds 'are not "Articles of belief" or a system of doctrine, but rather "confessions" summarizing the Christian story, or affirmations of the three "characters" in that story'.[6]

If these summaries are systematically ordered in a series of grammatical phrases knit together in a trinitarian syntax, they are also (or eventually became) intoned as part of an engaged ecclesial praxis. Just as the internalization of the Scriptures gave rise to creedal affirmations, so we learn the language of the creeds, internalizing their sense, and understand our experience by what they name and what they make sense of. It is that pedagogical engagement—which is not just rote memorizing, but enculturation—that makes the creed an act of worship, a confession writing what Christians believe within their emotions, thoughts, and actions. The engagement incarnates, radically, by eliciting our participation physiologically, emotionally, cognitively, and

---

[3] The debates of the origins of the creeds continue unabated since the mid-nineteenth century. See Wolfram Kinzig, Christoph Markschies, and Markus Vinzent, *Trauffragen und Bekenntnis. Studien zur sogenannten* Traditio Apostolica *zu den* Interrogationes de fide *und zum Römischen Glabensbekenntnis*, Arbeiten zur Kirchengeschichte, 74 (Berlin, 1998). For a quick guide in English on the *Apostle's Creed* see Wolfram Kinzig and Markus Vinzent, 'Recent Research on the Origin of the Creed', *Journal of Theological Studies*, NS, vol. 50, Pt. 2, October 1999, 535–59.

[4] Kinzig and Vincent, 'Recent Research on the Origin of the Creed' (n.3), p.541.

[5] Ibid., p.540.

[6] Francis Young, *The Making of the Creeds* (London: SCM Press, 1991), p.12.

spiritually. Every emotion has a behavioural effect, an autonomic effect and a hormonal effect. An engaged systematic theology must begin with, and continually return to, critical reflections upon that multi-affective and embodied pedagogy. The learning is complex and ongoing. It encompasses the history of the Church and churches. It constitutes the tradition and its traditions—that which is handed on, accumulated, redacted, reconstructed, and disseminated. And a thousand other languages meet and cross and inform every one of these processes. We can excavate only fragments of the complexity of that pedagogy that we inherit, confess, believe, understand (in part), and preach (in part).

The 'first "private" confessions of the faith, and since Antioch 324/5 C.E, also synodal creeds, can only be properly understood when they are read as reciprocal challenges and responses.'[7] Kinzig and Vinzent are writing particularly about the confessions of faith made by individuals who had been excommunicated in the light of the Arian controversy—Arius (responded to by Alexander of Alexandria) and Asterius (responded to by Marcellus of Ancyra)—and the subsequent synodal confessions that were issued at Antioch (based on the Arius–Alexander confessions) and Nicaea. I am extending the 'challenge–response' model by multiplying the different 'language games' in which these creedal confessions took place. This is not just a matter of ideas, even theological ideas. It is not just a matter of orthodoxy and heterodoxy. It is also a matter of complex discursive power in which what is believed can be held as believable and practised.

This was 'an age of effusive public language',[8] theological statements and later proclamations have to be situated within the circulations of public letters, panegyrics, orations, slogans, and iconography on coins and accompanying civic monuments. We will understand more about this discursive power as my argument develops and the engaged complexity of the contending theologies that emerge. To recognize how the Church and the churches learnt to speak in this creedal way, with this theological syntax, and learnt the barest of bones for a systematic theology, we need to appreciate not simply those 'reciprocal challenges and responses' but the wider contexts—cultural, historical, social, and discursive—from which they emerge. The professions are unique events in the life of the Church, the creation no less of a new literary genre, a new way of being theological, and inseparable from dense, nuanced networks of communication. Only Christianity, as a world religion, has such creeds. Pagans had no creeds; only ritual acts to perform. Since practices are liquid and always repeated non-identically, pagan rituals were always susceptible to syncretism and inclusiveness. The practices were not formally

---

[7] Kinzig and Vinzent, 'Recent Research on the Origin of the Creed' (n.3), p.553.
[8] Robin Lane Fox, *Pagans and Christians* (Harmondsworth: Penguin Books, 1988), p.657.

bounded by a text interpreting and delimiting them. Only Christianity circumscribes those who self-identify as Christians, through a prescribed *credo*
that took four centuries in its devising (and much, much longer in its legitimation) by ecclesial authority.

The creeds were enacted before they developed reflections upon that enactment. And as there were increasing reflections upon the enactment then the
enactment changed. Theological reflection cannot neatly be divided into first
and second order activities; that analysis is a distortion of what theology is
and the effect it has. And I shall return to that in Chapter 4. For the moment
I want to explore the structured and systematic unfolding of the creeds,
because in this they differed from the more loosely formulated *regulae fidei*.
Although even here, and as late as 340/1 C.E, in Marcellus of Ancyra's statement of the faith (in his letter of defence against excommunication written
to the Emperor Julian) the theo-logic meanders, and focuses (as one might
expect given the grounds for the excommunication) on Christological issues.[9]
The 'Christological summary and a trinitarian formula ... were originally
independent of each other.'[10] The structure that arose did so out of a specific
liturgical practice that returns us to the injunction to teach and baptize in
Matthew's Gospel: the so-named *interragotiones de fide* put to and answered
by neophytes at or before their baptism. *Do you believe in God the Father
Almighty? Do you believe in Christ Jesus, the Son of God? Do you believe in
the Holy Spirit?*[11] Tertullian attests to this baptismal practice at the end of the
second century, as does Novatian in the mid-third century. But, and here we
return to the politics of discursive power, the arrival at what we now confess
as the Apostolic Creed or the Nicene Creed was not a simple matter of putting
three 'building blocks' together (the *regulae fidei*, the *interrogations fide*, and
the 'private' statements of faith). Intellectual, political, and frequently physical battles took place in order to arrive at those condensed points: about the
one creator God and the nature of that creation, about the incarnation of
that God in Jesus the Christ, about the Spirit of God operating in the world
to bring about its sanctification, its healing, its redemption, and about the
Church as the body of Christ working in and through the Spirit for that same
sanctification, healing, and redemption. One relation binds these condensed

---

[9] See the Letter in James Stevenson (ed.), *Creeds, Councils and Controversies: Documents
Illustrating the History of the Church AD 337–461*, revised version (London: SPCK, 1989),
pp.5–6.

[10] Kinzig and Vinzent, 'Recent Research on the Origin of the Creed' (n.3), p.537. See also
Christoph Markschies, 'Apostolicum', *RGG* 1 (1998), 648–9.

[11] See J.N.D. Kelly, *Early Christian Creeds* (London: Longmans, Green and Co., 1950), ch,
II. More recently: Markus Vinzent, ' "... natum et passum etc." Zur Geschichte der Tauffragen
in der lateinischen Kirche bis zu Luther', in Kinzig, Markschies, and Vinzent, *Tauffragen
und Bekenntnis* (n.3), pp.75–183 and *Der Ursprung des Apostolikums im Urteil der kritischen
Forschung*, Forschungen zur Kirche—und Dogmengeschichte 89 (Göttingen, 2006).

points: the Creator God's relation to that creation. It is the story of this relation that is confessed, lived, and inscribed within the practices of the Church; a story of the one Triune God and the many—the author and the script for trillions of created participants.

Even when this story starts to get presented systematically, the statements of faith are not dogmatic systems but frameworks for the difficult work of faith as it seeks its understanding. In his Sermon 213, preached to those about to receive baptism, Augustine advises: 'First believe, then understand'.[12] Irenaeus, earlier in the second century, who spoke of a 'canon of truth' and a 'rule of faith' passed down from the Apostles and who makes his own summary of the core *kerygma* of the Christian faith[13] describes how 'the work of the tradition' bore the same gospel everywhere. His Greek is telling: *hē dunamis tes paradoseos*—truth, the faith, is actively disseminated down through the various churches, their contexts and their languages, while remaining the same. This dynamic understanding of the operation of the faith, which had yet to be developed theologically through a pneumatology and a doctrine of Providence, is an important aspect of an engaged systematics. The Old Roman Creed (the basis for the Apostles' Creed and closely resembling formulae found in Marcellus of Ancyra's Letter to Julian) only came into existence half way through the fourth century. The Apostles' Creed as we have it today was not fixed until sometime around the eighth century. As Kinzig and Vinzent conclude their investigations in the origins of the creed: 'Until well into the time of the Imperial Church of the fourth and fifth centuries the literary form resulting from the piecing together of the "building blocks" appears to have been comparatively loose. This allowed for considerable freedom in rearranging and recombining the pieces.'[14]

In these proto-creeds a story is presented of the divine engagement from creation to the last things (death and resurrection). The details describing the work of the three divine Persons invoked in the baptismal interrogations were culled from Scripture in the struggles to maintain there was one God, not three; a Son of God who was also Lord and, being born of a woman and dying under a particular Roman commander, became incarnate; a Spirit of God who inspired the prophets and taught the truth down through the various divine dispensations. Behind the choice of these particular details lie polemics and apologetics going back to the Apostles and Gospel writers themselves: distinguishing Jewish beliefs from Christian, Jewish-Christians from 'pagans' (a Christian term for those not baptized) and Christian beliefs from

[12] Augustine Sermon 213.4.
[13] Irenaeus, *Against Heresies* 1.10, 2 in *Ante-Nicene Fathers*, vol. 1, ed. Alexander Roberts and James Donaldson (Peabody, MA: Hendrickson Publishers, 2004), pp.331.
[14] Kinzig and Vinzent, 'Recent Research on the Origin of the Creed' (n.3), pp.555–6.

various docetisms, mysticisms, and gnosticisms. The gospel had to announce itself from within myriad belief-systems, ideologies, and superstitions. It had to employ the languages available at the time, turning words, concepts, ideas, and phrases to its own account. These religious beliefs, in the old gods, say, were world-views embedded in and expressive of complex cultural, political, and economic relations. They could not be extracted from life lived and made sense of in and across a great spectrum of social forces. So when Christian creedal beliefs were 'received ... meditated ... and ... held' (Augustine) they 'brought other fundamental changes, in people's self-awareness, in their opportunities and social organization. The Church and its careers and ever-growing processions became major new forces in economic and social history. Its form of worship distorted town plans of established cities and created new centres which showed new types of hospitality.'[15]

One of the most significant aspects of accounts of how the creedal formulae were arrived at,[16] and the complex histories that led to Nicaea (325 C.E.), Constantinople (381 C.E.), and Chalcedon (451 C.E.),[17] is the way Scriptures were being interpreted (while the Scriptural canon was being formed) and Christian teachings arrived at in contexts that were culturally and linguistically diverse (the West, the East, North Africa). The histories, politics, sociologies, ethnographies, philosophies, religions, and economics of this region around the Mediterranean are never far from the surface in the struggles to *make* Christian orthodoxy through the creeds, to circumscribe a space

---

[15] Robin Lane Fox, *Pagans and Christians* (n.8), p.22.

[16] Kelly opens his classic account of the development of the Creeds with the legend that it was the Twelve Apostles themselves who, inspired by the Spirit as it fell on the day of Pentecost, each prophesied an article. The story comes from the writer Tyrannius Rufinus at the turn of the fifth century and provides one of our primary sources for the Old Roman Creed (the precursor to the Apostles' Creed). The legend, repeated throughout late antiquity and the early medieval period, legitimated the authority of the Apostles' Creed. But Kelly emphasizes that some form of teaching was handed down from the earliest times and form criticism has pointed to elements of agreed *formulae* (as possibly fragments of baptismal hymns) in Paul's own letters.

[17] Several of these studies take a narrative form—the development of doctrine. For example, Henry Chadwick's, *Early Christian Thought and the Classical Tradition* (Oxford: Oxford University Press, 1966), Jaroslav Pelikan's *The Christian Tradition: A History of the Development of Doctrine*, Vol. 1: *The Emergence of the Catholic Tradition (100–600)*, J.N.D. Kelly's *Early Christian Doctrines* (London: A. & C. Black, 1977) and Frances Young's *From Nicaea to Chalcedon* (London: S.C.M., 1983). More recently, the narration of this 'development' has begun to appear less linear and far more nuanced, in studies like Rowan Williams, *Arius: Heresy and Tradition* (London: Darton, Longman & Todd, 1987), Rowan Williams (ed.), *The Making of Orthodoxy: Essays in Honour of Henry Chadwick* (Cambridge: Cambridge University Press, 1989), John Behr, *The Way to Nicaea: The Formation of Christian Theology* Vol. 1 (Crestwood, NY: St. Vladimir's Seminary Press, 2001), Lewis Ayres, *Nicaea and its Legacy: An Approach to Fourth-Century Trinitarian Theology* (Oxford: Oxford University Press, 2004) and John Behr, *The Nicene Faith: The Formation of Christian Theology* Vol. 2, Part 1 and Part 2 (Crestwood, NY: St. Vladimir's Seminary Press, 2004).

within which some differences of emphasis were possible so a catholicity was maintained and other differences (opinions, in Greek *heresiae*) were excluded, condemned, even prosecuted. It is impossible to work in patristic theology without being engaged; without recognizing how Christology, pneumatology, the doctrines of the triune God, creation, theological anthropology, sin and atonement, eschatology and ecclesiology were all enmeshed in other debates: in territorial claims, in dynastic entitlements, in ethnic minority or majority statuses, in hierarchies and proto-democracies, with charismatic figures, demons, angels, powers, and principalities.

To extract dogma from such engagements is radically to reduce, to the point of distortion, the seeking to understand the faith that is the dynamic for theological enquiry. At best the creeds were for beginners, those receiving catechism. They were grammars for the faith; maps of the territory to be explored existentially and intellectually as one grew and was formed in the faith. Within the overarching belief–structure further teaching of the faith could occur—through preaching, Scriptural reading and exegesis, instruction by letters and catechetical lectures coming down from bishops. That is not to say the creeds lack adequate theological content. They certainly don't. But that theological content is interpretatively open. Taking the Apostles' Creed: to call God 'Father', while it has Scriptural authority, opens a question in the context of a creedal article as to whether He is Father because He is *maker of heaven and earth* or because He is Father of His *only Son* or both. To call God 'Almighty' also has Biblical precedence but the Latin term here is '*omnipotentum*' which is not the same as the Greek term '*pantokratora*'. The Greek suggests sovereign control over a realm; the Latin suggests God can do anything (except 'He cannot die. Cannot be deceived. Cannot lie . . . Cannot deny himself').[18] The alternative Latin term would have been '*imperium*'—which would not have done at all because it would court the unwarranted attentions of the Emperor and the Imperial cult. We could further excavate the implicitly diverse theologies within the creeds by examining the terms 'only begotten', 'Son', and 'Christ Jesus' (rather than Jesus Christ) in the second article. Furthermore, while having a theological content that is interpretatively open, the Apostles' Creed tells us nothing, for example, about Christ's own teaching or the relationship between that teaching and the three theological *loci* the creeds do focus on: incarnation, soteriology, and eschatology. Unless we emphasize the Greek '*monogenes*' that translates 'only begotten' rather than the Latin '*unicus*' which has no sense of generation, then there is nothing about the pre-cosmic and eternal generation of the Son from the Father, and how that generation still maintains the one God. There

---

[18] Augustine, *Sermon* 213.2.

is nothing in the Apostles' Creed, or any of the early Latin Creeds, about Trinitarian relations (or degrees of distinction) at all.

The creeds provide us with a series of basic theological pieces to be interpreted but what is missing are the connections, how the pieces fit together, how they dovetail with or rub against each other. The oneness of the Godhead is not apparent in the early Latin creeds so how does the Father relate to the Son? How does the Son achieve the *forgiveness of sins*, the atonement? How does the Holy Spirit relate to the *holy catholic church*? We surely do not believe in the Church in the same way we believe in the Holy Spirit. How does the resurrection of the flesh occur? How is the oneness of the Godhead maintained across and through the operations of the three Persons? If the Creed as a summary of the faith was for preparation for baptism, what is the relation of this sacrament to the Eucharist? There is no mention of the Eucharist. There were genuine struggles among Christian theologians with understanding and explaining the 'hows' of this divine economy. This is evident in the different expressions for Christ being born of Mary. The Latin creed known to Augustine (closely related to the creed known to Ambrose) confesses a Christ *'qui natus est de Spiritu sancto et Maria virgine'*; born, then, *of* or *from* both the Holy Spirit and the Virgin Mary. Mary's agency in giving birth is explicitly correlated with the Holy Spirit's agency in the same birthing. But in three other Italian creeds (Aquileia, Ravenna, and Turin), the confession runs: *'natus est de Spirito sancto ex Maria virgine'*; born, then, *of* the Holy Spirit *through* or *from* or *out of* the Virgin Mary. Here the prime agency lies with the Holy Spirit and Mary is more a vessel for the Spirit's work of incarnating. Other creeds have *'natum ex Spiritu sancto et ex virgine Maria'* (Remesiana) or *'natum de Spiritu sancto ex utero Mariae virginis'* (Mozarabic), while Gallic creeds formulated it as *'conceptus est de Spiritu sancto, natus ex Maria virgine'*. As John Behr states: 'very similar sounding formulae are used to tell very different versions of the "Christian story"'.[19]

What is evident in the variety of these expressions is the range of local variations that were in use in the West, all still patterned on the Old Latin Creed coming out of Rome. Similar differences are evident in the creeds used in the East, which were often much longer, more detailed and theologically richer. And although the Nicene Creed, agreed upon by the council of 318 bishops, did stabilize a wording for the 'rule of faith', appended by a list of anathemas for those straying beyond the bounds of orthodoxy, it does not appear to have been used in the churches until around the second half of the fourth century; with Hilary of Poitiers not knowing of its existence until much later! The most extensive contemporary account of the Council, by Eusebius of Caesarea in

---

[19] John Behr, *The Formation of Christian Theology* Vol.2, *The Nicene Faith Part One*, (n.17) p.11.

his *Life of Constantine* (Book III. 4–24) is embarrassingly thin of any creedal formulation at all. Furthermore, new creeds followed the Nicene Council. For example, at the Council of Antioch in 341c.e, brought together in part to celebrate the opening of an octagonal church begun under the orders of Constantine, four creeds were produced and not one of them mentioned the word fought over so contentiously at Nicaea: the homoousion! Furthermore, what we call the Nicene Creed, and recited at our Eucharistic celebrations a such, is not at all the creed ratified by the 318 bishops in 325 c.e. The creed we recite is one that comes down to us from the Council of Chalcedon—and much ink has been spilt over trying to understand why the creed presented then, alongside the original Nicene Creed, was formally accepted *as* the Nicene Creed![20] If, following the Council of Chalcedon the creed now became truly catholic and ecumenical, this was only until the end of the eighth century and the formal insertion of the *filioque*—the defence of which was taken up by no less a figure than Charlemagne.

Although there was 'flexibility of usage'[21] and 'fluidity of credal formulation',[22] the 'Nicene' Creed as adopted at Chalcedon, *did* articulate Trinitarian relations through a series of technical theological terms: the Son as eternally *begotten* or *generated* from the Father and being of *one substance* with Him, the Spirit was defined as *proceeding*. The Spirit still swings loosely from this relationship and many theologians would say the Spirit continues to do so, particularly in the Western tradition following the *filioque* though beginning earlier with Augustine—for whom the Triune God appears to be two Persons and a relation. But what is more significant for the future of systematic theology is that the articulation of the faith in the Nicene Creed was increasingly detached from its liturgical basis in baptism. It was incorporated later into the Eucharist, but the creed now becomes, more significantly, the framework for the theological exposition of the Christian faith.

As for the Apostles' Creed new doctrinal items continued to be added, like the *descent into hell*, which first appeared in the Fourth Creed of Sirmium in 359 c.e. and *the communion of the saints*, which is attested in 394 c.e. in the 'resolutions of the synod of Nîmes'.[23] What was understood though by the *communion of the saints* was fluid, as 'the fluctuating meanings which were read into *sanctorum communio* in the patristic and medieval periods' attest.[24]

---

[20] The Council of Constantinople ratified the second creed presented at Chalcedon in 381; a Council not attended by Western bishops. For a detailed discussion of the various interpretations of how the second creed was accepted as the Nicene Creed see J.N.D. Kelly *Early Christian Creeds*, (n.17) pp.296–331; R.V. Sellers, *The Council of Chalcedon: A Historical and Doctrinal Survey* (London: SPCK, 1953); and L. Ayers, *Nicaea and Its Legacy*, (n.17) pp.253–8.

[21] J.N.D. Kelly, *Early Christian Creeds* (n.17), p.323.

[22] L. Ayres, *Nicaea and Its Legacy* (n.17), p.162.

[23] J.N.D. Kelly, *Early Christian Creeds* (n.17), p.389.   [24] Ibid., p.394.

LEARNING AND DEPLOYING A LANGUAGE
OF FAITH

The language of the faith being learnt and taught was not the same language, and even when it was the same language (Latin, say), there were still variations of expression and, furthermore, the semantic field of the words employed changed over time. No one finally controls what a number of recent anthropologists have come to call 'the natural histories of discourse'.[25] An example will assist us. Just as the development of Logos–Christology owes its basic concepts to the natural theology of the Stoics, so, for example, the language of 'peace' ran deep in Graeco-Roman political discourse. The Romans had made Concordia a goddess 'invoked at private wedding ceremonies, at festivals by whole cities, and the rulers of the Roman Empire'.[26] Peace was extolled as a divine power 'that yokes the universe and upholds world order'.[27] The language of 'peace' also had long and strong roots in the Jewish and Christian Scriptures, with Christological, pneumatological, eschatological, and ecclesial resonances. It announced a cosmic order for Graeco-Roman culture and Christianity alike. So when, in his letter to the diocese of Caesarea, Eusebius gives an account of the Council of Nicaea and tells them that the introduction of the word *homoousion* was assented to because 'peace [was] the object',[28] we cannot understand 'peace' (and indeed the Council and its creed) outside of those ancient traditions and contexts. But it is also a word with a very particular historical background, given Constantine's victory in the war against Licinius for control of the Eastern part of the Roman Empire. The *Pax Romana* made famous by Augustus did not extend to the eastern provinces. Indeed, because Christians were persecuted Constantine himself in his *Edict to the People* following the death of Licinius, speaks of 'civil war' and 'civil

---

[25] See Michael Silverstein and Greg Urban, eds. *Natural Histories of Discourse* (Chicago: University of Chicago Press, 1996). Silverstein and his colleagues demonstrate that 'texts' (like the creeds) arise from 'labile and mercurial insubstantiality' (p.4) associated with social interactions. They develop a number of terms to facilitate an account of the process 'entextualisation' (those social interactions that produce texts and the social institutions that stabilize and legitimate them as authoritative), paying attention to the 'metadiscursive' or 'dynamic and contingent social properties from which [the text] was assembled' (p.13). In this way they investigate the 'entextualizing processes in which the text is but one moment, and indeed, in which the text is sometimes only implicit in an aesthetic of transposition, transduction, and translation' (p.14). It is in this way that all texts have a natural history.

[26] Werner Jaeger, *Early Christianity and Greek Paideia* (Cambridge, MA: Harvard University Press, 1961), p.13.

[27] Ibid., p.14.

[28] The Letter is embedded in Athanasius's defence of the Council composed, *De Decretis*, written probably between 351–355 C.E. My reference is to the *Epistola Eusebii* prepared by Archibald Robertson in the *Nicene and Post-Nicene Fathers*, vol.4: *Athanasius: Select Works and Letters*, ed. Philip Schaff and Henry Wace (Peabody, MA: Hendrickson Publishers, 1994), p.75.

strife'. The language of peace, unanimity, harmony that pervades the accounts of the Council was learnt in a highly political context. If Christianity as a discourse and a set of institutions disseminating and authorizing such discourse plays a key role in that context then that role is multiple and complex.

Eusebius himself (along with other Christian historians like Socrates, Sozomen, and Lactantius) recounts some of the complexity of that context. Where in the west, following Constantine's conquest, synods of bishops were convened, under first Maximian, then Maximin, Christians in the east were undergoing persecution. Licinius, a colleague of Constantine's, his brother-in-law and co-author of the *Edict of Milan* granting Christians the right to practise their religion openly, took control on the death of Maximin in 313 C.E. But he too persecuted the Christians, according to Eusebius: disallowing synods of bishops to meet and agree on issues concerning the faith, confiscating property, curtailing inheritance rights, dismissing Christians from office in the military and in the civil administration. So when the *Pax Romana* was extended to the eastern provinces on the defeat of Licinius is 324 C.E., Constantine put an end to civil strife and began a project of both restoration and restitution on behalf of those persecuted and exiled. The imperial treasury itself made funds available for such a project in which 'all things whatsoever which shall appear righteously to belong to the churches, whether the property consists of houses, or fields and gardens, or whatever the nature of it may be, shall be restored in their full value and integrity, and with undiminished right of possession'.[29] In a telling personal letter to Eusebius, Constantine writes: 'We also empower you, and the other [bishops] through you, to demand what is needful for the work [of the restoration and extension of the churches], both from the provincial governors and from the Praetorian Praefect.'[30] The Church was now on similar footing, and in some matters, a higher footing, to the military and bureaucratic personnel that administrated the eastern provinces. In fact, the higher footing is in line with Constantine's theological understanding of God as the administrating judge par excellence and his requirement that bishops acted as judges in their episcopal courts.[31] Although there are debates among scholars concerning Constantine's

[29] From Constantine's 'Law respecting Piety towards God, and the Christian Religion' cited in Eusebius's *Life of Constantine*, translated by Rev. Arthur Cushman McGriffert in the *Nicene and Post-Nicene Fathers*, vol.10: *The Church History of Eusebius*, ed. Philip Schaff and Henry Wace (Peabody, MA: Hendrickson Publishers, 1994), p.510.

[30] Ibid., p.511.

[31] Note in his *Edict to the People* Constantine's description 'the most high God is himself the administrator of judgement [*tēs de kriseōs authentei*]', ibid., p.512. Eusebius, who cites this document, in his *Vita Constantini*, emphasized 'Constantine's role as the new Moses leading the Christian people out of the tyranny of persecution'—'Introduction' to *Life of Constantine*, trans. Averil Cameron and Stuart G. Hall (Oxford: Oxford University Press, 1999), p.7, also pp.35–9. Constantine as the new Lawgiver presents himself in the *Edict* as God's viceroy on earth, in line with 'Middle Platonic ruler-theory' (ibid., p.35) and in line also with Eusebius's presentation of the Emperor as the fulfilment of Scriptural prophecies. The translation of 'administrator' is not accurate. An administrator as the manager of an operation would be

imperial injunctions to bishops and how they were understood and exercised *in situ*.

'Peace' then in this context is not simply a theological word, and neither is 'salvation',[32] because the ramifications of Constantine's conquest of the eastern provinces involved major redistributions of economic, political, social, and cultural power. The social revolution that takes place now in the eastern province has to be understood against the background of shifts towards the increasing gentrification of Christianity that had begun from around the beginning of the third century. Converts were not necessarily from among the humble and poor any more. The demographic of believers included more lower middle-class and respectable artisans.[33] A new *arriviste* class was emerging as a new Hellenism was fostered to safeguard a liberal elite. Christian leaders, particularly bishops, absorbed this new cultural elitism, while developing Christianity as the true *paideia*—the true enculturation process. The Church in the west had already been provided with opportunities for social advancement; this was now extended to the east. The sons of soldiers, butchers, and farmers could rise to episcopal splendour.[34]

City life was fractious under these emerging conditions with local tensions between the upwardly mobile and the traditional classes, new landowners, administrative and military personnel, and the ruling oligarchies. During the persecution the Church had been the outcast, but now it had to be recognized as a major political and economic force in local government.

---

oikonomos. The translation here is more accurately '[the God who] authors (or has full command over) judgement'—that is, God as the plenipotentiary and ultimate executioner of judgement. Cameron and Hall translate the phrase precisely: 'judgement is exercised by the most high God' (ibid., p.112). It would though be interesting to speculate on what Constantine's Latin would have been that Eusebius or some secretary in the palace translated into Greek. The language of 'economy' that permeates Trinitarian theology of the fourth and fifth centuries was culled from St. Paul, reinterpreted by Hyppolitus and Tertullian, and employed by bishops involved in the administration of the empire and the executioners of ecclesial judgements to indicated God's governance of all things. See Giorgio Agamben, *The Kingdom and the Glory: For a Theological Genealogy of Economy and Government*, trans. Lorenzo Chiesa (with Matteo Mandarini) (Stanford: Stanford University Press, 2011). It is doubtful bishops exercised a superior judgement to their civilian counterparts and in fact in episcopal courts the 'language employed is that of healing, not judgement. The bishop is a physician'—Jill Harries, *Law and Empire in Late Antiquity* (Cambridge: Cambridge University Press, 2001), p.201. Nevertheless, though their powers did not extend to sentences of execution, a bishop could authorize a punishment involving violence when giving his judgement (see John C. Lamoreaux, 'Episcopal Courts in Late Antiquity', *Journal of Early Christian Studies*, vol.3, no. 2 (Summer 1995), 163–4.

[32] If God is frequently referred to by Constantine as Saviour (*soter*), then this has much to do with the military victories God, in His good providence, vouchsafes for the Emperor. Constantine's banner (*labarum*) of the cross was an ensign for battle, his enemies God's enemies. The spiritual restoration of right relationship to God through the Christ's atoning death on the cross (which is at the heart of salvation as 'healing'), plays no part in this theology.

[33] See Peter Brown, *The World of Late Antiquity* (London: Thames and Hudson, 1999), p.62.

[34] Few, like Ambrose of Milan, came from the old senatorial class.

Bishops, particularly metropolitan bishops, attained positions as local patrons of the city from which they could accumulate and consolidate economic, social, and cultural capital.[35] Their economic capital lay in the monies donated and tithed by ordinary believers, in lands given to them, offerings based on the first fruits of crops and produce, and certain fiscal privileges.[36] Constantine himself was lavish in the monies he dispensed for the building of churches across the eastern province. Diocesan economic power lay in the distribution of some of this income, dispensed as charity, proffered as bribes: 'A bishop who lost touch with his laity would find himself financially weakened and eventually with no funds for the task.'[37] Their social capital came from the network of allies they could foster locally from the rivalling factions of important landowners, in the church through ties to other bishops in the province and beyond, and in the empire through connections to the imperial court, the praetorian prefects or the provincial governors who all had armies at their disposal. Their social power came from their ability to ordain (deacons and priests), consecrate (other bishops), excommunicate, depose and pardon, and come to the aid of the poor in particularly desperate times like food shortages. The cost of the much-feared excommunication was high: confiscation of property and status, exile or deportation (to the salt mines), even lynching and imprisonment. Because of the well-known Christian care for the poor, the 'bishop's support of the poor led to the poor's support of the bishop and made the bishop a leader of a great part of the urban population. The common people added considerably to his political influence within the urban community.'[38] Their cultural capital came from the way they were recognized as holding the keys to salvation. It also came from their role in arbitration and conciliation, and their monarchical position between the earthly city and the heavenly. Their cultural power was exercised through the status with which they were regarded as those to whom obedience was due; as those with authority, divinely sanctioned, to legitimate.

The early years of Athanasius as bishop of Alexandria demonstrates the plots and counterplots, the allegations and counterallegations, the accusations and counteraccusations that could ferment from the complex interweave of these various capitals and powers, and the various commissions of enquiry, imperial hearings and councils that followed. His reign did not start

---

[35] See J.H.W.G. Liebeschuetz, *The Decline and Fall of the Roman City* (Oxford: Oxford University Press, 2001), ch. 4.

[36] See Lizzi Testa, 'The Bishop *vir venerabilis*: fiscal privileges and status definition in late antiquity', *Studia patristica* XXXIV (2001), pp.125–44.

[37] Robin Lane Fox, *Pagans and Christians* (n.8), p.505. Hence we can appreciate the complexities that arose for the bishop's role when the episcopal court acted as a judiciary.

[38] Jan Willem Drijvers, *Cyril of Jerusalem: Bishop and City* (Leiden: Brill, 2004), p.69.

well: on the death of Alexander the bishop of Alexandria, Athanasius, then his trusted deacon and emissary, hurried to the city

> to find fifty-four bishops, supporters of both Alexander and Melitius, deliberating over the choice of a bishop to heal the schism. On 8 June 328, before a common decision was reached, six or seven bishops went to the Church of Dionysius and consecrated him bishop of Alexandria.[39]

Order and disorder, 'peace', depended upon any number of local, ecclesial, theological, and imperial variables; and these were changing continually. The stakes were high, vendettas and vindications inevitable, as Athanasius strove to assert his episcopal powers in the face of a growing faction around the one-time excommunicated bishop of Lycopolis, Melitius, and a second multiplying faction circling around the still excommunicated priest of Baucalis, Arius. Theology was only one of the weapons he wielded as he fought off being deposed and exiled. But the exile (his first of several) came, on Constantine's orders, in 335 C.E.

Whether the accusations were true or false the picture of power-wrangling among bishops remains clear and the case of Athanasius was not an isolated one. The same Marcellus of Ancyra whose statement of faith we noted earlier had fled his see to present his statement to the Bishop of Rome. His accusers, among them Eusebius of Caearea who wrote two books *Against Marcellus*, speak of Marcellus returning from a previous exile to Ancyra to eject the bishop, Basil, who had been appointed in his place. There was rioting, fighting, and looting as Marcellus repossessed his church by force. 'His enemies later complained that priests of the opposing faction were dragged naked to the forum, Basil was ejected from the sanctuary and thrown into the street clutching the consecrated host, and holy virgins were stripped bare and exposed to public gaze.'[40] However much this might sound like scenes from a Baroque melodrama, the picture of the intricate and unstable relations between politics, economics, and ecclesiology are all too clear. Marcellus' 'creed' is only the theological surface of a much more profound power brokering. The long letter Julius, the bishop of Rome, wrote in defence of both Athanasius and Marcellus reveals similar atrocities in Alexandria when the bishop appointed to replace Athanasius, Gregory, took possession of his see—though the details of the atrocities came from Athanasius himself.

The Church's fortunes and stability were related to imperial fortunes and stability more generally, and after the death of Constantine, the internal politicking between his three sons (Constantinus, Constantius, and Constans) in a divided Empire meant problems were bounced from one court and council

---

[39] Timothy D. Barnes, *Athanasius and Constantius: Theology and Politics in the Constantinian Empire* (Cambridge, MA: Harvard University Press, 1993), p.18.
[40] Ibid., p.56.

to another.[41] What is evident is that this was a period of transition in which Roman civil religion was being translated into Christianity as a civil religion. To define ecclesial heterodoxy was to define political disobedience.[42] For Constantine, God's truth is 'described as Law (*nomos, lex*) a concept which embraces in varying mixtures the laws of nature, the books of the Bible, and the religious system of Christianity'.[43] This increasing conflation of imperial and ecclesial jurisdiction advanced at a time of unprecedented expansion in court life; the development of a new managerial culture. And the Church had fostered a large labour force that was networked, educated (or semi-educated), for the most part disciplined and accustomed to hierarchical organization. We know from accusations against Athanasius that the bishop of Alexandria controlled grain supplies into the country from the Emperor (for distribution to the poor) and out of the country for Constantinople (to forestall riots). Bishops acted as judges, 'presided over the manumission of slaves in church, and they soon began to act as ambassadors. In significant ways the Christian bishop was now outside the normal legal system.'[44] But this new ecclesial prestige did bring with it one requirement that returns us to Eusebius's letter on the Council of Nicaea to his diocese: 'peace being the object which we set before us, and steadfastness in the orthodox view'. That requirement was an

[41] At the Council of Sirmium in 351 c.e Athanasius was accused of high treason for setting the two caesars, Constantius and Constans (Constantinus had by this time been murdered and erased from imperial histories) against each other. See Athanasius's *Defense before Constantius*, written in 353 c.e, chs.2–5. For the historical background of the internal politicking see T.D. Barnes, *Athanasius and Constantinus* (n.39), and David M. Gwynn, *Athanasius of Alexandria: Bishop, Theologian, Ascetic, Father* (Oxford: Oxford University Press, 2012), ch.2.

[42] This is seen most clearly at the Council of Chalcedon later, in 451 c.e. While the congregated bishops were reluctant to issue another definition of the faith (did they not already have the Nicene–Constantinople Creed?), the imperial court and its officers were insistent some 'definition' (Greek *horos*—land-mark) should emerge from the Council in order to bring 'peace' to the Church. For the important consequences and necessary compromises for the Church of this shift towards Christianity as a civic religion see Christos Yanneras, *Orthodoxy and the West: Hellenic Self-Identity in the Modern Age* (Brookline, MA: Holy Cross Orthodox Press, 2006) and Christos Yanneras and Norman Russell, *Against Religion: The Alienation of the Ecclesial Event* (Brookline, MA: Holy Cross Orthodox Press, 2013). According to Yanneras and Russell, this shift led, in the West, to the Roman dioceses as a state, the *civitas vaticana*, and in the East to a series of nationalisms.

[43] Cameron and Hall, 'Introduction' (n.31), p.43. See also Øyvind Norderal, 'The Emperor Constantine and Arius: Unity in the Church and Unity in the Empire', *Studia Theologica*, 42 (1988), 113–50, for a more detailed discussion of Constantine's theo-political vision.

[44] T.D. Barnes, *Athanasius and Constantinus* (n.39), pp.173–4. See also Henry Chadwick's lecture 'The Role of the Bishop in Ancient Society' and Peter Brown's response—both in Centre for Hermeneutical Studies, Berkeley: Colloquy 35, 1980, pp.1–22. Other historians, like Jill Harries, remind us not to overplay changes in the structure and operation of imperial power for Christians: 'Christian communities were not totally revolutionized by the imperial conversion' and the 'bishop's role as judge was to defy categorization in Roman legal terms'—J. Harries, *Law and Empire* (n.31), p.203. In fact, controversies and contentions concerning the nature and limits of episcopal courts rumbled on for centuries to come.

'imperial' orthodoxy.[45] Cities held the key to good governance. As we have seen, they were also sites for power-plays. Mobs could be hired and elections rigged. Riots could be incited and violences, on all sides, could be perpetrated. Peace was equated with civil order—that is, imperial order. Other Christians too, under the authority of the bishop, were appointed to civic and provincial office, particularly in the time of Constantius.[46] Christians as bishops, priests, deacons, and laymen were all corralled into a bureaucratic machinery, with military support, and learnt its ways of speaking.

'Peace' is only one theological word among many that we can map on to a number of intersecting discourses rooted in forms of living that were simultaneously religious, political, economic, social, and cultural. Much is often made of the borrowings and dependencies of these early Christian writers on language used in pagan rites and Greek philosophy, but, since the city and the empire and the Church were all conceived as bodies, then there might be other discursive terrains that could also be explored: medicine and physiology, for example. I might have chosen words that were frequently confused and with important theological implications in the discussions on the relationship between the Father and the Son and God's relation to the created world: *gennētos* and *genēta*. The first is employed to describe the Son as 'begotten' (*gennēthenta*) of the Father (who is *agennētos*—'unbegotten') as distinct from 'made' (*poiēthenta*) or created (*ktisthenta*); the second is used of the creation of things. As one scholar has noted, there are important theological differences and distances registered through these words, whilst also a relation: 'Correlative to God as *agennētos* is the begotten Son, *to gennēma* correlative to God as *agennētos* are all generated things, *to genēta*.'[47] Athanasius, writing against the Arians tries to make clear the theological and semantic differences: 'Therefore, if God be unoriginate (*agennētos*), his image is not orginated (*genētē*), but is the Offspring (*gennēma*), who is his Word and his Wisdom.'[48] But all this semantic shift-shaping, along with clarifications of what kind of a human body the Son took and whether He had a human or a divine soul, is made more complex and the debates around Christology given

[45] The phrase is used by Rowan Williams in the conclusion to his essay, 'Does it make sense to speak of pre-Nicene orthodoxy?' in R. Williams (ed.), *The Making of Orthodoxy* (n.17), pp.1–23 (p.23).

[46] Timothy D. Barnes, 'Christians and Pagan in the Reign of Constantius', *L'Eglise et l'empire au IV siècle* (*Entertiens sur l'antiquité classique* 34), 1989, pp.303–37.

[47] T. A. Kopecek, *A History of Neo-Arianism* (Cambridge, MA: Philadelphia Patristic Foundation, 1979), pp.90–1. The Greek has been transliterated.

[48] Athanasius, *Oration Against the Arians* in *Nicene and Post-Nicene Fathers*, vol.4: *Athanasius: Select Works and Letters*, ed. Philip Schaff and Henry Wace, p.325. Compare this to the 'Mopsuestia Creed' reconstructed and cited in Kelly, pp.187–8 where we have 'begotten [*gennēthenta*] of his Father' as a description of Christ's eternal generation and 'born [*gennēthenta*] from the Virgin Mary'. No distinction between the terms is made, which does not 'correlate' but 'conflates' one creation with the other.

greater understanding when placed in the circulation of discourses about sexual difference and reproduction as it was understood at the time.

The Aristotelian model maintained a notion of sexual distinction between male and female along the lines of active, efficient causality (the male) and passive, material causality (the female). While both contributed seed for the birth, the male seed was understood as both stronger and soul-bearing. Without 'the capacity to supply a sensitive soul ... it is impossible for face, hand, flesh, or any other part to exist. Without the sensitive soul the body was no better than a corpse or part of a corpse.'[49] Athanasius's accounts of the Virgin's conception seem to emphasize this Aristotelian model: the flesh coming from Mary. This still left open the question of the soul. But from the second century there was another model of sexual dimorphism and reproduction also in circulation, by Galen. He espoused the idea that the female was the physiological invert of the male—that females were males who because of a lack of heat were unable to push out the uterus that it might become the penis and the ovaries that they might become the testes. Furthermore, while there was some seed that came from the ovaries, it was insufficient in strength to the male sperm that was the cause of reproduction. Male perfection and the ability to fertilize were both formed through his excess of heat.

Whatever the contestations among medics in the late Antique world what is at stake is understanding the biological operations of fatherhood and, as Thomas Laqueur points out, 'the distinctions of "real" bodies in order to arrive at a notion of fatherhood—the defining capacity of males ... transcends divisions of the flesh'.[50] For present purposes this enquiry into sexual reproduction and its possible impact upon theological accounts of generation and incarnation is not necessary. We do know Galen's approach to physiology impacted upon a number of theologians in the fourth century, in part because medicine was included in a classical education.[51] Patristic theologians, wishing to emphasize the incarnational relationship between the physiological and the spiritual, drew explicitly on available accounts of sense perception and human anatomy: Clement of Alexandria, Lactantius, Gregory of Nyssa,

[49] Thomas Laqueur, *Making Sex: Body and Gender from the Greeks to Freud* (Cambridge, MA: Harvard University Press, 1990), p.30. He is citing Aristotle. See also Aline Rousselle, *Porneia: On Desire and the Body in Antiquity*, trans. Felicia Pheasant (Oxford: Blackwell, 1993), pp.4–46 on conception of the bodies of men and the bodies of women. For an exploration of Athanasius on the generation of the Son, see Virginia Burrus, 'Fathering the Word: Athanasius of Alexandria', *'Begotten Not Made': Conceiving Manhood in Late Antiquity* (Stanford: Stanford University Press, 2000), pp.36–79.

[50] T. Laqueur, *Making Sex: Body and Gender* (n.49), p.31.

[51] See Vivan Nutton (ed.), *Galen: Problems and Prospects* (London: Wellcome Institute for the History of Medicine, 1981) and particularly Michael Frede's essay, 'On Galen's Epistemology', pp.65–84. For the changes effected by the Galen medical camp with respect to the Aristotlean camp, see Joan Cadden, *Meaning of Sex Difference in the Middle Ages: Medicine, Science, and Culture* (Cambridge: Cambridge University Press, 1993), pp.13–53.

Theodoret of Cyrrhus, and Nemesius of Emesa.[52] For my own argument, it is sufficient to demonstrate the way the language of theological doctrine and its exposition was part of wider social and cultural relations (political, economic, philosophical, scientific) and contextualized practices that were not simply liturgical. Both learning the language of the faith and expressions of that faith drew upon a wide range of experiences not reducible simply to the religious, and in this way doctrine, and its shifting understanding, were lived as well as taught.

FROM CREED TO SYSTEM: CYRIL OF JERUSALEM'S CATECHETICAL LECTURES

The systematic arrangement of doctrines constituting the Nicene Creed, like the struggles to gain universal acceptance of a variation of that Creed, cannot be separated from an empire struggling to organize, govern, and define itself. '[A]fter 325 . . . Christian identity was in need of redefinition, now that the persecuted Church had come to power.'[53] Creeds were part of that redefinition. More generally, as we will see in Chapters 2 and 3, new developments in systematic theology are frequently associated with a redefining process that is social, cultural, and political. As we have seen, both the arrangement of doctrine and the organization of imperial administration were operations aiming at peace and human flourishing (*salus*). They sought to provide a framework for everyday life and a belief–system that made that life meaningful; they sought to develop a Christian *paideia*. As Averil Cameron and Stuart G. Hall conclude, 'It is best . . . to accept Constantine's attachment to the Christian God and to Christ as the response of one deeply committed to his imperial calling, who adopts and patronizes Christ precisely because he seems to bring 'salvation'—victory, that is, prosperity and peace.'[54] The systematic theology that arose from the making of orthodoxy was as much an imperial as an ecclesial project, a moral as well as a cultural project. It is not that Christian theology entirely lacked order prior to the creed—Clement of Alexandria's *Stromata* and Origen's *De Principis* were both attempts at ordering a body of Christian teaching—but now 'system' had become necessary as a precondition for ecclesial and political stability. The order of creation (later given detailed exposition by Basil of Caesarea and Gregory of Nyssa)

---

[52] See Susan Ashbrook Harvey, *Scenting Salvation: Ancient Christianity and the Olfactory Imagination* (Oakland, CA: University of California Press, 2006), pp.110–14.
[53] P.W.L. Walker, *Holy City, Holy Places? Christian Attitudes to Jerusalem and the Holy Land in the Fourth Century* (Oxford: Oxford University Press, 1990), p.16.
[54] Cameron and Hall, 'Introduction' to *Life of Constantine* (n.31), p.46.

was organically related to the Trinitarian order of the relationship of God as Creator to his creation, with the work of Christ, the Spirit and the body of the Church (Christology, pneumatology, and ecclesiology) as *topoi* mediating an eschatological destiny. What had begun as flexible rules of faith, morphing into private confessions of Christian belief, after the Council of Chalcedon (461 C.E) had become a public declaration of theo-political allegiance.

The Creed became integrated into the liturgy itself and in 'this way, the creed lost its *ad hoc* character and became a standard and universal point of reference, fixed even in its very wording'.[55] It becomes part of a continuing catechesis, first taught to catechumens prior to baptism and then rehearsed by the congregation within the baptism liturgy. A shift is evident that involves the creation of a new genre in theological discourse, the systematic exposition of the faith. The shift is evident between Eusebius of Caesarea's statement of faith brought to the Council of Nicaea and the first detailed exposition of a creedal proclamation in 348 C.E by Cyril of Jerusalem.[56]

The creed Cyril taught was not the Nicene Creed even in the form it was given at the Council, but it was close. The creed itself was not written down. It was to be memorized and internalized by those about to be baptized in order that they might recite it before the congregation at their baptism. Committing the creed to memory, was the means by which the Christian faith was to be internalized. It was not a matter simply of imparting knowledge, but participating in an ongoing understanding of the teachings of the faith through the practice of that faith—that is, enfolding one's experience of the world within the tenets of its teachings: being formed in and by Christ. Cyril's lectures on the creed were first given as orations. Later they were transcribed and circulated, but we are unsure when and how. They were delivered on or close to the site of Golgotha because Cyril continually emphasizes the location of his teaching. Place is important or becomes important. The metropolitan bishopric of Palestine was Caesarea, not Jerusalem. Jerusalem did not get recognized as autocephalic until the Council of Chalecedon. But Constantine recognized the powerful symbolics of place: of Constantinople as the executive heart of the empire and Jerusalem as its spiritual heart. Cyril, though much younger than Constantine, concurred. Place mattered (literally)—and what it mattered or materialized was holiness. With Cyril, Jerusalem was not simply a place of historical importance. It was a place of theological importance

---

[55] John Behr, *The Way to Nicaea* Vol.2, Part One (n.17), p.151.

[56] Other catechetical lectures followed, not necessarily owing anything to either Cyril or each other: Ambrose of Milan, Theodore of Mopsuestia, and John Chrysostom. For a study of each of these series see Hugh M. Riley, *Christian Initiation: A Comparative Study of the Interpretation of the Baptismal Liturgy in the Mystagogical Writings of Cyril of Jerusalem, John Chrysostom, Theodore of Mopsuestia and Ambrose of Milan* (Washington, DC: Catholic University of America Press, 1974).

because of the universal *salus* that had been won here and the transformation to be affected in the consummation of the New Jerusalem. Place for Cyril evoked. Time here was multidimensional: liturgies translated the present city, re-established by imperial patronage and the building of the Basilica, back into the city of King David and the city where Christ was crucified and buried, and forward towards the city that was to come down from above at the consummation of the age. Time zones were crossed and recrossed as they bent into each other. As such, Jerusalem as a place was an aid to sanctification because it was an intensification of the holy. It was a site of God's presence, of sacramental and ontological value.[57] A Stargate, if you will.

Cyril's teaching of the faith was conducted within the church. Material space—built with magnificence by Constantine and housing both Golgotha and the Resurrection tomb. It was a place where the physical bodies of the communicants, the city as a civic and military corporation, the Eucharist and the theological body of Christ overlapped and interwove.

What is significant about the *Catechetic Lectures* is that of the eighteen given, it is only from lecture VI that Cyril expounds the theology of the creed he is teaching. The creed then, and the systematic theology issuing from it, is not a stand-alone declaration. It cannot be separated from the overall catharsis necessary as liturgical preparation for admission into belief. *Lex credendi* cannot be separated from *lex orandi*; nor, and I will say more about this in Chapter 4, is *lex credendi* a 'second order' reflection upon *lex orandi*. The practices of prayer and liturgical participation embed the teaching—mentally, spiritually, and corporeally. Each lecture moves towards a concluding doxology and the engraving upon the heart of what is delivered is understood as foundational for a continuing, Spirit-led, Christ-centred, Trinitarian pedagogy. As Cyril puts it in a 'Procatechesis' introducing the course of lectures: 'Prepare thine own heart for reception of doctrine, for fellowship in holy mysteries.'[58] The doctrine is part of a reception into a holy fellowship. And although it will require a voluntary and intellectual assent, it is received into the heart. As with the sacrament of baptism itself, doctrine is a means of grace. It is, to use a phrase used much later by Aquinas, 'holy teaching' that disposes those who are taught towards sanctification (which is a formation in Christ). Doctrine is a therapeutic operation upon the senses, the mind and the heart that facilitates the shift from Catechumen to Believer. 'Thou art

---

[57] For much more on Cyril's theology of place (and its distinctiveness from Eusebius' theology of 'holy sites'), see P. Walker, *Holy City, Holy Places?* (n.53). Cyril not only developed liturgies for pilgrimage and the spirituality of holy places, but building on a long Biblical tradition he made Jerusalem the first major 'heritage centre'.

[58] Cyril of Jerusalem, *The Catechetical Lectures*, trans. Edwin Hamilton Gifford, in *Nicene and Post-Nicene Fathers*, vol.7, eds. Philip Schaff and Henry Wace (Peabody, MA: Hendrickson Publishers, 1994), p.5. (The Greek text can be found in *Patrologia Graeca* vol.33.)

transplanted henceforth,' he tells them, 'among the spiritual ... made partaker of the Holy Vine.'[59]

Before, then, any doctrinal content is expounded, Cyril prepares them for the *salus*, the salvation, the healing, that is to take place. It is in fact already taking place for those who are receiving his words in a correct manner since the conversion, the *metanoia*, the repentance is a turning to Christ in enquiry. Lecture II concerns that 'turning towards' and it is mainly an exposition of examples from the Hebrew Bible of those who made that same turning to God themselves. The *exempla* are illustrative, but while a rhetorical technique *exempla* have also theological import with respect to conversion. The Patristic scholar, Lewis Ayres, has demonstrated how, in *Confessions*, '*exempla* constitute ... an initial step towards the refashioning of the soul' because 'the faithful practise their faith through imitation ... *Exempla* engage the reasoning faculties of the soul and thus shape the inner man.'[60] As stories received and memorized, they aid the shaping of desire and prepare the heart not just to receive the *sacramenta* but also to experience the sacramental in which the physical is recognized as also spiritual, the temporal as also eternal.

Lecture III introduces the sacrament of baptism. Again, Cyril's discourse is shaped by a series of *exempla* taken from Scripture, first from the Hebrew Bible and then from the Gospels. In this way he is inserting the Catechumen into God's story—a narrative of divine dispensation and providence. It is a Trinitarian story culminating in section 14 in Jesus's baptism that explicitly references the operations of the Father and the Spirit on the Son. But again what is striking is how Cyril enfolds those listening to him into a Trinitarian ontology: 'To Him belongs the "is", since He is always the Son of God ... He eternally "is", but thou receivest the grace by advancement [*ex prokopēs*].'[61] The Greek noun *prokopē* certainly means 'progress' or 'advancement'. But it is related to the verb *kopeō* that means 'to manure'—the *pro* is a prefix adding a sense of direction, even 'in favour of'. So what seems to be suggested here is 'growth' through fertilization and feeding. This rhetorical and theological enfolding then moves into an anticipation of their future state—'[a]ngels shall dance around you'[62]—and into Cyril's own doxological prayer. The Catechumens are brought into the very heart of the creed and its systematic theology though they have not been given either at this point. They are introduced into the way the creed and its theology are lived, before the content of what always remains 'holy mysteries' is disclosed.

[59] Ibid., p.7.

[60] Lewis Ayres, 'Into the Poem of the Universe: *Exempla*, Conversion, and the Church in Augustine's *Confessiones*' *ZAC*, vol.13, pp.263–81, pp.274–5.

[61] Cyril of Jerusalem, *Catechetical Lectures*, in *Nicene and Post-Nicene Fathers*, eds. P. Schaff and H. Wace (n.58), p.17.

[62] Ibid., p.18.

Lecture IV delivers 'The Ten Points of Doctrine', opening with the observation that the way of sanctification, the pedagogy of godliness, consists of both 'pious doctrines, and virtuous practice'.[63] One cannot be divorced from the other, for perfection lies in their dialogical operation: faith seeks understanding that greater faithfulness and so deeper understanding will follow. Understanding is a following after, a training, a discipleship. It becomes clear that what Cyril is inaugurating and creating is a pedagogical regime; an order, a discipline that educates and structures sensibilities through movements within the embodied soul. His rhetoric is both performative and generative. Playing upon their imaginations, he conjures not only descriptions of the eschatological state—'Henceforth thou art planted in the invisible [*noēton*—spiritual, intellectual] Paradise'[64] and 'enrolled in the armies in heaven'[65] [IV.37]—but what I would call a communal desire; the shared affect of an emotional community. This desire is key to the regime, it operation and its success. The bishop sat on his throne in the cavernous basilica with the candidates around him listening and entering imaginatively and emotionally into his vision of the kingdom.[66] There is an imitation, a mimesis, a passing on, a communication. What is personally experienced is socially shared. The bishop and the laity are bonded in the interpersonal communication that operates in, through, and with the all materiality of the basilica space, upon the soul as the *pnoē* [breath] of God; the soul as the image of God's Spirit as *pneuma*. Sound circulates, enters those who are receptive, and shapes thoughts, imaginings, and feelings. As such, this speech–act, in the basilica built upon the place where Christ was crucified and the tomb from which he was resurrected, anticipates the sacramental communion by bringing those who are listening into a foretaste of the body of Christ and the New Jerusalem. It is *not* the sacramental communion for these auditors are, as yet, unbaptized. Nevertheless, they are caught up in the dynamics of God's providential love as it works outwardly upon their ears and inwardly through their imaginations and the motions of the soul. It is this Trinitarian dynamic that will bring them to the sacramental communion, is in fact bringing them—for the communion is that nexus of interpersonal and Trinitarian relations. The pedagogical regime disciplines and reorientates the senses[67] and the appetites towards a piety that fashions various social behaviours. Its end is virtuous

---

[63] Ibid., p.19.   [64] Ibid., p.7.   [65] Ibid., p.28.

[66] For a broader discussion of the relationship between rhetoric, teaching and listening, Carol Harrison, *The Art of Listening in the Early Church* (Oxford: Oxford University Press, 2013), particularly chapter 4, 'Catechesis: Sounding the Theme', pp.87–116; also Carol Harrison, 'Augustine and the Art of Music' in Jeremy S. Begbie and Stephen R. Guthrie, *Resonant Witness: Conversations between Music and Theology* (Grand Rapids, MI: William B. Eerdmans, 2011), pp.27–45.

[67] Speaking of the fruitful olive-tree in Psalm 52.10, Cyril explains that this is 'an olive tree not be perceived by sense, but by mind [*ouk aesthētēt, alla noēti*]' [I.4].

discipleship through orientating the believer in, through, and towards worship. Its *telos* is ethical life.

We must add another level here so that we might appreciate more fully
how Cyril's teaching operates, and the theology of that operation. As a recent
scholar on Cyril observes: 'Cyril repeatedly emphasizes the voice of the
instructor.'[68] As I said, the creed promised to the neophytes is delivered orally
and they are explicitly told not to write it down. In the final lecture (XVIII.33)
they are told to tell no one of the instruction, the *disciplina arcani*, they have
received. In the catechesis which followed their baptism, conducted throughout Holy Week, and an example of which is found in Cyril's much later work
Mystagogic Catechesis, they are also explicitly reminded not to reveal the
teachings and practices of the Church concerning the sacramental 'mysteries' to those outside the church—not even to the Catechumens. The temporal
auditory effects of annunciation are to resonate in the memory.

The emphasis on the vocal reaches its climax at the Easter Eve Vigil and
the rite of initiation. In the darkness before dawn, those at the second stage
(between Catechumen and Believer), the *photizomenoi* (those being illuminated), assemble in the basilica and face west into the obscurity of the cave of
the crucifixion. From that obscurity a voice calls upon them to stretch forth
their arms and renounce Satan. It is only when they have done this that they
can turn east towards the rising sun and the site of the resurrection tomb
(the Anastasis). Then they walk towards the baptistery and strip naked. This
immersion within a liturgical materiality is continued as their bodies are
anointed with holy oil and they descend into the waters. On being baptized
they emerge and are given a white robe, then anointed again on the forehead,
ears, nostrils, and chest, this time with a perfumed holy oil (*muron*). The initiation rite sought to be 'awe-inspiring'; that is, it sought to evoke human wonder
at the incomprehensible depths of the Godhead.[69] Throughout his lectures,
Cyril demonstrates a 'concern for the emotive power of the liturgy'[70] in which
all the senses are engaged. The pilgrim known as Egeira, who witnessed the
Easter liturgies in Cyril's time around 380 C.E, describes the interior of the
cathedral, observing its ornate decoration: the gold, the silks, the embroidery,
sacred vessels, candles, candelabra, incense, the cries and groans of the congregation, the recitation of Scripture and the singing of Psalms and hymns as
they encounter that which transcends them. Listening to and following the
voice is part of an elaborate, theatrical, participative and profoundly theological pedagogy.[71] What Cyril defines as the sound structure of the teaching in

---

[68] Edward Yarnold, *Cyril of Jerusalem* (London: Routledge, 2000), p.39.

[69] For a more detailed appraisal of these rites, see Edward Yarnold, *The Awe-Inspiring Rites
of Initiation: Baptismal Homilies of the Fourth Century* (Slough: St. Paul Publications, 1971).

[70] E. Yarnold, *Cyril of Jerusalem* (n.68), p.51.

[71] See *Egeira's Travels*, trans. John Wilkinson (Oxford: Aris & Phillips, 3rd ed., 1999).
Scholars have drawn attention to the way Cyril draws upon the rites and rhetoric of the pagan

the way dogma is joined together systematically[72] is of a much lesser concern. The explicit teaching is governed by an overriding sense of the apophatic and an anagogical experience of that which cannot be spoken and cannot be known.

So while Lecture IV details the ten points of doctrine that provide a summary of the creed (that has still not been given to them), what is interesting and significant is the lineaments of a theological anthropology and a moral theology that follows the ten points and concludes the lecture. The anthropology and moral theology has the body as its central focus; for it is this body that will be resurrected (sections 30 and 31) and washed through baptism (section 32). The regime, which includes reading the Scriptures, aims at keeping the soul safe, cultivating Christ-like virtue through embodied practices, and protecting both body and soul from 'every diabolical operation'.[73] And, once more, instruction becomes exhortation and exhortation issues into an exordium that introduces a doxological ascent. The auditors are raised towards their heavenly crowns and encompassed in a vision of the eternal glory of Christ.

I am emphasizing here the way the theological teaching engages with material culture, human sensing and affections, the sacredness of the place, the complex temporal interweave of the place and the ecclesial space, encouraging participation. Participation in the divine is made visceral through sensory reception: hearing the voice of the speaker, seeing the light of candles, being touched by the sign of the cross and the water of baptism, tasting the salt given as a preliminary to admission, and smelling the scents of olive oil, incense, and the perfumed oils. The senses receive these impressions internally as they remain foundational for any knowledge or truth, but Christians were led towards understanding and recognizing their spiritual significance. And so, in a pedagogy of the senses, the spices of the baptismal ointment release the allusive and enchanting scent of Paradise that reforms the senses and the soul. *Apokatastasis*: 'a total renewal which brings about a return to the original paradisiac state.'[74] This was the incorruptible smell of creation

---

mystery cults and without any embarrassment, despite his clear criticism and refutation of paganism. 'The very terms "mystagogic" and "mystagogy" are borrowed from the pagan mysteries'—E. Yarnold, *Cyril of Jerusalem* (n.68), p.53. For a reconstruction of the Easter liturgies and Egeira's travelogue see J. Drijvers, *Cyril of Jerusalem* (n.38), pp.72–95. Cyril's use (both theologically and liturgically) of pagan mystery religions and the ascent towards true illumination or Gnosis can be found much earlier of course in work of Clement of Alexander. In *Protrepticus,* while disassociating the Greek mystery cults from Christianity (1–2), he draws extensively on the language of such cults for the development of his own account of Christian formation.

[72] *Procatechisis* (Yarnold's translation) in E. Yarnold, *Cyril of Jerusalem* (n.68), p.11.

[73] Cyril of Jerusalem, *Catechetical Lectures*, in *Nicene and Post-Nicene Fathers*, eds. P. Schaff and H. Wace (n.58), p.28.

[74] John H. Van Engen, 'Images and Ideas: The Achievements of Gerhart Burian Ladner', *Viator* 20 (1989), 85–115, 103. We will be meeting Ladner's influential work on 'reformation' throughout Part One of this volume.

that only Adam and Eve before the Fall had ever known—of flowers and trees, of rain water and fruit, of feathers and fields: the incense of the Kingdom. This was understood (and being understood recognized) both as the presence of God and the odour of sanctity. 'Fragrance and its source provided [Cyril of Alexandria] analogies for consubstantiality, incarnation, and hypostatic union within the Godhead, as well as for the way the human person could have knowledge of or participation in the divine while still preserving the complete distinction between divine and human natures.'[75] The participation involved a certain attunement or alignment of self with community, ritual with nature, and each facilitated an encompassing, spiritual envelopment that could be imaginatively appropriated and lived, but not intellectually plumbed. 'The scents of worship heralded the life-giving breath of the Holy Spirit.'[76] Participation here *is* revelation (see Chapter 4 for the way revelation comes to be distinctively understood as *in itself* a founding principle in modern theology, divorced from praxis and participation). 'Through the process of sanctification, the liturgy taught not only *how* to experience God with the body, but further, *what* to experience.'[77] Imaginations are fired, liturgical movements are performed, and the world outside (its seasons, its history, light and darkness) is enfolded into the world inside, written on the body and formed within the heart. The episcopacy of Jerusalem developed an elaborate stational liturgy in which holy sites and churches erected on or near them formed the basis for ceremonial processions that publicly and literally took possession of the topography beyond the Constantinian basilica: 'Processions going through the streets of Jerusalem and moving from one sacred site to another were an essential part of the presence and visibility of Christianity . . . Jerusalem's urban space became ritualized in this way.'[78] With Cyril we see the mobile frontiers between the historical sites, the reading and exposition of the Scriptures, doctrinal teaching, ecclesial liturgies, and spiritual operations.

We need not enter the lectures that explicitly treat each of the creedal formulas. The point has been made: the manner in which the truth that the body experiences becomes the truth that refashions the soul. 'For since a human being is twofold, being a composite of soul and body, the purification also is twofold: incorporeal for incorporeal, and bodily for the body. And the water purifies the body, and the Spirit seals the soul',[79] Cyril tells the neophytes. In

---

[75] S. Ashbrook Harvey, *Scenting Salvation* (n.52), p.118. Harvey reminds us that 'Corporeality and incorporeality were both forms of material existence' (p.102), for a number of fourth century theologians.

[76] Ibid., p.89.   [77] Ibid., p.62.

[78] J. Drijvers, *Cyril of Jerusalem* (n.38), p.77. For a more detailed account of some of this 'street theatre' see also John F. Baldovin, *Liturgy in Ancient Jerusalem* (Bramcote: Grove Books, 1989), pp.45–104.

[79] Cyril of Jerusalem, *Catechetical Lectures*, in *Nicene and Post-Nicene Fathers*, eds. P. Schaff and H. Wace (n.58), p.15.

the *Mystagogic Catechism*,[80] with respect to the Eucharist, Cyril writes: 'for as the bread corresponds to our body, so is the Word appropriate to our soul'.[81] The focus of his pedagogy, this *paideia*, is that the sensed becomes the spiritually sensuous: sweat glistening in the pre-dawn darkness of Good Friday in a procession of a thousand candles streaming down from the Mount of Olives to the Garden of Gethsemane. Sweat on the foreheads and the bared arms of those enrapt. And the pre-baptism anointing of olive oil on naked flesh, smoothed into intimate spaces. The point of the structured theology, as Cyril himself states in Lecture VI when he is about to begin his theological exposition of the creed, is to glorify the Lord, not to explain him: 'For we explain [*ezēgoumetha*—teach, interpret] not what God is but candidly confess that we have not exact knowledge [*ouk oidamen*] concerning Him. For in what concerns God to confess our ignorance is the best knowledge'.[82] His engaged systematics is orientated not primarily towards knowledge (though there will be understanding), because God is the Unsearchable and His works incomprehensible. Cyril's engaged systematics is oriented towards a pastoral and liturgical pedagogy that finds its fulfilment in doxology.[83]

When he begins his more detailed commentary upon the articles of the creed, from Lecture VI on *I believe in One God* to Lecture XVIII on the *Holy Catholic Church, the resurrection of the flesh, and the life everlasting*, he relates them to their roots in the Hebrew Bible and New Testament. Rarely speculative, rarely philosophical, rarely allegorical in his readings of the Scriptures, the creed is returned to texts in the Bible from which it drew its language and its authority. The present (and those present) is caught up with the whole of living history as the Bible records it. The creed can almost seem like a mnemonic

---

[80] There have been debates over the authorship of the *Mystagogical Catechism* since a manuscript with 'J' [John of Jerusalem, Cyril's successor] written on it was catalogued in 1574. We need not enter these debates because attribution has no impact upon this argument here. A detailed study of the authorship can be found in Alexis James Doval, *Cyril of Jerusalem, Mystagogue: Authorship of the Mystagogic Catecheses* (Washington: The Catholic University of America Press, 2001). Doval decides in favour of Cyril's authorship. The quotations from the *Mystagogical Catechism* are also taken from *Nicene and Post-Nicene Fathers*, vol.7, ed. Philip Schaff and Henry Wace (Peabody, MA: Hendrickson Publishers, 1994).

[81] A.J. Doval, *Mystagogical Catechism* (n.80), p.152.

[82] Cyril of Jerusalem, *Catechetical Lectures*, in *Nicene and Post-Nicene Fathers*, eds. P. Schaff and H. Wace (n.58), p.33.

[83] Ibid. There seems to be a hesitancy in Cyril towards theological contestation—even at time when such contestation is very much to the fore with the Arian controversies. In the Vth of his *Catechetical Lectures* when he explains how the teaching he is delivering will be a protection from heresy, the heretics named are the Jews, the Samaritans, and the Pagans. His sacramental theology, always insisting upon the material world, explicitly counters Gnosticisms, as does his Logos-Christology. But he does not mention the Arians. Some have thought this is because he was himself an Arian or semi-Arian sympathizer, but his late work, the *Mystagogic Catechism*, written after or around the Council of Constantinople 381 C.E shows him to be a defender of *homoousios* as much as Athanasius.

for an account of divine providence itself. For Cyril is not, like Origen earlier and Gregory of Nyssa later, searching the texts for their pneumatic meaning, rather (as he emphasizes in Lecture XVI and XVII on the Holy Spirit) he stays with the historical and literal sense, leaving the Scriptures to communicate their own spiritual meaning through the Spirit who is 'the True Enlightener'[84] and the 'great Teacher of the Church' (XVI. 19).[85] But the sole aim is doxology and an *anagogē* oriented towards the *monarchia* or divine unity of the Godhead. 'Ascend, I say, in imagination even unto the first heaven, and behold there so many countless myriads of Angels. Mount up in thy thoughts, if thou canst, yet higher; consider, I pray thee, the Archangels, consider also the Spirits; consider the Virtues, consider the Principalities, consider the Powers, consider the Thrones, consider the Dominions',[86] but 'inquire not curiously into [God's] nature or substance'.[87] Cyril seems to place his faith for the transportations and *morphoses* of his congregation in communication itself—both divine (through the Holy Spirit 'who gives wisdom of speech, Himself speaking, and discoursing')[88] and his own divinely inspired rhetoric. And thus the system and order of the creed itself becomes the vehicle for a participation in which those being illuminated glimpse their true destiny, eternal life. Deliberated upon, the creed performs a preparation of the soul to 'enjoy its spiritual and heavenly mysteries' and 'discover in each particular the greatness of the gifts bestowed on you by God';[89] it is part of a practice in the true *paideia*—the cultivation of a very Greek understanding of education that furnished the aesthetic, moral and religious values that best delivered the common good.[90] One could say that 'orthodoxy' for Cyril was less a matter of obedience to Nicene doctrine than of right worship.

CONCLUSION

We have learnt the language of the faith and the rules that govern its articulation, and we have found among its words the words of many other

---

[84] Cyril of Jerusalem, *Catechetical Lectures*, in *Nicene and Post-Nicene Fathers*, eds. P. Schaff and H. Wace (n.58), p.119.

[85] Ibid., p.120.   [86] Ibid., p.121.   [87] Ibid.   [88] Ibid., p.118.

[89] Ibid., p.142.

[90] The observation by Johannes Hoff on the way the uniqueness of Christianity in premodernity did not rest on 'revelation' or doctrine, but on the 'unifying dynamic of the body of Christ' is pertinent here. '[T]he creed did not function as a unifying *doctrinal* principle. Rather it was used as a *symbolon* in the literary Greek sense of this word—as an access code to the "body of Christ".' 'The Rise and Fall of the Kantian Paradigm of Modern Theology' in Peter Candler (ed.), *The Grandeur of Reason: Religion, Tradition and Universalism* (London: SCM Press, 2010), p.183.

languages: social, political, economic, and cultural. It's an old language, passed down to us through many mouths, renewed every time it is spoken afresh—and we continue to try and understand its grammar and vocabulary as it lives within us and shapes our thoughts and actions. We come to live within that language as we too now pass it on, differently. It is a language that runs deep and is stippled with many motivations. It fashions dispositions. And it is our language, a human language, replete with human limitations. But God created us that we might speak, and our language was spoken by the Word in and as Christ. It is a language that can take the impress of the divine—we can prophesy, and pray, and dream, and bless. It is more than just doctrine; it is life. God did not just enter our world. He entered our words; the words through which we compose our worlds. We learn the language of the faith because He spoke that language to us first and His Spirit leads us into all truth. Christ breathed in the world and breathed out the Holy Spirit. That's where our redemption begins; there, with the faith it inspires.

Nevertheless, we have learnt that the language of the faith, theology, is never pure; it is never innocent; it is never free from being ideological. It is written and spoken by human beings not angels; human beings embedded deep within very human situations, personal and collective. But it can be made to appear pure, innocent, and free from ideology in a Eucharist in the cathedral when the congregation turn east to sing the Nicene Creed or in a candlelit Evensong after the choir has sung a setting of the *Nunc Dimittis* and all turn east to affirm the Apostles' Creed. What an engaged systematic theology attempts to do is map and investigate and own the complexities of theology's discursive power. But it also attempts to do something more positive: to expose the various discursive grids out of which theological reflections emerge in order to inform and cast theological articulations in a new light. This may enable us to see what we hear differently, creatively. For we do yearn for the pure; we do yearn for the true. Through all the complexities and in all the vicissitudes of human existence we hunger for pure love, true religion, righteous judgement, and unspoilt beauty. Why is this when this innocence and simplicity is not what we find, not what we know, not what we recognize in the world around us? We will come to our own lost state soon. For now we smell the layers of the past as we sit in the pew and gaze at the embossed ceiling, and it is not nostalgia—for nothing is gone; nothing is remembered; nothing is regretted. There is nothing we wish to return to. There is no sadness; only a recognition of a deep, deep belonging and an equally deep, deep difference that presences itself in the carved features of an angel or a green man.

2

Summa

THE SEARCH FOR A NEW IDENTITY

The cathedral we entered in the opening of the last chapter had Anglo-Saxon origins, as I said. But the walls that compose it today are medieval. The stones were quarried, sawed into blocks and rough-filed in order to be fitted together by labourers working for the Austin canons around the tomb and the relics of a more ancient saint. The construction was part of a larger movement at the time of building in the Romanesque and later Gothic style. It was a new establishment in which the doctrine of the faith was reshaped, and learnt in different ways through liturgical changes, the meditative and studious practices of the cloistered quad, and the settled ways of Christians living together in community. The project was informed by a vision of the kingdom of God, a relation between Church and world, positioned close to but outside the high walls of a defended, fortressed town. It was a project that was to last until the kingdom came, each generation adding its own structures and design in a process stretching towards a future unseen. It remains unfinished.

Simply to name them today—after Marcel Proust has imaginatively recomposed northern France for us—is to walk through the fields lined with hawthorn in *Du Côté de Chez Swann* and to enter towns like Cambrai, Reims, Chartres, Bec, Angers, Tours, and Laon. These were medieval cathedral towns (except for Bec, where there was an abbey) in which schooling in theology was first systematically pursued; although 'theology' and 'theologians' were novel words in the early decades of the twelfth century. The conventional word for the intellectual study of God was 'divinity'.[1] Divinity concerned itself with reading the Scriptures; theologians, on the other hand, 'proceeded by reasoning from first principles'.[2] The Greek word *theologia* was available, and had been used earlier, but it was in the twelfth century that 'theology' and the profession of being a 'theologian' in the sense we have of these terms

---

[1] M.T. Clanchy, *Abelard: Medieval Life* (Oxford: Blackwell, 1997), p.264   [2] Ibid.

today emerged as one of the dominant characteristics of the twelfth century renaissance.[3]

We must not underestimate what was achieved here: it was, as the medieval historian R.W. Southern has shown, nothing less than the intellectual unification of western Europe that followed a time of conquest and invasion, insecurity and change.[4] The foundations for this vision of unity were laid in the teaching of the liberal arts, theology, and later canon law and 'the whole system, in its assumptions, its sources, its methods and its aims, expressed a coherent view of Creation, of the Fall and Redemption of mankind, and of the sacraments whereby the redeeming process could be extended to individuals'.[5] This is where our story of the journey from the *summa* to systematic theology must begin, and it is important to tell this story in order to situate the project being undertaken here within a context that makes evident both its distinctiveness with respect to those previous attempts to organize the 'rule of faith' as creeds, and also its continuity with them.

The painting of St. Jerome in his study by Antonello da Messina can help us. We'll meet it again in Chapter 7. Here it is the architecture framing the saint that draws our attention. It resembles a gothic church. Its windows and the light which floods the staged study emphasize that scholarship takes place semi-publicly. As I said, other than Bec, the schools of the eleventh and twelfth centuries that fostered early systematic theological teaching and writing were housed and supported by cathedrals. There was then a close relationship between civic life and intellectual enterprise. Intellectually, the human spirit was opening itself anew to the natural world, its history and its materiality. 'In the schools and in the streets and field's of men's minds had already been awakened the attentive observation of reality', the French ecclesiastical historian Marie-Dominque Chenu informs us.[6] As the urban environment developed through new techniques of production and commerce, as urban stone edifices began to appear, so a new 'religious metaphysics ... defined man as artisan (*homo artifex*) in relation to God's creative work (*opus Creatoris*) and the work of nature (*opus naturae*). The relationship to God's creative work conferred a religious significance upon human productive activity.'[7] This was

[3] Hugh of Saint-Victor in his *Didascalicon*, Book 2, ch. 2 comments upon the Greek term citing Boethius and Isidore of Seville: 'theology' means 'discourse concerning the divine' that 'with deepest penetration [discusses] some aspect either of the inexpressible nature of God or of spiritual creatures'. *The Didascalicon of Hugh of St. Victor: A Mediaeval Guide to the Arts*, ed. and trans. with introduction and notes, Jerome Taylor (New York: Records of Western Civilization: Sources and Studies 64, 1991) pp.62–3.

[4] R.W. Southern, *Scholastic Humanism and the Unification of Europe* (Oxford: Blackwell, 1997).

[5] Ibid., p.3.

[6] M.-D. Chenu, *Man, Nature, and Society in the Twelfth Century*, trans. Lester K. Little (Toronto: University of Toronto Press, 1997), p.10.

[7] Ibid., p.40.

a time in northern France when the population, trade and civic administration were expanding. Life teemed into medieval sides streets, the shambles, surrounding and pressing in upon the cathedral; the shops and market stalls that spilled over on to the cathedral pavements and steps. Secular life was becoming more esteemed, a new class of merchants was disturbing the older estates and these people brought with them new circulations of money and practices for its minting and storage (the strong-box or *archa*). Theology was taught in the cathedral schools, but it was thought through and lived in the streets and taverns of the towns.[8]

Hugh of St. Victor, in his famous treatise on the liberal arts, *Didascalicon*, delights in detailing the various forms of fabric making, armaments manufacture, trade in domestic and foreign goods, and even the 'science of entertainments' (which he called 'theatrics') that might keep people 'from coming together at public houses'.[9] Composed in Paris in the late 1120s, this is an appreciation of the new urban environment and all the contemporary arts and crafts that served humankind and their salvation. No form of knowledge was to be excluded from Hugh's pedagogical programme that sought to not simply train but form theological minds. The schools were serving local, diocesan, and increasingly royal and papal needs. Clergy who had undergone study of the trivium (grammar, rhetoric, logic) and quadrivium (mathematics, astronomy, geometry, and music), and later, theology, were able to function as executive administrators and managers in an ecclesiastically dominated civil service and legal system. This was especially so at a time when what was a broadly federal Church under the provincial administration of archbishops, bishops, and secular rulers (with the Pope as an ultimate but rather distant authority) was becoming a much more centralized Church with a uniform faith and a strong hierarchical organization (with the papal Curia at its operational apex).[10] It was a time also when the secular and the sacred were encountering each other in ways that blurred the former boundaries between the clerical and the lay. A renewed interest in the *vita apostolica* fostered lay communes and confraternities like the Humilitiati in northern Italy. This emerging urban class pursued lives of poverty and devotion which challenged, as the schools and mendicant

[8] We might note here that the relationship between city-living and theological discourse was not just a medieval phenomenon. The father of modern theology is often viewed as being Frederick Schleiermacher, and there is a strong correlation between his theological work and civic life in Berlin. See Graham Ward, 'The Making of Modern Theology and the Metropolis' in Nicholas Adams, George Pattison, and Graham Ward (eds.), *The Oxford Handbook of Theology and Modern European Thought* (Oxford: Oxford University Press, 2012), pp.61–82.

[9] *The Didascalicon of Hugh of St. Victor*, J. Taylor (n.3), pp.74–9 (p.79).

[10] At the Council of Rome in 1059, Pope Nicholas II set out a new procedure for papal elections that were now to be in the hands of the Cardinal–bishops and excluded the Emperor who had earlier had an important role to play.

orders also were challenging, the older feudal monastic ideals. In turn, the evangelical enthusiasm fuelled a strong anticlericalism. Amidst the growing complexity that had arisen from centuries of different codes of practice, different interpretations of Bible and creeds, different traditions and customary ways of handling matters, and archaic, labyrinthine modes of ruling, judging and deciding matters, there was a need for collation, recovery, harmonization, and reconciliation; a 'rationalization' even in today's management speak.[11] One of the first recoveries was the Latin language itself. Without the universal employment and development of Latin as the *lingua franca* of western European government imperial, ecclesiastical, and royal there would have been no Christendom.[12]

But there is something more we have to recognize in the architecture of these cathedrals, that also tells us something about social life and its relation to theology at that time. What still are today the astonishingly tall perpendicular upper windows, the elaborate tracery of their frames and their number, were all set high in the buttressed walls and, unlike in the painting by Messina, the doors were not flung open but rather heavily protected. The windows, reaching up to the vaulted gallery and clerestory, the fanned, barrelled or hammerbeam ceilings, were not windows upon the city as such, like the plate-glass transparency of more modern buildings. The light coming into the church could be immense, as we might witness at York Minster or Ely Cathedral, and set the pale sandstone or limestone ablaze. But it came in at a high level. On the more human scale, along the walls of the transepts, the ground windows, where there are any, are much smaller, like arrow slits through which archers shot. At the level at which all the offices and services within the church took place, the walls were thick, solid, and mainly windowless with doors of solid oak which firmly kept the outside world outside. In this way the walls resembled more the curtain walling of Medieval castles or the walls built around the town itself. We can again still witness this at York. No church-attendee, unless they climbed the tower in the manner of Victor Hugo's imagined refugee, Quasimodo, describing medieval Paris from the towers of Notre Dame—no church-attendee could view life in the city from where they stood to observe Mass being said.

The architecture, Romanesque or Gothic, is indicative of two states of affairs at the time. The first is that despite the cessation of invasions and conquests, the lands of France, Italy, and England were far from being stable. While many

---

[11] It is no coincidence that England, following the Norman Conquest by a people unfamiliar with the various languages and customs of the country, sent a number of men to be trained in the French schools in Latin and imported a number of others who had either been trained or had themselves been masters, like Anselm for example.

[12] The employment and development of vernacular languages had been on the increase in Europe prior to the eleventh century.

historians will speak of the twelfth-century Renaissance,[13] others will draw attention to dynastic anxieties, tyrannies, Saxon revolts, unrest over papal lands, the murders of Charles the Good in Flanders and Thomas á Beckett in England. In part, these were new disturbances caused by the economic and demographic changes: 'Violence, disorder, stress: the problems of traditional powers in western medieval lands arose chiefly from societal growth and change ... There was a confused old head on this young body, addled with conflicting venerable views of world order that had been incompletely reconciled in the compromise over investitures.'[14] The twelfth century was a time of rapid political development. Culturally, an emphasis can be found on order and hierarchy that was at once political, ecclesial, cosmic, and spiritual. If the theology that emerges appears optimistic in the grace-assisted overcoming of sin and aspirations that reached towards beatification, the dynamic behind the restoration was still insisting upon obedience and discipline. Being systematic was not only a theological project—it was the principle for social and political stability. Order was guaranteed by power, whether lay or spiritual. Secondly, while opening out and responding to the new civic and commercial life, theology was separated off from secular (in the medieval sense of that word) pursuits. Novitiate teaching at places like Saint-Victor and Sainte-Geneviève in Paris took place in the cloisters. Despite the growing evangelistic communities of lay people, probably because of them, both architectural and theological *poiesis* reflect here the growing separation of the clerical from the lay that followed the decree of the Roman council of 1059 making clerical celibacy mandatory for clergy above the rank of deacon. It was a separation the later Gregorian reforms and the extensive deployment of Latin encouraged. The impulse for reform was also an impulse towards the organization of ecclesial government (with respect to the powers exercised by newly organized lay government) that had its impact on the organization of the faith itself. Creeds gave way to elaborate systems as the world became reshaped.

SCRIPTURE AND THE REFORMING
OF THE WORLD

The theological and ecclesial changes that came in the wake of the reform impulse set new cultural and spiritual standards, new ideals. 'Throughout

---

[13] The most well known account of this 'renaissance' is R. N. Swanson, *The Twelfth Century Renaissance* (Manchester and New York: Manchester University Press, 1999).
[14] Thomas N. Bisson, *The Crisis of the Twelfth Century: Power, Lordship, and the Origins of European Government* (Princeton: Princeton University Press, 2009), p.9.

twelfth-century Europe, calls to reform stirred a wide range of people: not only monks and canons, but bishops, popes and the laity as well. Ideals of reform, their sources and their translation into both new and renewed modes of religious life, are subjects central to understanding the period.'[15] *Reformatio* was not merely understood institutionally (as a cleaning up or a clarification of pastoral practices and ecclesial functions), it became the central axis upon which a new theology of salvation was constructed. A new language for what it was to be a Christian emerged; to learn this language was to see the world in a new and ordered way. This soteriology drew together reflections upon the operative power of the Trinity, upon Christ as the Wisdom of God and His incarnation, upon human beings as plastic and fashionable under the restorative powers of grace, and upon the Church as participating in and as an extension of the mystery of life in Christ.[16] The *ratio* of restoration in Christ and through Christ developed an organic and dynamic approach to doctrine, its organization, its teaching and its role in the formation of 'the perfect man who loves what he believes'.[17] A balanced set of Latin clauses sums up a certain relation to the 'rule of faith' at this time: '*credamus quod diligere debemus, et diligamus quod credimus*' [that we may believe what we are bound to love and we may love what we believe].[18] Doctrine is caught up with the disciplining of desire such that it is impossible which is to have priority, the teaching or the desiring. The significant verb here is *debere*—to be obliged to, to be bound to, to be indebted to: belief and love are intrinsically related to and determine each other. True doctrine was a matter and consequence of right loving; and right loving was worked out and worked itself out in right living, virtue.

The word *universum* becomes frequent at this time: the world is one and it has a structure despite its seemingly unending multiplicity and mutability. This belief in the world's oneness was accompanied by a search for the overriding organization of all things human. And both the belief and

---

[15] Margot Fassler, *Gothic Song: Victorine Sequences and Augustinian Reform in Twelfth-Century Paris* (Notre Dame, IN.: University of Notra Dame Press, 2nd edition 2011), p.187. See also Giles Constable, *The Reformation of the Twelfth Century* (Cambridge: Cambridge University Press, 1996), p.45 on the application of *renovatio, reformatio, transformatio, reversio,* and *recreatio* to several writers of this period.

[16] See Jean Châtillon, *Le Mouvement canonical au moyen âge: réforme de l'église, spiritualité et culture* (Paris: Bibliotheca Victorina 3, 1992), pp.306–7. The Church as the body of Christ is understood to be inseparable from the salvific work of Christ in the world.

[17] Hugh of St. Victor, *De Arca Noe Morali* (*Noah's Ark*) 4.8. *Patrologia Latina* 176. 674. In *The Theology of Hugh of St. Victor: An Interpretation* (Cambridge: Cambridge University Press, 2010), Boyd Taylor Coolman takes Hugh's allegorical reading in his treatise 'Noah's Ark' as indicative of the architectural model that dominates his theology of spiritual formation. Hugh speaks of God as a craftsman (*artifex*) and the Holy Spirit as an artisan (*opifex*), and exhorts novices to regard the practices of stone-masons. Learning the language of the faith is a craft; the novice undergoes an apprenceship.

[18] Hugh of St. Victor, *Quid vere deligendum sit. Patrologia Latina* 177, 564–5.

the search were governed by a theological vision; a vision being examined, taught, and demonstrated through schools with ecclesial foundations. 'The order and disposition of things from the highest even to the lowest in the structure [*compage*—joined together] of the universe so it follows in sequence . . . that of all things that exist none is found unconnected [*nihil inconnexum*] or separable and external by nature,' Hugh of Saint-Victor wrote.[19] The *nihil* is an Augustinian echo of that from which the networked universe—*inconnexum*—was created. It's an echo also picked up by Arnold, Abbot of Bonneval, near the great cathedral school of Chartres, who wrote rapturously of the cosmic unity evident in the *Book of Genesis*: 'God distributed the things of nature like the members of a great body, assigning to all their proper places and names, their fitting measures and offices. Nothing is confused in God [*Nihil apud Deum confusum*].'[20] The language of being joined together is Pauline; Paul uses it in his letters to the Colossians and Ephesians to describe both the church and marriage. Disorder, confusion, and the chaotic were all characteristics of Fallenness; a state which is opposing God attempts to reverse *creatio ex nihilo*. The vision of God-created order in the world was of His goodness, justice (fittingness), beauty, and reasoned truth. Order itself was salvific, as was conformity to that order in terms of obedience and the exercise of discipline. Human beings were created, it was believed, with an in-built capacity to understand the nature of creation. This understanding was endemic to being human because they were the very centre of this ordered creation. Between the angels and the animals, human beings provided a microcosm of the created macrocosm, such that 'in coming to know the world he comes to know himself as well'.[21] This cosmic conception of being human offered new insights into what it meant to be made and then, in Christ, remade, in the image of God.

The consequence of the Fall (and from that Fall, original sin), as Hugh of Saint-Victor understood it, was a 'twofold corruption, namely, the mind with ignorance and the flesh with concupiscence'.[22] Ignorance is then a vice, such that carnal sense 'through corruption of the flesh . . . was deprived of its integrity [*integritate sua privatus est*], it can not drink in pure truth without a confusion of error [*puram sine confusione erroris veritatem haurire non potest*]'.[23] There's that confusion again that we have to struggle to keep at bay, and notice how *confusione erroris* is fittingly sandwiched between the adjective *puram*

---

[19] Hugh of St. Victor, *De sacramentis* I, 2.2. The Latin text is taken from the *Patrologia Latina*, the translation is by Roy Deferrari, *Hugh of Saint Victor on the Sacraments of the Christian Faith* (Eugene: Wipf & Stock, 2007), p.29.

[20] Cited in M-D. Chenu, *Man, Nature, and Society in the Twelfth Century* (n.6), p.9.

[21] Ibid., p.33.   [22] *De sacramentis*, I.7.32, R. Deferrari (n.19), p.133.

[23] Ibid., p.137.

and the noun it qualifies *veritatem*. Truth will eclipse error and confusion, but it involves a labour now, a labour extended over time as we are instructed 'to knowledge of truth through the forms of temporal and visible things'.[24] This is the theological framework for Hugh of Saint-Victor's high regard for pedagogy. So while the Fall damaged the capacity to understand, judge, and read the world aright; while the Fall pulled creation back into the confusion of the primary *nihil*—human beings, created in the image of God, remained open to God's remedial work. And while Hugh details the three forms of such work—namely faith, the sacraments, and good works—these are all activities that take place in the temporalities and visibilities of this world. So that now, following the appearance of Christ and the development of His Church, it was time to recover what had been lost.

A new sense of human intellectual potential and dignity 'promised not only an understanding of the plan of Redemption, but also a capacity to understand the natural universe, and at least in outline, the nature of God and the supernatural orders of being with which mankind is linked'.[25] The schools set about to achieve, slowly and meticulously, this encyclopedic synthesis of knowledge—sifting through the intellectual heritage that had been handed on to them—and their *summae* were the result. Gradually these intellectual labourers were to move out and acquire new sources— unknown works of Aristotle and the commentaries and philosophies of Muslims and Jews. Meanwhile, the Scriptures became the authoritative source text because it was understood to contain all knowledge. 'Since the content of Scripture is encyclopaedic, it calls for encyclopaedic knowledge in the student.'[26] So Hugh's examination of the liberal arts in *Didascalicon* was a preparatory work for the interpretation of the Scriptures, while the interpretation of the Scriptures was a preparatory work for reading the world aright.

READING THE WORLD

There is a new sense of labour: of studying and teaching and being taught. Learning the language of the Christian faith is now explicitly associated with literacy understood widely (so as to embrace both the cleric and his books and the peasant attending mass) as the interpretation of ordered signs. If Christ as the true Wisdom of God was the key to this interpretation (and order), the

---

[24] Ibid., p.138.
[25] R.W. Southern, *Scholastic Humanism and the Unification of Europe* (n.4), p.23.
[26] Beryl Smalley, *The Study of the Bible in the Middles Ages* (Oxford: Blackwell, 1984, 3rd edition), p.26.

Bible was the fundamental text whether in the form of statuary, bas-reliefs, stories in stained glass,[27] or through the words of Scripture.[28] From Origen onwards the Scriptures were recognized as a form of the incarnation of the Logos, the flesh now as sacred text.[29] The pneumatology necessary for the generation of Scripture was equally necessary for the interpretation of Scripture. As Smalley reminds us: 'The Holy Spirit speaks through the mouths of St. Gregory the Great and of St. Bernard of Clairvaux when they expound the Scripture.'[30] The reading of Scripture has agency to effect salvation; it is part of an ontological operation in the economy of the divine.[31]

It is important to understand, first, what is being attended to in approaching exegesis of the Bible and, secondly why, because this understanding has a bearing upon what is being attended to in the arrangement of the Christian doctrine in a *summa*. The text was important, fundamental, but what was being read was the world the text referred to—the objects, persons, history, and events the text attested to. And even these were not the main focus for the attention. These things themselves attested to Christ as the wisdom of God ordering creation in a certain way, operating within history in a certain way, dispensing grace for the salvation, healing, and restoration of all things in a certain way. What was paramount was the work of restoration in and through Christ. The words of the Scriptural text were only one form of signs among many other forms, objects among many other objects, through which the dynamic power of God in the world was recognized and performed. Put simply, interpreting the Scriptures provided a way in which the world could be seen and understood. To read symbolically—where the literal (historical or plain sense) retained symbolic significance accessed through allegorical and tropological readings of the texts—generated a world of symbolic meaning; a mode through which the world was seen and sense was made of it. 'How deeply the spiritual interpretation will penetrate language, thought,

---

[27] See the classic study by Emile Mâle, *The Gothic Image: Religious Art in France in the Thirteenth Century*, trans. Dora Nussey (New York: Harper & Row, 1958).

[28] The classic study of this subject is Beryl Smalley, *The Study of the Bible in the Middle Ages* (n.26). Chapters III and IV are devoted to Hugh, Richard, and Andrew of St. Victor. The Victorines viewed Biblical exegesis and study as a discipline through which formation took place. The most extensive and detailed study of Biblical exegesis in late antiquity and this period is Henri de Lubac's four-volume *Exégèse medieval: les quarter sens de l'écriture* (Paris: Aubier, 1959–64). See Volume III, pp.287–359, for a discussion of Hugh of St. Victor's contribution. *Medieval Exegesis: The Four Senses of Scripture*, trans. E.M. Macierowski (vol.3) (Grand Rapids, MI: William B. Eerdmans Publishing Company, 2009).

[29] Jean Daniélou, *Origène: Le Génie du Christianisme* (Paris: La Table Ronde, 1948), p.74. Texts Origen considered evidently symbolic were directly associated with the Eucharist.

[30] Beryl Smalley, *The Study of the Bible in the Middle Ages* (n.26), p.12.

[31] Jean Châtillon, *Le Mouvement canonical au moyen âge*: 'Between the Scripture and the Church there is an essential rapport that only the allegorical method is able to recognize and which the liturgy expresses' (n.16), p.301. There is no distinction made between Scripture and the Catholic tradition (of its interpretation).

politics, and finally everyday life,' Smalley opines.[32] The attention to the letter was an attention to the material body, the thing the letters signified in becoming a sign. The materiality of letter, word, and text was, of course, much more pronounced in a scribal culture, than in either a print or digital culture where there is an increasing distance from the physical labour of writing and transcribing. In the hands of exegetes of the Victorine school it was only by entering more deeply into the letteral/literal, into the material, that the spiritual wisdom of God might be recognized. In this way exegesis of the Scriptural word could be associated with consecration of the Eucharistic elements.[33]

How and what we see depends upon how we *think* we see (which depends upon how we are taught to see). The world as created by God was a different world because a differently understood world, for St. Paul, Cyril of Jerusalem and Hugh of St. Victor.[34] That understanding will impact upon doctrines of creation and salvation, which impacts upon the way life is lived, the values espoused, and how and what people are taught about that life. The way Scripture was read changed the way the world was experienced. So interpretation of the Bible was not an end in itself. It was implicated in any number of learning processes from the 'little clerk [who] learned his letters from the Psalter'[35] to understanding God's providential hand in history, its moral/pastoral (*tropological*) and its spiritual (*allegorical*) lessons. What emerges is a world that is itself sacramental; the material is symbolic. At every point a code is encountered, symbolically meaningful and symbolically related. Seeing and experiencing that world meant reading it correctly.[36] So reading becomes a craft as much as curing a hide, cooking venison, building walls, and sculpting statues, and the craft was initiated by appreciating what was being looked at and looked for in the material

---

[32] Beryl Smalley, *The Study of the Bible in the Middle Ages* (n.26) p.25.

[33] For an account of how this had implications for a realist understanding the Eucharist in both Paschasius Radbertus and Hugh of St. Victor, and constituted a resistance to over spiritualizing, see B. Smalley (n.26), pp.91–5.

[34] Martin Heidegger taught us the ways in which we continually see the world.

[35] Beryl Smalley, *The Study of the Bible in the Middle Ages* (n.26), p.xxx.

[36] In *De sacramentis* I.10.2, Deferrari (n.19), pp.165–69. Hugh of St. Victor correlates knowledge with three modes of seeing as Augustine did before him. For Hugh, there is seeing with 'the eye of the body' where the world outside is apprehended; there is seeing with the 'eye of reason' whereby what is apprehended is processed cognitively and cogitation itself sees 'those things within itself'; and then there is seeing with the 'eye of contemplation' whereby it sees 'God within itself and those things which were in God'. These three modes of seeing correspond to Augustine's corporeal, intellectual, and spiritual perception. As Boyd Taylor Coolman points out, for Hugh pre-lapsarian humanity possessed a 'perfect harmony between internal and external knowing'—*The Theology of Hugh of St. Victor* (n.17), p.169. Sight of this was lost through sin and had, through Christ, to be learnt again. But both the epistemology lost and that restored require an affective as well as a cognitive appropriation of grace. Love and knowledge cannot be separated.

at hand. The end of apprenticeship in such a craft was apprehending ultimate and universal values: the contemplation of God's wisdom, love and dispensations of grace. The books of Scripture and nature were books of life. The text of living was experienced and in being experienced digested, consumed.[37] The cosmos became liturgical for all things are recognized to by hidden with Christ in God.

THE *SUMMA* AND THE PEDAGOGY OF SALVATION

Neither the Scriptures and their interpretation nor the doctrine that issued thereby were ends in themselves; they were sacramental mediations of the work of Christ both in terms of knowledge and ethical living (love). 'The beginning of doctrine, therefore, is in reading, but its consummation is in mediation [*Principium ergo doctrinae est in lectione, consummatio in meditatione*],' Hugh of St. Victor tells us.[38] This, I would suggest, is another way of describing faith as it seeks understanding. For *doctrina* means 'teaching' and is translated as such by Taylor. *Doctrina* as a distinct object of attention and a substantive—the English 'doctrine'—is a late fourteenth century shift in the use of the word. The Latin *doctrina* is a description of a process, a practice, or the art of making someone learned—in line with the Greek understanding of *paideia*. Its consummation is 'mediation'. *Meditatio* here is not at all what we might understand after years of yoga practices and various forms of Buddhism. Hugh tells us that 'mediation' is sustained intellectual activity, cogitation: '*Meditatio est cogitation frequens*'. It is a prudent (that is, critical) investigation (*prudenter investigat*), seeking clarity. Its *telos* is gazing upon the 'wonders of God [*Dei mirabilia*]'.[39] Meditation is detailed, close study that is not trying to evacuate thought of content or transcend mind altogether. It is rather that intensive examination of content by the intellect. It is a practice of entering the world more deeply, not escaping it. For in entering into a reading of the texts of the world, most particularly Scripture, one enters into a participation in the mind of Christ, God's Wisdom. *Meditatio* is, then, being theological as a form of prayer. It is thinking deeply, where cognition is embodied; it is dreaming deeply. We will return to theology as deep dreaming in Chapter 5.

What is certain is that teaching requires schools and schools require textbooks. The origins of modern systematic theology lie in providing

---

[37] On the movement from Scripture, its memorization, the mediation it invoked and the moral formation it enjoined see Boyd Taylor Coolman, *The Theology of Hugh of St. Victor* (n.17), chapters 6, 7, 8, and 9.

[38] *Didascalicon*, III.11 (n.3), (Patrologia Latina) (n.19).   [39] Ibid.

textbooks for these new urban schools and later the universities of Paris and Bologna.[40] It emerges with a new attention to education. We will see this again with Philip Melancthon and dogmatics (Chapter 3)—a different understanding of what it is to education that produces different textbooks and different ways of presenting the Christian faith systematically. For Hugh, the Bible remained the central authority as revealed truth for all knowledge, and the monastic tradition had literally covered the Biblical texts with glosses that were eventually compiled into the famous *Glossa Ordinaria*. At the heart if not the origin of this compilation was Anselm of Laon, and new approaches to the systematic teaching of the faith arose through reading and commenting upon Scriptural glosses. 'The function of the schools was to collect, clarify and arrange biblical interpretations of the past, just as it was their function to collect, clarify and arrange the whole body of Christian doctrine and elucidate its consequences for human behaviour.'[41] In this way the schools facilitated the uniformity of faith and its practice throughout Europe. As Smalley points out: 'all the teaching of theology at Laon consisted in lectures on the *sacra pagina*.'[42] From these glosses *quaestiones* arose which led to a developing split between exegesis and systematic theology as the *quaestiones* took on an independent textual existence.

As we saw in the last chapter the Apostolic and Nicene Creeds provided summaries of the faith, the articles of faith. They provided a general structure in four main divisions: God as creator, salvation in and through the life and work of Christ, the activity of the Holy Spirit, and ecclesiology. One of the earliest *summae* we have is that by the Oxford theologian Robert Pullen. He had studied in Laon and then returned to Oxford to lecture. Begun between 1133 and 1139 (and therefore earlier than Peter Lombard's famous *Sententiae* written around 1150), Pullen's *Sententiae* follow roughly the creedal structure: the doctrine of God; Creation and Fall; Redemption; Man's place in the universe; Baptism; Marriage; Confession and Absolution; and Eucharist.[43] But Oxford was not, at that time, the place to launch a major work. Paris was increasingly becoming the scholastic centre of Europe, its reputation drawing students from beyond Europe. It was in Paris that Peter Lombard taught and produced the textbook that, much later in Oxford (around 1240), was rumoured to have replaced the Bible in

---

[40] It has been said that the first *summa theologiae* is John Damascene's *De Fidei Orthodoxa*. St. John of Damascus, *Writings: The Fount of Knowledge: The Philosophical Chapters, On Heresies, The Orthodox Faith*, trans. Frederic H. Chase Jr. (Washington: The Catholic University of America Press, 1958), pp.165–406.

[41] R.W. Southern, *Scholastic Humanism and the Unification of Europe* (n.5), p.118.

[42] Beryl Smalley, *The Study of the Bible in the Middles Ages* (n.26), p.73.

[43] For a more detailed account of this work see Francis Courtney, *Cardinal Robert Pullen: an English Theologian of the 12th Century, Analecta Gregoriana*, 64, 1954.

morning lectures.[44] Lombard's *Sententiae* were organized into four books and both summed up and glossed the doctrines of the faith found in the two primary texts of Biblical instruction, the *Psalms* and the Pauline Epistles. The first book was dedicated to the doctrine of God and the mystery of the Trinity; the second book treated creation; the third book the incarnation of the Word and redemption; and the fourth book was on ecclesiology, especially the seven sacraments, and the four last things (death, judgement, heaven and hell). We can see how closely he is following the structure of the creeds[45] and this becomes important for the development of an explicitly theological, rather than Biblical order.

The first major work governed by this theological rather than Biblical order was Peter Abelard's *Sic et Non*, the final version of which dates from 1132 although it began as early as 1120. Robert Pullen's work was directly responding to what he saw as Abelard's doctrinal heresy. *Sic et Non* was an arrangement of quotations from the Church Fathers on doctrinal issues in a manner that encouraged two educational methods developed by the schools: the *quaestio* and the *disputandi*. The 158 questions Abelard raised were supported by sets of contradictory answers found in the Fathers. The theological order is again mainly creedal, though it opens with four questions concerning faith itself. Then, in succession, there is: the doctrine of the triune God, the divine nature and attributes; creation and the fall; the incarnation and redemption; and the apostolic church which treats also the sacraments of Baptism, Eucharist, and Matrimony. A further set of twelve final questions on the nature of charity, grace, law, and sin completes the volume.[46] What was most alarming and original about *Sic et Non* was that Abelard gave no resolutions for the contradictory and juxtaposed citations he collected. The theological method aimed an invoking questions and disputes, and advancing an understanding of the faith through such a method. The text was an occasion for discussion, contestation, and the exercise of human reasoning; more like the script for a drama that would ensue. We will return to Abelard later.

Cardinal Robert Pullen was not the only theologian working to counter the effect of Abelard's teaching. Foremost among the theologians who countered

---

[44] On the Bishop of Lincoln's (Robert Grosseteste) letter of complaint to the theological masters of the university see R.W. Southern, *Scholastic Humanism and the Unification of Europe* (n.4), pp.103–4.

[45] Two recent studies have brought the work of Peter Lombard increasingly to scholarly attention; both are by Philipp W. Rosemann. The first is *Peter Lombard* (Oxford; Oxford University Press, 2004) and the second *The Story of the Great Mediaeval Book: Peter Lombard's 'Sentences'* (Peterborough: Broadview Press, 2007).

[46] See John Marenbon, *The Philosophy of Peter Abelard* (Cambridge: Cambridge University Press, 1997) and, for the influence of Abelard on other scholars such as Gratian, see D.E. Luscombe, *The School of Peter Abelard* (Cambridge: Cambridge University Press, 1969).

and corrected Abelard's errors prior to Pullen was Hugh of Saint-Victor.[47] This is not in itself surprising given the polemical offences that Abelard had launched against the founder of the Augustinian canons of Saint-Victor, particularly his former teacher (and who became Hugo's own teacher), William of Champeaux. William of Champeaux had been a pupil of Anselm of Laon, where, as I said, the teaching of theology and the exegesis of *sacra pagina* maintained their inseparable association. Hugh built upon this foundation. If Hugh had already attempted, in his *Didascalicon*, the systematizing of the liberal arts, then in his volume *De sacramentis* (circa 1132) he takes this labour one step further with respect to the Christian faith and his is the first of the great *Summa* of the twelfth and the thirteenth centuries. As the medieval historian David Knowles has pointed out, *De sacramentis* 'became the grand-mother of all the *Summae* of the following hundred years'.[48]

HUGH OF SAINT-VICTOR'S DE SACRAMENTIS

We have noted already that Hugh is concerned with order. There it was cosmic order and the pedagogically disciplined labour of coming to know. But in the composition of a systematic theology, the theologian is always faced with the questions of where to begin and why. We have seen, and will see further, various orders for the arrangement of the knowledge of the Christian faith, and in the light of these orders I will propose and justify my own arrangement. Order for Hugh is not just about structuring knowledge; neatly arranging doctrines as a series of interrelated propositional claims. Order for Hugh is related to rule, a right ordering, and reason—a theo-logic founded in God's own Wisdom. It is related also to discipline and theological method, to pedagogy as spiritual formation, to discipleship. The doctrines, and the relationship between them, are to be lived that they might be known: *doctrina* as a craft of making someone learned. As Boyd Taylor Coolman, in his study of Hugh's theology, observes with respect to meditative practices and *allegoresis*: 'At the very least this language [of building a structure within one's mind] gestures at the profound way in which meditative *allegoresis* entails an interiorization of theological thought, a personal appropriation of doctrine . . . The doctrinal construct is neither "ready made", nor an external system of

---

[47] For an interesting discussion of Hugh of St.-Victor's sacramentalism and realism with respect to Abelard's 'modal extremism' see Peter S. Dillard's analytical approach in *Foundation and Restoration in Hugh of St. Victor's* De Sacramentis (New York: Palgrave Macmillan, 2014), pp.43–63.

[48] David Knowles, *The Evolution of Medieval Theology* (New York: Ransom House, 1998), p.143.

doctrinal propositions disconnected from the believing exegete, remote from his lived experience.[49] While order need not be necessarily related to hierarchy,[50] order gives significance to one theological loci in favour of another in terms of what is being constructed, following from what came before, and with a view to what will be built upon later.

Order is related to government, and even justice. Hugh explicitly associates the order of creation as 'disposed in the way of justice'.[51] This is quite a distinctive approach to creation *ex nihilo*.[52] The recovery of recognizing the order, as an expression of both divine wisdom and divine *iustitia*, is the work of salvation and formation. Here, as with the word 'peace' that we examined both theologically and politically in the last chapter, we are concerned with learning a discourse. As the historian Thomas Bisson has shown, France at this time, along with most other countries now constituting Western Europe, was only just beginning to achieve a functioning government and judiciary. Law was based in 'custom', but frequently the extortion of monies or the ransack of estates and the filching of property was 'not by custom but by violence'.[53] New customs were often imposed, arbitrary violence by armed militia was regularly experienced as the jostle for lordship at the heart of a huge power struggle between kings and feudal counts, dukes and barons, made the exercise of sovereignty and the establishment of public order very difficult. There were only five juridical texts known across Europe between 1060 and 1150, but while 'they purport to address whole societies' there is no pretension that they had any 'legislative force'.[54] 'As late as Charles the Good, when records of curial judgments first multiply, there is no diplomatic of justice. Scribes wrote charters recording settlements or judgements, but not *iudicia* per se. Moreover, *iudicia*, however recorded, are very exceptional before about 1111.'[55]

The mention of the 'scribe' returns us to Hugh's theological exposition of divine *iustitia*, for these 'scribes' would have been trained either in the monasteries or the schools. The order Hugh of St. Victor announced (and he was not alone in this),[56] the 'way of justice and discipline',[57] was the

---

[49] Boyd Taylor Coolman, *The Theology of Hugh of St. Victor* (n.17), p.179.

[50] For an illuminating account of *ordo* and *hierarchia* in twelfth century theology and the influence of Pseudo-Dionysius, see M.-D. Chenu, *Man, Nature, and Society in the Twelfth Century* (n.6), p.80, fn.60.

[51] *De sacramentis*, I. Prol.3, Deferrari (n.19), p.4.

[52] See Peter S. Dillard, *Foundation and Restoration* (n.47) for an analysis of Hugh's understanding of creation *ex nihilo* compared to that of John Scotus Eriugena (from whom Hugh borrowed certain ideas), pp.27–41.

[53] Thomas N. Bisson, *The Crisis of the Twelfth Century* (n.14), p.136.

[54] Ibid., p.194.   [55] Ibid., p.149.

[56] See Roger Baron, 'L'Idée de liberté chez Anselme et Hugues de Saint-Victor', *Recherches de Théologie Ancienne et Médiévale*, 32 (1965), 117–21, for a comparison between Anselme and Hugh on justice and freedom.

[57] *De sacramentis*, I. Prol.3, Deferrari (n.19), p.4.

redemptive and restorative counterpart to the indiscriminate and arbitrary violences of 'custom' in the hands of any number of incipient and pretended lordships. His was not just a theology for the classroom, because several of those taught would have careers within the various baronial, ducal, and regal *curiae*. All of them would have had to position themselves with respect to kings, bishops, feudal families like the Senlis and Gardland, and deep conflicts between the old order and reform. Major property was at stake. In 1133 the abbey's royal patrons murdered the Prior of St. Victor for supporting the bishop of Paris and disregarding royal interests.[58] Hugh's teachings announced the way the Church might serve and service the world in the name of Christ and inculcate an ethical living beyond the monastery and into public life.[59]

Furthermore, it had been the Church that had preserved two other forms of law that became increasingly important in the unification of Europe: the Roman law of Justinian (the *Corpus iuris civilis* that would become the basis for civil law) and canon law (emerging from the glossators). The early twelfth century at Bologna saw work begin on providing Justinian's text with glosses and *apparatus*; the codification of canon law came much later.[60] The 'order' and 'justice' Hugh was seeking and teaching was conceived as providing universal structures through the Church for the world and its restoration. Gregory VII introduced the reformation of the Church, Hugh of St. Victor and theologians like him were facilitating the translation of that *reformatio* into an urban programme. It was nothing less than the fashioning of Christendom as a pan-European self-identification.

What is being attempted through Hugh's systematic ordering and relating of Christian theological *loci* is the articulation (and imitation in a strong sense of that word) of the operations of the divine; an articulation of the wisdom in such operations and the disposition of the created world for such a wisdom. In other words, the arrangement of the articles of the Christian faith in a systematic theology has itself a purpose; to mirror a divine design. For Hugh and those theologians of the twelfth century preoccupied with the universe, its unity and its singularity, order was an aspect of God's Providence, the operation of God's grace, and also the structure of creation itself. The purposeful ordering of *De sacramentis* is salvific, what one commentator (with respect to *Didascalicon*) has

[58] For an examination of this highly political dangerous context of change see Margot E. Fassler, *Gothic Song* (n.15), pp.187–210 and Robert-Henri Bautier, 'Les Origines et les premiers dévoloments de l'abbaye Saint-Victor de Paris', in *L'Abbaye Parisienne de Saint-Victor au Moyen Age*, edited by Jean Longère (Biblioteca Victorina, I. Turnout, 1991), pp.23–52.

[59] For Hugh of St. Victor's vision of the church as it arose from the tense political situation see Margot E. Fassler, *Gothic Song* (n.15), pp.211–40.

[60] For an account of these two processes see Hermann Kantorowicz's 'Note on the Development of the Gloss in the Justinian and Canon Law' in B. Smalley, *The Study of the Bible in the Middle Ages* (n.26), pp.52–5.

called 'an *effective* order or sequence of readings'.[61] And although this effective order had a pedagogical function for the students Hugh was teaching, such a pedagogy cannot be separated from both spiritual and ethical formation: reading and thinking as forms of meditation such that there might be a progress from what Hugh terms 'plain being to blessed being'.[62] 'Hermeneutic progress is progressive restoration and salvation.'[63] In this way Hugh's theological exposition is closely associated with his anthropology; an anthropology itself closely associated with his cosmology.[64]

Hugh does not follow the structure of the Christian faith in the Creeds. His orientation is far more biblical, but it is a theological presentation of the bible. Hugh's commitment is to history[65] and so *De sacramentis* is an early exposition what German Old Testament scholars in the 1950s called *Heilsgeschichte*. In an important section in Book I of *De sacramentis*, Hugh asks and answers the question 'Whether faith has changed according to the changes of the times'.[66] He concludes: 'let us not doubt that from the beginning through the succession of the times faith has grown in the faithful themselves by certain increases. Yet that faith of the proceeding and the subsequent was one and the same, in whom, however, there was not the same cognition [*eadem cognitio non fuit*], we thus unhesitatingly confess, just as in these whom we recognize as faithful in our time we find the same faith and yet not the same cognition of the faith [*non eamdem fidei cognitionem invenimus*].'[67] The verb *invenire* is interesting because it denotes not just the passive recognition, but the active discovery and acquirement. The theological and effective ordering of the Christian faith then has to accord with historical change; but it is a history orientated towards a future fulfilment.

That history for Hugh had a twofold structure (which mirrors the two books composing his treatise: creation or the foundation (*conditio*) and restoration (*restauratio*). Hugh's theological exposition of the Scriptures, the threefold dialectical method for that exposition (the literal/historical, the allegorical or doctrinal, the tropological or moral/spiritual) and the selection made among the Scriptures themselves are all framed by this structure. If this means that 'the inner-Trinitarian concepts and terms can seem tangential',[68] then it is

---

[61] Paul Rorem, *Hugh of St. Victor* (Oxford: Oxford University Press, 2009), p.28 (emphasis added).

[62] *Didascalicon* (n.3), p.54.   [63] Paul Rorem, *Hugh of St. Victor* (n.61), p.55.

[64] See Dominique Poirel, *Livre de la nature et débat trinitaire au XIIe siècle: le 'De tribus diebus' de Hugues de Saint-Victor* (Paris: Bibliotheca Victorina 14, Turnhout, 2002), p.261.

[65] See Grover Zinn, '*Historia fundamentum est*: The Role of History in the Contemplative Life According to Hugh of St. Victor' in *Contemporary Reflections on the Medieval Christian Tradition: Essays in Honor of Roy C. Petry*, ed. George H. Shiver (Durham, NC: Duke University Press, 1974), 135–58.

[66] *De sacramentis*, I, 10, 4, Deferrari (n.19), pp.173–8.   [67] Ibid., I.10.7. pp.177–8.

[68] Paul Rorem, *Hugh of St. Victor* (n.61), p.72.

because Hugh was responding to the cultural emphases of his time in urban Paris—the material universe, human psychology, and the historical boundedness of human existence.[69] He was also reacting against a raft of technical and philosophical terms for thinking through the nature of the Trinity which Abelard and his disciples were developing; though Hugh is not averse to some of these terms (probably culled from Boethius and John Scotus Eriugena) like causation.

At the centre of *De sacramentis*, as the axis upon which world history turned, and as the theological heart of Hugh's theology, is the incarnation of Christ. This is the longest section of the treatise and it opens Book II (while Book I details the creation of the world). If Book I concerns nature, then Book II concerns grace. But while there are two books, one examining creation and the other restoration, Hugh carefully avoids a sense of rupture. There is a radical, historical, and theological shift with the incarnation but it is part of a providential plan and a divine dispensation such that consummation is the fulfilment of creation even in its pre-Fallen condition. Creation, governed first by natural law (up to Moses), and subsequently by the written law (up to Christ) is governed now by grace. But however radical the shifts there is continuity such that graced living in and through Christ proceeds from the continuous flow of God's love, mercy, and goodness. There is a 'secret disposition [*secreta. . . . dispositio*] in the consummation of the good'.[70] With the incarnation all things enter into Christ more profoundly. The human soul, by *imitatio* is lead to *conformatio* such that sanctification is the realization of Christ's justification. Justification by faith is profoundly related here to participation in the Godhead and the economy of continuous flowing grace.

Hugh understands 'sacraments' (which was wider than the more ecclesial understanding of the sacraments which came later and followed a distinction between 'sacrament' and 'sacramentals') as efficacious signs, with an analogy between the material signifier and the spiritually signified, for the dispensation of God's grace. Sacraments were part of the divine dispensation from the beginning and continue throughout, though becoming more Christ-focused and ecclesially mediated following the incarnation, death, and resurrection. In Hugh's exposition of the opening chapter of the *Book of Genesis* attention is drawn to 'marriage' as a God-given sacrament prior to the Fall. And following the Fall God provided so-called 'sacraments of salvation' under both the natural law (like oblations and tithing)[71] and under the written law (like circumcision, the Sabbath, and the temple).[72] These earlier sacraments were

---

[69] See M.-D. Chenu, *Man, Nature, and Society in the Twelfth Century*, 'Theology and the New Awareness of History' (n.6), pp.162–201.

[70] *In Eccl.* Cited in Coolman (n.17), p.92.

[71] *De sacramentis*, I, 11, 1-9, Deferrari (n.19), pp.182–7.

[72] Ibid., I.12, 1–24, pp.187–204.

shadows of what would be fully realized by the coming of Christ: 'For the passion of the Saviour, which in the first place, sanctifies sacraments of grace to effect salvation (*effectum salutis*), through the medium of those sanctified also by those sacraments of earlier time so that salvation was the same both for those who by right faith venerated the signs of the future in the earlier sacraments and for those who receive the effect of salvation (*effectum salutis*), in these.'[73] Incarnation is intimately therefore associated with dynamic and creative energies of *effective* sacraments: 'The work of restoration is the Incarnation of the Word with all its sacraments, both those which have gone before from the beginning of time, and those which come after, even to the end of the world.'[74] Here is an operative, providentially disposed Word, the Wisdom with God from the beginning and through whom the world was created, in which the faithful participate.

The theological order of Book I interleafs a biblical exposition of creation and the Fall into disobedience (Parts 1, 2, and 6) with an historical account of life under the divine dispensations of natural law and written law, a doctrine of the triune God (Parts 3 and 4), the creation of the angels (Part 6), human beings, animals and the natural order, and an important discourse on the nature of faith. In an interesting foreshadowing of Calvin, it is faith (examined as a sacrament in Part 10) that is the created dynamic in the effectiveness of the sacraments (outlined in Part 9 and examined in detail in Parts 11 and 12). Entrusting response to the sacraments constitutes the necessary 'works' accompanying and expressing faith. It is faith that facilitates the restoration through grace, already begun immediately following the Fall (Part 7).

We can begin to notice Hugh's obsession with numbers as reflective of divine order—the triune God takes up Part 3, restoration begins in Part 7 (echoing creation in 6 days + the 1 day on which God rested), faith occupies Part 10 (an important number comprising 3 + 7 and associated with the ten commandments) and concluded in Part 12 (the perfect ecclesial number for the twelve tribes of Israel and the twelve Apostles).[75] He was not alone in this arithmetical obsession; it was an important characteristic of biblical exegesis at the time and a key to the way the Book of Nature and the Book of Scripture were correlated. Attention to the symbolism and correlations of number gave history not only its theology and purpose (as part of the economy of salvation), it gave history its sapiential design. The six days of creation, which corresponded to the six days of the human working week, became, for Hugh, the six epochs (*aetates*) of history itself—in this way both distinguishing and correlating time in nature and the time of human action (history itself). The

---

[73] Ibid., I.11, 2, p.183.   [74] *De sacramentis*, Prologue II, Deferrari (n.19), p.3.
[75] See Hugh's deliberation on the number four, its relation to the soul in *Didascalicon* (n.3), ii.iv pp.64–6, the body v, pp.66–7 and the *quadrivium* (instruction in arithmetic, music, geometry, and astronomy) in vi, p.67.

sixth age was the age of the incarnation—just as humankind came into being on the sixth day.

If Hugh keeps this theology of history within the limits of the Scriptural record, others who followed after him did not.[76] An examination of the time of the Church, from the Roman Emperor Augustus, to Constantine and then Charlemagne as the new Roman Emperor, issues into the first uses of the word 'modern' (*aetas moderna* or *modernitas*) in the twelfth century. What Aquinas would call 'revelation conceived as a system of pedagogy'[77] would furnish new messianic, eschatological, and even apocalyptic notes. Hugh did not speculate beyond his Scriptural limits, but in turning his back upon classical understandings of history as cyclic (a move already announced by Augustine),[78] towards an evolving dispensation of God's grace, he became an early exponent of the rise of the west over the east. Western flourishing was part of a divine dispensation that ushered in a new twilight in which the parousia would occur.[79] Rupert of Deutz, Anselm of Havelberg and, finally, Joachim de Floris would develop this eschatology in a Trinitarian direction, declaring three ages, two of which were over (the ages of the Father and the Son) and one of which was now the age of the Church (the age of the Spirit). Now the kingdom of God and the Church (and the Holy Roman Empire in some quarters) were synonymous. All this was to follow Hugh's transformation of Scriptural exegesis into the organized discipline of systematic theology. For Hugh what remained central was that despite epochal shifts in divine providence there was continuity: a sacramental dispensation with time conceived as progressive human activity from things visible to things invisible.

Book II of *De sacramentis* opens with Hugh's doctrine of Christ and salvation. Its focus throughout is the incarnation. He returns us to his earlier account of the Trinity, emphasizing Christ's 'sending' by the Father. There are moments here when a psychological analogy drawn from being human is transposed and put to work in an account of intratrinitarian relations. But the moments are few and any similarities are countered by repeated phrases such as 'we are not permitted to discuss' or divinity is 'ineffable'. Hugh's continual

---

[76] See Isabelle Guyot-Bachy, 'Les victorins et l'histoire: des maître sans disciples?' in *Bibliotheca Victorina XXII: L'École de Saint-Victor de Paris*, actes réunis par Dominique Poirel (Turnhout, Belgium: Brepolis: 2010), pp.179–96 for more details on this matter.

[77] *Summa Theologiae* IIa, IIae. q.1, a.7, ad. 2.

[78] See Augustine, *City of God*, trans. Henry Bettenson (Harmondsworth: Penguin, 1984), xii.14, pp.487–9. He emphasizes time is progressive for Christians—a progressive pilgrimage into the eternal. See also Richard Morris, *Time's Arrow: Scientific Attitudes towards Time* (New York: Simon & Schuster, 1985), pp.23–4 for an overview of ancient and medieval understandings of time.

[79] See Hugh of Saint-Victor, *Noah's Ark*, iv.9 and *The Vanity of the World* ii. For translations see *HUGH OF SAINT-VICTOR: Selected Spiritual Writings*, trans. and ed. Adred Squire (New York: Harper & Row, 1962).

appeal to Scriptural exegesis and his call to pray and meditate that there might be a greater understanding of what has to be believed, place limits on human reasoning. There is a wisdom in faith that is higher than knowledge but such faith only perfects human reasoning: 'Faith is superior in that its content is much wider than that of reason, but reason thereby does not cease to be an independent source of knowledge.'[80] Hugh's recognition of this, in part, is aimed at countering speculative and philosophical analyses of the divine through categories drawn from human nature found in Abelard[81]—though it was a generation of Abelard-inspired thinkers who developed such analyses to the point where a technical vocabulary developed a scholasticism leaving *sacra pagina* far behind, questioning revelation and exalting rational methods. 'Scholastic objectivity robbed traditional *meditatio* of its ends and dynamism,' Chenu observed.[82] The problem with Abelard's method, and the scholastic approaches it encouraged, was that the distinction between grace and nature all but disappears. Not only does a Pelagianism ensue but a spectre of ontologism arises in which, it might seem possible to know God directly by unaided human reasoning. Hugh's theology steers strongly away from either such Pelagianism or ontologism by being consistently orientated towards prayer and meditation, as in the tradition of the monastic *lectio divina*—the exegesis of and commentary on Scripture. But in the pursuit of the meaning (*sensus*) and then the deeper significance (*sententia*), both beyond the study of the *lettera*, then exegesis was giving rise to doctrine and doctrine could then be arranged systematically.[83]

Hugh's *De sacramentis* bears all the signs of a newly emerging genre of theological discourse inseparable from a newly emerging ecclesial confidence in the wake of the Gregorian reformation, and the newly emerging organization of public life across Europe. We can see the system clearly in Book I, ordered doctrinally through an historical exegesis of the Bible. In Book II, the systematic ordering breaks down, as if with the coming of the church nothing further historically can be said until the end of history

---

[80] John P. Kleinz, *The Theory of Knowledge of Hugh of Saint Victor* (Washington: The Catholic University of America Press, 1944), p.100. Kleinz's study provides an excellent account of the 'kind of certainty' that the soul has in faith, which is 'beyond opinion and short of knowledge [*supra opinionem et infra scientiam*]'—*De sacramentis*, I, 10.2, Deferrari (n.19), p.168. He points to the difference between this account of *certitudo* and Abelard's view of faith as *existimatio*. Abelard's questioning begins by putting everything in doubt. For Hugh 'faith is certain because it excludes doubt' (Kleinz, p.103).

[81] 'I first applied myself to lecturing on the basis of our faith by analogy with human reason and composed a theological treatise *On the Unity and Trinity of God*.' Abelard, *Historia calamitatum* in *The Letters of Abelard and Heloise*, trans. Betty Radice (Harmondsworth: Penguin, 1974), p.78.

[82] M.-D. Chenu, *Man, Nature, and Society in the Twelfth Century* (n.6), p.302.

[83] For an account of these three levels of exegesis see Hugh of Saint-Victor, *Didascalicon* (n.3), pp.147–50.

itself: individual human history (Part 16), world history (Part 17) and life beyond death (Part 18). So the incarnation (Part 1) gives way to ecclesiology (Part 2), both bound closely with a participative understanding of the body of Christ, and then into a clutter of discussions on ecclesial offices and power (Part 3), sacred garments (Part 4) and the dedication of a church (Part 5). With Part 6 we come to the first of the sacraments proper, baptism, Part 7 treats confirmation, and Part 8 the Eucharist. These follow a temporal order within the life of a Christian. But the order is interrupted again by discussion in Part 9 of sacramentals (from candles to curtains) and simony (Part 10). If there is a long account of the sacrament of marriage in Part 11, then between this sacrament and confession (Part 14) and the anointing of the sick (Part 15), we are given asides on the nature of vows (Part 12) and on vice and evil (Part 13).

This is not the organic system of the *summae* to come where articles of the faith are subtly expounded and internally related one to another. It is difficult to see Hugh's mathematical pedagogics at work in Book II. There were probably reasons for this. The work was revised over many years and its earlier forms circulated among students. The work is continually responding to the unfolding situation of reform in and around Paris. Book II details much of the ideology of the Reform movement, educating secular clergy in the symbolics of office and liturgy. The chapter on marriage evinces this most clearly. Even so the historical (though not the exegetical) method is clearly compromised or consummated in Book II (depending how you look at it). The overall theme of restoration is never in doubt, but it is as if time stands stills and the ecclesial mechanics—clerical offices and the cycle of liturgical rites—fill a space between the incarnation and the resurrection of the sanctified.[84] The Reformed Church was to be the eschatological Bride of Christ. For a theologian who recognized, in Book I, a development of faith, or at least cognitions of the faith, there seems to be no successive unfolding of the faith in Book II; no bold proclamation such as later Andrew of Saint-Victor would make, that with a living faith there was perpetual discovery (*inventio*), if not progress.[85] Hugh lacks the confidence implied in Bernard of Chartres comment on dwarfs standing on the shoulders of giants. Although Bernard's comment is still a humble recognition of the relationship between Scripture and the tradition of its interpretation, it is not a declaration of war between the ancients and the moderns.

---

[84] Not only theologians perceived time in this way. Honorius of Autun, for example, viewed ecclesial history as composed of five epochs, corresponding the five epochs of the Old Testament: apostles were followed by martyrs, then came the fathers, the monks and, finally, the Antichrist. See M.-D. Chenu, *Man, Nature, and Society in the Twelfth Century* (n.6), p.316.

[85] See the citation and translation of Andrew of Saint-Victor's commentary on Isaiah in Beryl Smalley, *The Study of the Bible in the Middle Ages* (n.26), pp.121–3 and 378–9.

But if we are attentive in Hugh's writing only to the relation of historical exegesis to theological doctrine and, on the basis of such attention, see the awkwardness of the structure of *De sacramentis*, we miss an important element of his pedagogy, the tropological. If the *telos* of his work, the *telos* of the restoration itself (Chapters 16–22 of Part 18 of Book II) is the vision of God, then paralleling the linearity of time is another dynamic, one of ascent. The tropological is intimately related to prayer and meditation upon the Scriptures—it details the pedagogy of the soul. The journey through the sacraments and sacramentals of Book II remains jolting and jerky but it imitates broadly the passage from baptism to last rites, birth to death in Christ. That journeying is correlated to the maturing soul in its pilgrimage towards the vision of God. With the vision of God the tropological, historical and doctrinal come together and find their consummation. The history of our restoration is perfected through and as the Church as the bride of Christ and the embodied souls of all the members making up the bridal body. Our knowledge is made perfect as 'we shall see all knowledge together at one glance [*uno simul conspectus*]' and the destined end of human beings is realized for 'He himself will be the end of all our desires [*desideriorum nostrorum*]', the Christian 'does not wish [*velit*] for more',[86] for we will love as we are loved. Knowledge and love are perfected as the objects of both are recognized as one. *De sacramentis* concludes its Scriptural exegesis then with: 'There we shall call and we shall see; we shall see and we shall love; we shall love and we shall praise. Behold what will be in the end without end! [*Ibi vocabimus et videbimus; videbimus et amabimus; amabimus et laudabimus. Ecce quid erit in fine sine fine*].'[87] The conclusion of the treatise is an invitation to go beyond the rationalism and affectivity of reading, through interpretation of that which is read, to the vision itself of God. The deictic 'There' places us, though at a distance, and the imperative 'Behold' opens our eyes to see and to desire.[88]

In this way *De sacramentis* mirrors the *lectio-meditato* of the *Glossa Ordinarium*, where text of Scripture and it exegesis, the seamlessness of the Bible and the tradition, opens reading to contemplation.[89] Faith grasps the

[86] *De sacramentis*, II.18.20, Deferrari (n.19), pp.474–5. The translation is accurate but misses some of the connotations: of *simul* and God's omniscience (whereby all things are seen and known simultaneously) in which we will participate; the use of the verb *desiderare* which suggests that something has been missing or lacking that we have longed for; and a variation on the verb *volo* which is to wish, but is related to the will (suggesting here the consummation of our willing).

[87] Ibid. II.18.22, p.476.

[88] On the importance of beholding in medieval meditative practice see Maggie Ross, *Silence: A User's Guide* (London: Darton, Longman and Todd, 2014), pp.100–25.

[89] For a fascinating account of the way in which the *Glossa Ordinaria*, compiled over several centuries from the ninth to the twelfth century, 'defies the possibility of the closure of meaning' (p.82) and invites the community of readers to 'a participation in God's self-knowledge' (p.89) through contemplation, see Peter M. Candler Jr., *Theology, Rhetoric, Manduction, or*

unseen as though seen through the seen. Earlier in Hugh's account of the vision of God he had raised the question of the difference between seeing and believing. Things 'present are seen, things absent are believed'. He then adds significantly: 'Indeed it is perhaps enough if by those things present we understand in this place the words which are at hand for the senses either of the soul or the body. Therefore too, when words are uttered they are called present.'[90] Words then mediate between presence and absence, visibility and invisibility—just as Christ as the Word mediates, by being God's utterance, God's presence to human beings; just as the Scriptures mediate witness and testimony through their liturgical utterance in the Church.[91] And now Hugh adds his glossary to those Scriptures, mediating also, through his own utterance, things absent and yet present.

Here is a performance; pedagogy as mimesis. What has been observed with respect to Aquinas's *Summa* finds an analogue in Hugh's much earlier *De sacramentis*: 'The teacher's vocation is to move the soul, by a participation in the movement of the intellect and the will whose agent is God alone. This makes the task of the teacher of sacred doctrine both more and less central: it is God alone who is the agent of understanding and good desire.'[92] This, for Hugh, means nothing more or less than that *De sacramentis* is a mirror in which its own articulation and pedagogic desire is reflected. It too participates in a sacramental operation. That means, that Hugh himself as author is being taught, is being transformed, by his own project. The project itself is being authored from above and beyond him, through him. We recall the primarily function of the sacramental is restoration following humankind's Fall into disobedience. Order and discipline become paramount. It is these things that have to be learnt. Sacraments are then pedagogical on two levels. First, on a theoretical level they enable the mind to understand in, and through, and by its participation in the mind of God[93], through Christ as God's Word and Wisdom. Secondly, on a practical, affective level, they enable a development of the virtues associated with such Wisdom, an *ascesis*; that is, a learning to

---

Reading Scripture Together on the Path to God (Grand Rapids, MI: William B. Eerdmans, 2006), pp.70–89.

[90] *De sacramentis*, II.18, Deferrari (n.19), p.472.

[91] The materiality of language, much more in evidence in a scribal and oral culture, mediates between any dualism between body and soul for Hugh. In a section concerning 'Hugh's Dualism', Peter S. Drillard (*Foundation and Restoration*, pp.145–54), doesn't appreciate the way this qualifies any dualism in Hugh's thinking, though Drillard is right to point out how different the body–soul model in Hugh is from Descartes'.

[92] Candler, *Theology, Rhetoric, Manduction* (n.89), pp.104–5.

[93] This is an Augustinian legacy. See Augustine, *De consensu evangelistarum*, i.xxiii, 35 (*Patrologia Latina* 34, 1058): 'we no not merely admit, we especially preach that highest Wisdom of God which, through participation in Itself, makes wise whatever soul becomes truly wise'. This participation and the restoration it affords is why the arts are so central to Hugh's theology. See also *Didascalicon* (n.3), II.i.

love properly, believe properly, and hope properly.[94] Pedagogy is inseparable here from *metanoia* and *anagogy*.

Hugh of Saint-Victor's *De sacramentis* presents a *Summa* in accordance with a logic of participation[95] that is simultaneously corporeal (embodied and affective) and spiritual, moral, and noetic, although that corporeality is not radical for Hugh. It cannot be because Hugh still holds a mode of dualism between body and soul. Not that sense perception is denied any participation in true knowledge. But Hugh regards personhood to be a matter of the soul not the body. 'What is man [*Quid enim magis est homo*]?' he asks, when discussing the nature of the incarnate Christ, and he answers: 'Man is a soul.'[96] It is this separation of personhood from embodiment that enables Hugh to write of Christ in the tomb 'not the whole man lay in the selpulchre, only one part of the man, the body only [*quia non totus homo in sepulcro jacuit, sed una pars hominis tantum corpus*] . . . the soul alone is rational substance'.[97] Being human is body and soul, but 'the basis of personality was entirely in the soul'.[98] Hugh no doubt hopes he can guarantee Christ's divinity with this distinction, but theologically it is difficult (bringing him close to Nestorianism),[99] and Aquinas will correct this by being more Aristotelian on this point. The difficulty lies in Hugh's understanding of 'person' and a confusion of human persons and Christ's person. Nevertheless the tenor of Hugh's logic is participative (ontological), semi-corporeal (semi-affective in human nature) and spiritual (noetic and pneumatological) because of the incarnation, and what the incarnation of Christ Jesus revealed about the restorative operations of the Triune God in the world and the history of the world. That's why the doctrine of the incarnation is so central to the volume. Although Hugh accords an important place for human reasoning—it is this which distinguishes human beings from plants and animals—on the grounds that such reasoning constitutes the image of God within us, then it has to bow beneath the superior reasoning of the Logos,

---

[94] The opening of *Didascalicon* (n.3), presents Wisdom as both efficient, ontological cause of humankind's knowledge and humankind's the moral goal. Aquinas will, of course, say something similar in the opening *quaestio* of the *Summa Theologicae* in his observation that all the other secular *scientiae* serve or are required for *sacra doctrina* (holy teaching) and that *sacra doctrina* is itself both a theoretical and a practical science; 'mystical union [for Hugh] is to be promoted through the pursuit and contemplation of truth on the one hand and the practice of virtue on the other'—Taylor, 'Introduction to *Didascalicon*' (n.3) p.29.

[95] The phrase belongs to Nicholas Adams who employs it in his book *The Eclipse of Grace: Divine and Human Action in Hegel* (Blackwell: Oxford, 2013) to describe the structure and character of logic for Hegel.

[96] *De sacramentis*, Deferrari (n.19), p.248. See also Hugh's treatise *De sapientia animae Christi*. In *Patrologia Latina* 176 (n.19), pp.845–56.

[97] *De sacramentis*, Deferrari (n.19), pp.239–43.

[98] Kleinz, *The Theory of Knowledge of Hugh of Saint Victor* (n.80), p.22.

[99] See Peter S. Dillard, *Foundation and Restoration* (n.47), for a 'thought experiment' conducted by Hugh that allows him to finesse any Nestorianism (pp.159–62).

Wisdom. Our reasoning bears a likeness to the operation of the mind of God, 'a likeness which is to us a form but to God is his nature'; nevertheless it is a form that can be 'conformed to the divine nature'.[100]

As a *summa De sacramentis* reflects the move beyond the monastic *Glossa Ordinaria* insofar as the Scriptural exegesis that constitutes both its foundation and its method created a text that stood apart from the intratextuality of the monastic glosses. It is a text, moreover, that gives a coherent structure to the doctrines of the faith; doctrines to be lived if they were ever to be truly and transformatively learnt. As a *Summa* it also distinguished itself from the more speculative rationalisms of Abelard's *Sic et Non* and *Theologia*, and the scholastic rationalisms which imitated it and developed the twin methods of *disputatio* and *questio*. But these applications of logic to the Wisdom of the Logos were the future of theology.

LOGIC AND THE LOGOS

An assessment of the relationship between logic[101] and the Logos—the first closely related to the powers of human reasoning, educated particularly through the *trivium* of grammar, rhetoric, and dialectic, the second to Christ as the incarnation of God's Wisdom and truth—touches the very heart of questions that preoccupied the theological debates of the twelfth century: the relationship between philosophy and theology, nature and grace, and the relationship between Christian doctrine and pagan logic. The questions concerning that relationship all revolved around establishing first principles. In his *Soliloquium*, a brief dialogue between one 'Peter' and 'Abelard' (whose name was actually Peter), Abelard refers explicitly to the Word of God as the Logos and then, somewhat fallaciously adds: 'Hence also, in accordance with the etymology of this noun, whosoever clings to this true and perfect Word through doctrine and love should truly be called 'logicians' and 'philosophers,' before concluding: 'Therefore no discipline ought more truly to be called "logic" than Christian teaching.'[102] This is a response to a statement made by Peter that pagan philosophers (he is probably thinking of Porphyry whose brief treatise on logic,

---

[100] *Didascalicon* (n.3), II.i, p.61.

[101] For a brief overview of the techniques of logic at this time see John Marenbon, *Later Medieval Philosophy (1150–1350)* (London: Routledge, 1987), p.35–49. For more in-depth studies see Martin M. Tweedale, 'Logic (i): from the late eleventh century to the time of Abelard' and Klaus Jacobi, 'Logic (ii): the late twelfth century' in Peter Dronke, *A History of Twelfth-Century Western Philosophy* (Cambridge: Cambridge University Press, 1992), pp.196–226 and 227–51, respectively.

[102] *Soliloquium*, trans. C. Burnett in *Studi Medievali* 25 (1984), pp.882–4, p.889. On Abelard's logic see John Marenbon, *The Philosophy of Peter Abelard*, pp.99–209.

Isogogy, was intensely studied by teachers of logic at the time) 'expounded the whole *summa* of faith in the Trinity more thoroughly in many ways than the prophets'.[103] But we if compare this set of claims to a bas-relief carved around 1140 over the west porch of Chartres Cathedral and the statuary in the north porch we can see an important difference between theologians like Hugh of Saint Victor (and St. Bernard of Clairvaux, who most assiduously took Abelard to task) and these theological appropriations of what became known as the 'New Logic'. Over the west porch, the seven liberal arts, represented by women, are either looking at the young Jesus held by his mother or looking out, like music, towards the west in rapture. The ancient philosophers are represented as looking down at their writings. They do not look towards the Word of God because they cannot see Him and resolutely do not see him. The prophets on the north porch stand alongside St. Peter staring straight in front of them. In his *Didascalicon,* Hugh had argued that philosophy and theology were almost synonymous since philosophy as the love of wisdom 'investigates comprehensively the ideas of all things, human and divine'. And even when he continued by making an important qualification that its object was 'that Wisdom which is the sole primordial Idea or Pattern of things'[104], this did not rule out Plato being a theologian. But Abelard's claim appeared to conflate faith and human reason or bring theology and philosophy into an accord much closer than orthodoxy could sustain.[105]

In his *Theologia Summi Boni* Abelard claimed: 'We do not promise to teach *the* truth, which, everyone agrees neither we nor any other mortal can know, but only a verisimilitude of it which accords with human reason and is not contrary to holy scripture. This we direct against those who boast that they impugn the Faith by human reason.'[106] But as one of the best scholars of Abelard comments: 'Abelard was not always so scrupulous . . . in distinguishing between "verisimilitude", which was humanly attainable, and "truth", which was not.'[107] As such the vision of God, God in his Triune being, is accessible insofar as it is understandable, by Abelard. When Hugh approaches

---

[103] *Soliloquium*, p.887.

[104] *Didascalicon* (n.3), I.iv, p.51. This position is reiterated again and amplified in Book ii, i, pp.61–2 and is immediately followed, in ii, with an account of theology.

[105] In *Didascalicon* (n.3), I.xi, pp.57–60, Hugh states that logic 'provides the knowledge necessary for correct speaking and clear argumentation' (p.60). It does not concern contemplation of the truth and there is no theological task given to it. But in fact in defining theology as a 'discourse' he cannot rule out the application of logic so conceived. Frequently Abelard emphasizes that this is what he is doing when applying logic theologically: commenting upon human speaking about divine things.

[106] *Theologia Summi Boni*, eds. E.M. Buytaert and C.J. Mews, *Petri Abaelardi opera theologica* III, Corpus Christianorum continuatio mediaevalis 13 (Turnhout, Belgium: Brepolis, 1987) p.123.

[107] M.T. Clanchy, *Abelard: A Medieval Life* (n.1), p.107. Abelard does not detail the relationship between 'verisimilitude' and 'truth'. Only a doctrine of analogy could do this.

the same subject it is ringed with apophatic negatives, as we have seen, and cautionary warnings that certain aspects of the faith can only be believed. Although in the concluding lines of *De sacramentis,* Hugh's 'Behold' conceals a possible realized eschatology that later Aquinas, who more clearly demarcated the lines between faith and reason, theology and philosophy, will place firmly as a *post-mortem* condition, beatification is not available in this life. But the tenses of the verbs Hugh employs are future. The eyes of our pre-lapsarian parents may have been about to see God directly, but, as Hugh explains, that is by an inspiration 'through the presence of contemplation [*per praesentiam contemplationis*]'.[108] We need grace and faith and will see only indirectly as thought turns to meditation and meditation to contemplation. 'Meditation is related to contemplation as movement to rest,' John P. Kleinz observes.[109] Thought, meditation, and contemplation are all modes of reasoning for Hugh, as we saw. 'Thus meditation is a certain power of the mind [*mentis*], curious and intellectually astute [*sagax*], dazzling in its investigation of the obscure and its unfolding of the unintelligible. Contemplation is that keen form of intelligence which, openly beholding all that is, comprehends with a clear vision. And so contemplation possesses what meditation inquires after [*quaerit*],' Hugh writes.[110] For Hugh, although there does appear to be a progressive trajectory from *lectio,* through *meditatio,* to the *visio dei* that is the result of being taught and seeking to understand, it is faith that seeks (*quaerit*) understanding by grace and participation in Christ as Logos. In this life there is only a 'foretaste'.[111] In the cases of both Hugh and Abelard we might say they are theological (and educational) optimists; the lostness of the human condition and its attendant epistemological darkness is rectifiable: by the numerous sacraments (including the liberal arts), for one, and by logic (embracing the first three of the liberal arts), for the other.

In his defence, Abelard could write (along lines reminiscent of Karl Barth on the task of dogmatics with respect to the proclamation of the Word of God) that what he was submitting to his logician's science was not God as such ('any question of perception is irrelevant [*supervacuus*] as far as God is concerned')[112] but human speech about God, and so helping theologians to clarify what was believed. Both Hugh and Abelard shared the conviction that human reasoning participated in the mind of God in some way and to some extent. This was the basis for their optimism and their attention to pedagogy. But neither had developed a language that could adequately define

---

[108] *De sacramentis,* I, 6, 14, Deferrari (n.19), p.103.
[109] Kleinz, *The Theory of Knowledge* (n.80), p.122. See the whole chapter VII (pp.105–25) for an examination of Hugh's understanding of the ascent to God.
[110] *In Salomonis Ecclesiasten Homiliae, Patrologia Latina* (n.19), 175, 117AB, my translation.
[111] *Didascalicon* (n.3), V.ix, p.132.
[112] *Logica Ingredientibus,* cited in Clanchy (n.1), p.106.

that participation; the language of analogy that emphasized a similarity and yet a greater dissimilarity. Hugh, I would contend, is closer to getting there, because his whole theology develops from an *analogia Christi* with respect to a doctrine of creation. And Hugh, in keeping closer to Scriptural glosses and emphasizing the pastoral objectives of moral development that must accompany spiritual understanding, came closer to an orthodox position. Abelard's position was much more equivocal, as his remark in *Theologia Summi Boni* that 'reason educates each single person naturally about God'[113] makes plain.

Even so, it was Abelard's method that would carry the day, despite the fact he was condemned to silence as a heretic by Pope Innocent II in 1140 with the formidable assistance of St. Bernard. His famous statement in the Prologue to *Sic et Non*, 'by doubting we come to inquiry and by inquiry we perceive truth',[114] brought the *quaestio* and the *disputio* to the forefront of theological method,[115] along with a set of terms drawn from Aristotle's categories and Porphyry's predicables. The originality of *Sic et Non* as I said above, lay in the way in which the antitheses, and paradoxes, and contradictions listed were allowed to stand in and for themselves. The questions could be endlessly multiplied. The *summae* that followed from the *quaestiones* and its method of disputation brought a new rational ordering and systematization of revelation and encouraged a new type of *intellectus fidei* in search of causes and reasons through a specialist vocabulary.[116] Being a theologian was fast becoming a profession. This method had the effect of 'desacralizing ... *sacra pagina*,'[117] challenging its authority, to the extent that Stephen, bishop of Tournai at the end of the twelfth century, could complain 'Scriptural studies have lapsed into a state of confusion in our time, for students applaud nothing but novelties.'[118] Chenu, as a good Dominican, saw the solution to this rich play of methodological variation was not going to be the Fourth Lateran Council

---

[113] *Theologia Summi Boni*, ed. E.M. Buytaert and C.J. Mews (n.107) p.201, lines 1346–7.

[114] *Peter Abailard, Sic et Non: A Critical Edition*, ed. B.B. Boyer and R. McKeon (Chicago: University of Chicago Press, 1978), p.103, line 332.

[115] See his observation in *Dialectica*, ed. and trans. L.M.de Rijk (Assen: Van Gorcam, 1970, 2nd edition) p.153, lines 24–5: 'The investigation of dialecticians is appropriate for those particular questions [*quaestiones*]—in which the principal business of this art consists.' Available on line: <http://www.forumromanum.org/literature/abelardx.html> accessed July 2015.

[116] On the later development of the *quaestio* in the thirteenth and fourteenth centuries see John Marenbon, *Later Medieval Philosophy* (n.101), pp.27–34. On Robert of Melun's *Quaestiones de divina pagina* and *Quaestiones* (produced in the 1140s) and the way in which they drew upon both the School of Saint-Victor and the School of Abelard, see Constant J. Mews,'Between the Schools of Abelard and Saint-Victor in the mid Twelfth Century: the Witness of Robert of Melun' in *Bibliotheca Victorina XXII: L'École de Saint-Victor de Paris*, actes réunis par Dominique Poirel (Turnhout, Belgium: Brepolis: 2010), pp.121–38.

[117] M.-D. Chenu, *Man, Nature, and Society in the Twelfth Century* (n.6), p.304.

[118] Ibid., p.311.

of 1215, which coincided with the publication of the founding statute for the University of Paris by the papal legate, Robert Courçon, but Thomas Aquinas.

CONCLUSION

It has often been remarked that cathedrals like Chartres are *summae* in stone. The order of the similitude cannot be easily reversed. Even before the establishment of the 'university' (at Paris and Bologna), theology was beginning to edge beyond its ecclesial setting. In doing so it became, for a time, an important public and trans-national discourse, a *lingua franca* that could bind newly emerging societies, cultures, politics, and legislations in a certain commonality. It gave Western Europe a particular identity as it rose to become the 'queen of the sciences'. It bore a vision of universal hope that could easily become triumphalist, crusading. But its roots in pedagogy, formation, and participation in a grace continually given and responded to, secured the imitate association of doctrine and liturgical practice; teaching as a practice that fostered right relations in a right order in a doxological affirmation of the Good. The Christian faith in its ongoing search for understanding concerned ethical life; doctrine was to be lived. And knowledge was intellectual and affective only to the extent that it was spiritual and moral. But new purely intellectualist notes were being tried out that provided seminal means for the procreation of secular reason.

3

Dogmatics

READINGS OF TIME

Events in time are fixed—things happen—but the telling of history is plastic and pliable. Histories of the West in the nineteenth century viewed the Reformation as a 'success story'. Reform meant improvement. For Hegel, in his *Philosophy of History*, the Reformation was a providential advance in which the hand of God, particularly in Germany, was manifest, and the operation of the Spirit's teleological working towards Absolute freedom was made plain (for Hegel, anyway). With Protestantism the Spirit of God is reconciled with the history of the world, as 'Spirit perceives that Nature—the World—must also be an embodiment of Reason, for God created it on principles of Reason [*Der Geist erkennt, dass die Natur, die Welt auch eine Vernunft an ihr haben müsse, den Gott hat sie vernünftig geschaften*].'[1] 'Man becomes Man' and '[i]t is now perceived that Morality [*Sittliche*] and Justice in the State are also divine and commanded by God, and that in point of substance [*dem Inhalte*] there is nothing higher or more sacred.'[2] We will have more to say about *Sittliche* and *Sittlichkeit* or ethical life at the end of this volume.

We will also return to Hegel's concept of Reason. Hegel writes history as theodicy: all things in the multiplicity of their creation, issuing from the One (but abstract God) will return to their concrete unity in God through the movement of the Spirit of Christ, the Spirit of the Logos or Reason, through time and the labours of cultures, communities, and civilizations. There was one universal story and Hegel was able to tell it. So even when Hegel,

---

[1] G.W.F. Hegel, *The Philosophy of History*, trans. J. Sibree (New York: Dover Publications Inc., 1956), p.439. *Vorlessungen über die Philosophie der Geschichte*, Werke 12 (Frankfurt am Main: Suhrkamp, 1986), p.521. The German says nothing about 'principles', and 'embodiment' is too corporeal for what is an inner working of Reason within the World that the World necessarily possesses.

[2] Ibid., p.422/502.

contemplating the Reign of Terror in the aftermath of the French Revolution, describes History as a 'slaughter-bench', nevertheless the divine operation will have its way; all the parts (bloody as they may be) will be brought into the whole. Redemption is reconciliation; and the Reformation opened a new chapter in the working towards that reconciliation of the spirit of man with the Spirit of God. The point is clear: History had a God-guided shape, and cultural changes such as the Reformation were revelations of what was taking shape in and through the divine. Through the emergence of cultural epochs the ways and thoughts of God were made known; and the optimism is paramount despite the Biblical injunction that God's thoughts are not our thoughts and God's way not our ways. Hegel had a way of conceiving the apophatic as just human ignorance; things were getting clearer, even though for him, the Enlightenment was not nearly as enlightened as it was becoming (through him).

This was, of course, a Protestant writing about the triumph of Protestantism, much in the same vein as both Luther and Melanchthon who found a legitimation for their protest and demands for *reformatio* in the operation of divine providence.[3] For all three history was a form of revelation. In fact, the intimate relationship between history and revelation has continued to be a very German theme in the theologies of von Balthasar and Pannenberg. This is no doubt one further outworking of the way Protestantism pioneered the invention of modern history. Hegel was only following a line of thinking about providential history opened in the early decades of Protestant publications with Philip Melanchthon's edition of *Carion's Chronicle* in 1532. History was a record of God's work and the Reformers were the true successors of the apostles. '[I]t was Melanchthon who became the real promoter of the study of time and history among Protestants in general.'[4] The great historians and historiographers of the nineteenth century, who laid the basis for the scientific study of history—Leopold von Ranke (no friend of Hegel), Johann Gustav Droysen, Jacob Burckhardt, Wilhelm Dilthey—were all Protestant, and nearly all German (Burckhardt was Swiss). There were German Catholic historians, composing multi-volume studies—notably Count Leopold von Stolberg and Johann Adam Möhler. But the former concluded his fifteen volumes in 430 and the latter his own fifteen volumes in

---

[3] Although *reformatio* had had a long history, as we saw in the last chapter. The classic text for the history and meaning of 'reformation' is Gergart H. Ladner, *The Idea of Reform: Its Impact on Christian Thought and Action in the Age of the Fathers* (Cambridge, Mass: Harvard University Press, 1954).

[4] Andrew Cunningham and Ole Peter Grell, *The Four Horsemen of the Apocalypse: Religion, War, Famine and Death in Reformation Europe* (Cambridge: Cambridge University Press, 2000), p.49.

1378. The Reformation was off their agenda or outside the professional possibilities of one historian's lifetime.

Yet, from the late decades of the twentieth century, a number of theologians (John Milbank[5] particularly), social theorists (like Alasdair MacIntrye[6] and Charles Taylor[7]), and one or two historians (such as John Bossy[8] and Eamon Duffy[9]), have been making a counterclaim about the Reformation. The French Jesuits Henri de Lubac, Jean Daniélou, and Michel de Certeau had done some of the theological and historical spade-work earlier in the twentieth century. In *Surnaturel*[10] and *Corpus Mysticum*,[11] de Lubac drew upon Patristic sources to point to theological shifts in the late Medieval and Early Modern Church that had become unhelpful corruptions—separating grace from nature, for example.[12] His *confrére*, Jean Daniélou, added to de Lubac's retrieval of the early Church Fathers and the Christian metaphysics they articulated. His work culminated in a detailed three-volume study: *Histoire des doctrines chrétiennes avant Nicée*.[13] Their student, Michel de Certeau, took up their approach, not with respect to Patristics but rather early modern theologies. In particular he was interested in changes in the history of spirituality. In *La fable mystique* he set out to demonstrate how the nominalist 'opacity' inherited by the scholastics from William of Occam generated a cultural crisis in early modern Europe that led to dramatic forms of emotional extremism—the cries of the possessed and the mystic's ecstasy—and a plethora of publications on spiritual guidance.[14]

---

[5] See John Milbank, *Theology and Social Theory* (Oxford: Blackwell, 1999).

[6] See Alasdair MacIntyre, *Three Rival Versions of Moral Enquiry* (Notre Dame, Ind.: University of Notre Dame Press, 1990).

[7] See Charles Taylor, *A Secular Age* (Cambridge, MA: The Belknap Press of Harvard University Press, 2007).

[8] See John Bossy's influential *Christianity in the West 1400–1700* (Oxford: Oxford University Press, 1985).

[9] See Eamon Duffy *The Stripping of the Altars* (New Haven: Yale University Press, 1992).

[10] Henri de Lubac, *Surnaturel: études historiques*, (1946). A new French edition has since been (Paris: Desclée de Brouwer, 1991).

[11] Henri de Lubac, *Corpus Mysticum: Essai sur L'Eucharistie et l'Église au moyen âge* (Paris: Aubier, 1944).

[12] For a survey of this trajectory in Catholic thought that paved the way for Vatican II, see Fergus Kerr, *Twentieth Century Catholic Theologians: From Neoscholasticism to Nuptial Mystery* (Malden, MA; Oxford: Blackwell, 2007).

[13] Jean Daniélou, *Histoire des doctrines chrétiennes avant Nicée*, 3 vols (Paris: Desclée, Éditions du Cerf, 1958–1978).

[14] Michel de Certeau, *La Fable Mystique.* vol. 1, XVIe-XVIIe Siècle (Paris: Editions Gallimard, 1982). See also de Certeau's earlier study *La Possession de Loudun* (Paris: Editions Gallimard, 1970). For an introduction to Michel de Certeau's work more generally, see Graham Ward, *The de Certeau Reader* (Oxford: Blackwell, 1999). We will return to de Certeau's work in Chapter 8.

This critical evaluation of ecclesial history, and retrieval of the resources of the tradition was not simply a Jesuit concern. At the same time two Dominicans, Yves Congar and Marie-Dominique Chenu, were also drawing attention to the 'baroque theologies' that had emerged from scholastic nominalism and the need to overcome them for Catholic theological renewal.[15] We met Chenu in the last chapter.

These French theologians, whether Jesuit or Dominican, were each reacting to a Neo-Scholastic Thomism that had come to dominate Roman Catholic theology. Out of its fears and denunciations of 'modernism', this scholastic trend disembedded theological enquiry from history, context, and embodiment in pursuit of timeless perennial abstractions in which theology could be understood as a rational science. Faith was a contractual matter of the will's intellectual consent to true propositions. These truths had no basis in human experience but rather conformed to objective reality. So although this Catholic position espoused Aquinas's conception of the single composition of body and soul, it privatized spirituality, relegated the role of the Bible and reduced dogma to clear statements. The *lapsus,* which Congar laid more at the feet of the Counter-Reformation's response to the Reformation crisis than receptions of, and revisions of, Aquinas, called for an enquiry into the processes by which the Church received its truth.[16]

The work in English, then, by theologians, social theorists, and historians in the last decades of the twentieth century arose within the context of debates within Roman Catholicism that began much earlier. The most exhaustive treatment of this genealogy of a *lapsus* and a desire to re-evaluate premodern theology came with the publication of Charles Taylor's *A Secular Age* in 2007, and that is where we will take up the story.[17]

---

[15] More recently Olivier Boulnois, the historian of medieval philosophy has covered similar terrain in his short essay 'Reading Duns Scotus: From History to Philosophy' in *Modern Theology* 21 (2005), pp.603–8. More substantially, see: Adrian Pabst, *Metaphysics: The Creation of Hierarchy* (Grand Rapids, MI: Eerdmann, 2012).

[16] See Yves Congar's seminal essay: 'La "réception" comme réalité ecclésiologique', *Revue des Sciences Philosophiques et Théologiques* 56 (1972): 369–403.

[17] Taylor's call for a re-evaluation is complex. It does not emerge in his genealogy of the secular, but later in the thesis. The earlier part of the book is governed by a more sociological and historical method, but later his own Catholic views are increasingly pronounced. As I go on to point out, the great change that occurred as a result of certain neoscholastic debates between what Chenu would call Dominican and Franciscan spiritualities (Aquinas and Bonaventure, Scotus and Occam) is part of an ongoing Christian 'disembedding' of religions of the Axial Revolution. Most of the book treats this long and many-headed development. It is only later in the book that his method becomes more confessional and theological. Then he begins to define what Christians need to 'recover'. For a discussion between Taylor's Christian proposals and the theology of Radical Orthodoxy see John Milbank's essay 'A Closer Walk on the Wild Side' in Michael Warner, Jonathan Vanantwerpen, and Craig Calhoun (eds.), *Varieties of Secularism in a Secular Age* (Cambridge, Mass: Harvard University Press, 2013), pp.54–82.

THE GREAT DISEMBEDDING

Taylor begins with the conditions for believing in God in the premodern period. They are threefold: it was held that the natural world was created and was a testimony to 'divine purpose and action'; that the social world, and the very existence of society, was divinely ordered; and that people 'lived in an "enchanted" world'.[18] It is a world that had undergone centuries of Christianization, while folkloric vestiges remained—like the belief in fairies. The literary historian, Andrew Greeley perhaps gives the best theological description of this world: 'Catholics live in an enchanted world, a world of statues and holy water, stained glass and votive candles, saints and religious medals, rosary beads and holy pictures. But these Catholic paraphernalia are mere hints of a deeper and more pervasive religious sensibility which inclines Catholics to see the Holy lurking in creation. [. . .] This special Catholic imagination can appropriately be called sacramental. It sees created reality as a "sacrament", that is, a revelation of the presence of God.'[19] An account of this 'enchanted', sacramental view of the world as evident in Hugh of St.-Victor is given in Chapter 2. It was a world of pluriform relations between people, times past and future, objects, divinities, and acts given expression through the symbolic imagination. It found expression in analogy, emblem, allegory, and liturgy. The liturgy, as we saw, was of utmost significance both to Cyril's and Hugh's understanding of doctrinal development. To live within the enchanted world was to develop the 'art of ascertaining multiform truth'.[20]

Taylor views the shift from the enchanted to the disenchanted world in terms of a 'longue dureé'.[21] Enchantment is a key characteristic of religion in the Axial revolution in which participation and being embedded socially, cosmically, and morally were cultivated. Nevertheless Christianity, for Taylor, was also one of the main drivers in the post-Axial age development and the shift away from being embedded, with its calls to belong to a Kingdom not of this world and for allegiances more fundamental than kinship and *cultus*. It is then from within Christianity that the 'great disembedding' is promoted.

---

[18] Charles Taylor, *A Secular Age* (n.7), p.25.

[19] Andrew Greeley, *The Catholic Imagination* (Berkeley: University of California Press, 2000), p. 5. See also John Bossy *Christianity in the West 1400–1700* (n.8): 'a universe where the physical domain was subject to the governance of the social, to wrath and love emanating from God or man, or from intermediate beings like saints or demons.'

[20] See 'Introduction', Theodore Bogdanos, *Pearl: Image of the Ineffable: A Study of Mediaeval Poetic Symbolism* (University Park: Pennsylvania State University Press, 1983).

[21] The term was developed by French historians of the Annales School and described a long term movement structuring a number of historical events. It was pioneered by Marc Bloch but finds one of its most important expressions in Fernand Braudel's *The Mediterranean and the Mediterranean World in the Time of Philip II* in two volumes, trans. Sian Reynolds (Berkeley: University of California Press, 1995 and 1996).

In particular—and here Taylor is extending the project of his earlier volume, *Sources of the Self* (1989)—it fostered 'the primacy of the individual',[22] itself the outcome of a new voluntarism emphasizing the freedom of the will and opening a cultural space for self-fashioning. Purpose was no longer viewed as an intrinsic, teleological operation within creatures and creation towards divine fulfilment, but was understood now to be extrinsic and a form of efficient causation. The mediations of the transcendent by spirits, angels, demons and 'embedded in things: relics, sacred places ... [notions of] higher time'[23] ceased to be believed in. The world could be conceived as a self-regulating machine and 'disenchantment, the active instrumental stance'[24] towards it. The reforming programme of the medieval Church became internalized as self-discipline, for both the laity and the priests. The immanent order, given greater sense of itself through the Stoic development of 'nature' and 'natural law', was separated from the transcendent and the divine, collective belonging, and agency morphed into the self as agent. Social atomism ensued. Human flourishing was no longer dependent upon nor perfected by divine operations beyond the human condition as such. The deepening of personal religious conviction, the need for such a personal piety, brought shifts towards 'covenantal' belonging to a religious group or denomination and a 'break away from the established solidarities'.[25] Here there were collections of independent believers committed to 'the disciplined remaking of behaviour and social forms through objectification and an instrumental stance'.[26]

Taylor's account of the *lapsus* then is, in many ways, more profound, and perhaps more pessimistic, than any simple narrative of a cultural and theological *lapsus* within Christianity beginning with a medieval scholasticism that set the trends brought to completion in the Reformation, Enlightenment, modernity and the triumph of the secular, immanent frame. Taylor does not deny some of the benefits and progresses made in the name of Enlightenment and modernity more generally. But the 'great disembedding' is, like the accounts by the other scholars I have named, marked by the descent into nominalism and disenchantment, the fermentation of social atomism, the fashioning of the 'buffered self', and the privatization of religion that created the social space for the advance of secularism.

The theological projects of *Nouvelle Théologie* and, more recently, *Radical Orthodoxy*, have been viewed as champions of this view of the history of the West. These historical and genealogical projects are much more subtle than they are often given credit for. Taylor's 'history' is not one of simple decline.

---

[22] Charles Taylor, *A Secular Age* (n.7), p.146.   [23] Ibid., p.150.   [24] Ibid., p.98.

[25] Ibid., p.158. For a more in-depth enquiry, see Andrew Pettegree, 'New Solidarities', Chapter 8, *Reformation and the Culture of Persuasion* (Cambridge: Cambridge University Press, 2005), pp.185–210.

[26] Ibid., p.155.

It is many-layered and attentive to numerous currents and counter-currents. More recently, John Milbank, in defending himself from the criticism of 'nostalgia' in his account of 'the secular as an internal corruption of the theological', an apostasy leading to the 'dereliction of the sacred',[27] takes pains to demonstrate the complexity and heterogeneity involved in the cultural and historical shifts. He makes the striking observation—which is certainly open to challenge and in need of clarification—that 'we remain caught within a "certain Middle Ages"'.[28] Nevertheless, it at this point in my analysis of the development and nature of systematic theology, that several, no doubt, will interpret this present work as endorsing that historiography of the *lapsus*, and the critique of nostalgia for a lost Christendom will be invoked. So let us proceed carefully, and come to conclusions slowly.

If Hegel flies pretty close to the sun on wax wings, then the more contemporary swing towards interpreting the demise of Christendom in terms of a falling away from true Christianity is not without its own problems. The problems are not necessarily historical or sociological. No one with an eye for advertising logos from Disney to Sweaty Betty can doubt the triumph and advancement of nominalism, where names are arbitrary tokens for a reality that has been constructed for shoppers by market advisors and brand-name managers. Neither could anyone paying fees to a life-style instructor or an image consultant doubt that the 'buffered self' has morphed into hyperindividualism. The turn out for elections at local and national levels presents a strong case for social atomism and disenfranchisement (among other things) and the increasing move towards management methods governing any modern (and financially successful) institution points to the cultural dominance of instrumental reason disenchanting the world. Furthermore, however much secularism is being fast recognized as an ideology, churches are, in the main, struggling to find and foster a congregation, and multiculturalism has brought other pieties to the fore so that few today speak about Christendom; except that is new atheists who continue to attack it. Neither as history nor genealogy nor sociology then are these 'counter' interpretations of the history of the Church wrong.

The problems are raised at the level of theology. Hegel's philosophy of history was robustly, if somewhat hot-headly, supported by a theology of history. His story was God's story; but in being God's story it was also a story of universal salvation. Many have argued that Hegel secularizes that salvation, making it an immanent though nevertheless divine process. I think things are more ambivalent, and have argued so elsewhere.[29] We will

---

[27] John Milbank, *Beyond Secular Order: The Representation of Being and the Representation of the People* (Oxford: Wiley Blackwell, 2013), pp.15–16.

[28] Ibid., p.40.

[29] See Graham Ward, 'How Hegel became a Philosopher: Logos and the Economy of Logic', *Critical Research on Religion*, December 2013, vol. 1 no. 3, 270–92.

return to Hegel's philosophical theology in the final part of this volume. The point here is that Hegel *has* a story. It is difficult to see what God's story might be in the *lapsus* scenario. Does Providence stop with Duns Scotus? Does its operations cease with William of Occam? Why should redemption become all the more difficult because of an influential human philosophy? What is at stake here is our salvation; not simply the influence and impact of certain theological thinkers. That the Church, in a reforming zeal that, as we have seen, goes back to the eleventh century and Pope Gregory VII, in advancing a scholastic philosophy conflating physical causation with instrumental reason, and an emphasis on divine and human voluntarism, should bring about its own demise, is an irony not lost on several of the *lapsus* proponents (particularly Michael J. Buckley,[30] John Milbank, and Charles Taylor). But, theologically, while the movement towards the apocalyptic and the eschatological cannot be elided with any Enlightenment notion of 'progress', nevertheless the Scriptural notion of the Kingdom of God and the victory of Christ's salvation for the world is an ongoing *adventus*. And although the Church mediates and participates in this salvation history, the operations of redemption reach beyond the Church into secular history and creation. Unless we want to adopt a clear supercessionist and exclusivist line—a line *Lumen Gentium* only narrowly avoided with its recognitions that the Roman Catholic Church a) 'is linked with those who, being baptized, are honored with the name of Christian', and b) that there are non-Christian peoples 'related to the people of God in various ways'[31]— then we have to accept that the Church (whatever that means in terms of the churches today) has no monopoly on salvation (or God's grace).[32] Its continual coming—announced in the present continuous uses of the verb 'to come' (*erchomai, erchou*) of the penultimate verse of the New Testament— is profoundly related to the movement of the Spirit, human faith seeking understanding and the 'hope that is in us' for which Christians are accountable (1 Pet.3.15). However destructive the persecution, however dark the night, however profoundly we are lost and bewildered by the times we live in, the witness continues because there is an operation of grace that

---

[30] See Michael J. Buckley, *At the Origins of Modern Atheism* (New Haven: Yale University Press, 1990). For a more recent account of the cultural developments that led from the Renaissance to the Enlightenment, see Michael Allen Gillespie, *The Theological Origins of Modernity* (Chicago: University of Chicago Press, 2008). Gillespie too makes nominalism an important fulcrum for change (pp.19–100).

[31] *Lumen Gentium*, §15 and §16, available at <http://www.saintwiki.com/index.php?title=Catholic_Primer_Library>, accessed August 2015.

[32] Edward Schillebeeckx: 'Salvation history cannot be reduced to the history of religions or to the history of Judaism and Christianity. For the whole of secular history is itself already under the guidance of the liberating God of creation.' Trans. John Bowden, *Jesus in our Western Culture: Mysticism, Ethics and Politics* (London: SCM Press, 1986), p.7.

commits to *metanoia*, ameliorative change; towards the future realization of a divine promise.

So, in some sense theologically, all the social, historical, philosophical, and cultural consequences of the 'great disembedding' or what, for a shorthand, we might call Western modernity, must either be within the Providence of God's love and mercy towards us or we allow fallible human beings to have power to swing the Kingdom off its course. That does not mean Christian theology cannot find, as it has always found, resources for its present seeking in its pre-modern past. That does not mean that some of the consequences of the secularizing 'disenchantment' and the turn to what Charles Taylor has called 'the immanent frame' for understanding ourselves and our world, cannot be critiqued and resisted as fostering powers and principalities working against the operations of divine salvation. But it does mean that the cultural transformations of early modernity have to be understood theologically as in some sense in continuity with the preceding work of Providence and not as a radical break or interruption. If as theologians we exaggerate the *lapsus*, then we are only countering Hegel's story of the *deus revelatus* with a story of the *deus absconditus*. And this would be a very modern move that followed in the wake of Luther's later theology. What the *lapsus* thesis calls for is deeper and more analytical histories and genealogies of cultural changes, continuities, and transformations.

For sure, with this chapter on Reformation theology we enter now a force-field of disputes that have defined and dominated modern theology. They generated a number of significant binaries (nature/grace, immanent/ transcendent, law/gospel, works/faith, *deus revelatus/deus absconditus*, sacred/secular, freedom/determinism, private/public, among others), libraries of polemic (evangelical, liberal, conservative, traditionalist, process pantheism, 'revelatory positivism'[33] etc.) and even war (civil and international). Of course, there have been disputes among Christian thinkers before, as we have seen—Gnosticism, Pelagianism, Arianism, Nestorianism, among others. The Church has never been just a 'fair field full o folk' (Langland) and we will have to explore this more closely when developing a doctrine of the Church (in Volume III). Theology has been created through these disputes; doctrine has changed, developed, deteriorated (depending on your standpoint): while faith has continually sought understanding in all the materiality of cultural circumstance.

[33] This a phrase first used by E. Seeberg in his book on Luther published in 1929. A slightly different version of the concept was, more famously, taken up by Bonhoeffer (who's doctoral work was supervised by Seeberg's son) with respect to the theology of Karl Barth, in three letters he wrote in 1944 (April 30th, May 5th, and June 8th). For a detailed examination of this idea see Ralf K. Wüstenberg, *Bonhoeffer and Beyond: Promoting a Dialogue between Religion and Politics* (Frankfurt am Main: Peter Lang, 2008), pp.43–44.

But a difference remains between what is or was, and what is the construct-ive interpretation of what is or was (either by participants at the time or his-torians later). In other words, no one doubts the system of binary dualisms that emerged in and were developed by modernity, but there is a legitimate question of how socially and culturally these binaries effectively operated. The binaries sought to separate and define certain distinctive concepts, intel-lectual and disciplinary terrains, or operations, rather like the early distilling processes in chemistry at the time. But given that pure distinctions cannot be isolated because of the nature of communication itself (its drifts and shifts), then socially and culturally we find the binary separations are always com-promised. Religious discourse and behaviour cannot be contained within a private as distinct from a public sphere, for example.

HAVE WE EVER BEEN MODERN?

In 1991, the French social theorist, Bruno Latour pointed out these compromis-es in the foundations of modernity, in his controversial book, *We Have Never Been Modern*. The project of modernization, he claims 'has made the work of [modern] purification less plausible and the contradictions more vis-ible . . . There are so many hybrids that no one knows any longer how to lodge them in the promised land of modernity.'[34] Admittedly, Latour begins from a highly specific and some would say reductive understanding of 'moder-nity'. The modern as a project involved two sets of entirely different practices according to Latour 'which must remain distinct if they are to remain effect-ive'. On the one hand, there is the establishment of the binaries; practices con-cerned with separating into two 'distinct ontological zones' human beings and nonhumans.[35] On the other hand, there was a set of practices 'creating mixtures between entirely new types of being, hybrids of nature and culture'. He calls these two distinct practices 'translation' (from one *to* another) and 'purification' (of one *from* another). 'Without the first set the practices of purification would be fruitless or pointless. Without the second, the work of translation would be slowed down, limited, or even ruled out.'[36] The work of purification was the task of critique or 'the critical stance'. It is evident then that, since one set of practices (the purifying) has to work as the condition for the possibility of the other (the translating to form the new hybridiza-tions), then as the distinction between the two practices collapses so does the

---

[34] Bruno Latour, *We Have Never Been Modern: An Essay in Symmetical Anthropology*, trans. Catherine Porter (London: Harvester Wheatsheaf, 1993), p.131.
[35] Ibid., pp.10–11.   [36] Ibid., p.11.

concept of our being modern. The binary construction of nature as distinct from culture implodes and syncretisms, interbreedings, and contaminations become the order of the day.

Now, as is evident from Latour's language, he is not treating binaries as they were produced and used in religious practices. His argument rests upon an examination of scientific and political practices. Nevertheless, habits of thinking and construal accrue from practices that cannot be simply scientific and political. Views of nature and culture emerge fostering specific sets of beliefs about the way things are, and they relate to and impact upon theological worldviews. The public is 'educated' into these hegemonic beliefs[37] and Latour emphasizes that modernity's whole paradoxical edifice rests upon what he terms the 'crossed-out God' [*le Dieu barré*].[38] The disbarment of the divine from the public realm is, for Latour, the fourth and final guarantee of there being a conception of the modern at all. Let's follow this more closely, because it's important in understanding the 'disenchantment' brought about in and through the use of these binaries.

For Latour the first guarantee for modernity is: 'even though we construct Nature, Nature is *as if* we did not construct it' (emphasis added). The second guarantee is: 'even though we do not construct Society, Society is *as if* we did construct it'. This leads to the third guarantee: 'Nature and Society must remain absolutely distinct; the work of purification must remain absolutely distinct from the work of mediation,'[39] or translation. So, he continues, the 'fourth guarantee had to settle the question of God by removing Him for ever from the dual social and natural construction, while leaving Him presentable and usable nevertheless . . . God becomes the crossed-out God of metaphysics, as different from the premodern God of the Christians as the Nature constructed in the laboratory is from the ancient *phusis* or the Society invented by sociologists from the old anthropological collective and its crowds nonhumans.'[40] This did not mean that people didn't believe in God. Rather it meant that God was conceived as outside, exterior, extrinsic, and wholly other— *debarré* (off-side). This produces the all-important binary upon which the modern (and the secular) is built: the immanent and the transcendent.

The upshot of Latour's thesis for my argument about the system of binaries modernity invests in is that distinctions are always melding into each other. Socially and culturally, however much they were used and declared (often in polemic, as we will see), the actual historical situation itself was much more complex. The constitution of modernity was so unstable and paradoxical that

[37] For a more developed understanding of what is at stake here in terms of making a belief believable see Graham Ward *Unbelievable: Why We Believe and Why We Don't* (London: I.B.Taurus, 2015).
[38] Bruno Latour, *We Have Never Been Modern* (n.34), pp.32–5.   [39] Ibid., p.32.
[40] Ibid., p.33.

cause and effect become increasingly problematic to distinguish, and become hopelessly entangled in the inability to maintain a separation between hybridization and purification. This confusion of cause and effect in fact leads to what Latour describes as 'impossible modernization'.[41] Ergo: the 'great disembedding' may not have been so 'great' as might first appear; nor the *lapsus* so dramatic either. That is important, as I said, theologically: Reformation theology is not such a radical break from the theology that came before it[42] —but there were significant changes that led to conceptions of systematic theology that this study wishes to resist (and correct). We need deeper historical studies to unveil the complexities here between enchantment and disenchantment. This is not the last time we will encounter Latour's work.[43] His attention to hybrid processes and the irreducibility of facts to static entities will be revisited again with resepect to ecclesiology in Volume III.

1521: DÜRER, HOLBEIN THE YOUNGER, AND CRANACH

It's 1521 and the Ottoman Turks, under Süleyman, have encroached upon European borders taking Belgrade. By 1529 they will have besieged Vienna. Luther, summoned to recant his opinions at the Imperial Diet of Worms, flees the city around 19 April, is kidnapped by the Elector of Saxony for his own sake and hidden in the castle at Wartburg. Bereft of his friend and mentor, in the small town of Wittenberg, Philip Melanchthon composes the 'first

---

[41] Ibid., pp.130–2.

[42] Since the Finnish School of Lutheran studies, there have been attempts to recover the ontological and metaphysical in Luther's early work, and trace the decline in the notion of 'real presence'. See Risto Saarinen, *Gottes Wirken auf uns: Die transcendentale Deutung des Gegenwart-Christi-Motivs in der Lutherforschung* (Stuttgart: Steiner Verlag, 1989) and, more generally, Carl E. Braaten and Robert W. Jenson (eds.), *Union with Christ: The New Finish Interpretation of Luther* (Grand Rapids, MI. Eerdmans, 1998). I have not engaged with this work because I am following trajectories opened by Melanchthon rather than Luther, who was a more systematic thinker.

[43] Increasingly, Latour has become interested in religion. After many years critically examining the turn to the scientific modelling of the world, the methods that facilitate this and the emulation of such methods in the establishment of other social sciences (like politics), religion is recognized by Latour as a distinct 'mode of existence'. See 'Thou Shalt Not Freeze-Frame: or How Not to Misunderstand the Science and Religion Debate' in James D. Proctor (ed.), *Science, Religion and Human Experience* (New York: Oxford University Press, 2005), pp.27–48. His most ambitious project to date situates religious practices in the socio-historical complexities he has been outlining: *An Inquiry into Modes of Existence: An Anthropology of the Moderns*, trans. Catherine Porter (Cambridge, MA: Harvard University Press, 2013). There is an accompanying platform available at <http://www.modesofexistence.net>, accessed August 2015.

Protestant dogmatics'.[44] In probably Antwerp, Albrecht Dürer is finishing a fine, but punishing sketch of 'Christ on the Mount of Olives'. In Basel Hans Holbein the Younger is painting the canvas that shocks Dostoyevsky to the core over three and half centuries later, 'The Body of the Dead Christ in the Tomb'. Meanwhile back in Wittenberg, Lucas Cranach publishes his famous and highly influential illustrations (with comments by Melanchthon), *Christi und Antichristi*. There is something new and dangerous in the European air. This isn't just about Martin Luther; he too is born into a circulation of social, cultural, and historical energies, unspoken, unconscious axioms, and sensibilities. Süleyman's advance from the East will considerably help his own cause by raising levels of anxiety across Europe. There is no Reformation or Protestantism as yet—just an increasingly vociferous 'protest' that something is 'out of joint'. Shakespeare's metaphor in *Hamlet* is telling: it is the social body itself which is discalculating, like the skeleton of a long forgotten corpse tossed into a charnel house but with the no hope of resurrection. It is as if the human race has grown tired of waiting for the returning Messiah. Later, there will be a wave of speculative works on the timing of the Second Coming beginning in 1544 with Andreas Osiander's *Conjectures on the Last Days and the End of the World*.[45] For now there is only a sense of destitution for which Christians have only themselves to blame. But they are not sure what they have done. Sinned, they conjecture. But they are not even sure what that means anymore, or how to atone, or, more concretely, put things right. There have been calls for reform and prophecies of a Reformer, and it is looking like Luther, or his patron Fredrick the Wise of Saxony, might fit the bill.

In his sketch Dürer's Christ has turned his back on us. There is no presentation of an iconic face any more; no meditations like Nicholas of Cusa's, in the previous century, on the eternal meaningfulness of Christ's gaze. His face is pressed deeply into a rock ledge. It is as if he is or is about to be petrified, and his arms are outstretched in a paralysed mimicry or intimation (it's not clear which) of being crucified. His body is splayed diagonally across the scene from left to right. He might already be dead. Dürer had visited this scene in the garden of Gethsemane many times previously—for example, in a dramatic engraving of 1508 and for his *Large Passion* and his *Small Passion* series

---

[44] 'Editor's Preface' to Melanchthon's *Loci communes theologici,* William Pauck (ed.), *Melanchthon and Bucer* in *The Library of Christian Classics* (Louisville: Westminster John Knox Press, 1969), p.xix. I have called this chapter 'Dogmatics' to distinguish a genre of writing on systematic theology distinct from the medieval *summa*. It is somewhat anachronistic because 'dogma' did not enter the English language until around 1600 and was taken from the Greek *dogma* meaning 'opinion' but now coming to be used as 'philosophical tenet'. Dogmatics as a 'system of theological principles' is a much later adaptation of the term (around the mid-nineteenth century).

[45] Andrew Cunningham and Ole Peter Grell (eds.), *The Four Horsemen of the Apocalypse* (n.4), p.50.

(both completed in 1510).[46] In these pictures Christ kneels, his face visible and the three disciples sit sleeping in the foreground. It is they with whom we are to identify. We are part of their group. There is a graphic contrast between the energetic agonies of Christ and the supine inactivity of his disciples. In the National Gallery of Art in Washington another woodcut can be found dated 1509/10 in which Christ *is* depicted in a similar pose to the 1521 sketch. But he lies horizontally across the middle of the etching while beneath him, in the foreground, are again the three sleeping disciples. In distinction to this woodcut, the 1521 sketch displaces the disciples to the left, beneath Christ's feet. Only two faces are visible, and an inert bundle that is probably the third. They lie beneath a tree, and of the two faces one is looking up and away from Christ and the other looking down towards his knees. There is a striking disengagement from the Christ. The rock ledge upon which Christ lies (as a much larger human form than his disciples) is given special prominence. It inclines, sliding down towards the bottom left-hand corner. Almost centring the whole image are the soles of Christ's exposed, naked feet, extending flush with the rock incline. The white surface upon which the sketch has been executed presents a light that bleaches, flattens, and oppresses the whole scene, accentuating Christ's splayed figure. It renders the landscape claustrophobic. It locks the people and the natural environment in a stasis that heightens the lethargy and enervation.

There is no hope for the future of the Church in this sketch. The crucifixion is an impotent surrender to natural forces. The image announces a state deeper than despair—the catatonic paralysis of trauma. This is a pre-apocalyptic vision that 'the world was in its last, decrepit and old age'.[47]

We find a similar representation in Hans Holbein the Younger's 'The Body of the Dead Christ in the Tomb'. A reproduction of the picture hung in Parfyon Rogozin's house in Dostoyevsky's novel *The Idiot*. Rogozin had seen the picture when he was abroad and 'I can't forget it', he tells Prince Myshkin. The Prince is shocked at what he sees. 'Why, some people may lose their faith by looking at that picture!' he exclaims. Rogozin concurs: 'Aye, that also may be lost,' he replies.[48] Loss is profoundly announced by the painting. It measures the length of a man's body but it is exceedingly narrow; for this is Christ laid out in his stone coffin. Christ as no one has seen Him. The slab of the coffin lid compresses the space within which the frigid, bruised, and mutilated corpse has been placed. Again, as with the Dürer sketch, there is a claustrophobia and the weight of a suffering that presses the Christ figure deeper into the

---

[46] See Erwin Panovsky, *The Life and Art of Albrecht Dürer* (Princeton, N.J.: University of Princeton Press, 1971, rev. edn.) and Dagmar Eichberger and Charles Zika (eds.), *Dürer and His Culture* (Cambridge: Cambridge University Press, 1998).

[47] *The Four Horsemen of the Apocalypse* (n.4), p.74.

[48] *The Idiot*, trans. David Magarshack (Harmondsworth: Penguin Books, 1955), p.251.

stone, the earth, death. Later in *The Idiot*, Dostoyevsky has a minor character (Ippolyt, the nihilist) give his own impression of what he sees: 'The picture seems to give expression to the idea of a dark, insolent, and senseless eternal power, to which everything is subordinated, and which controls you despite yourself.'[49] Certainly, God is dead, though there may be just the slightest of gesture towards resurrection: the index finger of Christ's right hand is pointing away from the body; pointing forward, though pointing down. The gesture is ambivalent, as are the lengths of stiffened hair hanging down from the linen cloth lining the base of the coffin. Does the finger 'reach towards the beholder'? Do the lengths of hair 'look as if they are breaking through the surface of the painting'?[50] Maybe. Although we behold as observers of the painting, we are not included, like the sleeping disciples in Dürer's sketch. Christ is terribly and yet intimately alone. We intrude into an impossible space and upon an impossible sight. Here is a nominalist emptying of the meaningfulness of the sign. The incarnation is cynically reversed: the flesh is no longer the Word. In this, the painting shifts away from Gothic expressionism toward a Mannerism that 'exhibit[s] an irrealism of objects ... which create[s] an irrealism of space itself'. A word deviates from its signification and '[t]his process of *deviation* is no longer based, as was traditional allegory, on an analogy and an order of things. It is exit, semantic exile ...'.[51] Here is a disenchantment that predates the iron cage of instrumental reasoning that characterizes Weber's sociological notion of 'disenchantment' (that Taylor employs). Only the irony, the chromatic intensity of the dark blues, greens, and browns, and the sheer facticity of the composed image keep the nihilism at bay.[52]

It is thought that Holbein converted to Protestantism in 1530; earlier he was more critical as can be seen from his woodcut 'Luther as Hercules Germanicus' (1522).[53] Both Luther and Melanchthon were angered by this aggressive and destructive portrayal of Luther as an intellectual iconoclast. It is known that Dürer had become a great admirer of Luther by 1521. They shared the same patron in Fredrick of Saxony. But even though Holbein fled

[49] Ibid., p.447. See also Julia Kristeva, *Black Son: Depression and Melancholia*, trans. Leon S. Roudiez (New York: Columbia University Press, 1989), pp.105–38.

[50] Oskar Bätschmann and Pascal Griener, *Hans Holbein*, (London: Reaktion Books, 1999), p.88.

[51] Michel de Certeau, *The Mystic Fable: Volume I, The Sixteenth and Seventeenth Centuries*, trans. Michael B. Smith (Chicago: University of Chicago Press,1992), p.141–2.

[52] I evidently differ here in my interpretation from the art historian John Rowlands that of 'Far from conveying despair, [the painting's] message is intended as one of belief, that from the decay of the tomb Christ rose again in glory on the third day.' John Rowlands: *Holbein: The Paintings of Hans Holbein the Younger* (New York: Phaidon, 1985), pp.52–3.

[53] Fritz Saxl, 'Holbein and the Reformation', in *Lectures* (London: Warburg Institute, University of London, 1957), vol.1: 277–85. Saxl suggests that Holbein's stance towards the *reformatio* was more in line with Erasmus's. The wording beneath the woodcut calls for reform of the Church, but not with Luther leading it (282).

Basel during a spate of Protestant image smashing between 1521–3, both painters display a form of iconoclasm in their utter erasure of the iconicity of the Christ. The face of Christ, both seen from the front in Holbein's 'Christ as Man of Sorrows' (1519) and seen side-on in 'The Dead Christ in the Tomb', defies any intimation of divinity. The mouths in each depiction are open in a paroxysm of despair and abandonment. For all the apocalyptic and millenarian language of prophecies and astrological predictions, of Savonarola's earlier preaching and Luther's evocations of the Last Days and an impending judgement, there is nothing messianic in these representations. No Second Coming of Christ on a white horse is expected. In fact, in both Dürer's sketch and Holbein's painting there is an overriding expression of inertia.

Both artists evoke a certain cultural mood: 'certain' is vague because moods are understood as more vague than emotions. Emotions have intentionality, they have objects and they bear judgements about affects and feelings. I will have much more to say about embodied emotional states as we proceed through the four volumes. Moods, distinctly, have no intention, no particular object (they may have a universal or general one) and if they are interpretations or judgements about situations such cognitive judgements are weak, lower order perceptions. The mood is negative, nonlibidinal (lacking in desire or articulating a listlessness) and pervasive. Moods are given rhetorical and stylistic expression as 'tone'; given aesthetic form, the tone amplifies the mood.[54]

The tone of Lucas Cranach's 1521 woodcut series *Christi und Antichristi* is markedly different from that in the Dürer sketch and Holbein painting.[55] As court painter to the Elector of Saxony and residing in Wittenberg, Cranch was at the forefront of Luther's revolution[56] as he was also at the forefront of a revival of eroticized paganism.[57] His work in this series shares much with the viral polemics of Luther's early writings and, as we will see, with Melanchthon's *Loci communes*. The pamphlet that he illustrated with the series is a blatant

---

[54] For relationship between aesthetic tone and affective investment see Sianne Ngai, *Ugly Feelings* (Cambridge, MA: Harvard University Press, 2005), pp.38–88. See also Lawrence Grossberg, *We gotta get out of this place: Popular Conservatism and Postmodern Culture* (New York: Routledge, 1992), who views tone as 'the affective investment which enables ideological relations to be internalized and, consequently, naturalized' (p.83). On 'moods' see N.J. Frijda, 'Moods, emotion episodes, and emotions' in Michael Lewis and J.M. Haviland (eds.), *Handbook of Emotions* (New York: Guilford Press, 1993), pp.381–403.

[55] The twenty-six woodcuts are reproduced in Gerald Fleming, 'On the Origins of the Passioni Christi und Antichristi and Lucas Cranach the Elder's Contribution to Reformation Polemics in the Iconography of the Passional', *Gutenberg Jahrbuch* (1973), pp.351–68.

[56] Cranach etched and painted Luther on numerous occasions as part of a conscious public relations exercise as the Reformer came to represent a movement, often in idealized portraits. See Martin Warnke, *Cranachs Luther: Entwürfe für ein Image* (Frankfurt: Fischer Taschenbuch Verlag, 1984).

[57] See Joscelyn Godwin, *The Pagan Dream of the Renaissance* (London: Thames & Hudson, 2002), pp.15–16.

piece of satirical propaganda pitching aspects from the life of Christ into dramatic and ironic tension with aspects from the activities of the pope (viewed as the Antichrist). We know from paintings like the dramatic *Christ Crowned with Thorns* (1510) that Cranach could execute work of remarkable realism and poignancy. But there is no realism in these rough cartoons. The detail is there but it bends towards caricature.[58] Take the two woodblocks illustrating Christ cleansing the Temple and the pope as Antichrist on his papal throne signing Bulls, indulgences, and disposing bishoprics for money. They situate and juxtapose economics and the apocalypticism: the appearance of the Antichrist, often conceived as preceding the return of the Messiah and the establishment of a thousand year reign for the Kingdom of God. Both themes were at the forefront of evangelical protest and the demand for reform. This is an apt set to draw attention to because Christ cleansing the Temple was a metaphor for the Reformer's call for a 'pure gospel' (*rein Evangellium*) as it was perceived to be lived by the primitive Church. The drawings are awkward. In the depiction of the Scriptural scene the Temple background shows the thin Corinthian pillars of a Romanesque church but, Escher-like, the arches are distorted in their spatial representation so that there is no association of the curves with each other. Christ's robes are baggy, crumpled, and incongruous. Faces scowl grotesquely—whether these are the faces of the disciples huddled to the right in seeming dispute with one another or the traders and bankers bent and collapsing into each other in the left hand corner. If the face of Christ looks hollow eyed and reluctant to be doing what he is doing (flagellating them),[59] his left hand is a claw of anger, the muscle of his raised forearm is attenuated, his knees are bent forward forcefully and his toes grip

---

[58] Cranach in fact became famous for his title-page designs that framed the title in a detailed and ornate border. This quickly became the 'trade-mark' of a printing-shop Cranach owned that handled Reformation *Flugschriften*. See Jutta Strahle, *Cranach im Detail: Buchschmuck Lucas Cranachs des Ältens und seiner Werkstatt* (Wittenberg: Drei Kastanien, 1994). Also: Max J. Friedländer and Jakob Rosenberg, *The Paintings of Lucas Cranach* (New York: AbeBooks, 1978), first published in 1911.

[59] Fraternities employing flagellation in dramatic processions of public purification began to emerge following the Black Death. See Norman Cohn, *The Pursuit of the Millennium: Revolutionary Millenarians and Mystical Anarchists of the Middle Ages* (London: Paladin Books, 1970), pp.127–48; and more recently Nicholas Terpstra, *Lay Confraternities and Civic Religion in Renaissance Bologna* (Cambridge: Cambridge University Press, 1995), pp. 61–4, 139–44. In Latin, *flagella* was associated with scourging and the act of penitence. This is an important image then for a key Lutheran idea—the punishment is wrought by Christ, it is a visitation of the wrath of God, as distinct from ecclesial penance shown in the Antichrist depiction. The people Christ is whipping have their back to him and they are not actively involved in the receiving of the scourging. They are simply accepting the *flagella Dei* as God's just punishment. In terms used in an important debate at the time that related to indulgences and the penances, the scene represents *poenitentia passive* (the equivalent of 'by grace alone'), as distinct from *poenitentia active* which is that which we do (for Luther this is a neopelagian notion).

the floor tightly. There is an energy here that is both vicious and controlled, both unleashed by the Christ and restrained (almost wooden) by the artistic expression. The effect overall is jarring.

The scene of the enthroned pope in a cathedral is far more sedate. A demonic looking dog sits in the left hand corner, like a witch's familiar, and above it the pope sits on a large, fat cushion, wearing his tiara and dressed in the heavy folds of an ornate habit. The dog is interesting. He is alert and facing out towards where the imagined artist is sketching and may indeed figure the diabolic.[60] The Corinthian pillars and arches curve elegantly, framing a candlestick on the left hand side of an altar—the rest of the altar lying outside the picture. The baldachino above the papal throne is proportioned correctly and three dimensionally. The ecclesial focus is not on the sacramental dispensation of Eucharistic grace, but papal authority. It is an authority in which God the Son (Christ) has been replaced as God the Father in the figure of the pope who (the commentary informs us) '*erzeigt sich als Gott* ["appears" or even "presents himself" as God]'. The faces are benign—whether they are those of the cardinal, bishops, and friar at the far side of the pope or the supplicants handing over or laying down money on a linen-covered altar in front of the throne that is more like a common table. The pope seems to be both in conversation with the cardinal and keeping his eye on the money coming in.[61] One face only among the supplicants, a man, appears lined with consternation. He is looking directly at the pope with what may be dismay or anger or even adoration.

The real 'drama' lies in the dynamics between the two representations made vivid and immediate through the black and white of paper and printing ink. This is an action that has to be constructed by the observer—reading the iconic details in each scene, cross-referencing and contrasting them to allow the tensions to emerge. The tensions are tonal, counter-punctual, but they create a cognitive, rather than simply emotional, dissonance. The antithetical, even dialectical, presentation is a cerebral one aimed at generating recognition, sardonic laughter, and discussion rather than incitement to action. There

---

[60] In *The Occult Philosophy in the Elizabethan Age* (London: Ark Paperbacks, 1983), the cultural historian, Frances Yates, points out that hunting dogs were classically identified with the senses. She draws attention to Cranach's later painting '"The Melancholy Witch" (1528), modeled on Dürer's "Melancholia I" (1514)'. The dog in Dürer's work is asleep, showing the figure of the woman in a trance, the dog in Cranach's painting very much awake and therefore implicated in the evil of the devilish Sabbath in the top left hand corner of the frame (pp.58–9).

[61] On Leo X's desire to complete St. Peter's Basilica in Rome, the papal Bull *Sacrosanctis* extending the sale of indulgences, the pope's negotiations with Jakob Fulger, the European banker and the machinations of Albrecht, Archbishop of Magdeburg, on behalf of the pope to secure the finances and secure also the Archbishopric of Mainz (and a Cardinal's hat), see Diarmaid MacCulloch, *The Reformation* (London: Penguin Books, 2005), pp.120–3. These events no doubt lie behind Cranach's woodcut as they lay behind Luther's explosive response in the 95 Theses (1517).

is a polemic, the radical apposition of two distinct ideologies, but the satirical irony operates intellectually. The similarity of the architectural backgrounds dehistoricizes; this is not about a difference in time and place (Jesus's historical context and the contemporary papal context). We are not concerned here with temporal change, but with the pure (and purification) and the impure (and unholy), the Second Coming and the Antichrist, the sacred and profane. There are no ambivalences here; the opposition is stark and total between (to use the words of the commentary beneath them) benediction and malediction. The two images are synchronic, rendering both the actions represented contemporaneous and abstract. One might even speak of each image as offering an allegory. For the lack of realism foregrounds the *act* of representation as distinct from *what* is being represented; a disjuncture between the image and its content/meaning. We could relate this back to the early intimations of Mannerism (and the impact of nominalism) that we observed in Dürer.[62] The form of the representation distances the reader/viewer from what is read or viewed. The construction of the antithesis is an intellectual act following the series of recognitions concerning the iconic elements (the papal tiara, for example, or the flagellant's whip). As one historian comments: 'The conscious lack of adornment was indeed part of the polemical agenda. It sought to engage the intellect, not the sense.'[63]

There is no mediation between the antitheses (and this lack of mediation is something we will return to). This produces a complex violence: the pictorial violence of Christ and the violence in the construction of the iconoclastic confrontation by the reader/viewer. The violence, when registered, is immediate for even the commentaries do not mediate and relate one image to the other. The antithesis vividly presents a binocular dissonance; it is the registration of this dissonance that generates the violence (albeit cerebrally). But one of the important points to recognize here—a point that we will return to—is that Cranach's dualisms are strategic and inseparable from the rhetoric of polemic. They are not, here, related to the Pauline binaries—theological and metaphysical—that both Luther and Melanchthon cull from their readings of Paul's *Epistle to the Romans*. Later, between 1526 and 1530, Cranach did develop the motif of an explicitly theological antithesis, Law and Grace, probably with the assistance of Melanchthon.[64] But what Cranach's *Christi und Antichristi* achieves is the distillation of Luther's early theology around two ideas—the gospel and the corruption of the papacy. And it is these two

---

[62] Cranach often was drawn to allegorical figuration, as was Dürer.

[63] Andrew Pettegree, *Reformation and the Culture of Persuasion* (n.25), p.106.

[64] See, Günter Schuchardt, *Gesetze und Genade: Cranach, Luther und die Bilder* (Torgau: Wartburg Stiftung Eisenach, 1994). See also Andrew Pettegree, '"The Law and the Gospel": The Evolution of an Evangelical Pictorial Theme in the Bibles of the Reformation', in Orlaith O'Sullivan (ed.), *The Bible as Book: The Reformation* (London, 2000), pp.123–35.

ideas—rather than the more complex theology of 'justification by faith' or 'salvation by grace alone'—that attempt to capture the popular imagination.[65]

If, as I said, the economic and apocalyptic are at the forefront of the contrast, these themes and their subsequent practices lie nested within a more complex network of other tensions. The legends above the scenes and the commentary by Melanchthon below them are in vernacular German. There is a class struggle here, as the illustrations and the printed pamphlet are aimed at mobilizing ordinary people, the laity. Those people may not be able to read, but certainly could see. If they couldn't read then they could have the legends and commentaries read out to them in a language they understood and spoke.[66] The syntax of the German is overwrought—Melanchthon the humanist could do no other—but the structure of the accumulated clauses is simple, nouns pile up, the vocabulary is non-technical and the text refers continually to where 'further reading' can be found: in the Scriptures. The Scriptures offer an authority of their own[67] that attests to and reinforces the authority behind Christ's action just as they offer a condemnation (a negation of authority) of the papal action. The polemical theology, which is thin Christologically but thick ecclesiologically, is not wrapped in a disenfranchising Latin (as the *Loci communes* is).

THE RHETORIC OF REVOLUTION

Luther's Latin and German display the same abruptness as Cranach's woodcuts; the same love also of polemical irony and paradox; and the same

---

[65] Albrecht Dürer may have come to a conviction of the truth of Luther's theology through understanding 'justification through faith' as Luther defended it at the Heidelberg Disputation (as he testifies). But having examined the number of editions printed of Luther's early writings and the public interest they stirred, Andrew Pettegree concludes: 'what seems to have made the greatest impact was the excoriating criticism of the corruptions of the priesthood (and particularly the papacy) and the doctrine of Scripture alone'. *Reformation and the Culture of Persuasion* (n.25), p.169.

[66] There is much debate about the widespread 'reading' of these pictures and commentaries and their impact upon fostering the Reformation. The classic discussion on German woodcuts, see R.W. Scribner *For the Sake of Simple Folk: Popular Propaganda for the German Reformation* (Cambridge: Cambridge University Press, 1981). He views them as an important bridge between literate, semi-literate, and illiterate classes. This has been challenged: 'there is little evidence that such reading actually played a substantial part in the dissemination of the text'. Andrew Pettegree, *Reformation and the Culture of Persuasion* (n.25), p.119.

[67] We can observe a movement here from the *lectio divina* of the eleventh and twelfth century monks towards an independence of the Scriptural text from the tradition of glosses; a movement from Scripture as an ecclesial text to a secular literary text to be read by the individual and interpreted through a Holy Spirit who was also independent of the work of the body of Christ as the Church.

dialectical structure of question and answer along with balanced formalisms. In his 'Address to the German Nobility' for example, Luther writes of not dealing 'with men in this matter, but with the princes of hell [*wir in dieser Sache nit (sic.) mit Menschen, szondern (sic.) mit den Fürsten der Hölle handeln*].'[68] The contrasts are startling (*Menschen/Fürsten*), the alliteration pugnacious (*Hölle handeln*) and the assonance of the denunciation total (*nicht mit*). The tone created is one of demagogic assurance and righteous anger; even when advocating peace and humility. The effect is visceral and confrontational. Statements like this demand a response. Luther's Latin can be more measured. Thesis 82 from *95 Theses* (1517) reads: '*Papa . . . infinitas animas redimit propter pecuniam funestissimam ad structuram Basilice ut causam levissimam*' ['The Pope . . . redeems innumerable souls on account of money, a most perishable thing, with which to build St. Peter's church, a most trivial purpose'].[69] The assonance and alliteration here combines with antithesis (*pecuniam/structuram*) and internal rhyme (*funestissimam/levissimam*). The rhetoric is showy but controlled by the pithiness of both content and syntax. The effect is a muted anger, more intellectual and formal than emotional. But the Latin of 'On the Babylonian Captivity of the Church', particularly the opening pages before he slides into teacher-mode on taking communion in both kinds, is caustic as Luther derides the 'drivel' of his critics from some gargantuan height. 'I pass over other matters lest I drown you in the sludge of this foul drain'[70] is a very polite translation of the Latin *te enecem sentina huius graveolentissimae coacae* ['lest the overpowering stench of shit in this sewer deprives you of life'].[71] Luther was writing about emotional experience and *affectus* from 1513 in his lectures on the Psalms,[72] but the emotional or affective as such is not the object of Luther's theological attention, and he does not employ a wide technical vocabulary for human emotional life.

I point this out because what is striking about Melanchthon's *Loci communes* of 1521 is the way the Latin flashes and flares incandescently, while

[68] 'Address to the German Nobility', trans. Charles M. Jacobs in *Luther's Works*, vol.44: *The Christian in Society I*, ed. James Atkinson, gen. ed. Helmut T. Lehmann (Philadelphia: Fortress Press, 1966), pp.115–217, p.125. German text: *Martin Luther: Studienausgabe*, Band 2, Hans-Ulrich Delius (hrsg.) (Berlin: Evangelische Verlagsanstalt, 1982), p.98.

[69] 'Ninety-Five Theses', trans. Bertram Lee Woolf, *Reformation Writings by Martin Luther* (London: The Lutterworth Press, 1937), p.30. The Latin text is available on <http://www.luther.de/en/95th-lat.html>, accessed August 2015.

[70] Translated 'On the Pagan Servitude of the Church' by Benjamin Lee Woolf, *Reformation Writings of Martin Luther* (London: Lutterworth Press, 1952), pp.212–13.

[71] Latin text in Hans-Ulrich Delius (hrsg.) *Martin Luther: Studienausgabe*, Band 2 (Berlin: Evangelische Verlagsanstalt, 1982), p.168. Luther is indeed famous for his scatology metaphors, but they are not as gratuitous or hyperbolic as they might seem. Woodcuts at the time show a close association between shit and the Satanic: witches kiss the anus of defecating goats and bishops are seen emerging for the arse of the Beast itself.

[72] I owe this observation of Dr. Simeon Zahl. See his essay, 'The Bondage of the Affections: Willing, Feeling, and Desiring in Luther's Theology, 1513–25' in Dale Coulter and Amos Yong

remaining polished and eloquent, and emotion is at the forefront of his argument. This is crucial for understanding what happens to systematic theology in the hands of this Reformer and why. It is significant here to note that both Luther's early deliberations on *affectus* and Melanchthon's forensic employment of the term in his 1521 treatise both emerge from a late medieval practice of *lectio divina*: meditative commentaries on the Psalms in Luther, an humanist's examination of Paul's *Letter to the Romans* in Melanchthon. The further theology, in its pursuit of being systematic, moves away from Biblical commentary, the more it becomes an intellectual, 'scientific' investigation.

But we have to begin by asking a more basic question: what is necessary to start a revolution? It is not clear from Luther's writings immediately following the *95 Theses* that he intended anything more than protest; and many had protested before (Savonarola) and were still protesting: Erasmus, for example. His open letter to Pope Leo in 1520 is placatory (or ironic): 'O most unhappy Leo, you who sit on the most dangerous throne of all, truly I am telling you the truth, for I yearn for your good.'[73] In this he seems concerned for Leo's personal well-being, as if as Antichrist he were possessed by the diabolic but didn't realize it. Some scholars have argued that Luther had no intentions of forming his own church but rather reforming the existing one.[74] This receives backing from even the boisterous 'On the Babylonian Captivity' that reads more as an indictment against Roman despotism and the toadying that reinforces it than striking out as a pioneer of a new ecclesia. How could such a new ecclesia be conceived? Some even see Luther as optimistic of a secular peace-settlement, following the Peasant's War and its concluding Treaty of Weingarten (1525).[75] Both these views are debateable. My own sense, in line with Heiko Oberman, is that although Luther was not chiliastic, his commitment to predestination and his sense of himself as a 'prophet' suggest his mission was to accentuate the work of Antichrist (the papacy) so that the 'elect' might be called forth from the mayhem. He heads into a storm he knows he has to continue to awaken. He takes every opportunity to propel himself into the public eye. This was his calling, as he understood it. Works like his *Sermon on Indulgences* (1520), being in the vernacular, are feisty and picking a fight, and there can

---

(eds.), *The Spirit, the Affections, and the Christian Tradition* (Notre Dame, IL: University of Notre Dame Press, forthcoming). It is explored also in Steven E. Ozment, *Homo Spiritualis: A Comparative Study of the Anthropology of Johannes Tauler, Jean Gerson, and Martin Luther (1509–16) in the Context of their Theological Thought* (Leiden: E.J. Brill, 1969), particularly pp.87–138 and 168–74. See also Günter Bader, in his *Psalterium affectum palaestra: Prolegomena zu einer Theologie des Psalters* (Tübingen: Mohr Siebeck, 1996), pp.155–86.

[73] 'An Open Letter to the Pope (1520)', Benjamin Lee Woolf, *Reformation Writings* (n.70), p.43.

[74] I. Höß, 'Humanismus und Reformation', in *Geschichte Thüringens*, H. Patze and W. Schlesinger (eds.), vol. III (Köln, 1967): 71–84.

[75] J. Wallmann, 'Luthers letztes Wort in Bauernkrieg' in *Der Wirklichkeitsanspruch von Theologie und Religion*, D. Henke *et al.* (eds.) (Tübingen, 1976), pp.57–75.

have been nothing so dramatic as the spectacles of Luther in dispute with the Augustinian Chapter (in Heidelberg), his confrontation with one of the leading theologians of the day, Cardinal Cajetan, at Augsburg, the disputation in Leipzig, and going head to head with Charles V, the Holy Roman Emperor, at the Diet of Worms. To say nothing of the notoriety of having a Papal Bull issued by Pope Leo X excommunicating him (*Exurge, Domine*, 1520).

There was popular sentiment and considerable exposure to the kind of social media available at the time to create celebrity. But, as Diarmaid MacCulloch points out: 'The old church was immensely strong.' MacCulloch, as an Oxford don, goes on the express his view that this strength 'could only have been overcome by the explosive power of an idea'.[76] But the idea he has in mind is 'justification'—a complex theological notion, indeed. I am not convinced. The question of justification and its relationship with predestination was common at the time, both within Luther's Wittenberg circle and beyond. It didn't provoke the furore that the Reformation unleashed, even in the hands of the belligerent Andreas Bodenstein von Karlstadt, a teacher also at Wittenberg, who also preached a strong version of justification by faith.[77] It was only much later, and under Melanchthon's guiding hand, that the 'idea' of justification was distinguished from sanctification, and was 'imputed' to the believer instantly by divine fiat.[78] If there were a single driving force then I would put my money on the liberation of Scripture made possible by printing. Either way, Luther did seem genuinely overwhelmed by the response his polemics were receiving, and probably saw the dawn of the apocalypse rather than the evangelical church as the *telos*.[79]

Melanchthon, on the other hand, seems more clear-sighted. Sermons, pamphlets, broadsides, *Flugschriften,* are all ephemeral literatures: they are occasional pieces. The hymns and metrical translations of the psalms were less occasional and formed the basis for a distinct Protestant liturgy, as did Luther's translation of the Bible into German for Scriptural readings, though these appear in the years that follow 1521. But there is nothing at all occasional about *Loci communes*: it is a new approach to dogmatic theology, a book-length systematics that puts the main joists in place for what, nine years later, will become the Augsburg Confession for the Lutheran church.

---

[76] D. MacCulloch, *The Reformation* (n.61), p.110.

[77] See Heiko A. Oberman's essay 'Wittenburg's War on Two Fronts: What Happened in 1518 and Why' in his *The Reformation: Roots and Ramifications* (Bloomsbury: T&T Clark, 2004), pp.117–48.

[78] The increasing move towards formalizing the doctrine of justification by faith was given considerable impetus in the Osiandrian controversy during the 1540s and '50s. It reached its final, confessional, usage in the Formula of Concord in 1580. I owe this observation to Dr. Simeon Zahl.

[79] See Gordon Rupp, 'Luther against 'The Turk, the Pope and the Devil' in Peter Newman Brooks (ed.), *Seven-Headed Luther* (Oxford: Oxford University Press, 1983), pp.255–73.

Melanchthon seems more clear-sighted about what a break with Rome would mean, and perhaps less apocalyptic than Luther. When it was not at all self-evident to the general public what was being demanded by Luther's confrontation, Melanchthon set out a new theological grammar. There is something programmatic, even manifesto-like, about his *Loci communes*.

But to return to my question: what is necessary to start a revolution? Major social changes were already significantly apparent: there was a rise in population following the dearth of the Black Death; there was a weakening of the structures of feudalism with a growing middle class, the organization of an independent work force within the gilds, and the formation of a new social order that was neither ecclesial nor aristocratic; there was a considerable move towards urban life, civic culture, and governance by secular magistrates; and there were reforms of lay piety that were levelling the hierarchy separating priests from ordinary people. But the people affected by these changes needed to be mobilized in order to shape new communities of belief. Furthermore, an alternative social and ecclesial existence had to be conceived. In Charles Taylor's words a new social imaginary and moral order had to be envisaged.[80] The immense strength of the old Church lay in its monopoly of symbolic and financial resources: churches and aesthetic treasures, authority and institutional structures, a network of relations with the ruling classes, considerable revenues, and over a thousand years of the consolidation of Christendom. But there were two resources not completely under the control of the old Church. Each of them had the potential to engender a new social imaginary and a moral order. Luther and Melanchthon recognized and deployed them to create new religious allegiances: the Bible and religious emotion. The key to marshalling support was a way of articulating a theology, orally and scripted, that was viral; that is, getting their belligerent German and visceral Latin into the life-stream of cultures, giving urgency to religious conviction. It energized; it enthused. The torpor we found in Dürer's 'Christ on the Mount of Olives' and Hans Holbein the Younger's 'Dead Christ in the Tomb', the malaise and ennui of the high Middle Ages, was shaken and galvanized.

LOCI COMMUNES

Loci communes[81] (1521) structures what Melanchthon understood as the core doctrines of the Christian faith in accordance with a new religious education

---

[80] Charles Taylor, *A Secular Age* (n.7), pp.159–218.

[81] I have benefitted enormously from being able to discuss both Luther and Melanchthon's interest in the affective with my colleague at Oxford, Dr. Simeon Zahl who is preparing a monograph on this topic, and allowed me to see a draft of his chapter on Luther and Melanchthon,

of the emotions. The language of the faith it professes is performative.[82] This is important because while no doubt Charles Taylor is correct to see the four forces behind the disenchantment of the world as activism, uniformatization, homogenization, and rationalization (that establish new moral, social and ecclesial orders),[83] paradoxically the disembedding process is profoundly corporeal in its early stages in so far as it relates to pedagogies of affect and experience and, as I will demonstrate, it certainly doesn't leave 'enchanted' reality behind.

Throughout his work, whether theological or scientific, Melanchthon consistently shows how 'things need to be known by experience'.[84] The core of *Loci communes* (1521) is a dialectic at once physical (carnal because all affect is embodied), intellectual (having a logical development) and theological (a persuasion of and participation in the efficacy of faith). Fundamentally, the economy of that dialectic is emotional, existential, and experiential; informing our understanding of the personal, the social, and the created orders, and our subsequent behaviour. And so, the passionate disorders of sin are exposed by the power of law with respect to 'dispositions [*affecti*]' and 'affections [*affecti*]',[85] and this opens a space for faith, the promise of the gospel and the emotional re-ordering by grace. In fact, *being affected*, 'this experience [of] the will of God [*experti voluntatem dei*]',[86] is an indication of the operations of grace and evidence that one is among the Elect (those who 'truly believe . . .

and pointed to places and people who could supplement my own reading. Dr. Zahl observes: 'the single most reliable place to find affections language in the writings of either figure is in relation to law and gospel'.

[82] The focus on teaching and rhetoric, like the method of finding the central and fundamental axioms of a subject (*capita communes* or *loci communes*), were key characteristics of fifteen-century humanism, more widely, and popularized by Rudolf Agricola's *De inventione dialectica*. The 'topic' now becomes the basis for the construction of knowledge, whether in law or theology. See Melanchthon's oration on Agricola, who he commends to students for his 'method of learning' in Philip Melanchthon, *Orations on Philosophy and Education*, ed. Sachiko Kusukawa, trans. Christine F. Salazar (Cambridge: Cambridge University Press, 1999), pp.227–35. It is interesting to note the association, because Melanchthon's use of '*loci*' 'often bear a close resemblance to similar juridical models'—Cesari Vasoli, '*Loci communes* and the Rhetorical and Dialectical Traditions' in Joseph C. McLelland (ed.), *Peter Martyr Vermigli and the Italian Reform* (Waterloo: Wilfred Laurier University Press, 1977), pp.17–28, p.24. The *methodos* was pedagogical and instrumental in its orientation, aiming at accuracy and efficiency.

[83] Charles Taylor, *A Secular Age* (n.7), pp.86–8.

[84] Oration 'On Atronomy and Geography' in *Orations on Philosophy and Education*, ed. Sachiko Kusukawa, trans. Christine F. Salazar (n.82), p.118.

[85] *Loci Communes Theologici* (1521), trans. Lowell J. Satre, revised and edited by Wilhelm Pauck for the Library of Christian Classics, *Melanchthon and Bucer* (Louisville: Westminster John Knox Press, 1969), pp.18–152. For the Latin text I have consulted Robert Stupperich, *Melanchthons Werke*, Bd.II/1, Hans Engelland (hrsg.) (Gütersloh: C. Bertelsmann Verlag, 1952). When the Latin makes an important difference, then the first reference is to the English and the second to the Latin text: p.56/48–9.

[86] Ibid., p.94/95.

really believe [*vere credunt*][87] in their heart.[88] The 'heart' (Melanchthon uses 'soul' sparingly at this point in his career), its inner movements and dispositions, is the theatre for a theo-drama.

This emotional economy or regime[89] forms the deep structure that organizes and dialectically relates the specific *loci* treated. The text creates, by calling out those who share the same emotions, the feelings Luther's work had been arousing, and thereby creates an emotional community.[90] Theologically, it is conceived in terms of a pneumatology (the Spirit as the cause of emotional transformation) that is dynamic and energizing, but there are sociological,

---

[87] Ibid., p.100/101–2. The role of *affectus* in the 1521 *Loci communes* has been given extensive attention since Wilhelm Mauer's seminal essay 'Zur Komposition der Loci Melanchthons von 1521: ein Beitrage zur Frage Melanchthon und Luther', *Luther-Jahrbuch* 25 (1958), 146–80. Detailed research has also been undertaken on the model and role of affect at this time. See Karl-Heinz zur Mühlen, 'Die Affektenlehre in Spätmittelalter und in der Reformationszeit' in Johannes Brosseder (hrsg.) *Reformatorisches Profil: Studien zum Weg Martin Luthers und der Reformation* (Göttingen, 1995), 101–22; and, by the same author, 'Melanchthons Auffassung vom Affekt in *Loci communes* 1521' in Michael Beyer and Günther Wartenberg (hrsg.) *Humanismus und Wittenberger Reformation* (Leipzig: Evangelische Verlagsanstalt, 1996), 327–36. See also the more wide-ranging essay by Bernd Wannenwetsch, 'Affekt and Gebot: Zur ethischen Bedeutung der Leidenschaften im Licht der Theologie Luthers und Melanchthons' in *Passion, Affekt und Leidenschat in der Frühen Neuzeit*, Bd. 1, Johann Anselm Steiger (hrsg.) (Wiesbaden: Harrassowitz Verlag, 2005), 203–15. In English, see Gregory B. Graybill, *Evangelical Free Will: Philipp Melanchthon's Doctrinal Journey on the Origins of Faith* (Oxford: Oxford University Press, 2010), pp.81– 105 and pp.246–9.

[88] Both sin as unbelief and faith as true belief 'enters into all the vicissitudes of our life and death because we use no creature rightly unless we do so through faith, and we abuse all creatures by unbelief, that is, if we do not believe that in using the creature we are pleasing God, and if we do not believe in the mercy and goodwill of God toward us while using the creature'. *Loci*, (n.85), p.103.

[89] In their book *The Sociology of Religious Emotion* (Oxford: Oxford University Press, 2010), Ole Riis and Linda Woodhead define an 'emotional regime' as serving 'to bring together the personal, symbolic, and social aspects of emotion, and captures the way in which emotions related embodied agents to their wider social and material-symbolic interactions, anchor and communicate the emotional agenda, and serve as normative points of reference' (p.69). This is highly pertinent because it points to how intersubjective such regimes are. They are not simply personally and subjectively experienced. All religions involve emotional programmes.

[90] 'An emotional community is a group in which people have a common stake, interests, values, and goals. Thus it is often a social community. But it is possibly a "textual community," created and reinforced by ideologies, teaching, and common presuppositions.' Barbara H. Rosenwein, *Emotional Communities in the Early Middle Ages* (Ithaca: Cornell University Press, 2006), pp.24–5. These communities arise because of the social and relational nature of emotions. In his own book on this area, *Best Laid Schemes: The Psychology of Emotions* (Cambridge: Cambridge University Press, 1992), Keith Oakley views social emotions as helping to 'manage transitions to new joint plans and help to maintain them' (p.178). In this way they become part of 'regimes' following and changing goals for living. For the way emotions were important aspects of religious piety, sermons and liturgies at the time of Melanchthon see Susan Karant-Nunn, *The Reformation of Feeling: Shaping the Religious Emotions in Early Modern Germany* (Oxford: Oxford University Press, 2010).

physiological, and psychological correlates for this pneumatology that brings it close to an earlier sacramental realism.[91]

The existence of a newly galvanized emotional community was expressed graphically in Melanchthon's problems with the Zwicklau 'prophets' and the fanaticism of Müntzer's Anabaptist movement in Münster. These were events that followed the publication of *Loci* and had a close association with the emotional energies released by Luther's writings. Religious emotional programmes energize in ways that are contagious and antinomian.[92] Theologically, a pneumatology has to be firmly locked into accounts of the Trinitarian Godhead, the work of Christ and human sinfulness. *Loci* is not without such accounts— particularly of human sinfulness; but neither the Trinity nor Christology are foregrounded in 1521. They are given much more attention, in the wake of the violence and troubles that ensue, in latter revisions of *Loci communes*. In 1521, the emotional economy is founded upon sin–law–grace: soteriology is what is keenly at stake. These are not distinct theologoumena set within a web of modern dualisms and binaries (flesh/spirit, law/gospel, sin/grace, even occasionally philosophy/theology). They are related to each other and each side of their opposite is necessary and intrinsic to the dynamic relations. Hence Melanchthon sees the inability of the Spirit to be received by human flesh and yet, by faith, is received; the operation of law and gospel through the Old as well as the New Testament; the revelation of sin as the prelude to the reception of grace. He is uncovering here a *Grundlage*, a divine order and a divine rhythm through which salvation is always present and working, with the coming of Christ as the final and full expression of a promise given to Adam and Eve. A distinction remains: between God as creator and redeemer, and creation. But the invisible interpenetrates the visible and those who entrust themselves by faith to God recognize and experience both the distinction and the interpenetration. In reading and interpreting Scripture Melanchthon is listening for the divine communication, the eternal *sermo*, a sacred rhetoric. We can, then, see Melanchthon advocates what John Milbank has described as 'a theory of human being as a linguistic being which participates in the divine linguistic being'.[93]

Since the ground-breaking work of Quirinus Breen in 1947 and Hans-Georg Geyer's work in the mid-1960s, we have come to understand more clearly how

[91] This is what the Finnish School of Lutheran studies has drawn attention to, relating it to Aquinas's 'realism', though I would suggest Augustine is the theologian most evident (see n.42).

[92] See Randall Collins, *Interaction Ritual Chains* (Princeton, NJ: Princeton University Press, 2004).

[93] John Milbank, *The Word Made Strange: Theology, Language, Culture* (Oxford: Blackwell, 1997), p.2.

the concept of *loci communes* is related to strategies in rhetoric and logic developed by humanists such as Rudolf Agricola and Erasmus.[94] Attention has been drawn to earlier uses of the term *loci communes* within Melanchthon's developing philosophy of language, logic, and meaning. Melanchthon is pursuing and examining the naked persuasive force of communication itself, and it is in that context that *loci communes* become significant as a rhetorical, logical and existential category. In Melanchthon's *De rhetorica libri* (1519) this pursuit was understood as *inventio*—finding the appropriate genre and structure for the subject of an argument. But the power of the persuasion lies in relating *inventio* to a 'study of the *loci communes* . . . by which they [the orator] might observe the nature and pure, deep power of these subjects'.[95] The *loci communes* were the basic, foundational truths, 'certain universal rules of living [*regulae quaedam vivendi generales*], established for men by nature [*natura hominibus persuasae*] which not for nothing I have called laws of nature'.[96] We can hear in the Latin the association of 'living', 'nature', and *persuasae* ('fixed' or 'established' as a perfect passive participle, but from the verb *persuadeo*, to convince or persuade). The force of conviction can be unleashed by the right rhetoric. Melanchthon's *De rhetorica* 'gave systematic expression to a deeper view of the ontological *status* of thought and language. A properly sharpened and focussed linguistic method captured the power of the created universe.'[97] *Loci communes* was structured around finding this rhythm of ontological truth in the syncopating counterpoint of sin–law–grace, the divine order of things. In doing this, the vivacious eloquence of the treatise imitated and bore witness to the vivaciousness of Scripture as sacred oration, itself an *imitatio* and testimony to the Word of God, the divine *sermo*. By faith, the operation of these three levels of communication—Scripture, the Christ event, and divine *sermo*—becomes revelatory and authoritative. All three levels inspire and arouse the affections. We are not just told and taught; we are con-formed by and inserted into 'the speech and diction [*sermonem ac phrasin*] of Scripture'.[98] In and through *Loci communes*, Melanchthon is teaching the 'teaching of the Spirit [that] cannot be drunk in purity except from Scripture itself [*doctrina spiritus pure*]'.[99]

'By faith' is the theological fulcrum upon which the argument of *Loci communes* rests. *Sola fide*, as Heiko A. Oberman, points out, is 'another spearhead aimed at the claims of reason (*ratio*)'[100]—that is if *ratio* is understood in terms of neoscholastic metaphysical logic-chopping and human

---

[94] For Qurinus Breen see 'The Terms "*Loci Communes*" and "*Loci*" in Melanchthon', *Church History* 16 (1947), 197–209. For H.-G. Geyer see his *Von der Geburt des wahren Menschen* (Neukirchen, 1965), pp.49ff. More recently, see John R. Schneider, *Philip Melanchthon's Rhetorical Construction of Biblical Authority* (Lampeter: Edwin Mellen Press, 1990).

[95] Cited and translated from *De rhetorica* in Schneider (n.94) p.73.   [96] Ibid., p.76.

[97] Ibid., p.77.   [98] *Loci* (n.85), p.41/31.   [99] Ibid., p.152/163.

[100] Heiko A. Oberman, *The Reformation: Roots and Ramifications* (n.77), p.12.

reasoning. For this is Melanchthon's first enemy in the *Loci*—the university curriculum pursued through so much Aristotle and scholastic commentaries on Thomas (by Petrus Tartaretus), on Scotus (by Antonius Sirecti), and on Gregory of Rimini (by Christopher Scheurl).[101] This *ratio* is philosophical (rather than Scriptural) and it has only a qualified value (*aestimatio*) for it is only 'the judgement of human reason [*ab humanae rationis aestimatione*] . . . [by] writers of commentaries [who] did not supress their mental faculties [*to psuchikon*]'. Melanchthon wishes to pursue 'spiritual judgement', that which is 'spiritually breathed or inspired [*pneumatikon spirarent*]'.[102] As Timothy J. Wengert points out this pursuit and pneumatic activity is mediated through experience: 'in 1535 [when Melanchthon revised *Loci*] he summarized the list [to drive away doubts; fear God truly; conceive true trust; perform true obedience . . .] under the rubric "spiritual affections." This term seems to have come from a parallel comment in 1533 [lectures to students], which mentioned "interior motions in accord with the law of God".'[103] But the pursuit of spiritual judgement and spiritually informed inner motions does not conceive of another form of human reasoning, and faith is not opposed to reason as such (otherwise there is no argument to be made, by Melanchthon or anyone else).

Debates have raged around the reason/faith issue in *Loci*. I am not entering those debates directly but rather wish to show that there are not two poles—rationalism, at one end, fideism, at the other. Some commentators have recognized 'their mutual interpenetration'.[104] One has gone further, arguing, 'there was, for him, no distinction between faith and reflective reason'.[105] I wish to put the issue of reason and faith in Melanchthon differently. In the dedicatory letter, Melanchthon tells Tileman Plattener that what he desires is for all Christians to be occupied by the divine Scriptures 'and be thoroughly

[101] For a detailed account of the curriculum at the University of Wittenberg and the changes of reform that Luther and Melanchthon, among others, were demanding, see Sachiko Kusukawa, *The Transformation of Natural Philosophy: The Case of Philip Melanchthon* (Cambridge: Cambridge University Press, 1995), chapter 2, and D.C. Steinmetz, *Luther and Staupitz: An Essay in the Intellectual Origins of the Protestant Reformation* (Durham, NC: Duke University Press, 1980).

[102] *Loci* (n.85), p.19/4. It is significant that Melanchthon's earliest reform programme, announcing in his inaugural lecture (that first drew Luther's attention to the young man) was pedagogical.

[103] Timothy J. Wengert, 'Philip Melanchthon and the Origins of the "Three Causes" (1533–1535): An Examination of the Roots of the Controversey over the Freedom of the Will' in Irene Dingel, Robert Kolb, Nicole Kuropka, and Timothy J. Wengert, *Philip Melanchthon: Theologian in Classroom, Confession, and Controversy* (Göttingen: Vandenhoeck & Ruprecht, 2012), pp.183–208, p.192.

[104] Heinrich Bornkamm, 'Melanchthons Menschenbild', in Walter Elliger (hrsg.), *Philipp Melanchthon: Forschungsbeiträge zur vierhundertsten Wiederkehr seines Todestages dargeboten in Wittenberg, 1960* (Vandenhoeck & Ruprecht: Göttingen, 1960), pp.76–92 (p.87).

[105] John R. Schneider, *Philip Melanchthon's Rhetorical Construal*, (n.94), p.247.

transformed into their nature [*in illarium indolem*]'.[106] It is the transformation of reason through that engagement with the inner and generic quality [*indoles*] that the Scriptures possess (through the Spirit)—an occupation that must be undertaken in faith (otherwise there is no transformation possible and the text is simply dead letters)—that opens the way to seeing, thinking, and experiencing anew. The transformation is possible by grace operating upon that which is at the human root of both reason and faith: embodied dispositions. Once the heart has been changed through faith and the work of the Spirit as the 'living' will of God, the 'living' law or order of things,[107] then a new understanding follows tracing the proper theo-logic of both creation and salvation. Reason and faith are only polarities if they are understood as disembodied intellectual (and anti-intellectual) operations.

The reference to the Greek word *to psuchikon* above, and the use of other Greek words throughout the text, is important and shall lead our exploration into this seminal text that not only articulated 'something radically new in theological science—a system of doctrine drawn from the Scriptures', but also for a 'hundred years ... was a textbook of dogmatics in the schools of Germany'.[108] Its influence can even be discerned in Calvin's admiration for the book and the structure of his *Institutes*. There are three uses of the Greek noun *psuchikos* in Paul's *First Letter to the Corinthians* 15.44 that are relevant. The first is 2.14 and where it qualifies 'human being' (*psuchikos ... anthropos*): 'But the natural man does not receive the things of the Spirit.' The second time it is used is when Paul refers to a pre-resurrection body (*sōma psuchikon*) as distinct from a resurrection body (*sōma pneumatikon*) (15.44 and 46). Despite certain English translations *psuchikos* has nothing necessarily to do with mental faculties. Rather it refers to the natural human condition, particularly the physiological condition. It is a Hebrew conception of human being as living through being governed by the breath (*psuchē*) of God. It is used elsewhere in Greek literature to describe the sensual and appetitive nature of human life. The *ratio* of the philosophers then that Melanchthon is describing is not truly rational at all. In a letter to John Lange, written by Melanchthon in July 1519, he approaches what I understand him to be pointing to in the opening of *Loci*. He is answering a query about the way the Church Fathers interpreted the Bible. 'All of us interpret Scripture differently, because we have had different experiences and feelings.' The Fathers did not always read them aright, hence their views conflict. 'Their emotions often led them astray and they abused the Word.'[109] That is why an understanding of spiritual judgement demands a new religious education of the emotions.

[106] *Loci* (n.85), p.19/4.   [107] Ibid., pp.123–4.
[108] Clyde L. Manschreek, *Melanchthon: The Quiet Reformer* (New York: Abingdon Press, 1958), pp.82–3.
[109] Ibid., p.50.

And so we will not fully appreciate what Melanchthon is trying to do in *Loci* without recognizing the relationship between truth, rhetoric, and medicine (because emotional life was the concern of medical science).[110]

Before doing that two further, clarifying points need to be made. First, the insertion of the Greek word indicates for whom this book is written. At Luther's insistence and in Luther's absence, Melanchthon has begun to lecture on Paul's *Letter to the Romans*. An outline for Paul's key teachings in the *Letter* had been circulated to students and, without Melanchthon's permission, published. *Loci* was written to correct that earlier publication. It was composed then for students, although probably not just at Wittenberg since the university there was networked with other universities in Germany and Switzerland (Erfurt, Basel, and Leipzig, for example). The significance of this is that while *Loci* is a programmatic articulation of Luther's theology is was not intended for the general public. Earlier I cited one of Luther's ninety-five theses to point out the formalism of the Latin style, but although Luther explicitly states his aim is to provoke an academic debate, most historians now accept that the aim of the work was to be 'an out-and-out manifesto . . . Now he is conscious of an educational responsibility that extends out and over the walls of the university into the Church as the "congregation of the faithful".'[111] Hence Luther sent a copy of the theses to the Archbishop of Mainz, allowed their rapid circulation and, within three months they were translated into German, printed and distributed. Melanchthon's aim was first and foremost educational. The treatise has to be viewed in the context of an educational reform at the university that he had announced in his inaugural lecture delivered four days after his arrival in Wittenberg, 'On Correcting the Studies of Youth'.[112] He saw it as a textbook. The emotional pedagogy he advanced was for university students of theology. The dangers of theology, written in this way, with this emphasis upon the emotional, would come across all the more clearly in the light of the spiritual madness unleashed in 1522. The book was translated into German by Georg Spalatin, in 1522, but Spalatin was not at the university—although he did have the ear of the Elector with respect to the new university he had founded, as letters between him and the professors at the university demonstrate. He was court chaplain and secretary to

---

[110] Melanchthon's interest in medicine and the 'virtues' of certain plants is well attested. See his orations 'On the Merit of the Art of Medicine' (pp.169–74) and 'On the Life of Galen' (pp.212–20) in *Orations on Philosophy and Education*, ed. Sachiko Kusukawa, trans. Christine F. Salazar (n.82).

[111] Oberman, *The Reformation* (n.77), p.119.

[112] A translation of this lecture can be found in *A Melanchthon Reader*, trans. Ralph Keen (New York: Peter Lang, 1988), pp.47–57. In his 1520 'Oration of Thoman Rhadinus Agaainst the Heretic Martin Luther', Melanchthon echoes Luther's call for the overthrow of the Antichrist in order to be rescued from Babylonian captivity, but this was to begin with reform within the universities with respect to a theological curriculum founded upon scholastic philosophy and commentaries.

Frederick of Saxony, accompanying his master to both the Diets of Augsburg and Worms. Spalatin, while translating *Loci*, knew where Luther had been hidden while Melanchthon still believed his friend had been murdered.

Secondly, the Greek word in the Dedicatory Letter strikes an opening note in the *Loci* which, having acknowledged and rejected the structures of other *Summae*, opens with the nature of being human.[113] All that follows—about the nature of sin, the intensification and consciousness of sin brought about by the law, the utter dependence upon grace for deliverance from the law of sin and death, and the court-room account of atonement that demonstrates how we are justified only by faith in what Christ achieved upon the cross—follows from Melanchthon's account of the human condition under the bondage of *affectus*. This he takes directly from Paul, and Paul's own use of *to psuchikos*.

Of course, renaissance humanism—the precursor to what Taylor calls 'exclusive humanism' (exalting human potential to the point that no longer required God to explain or better the human situation and radicalizing the immanent resources for moral life)[114]—gave credence to human beings being a little lower than the angels. But as Melanchthon's later remarks on Pico della Mirandola clarify, and the opening section of *Loci* illustrate, 'man is evil ... [and] all the works of men ... are actually corrupt'.[115] Melanchthon, on at least two occasions critiques Mirandolla, though not for his account of the human condition. The two occasions are noteworthy. Melanchthon critiques Mirandolla's view of eloquence as mere rhetoric in his *Elementorum rhetorices libri duo* (1547). Melanchthon contends, on the contrary, that eloquence [*Ausdruckskraft*—that which is expressive] is the 'original and not the unnatural form of language'.[116] The second occasion was in a study and defence of astrology and astronomy prefixed to the 1531 edition of Sacrobosco's *De sphaera* in which he takes Mirandolla to task for his attack on astrology.

Why are these critical remarks about Mirandolla important in the light of Melanchthon's acceptance of human nature as utterly depraved and fallen? First: because what emerges is Melanchthon's conviction of the power of language—which returns us to my remarks on style in his and Luther's polemics. The 1521 edition of *Loci communes* ends by citing I Corinthians 4.20: 'for the kingdom of God does not consist in talk [*en logo*], but in power [*en dunamei*]'. There is an important relationship between eloquence, proclaiming the gospel and power. Secondly, we begin to see a background for understanding why, in the opening section of *Loci*, Melanchthon attacks the

---

[113] In a manner reminiscent of Cyril of Jerusalem, Melanchthon states that there is no need to labour through the doctrine of the unity of God, the Trinity, Creation, and the Incarnation, for we 'do better to adore the mysteries of Deity [*mysteria divinitatis*] than to investigate them'. *Loci* (n.85), p.21.

[114] Charles Taylor, *A Secular Age* (n.7) pp.242–69.   [115] *Loci* (n.85), pp.34–9.

[116] *Elementa rhetorices*, ed. Volkhard Wels (Berlin: Weidler Buchverlag, 2001), p.81.

notion of human beings having a free will (*arbitrium*) and emphasizes everything occurs by 'divine determination [*in destinationem divinam*]' such that predestination must be discussed 'at the very outset of my work'.[117] We will return to this.

First we must understand that *affectus* (which is a broad term covering emotions, moods, dispositions, and attitudes) governs all human thinking and acting. It was Seneca who began to use this term for the emotions, often using it alongside the will as *voluntas*. After Augustine, Melanchthon views the dominant affection as self-love and this distorts every act of the human will (*voluntas*). In his critique of human beings in possession of free will, Melanchthon does not deny us some ability to will, but he distinguishes between the Pelagian fantasies of *arbitrium* and the limitations and perversions of *voluntas*.[118] In Latin *arbitrium* is associated with decisive acts; it emphasizes decision-making and intellectual judgement. *Voluntas* can be a synonym, but also carries the sense of 'I wish' (*volo*), 'I desire', 'I incline towards' or 'choose'. With Augustine *voluntas* is caught up in the movements of emotion (*motus*). The orientation of the will towards *amor sui, cupiditas*, and *libido dominandi* will mean that the emotions are totally disordered and so, therefore, are the acts that follow from such a will. So if 'the will [*voluntas*] is wrongly directed, the emotions will be wrong; if the will [*voluntas*] is right, the emotions will not only be blameless, but praiseworthy. The will [*voluntas*] is engaged in all of them; in fact they are all essentially acts of will [*voluntas*]. For what is desire or joy but an act of will [*voluntas*] in agreement [*consensione*] with what we wish for [*volumus*].'[119] If the will is orientated towards loving God (*amor dei*) then the emotions and acts are good and true. *Voluntas* is not simply a cognitive decision in Augustine—it operates within a spectrum of love, self-focused or God-focused. Melanchthon seems to take over this notion of the will as *voluntas* and emphasize its inability to make a right judgement at all where it is caught up within the emotional stews of sin. 'I deny that there is any power in man which can seriously oppose the affections, and I think that acts which are evoked [*elicitios*] are nothing but

---

[117] *Loci* (n.85), p.25.

[118] There has been much recent attention to the freedom of the will in Melanchthon's theology, mainly in the light of the debates that followed in the Reformed tradition. I have already mentioned Wengert's article (n.103) and Graybill's monograph (n.87); Wengert challenges Graybill's interpretation. See also Timothy J. Wengert, *Human Freedom, Christian Righteousness: Philip Melanchthon's Exegetical Dispute With Erasmus of Rotterdam* (New York: Oxford University Press, 1998). See also Mühlen, 'Melanchthons Affektenlehre' (n.87). For a deeper and more wide ranging examination of this issue see Risto Saarinen, *The Weakness of the Will in Renaissance and Reformation Thought* (Oxford: Oxford University Press, 2011).

[119] Augustine, *City of God*, trans. Henry Bettenson (Harmondsworth: Penguin Books, 1984), p.555 (Bk.14.6).

a feigned thought of the intellect [*fictitiam cogitationem intellectus esse*]. For since God judges hearts, the heart and the affections [*cor cum suis affectibus*] must be the highest and most powerful part of man.'[120] Only the grace of divine illumination can free human beings from the delusions and perversions of *affectus* (though not affectivity as such). But since this faculty is the highest and most powerful, then grace does not erase but reorient it as 'the Spirit of God renews and illuminates [*illuminante*] our hearts'.[121] We respond, in faith, to that illumination and we receive an emotional transformation: grace 'first calms our hearts and then inflames [*accendit*] us to give thanks'.[122]

This puts religious experience at the forefront of Melanchthon's soteriology and pedagogy; experience culminating in doxology. In this he stands in the tradition of Cyril and Hugh. He is cautious in describing the transformation from the affects of deceit and treachery to the positive affects of trust, gladness, comfort, strengthening, and assurance.[123] When he writes about the 'experience of the will of God',[124] the affects of God's mercy or the operations of the Spirit of God, it is to the Scripture that he refers. Nevertheless, the fruits of the Spirit are 'spiritual affections [*spiritualibus affectibus*]',[125] just as avarice, ambition, hatred, envy, strife, lust, and anger are 'the chief passions [*principes affectus*]' of sin.[126] They are actual, historical, and existential, for they are 'marks [*indicia*—indices], testimonies and signs of his presence [*signa spiritus sunt*]';[127] 'living faith is that efficacious, burning trust [*vivam fidem efficacem … et ardentem fiduciam*]';[128] for there is a 'longing [*desiderio*] of the spirit'.[129] Nevertheless, as Melanchthon points out later in *The Book on the Soul* (1553), 'now in fact the order of emotions is upset in this depravity of nature'[130] that is a result of human beings being fallen and sinful.

---

[120] *Loci* (n.85), p.29/15. The heart and the affections are not two distinct entities, the heart 'with its affections' is better. It produces fanciful and delusory thoughts that human intellect then works upon.

[121] Ibid., p.92/92. There is a rich medieval tradition of Christian reflection upon divine illumination, particularly with Augustine. See Lydia Schumacher, *Divine Illumination: The History and Future of Augustine's Theory of Knowledge* (Oxford: Wiley-Blackwell, 2011).

[122] Ibid.

[123] We will return to affect in the next volume when I discuss the process of sanctification. There I make more complex the distinction between positive and negative affect in relation to the operation of the Spirit. There are what cognitive psychologists and neuroscientists call negative affects that, understood in terms of being redeemed, have positive effects. Melanchthon will draw attention to the salvific work done by sorrow, shame, and a conscience that is terrified in repentance, for example. Later, in his treatise 'Commentary on the Soul' (1540) he will distinguish between those emotions that 'aid nature, others [that] destroy it', clarifying that negative affects like anger and sadness 'destroy nature when [they do] not agree with wisdom and the divine norms'—translated and in Ralph Keen, *Melanchthon Reader* (n.112), p.244.

[124] *Loci* (n.85), p.94.   [125] Ibid., p.113/117.   [126] Ibid., p.33/21.

[127] Ibid., p.109/112.

[128] Ibid., p.112/116. In Latin there is a semantic association between faith and trust.

[129] Ibid., p.145/155.   [130] 'Commentary on the Soul' (n.112), p.244.

PROTESTANTISM AND WHITE
MAGIC: A LINGERING ENCHANTMENT

We will return to this emotional disorder when we consider sin, for now we need to re-examine Melanchthon's remarks on Pico della Mirandola. Mirandola himself is incidental, but his name opens a series of interesting connections within which Melanchthon sits and which impact upon that shift remarked upon at the beginning of this chapter between enchantment and disenchantment. The connections go back to his great uncle, Johannes Reuchlin, who saw to Melanchthon's education and was directly responsible for his appointment at Wittenberg. In 1517 Reuchlin published his infamous *De arte kabbalistica* as a contribution of his own to the humanist rejection of scholasticism. It was dedicated to Pope Leo X and opens with an account of his meeting with Mirandola.[131] There was a dramatic break between Melanchthon and Reuchlin concerning the former's involvement with Luther in 1519—as a result of which Melanchthon would not inherit the fabulous library his great uncle had collected and promised to give him when he died. But there is no doubt Melanchthon knew his relative's work on Christian Kabbalism; and it must be recalled that it is from Melanchthon that we have one of the oldest forms of the Faust story.

The title of Reuchlin's previous publication indicates an important interest within Christian Kabbalism. *De verbo mirifico* was written and published in 1494. This and his later publication both emphasized the 'wonder-working' power of language, particularly the Hebrew language, the divine Names, and the name of Jesus as the Messiah. There has been some speculation on Reuchlin's influence upon Melanchthon, particularly as his studies of both the nature of being human and astrology deepened in his development of a natural, Christian philosophy.[132] No one, to my knowledge, has examined any connection between Reuchlin's account of language and power and Melanchthon's interest in the relationship between eloquence, the proclamation of the gospel and that final *dunamis* on which the *Loci* concludes. But rhetoric for Melanchthon, as we have seen, is a dynamic communication that impacts simultaneously on the rational and the emotional. In his examination of the hermeneutics of Reuchlin, Thomas F. Torrance recognizes the great importance for the history of Christian thought of Reuchlin's 'new understanding of the Word for which

---

[131] See Frances Yates, 'The Occult Philosophy in the Reformation: Johannes Reuchlin' in *The Occult Philosophy of the Elizabethan Age* (n.60), pp.23–7.

[132] See Sachiko Kusukawa, *The Transformation of Natural Philosophy* (n.101), p.70 for Reuchlin's possible influence on Melanchthon's acceptance of innate ideas. See also Guido Kisch, *Melanchthons Rechts—und Sozialehre* (Berlin: Walter de Gruyer & Co., 1967), p.45.

he had struggled so hard in attempting to set it free from the sophistica-
tions and syllogistic thinking of the Schoolmen ... The Scriptures must be
read and interpreted in a new way in which we let God himself speak to us
through them directly.'[133]

Three aspects of Reuchlin's *De verbo mirifico* bear examination with
respect to Melanchthon's early dogmatics. First is the emphasis on hearing
the voice of God, listening to the ineffable, which Reuchlin drew from Jewish
sources. His character Baruchias affirms, 'That in which nature chiefly practices magic, is the voice of God [*Illud autem in quo potissimum Magicam
exercet natura, vox est dei*],'[134] which is a direct quotation (not assigned) from
Mirandolla.[135] It is this voice that facilitates a seemingly direct communication between Scripture and the human reader.[136] God's Word is self-revealing
and so hearing it becomes self-authenticating and self-validating. Secondly,
the Holy Spirit is given the operative function in this divine communication. This is summed up in Reuchlin's phrase, *Deus enim spiritus, verbum
spiratio, homo spirans.*[137] It is from and because of God's self-communication
that human beings speak at all. But then all of nature speaks as it 'practices

---

[133] 'The Hermeneutics of John Reuchlin, 1455–1522' in *Church, Word, and Spirit: Historical
and Theological Essays in Honor of Geoffrey W. Bromiley*, ed. James E. Bradley and Richard A.
Muller (Grand Rapids: Eerdmans, 1987). Torrance tends to overemphasize Reuchlin's evangelical orthodoxy. It is true that Reuchlin does emphasize the importance of faith as a *vin-
culum* that enables our participation in the divine, that God in Christ is prime agent in the
wonder-working nature of the Word (the Pentagammaton of IHSUH), and that creation *ex
nihilo* renders the difference between creator and creation unbridgeable from the side of we
creatures, but Torrance underplays Reuchlin's engagements with the contemporary debates on
magic and theurgic practices. See John Webster's chapter, '*Verbum mirificum*: T.F. Torrance on
Scripture' in *The Domain of the Word: Scripture and Theological Reason* (London: Bloomsbury,
2013), pp.86–112. Webster puts Torrance's Reuchlin essay in a wider context in which Torrance
was searching for a way to repair 'the ontological relation of the mind to reality' (Torrance's
words) through understanding Scripture 'as sign—that is, with Scripture's ostensive functions'
(Webster's word) (pp.86–89). Reuchlin himself seems to be attempting to find a way between
Pedro Garcias's condemnation of Pico della Mirandola's Christian Kabbalism and Mirandola's
own defence of *magia naturalis*. Torrance's insightful essay needs to be counterbalanced by
Charles Zika's stunning research in 'Reuchlin's *De Verbo Mirifico* and the Magic Debate of the
Late Fifteenth Century', *Journal Of the Warburg and Courtauld Institutes*, vol. XXXIX (1976),
104–38.
[134] There is no English translation of *De verbo mirifico*, but there is a superb new German
edition of the Latin text with a German translation: Widu-Wolfgang Ehlers (hrgs.) *Johannes
Reuchlin: Sämtliche Werke* Band I,1, *De verbo mirifico/Das wundertätige Wort* (Stuttgart: Bad
Cannstatt, 1996), p.186.
[135] Pico della Mirandola, Magical Conclusion (15) *Opera Omnia* (Basle, 1557), p.105. There
is a slight difference. Pico's thesis reads '*illud in quo primum Magicam*'. See also Charles Zika,
Exorcising Our Demons: Magic, Witchcraft, and Visiual Culture in Early Modern Europe
(Leiden: Brill, 2003), p.49.
[136] See Graham Ward, 'To be a Reader: Bunyan and the Language of Scripture', *Literature
and Theology* (vol.4), March 1990, pp.29–49 where I trace the psychological difficulties that
ensue for the evangelical tradition from this verbalization of the text.
[137] *Sämtliche Werke* Band I,1 (n.134), p.160.

magic'.[138] This emphasis upon pneumatology is key to Reuchlin's Christian understanding of the Word, its operation, and its power to effect. 'What emerges most clearly through this maze of discussion [in *De verbo mirifico*] is the central and continual concern with "operation"—that is, a concern to make the words and philosophies of men and the names of the divinity potent and effective, both within the souls of individuals, and among men moving in the broader sphere of society'.[139] Through this wonder-working Word, human beings perform external miraculous activities in the world releasing the 'virtues' in nature. This, thirdly, raises the question of the status of Reuchlin's own act of communication, the trilogue that composes *De verbo mirifico*. The text is riddled with ritualistic references. The 'Prefatory Letter' to the Bishop of Worms speaks of entering 'such great darknesses [*tenebrae*] and obscurities concerning sacred matters, indeed the hidden places of secret words [*immo secretorum verborum latibula*]'.[140] The conversation takes place over three days, with initiation, purification rites and formula only to be verbalized by the initiated. So while 'Reuchlin himself at least does not conceive of the *sililoquia* as a magic procedure',[141] the rhetoric plays with the possibility of a corporate and incorporating mystery, a *theurgia*, and the whole movement of the text is towards the revelation of the true Word in Christ and the transformation of Sidonius and Baruchias. The words do *affect* then. There is a pedagogy of affect through listening to the voice of God being spoken and communicated through the Christian Kabbalist, and leading to conversion. And it is this that returns us to the role of humanist rhetoric and the power of language with respect to transformating *affectus* in Melanchthon's *Loci communes*, 1521.[142]

There was another prominent member of the Christian Kabbalistic circle close to Reuchlin and a group of friends associated with Luther and Melanchthon, Cornelius Agrippa. Agrippa gave a series of lectures on *De verbo mirifico* at Dôle (eastern France) in 1510. Agrippa was a close friend of Georg Spalatin who translated *Loci communes* 1521 into German. On September 17th, 1532, Cornelius Agrippa wrote to Melanchthon, as he had written to Erasmus four days earlier, to elicit his support for a publication in which he denounced

[138] Reuchlin, like Pico, distinguished bad magic from good magic on the basis of using the divine names.
[139] Charles Zika, 'Reuchlin and Magic Debate' (n.133), 134–5.
[140] *Sämtliche Werke* Band I,1 (n.134), p.10.   [141] Ibid., p.135.
[142] There is a key difference. Reuchlin is concerned with Scripture as 'theurgic' only tangentially. It is naming, and particularly the name of God as it becomes incarnate in Christ, which is effective. Melanchthon's Scriptural ontology, actualized by the Spirit and with reference to the redeeming work of Christ, circumscribes divine *dunamis*. There is evidently work to be undertaken between Christian Kabbalistic attention to the creative power of God through the Hebrew language and the origins of early Reformation emphasis upon a pneumatological Christology.

those conservative theologians opposed to humanism.[143] Later, in the 1550s, Melanchthon, castigating Faustus as a second Simon Magnus, mentions Agrippa explicitly as belonging to the same camp.[144] Even so, as Frances Yates observes, and as his letters cited above attest, Agrippa sought to be named among the reformers: 'His attempt to combine what he believes to be Erasmian evangelicalism with a magically powerful philosophy makes Agrippa a reformer of a strange and interesting kind.'[145]

Luther digested the work of Reuchlin and Agrippa, along with a number of his followers closely associated with Melanchthon, not least Dürer and Cranach.[146] One of the influences of Christian Kabbalism on these painters is explicitly with respect to the relationship between affect and astrology.[147] The discipline that was most concerned with this relationship was one in which Melanchthon took an increasingly keen interest: medicine. It would be accurate to say Melanchthon saw theological doctrine as a therapeutics;[148] salvation as a healing. His coat of arms, adopted in the 1520s having been granted the coat by Maximilian I, bore the emblem of the bronze serpent (from Numbers 21), a figure for Christ on the cross.[149] The emblem decorated the title page of the 1552 *Liber de anima*.

---

[143] Cited in Marc van der Poel, *Cornelius Agrippa: The Humanist Theologian and His Declamations* (Leiden: Brill, 1997), p.122.

[144] See Michael Keefer, 'Cornelius Agrippa's Double Presence in the Faustian Century' in James M. van der Laan and Andrew Weekes (ed.), *The Faustian Century: German Literature and Culture in the Age of Luther and Faust* (Rochester, NY.: Camden House, 2013), pp.67–92.

[145] *The Occult Philosophy*, pp.39–40. See also Charles G. Nauert, *Agrippa and the Crisis of Renaissance Thought* (Urbana, IL: University of Illinois Press, 1965), pp.35 ff. See also Paola Zambelli, 'Magic and Radical Reformation in Agrippa of Nettesheim', *Journal Of the Warburg and Courtauld Institutes*, vol. XXXIX (1976), 69–103. Zambelli argues in detail for Agrippa's close association with the more radical, Spiritualist (Anabaptist) Reformation. What is foremost, in his hermeneutics, theology, and magic is pneumatology: 'the spiritual interpretation of Holy Scripture, or rather opposition of Spirit to Letter ... and the reduction of the sacred text to a testimony which only inspiration given to each of the faithful makes it possible to render meaningful' (p.83).

[146] Heiko A. Oberman, 'Three Sixteenth-Century Attitudes to Judaism: Reuchlin, Erasmus and Luther' in *Jewish Thought in the Sixteenth Century*, ed. Bernard Dov Cooperman. Cambridge, MA: Harvard University Press, 1983.

[147] See Frances Yates, 'The Occult Philosophy and Melancholy: Dürer and Agrippa', *The Occult Philosophy*, pp.49–59 (n.60), where Cranach is also referred to.

[148] Wengert, 'Three Causes' (n.103): 'It was this concern—that theology was not merely about definition but also about effect—that drove him here to preach law and gospel,' p.202.

[149] For the view that the emblem speaks of the dichotomous relationship between the cross (the gospel) and philosophy (the serpent), see H. Ashby Hall, *Philip Melanchthon and the Cappodocians* (Göttingen: Vandenhoeck & Ruprecht, 2014), pp.18–20. Hall observes an association of the bronze serpent with the healing staff of Asclepius. There is another interesting connection here. The book *Ascelpius* was thought to have been written by Hermes Tristmegistus. It became the basis for one of the most widely read books by Marsilio Ficino, *De vitae coelitus comparanda* (1489) describing how the Egyptians attract celestial influences into the statues of their gods. We know Dürer was influenced by it—see Frances Yates (n.60). There were exchanges between Reuchlin and Ficino that Melanchthon 'had acquired' (*übernommen hat*). See Wilhelm Maurer, *Der junge Melanchthon. Band 1* (Göttingen: Vandenhoeck & Ruprecht, 1967), pp.89–96, 99–104. Melanchthon would have also known of Ficino's work through his

Emblems also could bear 'magical' import among the Christian Kabbalists.[150] They were involved in a *theurgia* that drew down either the divine/angelic powers of protection or the Satanic/demonic forces of destruction. Reuchlin, in *De Verbo Mirifico*, employing the name of a character Capnion (a Greek translation of his name, like Melanchthon's own), spoke of the power by which wonders were worked through words and signs in the Hebrew Bible, drawing attention to the bronze serpent.[151] In a rite announcing the ultimate revelation of the 'wonder-working word', a rite described in the book, Capnion draws together his dialogue partners Sidonius and Baruchias, and, swearing them to silence, breathes on them the secret word of the cross.[152]

Melanchthon is again on the edge of the debates about *prisci theologi* and the relationship between philosophy, magic, and religion, though his humanist's interest was focused on Galen and Pliny (rather than Orpheus, Apollonius of Tyana, and Hermes Tristmegistus). A detailed account of physiology according to Galen takes up a large opening proportion of *Commentarius de anima*, a work begun in 1530, published first in 1540 as if it were (which it isn't) a commentary on Aristotle, and revised for publication in 1552 as *Liber de anima*. Although Melanchthon seems unaware of it, his appeal to, and reliance on, the medical framework provided by Galen, places him in the tradition of patristic theologians who, in wishing to emphasize the incarnational relationship between the physiological and the spiritual drew explicitly on Galen's work: Lactantius, Gregory of Nyssa, Theodoret of Cyrrhus, and Nemesius of Emesa.[153] As one scholar has noted: 'Within this [Melanchthon's understanding of how divine law is a pedagogy of affect] psychological system the perceptions of the divine law are set down as emotions, parts of the appetitive faculty, thus creating, for moral philosophy, a dialectic between thought and emotion analogous to that between cognitive and appetitive faculties in the *Loci*.'[154]

teacher in astrology at Tübingen, Johannes Stöffler. It is interesting, and possibly significant, that Ficino's Platonism emphases the work of 'divine love' in terms of a frenzied inspiration (*furor*). In his famous letter to Peregrino Agli, in which Ficino speaks *de divino furore*, he tells Agli that the 'powerful emotion and burning desire which your writings express prove, as I have said, that you are inspired and inwardly possessed by that frenzy'. Melanchthon, when expressing the work of Spirit time and again uses the words 'inflame' and 'burn'—see *Loci* (n.85), pp.40, 54, 69, 92, 112, 131, 133. It is a mark of the Spirit's presence and operation within us. Does Melanchthon's understanding of pneumatology, and the energies of his own writing, owe something indirectly then to Ficino's Platonism? Ficino's was famous for his emphasis upon the mediating role of *spiritus* in the relationship between theology, magic, and medicine.

[150] See Michael Bath, *Speaking Pictures: English Emblem Books and Renaissance Culture* (London: Longman, 1994) and Michael Bath and Daniel Russell, eds. *Deceitful Settings: English Renaissance Emblem and its Context* (New York: AMS Press, 1999)—especially the essay by Peggy Muñoz Simonds, 'The Aesthetics of Magic'. For an exhaustive treatment, see John Manning, *The Emblem* (London: Reaktion Books, 2002).

[151] *De verbo mirifico* (n.134), pp.340–2.   [152] Ibid., p.408

[153] See Susan Ashbrook Harvey, *Scenting Salvation: Ancient Christianity and the Olfactory Imagination* (Oakland, CA: University of California Press, 2006), pp.110–14.

[154] Keen, *The Melanchthon Reader*, 'Introduction' (n.112), p.28.

In terms of classical, medieval, and renaissance medicine the affective and the astrological are related through the operations of the moon, stars, and planets upon the four humours. Astronomic conjunctions controlled temperaments, such that Melanchthon commented that his own daughter, Sabinas, was headstrong and not willing to listen to advice because she was born under the influence of Saturn (governing levels of black bile and melancholy) and Mars (governing levels of yellow bile and anger). In his rejection of Copernicus and espousal of the heliocentric view of creation, he speaks on the sun and 'its stewards, the moon and Venus, for these especially dominate in exciting the humours by which bodies are main-tained'.[155] In 1535 Melanchthon, to much criticism, published an oration 'On the Dignity of Astrology' and because he viewed astrology as an aspect of the study of the natural world (*physice*), the subject formed an import-ant part of his textbook *Initia doctrina physicae* on 1549.[156] Divine provi-dence acted through planetary motions, establishing the humoural basis for character and thus predetermining human action. In fallen human beings, ignorant of God and impervious to God's love and mercy because lacking in faith, the bondage to sin and of sin was adamantine. It was ori-ginal and manifested an *energia* ('an intensely alive force [*vivax quaedem energia*]').[157] That is the point. The fruits of such sin are 'vices'. He uses the Latin *vitia* aware of its negative associations with 'life' (*vita*). Unaided, the human person 'desires [*cupiat*] and wishes for nothing but carnal things [*carnalia*]. It despises God ... It is impossible that flesh love spiritual things [*Fieri nequit, ut spiritalia amet caro*].'[158] 'Punishment is inborn with us, as both the fear of evil to come coerces us and sadness from past evil is a defense and punishment of sins and a witness to the judgement of God,' he writes.[159]

Melanchthon was no natural theologian because he did not have a purely materialist account of nature. In fact, natural theology only emerged towards the end of the sixteenth century as the metaphysics informing Christian Kabbalism and the Scotist univocity of being formed the basis for what, later, Heidegger would call 'ontotheology'.[160] His medical astrology is only part of

---

[155] Cited in and translated by Sachiko Kusukawa, *The Transformation of Natural Philosophy* (n.101), p.130.

[156] Ibid., chs. 3 and 4 for a detailed study of both Melanchthon's work on the soul and his natural philosophy (*physica*).

[157] *Loci* (n.85), p.33/21.

[158] *Ibid.*, p.31/18. *Factum infectum fieri nequit* is a Latin proverb possibly going back to Plautus. It means 'what is done can never be undone'. Melanchthon's *'fieri nequit'* here had considerable force.

[159] 'On the Soul' (n.155), p.245.

[160] See Jacob Schumtz, 'La Doctrine médiévale des causes et la théologie de la nature pure (XIIIe-XVIIe siècles)', *Revue Thomiste*, special issue on the *Surmaturel* (Jan.–Feb. 2001), 217–64.

the cosmic circulations of divine motion[161] and what he calls (reminiscent of the medieval and Ignatian understanding of sense perception directing 'motions of the soul') 'movements of the heart'.[162] It is a key aspect of his understanding of law as distinct from gospel, and the pedagogy of affect that acts as the deep structure of *Loci communes 1521*.

Today, in the wake of the work done on in the neuro- and cognitive psychology of the emotions, Melanchthon's 'psychology' could be called and investigated further with respect to 'embodied cognition'.[163] Flesh is that physiological condition for embodied cognition that lacks the Spirit of God. Later, following more work on anatomy and Galen, Melanchthon will point to the mark of God's presence in the design and craftsmanship of embodiment. He will render the divide between nature and grace more porous by showing how divine law is written into the nature of things and can be divined[164]—only sin obscures our ability to comprehend it. The account of grace does not issue, as a systematic theology might, into an ecclesiology (though certain ecclesial topoi are engaged: the sacraments of baptism, confession, and the eucharist). Rather grace issues into social and political ethics: *Sittlichkeit*. Ethical living announces and incarnates the actualization of divine law by the operation of love that is a work of grace. I emphasis 'actualization' rather than 'fulfilment', for the gulf that separates the human from the divine in Melanchthon, because of sin, does not allow for grace to be the perfection of human reason or those natural dispositions (*affectus*) that are innate because they are 'implanted [*insitos*]' in us,[165] in the manner of Aquinas.[166] But there is something more to be said here which returns us to the 'transformation' in embodied understanding following the work of grace in faith. For the truth of the divine order and the wonder at beholding nature in terms of the creator, both of which lead to worship of God, is always present. Sin and unaided human reason obscures it from view. So

---

[161] See Simon Oliver, *Philosophy, God and Motion* (London: Routledge, 2013). Melanchthon's attention to motion, owing much to an Aristotle he rediscovers beyond scholasticism and following the writing of *Loci communes 1521*, is in line with Aquinas's own conception of it as detailed in Oliver's book.

[162] 'On the Soul', p.243 (n.155). See my essay 'The Body of the Church and its Erotic Politics' in Graham Ward, *Christ and Culture* (Oxford: Blackwell, 2005), pp.92–109.

[163] For a good critical survey and influential systematization of embodied cognition see Lawrence Shapiro, *Embodied Cognition* (New York: Routledge, 2010); see also Anthony Chemero, *Radical Embodied Cognitive Science* (Boston: MIT Press, 2011).

[164] Melanchthon shows a respect for 'divination', aware this would be controversial among other evangelical theologians at the time. He may even have practised divination. Strictly speaking, reading Scripture aright was an act of divination.

[165] *Loci* (n.85), p.51/42.

[166] It was suggested by Franz Hildebrandt in *Melanchthon: Alien or Ally?* (Cambridge: Cambridge University Press, 1946) that Melanchthon sailed 'suspiciously near to Thomas Aquinas' (p.25). The comment was intended to be negative and in line with Karl Barth's rejection of *analogia entis*. It shares Barth's misunderstanding about the nature of analogy in Aquinas.

the actualization is ours, not God's. To employ later terms Melanchthon did not employ: the supernatural clings to the natural though only grace can reveal it to those who believe. In this sense we might talk of a 'perfection' of the natural by grace, just as, in human beings, there is a sanctification that follows justification. Melanchthon himself uses the term perfection: 'our sanctification is not yet perfect [*nondum in nobis consummata sit*]. For our sanctification begins as an act of the Spirit of God, and we are in the process of being sanctified [*Coepimus enim spiritu dei sanctificari sanctificamurque, dum caro illa prosus enecetur*].'[167] It would seem, then, or is at least arguable, that for Melanchthon nominalism is the *episteme* of the sinful. The analogical world is there, emphasizing properly the distance and difference between the human and the divine. But it has to be slowly recovered and beheld in the ongoing perfection of sanctification. The opacity of the nominal world gives way to the translucent order of sacred things. If I am correct, then this theological position would qualify notions of participation along Thomist lines—though by how much would be interesting to clarify. Participation, for Melanchthon, is only possible for the justified.

Sittlichkeit is nevertheless rooted in the three laws that pertain properly to human beings: the worship of God (divine law) becomes a social disposition that demands nobody should be harmed (natural law); a social condition that requires 'we make common use of all things' (civic law).[168] All three laws can be and are explicitly Scriptural and deducible from the Decalogue. But, as Melanchthon's thinking advanced, he came to realize that to develop both a moral and natural philosophy (something he was more keen to do than be a theologian) he needed the resources of a number of the philosophers (Aristotle in particular) he castigates in *Loci communes 1521*.

If some have critiqued Melanchthon[169] for seemingly conflating natural, civic, and divine law—for the law of magistrates in attempting to maintain public peace and administer a state orientated towards the common good is a reflection of both natural and divine law—then they have not adequately appreciated that Melanchthon's thinking remains framed by the more ancient microcosm/macrocosm analogy between the human, the social, and the cosmic body. Melanchthon's attention to *Sittlichkeit* as it pertains to divine law and is actualized by grace demonstrates how far he is from Charles Taylor's notion of the 'buffered self'. For all the attention to affect and being affected, there is a strong social aspect to his sense of personhood, to the point where

[167] *Loci* (n.85), p.130/136. The phrase 'sanctificari sanctificamurque' has a distinctly liturgical resonance to it.
[168] Ibid., p.51. For an in-depth study of Melanchthon's social and political ethics in *Loci* see Rolf Schäfer, *Christologie und Sittlichkeit in Melanchthons frühen Loci* (J.C.B. Mohre: Tübingen, 1961).
[169] For example, Keen, *The Melanchthon Reader*, 'Introduction' (n.112), p.25.

he fulminates against 'sophists' who advocate that it does 'not seem right that the possessions of all should be shared so no one could look out just for his own rights [*non liceter vindicare suum cuique*]'.[170] This position qualifies theological anthropology as a doctrinal *locus* in and for itself—a modern theological occupation from Schleiermacher to Rahner. The existential attention to sin, grace, and faith is turned towards the human, experiencing subject, but it is not a subject possessing its own theological importance. The human person is significant *because of* the salvific work of Christ and the operations of the Spirit. The human person has theological value because God, in creating and loving it, values it. Having said this, there is a certain move in Melanchthon towards Taylor's notion of 'absolute humanism', since his arguments quite explicitly pertain 'to the human race as a whole [*universum genus humanum*] ... [and] the whole world [*universae naturae*]'.[171] The Scriptural emphasis on Adam, original sin, and the proclamation of the gospel, an emphasis as Augustinian as it is proto-Protestant, foregrounded the universalism of the human condition beyond ecclesial frontiers; ecclesial frontiers that were, at the time, having to encounter species of human being and a variety of religious cultures in the 'new world'.

CONCLUDING OBSERVATIONS

What is significant with the dogmatics presented in *Loci communes 1521* is that doctrine is not propositional. Melanchthon uses a variety of Latin terms: *sententia*—opinion, judgement, thought; *disciplina*—instruction, training, education; *doctrina*—teaching, learning. Each of them cannot be dissociated from practices; just as they issue from the practice of the exegesis of Scripture that speaks and energizes in the affections. Only once does Melanchthon refer to articles of the faith (*de fide*) and this too, like Cyril of Jerusalem and several of the bishops at Nicaea, he relates to Biblical interpretation. Sin, law, and grace as rhetorical *loci* are the existential roots of doctrinal expression; conditions of being. Other doctrines have to emerge from and build upon these fundamental *loci*. But 'Scripture' itself is isolated and reified as text apart from other texts. It is loosed from its ecclesial origins. Furthermore, in future years the pressure was on to be more systematic, more instrumental, more summative concerning doctrine. The subtle, rhetorical even metaphysical, appreciation of Melanchthon's understanding of *loci* was not available to many. There is a complex move (historical as well as stylistic) towards confessionalism: the 28 articles of Augsburg Confession (1530); the

---

[170] *Loci communes* (n.85), p.58/51.   [171] Ibid.

27 articles of the Helvetic Confession (1536); then 6 (1539), then 42 (1552) and finally 39 articles (1563) of the Anglican Church.

Although these confessions look back to the Creeds of the Councils between Antioch and Chalcedon (with articles often appended with 'anathemata'), they function more like contracts of allegiance or loyalty. They circumscribe the parameters of orthodoxy, with a clear sense of the 'enemy' outside (Roman Catholicism). They are ecclesial documents, but where the church is one social institution among others. They become the equivalent of a corporation's policy and mission statement. They are not liturgical documents. Nor are they promulgated as such. They announce: 'This is what our church believes'; with the silent corollary that there are other churches who do not believe these things in the same way. In a time of nation building and *cuius regio eius religio*, they are forms of ecclesial constitution; legal documents. Furthermore, the creative dynamics of Scriptural interpretation increasingly move towards using the Bible as a source of 'proof-texts'. This is already apparent in *Loci communes 1521*. The 'proof-texting' (often used to translate the Latin *testimonium*, which is a legal term) provides a ballast to a plethora of personal readings that is turning the Scriptures into 'a nose of wax'.[172] But it is also fostering a decontextualizing and dehistoricizing of the Scriptures with the emphases upon God speaking immediately through them ('the voice [*in voce*] of the Gospel')[173] and on the teaching of St. Paul that the 'letter kills'. The Scriptures become de-narrativized. Any movement towards the privatization of religion came not from some anonymous secularizing civil society, but from Christians themselves in their hunger for the immediacies of religious experience; a hunger that drove them to conclude that liturgical practices of the faith were cosmetic externals. Attention to preaching as the major form of instruction meant Scriptural exegesis was still embedded within an albeit transformed liturgy, but the Scriptures were now disseminated much more widely and publicly. The Bible, as I have said, was the greatest single symbolic resource for the Reformers in the establishment of a new *ecclesia*, but investing it with so much authority led to it being fetishized. It was becoming detached from a catechesis and a schooling that cultivated a respect for its complexities and a recognition of the further complexities involved in its interpretation. The Scriptures were being understood functionally, and their textual, mediating character was being drastically oversimplified.

Melanchthon, in the facing the uncontrollable 'enthusiasm' and splintering *ecclesia* fulminates against 'unlearned theology' (*incrudita theologia*). The

---

[172] See Graham Ward, 'To be a Reader: Bunyan and the Language of Scripture' (n.136).

[173] Melanchthon, in J.A.O. Preus's translation, *The Chief Theological Topics: Loci Praecipui Theologici, 1559* (St. Louis: Concordia Publishing House, 2011), and Hans Engelland's Latin edition in Robert Stupperich, *Melanchthons Werke* (n.85), (p.31/204), p.21/189.

teaching of Christian doctrine has to become a *disciplina* within the universities. Those authorized to teach, those wishing to be authorized to teach, must form an accredited profession. The changes made to the various editions of *Loci* between 1521 and 1559 (mainly a reissue of the 1543 text) chart the move from a highly charged piece of eloquence to a more considered dogmatic manual.[174] The existential and rhetorical meaning of *loci* is embedded with the structures of a *summa* that Melanchthon sketched and then disregarded explicitly in the opening paragraphs of the 1521 *Loci communes*. There are now *loci* for God, Unity, Trinity, and Creation, prior to the anthropology that focuses on sin, law, and grace, for example. The teaching here is indebted to the early ecumenical councils of 'the ancient and pure church', with a Logos Christology and an emphasis upon the Spirit as a distinct hypostasis and activating motion within creation (*vim agitantem*)[175] but not of creation (*nec significant agitationem creatam*).[176] The emphasis throughout is constructing and teaching a grammar of the faith so that those being trained theologically are aware of how 'we must be careful in speaking properly and carefully (*diligentia proprie et recte loquendi*)'.[177]

No doubt the caution expresses Melanchthon's own troubles and debates among the Lutherans in the years following Luther's death. But it is also a teacher's caution. Throughout his academic career in Wittenberg teaching and reform had been of the utmost importance to him. He had been instrumental in both bringing about educational reform and facilitating changes in German gymnasia and universities. And perhaps this is where we see the greatest cultural transformation brought about by the Reformation. The curriculum of the later medieval educational system had left behind the pedagogical structure known and practised by Hugh of St. Victor—as training in metaphysics was now understood to be the foundation for what followed in physics and ethics.[178] Neither Melanchthon nor Luther would reinstate it. But both of them, while insisting on the central importance of the Scriptures, also recognized the education needed to support the reading of the Scriptures and the cultivation of civic virtues. In doing so they laid the foundations for modern education since the subjects they viewed as significant were literature, languages, history, rhetoric, music, and medicine. These were seen as fundamental for a learned piety.

---

[174] For a good account of the changes and the development of a Reformed dogmatics and how Melanchthon changed the order of the topics between the 1521 edition and that of 1543/59, see Robert Kolb, 'The Ordering of the *Loci Communes Theologici*: The Structuring of the Melanchthonian Dogmatic Tradition', *Concordia Journal* 23 (1997), pp.313–37.

[175] *Loci Communes Theologici*, (n.174), p.31/204.   [176] Ibid., p.32/205.

[177] Ibid., p.39/214.

[178] See Jacob Schmultz, 'Mediaeval Philosophy After the Middle Ages' in John Marenbon (ed.), *The Oxford Handbook of Medieval Philosophy* (Oxford: Oxford University Press, 2013), pp.245–66.

The enchanted world was still in place (with its demons, angels, and astral forces) and continued to be so as what became natural philosophy developed. For Melanchthon it is difficult to see any division between natural philosophy and a theology of creation. In 1553, when composing his *Book on the Soul*, a book as much about the anatomical design of the body as the animations and faculties of the soul, he speaks of the need to lay the foundations of this knowledge because 'the foundations are necessary for understanding the doctrine of the Church and for the guidance of life'.[179] Any mention (and they are few) of Scotus, Occam, or Biel are all negative.

But the opening paragraph of the *Preface* of the *Loci* of 1543/1559 strikes a new note. Almost a hundred years prior to Descartes' *Discourse*, Melanchthon speaks about 'method' (*methodum*) in philosophical (and natural philosophical) enquiry and its usefulness in demonstrations from first principles. As we observed, the use of '*loci*' as the foundation for constructing knowledge of a certain intellectual field on the basis of definitions and distinctions can be found in Rudolf Agricola's *De inventione dialectica* (1479). In his 1539 oration 'On the Life of Rudolf Agricola', it is Agricola's pedagogical 'method' that is singled out for praise,[180] whereas Melanchthon does not foreground the *inventio* approach in 1521. Furthermore, 1543 predates the rise of Peter Ramus's dialectical method. It was only in 1547 that Ramus published his highly influential *Institutiones Dialecticae*, reissued in 1548 as *Scholae Dialecticae*.[181] The foregrounding of method in Melanchthon's final *Preface* to *Loci* detaches it from the theology expounded. The method is extrinsic to the material; the formalism of the arrangement of that material is independent and not accountable *to* the theology. Put another way, *lex credendi* is now divorced from *lex orandi*. The pedagogy of affect (and sanctification) gives way to a mechanical technique for learning. This, in turn, changes the genre of the text—it no longer performs, it simply states, and puts a series of such statements into a logical order. *Doctrina* is no longer the art of making something known, a 'verbal noun',[182] but a proposition, a tenet. The mechanics of pedagogical technique now frame both the theological system and how it is presented.

Philosophy, Melanchthon continues in his *Preface*, seeks 'the causes of certainty (*causae certitudinis*)'. Theology, he emphasizes, does not employ such a

[179] Preface to the *Book on the Soul* 1553, trans. Christine F. Salazar in Sachiko Kusukawa (ed.), *Philip Melanchthon: Orations on Philosophy and Education* (n.82), p.154.

[180] In *Orations on Philosophy and Education*, ed. Sachiko Kusukawa, trans. Christine F. Salazar (n.82), pp.227–35.

[181] Ramus did first publish his new system in an earlier version of, *Institutiones Dialecticae* as *Dialecticae Partitiones* in 1543, though whether Melanchthon knew of this text is uncertain.

[182] See Peter Fraenkel on Melanchthon's understanding of 'teaching' (doctrina) as a 'verbal noun', in his essay 'Revelation and Tradition: Notes on some Aspects of Doctrinal Continuity in the Theology of Philip Melanchthon,' *Studia Theologica* 13 (1959): 97–133. As we saw in Chapter 2, *doctrina* for Hugh of St.-Victor was a description of a process.

'method'. 'For the teaching of the church is not derived or drawn from demonstrations, but from those statements (*sed ex dictis*) which God has given to the human race in sure and clear testimonies (*testimoniis*) ... the cause of certainty (*certitudinis causa*) is the revelation of God.'[183] The modern turn to a foundationalism based upon 'revelation' is not then just a reaction to Kant's epistemology. It's already in place embryonically. Kant himself came from somewhere. There is, for Melanchthon, a difference between *causa* with respect to philosophical (and natural philosophical) enquiry and *causa* with respect to revelation (and the certainties that flow therefrom). The language of causation, whether employed for philosophy or for theology, is still indebted to Aristotle at this point: investigations seek to explain things in terms of their final (and divine) purpose. But Aristotle's efficient causation is in the hands of the Spirit and God as self-revealing, and the divorce between the philosophical and the theological, announced through employing the same word (cause) and the same goal (certainty), point towards developments, clarifications, investigations, and debates that will follow.

Melanchthon is aware of the difficulties he sets up: on the one hand, he wishes to insist God's Triune presence is 'with his creatures, not in the sense of a Stoic god'[184] and that that presence sustains His creation while also giving more freedom to individual liberty 'subject to reason' to be obedient, and do good works.[185] On the other hand, he sets up a divide between God as primary cause and the secondary efficient causation (*causarum efficientium*)[186] that operates according to natural law and the contingency of human choices. This bears the hallmarks of a residual Thomistic position on primary and secondary causation, but there is no developed analogical view of the world to make this comprehensive. But neither is there an ontological difference so fundamental to later conservative and neo-conservative Reformers, since Melanchthon goes on to elaborate nine cosmological proofs for the existence of God as the grand Architect on the basis of secondary causation, and then affirms that God's mercy is found 'aiding and restraining secondary causes'.[187] But that doesn't resolve the theological issues.

Later two directions in theological thinking announce themselves: the theological metaphysics of Suarez, with God as *causa sui* and the plenitude of being; and the insistence of Quenstedt and the Lutheran scholastics of the seventeenth century on God's free and unfettered will acting extrinsically and arbitrarily. Melanchthon tends towards emphasizing this voluntarist deity: 'the relationship of the primary and secondary causes is to be considered to be as God, a free agent, wills it to be'.[188] Logically, from his understanding of the spiritual operation of divine grace in the Scriptures he is driven towards this voluntarism, just

---

[183] *Loci Communes Theologici* (n.174), p.6/168.   [184] Ibid., p.54.
[185] Ibid., p.50.   [186] Ibid, p.45/223.   [187] Ibid., p.41.
[188] Ibid., p.55.

as later in the seventeenth century the weight placed upon Scripture will force many leading Protestant voices towards doctrines of its inerrancy and direct, verbal inspiration. Each theological resolution provides a different account of how the light gets in; raises a question about univocity and equivocity; announces that the more traditional analogical view of the world is no longer intelligible; and bequeaths to modern examinations of theological anthropology the problem of the relationship between 'participation' and 'justification by faith'.[189] In turn these theological thickets increase the preoccupation with method, and the teaching of right method. Modern theology still lives with that preoccupation.

We are returned to Bruno Latour's question of whether we have ever been modern: to the work of purification (and the demand for certainty that it will provide) on the one hand, and the work of mediation and the production of hybrids. To employ Taylor's terms, Melanchthon's position is neither disenchantment nor quite disembedding. Though there is one shift between the *Loci* of 1521 and the *Loci* of 1543/59 that illustrates one of the characteristics of disembedding for Taylor: what he calls 'excarnation'. This Taylor defines as a 'disengagement ... seen as essential to Reason [such that] the body tends to fall away'.[190] The existential orientation of Melanchthon's earlier *Loci*—that looks towards later Pietism and Schleiermacher—is framed by a more cerebral approach in his later revisions. The emotional regime gives way to an abstract and more academic educational programme, suited to the professional training of a new clergy. Karl-Heinz zu Mühlen points out that there were two models for the logic of affect both of which impacted upon the nature of the will. The first he terms Neoplatonic–Augustinian tradition in which the will 'is itself the power [*Macht*] of affect'.[191] This is the tradition evident in the 1521 text, when 'Melanchthon adopts the Neoplatonic-Augustinian tradition, especially ideas from Ficino like "*raptus*" ... and "*exstasis*".[192] He is following in the footsteps of Reuchlin. The second tradition Mühlen calls Aristotelian–Scholastic. In the 1543/59 text 'Melanchthon turns once more to the Aristotelian–Scholastic approach [in which] there is control of the drives [*Triebekontrolle*] through the will mediated by reason.' Here 'the dominating power [*Kraft*] of sinful affect in the human heart is denied'.[193]

The academy still serves the church, but it is a quite separate institution concerned with a 'knowledge' divorced from a spiritual practice. Central to this shift in the logic of affect is a theological epistemology issuing from a doctrine of God as 'eternal mind [*aeternam mentem*]'.[194] An existential condition

[189] John Bossy's (n.8) insight here.
[190] Charles Taylor, *A Secular Age*, p.288 (n.7). See also pp.613–1.
[191] Mühlen, 'Melanchthons Affektenlehre' (n.87), p.331.   [192] Ibid.
[193] Ibid., p.334. But I do not wish to rest my case for the shift in Melanchthon's theology from a pedagogy of affect to a more intellectualist stand on a possible change in his understanding of 'free will'. This change is still contested. See Wengert, 'Three Causes' (n.103).
[194] *Loci Praecipui Theologici* (n.173), p.40/214.

lies behind this new emphasis—there is an ongoing struggle of and for the faith, for example, and the word 'doubt' echoes throughout the book as a pervasive cultural scepticism takes hold—but it is viewed in intellectualist terms. 'In the face of these doubts we must strengthen our minds [*confirmandae sunt mentes*],' Melanchthon writes.[195] But the corporeal language of *affectus* and *dispositio* is displaced by a language of 'pious minds [*piae mentis*]'[196] as distinct from the effect of original sin which is 'darkness on the mind [*mente tenebrae*]' and sinning as 'wandering and erring inclinations [*vagis et errantibus inclinationibus*]'.[197] The stage for spiritual conquest now is 'the human mind and this light [of reason and intelligence] which is planted in [*insita*] the mind ... as a special [*praecipium*] testimony concerning God in nature'.[198] It is 'our minds [that] will grow in learning and devotion [*proficient mentes et erudition et pietate*]'.[199] Faith is a 'sure assent [*fides certa assencio, elegchos*]' or 'firm assent [*firmam assensionem*]'.[200] *Elegchos* is the Greek for 'conviction' or 'judgement'. It refers to a cross-examination. It is a legal term. Nowhere is this shift more evident than with respect to 'conscience'. In the 1521 *Loci* 'conscience' is associated with an engrafted sense of divine law that defends or accuses. It is related to '"concreted attitudes" [*habitus concreti*]'[201] and the emotions of guilt, fear, shame, or consolation. By 1543/1559 conscience is associated more closely with the intellect and judgement.[202] There are several places where the Latin has been translated into English as 'emotion' and gives the impression of being in line with the religious emotional regime of *Loci communes 1521*: the Spirit 'revives new God-pleasing emotions [*novos motum Deo placantes*]'[203] or God 'sees the emotions of the heart [*motus cordium*]'.[204] But spiritual affections (*spirituales affectus*) are now '*motus spirituales*'[205] and the work of the Spirit brings a rather vague 'infusion of qualities [*infusion qualitatum*]'.[206] The language of movement remains, hovering between an Aristotelian and a later Newtonian view of motion; the one organic and the other mechanistic. The internal is affected by the external (*agitatio*), but the indomitable power of *affectus* is no longer emphasized. Similarly, though *voluntas* is still used rather than *arbitrium*, the will is allied far more closely with the intellectual powers of judging and choosing, rather than the corporeality of 'wanting' and 'desiring'. In brief: the language of the Reformer's faith is now no longer performative.

---

[195] Ibid., p.41/216.
[196] Ibid., p.46/224.   [197] Ibid., p.48/227.   [198] Ibid., p.44/222.
[199] Ibid., p.39/214.   [200] Ibid., p.7/169.   [201] *Loci communes* (n.85), p.50/42.
[202] Although, in his *Commentary on the Soul* (1540), Melanchthon is still insisting on our innate capacity to distinguish between what is proper and what is vile. Since such a distinction is the activation for conscience then whatever intellectual judgement conscience allows actually has its sources beneath all cognition.
[203] *Loci Praecipui Theologici* (n.173), p.18/185.   [204] Ibid., p.21/189.
[205] Ibid., p.62/241.   [206] Ibid., p.62/245.

This evident 'excarnation' is not the dualism of body and soul announced by Descartes (and then somewhat qualified in his final book *The Passions of the Soul*—see Volume II). The *Loci* of 1543/59 is a revision taking place in the context of Melanchthon's 1540 treatise *Commentarius de anima* which opens with a lengthy analysis of the human body, as I have said. But somehow, perhaps given the excesses of Münster, the Peasants' War, the continuing infighting among second generation reformists, and the politics of a fragmenting Holy Roman Empire, the mind is the best place to retreat to. As the English poet Edward Dyer was to write in 1588: 'My mind to me a kingdom is.' With both the ecclesial body and the civic body in disarray, the academy hauls up its drawbridge. Although, even here we cannot jump too quickly to the modern, secular instrumentalization of knowledge and university education. Melanchthon was never ordained and unlike Luther he was never a monk, but he was part of a class of professional humanists who viewed the universities as imitations of that other 'university in the heavenly companionship, where ... wisdom should be learnt for all eternity'.[207] The medieval monastery was once thought to be an imitation and intimation of the kingdom of heaven; for Melanchthon it was the university and the disciplined *paideia* it could offer.

---

[207] Preface to *The Book on the Soul* (1553), p.154.

4

So What is an Engaged Systematics?

This is the programmatic bit. In other words: this is where I reflect upon how I am both approaching Christian systematic theologies of the past and endeavouring to compose my own. It serves. It serves to clarify and explain what I'm doing—nothing more. It is not itself theological—which is why theologians like Karl Barth tried to do without the programmatic bit. But he couldn't really. However short—given the millions of words that were to follow—even *Church Dogmatics* has its 'Prolegomenon'.[1] Admittedly, it's a bit of a chicken-and-egg problem. The approach has to emerge through the theological emphasizes that create the organic coherence of the relationships of one topic with the others. Each topic has bearing upon the shape and direction of the development that the others will take. If it doesn't have the integrity of this coherence then the approach, or method, is 'outside' the system—and since we are talking Truth here (and God) then nothing can be outside the system. But at this point you have only the barest understanding of what my theological emphases are and what the shape of the entire project is. So I could leave this chapter until the end. In fact, you might decide to dive into the next section and leave reading this until the end. Though the end of the three other volumes, and a mountain of work, and a number of years yet of writing are quite a distance to travel. So here's a speed-camera shot of what I'm trying to do and how I'm trying to do it.

I have given more textual space in the last three chapters to Melanchthon and the emergence of Protestant dogmatics than to either the emergence of the creeds or the Medieval *Summa*. This is because it is at this point in the history of the Christian tradition that major changes seem to have occurred and from which modern Christian theology issued: the detachment of a theological science from *lectio divina*, the shift towards adversarial confessionalism, the professionalization of 'theologians' in the development of university education, etc. The 'engaged' approach to systematic theology is,

---

[1] See Sections 1–3 of *Church Dogmatics* I.1, trans. G.W. Bromiley, G.T. Thomson, and H. Knight (Edinburgh: T & T Clark, 2010).

in part, a corrective to some of the less benign effects of those changes that Melanchthon's later theology was just beginning to register. It seeks to relate theology to cultural and social life, most particularly the life of the Church. This chapter sets out to elucidate: a) the character of that corrective; b) define the nature of an engaged systematic theology; and c) explore some of its theological consequences.

AN ENGAGED SYSTEMATICS AS A CORRECTIVE

Certain abstracting trends developing within and contextualizing theological production are evident particularly in the later dogmatics of Melanchthon, as we have seen. These trends worked against older traditions excavated in Chapters 1 and 2 in which Christian doctrine, where meditation upon Scripture and the practices of everyday life worked together pedagogically and, as such, faith and the Faith were lived as well as taught. After Charles Taylor we might say theology was 'disembedded', although, as we have seen, even the more concept-orientated understanding of doctrine in Melanchthon's *Loci Praecipui Theologici* of 1559 could not transcend its complex contextual matrix. Theological discourse always comes from somewhere, is spoken by someone, and is legitimated or delegitimated by some institution implicated in particular sets of social and cultural relations.[2] But theological discourse can ignore its context. It can pretend it comes from nowhere. It can even announce that it comes directly from God. It can forget the multiple mediations that both effect and provide the possibility for its production. When this happens dogmatics becomes abstract and its truth-claims propositional. This manifests itself in confessionalism (Augsburg, 1530; Heidelberg, 1563; Westminster, 1646), and the systematic theologies that follow are crafted within the framework of these contractual self-identifications. The sclerosis of scholasticism turns systematic theology into a glass bead game. And often what is at stake in playing the game is not *theos* at all, but theo-logic gaining acceptance by imitating the dominating secular modes of reasoning of the day, *Wissenschaft*. This trend is most clearly evident in Biblical studies.

There is something deeply misguided, deeply wrong, in perpetuating confessional theologies. And I mean 'misguided' and 'wrong' not primarily in their moral, but in their theological sense. That is, they work against the Spirit of Christ. They do so because at base they are adversarial. The polemics

---

[2] Defining where theology speaks from, and understanding a theological standpoint in terms of other less theological and even non-theological standpoints involved in cultural processes, is the burden of Graham Ward, *Cultural Transformations and Religious Practice* (Cambridge: Cambridge University Press, 2004).

of Reformed, Protestant, Catholic, Orthodox theologies may have settled somewhat recently, but a residual violence of us against them still informs them: 'You are in error! We have the truth!' These adversarial theologies have dominated presentations of the Christian faith throughout modernity, even spiritual classics like Vladimir Lossky's *The Mystical Theology of the Eastern Church* or the irenic posturing of *Lumen Gentium*, are still informed by a fear of being seriously attentive to the other, to difference. Theologically, faith seeking an understanding of the God of love, mercy, peace, and justice, cannot traffic in *ressentiment* and, as I will argue in Volume II, the politics of fear, out of fear. Fear is the affective heart of sin. That does not mean that Christian theologians should suppress their fears and angers and aim for the sedatives of the banal. Good theology will always have a prophetic edge and not one of us, as seekers of understanding, are without error. We see partially, even in trying to be faithful. We stand to be corrected, and are accountable one to the other. But the fears and angers have to be faced honestly with hearts that are open and being continually opened by the Spirit of Christ. We need to be changed, transformed. We cannot continue to produce and so pass on the violences of denominationalism and sectarianism. That is not the Spirit of Christ. That is not the gospel.

There are signs things are getting better. Not through the work of ecumenism, as far as I see it, at an institutional level. Much of the energy for that kind of top-level ecumenism is disappearing like water into sand. There is a new ecumenism from below that should be listened to. People in the various churches on the whole do not share, perhaps because they have no memory of, traditional battle lines. There is increasing fluidity of persons across the traditions. There are also theological and liturgical borrowings across the traditions. The several generations of the uncatechized in the West has meant people coming to the faith or returning to the faith do not have some of the hang-ups of an erstwhile confessionalism. Some of the young professional theologians today are moving well beyond their own denominational boundaries in their search for truth. In this way, forty years in the wilderness of secularization may yet reap the blessings of milk and honey: the promise of reaching beyond dogmatic fences erected and policed by various ecclesial institutions, and pulling them down.

An engaged systematic theology aims to be a corrective to adversarial theologies. Engagement is an action that looks towards a catholicity to come as it looks towards a kingdom to come. Let me be clear. This does not mean that classical or even propositional dogmatics is without value. Far from it! To understand the contents of the Christian faith is foundational—that is, a beginning in a journey in which faith seeks, and in seeking is deepened in, understanding. The contents of the faith are the start of a biblical, liturgical, and ecclesial formation led in and through a life of embodied practices all of which can be summed up as prayer. The contents of the Christian faith are not an end in themselves—and it is one of the tendencies of confessionalism to make doctrine at end in itself. Conceptual content that is an end in itself is information, and theology is not the dissemination of information, but the offer of a training in becoming wise; a training in what Aquinas calls the virtue of *pudentia*. Neither are scholastic, fine-grained distinctions between, say, *analogia attributionis extrinisca* and *analogia attributionis intrinsica* (by seventeenth century Lutheran divines) or Aquinas's distinction between *creaturae realiter referuntur* and *secundum rationem* in God (in *Summa theologiae* Iª q.13 a.7) worthless. But such technical distinctions are important only because of the effects they make possible on the way the world is seen, experienced, and discerned.[3] That is, the way the Christian life is lived, and the effects such distinctions have of the way salvation is understood, recognized, appropriated, and realized materially, corporeally, intellectually, and spiritually. Otherwise the acts of making such distinctions have a tendency to become exercises in cerebral gymnastics; acts of purely rational or 'scientific' analysis.[4] This not only perpetuates adversarial theologies, but it also leads to idealist, if not gnostic, distortions—with implications for discriminations along the lines of class, gender, ethnic, and sexual orientation. (More of that in Volume III.) They promote the notion that we, the 'professionals', know what *we* are talking about and therefore more than *you* the *hoi poloi*. So *we* will do the thinking for you. Doctrine that is lived cannot be elitist or perpetuate an intellectual elitism.

Ratiocination is a very small part of what it is to be a living person, or a living community of persons when we want to talk of 'public reason'. Cognition is always embodied, and this embodiment is not simply personal it is social and cultural. I will explain more about this in Chapter 9 when I examine belief not simply as a cognitive but also as an emotional activity (not always either apprehended or comprehended), rooted in fundamental dispositions as much physiological as psychological; even possibly biological. But recall the internalization of the creed and the enactment of redemption in Cyril of Jerusalem's catechesis and mystagogical liturgies (Chapter 1). Recall, the processes of *memoria*, meditation, and moral formation in Hugh of St. Victor's *De sacramentis*—indeed, his understanding of what a sacrament is (Chapter 2). Recall what was striking about Melanchthon's *Loci communes 1521*—the appeal to *affectus* and the establishment of an emotional pedagogy (Chapter 3). Their

---

[3] On the importance of technical theological terms and the misconstruals that arise from the lack of them and reliance upon descriptive images borrowed from the natural world, see Sergius Bulgakov on Appollinarius of Loadicea in *The Lamb of God*, trans. Boris Jakim (Grand Rapids, MI: Eerdmans Publishing Company, 2008), pp.2–19.

[4] For the development of theology as a 'science' (*Wissenschaft*) in the German university system see J. Zachhuber's excellent study in the evolvement of the new paradigm, *Theology as Science in Nineteenth-Century Germany: From F.C. Baur to Ernst Troelsch* (Oxford: Oxford University Press, 2013).

presentations of Christian doctrine require comprehension, require rational thought, but they reach deeper into the human condition, into the pre-reflexive and pre-theoretical. 'The heart is deep,' the Psalmist tells us (Ps.64.6) and there is a 'wisdom of unknowing' (as Augustine and Nicholas of Cusa) taught.[5]

An engaged systematics is concerned with *lived* doctrine; *doctrina* as a verbal noun, the art of making something known. It works as a corrective to a whole set of binary distinctions bequeathed to, and dominating the production of modern theology: faith/reason, grace/nature, revelation/knowledge, theology/philosophy, immanent/transcendent, natural/supernatural, intrinsic/extrinsic, subjective/objective. These binaries increasingly became enshrined in a social imaginary that produced institutions separating public from private, the academy from the church. We can call this secularism if you like, but there was never any pure secularism since the inherited discourses of Christendom still retained their power, albeit in transfigured ways.[6] These binaries also produced distinctions *within* theology: fundamental theology/ biblical theology/practical theology; philosophical theology/dogmatics/public theology; homiletics/ecclesiastical history/ethics. The distinctions have produced 'expertises' and divisions of intellectual labour, and the academy has institutionalized (and often siloed) these distinctions. Doctrine that is *lived* is doxological in its orientation and liturgical in nature—where liturgy is

---

[5] For a fine genealogical analysis of the shift that followed the epistemological break which we now term 'modernity' and from which modern theology's fixation on the self-revelation of the divine and the personal encounter with Jesus emerges, see Johannes Hoff, 'The Rise and Fall of the Kantian Paradigm of Modern Theology' in P. Candler, ed., *The Grandeur of Reason: Religion, Tradition and Universalism* (London: SCM Press, 2010). Hoff demonstrates how the earlier 'truth which *demands* to be affirmed *as* incomprehensible' (p.171) becomes, in modernity and modern theology, 'the assent of faith ... subordinated to the theoretic identification of approved propositions about things or events. This is precisely the point where the concept of "revelation" becomes a basic concept of modern theology ... From here on, "revelation" will appear as a systematic theological principle, which marks the characteristic features of the Christian faith and legitimizes its validity claims with regard to secular reason or non-Christian objections' (pp.178–80). Hoff observes: 'There can be no *scientia* without the faithful attachment to makeshifts which becalm our confused and confusing apprehension that we do not *really* know' (p.172). We believe. For similar claims see also, John Milbank, 'The Grandeur of Reason and the Perversity of Rationalism: Radical Orthodoxy's First Decade', in Simon Oliver and John Milbank (eds.), *The Radical Orthodoxy Reader* (London: Routledge, 2009), pp.367–405.

[6] Hence Carl Schmitt's recognition in his sociology of legal concepts, like sovereignty, that they were ultimately all theological in provenance. See his *Political Theology: Four Chapters on the Concept of Sovereignty*, trans. George Swarb (Cambridge, MA: MIT Press, 1985) and *Dictatorship*, trans. Michael Hoelzl and Graham Ward (Cambridge: Polity Press, 2013). See also my analysis of Kant's last book *The Conflict of the Faculties* in 'The Myth of Secularism', *Telos* (vol. 167), Summer 2014, 162–79. If secularism is related to Weber's 'disenchantment' thesis, then we have already begun to see in Chapter 3, that it is difficult to assess when this became culturally dominant. In many ways 'enchantment' is displaced into other areas: literature, for example, painting, architecture, and music. It still remains in Christian theology in the pietist tradition.

not just something that goes on in church, but a way of being church beyond buildings, institutions, lectionaries, and orders of service. I will examine this understanding of *ecclesia* in Volume III, but I would like to make it plain now that I am not against institutionalism as such or the Church as various institutional corporations. But we need a sociology and psychology of institutionalism to appreciate what they are good for (facilitating salvation) and what they might impede (facilitating salvation). For now what is important to grasp is that an examination of doctrine that is *lived* will erase academic distinctions between sub-disciplines, because it will continually cross and recross parameters that institutions and the development of theology as a purely academic activity have created.

Furthermore, in working to correct the imbalances and infelicities of the epistemological conditions of modernity, an engaged systematic theology will refuse a *lex credendi/lex orandi* distinction in which doctrine is viewed as a 'second order' reflection upon 'first order' ecclesial practice. This understanding of theology can easily separate the theory from the practice—although recognizing the practice or the discourses involved in the practice (Scriptures, liturgies, creeds, hymns) as primary in generating the believer's experience. Push this reductive tendency further and we end up trying to articulate a 'pure theology' or view theology in functional, intellectual terms.

There is one significant version of this first and second order understanding of theology, though, that is more suggestive. One of the most sophisticated explorations of the relationship of *lex credendi/lex orandi* is found in Geoffrey Wainwright's *Doxology: A Systematic Theology*. Liturgy in this work is 'the primary locus of religious language for the Christian . . . *Theological* language belongs to the second order: it is the language of reflexion upon the primary experience.'[7] So, for example, in his own engagement with the creeds Wainwright defines them as 'first-order' language.[8] But the approach is sophisticated because he appreciates a dialectical quality between what he terms (after John Macquarrie) the 'architectonic' (first order) and the 'critical' (second order) in theological discourse, and he accepts that theological 'reflexion' informs liturgical practice and vice versa:

> The language of worship mediates the substance on which theologians reflect; without that substance, theological talk would have no referent. Yet the 'architectonic' and 'critical' functions of theological reasoning, secondary though that reasoning is in relation to substantial communion with God, play a proper part in shaping and pruning the continuing primary experience. . . For reflexive reason is part of God's endowment to humanity and must therefore be included

---

[7] G. Wainwright, *Doxology: The Praise of God in Worship, Doctrine, and Life: A Systematic Theology* (Oxford: Oxford University Press, 1980), p.21.
[8] Ibid., p.19.

in the total picture of human communion with God. The second-order activity of theology is therefore, at its own level, properly doxological: the theologian is truly theologian when, in his very theologizing, he is listening for the 'echo of a voice' and is contributing, even if indirectly, to the human praise of God.[9]

An engaged systematic theology would concur with much of what Wainwright articulates here, especially the doxological nature of theological reflection. Wainwright notes that the praise of God is called *theologia* 'in the approach to the *sanctus* in the liturgies of St. Mark and St. Basil'.[10] The differences between Wainwright's approach and the one offered here can be best viewed in relation to the examinations of the writings of Cyril of Jerusalem, Hugh of St. Victor and Philip Melanchthon's *Loci communes 1521*. The language of the creed for Cyril was to be absorbed, shape liturgical experience, and learnt as a means of describing and understanding that experience. For the creed was recognized as human *regulae* distilled from Scripture. If there was a primary discourse it was the discourse of Scripture. Furthermore, the performative nature of Cyril's *Lectures*, given in the basilica, fashioned liturgical events that led specifically to sacramental action. These events *were* theologically 'reflexive', but the rhetorical nature of reflexivity was inseparable from the spiritual pedagogy he was leading them into. It is difficult to see where any lines (certainly hierarchical lines in which one is primary and the other secondary) were to be drawn between experience, doctrine, and understanding. The teaching as an act was to be lived as an activity as its vocabulary was learnt. We saw, with Hugh, how Scriptural appropriation was fundamental in a reformation of the entire human person and the community in which that person dwelt. But the Scriptural appropriation was complex and non-reductive because the literal and historical sense gave access to the allegorical and tropological sense. The reader or listener moved in and through the signs to the God-given, Christ-centred, Spirit-led reality that they spoke of and gave expression to. The reflexivity was *lived* through meditation and participation, because Scripture was understood as an extension of Christ as the Word. The character of *Loci communes 1521* shares similarities with both Cyril's and Hugh's approaches. Here too theological teaching is a 'reflexion' upon the first-order Scriptural language (recognized as revelation). Here too the rhetoric and performativity of the theological discourse both concerned *affectus* and evoked *affectus* such that Scripture was to be absorbed into a pneumatological praxis, both intellectually understood and embodied, of transforming desire. But the last edition of *Loci communes* differed from this: the critical nature of theology is advanced and it has more of a theoretical (and policing) 'function'. It distanced itself from its own production; its own language-use.

---

[9] Ibid.   [10] Ibid., p.468.

It is not without significance that Wainwright is vague about the 'second order' activity of theology, doxological 'at its own level'. The contribution to 'first-order' language is 'indirect'. It is at this point that *we might disagree* or an engaged systematic theology wishes to *push further*. Wainwright too wants to emphasize corporeal and affective engagement, experience, and participation. And we would both agree on an 'indirectness', understood along the lines of the nature of analogy—human discourse with respect to God treats greater dissimilarities between creator and created, but nevertheless affords traces (never to be adequately grasped in this life other than by faith) of similarity such that theological language is not equivocal (and therefore knows nothing of God beyond its own projections). But for an engaged systematics the aim, intention, and *telos* of both liturgy and theological, discursive engagement is spiritual participation and pedagogy. Both are educative and wish to effect and transform. One is not simply a commentary upon the other, in either direction. Theological engagement is a continuation of the doxological endeavours within the liturgy, as Wainwight would agree, since the liturgical is a continuation of the doxological teachings of the Scriptures. The aim of all three—Scriptures, participation, and the pedagogy learning and speaking about God—is *salus*, salvation. And all three are human productions that, it is hoped, divine operations guide or ameliorate. Wainwright recognizes that our worship is always 'imperfect' as it strives towards the 'perfect service of the Father'.[11] There is a difference with respect to ecclesial authorization and the legitimation of the tradition; and this authorization and legitimation *do* prioritize. Theological reflection would have very little to reflect upon if we did not have the Scriptures, the liturgy, and the traditions of past theological reflection. But the lines between *sacra pagina* and holy teaching are not so precisely or hierarchically established.[12] So, given that all Christians have to be theologians, understand, and give an account of what they believe in terms of what they are experiencing, entering more and more deeply into the imaginative world of the Christian faith, where for a Christian theology does prayer end and critical thinking begin? Hugh's understanding of *meditatio* as it issues into *contemplatio* would see no distinction. For the Christian, there can only exist a line to be crossed between liturgy and living *if* liturgy was just that which went on in church, and church was just the activities that went on in this building and that institution. And that is not the case; or not simply the case. So the imaginative circulations of the Word ripple out towards one discourse (Scriptures), then liturgical discourse, and ripple out further

[11] Ibid., p.59.
[12] For an analysis of *sacra pagina*, *sacra doctrina*, spiritual pedagogy, and the task of the theologian see Fáinche Ryan, *Formation in Holiness: Thomas Aquinas on* Sacra doctrina (Leuven: Peeters, 2007), especially pp.143–74.

as faith seeks understanding. This would follow from Wainwright's astute endorsement of the 'Church as an "extension of the incarnation" '.[13] We will examine in Chapter 6 how these circulations are initiated and caught up in the circulation of the divine communication of love, what John Milbank has explored as 'a theory of human being as linguistic being which participates in the divine linguistic being'.[14]

So—the engaged systematic approach would wish to correct any overemphatic hierarchy between first and second order reflection. It would wish to underline the mediatorial character of all human discourse and give this mediatorial character a theological warrant: we as human beings are 'made in the image and likeness of God' and Jesus Christ is the Mediator par excellence. Its embrace of the dialectics of participation as the basis for this mediatorial activity means it cannot accept a Kantian philosophy that demarcates noumenal religious experience from the phenomenology of critical, theological reflection. Further clarifications will follow in Chapter 6 when I examine the nature of theology as prayer. Significantly, Wainwright concludes the observations cited above with the famous dictum by Evagarius of Pontus: the theologian is one who prays.

A further point needs to be made which has less to do with engaged systematics as a corrective and more to do with engaged systematics being an approach to theology done today: in the historical theologies of Chapters 1 to 3 I emphasized how something new emerged theologically at a point of cultural and historical dissonance. An old order was in conflict with, and giving way to, a different order in terms of class, economy, government, law, and overlapping jurisdictions. The creeds emerged in the changes occurring in the wake of the Constantinian conquest of the Eastern Roman Empire. The *summa* emerged in the changes occurring in the wake of Gregorian reform, the rise of urban living, the decay of the feudal system, and the beginnings of the juridical state. Dogmatics emerged in the changes occurring in the rise of the nation state, the growing self-confidence of the middle classes and civic governance, and the changes in education. New identities and allegiances were being formed out of cultural dissonance, new experiences of the world were becoming evident that demanded theological reflection and rethinking on the relation of the Church to the world, and both to salvation. Maybe then we can see an engaged systematics as part of the new response to the time in which we live. Certainly, what I am doing in these volumes chimes with what a number of other systematic theologians are attempting in learning the languages of other disciplines and speaking into and out of the

---

[13] G.Wainwright, *Doxology: A Systematic Theology* (n.7), p.71.
[14] John Milbank, *The Word Made Strange: Theology, Language, Culture* (Oxford: Blackwell, 1997), p.2.

cultural pluralism and intradependencies that are radically reconfiguring the Church–world interface.

WHAT IS AN ENGAGED SYSTEMATICS?

An engaged systematic theology is both a way of approaching theologies that have been composed and a way of composing such theologies. As such, it is a mode of theological interpretation and a mode of theological practice that places importance upon what Charles Taylor, in examining the nature of what he calls the 'immanent frame', has described as 'less a set of beliefs' and more 'the sensed context in which we develop our beliefs'[15] and learn our languages. As we will see in Chapter 9, believing is social and cultural, not simply personal. It also has a structure that, to simplify grossly, is both synchronic and diachronic. That is: whatever is believed and believable (and I am not just talking about theological beliefs at this point) is both historically, culturally, and socially specific (the synchronic axis) and always undergoing a transformative process (the diachronic axis). Religious faith, Christian or otherwise, is a practice of belief. Learning the language of what is believed is fundamental to that practice. Belief could not be articulated, would have no content, and therefore remain highly amorphous, if it were not communicated through gestures, images, concepts, narratives etc.: in a word 'discourse'. So it is with this life-long learning that we must begin our definition of an engaged systematic theology. Taking a concrete Christian account of a violent, even traumatic event can help us to assess just how essential and dramatic that learning is.

Polycarp was Bishop of Smyrna in the mid-second century. At the age of eighty-six he fell foul of the Roman authorities by refusing to burn incense to the Emperor and was burnt alive, publicly. Any violent death is shocking. The records of those soldiers who returned from the trenches of the First World War, the testimonies of Americans in Vietnam, civilian and military, who witnessed the victims of napalm bombing—even more the silences of those unable to record or suppressing what they have witnessed—attests to trauma. The body, its numerous emotional and somatic memories, cannot forget while the mind refuses to recall. Moments of flashback cause paralysis, breakdown, and aphasia. Here is an old, much loved, and much respected Christian man set on fire, by the imperial authorities, for all to see. The horror of the punishment was a judicial means of generating public fear: Imperial law will be

---

[15] Charles Taylor, *A Secular Age* (Cambridge, MA: The Belknap Press of Harvard University Press, 2007), p.549.

obeyed or there will be painful consequences. We have a witnessed account of that execution in the form of a circular letter sent by the church in Smyrna to the churches throughout Pontus in Asia Minor. And in the account, the *Martyrdom of Polycarp*, something remarkable happens because of the way a certain form of Christian language, Christian imagining, transforms what is witnessed—transforming even trauma into doxology.

> A great flame blazed up and those of us to whom it was given to see beheld a miracle. . . For the flames, bellying out like a ship's sail in the wind, formed the shape of a vault and thus surrounded the martyr's body as with a wall. And he was within it not as burning flesh but rather as bread being baked, or like gold and silver being purified in a smelting furnace. And from it we perceived such a delightful fragrance as though it were smoking incense or some other costly perfume.
>
> At last when these vicious men realized that his body could not be consumed by the fire they ordered a *confector* to go up and plunge a dagger into the body. When he did this there came out such a quantity of blood that the flames were extinguished.[16]

Of course, this is the genre of hagiography in which atrocity is transmuted into martyrdom. Martyrs and would-be martyrs were highly valuable commodities. Their bodies (and if still alive and awaiting their deaths, then their prayerful minds) were viewed as stargates between earth and heaven. Their insights and their wisdom were significant. That is: efficacious. Their remains became important foci for pilgrimage, veneration, and (without being too cynical because there is a devotion here) economic patronage. Nevertheless, as one historian notes in her exploration of the Christian appropriation of everyday scents in late antiquity and with reference to Polycarp's martyrdom: 'the Smyrean witnesses used their sensory experiences of the event to direct their attention away from this world, away from the earthly experience of suffering and injustice enacted before them'.[17] The transmutation of traumatic experience need not be escapist. Flesh baked and smelted in fire is seen, but it is seen *as*. I will return to the importance of seeing *as* and its relation to belief in Chapter 9. The burning is seen in terms of the Christian imaginary; the imaginative world opened up by the Christ event.

For now what is significant is that the seeing *as* is made possible through a series of Biblical intertextualities that lie at the level of suggestion. No explicit references are made to the story in the *Book of Daniel* (chapter 3) of Shadrach, Meshach and Abed-nego thrown into a furnace by Nebuchadnezzar because

---

[16] *Martyrdom of Polycarp* 15.1–16.1 in Herbert Musurillo (ed.), *The Acts of the Christian Martyrs* (Oxford: Clarendon Press, 1972), pp.14–15.

[17] Susan Ashbrook Harvey, *Scenting Salvation: Ancient Christianity and the Olfactory Imagination* (Oakland, CA: University of California Press, 2006), p.46.

of their refusal to offer worship and sacrifice to an idol; or to the mysterious god-like figure who appears alongside them. No explicit references are made to the crucifixion and the blood and water that pour from the side of Christ when a soldier thrusts a spear into it; or to Christ as the bread of heaven; or to the anointing of Christ's feet by Mary using a costly anointment whose fragrance filled the house—an act interpreted by Christ as prefiguring his burial. No explicit references are made to the martyrdom of Stephen where the saint gazes intently towards the vaults of heaven that open upon the glory of God (Acts 7.55), while he is stoned to death. There are no explicit references because the language of these stories, heard or read, have been internalized, memorized, and meditated upon. They have become part of the imaginative repertoire of those who composed the account of what they saw. As the Canadian poet and translator, Robert Bringhurst, reminds us about narratives: they mean

> much more than telling stories. [Narrative] means learning how to hear them, how to nourish them, and how to let them live. It means learning to let stories swim down into yourself, grow large there, and rise back up again. It does not—repeat, does not mean memorising the lines so you can act the script you've written or recite the book you've read.[18]

What might once have been citation or verbal recall of Scripture has become part of the language whereby Christians learnt to understand by faith the circumstances of their lives; even when the public face of those circumstances is violent and potentially traumatic.

This is what I mean by saying that learning the language is essential and dramatic. The languages we learn shape our imaginative understanding of the world and our experience of it. They enable the seeing *as* which takes in the sensed and transfigures it—even beneath the level of conscious interpretation (as we will see). I drew attention to this learning in Chapter 1 with respect to the Creeds and theological words like 'peace'; while, with Hugh, we treated 'justice' and, with Philip, 'justification'.

There are several different and overlapping dimensions to learning and speaking language. There is our education and the contexts within which that education takes place. The primary context here is the Church: its liturgies, its teachings, its Scriptures, its sermons, its catechism, its architecture and

---

[18] Robert Bringhurst, *The Tree of Meaning* (Berkeley, CA: Counterpoint, 2007), quoted in Maggie Ross, *Silence: A User's Guide* (London: Darton, Longman and Todd, 2014), p.45. From another perspective, that of painting, the British painter Oliver Soskice has written: 'existence is received as the unreachable beckoning horizon within stone, the sky, brickwork rained upon, daylight, pools of reflecting water, apples in a bowl. A painter may spend a lifetime trying to translate this strange, innermost utterance of visible things. Yet the inexpressibly other is not the same as inexpressibly alien, because the unknown pole of everything is precisely what imposes our humanity upon us.' 'Painting and the Absence of Grace', *Modern Painters*, issue 4 1991, p.65.

material culture, and the conversations that go on, official and unofficial (who draws the lines here?) between members of the Church. Talk of dialogue introduces a sociological dimension about the language communities to which we belong, their economic, their political, their ethical contexts, their geographies, their status, and their unacknowledged biases. All discourse, its learning and practising, takes place in and as social interaction, and all social interaction is implicated in social relations. So there is a sociological dimension to learning and speaking the language of faith. These social relations in the churches are variegated. They involve, among other variables, class, gender, ethnicity, clerical or lay status, and age. There are, then, 'social effects mediated by the utterances' produced.[19] Some of these 'utterances' are by gesture, clothing, and material setting. Many of them are probably not negotiated cognitively, so the social effects of the learning and speaking are mediated unconsciously. As the American anthropologist, Asif Agha, points out, it is

> therefore all the more important to see that utterances and discourses are themselves material objects made through human activity—made, in a physical sense, out of vibrating columns of air, ink on paper, pixels in electronic media—which exercise real effects upon our senses, mind, and modes of social organization, and to learn to understand and analyse these effects.[20]

Involved in this discursive materiality, as in social relations, is material objects themselves—their use, their circulation and their production. It is from social effects that the organization of social life, ecclesial life, emerges along with the distinctiveness of cultures. The discourses found and fostered in one social organization like the Church cross over and become transformed in other social organizations: the crucifix venerated in this place becomes the crystal studded piece of jewellery worn in that place. The Church has no monopoly on the language it uses. In fact, as the Church becomes more hegemonic and dominant culturally then its language infects more and more other discourses.

Today we may be living in a post-Christendom world but there remains, to a greater or lesser degree than in the past, a speaking of Christ that goes on elsewhere and outside Christian communities. When I write 'speaking of Christ' it must be understood that I am using that genitive subjectively and objectively—as a possessive (the primary speech is Christ's own) and in relation to an indirect object (the speaking we do *about* Christ). Christ can be both the one who speaks and the one of whom things are spoken. Christ's own *sermo* is heard, if heard at all, only in obedience to Him; only in listening. But that *sermo* can still be deployed and redeployed outside of those in

---

[19] Asif Agha, *Language and Social Relations* (Cambridge: Cambridge University Press, 2007), p.14.
[20] Ibid., p.3.

obedience in ways that can be interruptive and initiate critical reflection. The speaking about Christ is variegated. It may be affirmative. It may be negative. It may be difficult to judge. The possessive and indirect uses of the genitive need not be in opposition to each other.

In the past this speaking took form in the first extensive and critical treatment of the Christian faith by a pagan (Celsus's *On True Doctrine c.*177) and a cartoon of Christ as a crucified ass in the Alexamenos *graffito* (*c.*200). More recently that 'speaking elsewhere' took the form of Herbert Howells' *Hymnus Paradisi* (1938), Francis Bacon's *Crucifixions* (1942, 1962, 1965), Patrick White's novel *Riders in the Chariot* (1961), Bettina Rheims' and Serge Bramly's photoshoot *INRI* (1998) or Bill Viola's video installation *Emergence* (2002). None of these more modern presentations of the Christian faith are either negative or affirmative. And none of them present an orthodox faith.

In Bill Viola's *Emergence*, for example, Christ seems to rise from the tomb (in the form of a baptismal font overflowing with water) but it is a dead body that rises to be received by two grieving women who first kneel and then stand to support a form that evolves into a *pieta*. The dead body remains dead, so that what might have been a resurrection becomes a dramatic stillbirth. This is a powerful meditation on hope thwarted, and instigates a number of questions—some of them pastoral, since there are any number of Christian women who have to undergo the experience of stillbirths. While the water motif attests to Viola's attraction to the elemental and the mythic, it resonates deeply and imaginatively. Viola's installation, like those other artistic expressions I mentioned, plays within, imaginatively engages with, and improvises on aspects of the Christian *mythos*. Though some such work can get reinserted explicitly into an ecclesial context—like Viola's *Martyrs* (*Earth, Air, Fire and Water*) created for St. Paul's in London in 2014. And then the transplanted work takes on Christian theological resonance not necessarily in accord with Viola's own conception of the piece. (For who can control how anything is given or received, especially the Word of God?)

Nevertheless, all these cultural impacts of the Christian discourse transform in turn the contexts, and the tang, the taste, register, or inflection of the speaking of Christ within the sociological organization of the Church. The language of the gospel is being employed elsewhere and for other means than conversion to the faith or the formation of those in the faith.

Learning to speak of Christ, learning and practising the languages of the Christian faith, cannot then ever be a static enterprise because these languages are continually circulating and shifting: synchronically across global 'fields of cultural production'[21] and diachronically through time. There are semantic

---

[21] The term and the critical analysis it facilitated belong to Pierre Bourdieu. For an introduction to his work see Randal Johnston edited collection of essays by Bourdieu, *The Field of Cultural Production* (New York: Columbia University Press, 1993).

drifts as the meaning of words or phrases leans in this direction, bends in this translation and that citation, undergoes transformation that becomes intelligible in one context and unintelligible in another. Experience—personal (what happens to us), social (what happens to our communities), historical (what happens to our countries, our world)—changes how we learn and understand the languages we speak; even when we speak of Christ. No Christian theologian today in the West, for example, can write theology without sensing and recognizing the pressure of world Christianities that are sensitive to Western intellectual imperialism and the historical, Christian involvement in colonialism: the distinctive Pentecostal voices from South Korea and the Congo, for example. No Christian theologian today, anywhere in the world, can write theology without sensing and recognizing the pressure of other religious pieties, their evaluation and their public, mediatized profiles, practised by neighbours, friends, and even other members of their family both in regions where Christians are a minority and regions where they still maintain a strong cultural presence. So our personal, social, and historical experiences change the way we speak of the Christian faith, how we communicate it, to whom, for what reason.

Having looked at the emergence and practice of systematic theologies from the second century to the sixteenth, we can recognize how distinctive that speaking of Christ becomes across millennia and how 'out of date' that past speaking of Christ becomes for today. The writings bear the imprint of complex and multidimensional contexts that I don't share: I don't live under the persecutions, paranoias, and threats to my life that Athanasius lived under; I don't live with the violences, injustices, lawlessness, and calls for *reformatio* of Hugh of St. Victor's abbey in Paris; and I don't live with the demons, angels, antichrists, and apocalyptic scenarios of which Luther and Melanchthon spoke. Neither do I live with the elegant, bourgeois refinements and the brutal authoritarianism of Schleiermacher's Prussia. And when we come closer to our own time, the imprint of context still remains: I don't live with the enormous guilt of the Nazi holocaust out of which Moltmann's theology emerged, or the neoscholastic Thomism that was such a burden to de Lubac, or Chenu, or Congar. I don't live under the liberal, well-heeled intellectualism out of which the 1960s 'death of God' theologies issued. Each set of theological writings speak of Christ in a way that is dated now. Our theologies do date, just as the emphases within our theologies come and go out of fashion. Theologians may want to landmark their theologies with monumental systematic developments over several volumes. I'm no exception here. But their work will date. It may even be forgotten. It will certainly be received differently, and translate in ways unforeseen at present. The hermeneutics of Hans-Georg Gadamer has taught us all this. We use the names—Augustine, Aquinas, von Balthasar, Barth—I have used names in the last three chapters—Cyril of Jerusalem, Hugh of St. Victor, Philip Melanchthon—but we are trading in holograms.

We learn to speak of Christ in specific ways at specific times and within specific locations, that's the point, and an engaged systematic theology recognizes and critically appropriates that fact. Such an approach to theology does not mean we cannot learn important theological observations from older theologies—about social relations as ecclesial relations through Schleiermacher, about the Jewish Christ suffering in solidarity with us through Moltmann, about the relationship between nature and grace through de Lubac and the immanent process of divinity in history through the 'death of God' school, for example. An engaged systematics does not undo our on-going learning from the tradition. In fact, it acknowledges it and acknowledges certain theological continuities with the past. It augments, even as it translates and recites these continuities, so that the imaginative dynamic of the tradition moves towards new appropriations and integrations of present experience with the past as it points continually, eschatologically, towards the future. And that does not mean the Christian truth is relative, for there is no position from which one could view all cultural variations. The concrete locatedness of any standpoint within the nexus of Christian discourse vitiates 'any form of radical relativism that presumes the perfect intersubstitutability of social "positions"'.[22] What the practice of an engaged systematics does mean is that the catholicity of the gospel continuously expands as all Christian words are gathered, by the Spirit, into the Word of God. And it's exceptionally valuable that we do so speak and change and develop our speaking—because faith is a living relationship.

Speaking of Christ is part of that living relationship with Christ. As the Dutch theologian, Edward Schillebeeckx, reminded the church: 'The "universal significance" of Jesus' message which is affirmed in particular situations therefore of course requires to be made a reality ("actualized") in changed circumstances.'[23] This is a logic that follows from a commitment to incarnationalism not simply as an event in history but the revelation of a divine principle—God *for us*—which cannot be separated from a Trinitarian understanding of God *in Himself*. The Word is continually given; it always has been given. The nature of love is to communicate. Our response and answer to that abiding address by divine love is also continually given; and given afresh. Schillebeeckx again: 'The church community alive today bears witness to the living actuality here and now of Jesus' gospel, which found its definitive account in the scriptures . . . but the church communities make the text a living word.'[24]

---

[22] A. Agha, *The Language of Social Relations* (n.19), p.5. He is referring here to all discourses and the knowledges they produce. It is I who relate this point specifically to Christian discourse.

[23] Edward Schillebeeckx, *Jesus in our Western Culture: Mysticism, Ethics and Politics* (London: SCM Press, 1986), p.40.

[24] Ibid., p.41.

It is not just the church communities that make the text of Scripture a living word. Jesus-talk, once culturally embedded and culturally pervasive, spills over into the streets. It is taken up elsewhere as we have seen: mouthed, mimicked, modified, cited, and recited in contexts beyond institutional or sociological boundaries. This is part of its dissemination. It goes viral. Christianity will cease, secularization will reach its apogee, once the circulation of religious language (Jesus-talk in this instance) dries up. But, theologically for Christianity, that would mean the cessation of the activity of Spirit with respect to the divine communication of love. So it won't happen. It cannot happen. And that means today secularism is just something some people, in some places, have told themselves and got others to believe is believable, even inescapable—a destiny. Elsewhere, I have explored the myth of secularism, observing how the ways in which its ideology is quickly exiting, if it hasn't already exited, what Foucault called the 'grids of intelligibility'.[25] Today, we need to appreciate and hear the ways Jesus-talk is circulating, and has, in fact, a life of its own, outside the ecclesia. Why is this important? Because, if we as the Church are to learn how to speak the Christian faith today, to speak of Christ today, and learn how to compose our systematic examinations of the faith today, in our times, in our places, in our sociocultural conditions—speak in a way that bears witness to a living, Spirit-led, faith—then we have to learn about how Christ is spoken elsewhere as well as how Christ speaks to us. As I said, there may be critical interventions here that the Church needs to acknowledge as valid. This is part of the learning and development processes involved in language transmission; part of that semantic shifting that is always occurring; part of the social circulation of discourse.

Two aspects of an engaged systematics become prominent in this learning to speak of Christ today. The first concerns attention to context and the second how our present seeking comes to understand; what philosophically is a concern with 'epistemology'. We will look briefly at each of these aspects.

1. Context

It might seem that what I am doing in the first three chapters is simply providing certain texts (creeds, a summa, a dogmatics) with a context; and to some extent that is exactly what I am doing. But I am also trying to do something else, and that is to explore discursive relations between text

[25] See Graham Ward, *Unbelievable: Why We Believe and Why We Don't* (London: I.B.Tauris, 2014), particularly Chapter VIII, pp.174–86. The 'grids of intelligibility' is a phrase Foucault employs in *The History of Sexuality*, Part One: *An Introduction* (London: Allen Lane. 1979), p.93.

and context. In the past 'context' was understood as that which framed the 'text'—the background. Context informed and situated the text within larger fields of enquiry and cultural endeavour. This tended to reify 'text'; set it apart. The creation of context in this model might highlight the distinctiveness of the text, it might reveal continuities and it might gesture towards understanding the text as an expression of the wider context (on a cause and effect basis). What this model of context did not do was examine the dynamics of the relation between the two points of reference. With an engaged systematic theology that aims at being non-reductive, then we have to appreciate how context is being used or, more particularly, the non-reductive nature of context itself.

A dialectical model of contextualization *did* attempt to do this. It would demonstrate how a text refigured the context and thereby altered it—even if the text established more firmly the status quo. Rather than in accordance with a logic of cause and effect, the dialectical model explored the reciprocal nature of the text-context relation. Marxist, feminist, post-colonial readings of texts might point both to the way the context impacted upon the text and also the way the text offered a critical reflection upon the context; a critical reflection that it was hoped would raise cultural conscious awareness to the extent that the context might be changed. And so, for example, in such a cultural transformation and social revolution, the validity of the suppressed or subaltern view is a means towards establishing a more just society. The work of the Frankfurt School understood critical theory to operate in this way.

With the advent of structuralism and greater attention to the semiotic, 'text' took on a much wider meaning. Cultures were themselves viewed as texts; discursive, symbolic systems. In their different ways the anthropologists Claude-Levi Strauss and Clifford Geerzt, and the philosopher Paul Ricoeur, each 'democratized' textuality because they saw it everywhere. This blurred any lines between context and text: for where did one end and the other begin if all cultural expression was a discursive code of one kind or another: a gesture, a rite, a poem, a dance, a system of gift-exchange? Everything was part of a flow of signs that could not operate outside of being related to an extensive grid of other signs that made the signs intelligible. And nothing lay beyond the text or outside it—well, at least for Strauss and Geerzt. Ricoeur was always pushing towards something more original and which provided the impulse for there being either texts, contexts, or signification at all. If texts became more difficult to distinguish from contexts and were indeed continually disseminating themselves through myriad semiotic channels, cited and recited in different forms, through different media, then this 'textual turn' engendered any number of complex analyses of the dynamic and unpredictable relations between texts and contexts.

Context, after structuralism, post-structuralism, New Historicism,[26] and Actor–Network theory[27] is made more complex: any bounded text or piece of semiotic action emerges from and returns to other texts or textualities that surround and inform it. Texts too have been made more complex, because they cannot be neatly severed from each other and disappear into some flat, homogenous landscape called a 'field' or a 'grid'. Some texts are more important than others. Some texts generate further texts more than others. I have already referred to the embedded intertextuality of Scripture in relation to the *Martyrdom of Polycarp*. The Bible, Shakespeare, the works of Freud, the paintings of Botticelli, the music of Bach—these have all generated and become embedded within other productions. Context spreads in wild and wonderful ways. Some publishers rejected J.K. Rowling's first Harry Potter novel, and the impact on literacy levels across the world might have been stopped right there.[28] But, thankfully, another publisher saw its potential!

Furthermore, some contextual backgrounds are readable and others are not. Contextualism can only treat those that are readable or have become readable through becoming texts. But there is much that is unreadable—informing the cultural imaginary, informing the presupposed social emotions, constructing our *habitus*. There is the terrain of what has been called the 'cognitive unconscious'—of which more in Chapter 9. Contemporary historians have turned attention on trying to articulate those unreadable backgrounds. Gathering fragments from numerous sources they construct histories of silence, of listening, of smelling. They attempt to excavate glimpses of the sub-textual and render it more available to us—giving us thicker accounts of texts and contexts.

Since the 1990s, and in part responding to the espousal of an all-embracing textual approach to culture, a group of linguistic anthropologists based in Chicago have been examining the 'social-interactional entextualization/ contextualization' processes.[29] In the struggle to find a language to express what no one has really examined before jargon (unfortunately) abounds. But basically, what they are examining are the social relations that give rise to texts—this is what they mean by 'entextualizing': not any single text but the

[26] For New Historicism see the ground breaking collection of essays by Stephen Greenblatt, *Renaissance Self-Fashioning: From More to Shakespeare* (Chicago: University of Chicago Press, 1980).

[27] For Actor–Network Theory see Bruno Latour, *Reassembling the Social: An Introduction to Actor–Network-Theory* (Oxford: Oxford University Press, 2005).

[28] The Harry Potter 'literacy phenonemon' is well documented. See <http://www.smh.com.au/articles/2002/09/19/1032054870385.html> accessed July 2015, for an account of its impact on school children in New South Wales, especially boys.

[29] Michael Silverstein and Greg Urban (eds.), *Natural Histories of Discourse* (Chicago: University of Chicago Press, 1996), p.8.

metamorphoses that produce textual transmissions and replications. These social relations, when examined, give rise to a 'metadiscourse'—identifiable categories outside or beyond discourse that make it possible at all. The text itself 'has the ability to freeze-frame past and future, eliminating the dynamic and contingent social properties from which it was assembled'.[30] It is the 'assembling' they wish to focus their examinations on—the transposition, transductions, and translations between gesture, talk and writing that betray shared cultures from which texts emerge. These examinations provide some remarkable observations: 'one cannot predict from the form of an utterance the aspects of its context that may be critical to its interpretation; nor can one expect the relevant aspects of context to be finite or bounded ... A communicative act has a relation to other acts, including the past, the future, the hypothetical, the conspicuously avoided, and so on, and these relations—intersecting frames, if you will—inform the participation structure of the moment.'[31]

So, Charles Taylor, in his research into the cultural shift from the enchanted to the disenchanted world, is right to demand an investigation into the 'context of understanding'. For beliefs are (and have) lived conditions for the possibility or impossibility of certain imaginative experiences of the world. '[A]ll beliefs are held within a context or framework of the taken-for-granted.'[32] Analyses of the way systematic theology was engaged in the life–worlds of Cyril, or Hugh, or Philip is attempting to discern the complexity of participation in the social relations that gave rise to the texts and their pedagogical deployment. Similarly, the practice of composing an engaged systematic theology works with, critically responds to, and elucidates the participations (theological, social, cultural, historical, political) in which it is involved and in which it is inducting others (primarily its readers) to be involved.

Thus, we are not simply talking 'context' here, unless we have a more nuanced understanding of what context means. We can always re-contextualize. We can colour in the background with historical details until we generate a three-dimensional image. But we are examining with an engaged systematics how the language was learnt and redeployed; how the form of doing and conceiving theology *in this way* and *with these emphases* was created; how we imagined that this was the way in which we should speak. And, then how we practised that speech in the numerous ways in which understanding is communicated in social relations and enriched. As the cultural anthropologist, Asif Agha, has detailed: 'cultural models are often normalized by social practices so as to constitute routine versions of (even normative models for)

---

[30] Ibid., p.13.

[31] Judith I. Irvine, 'Shadow Conversations: The Indeterminacy of Participant Roles' in M. Silverstein and G. Urban (eds.), *Natural History of Discourse* (n.29), p.135, see also pp.131–59.

[32] Charles Taylor, *A Secular Age* (n.15), p.13.

the social behaviours of which they are models.'[33] This process of cultural formation will become central to this project as a whole because it involves the way discursive activities embed values. An engaged systematic theology is an embedded and embedding theology. This will be one of its operational keys for the cultivation of ethical life and not unrelated, obviously, to all I said above about pedagogy.

As an embedded theology the criticisms of both syncretism and ideology have to be tackled head on. Embedded is embodied. Because of the nature of the dissemination of signs—and the circulation of social energies that meld text to context in myriad and complex ways—syncretism will never be avoided. And the purism sought by those wishing to avoid such syncretism is both a false consciousness and an impossibility. Ideology too cannot be avoided because we see from somewhere; our knowledge is freighted with human interests (personal and collective). There is no ideology-free zone and the idea there is, is again a false-consciousness just as all ideology is false consciousness. Our ideas are lived and changed and lived again differently, continually. Cultures are produced and transformed and reproduced again differently, continually. The same can be said of the beliefs, and hopes, and desires, and fears that inform all ideas and cultural productions.

2. Epistemology

An engaged systematic theology sets out towards a new epistemology. It will never get there. It will never have the certainty of truth that it seeks. Only God as Truth has that certainty. It will never realize the desires and dreams that lie behind secular reasoning: transparency, total accountability, pure reason etc. But the whole project is orientated towards and engages with a way of seeing and understanding the world differently, theologically; the world as God sees it. The pedagogy of the senses I pointed to in Cyril's *Catechetical Lectures* and the pedagogy of affect that I pointed to in Philip Melanchthon's *Loci communes 1521*, combine to foster and develop that embodied rationality of faith seeking understanding—seeking, that is, to know (where knowledge involves intimate participation of knower in what is being known) the wisdom of divine operations and the disposition of the created world for such a wisdom. This, as I argued, was the heart of Hugh of St. Victor's project. It is a *restauratio* and a *reformatio* of our sensing and feeling, distorted seeing and understanding, which both challenges and invokes engaged systematic theology to offer a new epistemology. As one theologian working herself in

---

[33] A. Agha, *Language and Social Relations* (n.19), p.5.

this embodied theological manner has succinctly put it: theology's 'epistemo-logical task [is] cleansing, reordering, and redirecting the apparatuses of one's own thinking, desiring, and seeing'.[34]

It is plain, as Cyril, Hugh, and Philip recognized, that the pursuit and orientation of such an embodied epistemology impacts on two directly con-nected and fundamental human activities. First, it will change the way we speak, how we name, what we imagine, and our understanding of what we are doing when we speak, name, and imagine. It opens new ways to imagine that are personal and collective; as collective, such changes to the imagination, our capacity to imagine, will have cultural and material effects. It will change the cultural imaginary.[35] Secondly, it will change the way we act. It will issue into, foster, and ferment ethical life. This is why the project as a whole takes on that title; it is the omega of an engaged systematic theology as it is the alpha, for this is life with Christ and hidden in God. Christ who is, simply (if we could see it clearly) life, 'our life', creative life, eternal life, the tree of life, by whom and through whom all things were created. As the Psalmist tells us: 'Whoso is wise, *and will observe these things*, even they shall understand the lovingkindness of the Lord' (Psalm 107.43, my emphasis). All theological knowledge, the Psalmist's observation of 'these things', issues from embodied cognition (even when it is divinely revealed), so just as there can be no actual distinction between first- and second-order theology, practice and belief, so there can be no hard and fast distinction, from the human point of view, between revealed and natural theology. In fact an engaged systematic theol-ogy questions what both 'revelation' and 'natural' are.

As I have said, this attention to embodied cognition will require rejecting any functionalist approach to doctrine—functional both in terms of teach-ing the 'five steps to salvation' and functional also in confessionalism that is really an expression of the secular politics of identity (and the cheap, con-sumer, 'imagined', and surveillanced communities they produce). The loyalty card and the sect are two expressions of the same functionalism, the same politics of the 'friend and the foe' (Schmitt), the same operations of the desire to dominate by disciplining (Foucault, Taylor), and the same fears borne of social atomism of having nowhere to belong, and no one to belong to or with. An engaged systematic theology pitches itself against the policing of the confessionalized sect and what John Milbank has described as the 'extrinsic

---

[34] Sarah Coakley, *God, Sexuality, and the Self: An Essay 'On the Trinity'* (Cambridge: Cambridge University Press, 2013), p.20.

[35] I have been concerned about the way the Christian faith can transform the cultural imag-inary since I wrote *Cities of God* (London: Routledge, 2000). I only realized that that was what I was trying to do as I worked on *Cultural Transformation and Religious Practice*, pp.159–72. There I develop the notion of changing the cultural imaginary, and explained how I am used the term 'imaginary'.

obedient response to revealed propositions'.[36] For embodied cognition there is no discernible divide between the extrinsic and the intrinsic at the level of experience (including the experience of grace).

In sum, then, the central axiom of engaged systematics as both a way of approaching theologies and a way of composing them is the understanding that doctrine is lived. That does not mean that doctrine cannot become propositional statements and declarations of belief. Clearly, as we begin to explore issues in Christology, Pneumatology, and Ecclesiology then I will be making and examining Christian teaching that has been passed down in propositional statements. Doctrine as lived, though, cannot reduce Christian teaching to the critical examination of propositions, of texts. Because, as we learn and modify the language of these Christian teachings within quite specific socio-economic, cultural, and historical contexts, then that language begins to shape the ways in which we feel *about*, understand *in,* imagine, and act *because of.* And some of our acts, in fact the majority of acts as responses *to,* are not consciously available to us.

WHAT ARE THE THEOLOGICAL CONSEQUENCES OF THIS APPROACH TO SYSTEMATICS?

The theological consequences of a method have to be the result of the theological emphases that have given rise to that method. Teaching, method and style must all co-inhere. The theological emphases in this work are Christological and Pneumatological, because what we know of God (which is always incomplete and inchoate) issues from the incarnation of God in Christ and the work of the redemption wrought in Christ through the Spirit. I give equal emphasis to both because it is to Christ we are conformed and through the Spirit that that conformity, that participation with Christ in the Godhead, comes about. This is not then a Christocentric, but rather a Christomorphic theology. There is nothing unmediated about our knowledge and experience of either Christ or the Spirit—the Scriptures *attest* to the Word of God and experience of the Spirit is only in through the categories we have available in the languages we have learnt and are continuing to learn. That a participation in the redeeming work of that Word and the Spirit can take effect through the human words of that attestation and a prayerful discernment of one's personal and collective experience is a matter of grace. It is grace that makes Scripture both 'holy' and

[36] John Milbank, 'A Closer Walk on the Wild Side' in Michael Warner, Jonathan Vanantwerpen, and Craig Calhoun, *Varieties of Secularism in* A Secular Age (Cambridge, Mass: Harvard University Press, 2013), p.71.

'inspired'. It is the Scriptural ontology announced by such grace that makes the theological experience of engaging the Scriptures[37] a touchstone for our deepening trust. I will have much more to say about this 'work of the Word and Spirit' in Part Two of this volume in treating revelation and its reception. (Volume II will explore Christology and Volume III Pneumatology.)

Other theological emphases follow from Christology and Pneumatology—doctrines of creation, being human, and the Church as the body of Christ. My understanding of the Trinity will take place in and through the examinations of the work of Christ and the Spirit. As for Schleiermacher, about whom much will be said, the Trinity is only partially a theological subject in its own right. As a lived doctrine it runs throughout and will be brought to a point of reflection upon the Father at the end of Volume III. All of these teachings come to a focus in Paul's statement, 'For you have died, and your life is hidden with Christ in God. When Christ, who is our life shall appear, then shall you also appear with him in glory' (Colossians 3.3–4). Death (*thanatos*), life (*zōe*), hiddenness (*kruptos*), with Christ (*sun tō Christō*), and in God (*en tō theō*) are all fundamental here; fundamental for defining what I mean by 'participation' and in what it is exactly that we are participating. If the Spirit isn't mentioned, its operations are part of what is hidden and which makes what is revealed possible. Just as the Spirit made the revelation of God in Christ possible with the incarnation in coming upon the Virgin Mary. The Spirit is there in the 'life' and the 'glory'. The Spirit is the *energia* in the economy that enables participation. In these two sentences by Paul the Christian faith is given a location (in God), a passage (from death to life), an epistemological condition (hiddenness), a Person who has both gone before and stands alongside (with Christ—a divine Person in whom the passage from death to life has opened the way for our own following by faith, through adoption) and a destiny (in glory). What it is to be human, truly human, is only to be found in that following and the relations that it establishes between Creator and creation. The concern with engagement gives emphatic weight to our being in relation and our *being receptive*; our being immersed in the world as God's desire for

---

[37] I am deliberately avoiding the language of 'religious experience'. Everything we know from neuroscience and physiology about the nature of sensing, being affected and the judgement that goes into the production of 'experience' informs us that experience is context dependent. It is an adaptive response to the specificities of our environment and the specificities also of the languages we have learnt to interpret what we sense and feel and make them meaningful. There is no generic 'religious' experience as there is no generic experience of being afraid. There are no doubt commonalities between experiences of a specific kind, but my experience of the divine as a Christian is not the same and cannot be the same as a Jewish experience of G-d or an Islamic experience of Allah, let alone a Buddhist experience of *karma* or a Hindu vision of *Atman*. It is this fact, of course, which makes comparative theology so difficult; and the difficulty (as nominalists and liberal theologians tend to think) does not lie simply at the level of naming.

humankind and the condition of our createdness.[38] In Christ, with God, all the possibilities of human personhood, its relations and its receptions, are realized and perfected. So a theological anthropology cannot be separated from Christology and a profound 'hiddenness' pertains to that humanity as to Christology. We are questions to ourselves (as Augustine saw), and to stare straight into that question is to encounter a fundamental wonder that is as terrifying as it is restorative. Deep peers into deep—and the Spirit enables that peering. Much more of this will be examined in Volume II, *Another Kind of Normal*.

From the emphasis upon participation it would follow that a systematics seeking to engage rests upon a pedagogy. *Conversio* (whatever form that takes, sudden or an evolving entrustment) that does not lead to *formatio* will lead to infantilism. To come to Jesus is only a beginning. There is a life-time of growth ahead of that 'coming' for we are always be-coming (a coming to be in the mystery of God as *principium et finis*). We have noted various forms such a pedagogy, or Christian *paideia*, takes in Cyril's creedal catechesis, Hugh of St. Victor's understanding of teaching as integral to a *reformatio* that makes possible *restauratio,* and Melanchthon's association of salvation with a change in the affections [*affectus*] following faith. Theologically, this pedagogy, as Melanchthon recognized, is inseparable from the operations of the Holy Spirit: the triune God shepherds His people into all truth by His grace, through His mercy, in His providential care. Only on the basis of this pedagogy is there participation and sanctification, as formation folds its *re-formatio* of the believer into a *con-formatio* with Christ.

As a pedagogy, an engaged systematic theology seeks to be performative. To adopt an image employed by Hegel: in order to swim one has to enter into the water rather than stand on the bank and try to work out the principle of swimming.[39] An engaged systematic theology wishes to act upon the minds, emotions, imaginations, hearts, and bodies of those who engage with it. Performative language is language rooted again in the body, like music and dance. Its aim then, is not simply to aid intellection[40] but also to foster discipleship and obedience to the work of the Spirit of Christ; and the cultivation of an ethics through the promotion of an ethos attuned to the God who

---

[38] For a translation of Aquinas's term for God's enfolding and infusing grace as it operates in and through human beings, *auxilium*, as 'engagement' see Eugene Rogers, *Aquinas and the Supreme Court: Race, Gender, and the Failure of Natural Law in Thomas's Biblical Commentaries* (Oxford: Wiley-Blackwell, 2013), pp.228–9.

[39] Georg Wilhelm Friedrich Hegel, *Enzyklopädie der philosophischen Wissenschften I, Die Wissenschaft der Logik*, section 10, trans. *The Encyclopedia of Logic*, T.F. Geraets, W.A. Suchting, and H. Harris (Indianapolis: Hackett Publishing Company, 1991), p.34.

[40] In terms that I will develop in Chapter 9 with reference to Iain McGilchrist's work, language aimed at intellection alone would simply feed left-hemisphere brain activity (that wishes to control and instrumentalize). Language appealing to the body and imagination is feeding right-hemisphere brain activity (which is empathetic and attuned to the world).

is Good and Just. Hence the orientation of this whole work is towards ethical life, towards that transformation and transfiguration that marks the turning of the 'heart of stone' into a 'heart of flesh' (Ezekiel 36.26–7).

It follows that an examination of that pedagogy and engagement requires drawing upon other languages and knowledges that, in their own way, teach us how to see things, provide us with vocabularies, enable us to interpret our experience, and explore engagement itself. We have seen how Hugh's commitment to formation began in understanding the role of the liberal arts (widely conceived). These provided tools and skills, the primary education, for the reading of the Scriptures. Already, I have been building my case with reference to history (Taylor), sociolinguistics (Agha), social anthropology (Silverstein), cultural theory (Bourdieu), and philosophy (Ricoeur). An engaged systematic theology is then necessarily interdisciplinary. That interdisciplinarity neither liquidates the intellectual discipline of dogmatics, nor suggests theology can be translated without remainder into any other intellectual field. Rather, interdisciplinarity enables the particularity of what Christian's believe to become more visible for what it is: enmeshed within networks of social relation, discursive effects, and cultural productions within and without. In fact, there is no strict within or without/insider and outsider perspective. That has implications for Church–World relations and how they are perceived. Theology is concerned with everything created and as such it necessarily draws upon every science (as Aquinas saw in the opening *questio* of his *Summa Theologicae*). It has to do this because theology has no proper object for its study. God is not available to us, as the economy is to economists, politics for politics scientists, human beings for anthropologists, or sexual mores for gender studies. As John Webster so perceptively observes, by entering into the terrains of other disciplines 'we do not leave behind the domain of the Word; we simply continue to trace its full scope'.[41] We come to appreciate even more the good and graceful hand of God's providence in creating us *as the creatures we are*.

I said an engaged systematic theology 'seeks to be performative' and so, like Cyril of Alexandria, Hugh of St. Victor, and Philip Melanchthon, it does not eschew rhetoric. But it has to pay attention, as we have seen, to its all too human limitations—being led into mystery is the Spirit's doing, as a merely human venture it will end up in obscurantism and obfuscation. Strategies of persuasion can be aesthetic or anaesthetic, edify or seduce, proffer healing, offer placebos or manipulate. But not to try to be performative is to lack the courage of one's convictions (and not follow through on one's theological method). An engaged systematic theology must then attempt to map and

---

[41] John Webster, *The Domain of the Word: Scripture and Theological Reason* (London: Bloomsbury, 2013), p.20.

investigate and own the complexities of theology's discursive power. But it must also attempt to do something more positive: to allow exposure to the various discursive grids out of which the theological reflections emerge in order to inform and cast those theological articulations in a new light. This may enable us to *see* what we *hear* differently, creatively, imaginately. That is the point. Above all, it is the imagination that has to be engaged; for the imagination moves between affect and cognition, and plays with the visible and the invisible. It ludically meditates as it mediates. There is no seeking in faith to understand that is not engaging the imagination. The pedagogy of the senses and the pedagogy of affect, the dynamics in the process of formation and sanctification in Christ, through the Spirit, (about which more will be said in Volume II), activate and discipline the imagination.

The injunction to be imaginative and so performative makes certain stylistic demands, as von Balthasar saw.[42] To engender life, engagement, and contention—and contention is important[43]—the style must be viral. An engaged systematic theology seeks then to become viral (irrespective of what it may achieve). The words (if words are the mode of its theological expression; there are, of course, many many other ways of communicating) issue from intimations and explorations of the invisible. This isn't as unusual as it might sound. We live with multiple forms of invisibility without accepting them as such. Thought, imagination, hope, and desire are all invisible until they materialize themselves. So are molecules of emotion, the work of neurotransmitters with respect to our autonomic life-systems, and dark energy. These scientific objects only offer themselves for inspection through complex, computerized mathematics. We who are creatures who have invented and live within symbolic systems, we who are a symbolic species to use a term understood by anthropologists,[44] have entrusted ourselves to invisibilities. Faith is such an entrustment: all the Christian concreteness we have lies in the stories of the historical Jesus, the histories of God's dealing with the Hebrews, the histories of God dealings with the saints, the martyrs, the theologians, God encountering us in the sacraments, the traditions of the Church and the ministrations of the angels, and our discernment of God's operations in our lives. But even in the depth of these realities there is an abiding invisibility that we seek to know and love. This is not at all nebulous. It indwells the very physicalities of providence and grace.

[42] See *Glory of the Lord*, Volume II: *Clerical Styles* and Volume III: *Lay Styles*, trans. Andrew Louth, *et al.* (Edinburgh: T & T Clark, 1986).

[43] On why contention is important see 'Introduction' in Graham Ward, *Politics of Discipleship: Becoming Postmaterial Citizens* (Grand Rapids, Michigan: Baker Academic, 2009), pp.21–5.

[44] See Terrence W. Deacon, *The Symbolic Species: The Co-evolution of Language and the Human Brain* (London: Allen Lane, 1997).

That very phrase—the very physicalities of providence and grace—and the commitment to relationality, pitch an engaged systematics against dualism. It rejects not only the nature/grace divide, but also the immanent/transcendent divide. It does not aim at transcendence. In wishing to go beyond self-conscious acceptance and recognition of the myriad relations that situate and inform us; in wishing to engage with God through Christ and in the Spirit: an engaged systematics is concerned with what is given or, rather, giveness. All is a gift but the gift itself has no tangible or even effable object. There may be objects—a tree, flaming in the autumn sunlight—but the intuition is far in excess of any phenomenological appreciation of intention (which resides within consciousness) and moves towards that which cannot be grasped. All that makes up our pre-conscious, unconscious cognition, the body's own knowledge, the deep mind, is involved in the engagement with giveness. But this is not transcendence as we have come to understand that term.[45] The given beyond, and grounding any possibility of, our self-consciousness goes deeper into our physiological, possibly biological and certainly spiritual condition in the world. Transcendence can all too often bear the sense of 'rising above' the body and the self. This rising above then becomes the object of a specifically desired experience. But while there may be intimations of what is deeply received of that which is given to us, there is no direct experience of it as such. There is a processing and a slow transformative learning and this can take years to recognize and understand. But then we experience none of our autonomic responses. We experience only the effects of those responses (an increase of heart beat, a flush of heat, a prickling skin, a fluctuation within the digestive system, etc.). An engaged systematic theology wishes to speak then of that which is radical (returning us to the roots of our spiritual and somatic condition before God) rather than of that which is purely transcendent. We have no access to the God who is *extra omne genus*.[46] After Erich Przywara, we might call this 'transcending immanence' and it is associated with the oscillations of *analogia entis*.[47] We begin an examination of *analogia entis* in Chapter 6 of this volume, but it will reoccur and develop throughout all the volumes.

Finally, given the commitment to engagement, life-long learning, and the lived nature of doctrine, the insights of an engaged systematic theology emphasize their provisionality. It is a theology expressive of the Christian faith at a certain point in the intersection of place, history, culture, and

---

[45] When the Church Fathers spoke about *anagogē*, when Hugh of St. Victor was speaking about 'ascent', these are metaphors. They are not terms within a geometric or topographical space.

[46] Aquinas, *Summa theologiae* I, q.4, a. 3, ad. 2.

[47] Erich Przywara, *Analogia Entis: Metaphysics – Original Structure and Universal Rhythm*, trans. John R. Betz and David Bentley Hart (Grand Rapids, MI: Eerdmans, 2014), p.239.

society. In this, one might say that an engaged systematics is like liturgy and the flows of tradition—tracing and expressing changes as one generation succeeds another within the wide arc of Christian truth. Like liturgies, all theologies, as I said earlier, are products of their time. This follows from a rejection of a purely epistemological approach into the contents of the Christian faith and a rejection of what Charles Taylor observes to be a fundamental cultural trajectory of secular modernity: excarnation.[48] An engaged systematics is radically incarnational. Each of the theological systems we examined in the last three chapters—the formation of the creeds, the first *Summa*, and the first Protestant dogmatics—was concerned with redefining Christian identity within a time of great cultural change: the Church as an imperial power; the Church as a spearhead for the revivals fostering the twelfth century renaissance; and the Church establishing itself over against Papal jurisdiction and allying itself with civil, secular authorities. An engaged systematics in effecting both a recovery and a corrective has a similar task: to shape and articulate a theological system re-expressing the Christian faith in the context of multiple networks and matrices of discursive power and the new visibility of religion that both drove and followed the implosion of secularism, bringing both the importance of world Christianities and other religious faiths to the fore. If we are treating life in Christ, then it is life today (with the past that we have inherited and are interpreting, with a future we conceive and move towards). This is a living faith. The truth of that expression of the faith today lies again both in Christ (as the truth of God revealed) and the Spirit (the operation of God's redemptive grace over time and in all our histories). This theological enterprise, like all theological enterprises, gains its relation to truth by becoming part of the unfolding tradition. And we have no access to the singularity and unity of that 'tradition'. We seek to understand, and all the judgements we make with respect to that seeking and that understanding lie within an eschatological remainder awaiting that 'appear[ance] with him in glory'.

BEING CHURCHED

We enter the Cathedral. It's the mother church of the diocese. The air is cool, the shadows deep and in the silence distant sounds reverberate. *I believe in God.* The place is scarred by the memories of past wars in which the Christian faith was deeply implicated. Dust settles on a wreath of poppies; threadbare flags hang limp in a side chapel. These are emblems of obscene violences in

---

[48] Charles Taylor, *A Secular Age* (n.15), pp.613–15.

the context of which we are churched. It's not just that the fallen of two world wars are commemorated here, the site of the main altar (with or without a rail, with or without a stepped elevation), the use or disuse of the side-altars, the way the chairs are arranged (facing each other in rows, gathered in semi-circles), the absence or presence of incense and bells, the empty niches where the statues of saints once stood, the use or disuse of copes and cassocks, the location of the pulpit and the lectern, whose memorial plaque or tomb is placed where in the building—all these attest to doctrinal wars, class wars, ecclesial sparring. Some of the wars have been put behind us—the boxed pews set aside for the wealthier patrons. Some of the wars still continue: the gender wars of who is allowed to celebrate or even be in the sanctuary or the wars over sexual orientation and who is and who is not given access to clerical office. And I say nothing of the fears surrounding the safeguarding of minors from sexual predators.

In learning the language of the faith we have learned these languages also. I have learnt here what holiness is and I have learnt also the ravages of sin not repented of, sin not forgiven, sin passed on, sin concealed in acts of self-justification and aggrandizement. And this is where an engaged system-atics has to begin—with what *is*, not with what we would like to be the case.

Part Two

How the Light Gets In

5

Where We Must Begin

THEOLOGY AS DEEP DREAMING

In the beginning there is no beginning. Not for us. We know about *Homo hei-delbergiensis* and *Homo erectus* and 'Lucy' (*Australopithecus afarensis*) and tool manufacture from around 2.2 million years ago, and the time when what developed into humankind split off from the other primates around 6 million years ago. The beginnings ricochet backward, endlessly, and regressively. I have written about this elsewhere.[1] Technically, God did not become man in Jesus Christ; He became *Homo sapiens*. We are not then dealing with history when we talk about theological origins. Nevertheless, we are dealing with something basic about the human condition with respect to God as creator when we treat the story of Adam and Eve. Irrespective of the J, E, P, D sources and rescensions, but following from them, Adam had more than one beginning. The first beginning was when he was kissed into existence by the breath from God's mouth and the second when he was conscious that he had been made and began to name the things around him. And then he slept. The Bible says God put Adam into 'a deep sleep' and the text doesn't tell us he ever awoke. So perhaps we, and all our theology, are part of Adam's deep dreaming. Then there was another beginning—with Eve, the bone of his bone and the flesh of his flesh. But none of those beginnings do we know now unless as a part of our dream, buried deep with our imaginations. The French philosopher and scientist, Michel Serres, tells us: 'In the beginning is the echo. Background noise, fluctuation, echo. Everything begins on the threshold of the echo.'[2] Adam's multiple beginnings are echoes of the divine genesis itself; the *tohu wa bohu* of Genesis 1.2.

---

[1] See Graham Ward, *Unbelievable: Why We Believe and Why We Don't* (London: I.B.Taurus, 2015).

[2] Michel Serres, *Genesis*, trans. Geneviève James and James Nelson (Ann Arbor: University of Mchigan Press, 1995), p.119.

We know the beginning that followed that third beginning. When things began again after eating of the Tree of the Knowledge of Good and Evil. This is the human condition we are born into. 'Where are you?' God called out, as He walked in the garden in the cool of the day. That's where we begin. For God did not ask this because He who is omnipotent and omnipresent didn't know where Adam was. God asked this because Adam didn't know he was lost among the trees of paradise. He is lost in the confused multiplicity that surrounded him. 'The forest is multiplicity.'[3] It was Adam who didn't know where Adam was. God was telling him about his condition. Deep was calling to deep. Adam was lost. And we have been lost ever since. That's the beginning we know: being lost. And God could not tell Adam 'You are lost. Come to me.' Within the cloudy soul and darkened mind of Adam no direct communication was possible. God could only pose a question, or Adam could only hear the voice of God now as a question. Brittle were all relations; there could be only questions. It is from within this question—'where are you?'—from within the claustrophobia of that lostness, that Adam responded; because he was lost indeed among the oaks and elms of Eden.

THE BOOK OF THE DUCHESS

We cannot undertake a journey of faith—and this project is demanding such a journey—without first recognizing how profoundly we are lost. Recognizing that doesn't take much research: open a newspaper, download the news, take a walk round the centre of any city in the early hours of a Sunday morning, watch TV dramas like the British series *Shameless* (2004–2013) or the American series *The Wire* (2002–2008) or films like Lars von Trier's *Antichrist* (2009) or Uwa Boll's *Darfur* (2009). We, in Britain, in Europe and all those countries who have trading links with us, are in the midst of another crisis. If it's called the Euro crisis then, coming on the back of the global banking crisis of 2008 and the threats of recession, the fears of unemployment and negative growth, then this is a crisis of capitalism itself. Meanwhile, the pressure on basic natural resources (like water), the arguments over climate change and carbon emissions, and increasing consumerist demands continue. The British Astronomer Royal, Sir Martin Rees, has suggested that humankind may not last to the end of the twenty-first century,[4] while more and more government money is being invested into

---

[3] Ibid., p.56.
[4] Martin Rees, *Our Final Century: Will the Human Race Survive the Twenty-first Century?* (London: Arrow, new edition 2004).

research into 'posthuman' possibilities. Apocalyptic fears are countered by technological utopian explorations.[5] The opening decades of this new millennium will probably go down in history as a time of ricocheting crises: terrorist attacks, military counter-attacks and interventions, civil wars, the collapse of some regimes, the rise of others, and environmental disasters caused by changing weather patterns. And globalization, which wove countries and peoples into tight webs of exchange, dependence, exploitation, and accumulation, is now threatening to take down certain nations and sell off their assets, their people's assets, to forestall bankruptcy.

No, we don't need to look far to see how profoundly lost we are. And some of the things we turned to, to alleviate the sense of that loss, our entertainments and diversions, are becoming all too costly. So we have to come more clearly to a confrontation with our condition of being lost. And we do not need any TV series by that title to inform us about what happens to people and their relations with each other in such a condition: the fights over the limited supplies and the fears that take on mythic proportions concerning what might be 'out there' in the dark entanglement of a jungle that Joseph Conrad's Marlow responds to with the words 'Horror! Horror! Horror'.[6]

In the Middles Ages, when great swathes of northern Europe were still thick with deciduous woods that haunted the imaginations of its poets, the forest was a symbol for being lost. On the whole those who lose their way— Dante in the opening of the *Inferno* or Gawain in the forest of the Greene Knight, and later the lovers in the enchanted woods of *A Midsummer Night's Dream* or the Duke in *As You Like It* exiled in the forest of Arden—emerge from the woods at the end of a period of testing and purgation. They emerge as wiser men and women.[7] There are two notable exceptions, Chaucer in the *Book of the Duchess* and Descartes in his *Meditations*.[8] We will treat Descartes later (Chapter 9) when I discuss the nature of believing and how it changed with the onset of modernity, but because trees play such an important theme

---

[5] See Michael S. Burdett, *Eschatology and the Technological Future* (London: Routledge, 2015).

[6] *Lost* (TV Series 2004–2010) takes up a scenario with adults that William Golding took up in *Lord of the Flies* with children. Golding is more fearless in showing us what happens to the threat of the other in such a situation. It is not projected into 'monsters' out there in the jungle, but is rather on the demons within. The novel by Joseph Conrad I am referring to is *The Heart of Darkness*.

[7] These narratives have the structure of fairy-tales in which the 'forest ... symbolizes the place in which inner darkness is confronted and worked through ... when we succeed in finding our way out we shall emerge with a much more highly developed humanity' Bruno Bettelheim, *The Uses of Enchantment: The Meaning and Importance of Fairy Tales* (London: Penguin Books, 1991), pp.93–4.

[8] Those forests, of course, were not completely erased even in modernity. If Descartes remains lost in one so, much later, will Heidegger—whose later work is concerned with finding paths and traces that do not lead him out of the forest but only to certain clearings [*Lichtungen*] where some limited assessment of one's immersion can be made.

within this project, let's enter into Chaucer's forest and understand something about his condition and our own.

The poem opens with a description of Chaucer's personal distress[9]: he cannot sleep, he's listless, indifferent to everything, overshadowed by a 'sorwful imaginacioun' (14), standing as 'a mased [dazed, in a maze] thing' (13), and feeling as though he is always at a point of falling. He recognizes this melancholy heaviness is against nature—'ageynes kynde' (16)—but he is hopelessly in thrall to it. Furthermore, when he is asked what it is that is causing the insomnia 'Myselven can nat telle why/The sooth' (34–5). He can only conjecture he has some kind of sickness that no physician is able to heal. And then, in a curious, almost throwaway line, he states: 'Passe we over [that] until efte [later]' (41). Caught up in this mental and emotional labyrinth, Chaucer begins a highly complex set of narrations within narrations. The first is a story he reads to try and put his mind at rest and enable him to sleep. It is a story concerning the death of a husband at sea and a wife who, after a long period of waiting for news, prays that she may be told in a dream whether her husband's prolonged absence means he has drowned. The story triggers in Chaucer a prayer of his own and immediately he falls asleep, waking up in a dream.

All this is highly conventional for literature at the time. But on waking up he hears the preparation for a hunt, and rises to join the gathering of hunters, riders, and their dogs. They are hunting for a hart and it is in the hunt that they all enter the forest and Chaucer finds himself lost in a profusion of tall, thick trees 'so huge in strengthe' (421). He moves deeper and deeper into the 'grene greves [groves]' (417), hearing the hunt around him and the deer passing him in haste, but seeing nothing. Disengaged and immersed in 'shadwe overal under' (426) he suddenly comes upon a 'man in blak' (445). The man is bent over in sorrow, muttering to himself that death should have taken him. Even when approached by the poet the man cannot speak and appears not even to see him. The man, who has detached himself also from the others to be alone, cares nothing for hunting the hart.

It is at this point that the language and associations of loss ('lorn'), lost, and to loose emerge in the narrative. The man in sable 'hath myne understanding lorn' (565). He reiterates something of the poet's own mental and emotional turmoil in the opening of the poem, comparing himself to Sisyphus in hell. Employing a conventional extended metaphor the knight speaks of having played chess with Fortune and 'I have lorne' (685). The poet misunderstands the game of chess (he is not of a stable mind), interpreting the metaphor literally, but gradually, in a tale within a tale of dreaming, a third tale unfolds of how

---

[9] The edition of *The Book of the Duchess* I am using is found in the Fairfax manuscript (Fairfax 16. Bodleian Library, Oxford). It is reproduced in *Dream Visions and Other Poems: Geoffrey Chaucer*, ed. Kathryn L. Lynch (New York: W.W. Norton & Company, 2007). The bracketed numbers following the citations refer to the lines.

the knight lost his 'blisse' (748) with the death of his wife. At the end of his tale he says to the poet: 'I tolde thee that I had lorne' (1303). And in a matter of ten lines, the hunt returns, a bell in a castle strikes twelve, the poet awakes and the poem is concluded with the poet's resolve to write a poem about his dream ('sweven'). 'This was my sweven; now it is doon' (1335).

The ending of the *Book of the Duchess* only returns us to the beginning: the writing of the poem itself. We are caught up and lost in its telling and retelling such that the closing clause 'now it is doon' is ironic. It is not 'doon'. Furthermore, we have been untimely ripped from the narration: so many tellings within tellings are suddenly dissolved when the clock strikes twelve and day breaks in the real world or the world anyway of the 'mased' poet. And nothing has been achieved other than the complex telling of interlacing tales. The 'nothingness' is itself significant, as we will see. For the moment, the poet has slept, yes, but whether he has now defeated his insomnia, whether he has now overcome the intellectual and emotional turmoil that caused and perpetuated that insomnia, is unclear. Earlier (41) he had promised to return to his own condition and the reasons for it. He breaks that promise and the abruptness of the ending comes from nowhere, like the panic of denial; in the sable knight the poet is facing the endlessness of 'lorn', an endlessness that cannot be lived without repressing it entirely. The end of the poem is violent. It bears none of the tranquillity of the therapeutic. The 'man in blak' himself is left still immersed in his mourning. The poet, who earlier had suggested that by telling his tale to the poet the knight might bring relief to himself, is unable to comfort him. On hearing the knight's story, and on finally understanding it does not concern a game of chess which the knight had lost but the death of the knight's wife, he can only tersely respond: 'Is that your los? By God, it is routhe [a cause for pity]' (1310). And, rather strangely, in a cultural context steeped in Christianity and a poetic context in which God is reiterated in the casualness of conversational oaths, no resurrection hope is offered the knight, no afterlife is presented. This absence is significant; it relates to a theme of nothingness that haunts the poem; for the poem opens in negatives and negations: the poet can sleep 'nygh nought' (3) neither 'day ne nyght' (2) so that 'by my trouthe, I take no kep/Of nothing, how hyt cometh or gooth' (6–7) so that 'Ne me nys nothing leef nor looth . . . For I have felynge in nothing' (8–11).

I have drawn attention to the disorientation that issues from this insomnia, but what is lacking in the paralysis of this nihilism is direction. If the natural *telos* of human life is happiness and that happiness, or beatification, is contemplation of God, seeing Him face to face, as Hugh of St.-Victor, Aquinas, and other Christian medieval teachers believed[10], then the poet has lost his

---

[10] Aquinas, *Summa theologiae* IIaIIae, clxxx.4, *resp.*: 'That which belongs principally to the contemplative life is the contemplation of the divine truth, because this contemplation is the end of the whole human life... This contemplation will be prefect in te life to come when we shall see God face to face, wherefore it wll make us perfectly happy.'

way because he has lost the sense of the purpose for which human beings were created. At the same time, it was out of such nothingness that God created the world (*creatio ex nihilo*) and the poem itself issues from this negative capability, even though what it accomplishes (for both poet and the man he encounters) is negligible. The afterlife, the resurrection, beatification, the vision of God seem dreams too far, too deep, even in (may be especially within) a poem about deep dreaming.

So, in this poetic forest we remain like the sable knight lost, and aesthetic delight serves not to console but underscore the need for consolation. Unlike in Dante, the poet has no Virgil (or Beatrice) who can take him (and us) by the hand and lead him (and us) back to an understanding of perfect love. The condition of being lost is that we are 'out of relation'. That is what death accomplishes in this poem—the end of relations, the inability to be engaged or interested in any thing or any one. In the poem the only relations are in dreams and even then the poet and the knight speak past each other until the conclusion. When the poem ends the relations are broken once again—between the poet and the knight and between the poet and the reader. This is hell, as the knight tells the dreaming poet. In his play *Huis Clos*, Jean-Paul Sartre understood hell as other people. Other people are hell, as his three characters in hell recognize, because their presence to each other is a constant reminder of their inability to relate, and how one's isolation is 'ageynes kynde [unnatural]' (16).

The journey of faith begins here in the questioning maze of disengaged non-relations that pitch emotions and thoughts into a turmoil with corporeal effects; where God can only be spoken of obliquely and knowledge of God is unclear, unfocussed, or entirely absent; where knowledge itself is dream-like, prone to error, tales within tales; wandering among signs and the games of fortune and the hunting of the hart; where death that terminates both relations and their human meaningfulness has dominion.

It is believed that Chaucer's poem was written in the years of the Black Death, that Blanche, the first wife of John of Gaunt, had succumbed to the plague, and that this was a poem written for her husband and Chaucer's patron. The Black Death is estimated to have killed between 30 and 60 per cent of the European population. The forest is thick with the pall of death, but the loss of meaning is deeper than death. As the knight informs the poet twice: 'I have lost more than thou wenest [understand]' (1306). The loss is everything that the unnamed wife in the poem encapsulates: the perfection of body and soul, beauty, and a goodness that inspired goodness that the knight extols at length for the poet and sums up in: 'My lady, that is so fair so bright!' What is lost is paradise and human meaningfulness, and the wife is figured as its virgin queen in a devotion that is almost Marian. This is the profundity of loss from which salvation issues. Only faith in God can break through the endless circulations of the spell woven by the narrations; faith seeking understanding. Nothing in the poem announces anything about faith.

THE BLAIR WITCH PROJECT

The objects, textures, and the tonalities of loss, of being lost, change with time, but they are always shot through with fear. The fear in Chaucer is of death: 'drede I have for to dye' (24)—for this makes all things potentially meaningless. His eight-year melancholy has sapped the life out of him and no cause is given for it; it is his existential condition. The forest is his confusion following his 'lost . . . lustihede [merriment, enjoyment, desire to live]' (27). As I said, later we will enter Descartes' forest. Literature describes many others—like Fangorn, a dense and dark woodland situated north of Rohan in the lee of the Misty Mountains in Tolkien's *Lord of the Rings*. The forests that grow so thickly in Tolkien's fabulous worlds (there are thirty six of them, from Aldalómë to Woody End) still recall the dark, deciduous woods that once covered most of Europe. They are places of fear, entanglement, magic, confusion, and evil. They are liminal, threshold worlds that are entered, though not always exited. Chaucer does not encounter evil in his forest. He is not threatened, only exhausted, drained—as if the roots of the trees were sucking the blood from his body, and death was a parasite. The three film-students who enter the forests of Maryland to make a documentary, in Daniel Myrick's and Eduardo Sánchez's *The Blair Witch Project* (1999), do not exit. And the fear of death is palpable. Chaucer's psychological and imaginative wanderings become a contemporary gnostic nightmare where secular, liberal America encounters its demonic spiritual nemesis.

We are given little information; that is part of the menace created in the film as viewers are made to piece together fragments in order to try and *make* sense of a film that cuts rapidly from one scene to the next. The 'witch' is someone called Elly Kegwood, hung in the eighteenth century. Is this a film about atrocious injustices perpetrated in America's past history, like Stanley Kubrick's *The Shining* (1980)?[11] It's difficult to say because we are given so little information, and much of it is tied only very loosely together: the story of the five men ritually murdered in the nineteenth century on Coffin Rock; the memory of a young girl seeing an old woman covered in hair and whose feet did not touch the ground; the account of Rustin Parr, a hermit in the 1940s who lured five local children to his house before torturing and murdering

---

[11] We will return to Kubrick's *The Shining* in Volume II when we consider the nature and operations of fear.

them. There is no obvious moral order on the basis of which the supernatural atrocities are perpetrated. Only the Parr story is explicitly linked to the 'witch', who he said haunted him and told him to kill the children. So the confusion of the film-makers, amplified by the cinematic use of low lighting and hand-held camera footage, is played out in our own confusion. We all wander into the forest with little comprehension and a deepening apprehension that we are not only lost but being driven deeper into the condition of being lost. 'We're totally on track. I know where we are now,' the director tells the other members of the film crew. There's a map, there's a compass, there's a 'knowledge' that the outside world knows what they are up to and will come looking for them. 'It's very hard to get lost these days in America.' But reading the map and taking compass bearings do not return them to the car parked at the edge of the woods. 'We're lost.' 'I know we're not lost . . . I know where we're going.' They are led in circles and then, in a fit of madness the map is lost because one of the other characters steals it and secretly kicks it into the river. Anxiety becomes panic, and panic hysteria. 'We've been in the middle of no where for two days . . . We're in the middle of the woods . . . This is really fucked up!'

Again the fear for the film-makers is not being lost as such but dying; and then when they start to hear noises outside the tent, of being killed. And being killed not by the clinical machinations of a psychopath, but the unpredictable because unbelieved in powers of unknown and malevolent agencies, up close and personal. The fear invoked in us as viewers is that there are dark, inexplicable and supernatural forces just beneath the ordinary circumstances of our lives, and that we are living on a decorative surface. At any moment a demonic hand will catch our feet and pull us under. We are shaken from our secular securities, and left prey to the dark corners of our own imaginations. In Volume II, when I consider fear's relation to sin, we will return to why being made to fear has entertainment value and what that says about our contemporary condition. For now, I suggest the sharp arousal of adrenalin and stress hormones makes us most alive, aware and alert at the point where our survival is most in question. One by one the film-makers are isolated and picked off as relations between the three of them fray and, finally, break. We see nothing of what happens to them in their isolation. That is important—no hovering figures, mad-eyed men, knives, or axes. We hear though, as they plunge through the primal forest and deeper into their terror (and ours). The footage fragments, images blur, black out, and distort. The self-assured girl, the project's director and lead commentator, is the last victim of an undefined, not clearly articulated and unlocatable evil. The stalked victims will never escape the forest and the clutches of that evil, the film suggests. For like the tortured and murdered in other centuries they will now join Elly Kegwood's haunting of those woods. The evil has consumed and possessed them, eternally. There is no redemption, no redeemer; and death itself is vicious, indiscrimate, inhuman, and malevolent. The loss is total; and no one wakes up from this nightmare.

THEOLOGICAL FORESTS

There is something still reassuring about living in Chaucer's forest, or Dante's, or the forest in Paolo Uccello's painting *Hunt in the Forest* (*c.* 1470) where the colours of the horses, the riders, the servants and the orange lanterns among the black trees suggests something both apocalyptic and celebratory. In these forests, even Uccello's, there is not the abyssal horror of Joseph Conrad's *Heart of Darkness* or *The Blair Witch Project*: something so terrifying in the tenebrous pall that it extinguishes the future and cannot be contemplated. There is no Galadriel or Gandalf. Yet here is where the present project must begin; with a new hunting of the h(e)art and our primal terrors; terrors reaching deep towards trauma. To lose oneself here, indeed, becomes the first step in coming to oneself, as the prodigal son in Luke's parable understood. It has to do—otherwise there is nothing and it really is all meaningless. In the Christian Bible the lost garden of paradise becomes the garden of Gethsemane. Later it will become the garden of the empty tomb. But that's way off. The garden of Gethsemane is a forest of black and twisted olive trees; a dark forest reflected today in the dark interior of the Eastern Orthodox Church built there on the road down to Jericho. Gethsemane speaks of betrayal and the limitless violence within us that makes such betrayals possible. The forest Dante finds himself lost in, in the opening lines of *Inferno*, is akin to the garden of Gethsemane, for his journey begins on Good Friday. John's Gospel puts it dramatically: on the eve of his crucifixion, having washed the feet of his disciples, Jesus enters the garden of Gethsemane 'and it was night' (John 13.30). The inscription over the lintel of hell in *Inferno* famously reads:

> Through me the road to the city of desolation,
> Through me the road to sorrows diurnal,
> Through me the road among the lost creation . . .
> Lay down all hope, you that go in by me.[12]

---

[12] Dante's *Hell*, Dorothy L. Sayer's translation (Harmondsworth: Penguin, 1949), p.117.

6

What We Need to Get Started

Everything in this project follows from Christ's response to his first temptation (and the second statement he makes in Matthew's Gospel): 'human beings shall live from every word (*rēmati*) proceeding out from (*dia*) the mouth of God' (Matt.4.4). True life, about which I will say more in the final chapter, is utterly dependent upon being receptive to the divine communication of love. Even Christ here is speaking that which had already been spoken through the Spirit by Moses (Deut.8.3).

COMMUNICATIVE RELATIONS

Beginnings are necessarily untidy because they are always conventional and pragmatic. There are no beginnings as such, as I have said (and Michel Serres has said): there are only echoes. We only start, and already have started, in the middle of things. Beginnings are occasions, new encounters, new contacts. There is a mantra I am told among forensic scientists: every contact leaves a trace. Beginnings are not origins, they are riddled with all the traces that converge upon and diverge from that contact. All those traces are relations—to past encounters and exchanges with people, with objects, in places, in contexts, in the past looking towards a future. The webs of such relations constitute a living complexity into which I will now insert an opening question, abruptly. But the question is basic. What is Christian theology?

The abruptness of the question is sharp because it comes from being lost while assuming, even asserting, that we know where we are. From the condition of being lost any neat dictionary definition only calls forth more questions and further elucidations. Theology, it can be said, is a discourse. And here is where it gets difficult: is it a discourse *about* God (as an object), a discourse *in* God (because it participates in God's disclosure of Himself), a discourse *from* God (who is its author and origin), or a discourse *to* God (as faith seeks its understanding in a pilgrimage towards salvation)? And then there's a follow-up question: what kind of discourse? Is it descriptive, explanatory, information-bearing, ideological, analytical, didactic, polemical, doxological? Whatever it is, in an attempt to reach its most basis element, theology is a communication, and it is concerned with the Christian faith. In that communication theology is a presentation of that faith, a representation of that faith. But ambiguity, like water, begins to ripple around our feet; for 'presentation' and 'representation' can suggest different things, both singly and together. Is theology displaying Christian wares in a market for competing faith-claims? Is that what we mean by presenting? Or is it 'making present', mediating the divine, incarnating it among the secularities of the contemporary scene? And, again, is theology representing the articles of the Christian faith as if these articles were objects before which theology holds a mirror angled to the world? Or is theology actually re-presencing these articles afresh, once more mediating their truth, their promise, their significance?

Allow me to leave these questions hanging so we can get at something more fundamental about the nature of discourse, or language-use. The poet Robert Bringhurst, who I cited in Chapter 4, writes of being a poet:

> Language listens to the world. I listen with it. What I hear when I listen is a question, which is listening itself. The question often changes form, from silence to breathing to speaking to music to voices to visions to silence again. But that is my vocation. The trail it leaves, more often than not, is a text.[1]

Langauge is a response to, a trial, a trace of, a call that is prior to it. It picks up that call and gives it another and different voice. Theology, like poetry, announces a vocation, but the call, comes from somewhere deeper, hidden, and silent. In the silence in which we are immersed there is a signalling.

At the invisible, but nevertheless material, level—the molecular biological level—signalling and communicating is a matter of electro-chemical charges (positive or negative) that attract, repel, bind, and separate amino acids into distinctive protein conformations.[2] At the visible material level, a signal is an energy wave, a symbol, and a connecting relation; wave and pattern, difference, repetition: a bank of bruised clouds in a freshened wind, a fire on a hill, a spoken word. Communication comes only with the establishing of relations.

Natural symbols (the red sky at night), artificial symbols (the laying of a hearth and the intentional use of fire): the environment is always signalling; the world is continually communicating. *Pace* Wittgenstein: the lion *does* speak and we *do* know about it. Ask any lion tamer. The science of epigenetics is based on how organic life reads, receives, and regulates these signals. No

---

[1] Robert Bringhurst, *The Tree of Meaning* (Berkeley, CA: Counterpoint, 2007), p.63.
[2] This is known as 'signal transduction'. The standard text on this is Gerhard Krauss, *The Biochemistry of Signal Transduction and Regulation* (London: Wiley-VHC, 5th edition 2014).

one can say at what point natural signals morphed into artificial symbols; when the reading of one became the basis for the construction of the other.[3] What we know is that the 'more awareness an organism has of its environment, the better its chances of survival'.[4] Plants and animals both read and signal; communication is written deep into creation and life-possibility. The nervous system is the body's read and response organism; its communications centre. Of course, when I say the world is continually communicating then I am using a metaphor drawn from the use of language by human beings. The analyses of cell and development biology, immunology, and parasitology arose at the same time as informatics and computer sciences. The organic world becomes modelled according to complex and dynamically evolving information systems. This is the molecular biologist Candace B. Pert on 'receptors' (molecules on the membane of a cell that act like gate-keepers) and 'ligands' (smaller molecules that can 'unlock' the receptor gate, and pass on their contents to affect changes within the cell)—which provide the molecular basis for why an aspirin removes the pain from a headache: 'In the wake of discoveries in the 1980s, these receptors and their ligands have come to be seen as "information molecules"—the basic units of language used by cells through the organism to communicate across systems such as the endocrine, neurological, gastrointestinal, and even the immune system.'[5]

The inverted commas around 'information molecules' alert us here to a question about the nature of metaphor itself. Metaphor 'establishes' a homology between two fields, the 'vehicle' and 'tenor' in the literary parlance of I.A. Richards. I will explain why there are inverted commas around 'establishes' in a moment. A ship ('tenor') can plough ('vehicle') through the water, but the cultural and semantic fields of maritime transport and an agricultural operation remain separate. In molecular biology, and among evolutionists who want to speak of purpose but not of intelligent design or intention, the

---

[3] For some interesting accounts see Terrence W. Deacon, *The Symbolic Species: The Co-evolution of Language and the Brain* (New York: W. W. Norton & Company Inc., 1997); Donald Merlin, *The Origins of the Modern Mind: Three Stages in the Evolution of Culture and Cognition* (Cambridge, MA: Harvard University Press, 1991); and Robin Dunbar, *Grooming, Gossip and the Evolution of Language* (London: Faber and Faber, 1996).

[4] Bruce H. Lipton, *The Biology of Belief: Unleashing the Power of Consciousness, Matter & Miracles* (London: Hay House UK, 2008), p.9.

[5] Candace B. Pert, *Molecules of Emotion: Why You Feel the Way You Feel* (London: Simon & Schuster, 1998), p.27. We can take another field, cosmology, and find the same kind of descriptions occurring. According to Grand Unified Theories, there are three basic forces governing the behaviour of all matter. 'Each force of nature arises from the exchange of a different "messenger" particle, or boson. The messenger transmits a force between two particles, just as a tennis ball transmits to a player the force of an opponent's shot. At high enough temperatures—such as those when the universe was 10–35 seconds old—physicists believe the electromagnetic and strong and weak nuclear forces were identical, and mediated by a messanger dubbed the X-boson.' In Jeremy Webb (ed.), *Nothing: From Absolute Zero to Cosmic Oblivion—Amazing Insights into Nothingness* (London: Profile Books, 2013), p.7.

use of 'communication' metaphors come with a constant warning: this is a human way of seeing things; the way empirical observations and data have to be conceptualized.[6] It's 'intentional fallacy' according to Daniel Dennett. After all, no one see these ligands and receptors. A mush say, of pig's brain, is placed in a test tube with a radioactive chemical. The test tube is then shaken violently and filtered through a highly complex machine and a count of radioactive isotopes that have attached themselves to the ligands is read. A computer then provides a report, a series of mathematical figures, which get translated into identifying ligands that have attached themselves to the membrane's receptors and affected electrochemical reactions within the cell's nucleus. The mathematics are then read by the laboratory technician and the scientist, and translated into a written report of the finds. This is where the metaphor enters; with the writing of the report. They can be helpful, heuristic, have explanatory power; but they can also be misleading.[7]

Admittedly, metaphors *can* be misleading and the scientists *should be* wary of anthropomorphism. But who creates the categories of distinction here between signalling and receptive transformation at the molecular level and the sophisticated communication systems that some animal groups employ by instinct? After all, metaphors are not just defined by the differences they announce, but also by the suggestive comparisons (or homologies) they 'establish'; the semantic transmutations they perform. In other words metaphors have cognitive content; they give us something to know by inference.[8] They are not just 'expressive'. A metaphor is a linguistic act in which difference and similarity are negotiated through a silence, through an unexplained though nevertheless performed relation. It is the relation that 'establishes', and it is a relation about which nothing is said and everything is inferred. Some have seen a connection between what Noam Chomsky defined as the 'deep structure' of language and biological predeterminates that might favour the development of such a structure.[9] I raise the question. At the end of Volume II, when I treat the doctrine of creation, I offer something of an answer. But it will be only 'something'. I am not advocating any traditional Intelligent Design Theory (though I can see how the theory might emerge if the homology aspect of metaphor is overstated). And certainly the leap into

---

[6] See Michael Ruse, *The Philosophy of Human Evolution* (Cambridge: Cambridge University Press, 2012), pp.76–81 and 145–6.

[7] See George Lakoff and Mark Johnson, *The Metaphors We Live By* (Chicago: Chicago University Press, 1980) and, more recently, Mary Midgley, *The Myths We Live By* (London: Routledge, 2004).

[8] On the cognitive content of metaphor see Janet Martin Soskice, *Metaphor and Religious Language* (Oxford: Oxford University Press, 1985).

[9] See Steven Pinker, *The Language Instinct: How the Mind Creates Language* (New York: William Murrow, 1994). See also T. Deacon, *The Symbolic Species* (n.3) for a discussion of Chomsky and Pinker and his own view.

the symbolization of communication and then the development and manipulation of symbolic systems, belongs only to late hominid and human societies. Nevertheless, something remains (and remains unexplained) in the shifts from the communication of meaning in natural signs to reading and responding to them (whether as animal calls or human discourse).[10] To return to Bringhurst's observation: is the scientist in her report vocalizing a voice, a call, a communication that comes prior to our speaking, our sensing the world and our *making sense* of it? Whence comes what the psychiatrist Iain McGilchrist describes as 'the *urge* to communicate . . . that retains right-hemisphere empathetic elements'?[11] The urge is something evidently concerning the body's negotiation with the world; but it is also evidently concerning what both body and world are responding to. However the question is answered, we nevertheless 'assume that what confronts us offers the possibility of some kind of ordered speech'.[12]

All discourse, as distinct from, but nevertheless possibly related to, complex organic forms of communication, involves a making, a fashioning. In Greek, because this word is going to be important, the crafting of such discourse is a *poiesis*. I wish to introduce the 'poetic' element in such communication from the beginning (from the Greek verb to build, create, compose, *poieō*) because that informs us that the making of theology is creative and the creative is an ongoing process. Theology is a creative communication. It has to be, partly because in being lost, there is an active seeking that is part of communicating and partly because the object of such seeking is not readily available. I could be speaking of course in and from a silence that is just void, meaningless—like those snatches of broken conversation between the film-makers in flight in *The Blair Witch Project*. But it is not a void because, and only because, there is a speaking within which my theological speaking is situated. It is an understanding of this prior speaking that makes theological discourse distinctive. Theology would then begin with 'deep listening' (which could be a translation of the Latin *ob audere* from which we get the word 'obedience').[13]

---

[10] See T. Deacon, *The Symbolic Species* (n.3) for a detailed discussion of the differences between 'communication' at the animal level and the semantic leap into human symbolization. In this important book, Deacon attempts to sketch the evolution of the human power to symbolize, and discusses philsophers of biology who point towards 'proto-mentality' and 'teleosemantics'. See also Graham Macdonald and David Papineau (eds.), *Teleosemantics: New Philsophical Essays* (Oxford: Oxford University Press, 2006), and Ruth Millikan, *Language, Thought, and Other Biological Categories: New Foundations for Realism* (Cambridge, MA: MIT Press, 1984).

[11] Iain McGilchrist, *The Master and His Emissary: The Divided Brain and the Making of the Western World* (New Haven: Yale University Press, 2009), p.125 (emphasis added).

[12] Rowan Williams, *The Edge of Words: God and the Habits of Language* (London: Bloomsbury, 2014), p.31.

[13] This observation comes from Maggie Ross, *Silence: A User's Guide* (London: Darton, Longman and Todd, 2014), p.92.

THE VOICE

Theologically, communicative relations are established by God.

> The voice [*qôl*] of the Lord [*Y'hwāh*] echoes over the waters,
> The God of glory [*ēl-haKāvôd*] thunders.
> The Lord is over the mighty waters.
> The voice of the Lord is power.
> The voice of the Lord is majesty.
> The voice of the Lord breaks the cedars...
> The voice of the Lord makes flames of fire burst forth,
> The voice of the Lord makes the wilderness writhe in travail...
> The voice of the Lord makes the hinds calve
> And brings kids early to birth;
> And in his temple all cry 'Glory!' [*Kāvôd*]. (Psalm 29.3–9)

This Psalm frequently appears in the liturgy of the cathedral for the celebration of the baptism of Christ, along with the opening of the creation story in Genesis and a reflection upon Trinitarianism. The 'voice' of the Lord [Yahweh] is, of course, a metaphor with two semantic fields brought into play, the human and the divine, in the context of a strong and determinative insistence throughout the Bible that there is an unbridgeable distance between creature and Creator. But given the nature of the Hebrew language, in which concrete particularities have allegorical weight ('arm' for 'power', for example), then anthropomorphisms operate with an abstract *and* analogical ballast. While the voice or call are human descriptions, nevertheless there is *something* of a divine communication, divine revelation, not only referred to but operative. In fact, it is only by being referred to, in our speaking in response, that it announces itself.[14] There is a pedagogy involved in learning both this use of language and how to read its employment with respect to spiritual matters. Theologically we are concerned here with the nature of analogical participation, relations between creature and Creator, of which more will be said as we proceed.

Some have said 'the voice' is just a reference to the natural phenomenon of thunder. They say that Psalm 29 is one of the oldest pieces of writing in the Hebrew Bible and that it is probably modelled on Ugaritic hymns to Baal, the storm god. Hence the 'voice' is thunder. People have said that before (John 12.29). We are back with the martyrdom of Polycarp—what some *believe* they

---

[14] As the French theologian, Jean-Louis Chrétien, writes: 'We hear the call only in the answer, in a voice that has been altered by it, which utters the very alteration that gives it to itself as not belonging to itself, and which endures its own unsubstitutable disinheritance.' J.-L. Chrétien *The Call and the Response*, trans. Anne A. Devonport (New York: Fordham University Press, 2004), p.27.

see and what others *see–as*. The 'waters' in the Psalm describe the primal 'chaos' such that we are given an elipitical account of the genesis of creation. It is described as an echoing chaos or perhaps a chaos of echoes. But the word 'echoes' is not there in the Hebrew text; it is a poetic inference of 'many waters'. Michael Serres, at the end of his meditation *Genesis*, offers another suggestive description of this process, drawing upon quantum physics and the biological concept of emergence: 'Under the word and language, this wave, beneath the wave, the black *noise*. The unknown, the infra-subject of hate and multiplicity, open chaos, and closed simply under the numbers. At the seeding of the wave and the surge, as at the beginning of the world, is the echo of pandemonium. The word will be its messiah, and the idea will be the messiah of the messiah, awaited in the noise, hoped for in the raising up of the musical renaissance.'[15] Serres is attempting to describe the emergence of form. The Psalmist goes further: the power of the voice or divine call [*qôl*] is creative and destructive but it presences God's glory [*ēl-haKāvôd*], the only response to which is worship—a worship consisting simply in acclaiming and echoing the presence of that glory [*Kāvôd*]. God's glory is inseparable from God Himself; that's what *ēl-haKāvôd* expresses. There can be no other proper subject here other than *ēl*—which, in Hebrew is an aleph (the first letter of the alphabet) followed by a lamed. Any other subjects' 'glory', like the king's, is only a reflection and participation in what is properly only God's. 'Glory' is the beginning. It too, as a Hebrew word, has a concrete, physical root—heaviness. God's glory presses itself upon the present. It is not God, but what creatures apprehend in and as the presence of God. It is related to a later Hebrew word *Shekinah*. This word only appears as a verb in the Bible and is associated with dwelling, abiding—words picked up in John's Gospel as descriptions of the incarnation (John 1.14) and the presence of the Spirit (1.32).

What is also absent from Serres' scientific meditation on the birth of communicative form ('the word') from the echoes of chaos is the character of the operation. For energy fields have a character, a mood, a tone; they are not neutral, they cannot be produced from neutrality. Neutrality is entropy—the loss of energy. To see a man or a woman punched in the street, to watch a fight, is to enter into a force-field of anger and hate that floods the nervous system with adrenalin, even though we are a bystander. We experience that anger and hatred, internally. Neuroscientists will point to the 'mirror neurons' that enable this internalization.[16] The Psalmist exhorts the people of

---

[15] Michel Serres, *Genesis*, trans. Geneviève James and James Nelson (Ann Arbor: University of Michigan Press, 1995), p.139.
[16] 'Mirror neurons' were discovered by Giacomo Rizzolatti and his team of neurobiologists in the opening years of the twenty-first century. States perceived and experienced external to the body are mimicked within the body and the brain, such as reading a racey novel for example. They evoke 'simulation, in the body's brain maps, of a body state that is not actually taking place in the organism' and provide the biological basis for 'empathy' and the body loops

God to enter 'the beauty of holiness' (Psalm 29.2); a holiness which is God's first and ours by participation in its gift, its grace. The presence of God has an aesthetic dimension, a beauty. Furthermore, it comes us to because we are 'his people'. 'The Lord will give strength to his people; the Lord will bless his people with peace' (Psalm 29.11). The 'his' is the relation that *makes* the communication; that *seeks out* that contact, making possible all response. *For us* it becomes communication in making that response. Not that our words can become God's Word to us, but our words attest to a call that disinherits us of ourselves.[17] Even so, this divine presencing is characterized by love, and the belonging that love enjoins. It is because God loves that there is a communication. Love calls out. Love cannot refrain from calling out and establishing relation. This is a love that is not under the condition of being lost; a love that is free and freeing. Love under the ensign of being lost, of loss, *can* refrain from calling out and establishing relations—because it becomes turned upon itself autistically. We saw this with Chaucer's poet, burrowing deep within himself, preoccupied with his own anxieties, preoccupied with his loss of himself. *Amor sui.* We saw this with the film-crew in *The Blair Witch Project*—the evil starts by separating them: the arrogance of the director who insists she knows where they are when she doesn't, but she doesn't want to lose face; the lies and deception about who stole the map and what happened to it. Evil destroys relations. It murders the children. It gathers together the men on Coffin Rock and then it ritually slaughters them.

But love that is free from its own fears *cannot* refrain from calling out and establishing relations. Love and beauty characterize the operations of holiness and the presencing of glory. God created out of love. We will have more to say about this in Volume II when we relate revelation, Christology, and anthropology to creation. For now, the emphasis is upon the communicative relations that that love invokes and inspires, because good (that is loving) theology can only emerge in response to the character of this communication. Only in response to this loving invocation, the 'voice', the 'call', can theology be a *poiesis*. The opening lines of the *Letter to the Hebrews* are illustrative: the communication of the contents of the letter, the composition of the letter itself as a communication, issues from 'the many and various ways God spoke of old to our fathers by the prophets; but in these last days he has spoken to us by a Son, whom he appointed heir of all things, through whom also he created the world' (Hebrews 1.1–2). Theological speaking, theology, can only emerge

---

'as–if' system fundamental for the formation of beliefs. See Antonio Damasio, *Self Comes to Mind: Constructing the Conscious Brain* (London: Vintage, 2012), pp.102–3; see also: *The Feeling of What Happens: Body, Emotion, and the Making of Consciousness* (London: Vintage Books, 2000).

[17] The 'disinheritance' is what Jean-Louis Chrétien (n.14) refers to as uttering 'the very alteration that gives it to itself as not belonging to itself'.

as a making, a *poiesis*, from God, from within God's self-disclosure—as I, as a theologian, speak out of my own lostness, as a response to that which has been spoken by God. 'Where are you [Adam]?' As a purely human enquiry (and I am begging the question of whether there is any such thing as 'purely human', a being human that can be isolated from the divine, the animal, and the vegetative) it is a 'blind mouth' (Milton): it can vocalize but it cannot see, it cannot understand what it is vocalizing; it is a noisy gong or a clanging cymbal; it is caught up in the endless circulation of signs, in the endless circulation of interpretations: like the man in Jorge Luis Borges' story who dreams of making a man by dreaming him in the circular ruins of a burnt out temple where no god is worshipped.[18]

But it is God who has communicated God's self out of love: *theo-logos* (God-speech, God-eloquence, God-thought, God-deliberation) in creation and in Christ through whom all things were made that are made. He has spoken and speaks us to through His Spirit. What is communicated? Love. Love is communicated from that big bang out of nothing, that fiat out of nowhere: 'Let there be'. A big bang out of nothing that is prior to the Big Bang. Love cannot withhold itself; even in sacrifice it gives away. And that love stirs us with its energies into life, in a desiring that far surpasses sex and is far more frightening, driving to a deeper nakedness, a greater abandonment, an excessive generosity. We cannot seize upon this communication. It does not immediately put a full stop to our sentences; put an end to our questions, seeking, and groping. Rather, this communication establishes the sphere within which we glimpse at first (because sin has to be faced, acknowledged, and renounced) the depths of our lostness, and gives it articulation. It is God's communication that comes into the world to lighten its darkness; to enlighten our darkness. In and as creation, in and as Christ, through and by the Spirit, it establishes a communicative relation. The ongoing creative communication of the *theo-logos* is a *theo-poiesis* in which our theologies are a participative response. Anselm, reflecting upon Trinitarian relations, informs us that the Godhead is 'eternally mindful of himself . . . But, if he conceives of himself eternally, he expresses himself eternally.'[19] This expression is in terms of the conceptualization (God the Father), the proclamation of the Word (God the Son), and the breathing forth (God the Spirit). The whole Godhead is involved then in *theo-poiesis*. What I am doing now, in writing about *theo-logos* is responding to the communication, to that eternal expressiveness. But I do so from within the condition of being lost and seeking understanding. I do so only by an entrustment.

---

[18] Jorge Luis Borges, 'The Circular Ruins' in *Labyrinths: Selected Stories and Other Essays*, edited by Donald A. Yates and James E. Irby (Harmondsworth: Penguin Books, 1964), pp.72–7.
[19] *Monologium*, in *St. Anselm: Basic Writings*, trans. S.N. Deane (La Salle, IL: Open Court Publishing Company, 1962), chapter XXXII, p.141.

The question can be raised, has been raised by students in seminars where I have presented this opening for a systematic theology: is the lostness radical enough? Is the darkness not so profound that even the word 'God' loses its meaning? Does the word 'God' now speak at all to us? There is certainly a condition of being so lost that paralysis and aphasia freeze all the possibilities for signification; when the burden of confusion and exhaustion weighs the mind and body, and forces it down into numbness. Even suicide as an act only becomes possible with some emergence from this numbness. The darkness of such despairs does exist. It is experienced, both by saints and sinners. It exists also in those who perpetrate the violences that traumatize others. Those who terrorize, those who exploit, those who become vicious in defending what they believe is theirs, will be theirs—out of lust, out of greed, out of hatred, out of resentment. But theology cannot speak from such darknesses because it cannot speak into them. Yet in trauma and human evil grace *can* most reveal itself, for only the revelation of Christ Himself can speak in such situations.[20] We have to recall that even Christ descended on Holy Saturday into the terrifying silence of solidarity with those in hell.[21] Theology may testify, by inference from Scripture, to such a silence and to such a solidarity; but it cannot go there. It can only point to what Dante described as the terror 'awash in the lake of my heart' (*Inferno*, 1.20). This is the place where communication is bestial; the place of cries and sighs, groaning, moaning, howling. There is no apprehension of being lost because the darkness is so total that no situation can be made out at all. Perception always makes contact with the world. We can only ever enter the death of God, like Dante, with a guide. 'Seeing him near in that great wilderness,/to him I screamed "*Miserere*": "Save me"' (*Inferno*, 1.64–5). We have to see something, someone. We have to scream into the darkness 'Save me'. And that is where theology can begin, because a light has made it possible for us to see and the primal scream against perishing has revealed to us that we are still alive. The scream is a response that calls for a response; it is to enter again into communicative relations, even though Dante confesses: 'Surrendering, I'll say I'll come. I fear/ this may be lunacy' (*Inferno*, 1.34–5).[22]

---

[20] See Serene Jones, *Trauma and Grace: Theology in a Ruptures World* (Louisville, KN: Westminster John Knox Press, 2009).

[21] This is one of the most profound and pastorally important observations of Hans Urs von Balthasar in *Mysterium Paschale*, trans. Aidan Nichols O.P. (Edinburgh: T. & T. Clark, 1990). Christ enters into the aphasia of human trauma on Holy Saturday. This is the nadia of kenosis.

[22] Dante's 'guide' is not Christ, of course, but another poet who lived before Christ. But it is someone who has been sent and whose work, as Dante tells him, spoke of a future in which Christ would come and a city, Rome, founded upon St. Peter. The point is that even in Dante's darkness there is a providence that provides the response to his '*miserere*'. Here I am citing the translation of *Inferno* by Robin Kirkpatrick (Harmondsworth: Penguin Classics, 2006).

RESPONDING

Consider that 'responding' and what is involved in such an action. Responding is relational. I am involved at the level of interest and engagement with that to which I am responding: the creative and communicative act of God or *theo-poiesis*. In the Greek patristic tradition, the verb *theo-poieo*, described the process of deification—how human beings became divine in response to God becoming human.[23] *Theo-poieo* treats the soteriological import of the incarnation that situated God as both the primary efficient and final cause, in the language of Aristotle. The patristic use of this verb was frequently in association with an exposition of the *Letter of St. James*, which is no accident—because the only use in the New Testament of the Greek noun *poiesis* is found in that epistle, along with the noun *poietes* (doers, makers, poets) which is also found once in the Pauline corpus (Romans 2.13). Outside the New Testament, and in the Hellenic culture more generally, *poiesis* is an important term designating divine creativity (which was distinct from the activity of the demiurge in Plato).[24] And while there are differences between the way Plato employs the term and Aristotle, for both it is related to a new bringing forth or *genesis*. No one can place himself or herself at the origin of that *poiesis*. It is the surrender to the Spirit that makes contemplative prayer possible, and in the placing of oneself within the circumference of that origin any notion of 'I' is radically decentred. No human being is the source nor ever could be of that primary *poiesis*. The term is also frequently found in both the work of Philo and the *Corpus Hermeticum*.[25]

I want to take up these references to *poietes* and *poiesis* in the *Epistle of St. James*, because it explicitly relates them to the operation of the Logos. Its author writes, '[R]eceive with meekness the implanted word [*ton empsuton logon*] which is able to save your souls' (Jas.1.21). This reception enables what can be subsequently enacted, being 'doers of the word [*poietai logou*]'. Christian salvific praxis does not merely follow from the Christian's personal decision to act; it follows, and is in some distant accord with, a reception that is prior to that decision. Nevertheless what we are told is that what is received (the *Logos*) is also what is already implanted within the soul. Some

---

[23] See explicitly Athanasius, Book I, *Orationes Contra Arianos*, but the use of the verb can also be found in Clement of Alexandria, Origen, Cyril of Alexandria and Didymus of Alexandria. It then turns up in the writing of Basil, Gregory of Nyssa, and Maximus the Confessor.

[24] *Timaeus* 41d–42e. See also Giorgio Agamben, 'Poiesis and Praxis' in *The Man Without Content*, trans. Georgia Albert (Stanford: Stanford University Press, 1999), pp.42–57.

[25] See the important and influential article by Wilfred L. Knox, 'The Epistle of St. James', *Journal of Theological Studies*, OS-XLVI, 181–2 (1949), pp.10–17. Knox's observation has been affirmed more recently in Hubert Frankemölle, *Der Brief des Jakobus*, 2 vols. (Gütersloh, 1994), vol. 1, pp.305–20.

commentators have interpreted this as a contradiction, but I would argue that this is an example of the chiasmic, paradoxical structure of Christian agency: any action involves a movement that issues from both that which is received or revealed and that which is innate—that which is given and that which enables a response to what is given. I am empowered by the creative Word to perform a creative act in the name of that Word, an act that reveals that Word *as* Word, and the basis of that empowerment is both the grace of God and what Augustine describes as '*interior intimo meo et superior summo meo*'.[26] This constitutes a special relation, a relation to that divine *poiesis* in my response which bears witness to it. It is the relation that would have been possible if Adam had been able to offer, in answer God's question, 'Where are you?' the prophet Isaiah's reply, 'Here I am' (Is. 6.8).[27] Theology is involved in the constitution of that relation; what I am writing is involved in that relation, testifying to that divine communication, sheltering under the mantle of the prophet. And so theological writing is itself a making, a creative composition, a *poiesis*; but of a secondary and derivative order. Nevertheless: *if* the response is to convey something of the truth about the relation it bears to that to which it is responding; *if* there is to be something commanding in the interest and engagement of that relation that requires communicating; *then* the secondary or derived *poiesis* participates, in its own creaturely way, in its own creaturely responding, to that *theo-poiesis*.[28] In *De verbo mirifico*, a text we encountered earlier with respect to Melanchthon, Reuchlin puts this crisply: 'Because God is Word in Himself, he converses with creatures in words. It is from a source in God's creative speech that all man's ability to employ words is derived.'[29] Reuchlin then gives this observation a distinctly soteriological slant with the coming of Christ, for from the moment Christ

---

[26] *Confessions* Book XIII, 3.6.11.

[27] Emmanuel Levinas places great interpretative and philosophical weight on the French translation of this Scripture, '*me voici*'. In particular, he emphasizes how grammatically the 'I' is in the accusative. He reworks this grammatical point into the ethical subject who stands always accused before the other person (*autrui*) and the absolute other (*autre*). See his essay 'God and Philosophy' in *E. Levinas: Collected Philosophical Papers*, trans. Alphonso Lingis (Dordrecht: Matinus Nijhoff Publishers, 1987), pp.153–74, especially p.170. Levinas is correctly translating the Hebrew of Isaiah 6.8, where 'Here I am' is *hin'niy* (literally 'behold me'). We have already noted the importance of 'beholding' in Chapter 2, referring to Maggie Ross, *Silence: A User's Guide* (London: Darton, Longman and Todd, 2014), pp.100–25. 'Behold' is a receptive positioning that opens the self up for contemplation.

[28] For a much more detailed study of the *Epistle of St. James* and its importance for the writing of theology see Graham Ward, '*Kenosis, Poiesis* and *Genesis*: Or the Theological Aesthetics of Suffering' in Adrian Pabst and Christoph Schneider (eds.), *Encounter Between Eastern Orthodoxy and Radical Orthodoxy* (Aldershot: Ashgate, 2009), pp.165–75.

[29] Johannes Reuchlin, *De verbo mirifico*, 2.13. There is no English translation but there is a superb new German edition of the Latin text with a German translation: Widu-Wolfgang Ehlers (hrgs.) *Johannes Reuchlin: Sämtliche Werke* Band I,1, *De verbo mirifico/Das wundertätige Wort* (Stuttgart: Bad Cannstatt, 1996.

spoke to other human beings that divine speech was passed in to human speech and letters.

To take this further: it is necessary to have certain capabilities in order to make any response to what is communicated; in order to recognize that there has been a communication at all. As the Psalmist writes: 'He who planted the ear, does he not hear? He that formed the eye, does he not see?' (Psalm 94.9). Jesus' parables frequently end with a reference to having the ears to hear; signals require receivers otherwise there is no communication at all. The capacity to hear the *theo-logos*, like the capacity to hear any created sound, is not passive. We will be entering the somatic complexities of the senses later as we are drawn further into this communicative process. And 'hearing' in the phrase 'to hear the *theo-logos*' is not a metaphor; to hear within the soul, is to hear also within the body. They cannot be divorced. When we say that we hear ourselves think, the inner voice is not physically audible, but it is intellectually audible. The inner audition is not metaphorical.[30] The hearing is active, creative, and interpretative. This is deep listening. To respond is then to be in relation *and* to have the capabilities of being in that relation to respond—what, in the Epistle of St. James, is described as the implanted word [*ton empsuton logon*]. Of course such a statement already raises a formidable cacophony around the question of what is natural and what is graced.

Let me silence the cacophony of such debate, only to return to it later in more detail, with a brief riposte: I am not accepting the dualism of nature and grace. I accept there is a difference, though I doubt there is anyone who can designate the border where that difference becomes a difference. Erich Przywara, discussing *analogia entis* in Aquinas, observes: 'The supernatural "concerns the end itself" (*circa finem*)', while the natural is ' "underway" to the end (*ad finem*)' and all is sustained by God as Creator.[31] Since sin is *un*natural, the distortion of the natural, the closest we get to nature is probably the Pauline understanding of 'flesh': sensate physicality.[32] We sense. We

---

[30] One might refer at this point to the spiritual senses. The Dutch beguine, Hadewijch of Antwerp, frequently describes hearing in what has been called 'the paradox of loud sounds that are also silence'. See Bernard McGinn, 'Late Mediaeval Mystics' in Paul L. Gavrilyuk and Sarah Coakley (eds.), *The Spiritual Senses: Perceiving God in Western Christianity* (Cambridge: Cambridge University Press, 2012), pp.190–209, especially p.200. See also the French phenomenologist, Jean-Louis Chrétien, in the opening words of his volume *La Voix Nue* (Paris: Les Éditions de Minuit, 1990): 'Seule éclaire la voix nue. De la crypte de la gorge à l'intimité de l'oreille, souffle traversant l'air, c'est toujours un secret qu'elle porte et qui la porte, jusqu'à l'essouffler parfois et la suspendre, la faisant taire sans que le verbe puisse la délaisser,' p.7.

[31] E. Przywara, *Analogia Entis: Metaphysics: Original Structure and Universal Rhythm*, trans. John R. Betz and David Bentley Hart (Grand Rapids, MI: W.B. Eerdmans, 2014), p.227.

[32] The Council of Chaledon might be understood as called to attempt to stabilize the complexity of what *phusis* (nature) meant. As we know from the work of Cyril of Alexandria, the word was often used as a synonym of *ousia* (being).

take from and return back to the world with our senses. And what we take and give back compels us to go deeper into the given that our senses have taken from; the giveness of what is sensed that saturates all phenomena.[33] We can resist that compulsion and try and remain at the level of the sensual. But it will taste like ashes very quickly because it has been ripped from the flows of time and life in order to be possessed. Even so, if we go with the compulsion, we never experience the 'pure' saturation itself. We don't experience the excess of what is given as such.[34] There is no 'pure nature'. The sensed is, in intellectual terms, like the literal interpretation of Scripture. We are driven beyond that literal to what Hugh of St. Victor (and the medieval tradition of Scriptural exegesis more generally) would call the allegorical and the tropological. Nature, as what is immediately sensed cannot be isolated. Once sensed the sense is made sensible. We treat only mediations of the natural, mixed but not confused with the supernatural—like the hypostatic union itself. And as with the hypostatic union, only God knows the mixture and the non-confusion. But we were created in and by and through the Logos. That's why we share in, are an image of, in our own creaturely way, the incarnation. We were created to be in relation to that Logos. Ergo, unless that Logos is perversely masochistic, we were created such that we were capable of such a relation or at least responding to the call that puts us into that relation. The relation, the capability of relating and our createdness are all gifts; nature is already graced. Maurice Blondel puts this pithily: 'the very notion of immanence is realized in our consciousness only by the effective presence of the notion of the transcendent'.[35]

I am emphasizing this capacity of theology (my writing, my derived *poiesis*) to respond to the ongoing *theo-poiesis* communicating the *theo-logos*, to counter, again, a view of 'theology' as a 'second-order reflection'; theology as, in Karl Barth's words, *Nachdenken* (a thinking *after*).[36] In being only partly right, it is a distorted view of theology.[37] According to this teaching, dogmatics acts as a subsequent reflection upon the Church's teaching and ministry. Its role is regulatory. But, as we have seen in the opening chapters

---

[33] The best phenomenological accounts of this 'saturation' can be found in Jean-Luc Marion's explorations, particularly *In Excess: Studies of Saturated Phenomena*, trans. Robyn Horner (New York: Fordham University Press, 2004).

[34] This is where I would differ from Marion (n.33), who wishes to push his phenomenology towards a distillation of the 'excess' as such, the purely given.

[35] Maurice Blondel, *The Letter on Apologetics and History and Dogma*, trans. A. Dru and I. Trethowan (Edinburgh: T. & T. Clarke, 1994), p.158.

[36] See Chapter 7 for more on Barth's theological stance and its difficulties.

[37] One of the clearest articulations of this 'second order reflection' principle—which emerged through discussions in philosophy over the value of metaphilosophy—can be found in John R. Franke, *The Character of Theology* (Grand Rapids: Baker Press, 2005), pp.44. In Chapter 4, I treated the much more subtle account of first and second order discourse with respect to Geoffrey Wainwright's work.

in this volume, while *regula fidei* regulates all our speaking about God, it only affords the traces of what is communicated to us. It is living within the eternally proceeding communication itself, and responding to it, that reveals God to us. As such revelation is not some immobile and reified *depositum* to be spelt out in a number of doctrinal propositions. Nor it is some rupturing diachrony as with both Barth and Levinas. It is rather what Aquinas called 'holy teaching' (*sacra doctrina*) that calls for our continual participative response to be cognitive and affective, spiritual, and corporeal. Our response is our own speaking about God, theology, which circulates creatively, dialectically, in accordance with the three-fold regulations of the creeds: that God is Father, God is Son, and God is Holy Spirit.[38] So, while not denying the task of dogmatics is to examine the 'grammar of the faith' so that the Church might articulate its beliefs most clearly and use words like 'God', 'Lord', and 'creation', and 'salvation' in the best and most appropriate manner, that is not all that the discourse of theology is. What remains, and eclipses by far such epistemological cogitations, concerns theology as *poiesis*.

CONCLUSIONS

Three observations follow from what I have outlined.

First, *the* Faith as used in the 'articles of the faith' or *regula fidei* is a body of teaching communicated by God Himself as the first and only teacher, and the operations of God in Christ through the Spirit leading us into all truth. Our doctrine lives only in and as that communication that we may be, in the words of the Epistle of St. James, 'doers of the word [*poietai logou*]'. The 'holy teaching' is accommodated to human capacities such as the capacity to reason, but its source (its 'first principles' if we employ Aquinas's Aristotelian language) is in God's own continual self-disclosure. But faith is also an act, and an act that is not just an intellectual assent to this teaching. Faith is the gift of being able to entrust ourselves to this divine operation; an entrustment to a divine enfolding love. It comes from and returns us back to God. It is inseparable from the operations of call and response summoned by divine

---

[38] For such an understanding of the 'grammar of the faith' see Nicholas Lash, *Believing Three Ways in One God: A Reading of the Apostles' Creed* (London: SCM Press, 1992) and his essay 'When did theologians lose interest in theology?' in *The Beginning and the End of 'Religion'* (Cambridge: Cambridge University Press, 1996), pp.132–49. I am brushing over here differences between a more Protestant account of theology as a second-order reflection, which emphasizes the principle of *sola Scriptura*, and the more Catholic account of theology as parsing the grammar of the faith in which the Scriptures cannot be separated from the Church and the tradition. I am doing that at this point because later in this volume I will say much more about this difference and why my own theology belongs to the more Catholic perspective.

communication. The gift is not some extrinsic add-on but intrinsic to the circulations of the Holy Spirit in creation. Faith is then a participation in such circulations not just with respect to ourselves or even the Church. For God's operations concern salvation and that salvation is for the created world. Faith is spiritually dynamic within this divine and salvific operation. In seeking understanding faith is a way of life within the oscillations of mutability. It is a disposition, an inclination, a *habitus*. As a way of life and the development of a habit of thinking, imagining, and acting with respect to God (which is nothing less than a life of worship), then faith is a virtue akin to love and hope—it is the means by which our life-practices are shaped in accordance with 'thy will be done'. The theological task has to be recognized as a practice of faith in the formation of virtue—where virtue to con-formity with Christ. This is why faith seeking understanding is the motor-force at the creaturely level of ethical life.

Theological *poiesis* is not then just a 'second order' reflection; as an activity of faith it does not simply operate in a realm distinct from holy teaching itself. And the danger of making too clear-cut a distinction between holy teaching and faith seeking understanding is the situation we have now where the task of dogmatics can be sub-contracted to university departments of theology while the Church gets on with its ministry and teaching; a teaching that may or may not be informed by dogmatics. In this way we have institutionalized a split between theology as a rational practice of faith with respect to under-standing the contents of that faith, and the practices and work of the Church. Most of the theological research and writing conducted in universities is not done in the service of the Church. Time for such theological labour is not paid for by the Church. And the Church only receives from that labour drips and dribbles.[39]

Secondly, dogmatic theology as a discourse is a communication related to those theological communicative relations I described earlier. As faith seeking understanding, theology is mediation. It is not *a* mediation, because *a* media-tion is that which takes place between two discreet entities: an arbitration process between managers and unions; a diplomatic delegation between two

---

[39] It does not follow from this that theology as an intellectual discipline should *not* be con-ducted within the university. The university remains a benchmark for intellectual activity, with the quality of its teaching and research regularly examined so that the highest standards in intellectual endeavour may be maintained. It has a commitment to truth and to the exami-nation of the rigour of methods in attaining the truth. It also has a commitment to critical reflection and debate among those pursuing truth. But the present situation does raise the question of whether, if the Church is, or ought to be the direct beneficiary of such theological research it should be more involved (even financially involved) in its production and ensure the communication across the two institutions. The university, for its part, has also to recog-nize as a public body that it should and house and support such work. It does this for a variety of other public and corporate interests.

warring states. There is not, on the one hand, God's self-communication and professionalized interpreters, on the other, who pick up the divine transmissions and vocalize them in a response to God, on behalf of the human community. Theology is mediation through and through because there are not two immediately, self-present, discreet entities *between which* transactions flow back and forth. Theology is mediation because it is *poiesis* from start to finish. Yes, we never and cannot treat the nature of God as such. That is not so much because God withholds such a disclosure, but much more because we are created and dependent creatures who can only access the depths of the Godhead in a manner that befits our creatureliness and the nature of our creation. We see *as* through a mirror because we are made 'in the image of'.[40] Even in the comsummate fulfilment of the Kingdom, even in the resurrection, there will never be a grasping of God's nature as such. But we are not talking about theology grasping God's nature. We are talking about theology working within God's communication of Himself. This communication, because it is a relation and in relation, is not an object outside the theological process of mediation. Neither are we, who are hearing and in hearing responding, outside the process in seeking understanding. Our teaching is governed by God's holy teaching. And that doesn't mean that in our talk about God, in our making meaningful what it is to use the noun 'God', the God we speak about is not transcendent in a sense we can grasp. That which transcends is by definition infinitely transcending our ability to think. The mediation process is not just an immanent one—because the call is prior to and inaugurates the response. But it does mean that neither God in God's transcendence nor humanity is the formal object of theological discourse; neither the Trinity nor redemption is the primordial theme of theology. There would have been a faith seeking understanding had Adam not fallen; had human beings not been in need of God's redemption. Our creation *is* the establishment of a relation. Love is the only primordial theme of theology; and love is the communicative relation between the creative, triune God and His created humanity.[41]

At the end of Volume III of this project I will say something about the nature of the triune God, inferred from all we will have covered before that point. Such a consideration will draw together what we will have come to appreciate

---

[40] Przywara commenting upon analogy in Augustine puts this well: 'the *imago Trinitatis* implies the surrender of the mind's immanence to the infinity of incomprehensibility' E. Przywara, *Analogia Entis* (n.31), p.264.

[41] Of course the relation is asymmetrical because the line between creator and created cannot be erased. We need not get into the scholastic niceties of distinguishing between our 'real' relation to God and God's 'logical' relation (what Aquinas understood as the difference between '*creaturae realiter referuntur*' and '*secundum rationem*' in God in *Summa theologiae* I[a] q.13 a.7). We need only keep continually before us the *diastema* that separates creator from creation. It is with the scandal of God's action in Christ in becoming a creature that we will open the Christology in Volume II of this project.

about the nature of God's existence and God's attributes. Inevitably, such an undertaking will furnish only abstractions because whatever our capabilities for responding to God's self-communication, and whatever the process of our salvation and deification, nevertheless the distance between creator and creation will always remain. We will never grasp what God is in God's self, and our appreciation of the nature of God's existence and God's attributes will be analogical and Christological because we will never know as God knows. We only know God in Christ and the Spirit; though in knowing them we know the Father by inference. Similarly, humanity can never be separated from the created order itself. It has been endowed with capabilities that enable it to respond to God in ways that differ from other animals, from birds, from reptiles, from fish and vegetation. But humanity cannot be an object as such that can be grasped independent of both its relation to the rest of creation and the relation of that creation to God. We do not see ourselves as we are; we cannot. Only God sees and knows us as we are. And so, in brief: the nature of God remains a mystery and so does the nature of being human. Any knowledge of what we are as human beings and what God is as God can both only emerge in the pursuit of the theological relation itself—the ongoing theological communication that is a *theo-poiesis* in which, as human beings, we are called by that *theo-logos* to participate. Theology as such then, even dogmatics, is a genre of prayer; and that is why prayer (which is not subjective because that already presupposes we know what being a subject is and that there are such things as isolatable subjects) finds such a prominent role in this present undertaking.

We need to examine this further because, as an academic discipline undertaken in a secular university setting, the idea that theology is a genre of prayer would seem strange: to students of theology as to professionals teaching theology. But in part the strangeness of what I am suggesting has arisen through the processes of differentiation, specialization, and division of one expertise from another that modernity inaugurated. If this process is labelled 'secularization', then that is a misnomer. There is no reason why social and institutional development and differentiation should be viewed as a corollary of secularism. To accept such a logic is already to buy into the myth of secularism.[42] Institutional differentiation, specialization, and professionalization has a much older social history that is not simply ecclesial. We saw it in the twelfth century movement of *reformatio* that divided the clerical from the lay. That distinction has deepened over the centuries through a lack of ecclesial investment (time and attentiveness as much as money), even disinvestment in lay education. The call to the Christian faith is an active and ongoing one. It is

---

[42] On the myth of secularism and its instability during the Enlightenment see Graham Ward, 'The Myth of Secularism', *Telos* (vol. 167), Summer 2014, 162–79.

not like library membership. As Paul understood, the call is to 'work out your own salvation [*tēn eautōn sōtērian katergadzesthe*]' (Phil.2.12), where 'work' is 'to effect by labour' or 'to achieve one's object'. It is a Greek verb used both of agriculture and manufacture. Faith is a labour in and of faith, in a process of sanctification and formation in Christ.[43] And all Christians are called to such a work. As such all Christians, seeking an understanding of their faith in and through the experiences of everyday living, are theologians, just as Christians are all called to pray.

One of the characteristics of prayer that theology as a genre of prayer inherits is prayer's therapeutic action. To pray is to participate in the wholeness of the Godhead, the wholeness that makes us whole. Through and in prayer the Spirit of God circulates, breathing into us, with us and through us and out into the environments and neighbourhoods within which we are enfolded. Prayer is not just an interior subjective activity. It actually constitutes personhood. Prayer is always reaching beyond and behind consciousness transformatively. Prayer affects, and the effects of those affects colour our moods and emotions, our imaginations, our thinking and our doing. Prayer not only filters the world around us through who we are as individuals—our concerns, our pleasures, our stimulations, ennui, superficialities, and profundities—it affects that very world in and through our dispositions and actions. To change the way we think about the world in which we dwell is to change the world itself. The Spirit as it moves in and through prayer works the work of God with respect to salvation—both our salvation (as Paul indicates—and the 'your' is plural not singular and subjective), the Church's, and the extensive contexts we occupy. Theology as a genre of prayer inherits this therapeutic and transformative capacity. In its pursuit of truth it is a Spirit-led and Spirit-inspired activity. The acts of interpretation (of the Scriptures, of the documents of the Ecumenical Councils, of the Church Fathers and Mothers, the world, our experience, our relationship with God) which constitute doing theology are themselves therapeutic exercises. To interpret is to seek to understand; and to seek to understand is to seek a mental (physical and affective) equilibrium (one which minimizes confusion and dissonance).

---

[43] As we saw in Chapter 3, in the process of elucidating 'justification by faith', Melanchthon separated justification as the objective ground of salvation in Christ, from sanctification as the subjective ground of salvation in Christ. To my mind this is a false dichotomy born of an over-enthusiastic intellectualism. Justification is only one metaphor used in the New Testament to describe atonement (will be exploring several others in Volume II). Importantly, the range of metaphors points to our inability to grasp that transaction between God as Father, and God as Son, and the work of God as Spirit in atonement. What we can have some grasp of is the work of grace as a consequence of that atonement. The problem of having a doctrine of justification distilled out from the ongoing work of sanctification is how one participates in the atoning work of Christ.

Think, for example, of the emotional and intellectual turmoil we go through when we are profoundly attracted to someone but don't know whether what we feel is reciprocated. And then the further, perhaps even more profound turmoil that follows when there is some reciprocation but we are unsure whether there is an imbalance: I love them far more than they seem to love me. Every gesture, tone, word texted, item of clothing worn etc. is scrutinized to answer the questions bubbling up like indigestion, burning and sour within us. Until . . . either we are reassured or come to the difficult conclusion the relationship is not going to work. This is the very heat of interpretation. And 'heat' is the right word because at molecular and endocrinal levels of our embodiment energy is being generated and transmitted throughout this interpretative process. Yes, we can treat interpretation like code-breaking or solving cryptic clues in a crossword, but genuine existential acts of interpretation are transformative. Our well-being hangs in the balance. Nicholas of Cusa, writing a commentary on the phrase 'the father of lights', as it appears in the *Letter of St. James*, describes how 'the life of the intellect is understanding, and this is its desired being'.[44] The whole of Marcel Proust's epic novel, *Remembrance of Things Past* is a fine elaboration of the seductive, sometimes, feverish logics of interpretation. The opening volume, *Swann's Way*, which traces the torments of Swann's obsessive love for the prostitute Odette, is, in miniature, the theme of the whole novel series itself and Marcel's love for their daughter, Gilberte, and later Albertine. All the potential pathologies of love are caught up with the desire to understand, with interpreting and interpreting correctly. It is in this sense that the act of interpretation is therapeutic—it aims at a settlement and it fights passionately against the madness of semiosis (where meaning and the meaningful are endlessly open and constantly shifting). It would appear, as human beings, that we can neither cope with a world emptied of meaning (which brings boredom, ennui, and melancholia) nor a world where everything is saturated with so much meaning we are overwhelmed (which brings paranoia or autism).

Interpretation *is* a cognitive activity and sometimes it remains just at the level of cognition (reading a shopping list, identifying which toilet is for which sex). But there are modes of interpretation that are existential; they concern one's very wellbeing. Here reading and responding becomes meditation (as Hugh understood). And with these modes of interpretation we treat the biology, physiological, and emotional make-up of the act of interpretation. Theology, faith seeking understanding, engages such a mode of meditative interpretation. Witness John Bunyan, in his autobiography *Grace Abounding*

---

[44] Nicholas of Cusa, 'On the Gift of the Father of Lights', trans. Jasper Hopkins in his book *Nicholas of Cusa's Metaphysic of Contraction* (Minneapolis: Arthur J. Benning Press, 1983), p.372–86, 372.

to the Chief of Sinners, struggling to interpret what the Scriptures were saying about the state of his soul such that texts seemed to haunt, taunt, tempt,
and stalk him—until he comes to a place of understanding. The interpretive
practices that theology requires concern, like prayer, the very incarnational
processes of justification, sanctification, formation, and discipleship. They are
pedagogies that discipline our desire; that orientate and channel that seeking
installed by desire. As we saw in Chapter 2, medieval theologians, like Hugh
of Saint Victor, were aware that theology began with the interpretation of
Scripture; recognized that such interpretation began with the historical and
plain sense of the words (which required the exercise of grammar, dialectic,
and rhetoric—the *trivium*); but it didn't end there. Although the more recent
development of Scriptural exegesis in terms of historical and philological
skills does seem to stop with the letters and markings on the page, medieval
theologians saw the allegorical levels of interpretation exercised (and exor-
cised) the spiritual dimensions of being human and the tropological level of
interpretation worked upon human dispositions to act by encouraging and
fostering ethical modes of being. If the material content of Scripture is the
history of our salvation then that salvation is in part brought about by our
engagement with Scripture. It is in this sense that Scripture becomes, and
not simply attests to, the Word of God; and is therefore sacred. Interpretation
as such was once profoundly understood as being associated with pedagogy,
formation, and salvation itself. 'Hermeneutic progress is progressive restoration and salvation.'[45] I will have more to say about such pedagogies in Volume
II with respect to Christology and discipleship. Hugh sums up this cognitive,
spiritual, and affective operation: 'the start of learning, thus, lies in reading,
but its consummation lies in meditation'.[46] Like Hugh of St. Victor, I associate interpretation with meditation and contemplation, and it is as such that
theology as an interpretative practice is associated with prayer—and prayer
with moral and spiritual formation.[47] I cite, again, the theologian Evagarius

---

[45] Paul Rorem, *Hugh of St. Victor* (Oxford: Oxford University Press, 2009), p.55.
[46] *Didascalicon of Hugh of St. Victor*, p.93.
[47] There is no easy correlation between being a theologian and being a well-formed
Christian. There is an analogue here with Plato's philosopher king in his or her ascent to the
Good: intellectual and moral development should be related. But the relationship is not always
either evident or obvious. In an essay by the British theologian, Donald MacKinnon, discuss-
ing the relationship 'of moral goodness to intellectual insight' (p.129) in the work of Paul
Tillich and Gerhard Kittel, 'a dark theme' emerges. Major thinkers of ongoing importance like
Russell and Tillich led lives in open adulterous and serial relationships; others like Gottfried
Frege and Kittel were unabashed in their racism and bigotry (anti-Semites both). Masterfully,
MacKinnon concludes: 'All human faith depends upon, and is hardly decipherable *mimesis*,
of the *fides Christi*, the faith of Christ, that is itself human express of God's total fidelity to
himself and his creation. And this faith of Christ we have most painfully to see as something
that if we rest our hope upon it, and find in it the source of our flickering certainty, we must
affirm for what it was, and through the Resurrection, eternally is: response after the manner of God's being and of human need, no wilful wrestling of an unambiguous triumph over

Ponticus in the late fourth century, in his small sentences on prayer: 'If you are a theologian, you will pray truly, and if you pray truly, you will be a theologian.'[48]

And so every engagement with *theo-poiesis*, every theological enterprise as derived from that *poiesis*, mediating and participating in it to the extent that is possible as creatures, is constituted in and as prayer. It must be written insofar as it is prayed and it is to be read also insofar as such reading is prayed. This is hard work because the levels of attentiveness and discernment needed in prayer far exceed the levels of attentiveness required for reading; even when that reading is detailed and nuanced as in literary appreciation.[49]

Thirdly, and following directly from theology as a genre of prayer, faith seeking understanding cannot take place outside of contemplation.[50] The beginning and end of faith is the vision of God. Faith is drawn towards that vision, seeks to understand it more and more clearly, articulates what it contemplates and contemplates what it articulates. As I have emphasized above, such an articulation, handed on and communicated to others, is involved in the operations of God with respect to the Church and to the world. Theology

---

circumstance that will, by its seeming transparency, satisfy our own conceit' (pp.136–7). See Donald MacKinnon, 'Tillich, Frege, Kittel: Some Reflections on a Dark Theme' in *Explorations in Theology 5: Donald MacKinnon* (London: SCM Press, 1979), pp.129–37. The Christian life of faith, lived in Christ's own faithfulness, remains, this side of Resurrection and judgement, a walking on ambivalent waters and we are not easily slewed of our own conceit.

[48] 'On Prayer' in *Evagarius Ponticus*, ed. A.M. Cassidy (London: Routledge, 2006), pp.185–201, p.196, Sentence 61.

[49] This raises an interesting and not insignificant question concerning the difference between praying and reading well. It is significant because at several points in this work I shall be trying to read certain texts (theological, philosophical, literary, and Scriptural) in a manner that is honed through literary appreciation, or what in the School of English at the University of Cambridge was called 'practical criticism'. Reading well is a skill. It requires attentiveness and practice to move deftly between eisegesis and exegesis. The question here then is whether theological writing, if it is to be prayed and not just read, still invites the attentiveness of reading well. Is theological writing literary and is the attentiveness of good reading also in part the attentiveness of praying? I would say it was and, as a corollary of that theological writing should aspire to the very best form of communicative language: poetry. That is a tall order as Hugh of Saint-Victor understood when he said, 'the higher sacraments of faith must be treated reverently with a higher diction and a diction worthy of sacred things' (*De sacramentis*, Book II, Prologue, p.205). But, ultimately, if our derived *poiesis* participates in *theo-poiesis*, then theologians are called to be poets. No modern theologian has seen this better than the French Dominican Olivier-Thomas Vernard in his three-volume examination of the work of Aquinas: *Thomas d'Aquin poète théologien Vol.1: Littéature et thélogie: une saison en enfer* (Genève: Ad Solem, 2002); *Thomas d'Aquin poète théologien Vol.2: La langue de l'ineffable: essai sur le fondement théologique de la métaphysique* (Genève: Ad Solem, 2004); and *Thomas d'Aquin poète théologien Vol.3: Pagina sacra: le passage de l'Écriture sainte à l'écriture thélogique* (Genève: Ad Solem, 2004).

[50] For a discussion of theology as contemplation and contemplation as *theoria* see Jordan Auuman O.P., 'Appendix 2: Historical Background,' in St. Thomas Aquinas, *Summa Theologiae* vol.46: *Action and Contemplation*, Jordan Auman O.P. trans. (London: Eyre & Spottiswoode, 1966), pp.90–101. I am grateful for Frederick Bauerschmidt pointing out this reference to me.

is not some private meditation, just as it is not some purely intellectual exercise conducted in a university setting. Rather, theology undertaken as a
response to God's own communications must nurture and generate further
communication. It is this work of faith as inseparable from prayer, and in
which contemplation of the vision of God as the beginning and end of all
faith's activity, that I am emphasizing in describing theology as prayer. If holy
teaching and faith are both a way of life, then so is prayer. Prayer *is* faith,
hope, love as they are lived, as they find articulation not just in words, but also
in gestures, actions, choices, inflections of the voice, thoughts, imaginations,
blushes, and the beating of the heart.

Some theologians have composed their theologies as prayer: explicitly
Augustine in *Confessions* and Anselm in *Proslogium*. But I am not talking
here about prayer as a genre of writing. Theology can adopt any number
of different genres: Paul's letters, the biblical commentaries of the Church
Fathers, the poems of St. John of the Cross, the prose meditations of Thomas
Traherne, the *Sic et Non* deliberations of Peter Abelard, the novels of Flannery
O'Connor, the plays of Paul Claudel, the paintings of Georges Rouault, and
the academic writings of Barth or von Balthasar are just some examples. But
theology written in the genre of prayer gives clear expression to the creative
relationship between God and the person with faith. The I-Thou framework
for the discourse allows for an intimate communication of the inquiry into
theological understanding within which the reader is awkwardly positioned,
and constructed, as interloper. Secondly, the dialogical structure performs
the process of the seeking and the coming into illumination, often through a
series of questions asked of God and then critically examined so as to arrive
at an answer to the question aided by God Himself who gives the grace for
understanding. The first person singular can take on, at times, a first person
plural aspect. That is, the 'I' as it performs its coming to an understanding
can incorporate the implied and interpellated reader. The reader's reasoning
enters into, is mimetically in-formed by, the author's own reasoning. There
is a following, a discipleship, a teaching. In Augustine, this co-option of the
confessional genre also enables both he and the readers to be conscious of the
rhetorical production of the text. Such a consciousness allows for the continual recognition that we are handling human thoughts about God, not God's
immediate revelation of Himself. Such a consciousness installs a space for
critical and discerning judgement.

This project is more closely associated with the academic treatise insofar
as its examinations are not conducted within an I-Thou framework. I believe,
it is important that theology is voiced stylistically and that there can be a
conscious identification of that voice through the use of I. In that way faith
seeking understanding is held accountable to the one who is attempting to be
faithful. In being accountable, he or she is therefore open to being publicly
contested by his or her readers. But, this discourse is nevertheless addressed

as such to God in the way theology written in the genre of prayer is, because its emphasis is upon the nurturing and generation of further communication on the subject with which it is concerned: holy teaching—whether that further communication is in or outside of the Church. Nevertheless, in parts, it will also draw in other genres of theological writing.

The reason why it is necessary to have examined and qualified theological discourse as 'second order reflection' is that if we do not understand what is taking place in theology then we will not understand what it is that we are doing (and what is being required of us) when we are writing or reading books such as this one. The truth of the Christian faith is continually being created as it is continually being communicated. Otherwise we're just trafficking in dead things like diskettes from Amstrad computers. That doesn't mean that we create the faith anew every time we fashion the theological, for there is a *regula fidei*, articulated in the creeds, which regulates what is fashioned; but faith is created anew and our articulation of that faith furnishes the articles again, the same articles, but differently inflected; just as every celebration of the Mass or saying of Morning Prayer is a new celebration, a new saying—or it's a museum *tableau-vivant*.

Theology as prayer is presumptuous to announce; scandalous to perform; and yet, it is quite simply, the heart of the matter. Karl Barth, who did not see theology *as* prayer, though certainly recognized theology was rooted in prayer[51], states the problem of the dogmatic task with his usual dialectical audacity: 'Humanly speaking, it is a stark impossibility which here stares us in the face—that men should speak what God speaks; but it is one which in Jesus Christ is already overcome … Only by wanting to look at ourselves instead of Jesus Christ can we maintain this impossibility and set it against the truth of that identification.'[52] Barth points to the overcoming of the presumption and scandal in Christ, and I will take a similar stand by radicalizing that incarnation of God in becoming human being. For the moment, theology as prayer demands a recognition of two inseparable characteristics of theological praxis and the cultivation of a responsible disposition with respect to that recognition. Let me clarify.

The two inseparable characteristics of theological praxis are a) that it treats because it is a participation in truth, and b) that it is a proclamation or continuing dissemination of the communication of that truth. These inseparable characteristics demand the cultivation of discernment that combines the

---

[51] 'The human frailty of the Church's proclamation must be constantly borne in mind to the precise extent that we have to be clear that both those who speak and those who hear in this matter necessarily rely on the free grace of God and therefore on prayer', Karl Barth, *Church Dogmatics* I.2, trans. G.T. Thomson and Harold Knight (Edinburgh: T. & T. Clark, 1956), p.755.

[52] Ibid., p.749.

attentiveness of prayer with judgement, an active and responsive deep listening with a critical testing. I need to emphasize two aspects of this cultivation before we continue. The first concerns 'discernment'. It is related here to two activities: prayer, on the one hand, and making a judgement on the other. In the practice of theology these two activities have to work co-operatively. But in that co-operation I do not wish to suggest 'discernment' is some kind of ghostly activity. It becomes spiritual in the context of prayer—that is, prayer has to be Spirit-led and a continual appeal to being led in ways both affirming and interruptive. There is an attentiveness in discerning; an attentiveness to Christ since the content of what we discern must further a recognition of Christ. As a spiritual exercise it is a working of, and within, the Spirit of Christ. If we can't recognize Christ in what we discern, if the judgement we come to is not in accord with our relationship with Christ and our ongoing interpretation of the Christ event in the Scriptures, then considerable doubt has to be shed on the content to which our attentiveness is attuned in discerning. We can never forget the levels of human projection that Feuerbach quite rightly exposed for us. But doubt is not denial. What we may arrive at could be something new. Doubt then leads to further testing and testifying.

All this sounds immensely complex and as an embodied cognitive endeavour it is complex. But we should never lose ourselves in the complexity; the Spirit leads us into truth not obfuscation. And 'discernment' itself is a very ordinary cognitive activity. It is an activity related to the acquisition and organization of any knowledge, about any thing from faith, to fish, to fishfingers. Discernment is only the cognitive act of making distinctions, and distinctions are made with respect to what an object is not as well as to what an object is: this is a pear, it is not an apple. Making distinctions is basic in how we come to know and order our knowledge of the world—even if that ordering may not re-present the order of the world as such. So discernment is not some kind of ghostly process of detecting some invisible reality 'behind' what is in front of us; even when, as a cognitive activity it takes place in prayer. Hence we can, and I will, employ insights into the operation of cognition drawn from neuroscientists and cognitive scientists to help understand the processes involved in discernment—exactly because such processes are at work in prayer.

Secondly, I need to emphasize throughout this description of the synchronized activities of prayer and discernment that we are not talking about subjects in isolated cells here; we are talking about persons who are constituted as such within the context of various and variously networked relations that form communities (of which the ecclesial community in its local and catholic forms of belonging is first and foremost because, for the Christian, it is the mother of all the other communities). So I need to develop what I mean by truth, proclamation, and judgement as the basics before we can proceed further.

7

The Double Helix

Truth, Proclamation, and Judgement

TRUTH

If we follow what was said above about how the formal object of a theological investigation cannot be knowledge of God in Godself nor knowledge of humanity and its redemption; if all these theological objects of knowledge in the lostness of our condition are deep in mystery: then the question evidently is how can theology be a pursuit of the truth at all? What kind of knowledge are we being exposed to and acquiring in this pursuit of truth? Does theology have to be a pursuit of the truth? This is where dogmatics differs from the separately developed 'branches' in the modern study of theology like the interpretation of the Scriptures and the history of the Church. These disciplines are not concerned with the pursuit of the Truth with a capital T. They are concerned with getting the facts straight; they are concerned with accuracy of interpretation within a defined *Sitz in Leben*; they are concerned with philological issues concerning translation; they are concerned with weighing the evidence that constitutes and supports an argument and a critical review of previous scholarship. All these are proper concerns in the production of human knowledges (particularly textual analysis and historiography) and they are legitimately related to professional conduct in the field of disciplinary enquiry. Furthermore, these fields are composed of both a contemporary breadth of opinion and an historical depth of opinion, and so there is an understanding in undertaking such work that it is thoroughly hermeneutical as a scientific procedure and therefore its conclusions are all provisional and debateable. But *theo-logos* is Truth. And so theology is then concerned with this revealed Truth.

Anselm again:

> But if the very substance of the Father is intelligence, and knowledge, and wisdom, and truth, it is consequently inferred that as the Son is the intelligence,

and knowledge, and wisdom, and truth, of the paternal substance, so he is the intelligence of intelligence, the knowledge of knowledge, the wisdom of wisdom, and the truth of truth.[1]

Christ as Logos is the truth of the Father's truth and that is what Jesus proclaims in using the great 'I am' phrase when he states: 'I am . . . the truth' (John 14.16). And the Spirit who is sent, is sent to lead us into all truth. God, in being God, is truth. Truth is one of the names of God. And a name with respect to God is identical with God's nature. If *theo-poiesis* is concerned primarily with a relation—with a divine communication and response—and if Christ is the incarnation of God as the truth, and if our lives are hidden in Christ with God, then Kierkegaard is right when he gnomically informs us: 'the truth is obviously not to know the truth but to be the truth'.[2]

In context, Kierkegaard is commenting upon the scene of Christ before Pilate and Pilate's question to him: 'What is truth?' But the commentary itself, inserted within an exposition of Christ's claim in John 12.32 about drawing all people to Himself when he is lifted up, begins with prayer. Kierkegaard (under the pseudonym of Anti-Climacus) also conducts his theology here through and as prayer. Only Christ is the truth, but, as a follower of Christ, the truth in Him is redoubled 'within yourself, within me, within him, that your life, my life, his life expresses the truth'.[3] There is only truth in us through that relation. Of course, as Kierkegaard goes on the say, there is a knowledge necessary to being the truth ('[b]eing the truth is identical with knowing the truth').[4] But this is a knowledge acquired in and through the relation to truth itself; it is acquired through a conformity to the truth (discipleship). The object of such knowledge is not merely an intellectual comprehension. It is also an acquirement, a habit. In fact it is only an object of knowledge insofar as it is acquired. The truth has to be lived, physically, socially, cognitively, and spiritually. This knowledge, the knowledge of this truth, conflates any Aristotelian distinction between theoretical and practical that is anything more than just an aid to a better understanding, a propaedeutic. As Kierkegaard concludes: 'only then do I in truth know the truth, when it becomes life in me'.[5] That is, ethical life.

The knowledge we are treating then as theologians is partial, as all relational knowledge is partial; but it remains nevertheless knowledge of and in the truth. As St. Paul affirms: 'Now [*arti*—just now] I know in part.' But, continuing, Paul introduces another aspect of truth: 'Then [*tote*—at that time] I shall know even as I am known' (1 Cor. 13.12). The pursuit of truth moves

---

[1] *Monologium*, chapter XLVII, pp.157–8.
[2] *The Practice of Christianity*, ed. and trans. Howard V. Hong and Edna H. Hong (Princeton: Princeton University Press, 1991), p.205.
[3] Ibid.   [4] Ibid.   [5] Ibid., p.206.

from 'now' to 'then'. Truth is eschatological as far as we are concerned.[6] It will be incomplete until we are resurrected and with Christ, and even then we will and can know Christ only to the extent to which we will and can know ourselves. That paradoxical reversal of knowing only as we are known is fundamental. We cannot become the Logos, which would mean being dissolved into the Logos. We remain, most truly, created *in* the uncreated Godhead. This means that in the seeking of understanding that follows from *theo-poiesis*, that *theo-poiesis* which both calls for and galvanizes such a seeking, then the pursuit of truth proceeds through the partiality of knowledge as we acquire it over time ordered providentially to the vision of God.[7] 'Acquire' here needs some glossing. This knowledge, even in its partiality, cannot be grasped without also, simultaneously, being surrendered; grasped only in being surrendered. The knowledge is never ours because it is knowledge of ourselves as knowers who are known. The process of knowing and un-knowing is continual, the seeking is eternal, and that is both the exercise of faith and the work of faith. The process participates in the spiralling kenosis-pleroma choresis that is Trinitarian life itself—emptying out to fill and fulfill (or perfect). We live and acquire truth in and through the eschatological pursuit of the Spirit of truth.

Such a process has educational corollaries, as we shall see when we examine both the economies of sanctification and atonement in Volume II and the *paideia* and politics of discipleship in Volume III of this project. In brief: it is only in a lived-out and developing conformity of Christ's life to ours, over time, in which seeking, acquiring, and surrending is increasingly a conforming, that the truth is known. Seeking here is striving, intellectually, affectively, and somatically. We have seen with Melanchthon (who is the inheritor of an Augustinian legacy) that acquisitive faith operates at the level of disposition, desire, and inclination. It is only in and through the testing, struggling, demanding to understand, recognition, worship, humiliations, incomprehensions, and triumphs of a lived-out faith that we come to know. This is the very substance of our seeking; and our understanding is written within us, cognitively and emotionally, right down to the peptide chains that govern our endocrinal systems and neuro-tranmissions, that, in turn, coordinate our physiology and govern our moods, feelings, behaviour, and thought—the biology of the heart, we might say. There is not a molecule of us that does not need to be transformed. This is what it means to be a new creation in Christ

---

[6] It is not eschatological as far as God is concerned because, as Christ revealed, He is both alpha and omega, beginning and end.

[7] Erich Przywara, commenting upon Aquinas, writes: 'The vision of God is essentially a vision of "God through God," which is to say, by all appearances, the clearest case of God alone working all things.' *Analogia Entis: Metaphysics: Original Structure and Universal Rhythm*, trans. John R. Betz and David Bentley Hart (Grand Rapids, MI: W.B. Eerdmans, 2013), p.292.

who makes 'all things new' (2 Cor.5.17, also Rev.21.5).[8] The only way out of being lost is to be found and delivered. And inevitably acquiring that truth within us, *as* us, will entail suffering as well as jubilation; because unlike Chaucer we cannot wake up from the forest as from a dream. We are more like the man in sable, locked into his grieving isolation, with no memory of the possibility of resurrection life. But from the paralysis of our loss we need to be drawn again into both the beauty and the pain of relations and taught how to see and live those relations in the knowledge of Christ. And what is it that we will know? The truth of Christ, ourselves and the world in Christ; knowing ourselves and our world through his knowing of us and the world created through him.

In the Gospels the question Pilate poses to Christ—'What is truth?'— goes unanswered. It is a question, as Kierkegaard understood, impossible for Christ to answer. 'If Christ were to answer this question, he would for a moment, falsely, have to pretend he was not the truth . . . [because] it becomes untruth when knowing the truth is separated from being the truth or when knowing the truth is made identical with being it, since it is related the other way round.'[9] The posing of the very question exposes the terrifying depth of Pilate's ignorance. He is like a man in one of many recent films made around the theme of amnesia—*Momento* (2000), the *Bourne* trilogy (2002, 2004, 2007) and *Eternal Sunshine of the Spotless Mind* (2004)[10]—whose memories have been damaged, lost, or erased and is therefore unable to recognize the one person who might restore them to him. This is what it means to be truly lost. But how are we found? How are we drawn back into the world that makes sense again in the light of Christ? Pilate stares at the truth and he

[8] But then that molecular renewal is written into our evolutionary development. According to the Institute for Stem Cell Biology and Regenerative Medicine, at Stanford University, we renew our own skin every seven days and every cell of the body every seven years.

[9] *The Practice of Christianity* (n.2), pp.204–5.

[10] What are these imaginative explorations of amnesia suggesting about the contemporary psyche? On the one hand, a new beginning is possible because the past is obliterated; on the other, the past haunts and cannot be put aside. The body remembers. It still aches, throbs with pain and bears scars. There is a forgetting, but not a forgiveness. We can't begin afresh, but nevertheless we desire to. The films articulate that impossible desire, that impossible innocence. The recognition of its impossibility could be a first step towards a turning to God and an acknowledgement of sin. We can only understand sin as such from the point of view of redemption. Perhaps this is why all three films play with Christian imagery. This is most evident in the third of the Bourne films, *The Bourne Ultimatum*, where there are messianic echoes related to Bourne himself and the Project Blackbriar for which he was a recuit or a victim. His real name in David Webber and he is listed on his file as 'a Catholic'. In a total kenosis he is stripped of this identity because 'You wanted to serve and save American lives'. He acknowledges that he accepted to 'do anything it takes to save American lives'. At the end of the film, Bourne (apparently shot) dives into the Hudson River and the camera plays with his body floating there in a cruciform pose, seemingly dead. A television news item tells us 'after a three days search Webber's body was no where to be found' and immediately following this the body comes to life and swims away.

doesn't know it. Only love can affect the miracle of being found and drawn into the truth. The moment of hope for Pilate comes when he responds to his wife's dream that he should have nothing to do with this innocent man. Possibly here lies a tiny crack through which the light might enter. Only the story of Pilate's wife is not in John's Gospel; it is in Matthew's.[11] Often, of course, it is love that has led us into the forest. That is true of Chaucer's man in sable and Dante. It is the pain of love lost, love broken, love denied, betrayed, spurned, or simply love that is left to die, that brings us into the state of being lost. But nevertheless, it is still only love given once again that can begin the process of returning us to life—if it can be received. God's love calls continually. It is the reception and response that is key. Being loved will not affect the miracle, only being able to respond in love. In a sense Pilate has the answer to his question before him; in a sense that answer is offered to him. But he cannot or will not respond. It is this that installs what Kierkegaard describes as the 'infinite difference' between Pilate and Christ;[12] and there is something appalling in that word 'infinite'. In the Gospel of John, Christ is hidden from Pilate who wants truth to be an object to be intellectually examined. This Christ who is incognito, who is not recognized as such or even recognizable, Kierkegaard also famously develops,[13] but we will not be following him there at this time.

What I will be developing is the role 'hiddenness' plays in theology's pursuit of the truth; a 'hiddenness' that takes something both from the Greek *mustērion*, associated with what is secret and liturgies of initiation and discipline into that secrecy, and *kruptos*, associated with a necessary concealment. We saw something of the centrality of 'mystery' when we examined the teaching of Cyril of Jerusalem—the imagined and yet invisible Paradise and Kingdom within which Cyril seeks to install the catechumens. St. Paul brings the two terms *mustērion* and *kruptos* together in a way which suggests they are almost synonymous with the respect to the direct object of his sentence, the wisdom of God: 'we impart a secret and hidden wisdom of God [*laloumen theou sophian en mustēriō, tēn apokekrumenēn*]' (1 Cor.2.7). This is an interesting sentence indeed for the practice of theology. In the English translation secret and hidden are synonyms because they are both adjectives of the direct object 'wisdom'. But in the Greek, the wisdom is certainly hidden, but then that hiddenness plunges into an apophatic darkness all of its own; for the hiddenness of God's wisdom is hidden 'in mystery', *en mustēriō*.

---

[11] For an analysis of the political theologies of Pilate and Christ in John's Gospel see Graham Ward, *The Politics of Discipleship* (Grand Rapids, MI: Baker Academic Press, 2009), pp.285–93. Perhaps the difference between John's account and Matthew's lies in the authors' reading of the role of the Roman Empire with respect to the Jewish denial of Christ: a pessimistic collaboration in John, an exoneration from such a collaboration (and source of hope?) in Matthew.

[12] *The Practice of Christianity* (n.11), p.205.   [13] Ibid, pp.127–33.

The 'secret' is not an aspect of wisdom so much as a domain within which that wisdom itself resides; a realm even more impenetrable than concealment itself; the realm which Paul later describes as 'the depths [*ta bathē*] of God' (1 Cor.2.10), from which the concealment issues into revelation as the Spirit forages.[14] We will return to wisdom in a moment. But we cannot leave this sentence without paying some attention to that verb 'impart' (from the verb *laleō*—to talk, speak, even to teach). Hiddenness and secrecy are at the very heart of what Paul is teaching the Corinthians; they are inseparable from the communication, revelation and proclamation of God's wisdom. Nevertheless we do not treat and cannot treat God in Godself.

Before saying something more about proclamation and truth, allow me to add one more characteristic of theology's pursuit of the truth—revelation. Epistemologically, attention to knowledge that always remains partial and hidden is often related philosophically to scepticism. So, Aquinas, in the opening question of his *Summa* devotes articles 2–5 to questions related to whether theology is a science and if so what kind of science.[15] His paradigm for *scientia* is taken from Aristotle and is governed by Aristotle's four types of causation (material, formal, efficient, and final).[16] While Aquinas distinguishes between primary and secondary causation, historically and culturally, we seem to be in a different place: 'emergence', 'self-organization', and 'self-replication' (among the biologists) and 'eternal inflation', 'the cosmological constant' and 'chaotic states' (among the quantum and cosmological physicists) impact upon Aristotle's notion of the physical and the laws that govern it. Pier Luigi Luisi, an eminent biochemist and researcher on the origins of life, demonstrates how the debate is still continuing, amid so much that remains unknown, on whether 'life' is a matter of pure contingency or thoroughly determined. No scientist has been able to reproduce in a laboratory the prebiotic conditions for the emergence of life.[17] We will return to Luisi's work in the final chapter. For Aristotle, laws governed the physical, they were prescriptive, and took their ontological dynamics from a colourless God as the unmoved mover. They are determinative. Today, although there is something of a return to thinking through teleology,[18] there is a

---

[14] I will not pursue here the reflection by Martin Heidegger and later Giorgio Agamben on truth as *alētheia*—that which emerges from and cancels (the Greek sense of the privative *a*) *lēthē* or forgetfulness.

[15] Aquinas, *Summa Theologicae* Ia q.1 a.2–5.   [16] See Aristotle, *Physics* Book II.

[17] See Pier Luigi Luisi, *The Emergence of Life: From Chemical Origins to Synthetic Biology* (Cambridge: Cambridge University Press, 2006).

[18] The 'teleology' of contemporary biology is often termed 'teleonomy' because it does not involve movement towards some future state but rather a chain of activity coherent with and determined by the genetic programme within DNA. A. Weber, in his article 'The "surplus of meaning". Biosemantic aspects of Francisco J. Varela's philosophy of cognition' (*Cybernetics Human Knowing*, 9 [2002], 11–29), calls this 'internal teleology'—the internal logic of a system.

question about whether laws of nature can be anything more than approximate descriptions of certain regularities. This impacts upon any doctrine of creation in ways that are correlative to what we now can understand as a 'system' in 'systematic theology'; that is 'system' has always to be open and porous to the contingencies of circumstances.

Nevertheless, despite the cultural and historical differences separating Aquinas's understanding of the world from ours, Aquinas's understanding of knowledge acquired through a human science still holds. It is based on truth as a 'conformity' (*adaequatio*) of thing and intellect (*rei et intellectus*).[19] The 'conformity' arises because there is a distinction between intellect and thing with respect to truth: 'truth resides primarily in the intellect; and secondarily in things, according as they are related to the divine intellect (*secundum quod ordinantur ad intellectum divinum*)'.[20] The truth of divine science is, then, of a different order from knowledge in the human sciences, but divine truth does not render knowledge through the human sciences *inadaequatio*. Nevertheless, any conformity between intellect and thing that is not 'related (*ordinantur* – set in order) to the divine intellect', makes 'what is known through natural reason'[21] within the human sciences open as to whether it is true knowledge. The operational principles of a divine science are taken from God's knowledge, the truth, as it has been *revealed* to us. Our acceptance of this revelation—which, for a shorthand at this time we can call our 'faith', but much more will need to be understood about faith as we proceed—does not destroy but perfects knowledge as it is developed by the human sciences because it illuminates or clarifies any 'conformity' by ordering it with respect to divine truth. What has been revealed of divine *scientia* has been revealed in the world created by God, and so the science associated with holy teaching, theology, while treating 'His effects, either of nature or of grace,'[22] must also treat all forms of human knowledge for, as creatures, we are informed by the processes of natural reason as they abstract from what is given of things by the senses.

Highly significant is that the treatment of truth involved in theology as *poiesis* is not just a theoretical or speculative one; it is also, profoundly, practical. It is practical in two ways: first because it is concerned with human agency and, second, the very 'purpose of this science … is eternal bliss.'[23] The concern with human agency is a concern with ethical life; the concern with purpose returns us the Aristotle's 'final causation'. The pursuit of truth is itself governed by a teleological motion that is consummated in *visio dei*, 'eternal bliss'. As a science, then, theology as *poiesis* is salvific. It is not just

---

[19] Aquinas, *De Veritate, 1.1 resp.*
[20] Aquinas, *Summa Theologiae* Ia q.16 a.6, resp.
[21] Ibid., Ia q.1 a5, reply to objection 2.   [22] Ibid., Ia q.1 a.7, reply to objection 1.
[23] *Ibid.*, Ia q.1 a.5, *resp.*

about the systematic ordering of doctrine, nor about the explication of that doctrine which secures God-talk in the Church from error. It is also, and much more, an exercise itself of faith seeking understanding; a performance whose end is 'to come to his eternal joy'.[24]

Hence in the first article on why theology is necessary at all, Aquinas answers: 'man's whole salvation, which is in God, depends upon the knowledge of this truth [*veritatis cognitione dependet tota hominis salus, quae in Deo est*]'.[25] The Latin is even more expressive because it places both the 'knowledge of this truth [*veritatis cognitione*]' and the whole of human salvation, emphatically *in Deo* both spatially and, ending on that all-important Thomistic *est*, ontologically. *Veritatis cognitione* is not quite 'knowledge of this truth'. The English syntax suggests the knowledge and the truth can be independent. The Latin syntax makes it quite clear: *cognitio* is a becoming aware of, *cognitione* as the ablative is bound up with the genitive to which all the elements of the clause belong, *veritas; tota ... salus*. The subject of the sentence sums up what is possessed, 'all things that are healthy and for our well-being'. How they belong to truth is given in the verb, they 'depend'. There is then an active, acquisitive character to becoming aware of the truth, the corollary of which is, as I said above: the truth of the Christian faith is continually being created as it is continually being communicated in God, by God, through God. That is why it is a living truth issuing from Christ as truth, life, and love.

PROCLAMATION

We, and all creation, are enfolded within this transport of truth, its creation and communication in and as relations of love. Proclamation is not then a by-product of *theo-poiesis*: the creator God in creating establishes a relation and that relation communicates something of the creator to creation. Proclamation is intrinsic to the economy of truth, to the operations of God's unveiling of Godself within the world. Of course, this is returning us to the prayerful nature of faith seeking understanding. Proclamation is the active response to receiving the communication of Godself—which is why Augustine's framing of his middle theology within an act of confession elicited by and addressed to God is so very apt. But there are other genres of prayer and a diversity of forms of proclamation.

---

[24] This is the final line of the absolution following confession for Morning and Evening Prayer in the *Book of Common Prayer*.
[25] Ibid., Ia q.1 a.1 *resp.*

I pointed out in Chapter 4 that one of the significant contributions of the structural and post-structural attention to discourse is that we have come to appreciate texts, and semiotics more generally, as communications that are far more than thoughts. There is no immediate and direct association between a sign and what it signifies. Signs sit within shifting networks of other signs so decoding them is a complex activity, laced with ambiguity and brocaded with suggestion. Furthermore, attention to linguistic signs in early structuralism gave way quickly to the recognition of economies of communicative signification that were not just linguistic. Social and intellectual action was understood as forms of *écriture*; living came to be seen as scripted and scripting performances as we endlessly negotiate the signs and symbols that surround us.[26]

This social semiotics can take on a much richer theological provenance by relating it back to older reflections upon the textual nature of creation in the Jewish and Christian traditions. We have encountered Kabbalism and it association with wonder-working language with Johannes Ruechlin in Chapter 3. The Tree of Life became the central symbol for Jewish Kabbalism. Kabbalah is Hebrew for 'receiving' and what is received is that which emanates from the *Ein Sof* associated with all things. From the divine source ten *sefirot* are named, emanations that are attributes of God by which the universe is sustained. The Tree of Life arranges these ten *sefirot* in three columns like a trunk and two branches and there are twenty-two Paths of Connection between them. To each path is assigned one of the letters from the Hebrew alphabet. Creation was spoken into being by God; in God's oral action there is a writing out of Godself. In the Christian tradition, since the world was made by the Logos then all things not only speak of Christ they reveal Christ by signifying Him. Several early Church fathers spoke of creation as an act of writing by the finger of God. Stones, stars, trees, and streams all have a voice in the Psalms; they proclaim the hiddenness of things, show forth the glory of God, respond to God's presence and benediction and delight in their creation. All things rise from dust to doxology; we just have to learn how to read the world correctly.

---

[26] There are many examples that could be examined here from Claude Levi Strauss's and Jacques Lacan's adaptions of structural linguistics to the rites of social organization and psychology respectively, to Foucault's exploration of discourse's on the body and the bodies formed by them. One prominent example can be found in Michel de Certeau's well-known essay 'Walking in the City'—see Graham Ward, *The Certeau Reader* (Oxford: Blackwell, 2000), pp.101–18. Here, in an exercise of social semiotics, de Certeau points to the ways we write the city whenever we walk around it, but the writing always and only occurs within what the city has written for us to walk in the first place. For a more analytical approach to the shared hermeneutics of text and action, see Paul Ricoeur, *Du texte à l'action: Essais d'hermeneutique, II* (Paris: Editions du Seuil, 1986), translated into English by Kathleen Blamey and John Thompson, *From Text to Action* (Evanston: Northwestern University Press, 1991).

We can then recognize Christian proclamation as caught up within these economies of signification that speak the world to us and through us. Such proclamation is inseparable from seeking to read the world truly, and inseparable also from articulating its song of praise. As such it is responding to a call written into the nature of things. It is caught up within the dialectics of receiving, reiterating, and relating. It is in this way that proclamation is prayer, and the medium and the motor for the transformation of all things into the *doxa* (splendour, glory) that they have in God. Proclamation cannot be divorced from worship. As I have said, the beginning and end of faith is the vision of God. But given the multiplicity of the communications between things, between people, between creator and creation; given that all things signal to each other in complex webs and systems that continually adapt to the receptions they receive and respond to; then we can conceive prayer as continually being rehearsed by creation—since the *theo-logos* is continually being spoken. I need to explain that statement more fully because it will form the basis for the claim I am making and performing throughout this work: that the systematic presentation of theology as a human response to and participation in *theo-poiesis* cannot be divorced from ethical life. In *Church Dogmatics*, while Karl Barth does not see dogmatics and ethics as entirely separate enterprises, he does see the need among professional theologians for a division of labour such that the task of dogmatics adopts a mediatory position between the exegesis of Scripture, on the one hand, and practical theology, on the other.[27] For Barth, the reason for this division lies in the task of dogmatics: its pursuit of what he calls 'pure doctrine'. He allows that 'pure doctrine' is an aspiration and is caught up with all the movements of culture and history. But, given what we have been exploring about with 'hiddenness', 'mystery', the partiality and frailty of human knowledge, even the aspiration to pure doctrine has to be understood as delusional. Pure doctrine is an idealist's reduction. It functions like a regulative transcendental in Kant's philosophy. But doctrine is messy. It has to be, because life is messy. That does not mean we not should seek for order and pattern within this messiness while also not denying or reducing its complexity. But the danger of a concept of 'pure doctrine', like all abstractions, is that it is so divorced from life that it has no value whatsoever, theologically or otherwise. We cannot then take this pursuit for dogmatics and the way it has institutionalized the difference between intellectual disciplines within a university faculty of theology, and baptize it as truth. In his own systematic theology, Wolfgang Pannenberg goes even further than Barth. He wishes to divorce dogmatics from ethics entirely: 'It is a material distinction. Ethics deals with us and our actions, dogmatics

[27] Karl Barth, *Church Dogmatics* I.2, trans. G.T.Thomson and Harold Knight (Edinburgh: T. & T. Clark, 1956), pp.770–96.

with God and his actions even when dealing with creation or the church.'[28] Fortunately, in practice, Pannenberg's systematic theology continually transgresses the naïve reductionism of his 'material distinction'—and because of that his work remains a valuable theological resource.

We can glimpse what I mean by 'prayer as continually being rehearsed by creation' through examining a character in a novel. Characters in novels offer presentations of what it is to be human, and in the hands of a great novelist then every aspect of the presentation of that character speaks to and stands in relation to all other aspects of the novel in a manner, isomorphic I suggest, with the way in creation all things signal to each other.

Gustave Flaubert is a recognized master of the highly organized simulacrum of the world in the novel genre. In *Madame Bovary,* Emma Bovary is at the centre of a number of relations around which the plot is conceived: wife of Charles Bovary, lover first of Rodolphe Boulanger and then Léon Depuis, and mother of a young daughter Berthe. Charles is a provincial doctor and most of the novel is set in the market town of Yonville-l'Abbaye where he has his practice. Emma's life both issues from and is woven into a series of other relations to people in that town, some of whom have close professional relations with Charles (like the pharmacist Monsieur Homais) and some of whom she encounters in her daily business (like the shop-keeper Monsieur Lheureux). Flaubert, then, presents a character enmeshed in any number of interconnected networks and relations: familial, erotic, professional, economic, social etc. And each of these characters too is enmeshed in networks and relations of their own. Every detail of the plot emerges from these interlocking relations such that an action in Rouen will have implications in Yonville-l'Abbaye, and even Paris. Even objects play their part in these networks because relations are also exchanges and sometimes these exchanges involve objects. Emma's clothes, for example, are finely described—like the new riding costume she wears when she first goes out with Rodolphe and is seduced by him. Flaubert's detailed observations are separable from who Emma is, the mood she is in and the action that might follow from that mood: her clothes (their colours, fabrics, and cuts); the seal she buys Rodolphe bearing the motto *Amor nel cor*; a cigar-case first observed in the hands of an anonymous 'Vicomte' who flirted with Emma at an aristocratic ball and then is reproduced as another present for Rodolphe; the bottles and jars in Homais' pharmacy—are all communications and responses to communications travelling along these complex networks of relation. They express and they occasion actions, and simply because other people are inevitably involved or even tendentiously implicated in them such actions become ethical or have ethical implications. Emma

---

[28] Wolfgang Pannenberg, *Systematic Theology,* volume 1, trans. Geoffrey W. Bromiley (Edinburgh: T. & T. Clark, 1991) p.59.

will commit every sin in the bourgeois book (primarily adultery and financial mismanagement) and some of the top-shelf sins within Christian ethics
(despair and self-slaughter), but no one and no thing is innocent in *Madame
Bovary* because of the web of relations that binds everyone and everything
and every action. That does not mean Emma is exonerated because all is
determined. The complexity of the interrelations is so fine there is more than
enough room for individual choice.[29] But it does mean that Emma's whole
story emerges through these myriad lines of communication, one thing
speaking to another, feeding-back, and feeding-forward.

Her living is a speaking and on several occasions that speaking is openly
addressed to God. There are moments of manifest prayer in the convent
where she was educated and in the Cathedral at Rouen where she has her first
erotic assignation with Léon. The most dramatic prayerful scene comes when
she is seriously ill following the end of her relationship with Rodolphe. At the
height of the illness she asks for communion and, while her dresser is being
'transformed into an altar', she has a 'glorious vision':

> Her body, freed from its burdens, had become weightless, a new life was begin-
> ning; she felt that her being, rising up towards God, would dissolve into his
> love the way burning incense dissolves into vapour. The sheets of her bed were
> sprinkled with holy water; the priest took the white host from the holy ciborium,
> and, almost fainting with celestial bliss, she thrust forward her lips to receive the
> body of her Saviour. The curtain of her bed, like clouds, billowed gently around
> her, and the rays from the two tapers burning on the dresser looked to her like
> dazzling haloes. She let her head fall back, fancying that she could hear, coming
> through the ether, the music of seraphic harps, and that she could see, in a sky
> of azure, on a throne of gold, surrounded by saints holding branches of green
> palm, God the Father in all his majesty, gesturing to the angels with wings of
> flame to descend to earth and carry her in their arms up to heaven.[30]

Emma recovers from this illness and '[s]he aspired to become a saint'—that is,
until she meets up once more with Léon. Flaubert never allows us the luxury
of becoming absorbed in his representations. A gentle irony plays throughout this scene, an irony considerably sharpened when read in the context
of Emma's genuine death-bed scene following her swallowing of arsenic.
Nevertheless, Flaubert's irony is not the point here. The point here is that the
depiction of Emma that emerges from the expressive networks of communicative relations (which include the theological relations) and the creative
actions to which they give rise offer an illustration for what I mean when I

---

[29] For a theologically coloured argument about individual responsibility within complex
adaptive systems of communication see Nancey Murphy and Warren S. Brown, *Did My Neurons
Make Me Do It?: Philosophical and Neurobiological Perspectives on Moral Responsibility and
Free Will* (Oxford: Oxford University Press, 2009).

[30] *Madame Bovary*, trans. Margaret Mauldon (Oxford: Oxford University Press, 2004), p.189.

observe 'prayer as continually being rehearsed by creation'. What is spoken becomes prayer when these communications and actions are given their true reference point in God or, as Aquinas put it, *secundum quod ordinantur ad intellectum divinum.*

This reference point or ordering is never absent. It is not we who provide it. God's self-communication is the source and *telos* of all these signifying actions. This is why I have drawn attention to the fact that we can never be entirely secular; our language speaks of far more than any ideology can control.[31] In the twelfth century, John of Salisbury in a witty back-handed remark made at Plato's expense, wrote in a manner consonant to what I am suggesting here: ' "Poetry's lyre" plays in the name of truth, while the fictions (*figmenta*) of poetry, lovely without question, are lies that move us to relish truth for its full worth. Poets are liars, and the lies of poets are in the service of truth.'[32] The great Catholic historian of that period, Marie-Dominque Chenu, concludes that throughout the twelfth century, 'Poetry was [conceived to be] in the service of wisdom—of philosophical or theological wisdom.'[33] Something in a writer's honest groping to speak will always resonate with the proclamation of truth, respond to the divine communication and vibrate with the voice of creation itself. That's why, extending 'poetry' into *poiesis*, I frequently draw upon literature, art, architecture, film, and song as resources for theology, as forms of the proclamation of the communication of truth in God, as forms of prayer. For to whom are these communications addressed? And who can determine when or whether they are addressed to God or not? Legitimately, we might ask, given the webs of communicative relations issuing from *theopoeisis*, can there ever be a refusal to pray? The question of such a refusal, of an active resistance to God's communication of Himself, is like the silent scream in Edvard Munch's painting with that title: a terrifying paradox. It is a question to which we will return when we consider prayer in the light of sin and evil in Volume II.[34]

---

[31] Graham Ward, 'How Literature Resists Secularity', *Literature and Theology*, vol.21, no. 1 (2010), 73–88. See also the argument of Rowan Williams in *The Edge of Words: God and the Habits of Language* (London: Bloomsbury, 2014).

[32] There is a recent translation and edition of John of Salisbury, *Policraticus*, by Cary J. Nederman (Cambridge: Cambridge University Press, 1990), but unfortunately it does not contain this section of the text. This section (Book iii.6) can be found translated by J.B. Pyke as *Frivolities of Courtiers and the Footprints of Philosophers* (Minneapolis: University of Minnesota Press, 1938).

[33] *Man, Nature, and Society in the Twelfth Century* (Toronto: University of Toronto Press, 1997), p.100.

[34] There is a difference between literature and theology that *Emma* illustrates. Theology continually seeks to enter more deeply into the mystery of God; whereas literature seeks to enter more deeply into the mystery between God and creation. The American poet, Jane Hirschfield, expresses this when she writes: 'Poetry's fertility lives in the marriage of said and unsaid, of language self and unlanguaged other, of the knowable world and the gravitational

What, I hope, becomes apparent from this illustration, is that theological proclamation, which is inseparable from faith seeking understanding and which takes a multiplicity of forms, cannot be divorced from ethics. As itself an act of communication of the truth it will impact, as all communicative activity impacts, on everything and everyone else. And ethics here is not simply concerned with personal behaviour but also social behaviour; ethics and politics are inextricably tied into each other. I will come to what distinguishes the explicit proclamation of the truth in Scripture and liturgy in a moment. But at this point I just wish to add one more observation to the way proclamation conflates dualisms like theory and practice, overcomes academic disciplinary boundaries like the one between systematic and practical theology, and is therefore inseparable from ethics. That observation can be summed up in the word 'therapy'. If we return briefly to the Aquinas text I cited earlier: the knowledge of truth, which depends upon God, brings salvation, *salus*, health. As anyone who works with people having mental health problems—with the autistic, with the anorexic, with the profoundly depressed—and those who work with people who life overwhelms—those who have been traumatized, those who have been bereaved—knows, communication, slow, halting, painful as it may be, is restorative. The horror for the predicament of man in sable in Chaucer's *Book of the Duchess* lies in the fact that he is left in the forest, the poet gone, alone and silent like the ghost of Patroclus in Madeline Miller's acclaimed novel *The Song of Achilles*.[35] Communication is restorative because it is relational; it is orientated towards what is outside and expressive of an interest in and engagement with what is outside. The tightly coiled turmoil of the soul frozen and silenced by its own pain and impotence is relaxed in the circulation of breath and sign. The light, like the slow dawns on a winter's day in the northern hemisphere, gets in. Of course, there can be violent forms of communication, violent and aggressive acts. But these are abuses of proclamation that wound rather than heal. There lies evil. There lies sin. Communication is never a one-way street. There is no communication and no relation without a reception of what has been sent. That reception is everything. That reception can bring out a hope for better things, better relations, even from the most abusive and violent proclamations. Not easily. Not without a cost to the souls who receive in this way. But it is possible that from the bitterest act threads of something healthier, threads of *salus*, may be pulled.

pull of what lies beyond knowing.' Jane Hirschfield, *Nine Gates: Entering the Mind of Poetry* (New York: HarperPerennial, 1998), p.124.

[35] Madeline Miller, *The Song of Achilles* (London: Bloomsbury, 2011). The ghost is buried with his beloved friend in one grave but has to remain a homeless and wandering wraith because no one has inscribed his name upon the tomb. The book was awarded the Orange Prize for 2012.

If proclamation is not a by-product, but intrinsic to the economy of truth, then are there differences between types of proclamation? Or, more concisely, what is the valued-added of explicitly theological proclamation? There is one further and related aspect to this question significant for the present enterprise: in what relation does the practice of theological writing stand to the two other major forms of explicit theological-*poiesis*, the Scriptures and ecclesial liturgy (which would include preaching, the administration of the sacraments and the occasional offices)? The answer to these questions relates to ecclesiology, examined in Volume III of, particularly the relationship of the Eucharist to the other sacraments. Does the Eucharist trump all the other sacramental offices in the Church? Or is it just one among the others with equal weighting? My answer to these questions, like my answer to the questions regarding differences in explicitly theological proclamation focuses on two characteristics: what is more or less comprehensive and what is more or less explicit. It is not a matter of more grace being available in one (proclamation or sacrament) than another. How would we even begin to calibrate grace? God is given totally in all God's gifts and giving. That is what the gift of the incarnation announces: God gave His Son, He gave His very Self out of or in love. This is the character of all grace. But there are more comprehensive and explicit expressions of what is given in that grace that depends on our active reception, our co-operation in ordering what is expressed with respect to the divine.

If I treat Scripture first then that must not be understood along the lines of *sola scriptura*; that is, that the Scriptures as the only necessary means of salvation. There has been a tendency in certain forms of Protestantism to neat, sometimes mechanical, hierarchies: there is the Word of God in Christ, then there is the Word of God in the Scriptures which bear witness to Christ, and then there is the Church's proclamation (most emphatically in preaching) which interprets the Scriptures for the edification of the Church and, in doing so, can, by grace and the operation of the Spirit, participate in the dissemination of the Word of God. Thus the hierarchy installs a sort of proportional chain of truth: the revelation of God, the Scriptures as the witness to this revelation inspired by the Holy Spirit, and inspired interpretation of the inspired witness to this revelation. The Scriptures here are foundational, but they are not now seen as channelling Christ as the Word.[36] There has been a tendency

---

[36] There was a time within seventeenth-century Protestant scholasticism when the Scriptures did have this mediating role, when, quite contrary to Calvin's more subtle approach to human language and Scriptural interpretation, every Greek word, iota, and subscript were viewed as dictated by the Holy Spirit. That led to grave difficulties, psychological as well as institutional. Institutionally this led to increasing sectarianism as splinter evangelical groups were formed. Psychologically, the damage of this approach to revelation and the Scriptures can be seen in John Bunyan. He became paranoid because he could not distance himself from the hounding voice of Scripture that continually rang out his condemnation. See his autobiography, *Grace Abounding to the Chief of Sinners* (1666). For an account of how John Bunyan was

within the Catholic tradition to develop a more organic model: Christ as the revelation of God and the Scriptures as the inspired witness to this revelation are both mediated through the Church as the body of Christ, the dispenser of the incarnational graces of that embodiment and the interpreter of the Scriptures witnessing to that embodiment. There is a hierarchy here also, but its focus is internal to the Church (particularly the distinction between the priesthood and the laity). The Scriptures in the Catholic tradition are viewed as mediating the Word of God, but this mediation is via the Church and the Church's interpretation of the Scriptures. The internal hierarchy is developed pedagogically, with the bishop as the teacher *par excellence* and the laity as those being taught. Both fundamental theology, which in more recent Catholic theology centres upon an apologetic for why the Roman Catholic Church is *the* Church of Christ[37], and systematic theology are vehicles for teaching.

I don't wish to start another tradition here. As I am an Anglican priest and to a degree have been educated within an Anglo-Catholic tradition, then the theology that is being composed here is highly indebted to that formation. But I am not making any claims that I am composing an Anglican systematic theology.[38] Nevertheless, I do wish to provide a model for how the Scripture and the Church in its historical reflections, its liturgies and its ministries *might* relate. That *might* could be viewed as either Anglican hesitancy or humility. I leave that judgement to others. In fact, the observation of different traditions of theological endeavour open questions about the very place from which an academic theologian like myself speaks, along with the question by what authority such theologians speak. These questions need to be addressed, but I will address them in Volume IV when I treat world Christianities and the heterogeneity of the Christian tradition (I use the singular thoughtfully) as a way of opening up the question of inter-faith relations.

For now it must be noted that within both the Protestant and the Catholic traditions changes of emphasis have evolved. We saw that in the first three chapters. Cyril of Jerusalem concern for a creed that was indissociable from Scripture, in fact, a distillation of it; Hugh of St. Victor's *lectio divina*, attention

---

'saved' from his paranoia by learning that Scripture had to be read, and therefore interpreted, see Graham Ward, 'To be a Reader: Bunyan and the Language of Scripture', *Literature and Theology* (vol.4), March 1990.

[37] Karl Rahner draws attention to this tendency, and follows it himself, in *Foundations of the Christian Faith*, tr. William V. Dych (London: Darton Longman & Todd, 1978), pp.346–59.

[38] For the inherent difficulties of composing an Anglican systematics—in part because Anglicanism was an invention of the Victorians, partly because of the difficulty of its 'coherence'—see Mark D. Chapman, *Anglican Theology* (London: T. & T. Clark, 2012), pp.8–9. In a previous article, Colin Gunton raised the question of even the possibility of composing an English systematic theology: 'An English Systematic Theology', *Scottish Journal of Theology* 46 (1993), 479–96.

to the fundamental basis that Scripture provides; and Melanchthon's *sola Scriptura*. Each theologian views the Scriptures as the Word of God, while understanding the relationship to that Word, to Christ, and to mediation differently. Hugh, for example, views Scriptures as an extension of the Word of Christ and reading them as participating in God's salvific economy. More recently, there have been changes of emphasis among Protestant and Catholics as they have increasingly become more self-conscious of ecclesial divisions—which must always be scandalous, for there can only be one Church as there can only be one body of Christ and one truth. Both the historical need to understand, justify, and berate schism (depending upon one's ecclesial standpoint) and, more recently, developments in ecumenical theology, have wrought changes: the recognition of the centrality of the Church's sacramental ministry as complementing and adding something importantly distinctive to the Church's commission to preach, within Protestantism; greater emphasis upon the fundamental role of the Scriptures for the teaching office, the importance of the individual reading the Scriptures, and the office of preaching within the Catholic Church.[39]

But contrary to any reification or fundamentalist ideology of *sola Scriptura*, I would argue that the Church is enfolded within the Scriptures. The event of Christ emerged historically within the Jewish Scriptural tradition. The early Church in receiving the enormity of the truth of this event, following Christ's Ascension and the reception of the Spirit, had to find resources for both its own self-understanding and for its proclamation. These resources could only come from three sources: the teachings of Christ himself; the Jewish traditions within which both Christ and the Church lived; and the wider Greco-Roman cultural environment that was a dominant part of the *habitus*. It was these traditions and *habitus* that the writings of Paul and later Gospel writers like Matthew and Mark reworked and reread, in and through the Spirit, in order to assess this turning point in the history of human kind. We can only assume that that assessment, the reflections it called forth upon the three sources the early Church had to hand, took time and, to begin with, there was in a certain state of flux. Paul, in particular, faced with the reality of the Gentile response to the gospel and trained within the Pharisaic schools must have been driven deep into prayer and contemplation. As has recently been observed with respect to Paul's development of a theology of the resurrection on the basis of Jesus' own resurrection:

> The Christian hopes eagerly for the future moment when 'righteousness' will finally be accorded, for the full and final coming of the kingdom; present life in the Spirit is a genuine anticipation of this 'age-to-come' life. This is significantly different from anything we find in second Temple Judaism outside early

---

[39] See the Second Vatican Council document *Dei Verbum*.

Christianity (though it had some analogies at Qumran, precisely because there too we find an inaugurated eschatology); but it is only explicable as a mutation from within the worldview of the second-Temple Jews.[40]

The Jewish traditions and its Scriptures had to be completely reread and reworked for such a mutation of world-view. Luke bears witness to this reworking and rereading when, in the Emmaus story, he has Christ begin to expound in all the scriptures the things concerning himself beginning 'with Moses and all the prophets' (Luke 24.27). Luke repeats this narrative trope later in *Acts of the Apostles* when he has Philip expound to the Ethiopian eunuch the 'good news of Jesus' beginning with the passage from Isaiah that the eunuch had just read to himself.

The New Testament *and* the Christian Church emerge from these textual reworkings and rereadings following the event of Christ (His teaching, death, and resurrection). The Scriptures are then, both the Hebrew Bible and pre-eminently the New Testament, ecclesial documents. The Scriptures do not found the Church. Jesus Christ founds the Church, and the Scriptures are not isomorphic with the Word of God in Christ. In Hugh of St. Victor's view that the Scriptures were an extension of the Word, he never gives them equal weight. A distinction remains between the Person of Christ and the Spirit-inspired *sacrament* (in Hugh's understanding of that word) of Scriptures. But neither are the Scriptures simply ecclesial documents because they bear witness to the Christ-event and meditate upon it. This puts the Scriptures 'outside' the event of Christ itself.

To return to the communicative relations I outlined in Chapter 5: the Christ-event is a *theo-poiesis*; Christ himself is the *theo-logos*; the Scriptures as responses to both this *theo-poiesis* and *theo-logos* are expressive participations within the economy of divine truth. Though they are products of distinctive and concrete historical and cultural situations, though they are crafted from human words used in human ways, and in particular languages; nevertheless their origin lies in actively responding to and participating in Christ as Logos, the Word of God. It is in this way that neither their witness nor their meditations are outside the economy of divine revelation in which the Christ-event figures; both participate in that event, all that went before it and all that follows from that event's temporal unfolding. As such, the Scriptures receive their authority from their ultimate author as a revelation of God Himself; they are part of the ongoing event of the communication of the Creator's love for all that He created. They cannot be separated from that creation and ongoing incarnation of God's love. They

---

[40] N.T. Wright, *The Resurrection of the Son of God* (London: SPCK, 2003), p.225. For a rather different interpretation and emphasis see Margaret Barker, *King of the Jews: Temple Theology in John's Gospel* (London: SPCK, 2015).

are also, in their own distinctive way, the Word made flesh. And it is this that sets them apart for other literatures. The particular and scandalous incarnation of God with us in Jesus Christ is the consummation and intensificiation of that communication that was there in our being created at all. Understanding that is important not only for the Christology I will develop in Volume II, but the way I am employing the exegesis of the Scriptures throughout this project.

The Scriptures can certainly be examined as historical documents. They can be dated and different emphases between the Gospels, for example, can be noted. They can be placed within their reconstructed sociological, inter-textual, and philological contexts. Accounts can be drawn up about how they might have been edited or extended, what Jewish, Hellenic, and Imperial sources might be traced within them. Attention can be drawn to the politics of canonicity (what documents were included, the history of the debates about their inclusion, and what documents were excluded). Nevertheless, the Church interprets them as a *corpus* internal to its own constitution, and given as such through the Spirit for our instruction and edification. They are foundational for the Church and its teaching *as the canon they are* (although the Catholic Bible here is more inclusive than the Protestant Bible in terms of inter-testamentary texts). In fact, the formation of the canon is entirely an ecclesial matter because it took place as a post-apostolic phenomenon (that required time, attention, prayer, debate, and interpretative labour now largely hidden from us). The Church in interpreting Scripture can learn something from the enormous erudition and scholarship of those academics working on the Biblical texts, their historical contexts and dissemination, while recognizing history itself is not a precise science and academic autopsies and post-mortems are not intended now as forms of ecclesial service as once they were. But because the Scriptures are viewed as issuing from Spirit-led ecclesial reflection over a period of time and addressed to the Church, they are to be treated hermeneutically in a holistic manner. The Church is then free to reject (or accept) Bultmann's 'demythologisation' or the levels of redaction in the *Book of Isaiah* or *Mark*, or the debates over the Pauline and deutero-Pauline epistles, or whether *The Gospel of John* is structured according to a liturgical calendar, was the first or the last of the Gospels to be composed or written first in Aramaic and subsequently translated into Greek. The Church has this freedom because the foundational nature of the Scriptures means that their interpretation is governed by soteriological concerns and God's providential economy.

All our understanding of Jesus Christ as the Word of God issues from and returns us back to the Scriptures. But the Scriptures are a living text and the tissue of that textuality is woven into every aspect of the Church, the history of its mediations, its liturgies and its ministries—all of which are summed up in the word 'tradition'. And the 'tradition' is both single and simple, however heterogeneous and diverse, because its source is in God's communication of love. But, as a living text profoundly involved in the formation and history of the Church, the Scriptures never can be isolated (or reified). As Hugh of St. Victor understood: they are part of God's providential dispensation, a sacrament. As written they always remain texts among texts, but what they articulate has to be recognized as in continuity with a *theo-poeisis* written into creation itself. As Jesus tells the Pharisees complaining about outpouring of worship attending his entry into Jerusalem on a donkey: 'I tell you, if my disciples keep silence the stones will shout aloud' (Luke 19.40). Anything can speak of God, because everything is in God. As texts, the Scriptures are read and in being read, and read through the myriad reflections of the Church's past readings and interpretations, they are as much shaped by the history and present circumstances of the communities in which they are read as they shape the Church's understanding of that history and its present circumstances. What we interpret is not simply what is *in* in the text or what is *behind* the text. We interpret also what is *in front of* the text. We enter, as John Webster has recently and felicitously described it, the 'domain of the word'—where 'word' is also 'Word', all things being in Christ.[41] On this basis, the model of the relationship between the revelation of God in Christ, the Scriptures and the liturgies and ministries of the Church would be more like the double helix. If the nucleic acids of DNA and RNA, structured in a double, spiralling braiding with proteins and carbohydrates, constitute life, then the Scriptures and the Church can be likened to the same double, spiralling braiding that constitutes the circulations of life in Christ. That does not mean Christ is constituted only in and through the Scriptures and the Church because while, through the Spirit, they mediate Christ they also bear witness to Him as God, as transcendent. Christ is not subject to the immanent dynamics of Scriptural interpretation and the operations of the Church within the world. As the origin of both, as the Logos spoken by God into the world, as the Lord of 'all things', both the Scriptures and the Church serve the establishment of the divine communicative relation announced in the incarnation of Christ. Of themselves they have no authority and no claim to be either foundational or normative for any human being. Their authority is borrowed, their effectivity for salvation is Spirit led, and their operations are a matter of grace. Any understanding the Church has of Christ as God is utterly dependent upon the life of Christ that circulates in and through the interpretation of the Scriptures in and through the liturgies and ministries of the Church and the liturgies and ministries of the Church in and through the interpretation of the Scriptures.

---

[41] John Webster, *The Domain of the Word: Scripture and Theological Reason* (London: Bloomsbury, 2013), p.20.

BUT: that's the double braiding. And the spiralling recognizes that life in Christ is lived: it has a past, it has a future, and it exists in a complex manner in the present, as Augustine appreciated in his observations on the distensions of time. 'There are three times, a present of things past, a present of things present, a present of things to come. There are, indeed, in the soul these three aspects and nowhere else do I see them. The present considering the past is memory, the present considering the present is immediate awareness [*contuitus*], the present the future is expectation.'[42] References will be made to Augustine's theological appreciation of time at various points in this project. Here what is both interesting and important is the place of the soul as the *organon* not only processing the experience of time, but also intellectually accessing it [*contuitus*]; and the fact that the present [*praesens*] does not exist in and of itself for human beings. The present only exists in relation to past and future, and even then it is only *contuitus*. The suffix *con* (with) is annexed to the deponent verb *tueor* (to gaze upon, regard or even to care for). What is suggested here is that 'immediate awareness' is an attentive, protective beholding of the presence of Christ that only is possible alongside the past and the future. For Augustine, only God can be present and know Himself as the present as such, because the present is eternal and God is omniscient. The soul, then, as it processes, accesses, and reflects upon temporality *con-tuits*, in some deep manner, that which is eternal. In *De trinitate*, Augustine will considerably develop this understanding of the soul in terms of its relation to the Trinity and human beings made in the image and likeness of God. If, with Augustine, we have slipped into the anthropological and out of the ecclesial, then let me add tersely here (because it will be unpacked in Volume III) that the individual soul is a nodal point within the nexus or matrix of the soul of the Church; for if the Church is a body, indeed the body of Christ, it also has a soul; a collective soul. Furthermore, any theological account of what it is to be human can only be developed in terms of Christology and any account of Christ as both God and human being requires an enquiry into what we are.

The double helix model of the relationship between Christ, the Scriptures and the traditions of the Church modifies both the Protestant and Catholic theological positions, although it has to be understood here that there is not a model (approximating to the true relation) and then its manifestations. Both the Scriptures and the Church are living phenomena, participating in the living Christ. The extracted models for this continuing operation are only offered as metaphorical descriptions. The double helix description, then, modifies the two previous descriptions. It obviously modifies the Protestant description by demonstrating that the *sola Scriptura* dogma can abstract

---

[42] The translation here is mine, but modifies Henry Chadwick's highly readable translation in *Confessions* (Oxford: Oxford University Press, 1991), p.235.

Scripture from its inevitable hermeneutical spiralling and from its ecclesial context in ways that demotes the real participation in Christ that the Church participates in and through its engagement with Scripture. There cannot be a hierarchical distinction between Scripture and the Church such that the latter participates in an ontologically lower form of the living Christ. Yes, Scripture and the Church are independent realities: they cannot be conflated. The first is composed of a set of texts and the other a set of offices constituting a social institution that has both authored and then authorizes these texts. But neither can one be subservient to the other; both are subservient to Christ and the communicative relations of the Logos. Furthermore, Scripture can 'speak' to an individual who stands outside any ecclesial setting—though the Church cannot speak 'outside' of Scripture that governs the rule of its faith. In Chapter 4, discussing how the language of the Christian faith is spoken elsewhere and by those who are not necessarily part of the Church (or self-identify as Christians), I drew attention to the need for the Church to listen to this speaking about Christ from elsewhere. It reminds the Church that both Church and world are *en Christō*.

Augustine's *tolle lege* experience would be another example of this independence of Scripture 'speaking'. Although, it is not insignificant in this event in which Augustine is inwardly urged to pick up the Scriptures and read 'the first chapter I might find', that the verse upon which his conversion turns is not a self-disclosure of God, but a disclosure about himself that is so apt it can only come from God: 'I seized it, opened it and in silence read the first passage on which my eyes lit: 'Not in riots and drunken parties, not in eroticism and indecencies, not in strife and envy, but put on the Lord Jesus Christ and make no provision for the flesh in its lusts' (Rom.13.13–14).[43] It is also not insignificant that Augustine was surrounded by people who were members of the Church and had contact with Simplicianus, the priest responsible for baptizing Ambrose, later the bishop of Milan. In other words even the independence of Scripture 'speaking' and bringing a man to a conviction of his need to confess, repent, and submit himself to the authority of Christ, is not an operation entirely outside the communicative disseminations of the Church. Furthermore, the revelation Augustine received was not akin to Paul's revelation on the road to Damascus. God disclosed Godself in Christ to Paul; what was disclosed to Augustine was himself, and an injunction to 'put on the Lord Jesus Christ'.

Scripture then has a limited independence; its freedom is prescribed, but by grace. Scripture participates in God's own freedom just as the Church is composed of those set free to serve Him.[44] There is a tendency to forget this

---

[43] Ibid., p.153.

[44] Of course Scripture can and has been read as literature. In fact, this has become quite a preoccupation among post Second World War literary scholars from Eric Auerbach on

prescription in Protestantism. Barth, in his richly suggestive chapter on 'The Freedom of the Word', slides between the Word as Christ and the Word as Scripture in anthropomorphizing his subject. For example, 'Scripture itself is a really truly, acting and speaking subject.'[45] But the danger here, as in the danger with the verbal inspiration of Scripture (which Barth did not accept), is that the anthropomorphism is not read as a rhetorical trope but literally. And this is wrong. The Scriptures are utterly silent, signs on paper, locked between book covers and sitting on a shelf, until someone reads them. The reading speaks because it orchestrates and performs the silence of the signs. The Scripture itself has no independent agency. The Logos is the subject of all proclamation; the Scripture can never be a subject—that would reify it and turn it into an idol. And while the reader may be someone entirely outside the Church, still I doubt not that the reading bears the connotative weight of Church and cannot disassociate itself entirely from the Church; the text is still faintly redolent of incense and old wax.

The point here is that the double helix description of the relationship between Scripture and the Church with respect to the life of Christ and God's self-disclosure in that life has implications for the proclamation that takes place in theology as a *poiesis* called into being as a response to *theo-poiesis*; that is, for theology *as* prayer within the Protestant model. We can approach these implications through an analysis of Karl Barth's understanding of dogmatics. Because of the hierarchy of Word, Scripture, and the preaching of the Church (the threefold proclamation of God), then for Barth dogmatics has not 'the real and immediate task' of proclamation itself.[46] Theology's status is critical with respect to the preaching Church. Its position is one of hearing the Word of God in the Scriptures and acting in a therapeutic manner on what the Church proclaims. But its relation to proclamation is indirect (if not downright ambivalent). Its object is the content of the faith and the danger that besets it is intellectual abstraction. It is not itself a form and operation of faith. Barth announces that: 'If the human word of Christian preaching is to perform the service of leading to a hearing of God's Word, it must obviously have the quality of creating obedience to the Word of God, as it is itself

mimesis in the Abraham and Isaac story to Harold Bloom on the book of J. But when even the Scriptures are read as literature, or literature employs the Scriptures intertextually, it is often those who are involved in Jewish or Christian practices of piety who are among the first to appreciate what such readings and intertextual uses bring to the practices of the faith. Literary appreciation in itself, outside the context of pious reflection (and so in the context of a faith or a willingness to receive the gift of faith) is attentive only to aesthetic criteria not to the hearing of the divine Word. The same might be said of the work of much Biblical criticism. Scripture only becomes Scripture within the context of pious reflection that refers what is read to God. It is then always orientated as a sacred book towards that which makes it sacred, Christ and the Church that bears witness to and participates within the life of Christ. See n.36 for the difference between theology and literature.

[45] Karl Barth, *Church Dogmatics*, I. 2 (n.27), p.672.   [46] *Ibid.*, p.750.

obedient.[47] The human word in the Church's preaching must be as transparent a word as possible and dogmatic theology is commissioned to be the window-cleaner in this scenario. With its aspiration to pure doctrine it addresses itself to the transparency of the Church's proclamation. The distinctive separation here of Scripture and Church opens a critical distance not just with respect to the Word of God, but also to the role theology plays as a mediator between a reception of that Word (through hearing) in the Scriptures and the application of what is heard to the Church's preaching. Theology then is actually maintaining the separation of the Scripture from the Church. Its status is both privileged (as the hearer) and servile (as the one who serves the Church's preaching). Theology does not participate in *theo-poiesis* and as such it, in part, maintains the hierarchical distinctions between the Word of God, the Scriptures and the Church's proclamation and, in part, installs them. We are back with first and second order reflection. But, from the point of view of the double helix description, the individual theologian here is absolved from the scandal of his or her responsibility; the responsibility of being a bearer of the Word, having in Barth's terms 'a real and immediate' relation to its proclamation. The theologian acts paternalistically towards the Church if its proclamation is not as pure as it should be, wagging his or her finger and saying 'I told you so' or 'Be warned'. Although, equally, the theologian is open to judgement if the windows of the Church's proclamation are not clean enough. But judgement from whom? It can only be judgement from the Church: you did not do properly the job assigned for you to do which was to keep the windows clean. The theologian might then reflect that he or she had not heard the Word in the Scriptures properly or adequately, but then that assumes that there is an access to the Word in the Scriptures independent of being involved in the Church's proclamation.

Let me emphasize that we are talking about descriptions of activities and operations here. That is not to say that the descriptions bear no relation to institutional organization and or even ideologies supporting that organization. Both the Protestant and the Catholic Churches institutionalize the relationship they believe pertains with respect to Scripture and the Church and, in their defences for such a relationship and its institutionalization create ideologies that support it. And we know that ideologies are not passive. Enshrined in practices they interpellate us in ways such that we identify ourselves with them.[48] Nevertheless descriptions of what is the case *at the level of operation* always differ from what the institution provides for and announces

---

[47] Ibid., p.764.

[48] The work of Louis Althusser and Michel Foucault, along with Judith Butler on performativity, is all-important for revealing the operations of institutionalized ideologies. These works and figures have been written about on numerous occasions and with reference to ecclesial practices. As only one example, see Graham Ward, *Cultural Transformation and Religious Practice* (Cambridge: Cambridge University Press, 2004), pp.117–74.

is the case *at the level of ideology*.[49] At the level of a description of what actually takes place in the working relationship between the Word of God, the Scriptures, and the Church, the description offered by Barth is confusing, begs more questions than it answers, and is inadequate. As a description it is also inaccurate with respect to Barth's own practice. *Church Dogmatics* is conceived as (and reads as) an extended theological sermon. It *is* the Church preaching. Theology as prayer, theology as bound up with *theo-poiesis*, theology as itself an act of faith and a recipient of grace, is a theology that has to find its place within the double-braiding of Scripture and Church. The theologian bears a responsibility before God because theology, as a Church activity *does* 'perform the service of leading to a hearing of God's Word' and 'must obviously have the quality of creating obedience'. He or she stands under the judgement of God alongside all the others bearing different offices within the Church. This responsibility is only bearable in the context of a vocation and calling; that is, as a continual deep listening to grace given and received for this particular office, grace that must be passed on so that more grace might be given. Only in Christ, only as part of His body in whom 'the whole fullness of the deity dwells bodily [*to plērōma tēs theotētos*], and you have come to fullness of life in him [*kai este en autō peplērōmenoi*—literally, in him you are those who are being filled]' (Col.2.9–10), can this office be held and fulfilled. Theology as prayer issues from and returns to a divine rhythm running throughout incarnation of emptying (*kenosis*) and filling (*pleroma*); that circulation of grace which is life in Christ: from the fullness of His divinity we are continually being filled. As such, I say again, we are all theologians.

When we examine the double helix description with respect to the relations between the Word of God, the Scriptures, and the Church in its present and past proclamation in Catholic dogmatics, a further aspect of the Protestant description becomes evident. That is, the tendency within the Protestant description to prioritize the present proclamation of the Church rather than placing any present proclamation in the context of both what the Church has already proclaimed and its future trajectory. In Protestant dogmatics the priority given to present proclamation emphasizes rupture; in Catholic dogmatics what is emphasized is continuity. The emphasis upon the purity of the present as such in Protestant dogmatics runs counter to the Augustinian theological understanding of time outlined above. On Augustine's model the

---

[49] By 'ideology' here I mean dogmatic assertions about *what is the case* that are divorced from *what actually takes place*. Ideology arises from the division between the idea of what should be and the practice of what is. What social theorists and philosophers like Louis Althusser reveal is how the ideas of what should be can find institutional bases that socialize subjects to the extent that the ideology becomes a *habitus*, a way of thinking and living that is pre-critical and pre-reflective. When I speak then of the denominational creation of ideologies I am pointing to this disjunction between a dogmatically held position (on the relationship between Scripture and the Church) and what in fact practically takes place.

danger here is a reification of the present [*praesens*] that would in fact be a usurpation of a divine prerogative. That would be a form of false consciousness. Modernity is frequently understood as idolizing the present, the *modo*.[50] Only God is truly present because the present as such is eternal life. In the language of Erich Przywara, God is 'eternal actual'.[51] The nearest approximation to this living in the present from a creaturely perspective is animal and vegetable life. Like other animals, the human body knows nothing of time. It responds to what has happened in our past and our future hopes and desires, but in its own functioning there is neither past nor future.

The Catholic description maintains not only a continuity of relation between Scripture and Church, but also a continuity in that relation in and across time. Indeed it accepts those continuities as proof of it being the true Church of Christ. The double helix description is more adequate to what is the case here in what is a symbiotic relation between Scripture and Church, and an affirmation that the Word of God is not solely to be equated with the Scriptures.[52] Where it differs is with reference to the internal hierarchy of what we might term the knowledge economy. The structural distinction between the clerical and the lay offices forms the basis for a further distinction between the teaching Church and the learning Church. The teaching Church is institutionalized as an office whose catechetical work has binding authority upon its members. This office is headed by the Pope himself and the doctrine of Papal infallibility (although this is only claimed in certain circumstances), and the college of bishops.[53] The teaching that issues from the symbiotic relation of Scripture and Church comes down, then, through this office to the Church as a whole, both clerical and lay.

---

[50] See here Jean-François Lyotard, *The Postmodern Condition: A Report on Knowledge*, trans. Geoff Bennington and Brian Massumi (Manchester: Manchester University Press, 1984), pp.81–2 and, for its theological implications, Hans Urs von Balthasar *Glory of The Lord*, Volume V: *The Realm of Metaphysics in the Modern Age*, trans. Oliver Davies *et al.* (Edinburgh: T. & T. Clark, 1991), pp.9–47 and Graham Ward, *Cities of God* (London: Routledge, 2000), pp.156–70.

[51] Erich Przywara, *Analogia Entis*, (n.7), p.121.

[52] There is now, though, a certain lack of emphasis in Catholic dogmatics upon the Scriptural 'fold' within which the Church emerges. That is, the way the Church's understanding of itself and even its inner organization issue from Judaism and the Hebrew Scriptures. The Gospel writers each in their own way map their accounts of Jesus upon the fulfilment of Promises in the Hebrew Bible. Paul's letters speak of the use of Psalms in the earliest of Church liturgies. Furthermore, there is some possibility, pointed to by a large number of biblical scholars, of an awareness by the writers of what became the New Testament of inter-testamental works such as the *Wisdom of Solomon*, the *Testaments of the Twelve Patriarchs* and the explicitly Messianic texts of the *Testament of Levi* and the *Testament of Judah*. Catholic dogmatics tends to emphasize the Church as an entirely new entity. The *lectio divina* tradition has been somewhat diminished.

[53] There is a tendency in Protestant theology which defines itself over and against Catholic theology to exaggerate Papal infallibility. In fact, that mandate has only been used twice and on both occasions did not concern the articles of the faith.

We can see this order clearly outlined and supported in Karl Rahner's *Foundations of the Christian Faith*. The book was clearly conceived as both a dogmatic work (recalling for the Church its doctrinal foundations) and an apologetic work (addressed to other Christian churches and the contemporary religious and secular scene beyond)—a work, then, in the context and spirit of the Second Vatican Council. Rahner organizes his book around three inter-related doctrines: theological anthropology, Christology, and ecclesiology. Because of the attention to the dynamics of the reflective dialogue between Scripture and Church, then the book also is concerned to map these doctrines on to an historical spinal cord: the history of salvation, an understanding of the universality of revelation and its operation in concrete particularity, and eschatology. His reflections upon ecclesiology follow immediately upon his Christology on the theo-logical basis that the Church is founded by Jesus Christ. What then follows is an apologetic for the Catholic Church as the true Church based upon its continuity with the origins of the Church itself as they are evident in the New Testament. This examination leads clearly into a nexus of issues on Scripture/Church relations all thought through on the basis of the ecclesial nature of Christianity. It is important to understand a connection here that Protestantism would not accept—that there is an essential relation between the Church and Christianity, not merely an institutional or pragmatic one. The Church is obviously not the essence of Christianity, that can only be Christ, but 'the church must be understood in such a way that it springs from the very essence of Christianity as the supernatural communication of God', and, as such, the Church 'is part of Christianity as the very event of salvation'.[54] The Church and the history of salvation are co-extensive. The Church is not extrinsic to Christ and the operation of God, which is His grace, it is essentially implicated in the historical and social mediation of Christ and salvation in Him. That does not mean that the Church prescribes the freedom of God. The work of God's grace is not limited to the Church. But it does mean that the Church as the body of Christ offers the clearest witness to, expression of *and vehicle for* what is being offered in God's grace to the world. The New Testament is the first verbalization of that witness and expression and as such it is a thoroughly ecclesial document.

We must observe here that this position demands that dogmatics cannot ever be separated from apologetics, because intra-ecclesial reflections upon the teachings of the Church have extra-ecclesial implications with respect to the world if the Church is part of the ongoing economy of salvation. Evangelical Protestantism because it would not admit the Church's *essential* (that is, ontological) role in salvation makes a sharp distinction between

---

[54] Karl Rahner, *Foundations of the Christian Faith*, trans. William V. Dych (London: Darton Longman & Todd, 1978), p.343.

apologetics and dogmatics. But given that the 'church and its proclamation existed before scripture and scripture is based upon them'[55] and given that the Church has an eschatological role to play, Rahner then proceeds to the Church's teaching office.

The argument has a logic but, at times, the logic does not seem entirely *theo*-logical. For example, consider:

> From this perspective, the perspective of this eschatological situation which is the situation of Christ himself, the Catholic understanding of the church saw that when the church in its teaching authority, that is, in the whole episcopate along with the Pope, or in the personal head of this whole episcopate, really confronts man in its teaching with an *ultimate* demand in the name of Christ, God's grace and power prevent this teaching from losing the truth of Christ.[56]

If we follow this through the Church can never be in the wrong because the Church is so identified with Christ and the operations of God's grace it is providentially 'covered'. The hierarchy of its teaching office is not only of the order of the truth itself, it is also the promulgator of such truth.[57] What is missing here is the mediation, and accommodation, that is so central to the incarnation. Christ came in human flesh that human flesh might be saved, and human flesh is undergoing that salvation until the consummation of all things in Christ at the end of time. The Church, as human flesh and the workings of human flesh; the Church as composed of those who are being saved by Christ, as an institution involved in the complex mediation of the historical and the social: this Church cannot be itself the embodiment of eschatological perfection. The Church is not isomorphic with the Kingdom of God. The Church too is on the way. Later in his volume, in sketching the Church's teaching on eschatology, Rahner will call our attention to the double structure of the now and the not yet, the present and the future, the temporal and the eternal.[58] It is this structure that constitutes eschatology and in so doing announces a difference between Christian hope and utopianism. Only in its complete history, in its complete formation as the bride of Christ, is the Church the realization of this hope. Prior to the consummation of all things the Church is to be wholly orientated towards this future, but at present it

---

[55] Ibid., p.363.   [56] Ibid., p.381.

[57] In the Encyclical *Faith and Reason* John Paul II, alluding to the Second Vatican Council's *Dei Verbum*, speaks of 'the unity created by the Spirit between Sacred Tradition, Sacred Scripture and the Magisterium of the Church, and these three all imply one another and cannot be separated from each other' in *Restoring Faith in Reason*, eds. and trans. Laurence Paul Hemming and Susan Frank Parsons (London: SCM Press, 2002), p.93. Although not explicit, this 'triple-braiding' outlines a triune structure that appears to be an analogue of the Trinity itself.

[58] Karl Rahner, *Foundations of the Christian Faith* (n.54), pp.431–47.

'lives by faith as a pilgrim [*peregrinator ex fide vivens*]'.[59] It has a reality, at present, entirely based upon a continuous act of faith. As an act of faith it makes judgements and takes decisions, but it has to remain open to being corrected. Christ alone knows because He is the truth. What may be deemed an act of faith may in fact be an act of hubris. And Christian human reality, which still sees through a glass darkly, participates in that wrestling between the need to act in faith and make a judgement, and the need to declare an ignorance such that its acts are potentially always acts of hubris. Here lie the degrees to which the truth of Christ is lost, or obscured, or perfected. If the Church was not caught up with this wrestling for the truth then there would be no mystery, no hiddenness—and mystery is so very dear to Rahner's theology. Only in the final judgement will the truth be known. The Church remains composed of sinful human beings; an office can be no guarantee of grace and does not obviate the need for our ongoing *metanoia*. This is will be examined further when I undertake an examination of ecclesiology in Volume III.

The Catholic teaching hierarchy, with its top down model for the dissemination of knowledge, can give the impression of degrees of proximity to revelation in a similar way to the Protestant model. Only there, as we saw, the proximity to revelation was based upon a separation of Church from the Word of God in Scripture. Here the hierarchy is internal. The double helix description of the relation between Scripture and Church does not in itself prescribe against such a hierarchy, but I wonder again whether there is something counter-factual about such a teaching hierarchy. Before I give my reason let me make clear that, politically, the situation has nothing to do with either feudalism or democracy; and the rejection of the former in favour of the latter. This is not about political organization as such. In fact both our notions of feudalism and modern democracy are heavily indebted to Christian ecclesiologies.[60] My reason for raising the question of whether the teaching hierarchy is counter-factual is to return us to the model I proposed earlier concerning communicative relations, truth, knowledge, and networking communities. The Church is not an hermetically sealed entity. It finds itself always in the context of the world and implicated in any number of

---

[59] Augustine, *City of God*, trans. Henry Bettenson (Harmondsworth: Penguin Books, 1984), Preface, p.5. Bettenson's translation has been amended. He translates *in hoc temporum cursu* less literally as 'in this world of time' and *peregrinator* as 'stranger'. For in-depth studies of the pilgrim trope, and the possible ways of translating *peregrinator* in Augustine see M.H. Clausen, ' "Peregrinatio" and "Peregrini" in Augustine's *City of God*', *Traditio* vol.46, 1991, pp.35–75; Manuela Brito-Martins, 'The Concept of Peregrination in St. Augustine and Its Influences', *International Mediaeval Research: Exile in the Middle Ages*, Laura Napran and Elisebeth van Houts, eds., pp.83–94. More recently there has been a full length study by Miles Hollingworth, *The Pilgrim City: St. Augustine of Hippo and his Innovation in Political Thought* (London: T. & T. Clark, 2010), pp.71–2, 133–4.

[60] As Carl Schmitt recognized in his early monograph *Dictatorship*, trans. Michael Hoelzl and Graham Ward (Cambridge: Polity Press, 2012).

relations with that world. Any notion of its self-understanding emerges in and through such relations. Some of those relations may be confrontational, some downright aggressively negative, some affirmative and some indifferent. It is difficult to understand the changing character of Roman Catholicism under John Paul II, or the changing character of international relations at that time, without examining the way the Pope paid official visits to various countries throughout that papacy.[61] Similarly, albeit negatively, the more recent attention to cases of paedophilia and the Catholic Church, and the political use made of it by former Catholic countries whose governments wish to push through secularization policies, reveal levels of action and interaction between the Church and the context in which it operates. The extensive and lateral networks of communication will always present established hierarchies with problems. Not only will no teaching office ever be able to control the dissemination, reception, adaptation, and citation of the truth it hands down, but any such *ecclesia docens* will also, necessarily be what Karl Barth called an *ecclesia audiens*.[62] The top down account of knowledge and its communication fails to pay adequate attention to the way all communication before, after, and during being given is also received.

To clarify this point with respect to the Catholic Church, let us take, as one example, the Papal Encyclical *Faith and Reason* which appeared in 1998. It origins lay not only in the inner debates and concerns of the Curial Congregations like the Congregation for the Doctrine of the Faith, and Pontifical Commissions, its origins also lay in the teaching of philosophy and ethics by Karol Vojtyla in Lublin, Poland. Furthermore, the Encyclical emerged following a number of seminars conducted at the Castel Gandolfo in the 1980s, seminars to which a series of international philosophers were invited. When the Encyclical finally appeared although it was addressed to the Bishops, it also explicitly addressed a number of other recipients like those involved in the training of future priests and moral theologians. However much it was a document from the Magisterium, in being published it was released not only to the Church in all its various forms and denominations but also to philosophers more generally. Whatever the inner process of discernment within the Magisterium and its subsequent judgements in the Encyclical, it then underwent a critical reception in any number of

---

[61] For a more detailed study of this interaction between the Church and the world, see U. Columbo Sacc, *John Paul II and World Politics: Twenty Years of Search for a New Approach 1978–1998* (Leuven: Peeters, 1999).

[62] It is interesting to note John Paul II, in his Encyclical *Faith and Reason* alludes to how 'the requirements of the Magisterium have not always been followed with the readiness of spirit desired' in *Restoring Faith in Reason* (n.61), p.101. The Encyclical also demonstrates the way the Teaching Office has to engage, with modern philosophies in this instance, in order to come to a proper judgement and even, if necessary, exercise censorship. It is an active Office only insofar as it is also a responsive Office.

countries throughout the world that constituted another discernment process and further sets of judgements. To name only some of the more prominent publications in English, the Encyclical was reviewed in *The Tablet* in the summer of 1999[63] and, in September 2000, *New Blackfriars* published a special issue dedicated to the issues raised and invited essays from leading Catholic thinkers. A further collection of essays was edited in the States by Timothy L. Smith and published in 2001.[64] Then a new translation of the Latin text into English was prepared and a further volume of critical essays and comments appeared in 2002.[65] And I am literally only skimming the surface here. But these critical essays drew attention to issues such as: the relationship between the Pope's ecclesial statements and the individual philosophical viewpoint of Karol Vojtyla; the unnuanced account of truth; the multiple and different ways in which the term 'philosophy' was being used; the modern genealogy of the whole faith and reason debate; and the naming of certain accredited 'philosophers' such as John Henry Newman and Edith Stein, who had either recently been canonized (Stein) or were in the process thereof (Newman).

As I said the Church is not an hermetically sealed entity. Any publication leaves the control of its authors and is catapulted well beyond any circumscribed intentions by those authors. That is the nature of communication.[66] And the truth or lack of it within that communication is either forgotten because it fails to raise the interest of a sufficient number of people or it is publicly discussed and evaluated (with no one conclusion being draw). No one can police the boundaries of a communication. So any theological pursuit for 'pure doctrine' is in effect the chasing of rainbows, this side of the eschaton. We can never overcome the God-given finitudes of human thinking and language. And the God-given nature of these finitudes requires more humility in any theological task about what can be achieved. Anticipating an analysis I will undertake in a moment, we could say, like Paul, that with the Encyclical *Faith and Reason* we have an example of 'the word of God, which is at work [*energeitai*—is energizing] in you believers' (1 Thes.2.13).

---

[63] By Anthony Kenny, *The Tablet*, 26th June, 1999, pp.874–6.

[64] *Faith and Reason*, ed. Timothy L. Smith (Chicago: St. Augustine's Press, 2001).

[65] *Faith in Reason* (n.61). This collection of essays included contributions from other Churches—the Lutheran Church and the Orthodox Church.

[66] Of course, such a view does not prevent a Church with the binding authority of a Teaching Office from exercising its powers of exclusion through various means: dismissal from a job being paid for, financially supported by or closely associated with the Church; placing publications on an *Index liborum prohibitorum*; refusing to grant a licence to teach; ultimately, excommunication. But it is instructive, and relevant to the processes of discernment that I have been drawing attention to, that Marie-Dominique Chenu's book *La Saulchair: Une école de la théologie* (Paris: Étoiles, 1937) was placed by Pope Pius XII on the *Index* in 1942 only later to be taken off by the Fathers of the Second Vatican Council.

As I said, the double helix description of the life of Christ proclaimed and worked out through the double-braiding of the Scripture and the Church does not prescribe for or against any particular form of Church government. But within the context of the communicative networks of relation whereby neither Scripture nor Church can be isolated objects or activities, the double helix description would point to the seepages and syncretisms (evolutionary biologists would say 'adaptations') that greatly qualify any hierarchical control within the circulations of continual cultural, historical, and geographical transformations. Top down theological communication is always already infected by bottom up communications and myriad tangential relations. Theology, in the way I have defined it in terms of and in the context of prayer knows neither hierarchy nor distinction between clerical and lay persons. But I recognize this does raise the question of authority, which is the third of the basic elements of *theo-poiesis* I need to outline.

RECAP

Allow me to recap, for we have travelled some way here. In Chapter 5 I spoke of two inseparable characteristics of theological praxis: a) that it treats because it is a participation in truth, and b) that it is a proclamation or continuing dissemination of the communication of that truth. We have examined now something of both the character of that truth and proclamation—though there is always more to say. But I also said that these inseparable characteristics demand the cultivation of a discernment that combines the attentiveness of prayer with judgement, an active and responsive listening with a critical testing. The reason why the hierarchies are important to the Protestant model of the Word of God and the Catholic model of the teaching office is that they each establish an authority governing the relationship between truth and its proclamation. In offering an alternative description of that relationship—a description that I would argue equates more to what in fact occurs (irrespective of institutional governance and the ideology that support it)—where does the authority lie?

JUDGEMENT

If proclamation is intrinsic to the communication of truth, the double-braiding of Scripture and the Church provides the most comprehensive and explicit expression of that truth insofar as the truth is Christ, the Word of God, and the life of Christ that circulates within and constitutes this double-braiding.

All other proclamations have to be weighed and judged by this proclamation by the Scriptural Church. We can only speak in the singular here—of *this* proclamation—because the unity of all the different proclamations by the Scriptural Church find their unity in the single truth that is Christ and the single teaching of this truth by the Spirit of Christ. *Theo-poiesis* has its source, subject, and object in God. Theology as prayer—insofar as it is a response, returning to God that which proceeds from Him while participating in the spiralling operation of His grace—can only concern itself with this Word, the revelation of God by God. But theology even as prayer produces its truth in the flux and flow of human words. It too cannot be extracted from the webs of communicative relations that compose our understanding of the world and our experience within it. Therefore there has to be a continual judgement of human speaking. The truth is learned. It is learned as it is lived. That is the beating pulse of Christian discipleship. As it is learned so there must be a deepening of discernment, a continual reading of the world in the light of Christ and by the breath of the Spirit. Prayer is that activity whereby we bring the world to Christ and Christ to the world; for we live in Christ and our life is hid in Christ insofar as we are submitted to Him who lives in us. The knowledge and the proclamation of theology as prayer find both their source and object in Christ. Theology as prayer is an act of faith, faith that is itself a gift from God to which we entrust ourselves. But this act of faith cannot be totally divorced from other human acts because as faith seeks understanding it must necessarily engage all those human facilities which enable any understanding: sensory perception, emotional experience, imagination, intuition, will, memory, reasoning etc. Illumination does not by-pass the nature of being human; it perfects it.

In his Encyclical *Faith and Reason*, John Paul II, writes: 'Faith permits us to enter the inner mystery [of truth in Christ] and from there develop a coherent comprehension [*cuius congruentum fovet intellectum*].'[67] *Congruens* is an important adjective emphasizing 'suitability'; the comprehension or intelligence developed is suitable or appropriate to our human nature—a nature created by and for God and the truth of His Word.[68] The Encyclical takes

[67] *Faith in Reason* (n.61), p.23.

[68] *Congruere* here parallels the term used by Aquinas that is related to the nature of analogy: *convenire*. The substantive, often translated 'fittingness', is *convententia*. It is a form of argumentation or explanation, *argumenta ex convenientia*, particularly concerning events in salvation history; it points to how things had to be this way rather than any other. Fittingness is then related to necessity and God's providential wisdom. That is, given the nature of God and the limitations of human beings, then it is in this form that God reveals Himself to us as human beings. Seeing what is fitting, like analogical understanding, is a seeing in accordance with faith. We will meet this again with Anselm in the next chapter. For the relation of *secundum convenientiam* with analogy see Gregory P. Rocca, *Speaking the Incomprehensible God: Thomas Aquinas and the Interplay of Positive and Negative Theology* (Washington: Catholic University of America Press, 2004), p.144. On the fittingness, for example, of the manner in which Christ died see Aquinas *Summa theologicae* III[a] q.46 a.4.

great pains to emphasize that since God has made both human creatures and the world, and Christ came as a man into this world, speaking our human language, then there is a divine accommodation to our condition that associates the very human desire to know truth with the revelation of truth in and as Jesus Christ. The act of faith can be understood as a God-given exercise and expansion of our human capacities to feel, imagine, think, reason and understand. As one scholar has observed, this position 'would imply that the very idea of nature involved an openness to fulfilment by grace (and therefore a grace that grace is constitutive of nature)'.[69] There are two necessary caveats here. First, there is an apophatic caveat that God's thoughts are always infinitely beyond our thoughts. Secondly, there is a theologico-existential caveat that grace is 'constitutive' of nature insofar as nature is a God-created phenomenon. But when the creator is excluded from an understanding of creation, which is what takes place with sin (and secularism), and nature can no longer be recognized as a gift, as a *sacramentum*, then although we do not have two different natures, we do have two different understandings of nature: God's view and the human view in which God's view is occluded. Faith operates between these two views, analogically. It cannot attain God's view of nature. Christ is the key to this view, but however much the *telos* of discipleship is deification we do not become Christ. And yet, faith affirms nature as God's gift and seeks to understand as fully as possible God's view of that nature in and through Christ. Beyond the knowledge to be obtained about the nature, composition, and order of things in this world, there is a further knowledge that is hidden. Hidden, that is, because it lies beyond all accommodations possible to human capabilities. Only faith enters into that which is hidden and can only be revealed to us, and in this way it perfects those very human capabilities themselves. As such, the theo-logic required in theological discourse as prayer is not of a different order of logical analysis than might be required in disciplines as diverse as philosophy or theoretical physics; but it is a logic orientated towards thinking through questions and examining notions which are given in and through faith in Christ.

If human beings are by nature creatures who desire to know and to understand, in fact possibly among all other creatures the only creatures who know they know and understand themselves understanding; if through the rise and fall of numerous civilizations and countless languages human beings have developed sophisticated sign systems for the communication, sharing, examination, and investigation into meaning; and if truth is written into the very fabric of creation by the Creator whose initial acts were the very communication of His love—then all the expressions of this human desire and this hidden truth, expressions as various as poetry, mathematics, and the design

[69] *Faith in Reason* (n.61), Eilert Herms, 'Objective Truth: Relations between Truth and Revelation in the Encyclical *Fides et ratio*', pp.206–24, p.200.

of buildings and cities, are responses and participations in a vast circulation of communicative relations which find their apex and answer in Christ. From Aristotle to René Girard, philosophers have recognized that human beings are imitative creatures; that is, we learn, understand, and communicate through representing, copying, and exchanging. In the last chapter I alluded to mirror-neurons as the biological basis for such imitative behaviour. Theology as a discourse enters into and expands that circulation and imitative exchange by making manifest, by the Spirit, what is hidden; by drawing, by the Spirit and in faith, all things back to the whence from which they came; by guiding, by the Spirit of truth, all things deeper into truth. Faith requires us to understand; belief seeks the certainty of knowing. As I said, we cannot attain such certainties, but 'the dynamic force which exists in faith itself'[70] cannot come to rest until in finds its rest in the truth of God.

What this means is that every Christian as a bearer of the Word is called to be a theologian. Every Christian as a bearer of the Word is called to be both a teacher and a hearer of the Word. Every Christian as a having faith in that Word seeks to understand the meaning of that faith, the substance of what is hoped for and believed. In obedience, which is an entrustment to listening to and discerning the call, there is a commission and a duty. And yes, there are people specifically trained for the office of teacher, those who have shown they possess certain providential gifts and the vocation. There is a training; intellectual disciplines that can be learnt and which facilitate our understanding of the faith. And those so trained can assist other members of the Church in seeking to understand their faith and assist also in making judgements about the myriad communications within which we are all involved; enabling a process of discernment. But we are all called to pass on that which we have received; to proclaim the good news; to speak the truth publicly. In being called we are also sent. And who knows who speaks more truly, who teaches more effectively, who judges more accurately—the silent widow who Jesus pointed out in the Temple who gave away all she had and became as testimony to devotion and trust that overrides the specificities of time and culture (Mark 12. 41–4; Luke 21.1–4), or the theologian with his multi-volume dogmatics, or even, dare we say, the Pope with his encyclicals? Only God can answer this.

We can appreciate something of what I am trying to convey here of the non-hierarchical reception, response, calling out and sending forth in the opening of Paul's *First Letter to the Thessalonians*:

> For we know, brethren beloved by God, that he has chosen you [*tēn eklogēn umōn*]; for our gospel came to you not only in word [*en logō*], but also in power and in the Holy Spirit and with full conviction [*plērophoria pollē*] . . . And you

---

[70] Restoring *Reason in Faith* (n.61), p.151.

became imitators [*mimētai*] of us and of the Lord, for you received the word [*logon*] in much affliction, with joy inspired by the Holy Spirit; so that you became an example [*tupos*] to all the believers in Macedonia and Achaia. For not only has the word of the Lord sounded forth [*exēchētai o logos tou Kuriou*] from you in Macedonia and Achaia, but your faith in God has gone forth [*exelēluthen*] everywhere, so that we need not say anything. (1 Thes.1.4–8)

The Church is immersed in the world in all its temporal and topographical materiality. It is constituted in and through multiple forms of relation, as also are each of its members. Clusters and conglomerations of these relations are drawn out by God and drawn together to compose the *ekklesia*—those, literally, who are called out. Again the Greek is included here not to be clever but to demonstrate important Pauline nuances that are not available in the translation.

Observe that philological and auditary association between those who are God's chosen *eklogē* and the *logos*—the choosing is an act within the Logos itself, the Logos externalizing and communicating itself, if you like, in and as mission. As Christ was sent so we are sent; as the Spirit proceeds from both the Father and the Son, so, in the Spirit we process outwards.[71] And *logos* reverberates throughout this passage: as the words spoken by Paul and later as the word of the Lord such that those who are the externalization of the Word (*exlogē*) become those who 'sound forth' (*exēchētai*) the word of the Lord to people in the rest of Macadonia and the more southern province of Achaia, and whose faith 'has gone forth' (*exelēluthen*) everywhere. It is not just the logos reverberating throughout this passage it is also the dynamic of sending out (*ek*). The verb *exēcheomai* from which we get *exēchētai* picks up on the auditory associations in Paul's very language, only the sounds are now amplified and emitted. This is the deponent form of the verb to publish, *exēcheo*. Etymologically, this verb is also associated with the homonym *ekcheo*—to spill, to pour out, to stream out. It relates to the other liquid metaphors often used by Paul to describe the economy of salvation within Christ himself. That is, the pouring out (*kenosis*) of Christ in the incarnation and the filling up of Christ (*plēroma*) in the fullness of the Godhead. The activity of the Church at Thessalonica, the imitation of both Paul and the Lord, is a participation in this liquid circulation of the Logos. This gives a spiritual gravitas to 'imitation'

---

[71] In this way, of course, Christian proclamation is inseparably bound with the Trinitarian perichoresis of *missio* and *processio*. In his Trinitarian theology, von Balthasar strongly emphasizes that *missio* proceeds from *processio*, and that this is at the very heart of what it is to pray. '[T]he Son's *missio* is his *processio* extended [through desire, *verlangert*] in 'economic' mode; but whereas in his *processio* he moves towards the Father in receptivity and gratitude, in his *missio* ... he moves away from Him towards the world.' *Theo-Drama: Theological Dramatic Theory* III, trans. Graham Harrison (San Francisco: Ignatius Press, 1992), p.332; *Theodramatik: Zweiter Band* (Einsiedeln: Joahnnes Verlag, 1978), p.356. It is Christ who, in this perichoretic movement, prays, and all our prayer takes place within His.

[*mimēsis*]. It does not signify just copying, but enacting, performing, participating. What is translated as 'became imitators' is more 'became those who
echo albeit in their own fashion the actions seen in and expressed by' Paul
and the Lord.[72] But these imitative performances are done in and through
the Word and bring forth further amplifications of that Word. The communicative relations of this church are folded within the divine communication
whose work is governed by relational movement expressed in the prepositions ('to', 'in', 'with', and 'from'). The final verb *exelēluthen* is the perfect
indicative tense of *exercomai*. It suggests an ongoing event like the expanding
concentric ripples in a pond when a pebble is dropped, a reaching out which
creates new possibilities for becoming. The faith of the Thessalonians goes
'everywhere', permeating all aspects of the pagan and secular world, and in
this way transforming them.

The church at Thessalonica did, in all likelihood, possess an internal structure with a leader. But it is the activity of the Church as a whole which Paul
calls attention to. The disseminating work of the Church takes its authority to
act only in part from the authority of Paul. Earlier I pointed to a phrase that
Paul uses to describe the Church at Thessalonica in which he explicitly tells
them it is 'the word of God, which is at work [*energeitai*—is energizing and
actualizes[73]] in you believers' (1 Thes.2.13). It is the dynamism of a responsive
faith to the directions of the Spirit that authenticates the activity, and this well
before there was any New Testament canon—although there was a gospel, a
message of salvation in Christ. The form and nature of this 'Gospel' is still a
matter of debate. There were certainly collections of the Lord's sayings, oral
testimonies by the apostles and probably the narrative beginnings of what
would become the Gospels. The seal of this activity's truth—for ultimately
all authority is Christ's—is the power that accompanies the word, that energizes and actualizes it, and the 'full conviction' that evidences the presence
and activity of the Holy Spirit. The Greek here, *plērophoria pollē*, is rich with
spiritual suggestiveness and a poetic gem for its assonance and alliterative
rhythm. If we break it down: *pollē* is the intensifier—many times over, multiple: a multiplicity in the way Michel Serres uses that biological and quantum
understanding of the word to explore creation itself (see Chapters 5 and 9).
Then we have another association back to Paul's pneumatic vocabulary cen-
tred upon the divine *plerōma* with the noun *plērophoria*. The noun occurs
four times in the New Testament (here, Col.2.2, and Heb.6.11 and 10.22).
The verbal form *plērophoreo* is found six times (Luke 1.1, Rom.4.21 and 14.5,
Col.4.12, 2 Tim.4.5 and 4.17). The verb carries the meaning of things to do or

---

[72] In 1 Thes. 2.14 the 'imitation' is also of other churches of God in Judea all of whom are 'in Christ'—the 'in' is a locative dative: Christ is a realm.

[73] In Aristotle, *energia* expresses 'actualization' in distinction to *dunamis* which expresses 'possibility'. See *Metaphysics* Book IX, 6, 1048a, 37, 6–10.

accomplish (Luke 1.1, 2 Tim.4.5 and probably 4.17), but in Paul it is always both an affective and cognitive activity associated with truth: to be totally convinced, to be completely persuaded, to be fully assured. The word is nearly always found in relation to a work of God (Rom.4.21, Col.4.12). But let me add one more connotative layer here. The English words 'euphoria' and 'dysphoria' each add a prefix to a Greek word which derives from the verb *pherō*—to bear, endure, carry (away), bring (forth). With *plērophoria*, I suggest, we have word concerning participation in the Christ, the fullness of God. There is an unmistakable recognition, a knowledge, carried within, borne by, brought forth in Paul's word because of the way that word participates in the *plerōma* of Christ. This recognition, that is both affective and cognitive, is the sign of that word's authenticity and its truth.

No ecclesial office and no sacred text can bestow this recognition, this religious experience. It only issues from and in a right relation to the truth itself. But the Church, and all its ecclesial offices, is absolutely central to the discernment of this recognition and the Scripture is absolutely key to identifying the characteristics of such a recognition for it is the testimony of those who have themselves experienced and been in that right relation to the truth. As I said, the 'recognition' is not only cognitive it is affective; that is, it bears an emotional charge, it creates an emotional community. We will be treating emotions and experience throughout this project, for the moment it is only necessary to appreciate the way emotion concerns our embodied conditions in profound ways. To be affected is a somatic condition. I have drawn attention to the affectivity in Paul's language (as I did in the earlier chapters with respect to Cyril of Jerusalam, Hugh of St. Victor, and Philip Melanchthon). Paul's language is one of assurance, the language of being energized, the language of power: the church at Thessalonica receives the word 'in much affliction' and with joy.

If the 'recognition' of truth was not just a personal relation, if it were a matter for cognition, then criteria could be drawn up concerning such cognitions and their translation into propositions. And the propositions could then be ordered into a doctrinal confession. But this is not the nature of the truth we have been examining, and this affective operation accompanying 'recognition' makes discernment by the Church and by the Scriptures necessary. It cannot be just a subjective matter—there is any number of pathologies generated by the passions and manifest in the passions, as Melanchthon was aware. Religious enthusiasms and fanaticisms are all rooted in the affective conditions of being human. There needs to be a process for distinguishing between the visions of Joan of Arc and the schizophrenic voices of the serial killer Peter Sutcliffe.

Of course Joan of Arc was burnt at the stake for heresy and one might think, then, that the discernment process went awry. But who knows? In the closing scenes of Jean-Luc Besson's film, *The Messenger: The Story of Joan of*

Arc [1999], Jeanne starts to receive visitations from a dark supernatural figure (played by Dustin Hoffmann). He shows her he can appear as the Christ-figure of her earlier visions, but now he accuses her of pride and puts her visions down to psychological disturbance. In the Cast List he is named Conscience, but he is far more complex than such an inner moral faculty. As her trial begins, this figure acts internally to intensify her torment and self-doubt to the point that she confesses to him that all her actions did proceed from pride and that she had sinned gravely. He then asks her a simple question—'Are you ready?'—to which she answers that she is. He absolves her and the scene that follows shows her being driven away in a cart and burnt at the stake in agony. But the film does not end there. Had it ended there then we have all been deceived by how Jeanne's life has been presented within the film, the ardour of her conviction and the miracles that have been wrought through her for France, the national body, through and upon her physical body. And the Devil has won. But, filming through the flames that have just enveloped her face, the camera's final shot is a slow zoom towards a close-up on an old stone crucifix on a church roof. The film fades out. In the silence that follows and on a black screen, white lettering fades in and out again, three times. The first fade in: 'Joan of Arc was burnt on May 30th, 1431. She was nineteen years old.' Second fade in: 'She was canonized by the Vatican . . .' Third fade in: 'five hundred years later'. The discernment of the truth, the emergence of the truth from its hiddenness, Heidegger would say (for in Greek, truth is *alētheia*, a negative of *lēthē*, forgetfulness), can take a long time.

From Chapter 2 we can recall Beryl Smalley's observation on the medieval view that 'The Holy Spirit speaks through the mouths of St. Gregory the Great and of St. Bernard of Clairvaux when they expound the Scripture.' This too can be understood as an interpretative possibility only on the basis of a discernment over many years (not quite so many in the case of St. Bernard) of a divine speaking to the Church in and through these authors.

It would seem that an application of the Scriptural observation that 'by their fruits you shall know them' a judgement might be easily arrived at. But I am not treating all actions at this point, I am only examining the necessary discernment processes for theology as prayer; the discernment with respect to that theology's recognition and dissemination of truth. What I am trying to clarify and demonstrate is that two descriptions for this discernment, the Protestant one and the Catholic one, are not adequate descriptions. That the doctrine of *sola Scriptura*, on the one hand, and the Teaching Office, on the other, are reductive forms of the complex issues involved in the networks of communicative relations within which both readings of the Scriptures and the operations of the Church circulate. Theology that offers itself as prayer, as a participation in the relation with truth established by *theo-poiesis*, has to be discerned across these networks of communicative relations. The only authority it has must be an authority it bears, carries, and brings forth in the transformative *plērophoria pollē* it affects in its 'sounding forth' and in its 'imitation'. Proclamation, which issues from the life of Christ within that double-braiding of Scripture and Church, a life which is shared with all of creation even though there may be little recognition of the creation and maintenance of that life in God,[74] is *kērygma*—and *kērygma* is the summons to conviction, conversion, and change.

To employ a judicious term by Jean-Luc Marion, discernment, like faith seeking understanding, is an 'endless hermeneutics'[75] or perhaps more accurately an ongoing hermeneutics within an eschatological trajectory. It is a knowledge accumulated through the praxis of prayer which is, in turn, an *imitatio Christi*. In short, discernment is inseparable from discipleship and cannot be divorced from spiritual development or sanctification. In this way it both employs reasoning with respect to embodied and affective experience. The seventh-century Christian ascetic, John Climacus, in his famous treatise *The Ladder of Ascent*, treats the ascetic life and the acquisition of the virtues in twenty six steps. The final step is a chapter called 'Discernment'. As Climacus defines it: 'discernment is ... a solid understanding of the will of God at all times, in all places, in all things ... an uncorrupted conscience. It is pure perception.'[76] Discernment concerns attunement—a term that will be used frequently and developed when I discuss our 'immersion' in the world in Volume II. The attunement here is between our understanding and willing and God's; our seeing and the way God sees. It is thoroughly analogical because there is neither univocity or equivocity between our understanding and willing and God's; our seeing and the way God sees. There is similarity within an ever deepening dissimilarity. Discernment is not a solitary but an ecclesial practice. The discernment of a vocation to the priesthood, for example, demands the submission of one's life to an inspection by others with experience of discerning past vocations, as well as our own introspection. What is being discerned is the calling upon and within our life; not just to be Christians and follow Christ but how that being a Christian and following Christ is being worked out in the practices of everyday life: family, friends, employment, inconveniences, tiredness, blessings etc. Theology that offers itself as prayer, as proclamation, as participation in the unfolding of truth in the Church, in the world, has to undergo the same inspection. The work has to be judged. As I said, all Christians are called to be theologians insofar as, first, there is a commission to speak out boldly (what, in Greek for both the writer of the

---

[74] Although life is shared with all of creation, there must be a qualitative difference of 'life' in Christ. This is resurrection life, eternal life, whereas the life shared by all creation is a fallen life, a life affected by sin. I return to this in Chapter 9.

[75] See Jean-Luc Marion, 'The Face: An Endless Hermeneutics', *Harvard Divinity Bulletin* 28, no.2–3 (1999), 9–10.

[76] John Climacus, *The Ladder of Divine Ascent*, trans. Colm Luibheid and Norman Russell (New York: Paulist Press, 1982), p.229.

Gospel of St. John and Paul call *parrēsia*) and, secondly, because faith is not irrational but a use of a theologically ordered reasoning in groping to understand more fully what is given in faith.

In the Chapter 8 I will elaborate further on both these aspects, for the moment I only wish to emphasize, going back to what was said earlier about truth and proclamation, that everything we do, say, write, and relate to (from the way we each drive a car and interact with other people to the clothes we wear and the gestures we make) 'speak' and in speaking add to the circulation of communicative relations. The Christian 'speaks' theologically; they can do nothing else not only because of a commitment to following Christ, but the fact their lives are hidden in Christ.[77] That speaking will involve truth-claiming, proclamation (*parrēsia*) and faith's ongoing conversation with understanding. But then there are some of us whose ministry to everyone else in the Church lies in trying to describe in the best use of language we can (which is a language straining towards poetry because poetry is the most precise use and complex understanding of language there is) that speaking which all do in relation to the journeying of faith towards a more perfect understanding. What I am saying about judgement and discernment is that both the call to minister in this distinctive way to the Church, and the product, the *poiesis*, of that ministry (the theology we write, the theology which cannot be divorced from prayer) has to be submitted to the Church for its attention. That attention may be affirmative, critical, negative, wish to add supplements or caveats or a mixture of these responses. But all the responses are the practising of discernment, the practising of judgement, with respect to whether or to what extent the transformative operation of *kerygma* can be found in the work. The authority for doing the work, then, is both Scriptural and ecclesial for it is based in a 'calling' that can only come from the Word of God and be discerned as such by the Church. The discernment and judgement of the work is also both Scriptural and ecclesial (though that does not exclude other institutional bodies from engaging with the work and aiding the process of discernment). And the Church here is evidently all Christian denominations; for the dissemination of the work, by a publisher, is global. In that sense the project *becomes* ecumenical; though its origins lie in a distinctly Anglo-Catholic standpoint: mine.[78] Within the ambit of published work also lie a whole spectrum of others—Gnostic, agnostic, of other faiths, and none. Their discernment too, which cannot have the authority of Scriptural and ecclesial discernment, may nevertheless yield important and even formative insights.

---

[77] Of course, that does not mean as Christians all our 'speaking' is righteous. We remain sinners; we can then 'speak' sinfully in ways that demand repentance and no amount of self-justification will deliver us of the disturbance in *our* relations to Christ that results from sin. I italicize 'our' because even our sin does not disturb Christ's own relation with us.

[78] On the complexity of theological standpoint see Graham Ward, *Cultural Transformation and Religious Practice* (Cambridge: Cambridge University Press, 2004), pp.72–116.

As a coda to and a development of that last point: if then creation proceeds from God through and by His Logos; if then all things exist in Christ and refer to Him as the revealed truth of God; if all communication, and relations in and through communication, bear an implicit witness to this truth, a witness made explicit when communication and relations are orientated by faith in him; and if, finally, this proclamation is disseminated such that the Church hears, receives, and makes its judgement with respect to the truth that is Christ, the Church universal—then this has profound methodological implications for theological *poiesis*. Of course Scripture and the writings that have proceeded from the Church have, as I have said, priority—because they bear the most explicit and comprehensive witness to the truth in and as Christ. But truth can be gathered from a thousand planes, among myriads of flowering sources: literature, film, architecture, philosophy, painting, sport, advertising, song etc. Theology as a discourse can move across these planes; as a discourse it is already implicated in the intertextuality of all speaking and writing, all communication and relation. But, more significantly, theology need not be sectarian and can be prevented from being sectarian by realizing the textual economies within which it operates. To capture this nexus of communicative relations theology has to be engaged (see Chapter 4).

Consider the depiction of St. Jerome in his study by Antonello da Messina, painted in 1475 that I alluded to in Chapter 2.[79] Lodged solidly in the centre, Jerome sits upright in robes of a cardinal red, book in hand resting on a wooden desk. Behind and in front of him there is shelving and cupboards of a similar wood. But the study is like a stage set. It stands on a raised dais and has to be reached by a short stairway from the tiled floor. The study is framed by the interior of a church or a monastery. On the right, there is a colonnade of pillars that leads down to a window opening on the green hills outside. On the left, the shelving and cupboard in front of Jerome forms an arch and through that arch we see another window with an open view of the same countryside. Above the study, in a stone vaulted ceiling, clerestory windows view a hyacinth sky. An arched window through which we are peering frames the whole theatrical scene. Two birds and a bowl stand on the window ledge. The stylization, focussing the red-robed figure at the very centre of the painting and the white pages of what are no doubt the Scriptures, sums up what I have been presenting not only as the relationship between Scripture and the Church, but theology as open on all sides to the world. Theology, which is depicted here as the theologian reading the Scriptures in the lofty structures of the church, receives the world from all sides into the cool, but warmly

---

[79] I owe both this reference and this idea to John Perry who used the painting for the cover of the programme for a conference at the McDonald Centre in Oxford in 2012 on 'Christianity and the Flourishing of Universities'.

coloured stone of its structured and even geometric interior, as if what is corporeally sensed passes over into what is spiritually sensed. That openness is significant. In such an openness, that must always bear the risk of being violated, being deceived, being used, there is no space for denominations as gated communities. There is no space either for continuing self-illusion. There is a vital need, as we shall explore in Volume III, for cultivating a sense of belonging, for the structures of specific locations and the materiality of place, but the theologian cannot prescribe, as Karl Barth once did, that 'as Evangelical dogmatics it will necessarily involve opposition both to Roman Catholicism and also to the Neo-Protestantism which is repudiated by the decisions of the Reformers. And it will continually have to unfold this opposition at every point.'[80] The theologian must, as Barth goes on to state, employ all means 'to the end of awakening the Church to a new obedience to its Lord and a new loyalty to itself',[81] but not by way of creating mythic, reified enemies. In Christ there are no denominations and a theology orientated towards a creative *poiesis* that, by grace and faith, participates in Christ's own *theo-logos* and *theo-poiesis* must bear an ecumenical witness that confronts the brokenness of the Church with all the sternness of the face of the Pantocrator who judges from above.

Theology, as that reading of the Scriptures in and through the Church, the universal Church, must allow itself to be led by the Spirit to engage with the world with all its intellectual inherited resources, whether Catholic, Protestant, or Orthodox, and engaged with and alongside the other monotheistic traditions into which it is folded, Jewish and Islamic. We will treat this more fully and systematically in Volume IV. Barth continues: 'If dogmatics treats Roman Catholicism and Neo-Protestantism and, reaching further back, Arianism and Pelagianism as heresies, it does not do so, of course, without independent examination and judgement.'[82] That examination and judgement is necessary, as I have pointed out. But it belongs to the universal Church as it earnestly and endlessly seeks to be obedient to the truth in Christ to undertake such an examination and make such a judgement. Only then can a 'heresy' be declared.[83] The pivoting fulcrum here is the labour of discernment in and through prayer, across the histories and geographies traversed by the Spirit that leads the Church into all truth. As Barth rightly said, 'dogmatics ha[s] always been on the watch';[84] it always will be. But the

---

[80] Karl Barth, *Church Dogmatics*, I.2 (n.27), p.810.   [81] Ibid.   [82] Ibid.

[83] See Maggie Ross, *Silence: A User's Guide* (London: Darton, Longman and Todd, 2014): 'If orthodoxy in early Christianity is about maintaining the paradoxes, then the concept of heresy is itself heretical; linear doctrinal and dogmatic statements destory the paradoxes ... Any doctrinal statement is virtual and dead, a product of self-conscious language; it flattens ... the polyvalent insight of the deep mind into two dimensions and kills it' (pp.84–6).

[84] Karl Barth, *Church Dogmatics*, I.2 (n.27), p.807.

dogmatician watches, like Jerome, by keeping his and her eyes reading the Scriptures in and through a Church that is open to the world. And that means that sometimes the Church has to hear and receive a judgement upon itself made by that world; because the Spirit blows where it will.

Our theologies, like all our creaturely productions, are culturally and historically informed. That is why, in seeking after the truth that is universal and eternal, we must always seek afresh, hearing and receiving, responding, and relating to what is God doing now in our time. That means theology, like all creaturely productions, inevitably bends towards what is in fashion, what is fashionable. At times there has been an emphasis placed upon sacramental life, at times upon Christology; at times the Trinity has received more attention, or theological anthropology or ecclesiology. At the moment, for example, the plethora of books being published on political theology and pneumatology is a sign of the times in which we Christians live. But the Church in its labouring to discern and in its passing of judgement has always to recall its ignorance, the fragility of its discernment, the necessary limitations of its judgements.

8

Faith Seeking Understanding

Life

The Psalmist prays: 'In thy righteousness, give me life!' (Psalm 119.40)

If theology is a proclamation of life in Christ, as that life issues from the double-helix of Scripture and the Church, then the oxygen and blood which sustains that life is faith seeking understanding. There is no animal life without oxygen and blood, and the symbiotic relation between them. There is no life in Christ—where my breathing is also the breathing of the Spirit of God within me—without participation by faith in Christ; and that participation 'seeks'; and what it seeks is to understand what it is to be more deeply hidden with Christ in God. In that hiddenness there is knowledge and understanding. The main title of this chapter is a translation of Anselm's *fides quaerens intellectum* which we will go on to examine, and it appears in a slightly different guise in Augustine's Sermon 43: 'Believe that you may understand (*Crede, ut intelligas*)'. Concepts like faith, understanding and their conjunction have a history, just as they have a language and a grammar from which they emerge. We might call these the historical and philological contexts of the concepts. But as concepts I wish to emphasis that we are naming actions and processes. As, we observed in Chapter 1, faith can be a substantive when we talk about 'the Faith' as the contents of what the Christian Church believes (summed up in one of the Creeds or the Articles of the Faith). But neither faith nor understanding here are substantives in this way. They are governed by the verb 'seeking'; they are active and engaged, physically, emotionally, intellectually, and socially. Viewed as such these concepts have and generate an operational context. I want to map something of that operational context before exploring the other historical and semantic contexts, because the operational context picks up on and develops a number of other themes that I touched upon in the last chapter and indeed the central claim throughout this project: that doctrine is lived.

HIDDENNESS

The first theme is 'hiddenness'. *Quaerens* is the present participle of the verb *quaero* that is to seek as in to enquire after, to strive for, to win by effort, to ask, desire, require, or demand. These are all intellectual, affective, and therefore somatic operations with respect to what is not self-evidently there: the invisibilities that we continually negotiate.[1] A verse from the *Letter to the Hebrews* puts this succinctly: 'Now faith is the substance [*upostasis*] of things hoped for, the evidence of things [*pragmatōn elegchos*] not seen' (KJV). In Greek, there are juridical associations with 'evidence' (*elegchos*) in keeping with a letter concerned about the Jewish laws of sacrifice and priesthood, and their fulfilment in Christ. It is evidence as proof, as a test of the validity of something that is being alluded to. The noun can even mean 'conviction' and 'judgement'. *Pragmata* also belongs to this semantic province. It is a business word, an official, public office word. It can mean 'matter', or 'reality', or 'doing'. In the context of what is not seen these two words compose less a paradox (which most English translations suggest) than a suggestion of an image on earth of a truth in heaven. If this appears quite Platonic in background, then again it is in keeping with an epistle concerned with types and realities. The image is a participation in the 'substance' (*upostasis* or 'real nature') of that truth, a form or *Gestalt* (to use von Balthasar's language) of the truth. In the same *Letter*, the Jewish temple on earth is an image or form of the heavenly Temple and the Levitical priesthood on earth is an image or form of the heavenly priesthood of Christ 'after the order of Melchizedek'. What this suggests is that faith handles certain manifestations of heavenly truths accommodated or fitted to earthly means. This develops what I said in the last chapter about Pope John Paul II's use of *congruere* and Aquinas's use of *convenire* and 'conformity' (*adaequatio*). These 'evidences' are not themselves visible to the human eye. In fact, to the human eye they are not then 'evidence' of anything; just things themselves. But through the eye of faith things themselves become evidences; visible traces of what is as yet invisible. Faith is not then some intellectual suicide leaping into the void, but an intellectual and affective, somatic engagement with the invisible in the visible. We saw

---

[1] These invisibilities are manifold. They range from the empirical invisibilities of our life on this planet to the intellectual invisibilities of thought, imagination. Those sciences leading current investigations into the nature of things are leading to an implosion of scientific realism. They are treating the very molecules of emotions and the dark energies of the material—neither of which is visible as such. They are made visible through highly abstract and computerized mathematics. Similarly, increasing attention in neuroscience to the complex operations of neurotransmitters with respect to thought, feeling, and the autonomic regulation of our bodies, has shown how much is pre-conscious and unconscious. For a deeper investigation into these invisibilites see Graham Ward, *Unbelievable: Why We Believe and Why We Don't* (London: I.B.Taurus, 2015, pp.192–200. I am using some of the material in that investigation in what follows in this chapter and Chapter 8.

this sensing of the invisible when we examined Cyril of Jerusalem's pedagogy as embodied in the liturgy of baptism. What is crucial about hiddenness as mystery—and *musterion* in Greek becomes *sacramentum* in Latin—is that it is an aspect of this world.

The philosophical project of phenomenology begins here. In his ground-breaking *The Idea of Phenomenology*, Edmund Husserl defines the philosophical approach along Kantian lies: phenomenology 'questions things [*Sachen*] themselves'.[2] It creates an empty space in order to arrive at that which makes the consciousness by which intuitions are grasped possible, through a foundational bracketing out of content and context (*epoché*). When we arrive at his late work, *The Crisis of European Sciences*, Husserl presents the new philosophical approach as 'starting from natural world-life, and . . . asking after the how of the world's pregiveness [*der Vorgegebenheit der Welt*]'.[3] To approximate to this 'pregiveness' phenomenology performs a series of reductions aimed at recovering the primordial that is not immediately evident. It is in this way that phenomenology concerns itself with 'hiddenness'. Theology pushes this phenomenological enquiry further, but it can do so only by taking the phenomenological method and developing it, as we will see.[4] As Michel Henry, in his own Christian phenomenology, clarifies: phenomenology concerns itself substantially with 'donation, monstration, phenomenolization, unveiling, disclosure, apparition, manifestation, revelation. It cannot go unnoticed that these key words of the discipline of phenomenology are, to a great extent, those of religion—or theology.'[5]

In an important lecture to the *Société française de philosophie* in 1946, the phenomenologist Maurice Merleau-Ponty, having outlined the thesis of his previously published work *The Phenomenology of Perception*, emphasizing the relationship between the visible and the invisible, the transcendent horizons within the immanent, draws a direct comparison between phenomenology and the Christian worldview:

> My viewpoint differs from the Christian viewpoint to the extent that the Christian believes in another side of things where the '*renversement du pour au contre*' takes place. In my view this 'reversal' takes place before our eyes. And

---

[2] Edmund Husserl, *The Idea of Phenomenology*, trans. L. Hardy (Dordrecht: Kluwer Academic, 1999), p.35.

[3] Edmund Husserl, *The Crisis of European Sciences and Transcendental Phenomenology*, trans. D. Carr (Evanston, IL: Northwestern University Press, 1970), p.154.

[4] For a more detailed account of the way theology pushes phenomenology further and, not illegitimately, in terms of phenomenological method itself, see Graham Ward, 'The *Logos*, the Body and the World: On the Phenomenological Border' in Kevin Vanhoozer and Martin Warner, eds., *Transcending the Boundaries in Philosophy and Theology: Reason, Meaning and Experience* (Aldershot: Ashgate Publishing Company, 2007), pp.105–26.

[5] Michel Henry, *Incarnation: Une philosophie de la chair* (Paris: Éditions du Seuil, 2000) p.37. My translation. The whole the first part of Henry's book concerns *le renversement de la phénoménologie*, pp.35–132.

perhaps some Christians would agree that the other side of things must already be visible in the environment in which we live.[6]

Indeed some Christian theologians would agree: to name Marie-Dominique Chenu and Henri du Lubac as just two of them. But for those theologians, and I would concur with their judgement, there is no *renversement* as such, for there is nothing *contre*.[7] Nevertheless, this is a remarkable statement by Merleau-Ponty—a statement that begins by distinguishing phenomenology from Christianity but ends up re-framing both intellectual projects. This was noted in the discussion that followed the lecture. Merleau-Ponty then spelt out one of the implications of his analysis: 'As to mystical experience, I do not do away with that either.'[8] If we accept the 'mystical experience' as the experience of what is hidden, the enigma of the material, then, on Merleau-Ponty's phenomenological terms, who a priori can decide whether with such an experience we are treating 'the effective passage to the absolute' (and therefore a mode of transcendence) or 'only an illusion' (and therefore a mode of immanence)?[9] In fact, throughout Merleau-Ponty's work the Catholic imagination proves difficult to 'bracket out'. It finds expression in phrases like the 'incarnate subject', the 'metaphysical structure of the body', the 'pre-existent *Logos* [a]s the world itself', 'perceptual faith', sensation as 'literally a form of [Eucharistic] communion' and a description of phenomenology's task as revealing the 'mystery of the world'.

In his last published essay, 'The Visible and the Invisible', Merleau-Ponty again insists he is not treating 'an absolute invisible . . . but the invisible of *this* world'[10], underscoring the immanence of his project. In this way he can distinguish between transcendence per se and intentional transcendence. To understand the difference we can take an example Edmund Husserl used in his early work, *Logical Investigations*: a cube.[11] It is an example Merleau-Ponty himself found helpful and used. When we see a cube we do not and cannot perceive its six sides. We can only see two or three. And yet we know that a cube to be a cube has to have six equal sides. In seeing the cube then we 'project' the missing sides in making sense of what we see. In Husserl's terms this apperceptive transcendentalism provides the conditions for the possibility of what is perceived to be, and meaningfully recognized as, a cube. The three of

---

[6] *The Primacy of Perception*, ed. and trans. J.M. Edie (Evanston, IL: Northwestern University Press, 1964), p.27.

[7] Both of these theologians, prominent among those called derogatively *nouvelles théologie* recognized in their readings of Aquinas that the boundaries between nature and grace were malleable.

[8] *The Primacy of Perception* (n.6), p.35.   [9] Ibid.

[10] Maurice Merleau-Ponty, *The Visible and the Invisible*, trans. A. Lingis, ed. C. Lefort (Evanston: Northwestern University Press, 1968), p.151.

[11] *Logical Investigations*, Volume I, trans. J.N. Findlay, ed. Dermot Moran (London: Routledge, 2001), p.310.

four invisible sides are actually present along with the other sides that we can see, but they are concealed *in* the visibility of what is seen. This 'projection' or 'expectation' that posits as co-present in an object that which is invisible *in* its visibility is intentional transcendence—because the meaningfulness of the object goes beyond what is perceived of the object in itself (if indeed we can even see any object at all in itself) to constitute the *idea* of the object.[12] Merleau-Ponty develops this recognition of intentional transcendence into what he calls 'perceptual faith' (*la foi perceptive*).

> Meaning is *invisible*, but the invisible is not the contradictory of the visible: the visible itself has an invisible inner framework (*membrure*), and the invisible is the secret counterpart of the visible, it appears only within it, it is the *Nichtsurpräsentierbar* [unpresentable] which is presented to me as such within the world.[13]

'Perceptual faith' is the seeing of meaningful form (what has been referred to as Merleau-Ponty's 'gestalt ontology')[14] through intentional expectation and projection. If it is a 'faith' in an invisible *logos* that opens horizons of meaning within *phusis*, it is not then some intellectual assent to the unknown that denies material reality. It is a 'faith' that is co-posited with perception itself. Commenting on the play of negativity in this citation from 'The Visible and Invisible' (employing the negative suffix *in* and the *Nichts* that qualifies *urpräsentierbar*),[15] one scholar has observed: 'Merleau-Ponty seeks the 'positive signification of negativity,' that which [. . .] belongs to 'the essence of Christianity'. Yet it is this same fecund negativity which he has missed in the theology he has called 'explanatory'. That kind of theology is thus stopped in its tracks in a tentative thought concerning the central mysteries of Christianity which do not respond to the dual requirement of contesting false absolutes and thinks the Incarnation through to its end'.[16] Thinking through incarnation 'to its end' is exactly the principle that will dictate the systematic theology presented in this project, as will become explicit in Volume II when

---

[12] The British philosopher and novelist, Iris Murdoch, pushes this notion in a Platonic and metaphysical direction when she attests: 'We see parts of things, we intuit whole things.' *Metaphysics as a Guide to Morals* (London: Chatto and Windus, 1992), p.1.

[13] *The Visible and the Invisible* (n.10), p. 215.

[14] See Arne Naess, 'Reflections of Gestalt Ontology', *The Trumpeter* 21, no.1 (2005), 119–28. For a definition of 'gestalt ontology' as it is proposed and sketched in Merleau-Ponty's early work see Forrest W. Williams, Appendix 1: 'Merleau-Ponty's Early Project Concerning Perception' in Maurice Merleau-Ponty, *Texts and Dialogues: On Philosophy, Politics and Cultures*, eds. Hugh J. Silverman and James Barry, Jr. (Atlantic Highlands, NJ: Humanities Press International, 1992), p.147.

[15] Strictly speaking *Nichtsurpräsentierbar* does not translate as 'unpresentable'. What the word points to is deeper that the 'unpresentable'. The German prefix *ur* in *urpräsentierbar* indicates an origin more profound than the unpresentable.

[16] Emmanuel de Saint Aubert, ' "Incarnation change tout." Merleau-Ponty critiques de la "theologie explicative" ', *Archives de Philosophie*, 71.3 (2008), 374.

I treat Christology. So we can learn something from the phenomenological approach that takes the material seriously in its pursuit of the meaningful.[17] Indeed, it can provide a basis for a doctrine of revelation.

The use of theological or quasi-theological language by Merleau-Ponty, even though its reference to the divine is disavowed by Merleau-Ponty himself in favour of immanence, opens the question of the cultural politics that closes off inquiry too early. This is especially so when Merleau-Ponty himself recognized that the phenomenonological enquiry is and will always be incomplete: 'the most important lesson which the reduction teaches us is the impossibility of a complete reduction'.[18] So while judgements always concern the immanent, the immanent itself cannot be a closed realm. And if the immanent is endless and can never be grasped as such, if the immanent is not contained and leaks, then towards what horizons does it tend? Quite simply, it cannot be divorced from and pitted against a construal of the transcendent. Later, Merleau-Ponty wishes to speak of the flesh of the world as 'a pregnancy of possibles, *Weltmöglichkeit*'.[19] One can admit, as Edmund Husserl does explicitly in #58 of his *Ideas*, that absolute transcendence or the transcendence of God must be excluded from the study of phenomenology, which treats only 'a field of pure consciousness'.[20] But theologians readily admit that God is not an object in this world; or a proper name for that matter. So if we take Gregory of Nyssa's view that the 'term "Godhead" is significant of operation, and not of nature',[21] who can draw the line between absolute and intentional transcendence and claim immanence begins and ends here? Who can strictly announce that the invisible is *only* the invisible of this world?

Consider the observation of a more recent French phenomenologist, Jean-Louis Chrétien, who, while respecting that the business of phenomenology is not to prove the existence of God, nevertheless wishes to examine, as early Heidegger did, religious phenomena phenomenologically: 'The invisible before which human being shows itself can range from the radical invisibility of the Spirit to the inward sacredness or power of the visible itself, like a mountain, a star, or a statue.'[22] Of course, the corollary in this line of thought is that what moves us beyond phenomenology and towards a theology of

---

[17] Merleau-Ponty is assisted here by the French language in which *sens* can refer to one of the five senses (the sensible), to that which is meaningful (making sense of), and to that which gives direction (*sens interdit* is a no-entry sign, a one-way street).

[18] *Phenomenology of Perception*, trans. C. Smith (London: Routledge & Kegan Paul, 1962), xv.

[19] *The Visible and the Invisible* (n.10), p.250.

[20] Edmund Husserl, *Ideas: General Introduction to Pure Phenomenology*, trans. W.R. Boyce Gibson (London: Allen & Unwin and Humanities Press, 1931), p.134.

[21] Gregory of Nyssa, 'On "Not Three Gods"', in *Selected Writings and Letters of Gregory, Bishop of Nyssa*, trans. W. Moore and H. Wilson (Grand Rapids, MI: Eerdmans, 1979), p.333.

[22] Jean-Louis Chrétien, 'The Wounded Word: The Phenomenology of Prayer', in *Phenomenology and the 'Theological Turn': The French Debate*, eds. D. Janicaud *et al*. trans. B.G. Prusak (New York: Fordham University Press, 2000), p.150. Translation modified as the

phenomena (which is nothing more or less than a doctrine of creation) is the corporeal itself, the mystery of embodiment, the mystery of flesh: radical incarnation. If, we took the human body rather than a cube as an object for intentional transcendence, then how much more complex and irreducible do the invisibilities become? We will return to this more fully in Volume II.

What is hidden does not belong to another realm behind or beyond this one. The language of 'transcendence' is misleading, as I have already observed in Chapter 4. Furthermore what is hidden is not hidden by divine intention. All things are disclosed, even the deep things of God. In Chrétien's felicitous turn of phrase, human being shows itself *before* this hiddenness: exposed, naked, accountable. As we saw above, when discussing the nature of truth: nothing of God's wisdom is held back from us. But not everything disclosed can be received; we cannot see, or hear, or taste, or smell, or touch clearly. The things of God have to be revealed to us; we have to be illuminated. In God the hiddenness is profound and ultimately impenetrable such that we only approach a comprehension through negation, the *via negativa*. But hiddenness, the invisible within the visible, is a fact of ordinary life and inseparable from the materiality of the world. Hence we believe far more than we know; the basis of certainty (as Wittgenstein understood) is the unprovable.[23] Neuroscientists inform us that our sensory perception and reception is far greater than our consciousness can process. Consciousness may work with only five per cent of what is taken in from the environments we inhabit so that only a tiny portion of the world is adequately lit for our examination and reflection at any one time. These philosophical

French *homme* denotes 'human kind'. Chrétien wishes to explore the 'promise' of transcendence within phenomenology, phenomenologically. It is a promise that traverses immanence. See here *Traversées de l'imminence* (Paris: Les éditions de l'Herne, 1989) and *La Voix nue: Phénoménologie de la promesse* (Paris: Les editions de minuit, 1990). The opening paragraph of this last book could stand as a description of the communicative relations I spoke of in Chapter 5 albeit from the human 'giving voice to' rather than the divine speaking of the Logos. It details the physiology of vocalization, locates speaking with respect to hand-gestures guided by the unknowable (*insaisissable*), and looking (*le regard*) oriented by the invisible. 'All human voicing responds, all inauguration lies in the suffering and the passion beneath the anterior voice which only understands in responding that which precedes and exceeds it' (p.7).

[23] What is an observation in John Paul II's *Faith and Reason*—'in human life truths that are simply believed are more numerous than those acquired by mean of personal recognition' (p.53)—is something of a truism after Gödel's demonstration that undecidables haunt all systems and Heisenberg's quantum physics established the uncertainty and intrinsic randomness that make all natural processes at the microlevel probabilistic rather than deterministic. See here Mark C. Taylor, *The Moment of Complexity: Emerging Network Culture* (Chicago: Chicago University Press, 2001) for an excellent inquiry into what contemporary biology, mathematics, and physics point to: a deeply aporetic reality. Taylor writes: 'The formulation of the laws of thermodynamics and the recognition of the role of probability in natural processes marks the beginning of the end of the dream of certainty that fuelled the modern imagination for over three centuries' (p.115). For Wittgenstein, see *On Certainty*, trans. Denis Paul and G.E.M. Anscombe (Oxford: Blackwell, 1974).

and physiological observations will be important factors when we come to examine the nature of faith (and its relationship to belief) and understanding (and its relationship to knowledge) in Chapter 9.

Nevertheless, from the phenomenological investigations of both Merleau-Ponty and Chrétien we can accept that there is a difference between hiddenness with respect to God and everyday forms of hiddenness. As we saw, Merleau-Ponty wants to make that difference into the stark contrast between absolute and intentional transcendence. For him, there is no striking through or traversal of such a difference. Chrétien, on the other hand, while accepting a difference between 'the radical invisibility of the Spirit' and 'the inward sacredness or power of the visible itself' admits the possibility of a traversal, though not a continuum. To admit of a continuum would be pantheism. This is why Chrétien describes the Spirit as *radically* invisible. The Spirit of God is not of this world; is not corporeal. The strict phenomenologist would judge Chrétien to have transgressed the boundaries of an intellectual science, smuggling in faith by smuggling in the Spirit. Such a venture sullies the purity of phenomenological description for Chrétien's Spirit is not only an interpretation rather than a pure description of the phenomenon, it is also an explanation: that Spirit as *radical* (from the Latin *radix* or 'root') is the explanatory origin of 'the power of the visible itself'. It is in this way that phenomenology opens up the question of revelation.

The idea that phenomenological project is being transgressed is at the heart of Dominique Janicaud's critique of phenomenologists like Chrétien (along with Jean-Yves Lacoste, Jean-Luc Marion, and Michel Henry—whose projects cannot be conflated) who have taken the phenomenological investigation into the terrain of theology and the *topos* of revelation. 'The phenomenologist is neutral, in the sense that he or she is open to the thing itself, without any teleological prejudice than the ideal of rational and scientific truth,' Janicaud writes.[24] But we need to examine the presuppositions of Merleau-Ponty and Janicaud's positions. For Janicaud the phenomenologist's 'neutrality' is an ideal, but the aim of his or her investigation is a description of what is given in the foundational intuition of 'the thing itself'. The illegitimacy of the 'theological turn' is that it violates the descriptive task insofar as the theological interprets the manifestation of the phenomenon, naming it theologically and teleologically (as given by and receiving its significance from God as the revelation of the inaccessible other). The violation of the descriptive task is a

<hr/>

[24] Dominique Janicaud, *Phenomenology and the 'Theological Turn'*, trans. B.G. Prusak (New York: Fordham University Press, 2000), p.48. Janicaud does however note that these theological investigations do go back to Husserl's own work, or more precisely 'the contradictions in Husserl's own *oeuvre*', p.96. For a more recent continuation of Janicaud's investigations into the limits and possibilities of phenomenology see his book *Phenomenology 'Wide Open': After the French Debate*, trans. Charles N. Cabral (New York: Fordham University Press, 2005).

movement beyond the phenomenon itself within its immanent horizons. The philosophical difficulty that Janicaud's conclusions raise is somewhat akin to the philosophical difficulty raised by Merleau-Ponty's conclusions insofar as they share a common assumption: that there is an hermetically sealed realm named the immanent (and this is not demonstrated as such by phenomenology, nor could it ever be demonstrated as I have already pointed out). The philosophical difficulty is this: how do we distil the experience of the phenomenon's appearance, its givenness to consciousness in this intuition (even embodied consciousness), from its representation to consciousness (in concepts, words, language)? As Kant recognized we would have no intuition at all, it would be blind, if it were not already represented to our consciousness. In brief: how is it possible to achieve a pure description that is not already interpreted by the very concepts called forth by the intuition? To be fair, Merleau-Ponty was aware of this fact from the beginning: the 'elementary event [of intuition] is already invested with meaning'[25] and concludes that perception must be 'understood as interpretation'.[26] We can then pose a question to both the radical and unbridgeable difference between in absolute and intentional transcendence in Merleau-Ponty and between 'neutral' description and interpretation in Janicaud: what would be the difference between a necessary and legitimate perception as interpretation, intention always being bound to representation, and the theological point of view as an unnecessary and illegimate interpretation?

The upshot of all this is that the radical and unbridgeable difference found in Merleau-Ponty and Janicaud is not rationally defensible. It is based on an undemonstrated assumption about the enclosure of the immanent and is a move to secure phenomenology as a secular philosophical science. For why should, a priori, the immanent be an end in itself, what Hegel termed a 'bad infinite'? If we follow, and further, Chrétien's phenomenological investigations into the invisible in the visible, the mystery or hiddenness *in* the world, the enigma pertaining to the material, then we need to understand the logic of the difference between common and everyday hiddenness and the hiddenness of the divine such that they are not part of a single continuum (which would in fact nullify the difference entirely in favour of a continuum).

ANSELM

The answer to this problem, in a nutshell, is analogy. Because analogy plays such a fundamental role in this theological project I need to unpack something of what I understand by analogy and show how it can perform its

---

[25] *Phenomenology of Perception* (n.18), p.11.   [26] Ibid., p.42.

necessary work with respect to knowledge of the divine. This will not be my final word on analogy and indeed a long chapter on the analogical world-view in Volume II will add more detail to what I have to say here. In this context, it is sufficient to develop an understanding of analogy that will further our investigation into the crucial role faith seeking understanding plays in the creative production of theological discourse, as a *poiesis*, and in the continuing exploration of that ineradicable 'hiddenness' which is both material and divine. And because the phrase *fides quaerens intellectum* belongs to Anselm and we will be developing an understanding of what is meant by that phrase first with respect to Anselm, let me turn now to Anselm's *Monologium* in order to say something provisional about analogy. I do so because I made a statement above which I did not demonstrate the truth of and yet the whole understanding of 'hiddenness' arises from the claim made by this statement. I claimed: All things are disclosed, even the deep things of God.

Now not everybody who employs the word 'God' would agree with this statement, even those who claim to believe in the Christian God. Certain process theologians and certain interpretations of Hegel's theology would commit the revelation of what is God by God as evolving over time, as subject to all the vicissitudes of history and cultural diversity. What Anselm's *Monologium* points out is that this is not how the word 'God' is used within Christian theology. He explicitly raises the problem of eternal truth and its temporal, spatial understanding by performing two logical demonstrations, one regarding place and one regarding time.

Of place: 'If, then, it [the supreme Nature of God] exists as a whole, in each individual place, then, for each individual place there is no individual whole ... How, then, can what exists as a whole, in any place, exist simultaneously, as a whole, in another place? ... Since, then, one whole cannot exist as a whole in different places at the same time, it follows that, for individual places, there are individual wholes.' But that then commits the Christian thinker to an absurdity because 'if the supreme Nature exists as a whole, at one time, in every place, there are as many supreme Natures as there can be individual places'.[27]

Of time: 'how can anything exist, as a whole, simultaneously, at individual times, if these times are not themselves simultaneous? ... that supreme Nature is in no wise composite, but it supremely simple, supremely immutable—how shall this be so, if that Nature is one thing, at one time, and another, at another, and has parts distributed according to times?'

[27] *Monologium*, in *St. Anselm: Basic Writings*, trans. S.N. Deane (La Salle, IL: Open Court Publishing Company, 1962). Latin text (with an amended translation), *A New, Interpretive Translation of St. Anselm's* Monologion *and* Proslogion, Jasper Hopkins ed., (Minneapolis: A.J. Banning Press, 1986), chapter XXI, pp.120–1.

In answering the question of how the whole truth about God can be both omnipresent and yet located, eternal, and yet temporal, Anselm distinguishes between the nature of God's existence in itself and creaturely existence. 'Hence, though of being of this [creaturely] class it is with all truth asserted that one and the same whole cannot exist simultaneously, as a whole, in different places or times; in the case of those beings which are not of this class [God whose existence is beyond what our intellects can represent[28]], no such conclusion is necessarily reached.' Because the divine ontological condition is such that 'place does not act upon it as place, nor time as time . . . [Therefore] what rational consideration can by any course of reasoning fail to reach the conclusion, that the Substance which creates and is supreme among all beings, which must be alien to, and free from, the nature and law of all things which itself created from nothing, is limited by no restraint of space or time; since, more truly, its power, which is nothing else than its essence, contains and includes under itself all these things which it created?'[29] One further logical demonstration returns us directly to analogy: 'For when the supreme Being is said to exist in space and time, although the form of the expression regarding it, and regarding local and temporal natures, is the same, because of the usage of language, yet the sense is different, because of the unlikeness of the objects of discussion.' And so: 'In no place or time, then, is this Being properly said to exist, since it is contained by no other at all. And yet it may be said, after a manner of its own, to be in every place and time, since whatever else exists is sustained by its presence, lest it lapse into nothingness.'[30]

Anselm admits both an apophatic difference between God's Being and creaturely existence and yet at the same time a traversal of that difference because all places and times are sustained by God's Being. The analogical relation pertains to 'the form of expression', 'the usage of language', and a saying 'after a manner of its own'. Anselm, to my knowledge, does not use the category of 'analogy'; he refers to a way language is being employed. In his work *Cur Deus Homo* he employs the word 'fittingness' to describe God's suitable accommodation to the human and created order. It is a word that announces a theological aesthetics associated with the analogical. It is also a word that returns us to John Paul II's use of *congruere* (and indeed Aquinas's use of *argumenta ex convenientia*).[31]

---

[28] See Aquinas, *De veritate* q.8, a.1, ad 8: '*quod Deus super illud quod de ipso intellectui nostro repraesentatur.*'

[29] St. Anselm, *Monologium*, chapter XXII, (n.27), pp.124–5   [30] Ibid., pp.126–7.

[31] For a more detailed examination of fittingness in Anselm's thinking see Michael Root, 'Necessity and Unfittingness in Anselm's *Cur Deus Homo*'. *Scottish Journal of Theology* vol.40, 211–30. For a careful and erudite exposition of Anselm's theological aesthetics, see David S. Hogg, *Anselm of Canterbury The Beauty of Theology* (Aldershot: Ashgate Press, 2004).

It is absolutely crucial that Anselm establishes what we might think of as a rule whereby we can understand and engage in theological *poeisis* because we recognize what can and what cannot be 'properly said'; that we are treating two different orders of being; and that these two orders are not entirely divorced one from another because the existence of one is derived as a gift from the supreme being of the other. If they were entirely divorced, if the 'form of expression' or the 'usage of language' were equivocal, then we could know nothing of God even if God revealed Godself. All our speaking, all our faith as it seeks understanding, would be empty babbling. Anselm, then, establishes this analogical rule at what is almost the centre of his *Monologium*, because it enables him to proceed in his discursive theological investigation into what is impossible to comprehend in and of itself: the Trinitarian relations between the Father, Son, and Spirit. And when we have moved entirely beyond the things that pertain to this created place and this created time we have entered the realms of faith. Analogical thinking is the operation whereby faith traverses reason and reason faith. It follows from this that analogical thinking is not either an alien or an illegitimate mode of reasoning. Indeed Anselm draws attention to the way 'we often express and yet do not express, see and yet do not see, one and the same object; we express and see it through another; we do not express it, and do not see it by virtue of its own proper nature'. This has implications for faith, reasoning and their relation, as we will see.

In Volume II, when I treat the analogical world-view I will extend 'analogy' beyond static rules for the use of language to a dynamic account of its rhythm in a Christological understanding of creation. For now we can return to the question of the difference between natural hiddenness and divine hiddenness, recognizing both how they differ and how also they are associated[32]; that all is given in the speaking of God's Word in and through creation and in and through Christ; but that there are both natural and spiritual mysteries that pertain to the reception of what is given that are in line with our finitude and the finitude of our own speaking. There will be more yet to say about hiddenness, but what is evident from the examination we have been following so far is that the seeking undertaken by faith that negotiates what is hidden, the mystery of the world, returns us to the importance of discernment. Discernment is the second theme for our examination of what I called the 'operational context' of *fides quaerens intellectum*.

[32] We can also conclude, on the basis of the analogical rule sustaining while traversing the difference, that process theologies, even Christian ones, which do not employ this rule in relation to their talk about the relationship between the Uncreated and the creature are not in fact speaking of the Christian understanding of the word 'God' at all. They are speaking ungrammatically.

DISCERNMENT

We have spoken already of discernment in the context of judgement and the Church's inevitable involvement in the processes of passing judgement. It is the same discernment process that we are treating here, but now I wish to explore more of its existential rather than institutional action. For this we need to return to the figure of the poet in Chaucer's *The Book of the Duchess* and appreciate the spirit and source of the seeking involved in faith and its under-standing. Discernment is inseparable from that seeking, as it is inseparable from coming to know the truth as doing it rather than just cognitively grasp-ing it. The question that is prior to *why* we must discern is *how* it is that dis-cernment arises as part of our experience of being in the world. I noted earlier that discernment is a process of reading; good, better, best discernment, then, is a matter of learning how to read well. The context of my earlier observa-tion was reading theological productions, but here I am talking about reading the signs, signals, and communicative relations that surround and impinge upon us necessarily as creatures in the world. And every created entity must necessarily, in receiving these signs, these communications, and responding to them, read them. As I said, neuroscientists inform us that consciousness treats only a very small proportion of what the environment communicates to us continually. Created entities not having consciousness (plants, for example) or have much lower levels of consciousness (animals), still have to 'read' what the environment tells them and respond appropriately. Not to respond, or to be unable to respond, is to die or, in some instances, to adapt. The reading I am speaking about then, in association with discernment, is not simply a matter of consciousness; the reading goes on at emotional and somatic levels not lit by consciousness. If I am brief and sketchy in my account here, it is because the account will be considerably added to as we engage with different theological *topoi* in subsequent volumes. Here I only wish to speak of what has been called 'emotional intelligence',[33] the pre-cognitive character of much of our reading of the world (and the hiddennesses of that world), and the primacy of affect.[34] Our minds are embodied, and much of the work done recently in both philosophy of mind and cognitive science, is returning us to that embodiment and informing us of operations that profoundly inform our

---

[33] For a highly readable introduction to 'emotional intelligence' see Daniel Goleman, *Emotional Intelligence: Why It Can Matter More Than IQ* (New York: Bantam Books, 1995). For a more academic and up to date study, see Michelle Maiese, *Embodiment, Emotion, and Cognition (New Directions in Philosophy and Cognitive Science)* (Basingstoke: Palgrave Macmillan, 2011).

[34] We will be treating the primacy of affect in much greater detail in the next volume with respect to sin and sanctification. One book that has certainly gained much attention in this field recently is Iain McGilchrist, *The Master and His Emissary: The Divided Brain and the Making of the Western World* (New Haven: Yale University Press, 2009).

reading of the world. We read the world continually; that is how we have sur-
vived, how we have adapted to our environments, and how we have been able
to recognize what would be needed for us to change the environment to better suit our needs. Discernment is then an ongoing and an inevitable aspect
of our physiological and mental welfare. It is an aspect of what neuroscientists call the 'cognitive imperative': the demand made by the brain to make
order, to search for causes, and to question. In an interesting article in *Time
Magazine*, Michael Brunton defines 'cognitive imperative' as '[t]he uniquely
human, hardwired instinct to link cause with effect that gave us a vital evolutionary advantage'[35] before postulating on the evolution of faith. Alluding to
the work of the London-based developmental biologist, Louis Wolpert, in his
book *Six Impossible Things Before Breakfast*, Brunton associates the 'cognitive
imperative' with our 'belief machine' and postulates an evolution of faith.
That same hardwired discernment is also an ongoing and inevitable aspect of
our spiritual welfare; and it is, essentially, what *quaerens* means.

   Discernment is then an experience with transformative affects. It is an
intrinsic aspect of being alive. We are all seeking that we might understand.
What provokes such seeking and the need to understand is what the world
presents of itself to us. Consider again what we explored with respect to phenomenology. As a philosophical procedure it brackets out from the phenomenon itself any historical, cultural, and biographical interests. It attempts, in
its reduction, to allow the meaningfulness of the phenomenon to emerge in
its naked givenness. But it only does this, its procedure is only made possible,
because what is given 'speaks', presents itself. Jean-Louis Chrétien describes
this as the 'call', the demand made up on us by the simple fact that the phenomenon exists. This kind of language returns us to where we began with the
theo-logos and the requirement that we respond. In another idiom, Charles
Taylor, writes about 'import'.[36] Recall, very little of what we receive through
our senses is cognitively processed. So what is it then that illuminates this
aspect of our environment rather than that? Taylor does not attempt to
answer this question, but he describes how certain phenomena have 'import'
for us, and that that is why we register and experience them. In turn, this
import tells us something about the kind of people we are: it announces our
inextricable interest and engagement in the world that, in turn, engages us. To
discern, to make, modify and reverse judgements, is part of what it means to
be human: we were born (and therefore created) in this way.

---

[35] Michael Brunton, 'The Evolution of Faith', *Time Magazine*, 1 April, 2006. One wonders
whether this 'cognitive imperative' is anything more than a development biologist's account of
what Augustine called 'curiosity'. Either way, discernment is inseparable from an intellectual,
appetitive, and somatic *desire* to understand.
[36] Charles Taylor, 'Self-Interpreting Animals' in his *Philosophical Papers: Volume I, Human
Agency and Langauge* (Cambridge: Cambridge University Press, 1985), p.58.

So, to return to Chaucer lost in a dream of being lost in a forest and a hunt in which he is playing no part: Our initial condition of being in the world is being lost because we are immersed in the plethora of phenomena that demand we respond to them; that is the condition from which all learning has to begin, even how we have 'learnt Christ' (Ephesians 4.20). We have to begin to make sense—with a strong emphasis upon that making. We only find the truth about the world by *making* that truth. And this is not a philosophical matter of constructivism versus empiricism. Both philosophies are highly reductive because they fail to correspond to the complexity of what *is* and how we negotiate that complexity in order to live and understand that living. Chaucer's poem points to an existential condition in which we are not just lost. The different objects and activities in which 'lorn' or 'lorne' appear in the poem convey our inability to know exactly what it is we have lost or rather our inability to recognize how having lost something or someone only points to a more profound condition of being lost ourselves. The upshot of such a condition is a persistent mourning. This is conveyed in the poem by the inescapable presence of the man dressed all in sable whose sorrow cannot be assuaged, whose predicament cannot be healed.

Being lost calls forth an infinite need for consolation; the infinite need to find objects in our loss that will either compensate for it or explain it to us (and in explaining will prevent the loss from sending us deeper down into our human predicaments). We cannot redeem ourselves—that's the problem, and yet there is an embodied knowledge that we are not what we ought to be. We are lacking some knowledge of ourselves and no DNA code, no trawling through our ancestors, and no dredging up of some traumatic memory tells us what it is. But the inner awareness of what is missing carves spaces of yearning. It is both a witness and an appeal to this yearning that we have films like Ridley Scott's *Alien* (1979) and *Prometheus* (2012).[37] There is a whence and a why which our foraging for answers cannot discover. Even in Chaucer's poem we are left wondering what the relationship is between the dream and the dreamer, and while we might offer a range of tentative suggestions there are no answers. We know, as in the poem, the spaces of yearning dilate, particularly with experiences of love and death; especially love that is unrequited or lost. And even love that is reciprocated can make us panic. We know our sense of loss deepens when communicative relations are broken;

[37] Wrestling with what it is that is human and where this came from is one of the abiding preoccupations of Ridley Scott's films. In *Alien* and *Prometheus* the enquiry is posed through putting human beings in the context of extraterrestrial activity; in *Blade Runner* (1982) it is posed through queering any line that distinguishes human beings from complex machines, androids; and in *Black Hawk Down* (2001) and *The Kingdom of Heaven* (2005) it is posed through putting human beings in extreme circumstances, the war in Mogadishu and the Crusades, respectively.

when we can no longer connect to the world, to other people, to a sense of ourselves. We know how we can snatch at physical contact to ease the pain of self-exploration and the haunting sense we are being explored by something other than our own introspection (graphically enacted in *The Blair Witch Project*). But we need to have revealed to us what it is that we have lost such that our knowledge of ourselves, and the worlds we make, are so radically incomplete. We need to know what it is we should be.

FIDES QUAERENS INTELLECTUM

In this condition, then, what is known above and beyond our knowing that we desire to know? We know our seeking. We know our yearning. Understanding is a venturing out; a time-laden labouring. This is the operational context out of which *fides quaerens intellectum* emerges: that which is hidden, and the ongoing, sometimes insomnia-fevered, processes of trying to discern. *De ratione fidei* is translated by Richard Southern as, 'Reason as the activity of faith'.[38] Anselm tells us in his Preface to *Proslogion* that the phrase itself was the working title for the treatise. Until around 1083, what was renamed *Proslogion* was *Alloquium de ratione fidei*.[39] The earlier text, *Monologion*, also had a provisional title: *Exemplum meditandi de ratione fidei*. So examining reason as an activity of faith was central to Anselm's theological concerns. It is important to recognize, at the very beginning of our investigation into the operation of *fides quaerens intellectum*, that we are not treating here any dualistic separation between reason and faith. Such a separation is the product of modernity, and particular the Enlightenment narrowing of what reason was.[40] As the nuanced phrase *de ratione fidei* demonstrates—a phrase that can also be translated 'on the consideration of faith' or 'on the matter of faith' or 'on reflecting upon faith' or 'on the reasoning of faith' or 'on the reasonableness of faith'[41] —the relationship between faith and reason is subtle and complex. Faith and reason are richly intertwined. Laying this phrase to

---

[38] R.W. Southern, *Saint Anselm and His Biographer* (Cambridge: Cambridge University Press, 1963), p.55.

[39] For details on the naming processes for each treatise see R.W. Southern's footnotes to Eadmer's *The Life of St. Anselm, Archbishop of Canterbury* (London: Thomas Nelson and Sons Ltd., 1966), pp.29 and 31.

[40] See here two helpful articles by Nicholas Lash: '*Visio Unica et Ordinata Scientiae*' in *Restoring Faith in Reason*, pp.225–37 and 'Anselm Seeking' in *The Beginning and End of 'Religion'*, pp.150–63.

[41] S.N. Deane's translation of *ratione fidei* from Anselm's Preface to the *Proslogium*—in *St. Anselm: Basic Writings* (n.27), p.48—as 'the Grounds of Faith' is misleading if not wrong. Significantly, the phrase is the Latin translation of Paul's exhortation in *Romans* 12.6 on using gifts 'in proportion to our faith [*analogian tēn pisteōs*]'. *Analogia* can mean 'proportion' as it

one side, *Proslogion* plunges into Anselm's own (and much earlier) version of Chaucer's forest in the middle of a hunt:

> O wretched lot of man, when he hath lost that for which he was made! O hard and terrible fate! Alas, what has he lost, and what has he found? What has departed, and what remains? He has lost the blessedness for which he was made, and has found the misery for which he was not made. That has departed without which nothing is happy. And that remains which, in itself, is only miserable.[42]

It is evident immediately that the language and the register of *Proslogion* differs entirely from the pared down minimalism of Anselm's Latin in *Monologion*. And that is because something quite different is taking place in this later thesis.

We have already dipped into *Monologion*, so named eventually 'because in this he alone spoke and argued with himself'. In this treatise 'putting aside all authority of Holy Scripture, he enquired into and discovered by reason alone what God's nature is, and proved [*probari*] by invincible reason that God's nature is what the true faith [*vera fides*] hold it to be.'[43] So writes Anselm's earliest biographer and pupil Eadmer. The Latin *probare* is not to prove in the way a detective brings all the evidence to bear upon a case of guilt or a mathematician proves a theorem. *Probare* is to make good, to approve, to make credible, and is therefore associated with discernment and judgement. '*Probare* . . . means to demonstrate through the work of the mind what is already the case . . . it means to bring myself, by means of the mind and by rigorous reflection, into what can be known.'[44] There is a circularity about such an enquiry, as Eadmer points out when he tells us that reason is acting upon what true faith holds to be the case. As I said, *Monologium* moves towards demonstrating the rational coherence of the Trinitarian (and the Western Trinitarian, at that) understanding of 'God'. That circularity is inflected differently in *Proslogion* because the whole of the reflection, as a meditation, takes place within both an exhortation to prayer addressed to his readers—the opening sentence bids the reader flee from his or her preoccupations and retreat into 'the inner chamber of the mind . . . seeking him'—and an act of a prayer on behalf of himself in the manner of Augustine's *Confessions*: 'And come now, O Lord my God, teach my heart where and how

---

can also indicate 'conformity' or 'correspondence'. It may be pushing the Greek too far, but I wonder if what is suggested here with Paul is a divine accommodation to human understanding that takes place in faith and that reasoning on the basis of faith participates in it. I drew attention above to a teaching on this accommodation in the papal Encyclical *Faith and Reason*. This would make 'faith' the most natural of human operations and reason as logic-tracing secondary. See Chapter 9.

[42] Anselm, *Prologium* chapter 1, p.50 in *St. Anselm: Basic Writings* (n.27).
[43] *The Life of St. Anselm* (n.37), pp.29.
[44] Laurence Paul Hemming and Susan Frank Parsons, *Restoring Faith in Reason*, p.ix.

it may seek thee.'[45] Hence, Eadmer tells us, the treatise was eventually named *Proslogion* 'because in this work he speaks either to himself or the God'.[46]

Eadmer is not always the most perceptive of readers. Anselm begins by an exhortation to his readers which in Latin states '*excitatio mentis ad contemplandum Deum*'. I point this out because *excitare* is to rouse, awake, incite, and stimulate. This embodied, energetic reasoning takes place *within* faith and it is a dynamic and creative intellectual experience, an act of contemplative prayer. The reader of the treatise is absorbed into the authorial 'I' as they set out on a quest.[47] The quest immediately delivers us to the exile of the human condition, its loss, its state of being lost, before emerging, at the end of that opening chapter of the *Proslogion*, at a redefinition of *fides quaerens intellectum* as: 'I do not seek to understand that I may believe, but I believe in order to understand. For this also I believe—that unless I believed, I should not understand [*Neque enim quaere intelligere ut credem, sed credo ut intelligam. Nam et hoc credo quia: nisi credidero, non intelligam*].' The last phrase '*nisi credidero, non intelligam*' is the Vulgate translation of Isaiah 7.9 and the *credo ut intelligam* is a direct echo of Augustine's Sermon 43. So this is not a new quest; this is a quest rooted in both the Scriptural and the ecclesial tradition. *Fides, credo, ratio,* and *intelligentia* are all kinetic operations and as such, although Anselm shies away from any account of embodiment that is not Christ's, they are embodied experiences; theological experiences. Given this, the modern borders which have been constructed separating the spiritual life of faith from the epistemology of knowledge, and both from metaphysical questions concerned with being, as we will increasingly see, are totally artificial to Anselm's medieval, theological mind. Furthermore, *credo* can also mean to discern, to come to an understanding; the verb attends to a process from which a final assent of 'I believe' issues.

It may appear perverse to skip over the argument that is so famously set forth in the *Proslogion*, the demonstration of the existence of God. In fact, Eadmer makes no reference to this 'argument' in his account of the *Proslogion*, only to the emotional and psychological difficulties Anselm experienced both before and during the process of producing the treatise. The astonishing intellectual attention to the 'ontological argument' has meant that readings of the treatise have been distorted. Only three out of twenty-six chapters of the *Proslogion* treat the necessary existence of God. To understand how the

---

[45] Anselm, *Prologium* chapter 1, p.49 in *St. Anselm: Basic Writings* (n.27).

[46] *The Life of St. Anselm* (n.37), pp.31.

[47] For an account of the striking originality of Anselm's own prayers, written for the use of others and circulated widely, and the changes in devotional needs in the eleventh century, see R.W. Southern, *St. Anselm and His Biographer* (Cambridge: Cambridge University Press), 1963 pp.34–47. In these prayers too the reader is assumed into the authorial 'I' in an act of devotion through identification.

argument belongs to the work as a whole we have to return to the loss and the condition of being lost: because what is lost, and creates the conditions of being lost, is our knowledge of God prior to the Fall, prior to sin. The loss is ignorance and the darkness which has overtaken our understanding, and has left us existentially disorientated: 'whence have we been driven out; whither are we driven on?'[48] The Scriptural Fool who says in his heart there is no God and with whom Anselm contends, is a figure then for all of us—even Anselm himself. All are Fools who have not received the illumination of the divine, the revelation of the truth of God. Hence the opening prayer expresses a longing and a desire: 'enlighten our eyes [*illuminabis oculos*] . . . enlighten us [*illumine nos*], reveal [*ostende*] thyself to us'.[49]

The burden of *Proslogion* is the construction of a theological epistemology, an epistemology at odds with modern epistemologies after Descartes and Kant that divorced themselves from ontology. The famous 'argument' establishes the ontological ground for the condition of a theological knowledge that is knowledge of the truth. That ontological ground is the difference between God's necessary being or what Anselm describes as 'to exist more truly than all other beings, and hence in a higher degree than all others [*verissime omnium et ideo maxime omnium habes esse*]' and we creatures who 'do not exist so truly, and hence in a less degree [*minus habet esse*]'.[50] The English translation here in terms of degrees of being is confusing, theologically, because it suggests a continuum or a proportionality of being that Anselm does not intend.[51] There is no continuum; the relation is analogical and it is made possible by a) the fact that God created us to see Him, fashioning our somatic and intellectual capacities in just the right way to be 'fitting'; b) we lost that ability to see Him through sin; c) and God restores that ability to see Him in exhibiting Himself and the grace of illumination. Theological reasoning is an act of faithful believing made possible by grace, and the operation of such grace is Trinitarian, for God has revealed Godself in Christ and the Spirit teaches us to understand the truth

[48] Anselm, *Proslogium*, I, p.51.

[49] Ibid. We can note that revelation is a verbally conceived—the process of illumination. The verb *ostendare* is to make clear, to display, to exhibit, to disclose. Revelation or illumination is not some rupturing and punctiliar breaking in of God, but the making visible of God's presence, God's light, that is always there.

[50] Ibid., p.55.

[51] Although one has to admit that the confusion over this ontological distinction was registered early and with someone who did read the Latin. The famous *In Behalf of the Fool* by the monk Gaunilo is clear evidence that some read Anselm as speaking about a continuum and a proportionality of *esse*. Gaunilo's reply is based on such an interpretation. Gaunilo is attempting to demonstrate the illogical nature of Anselm's 'argument'. His reply then is philosophical—and hence foreshadows Kant's rejection of the ontological argument. But, in fact, the more serious consequence of Gaunilo's misinterpretation of Anselm is theological: if the being God and the existence of human beings was only a matter of 'degree', then God only be a greater version of ourselves, and hence the whole structure of the soterological argument that runs throughout *Prologium* would be in jeopardy.

that salvation in Christ brings us to again. But observe how form and content marry in Anselm's writings; how prayer, theological reflection, and rhetorical persuasion work together to 'excite' the mediation and display the excitement into which we as readers are drawn[52]:

> Teach me to seek thee, and reveal thyself to me, when I seek then, for I cannot see thee, except thou teach me, nor find thee, except thou reveal thyself. Let me see thee in longing, let me long for thee in seeking; let me find thee in love, and love thee in finding [*Doce ne quaerere te et ostende te quaerendo, quia quaerere te possum, nisi tu docens, ne invenire, nisi te ostendas. Quaeram te disiderando, desiderere quaerendo. Inveniam amando, amen inveniendo.*][53]

The poetry of the prayer here—there is no other word for the mellifluous rhythms of the balanced syntax, antitheses, alliteration, and assonance—stirs the desire within us which is the very power of both the longing and the love. The longing, which commits us to a physiological and emotional process, is governed by 'thy truth [*veritatem tuam*]' which the 'heart believes and loves [*credit et amat*].[54] In this way we are invited not to remain 'outside' the mediation as philosophers. We can't remain outside because believing *is* loving. As readers/observers, we are to be participants in the mediation, having our reasoning disciplined by Anselm's reasoning, being brought through his teaching to that teaching which is inseparable from the operations of Trinitarian grace in God revealing Godself. It is God who 'give[s] understanding to faith [*das fidei intellectum*]'.[55] We are not then offered Anselm's teaching on such and such. We are invited into a pedagogical practice, into the experience of one who is being taught as he believes, prays for understanding, and receives illumination. The teaching is to be experienced and practised; experienced in being practised. We return to the verbal noun: *doctrina*. Hence the treatise is composed of questions which perform the seeking (*quaero* is closely associated with *quaerito*—to ask persistently). And the questions arise out of the paradoxical tensions that reveal the ontological difference between the attributes of God (all powerful, all merciful, just, good, eternal, omniscient), and our creaturely experience delivered through embodied epistemological processes (sense perception, conception, understanding, dialectical reasoning, knowledge).[56] Resolutions (often beginning 'Truly, then . . . ') are always provisional because continually Anselm reminds us that God surpasses our ability to understand fully, even to the point where he recognizes we can say things we don't actually have any knowledge about ('help me to understand

---

[52] R.W. Southern, *St. Anselm and His Biographer* (n.45), p.25: 'Even when his ideas seem wrong, they have a power of persuasion which seems independent of the truth.'

[53] Anselm, *Proslogium*, I (n.27), p.52.   [54] Ibid., p.53.   [55] Ibid.

[56] This ontological difference is existentially registered in terms of the effects of God and the affects of being human. See ibid., chapter X, p.63.

what I say').[57] The saying, the writing, is the embodiment of the thinking, the seeking, the coming to understanding as and in a pedagogical praxis.

PRAYER AND EPISTEMOLOGY

Anselm does not present us with an epistemology as such (unlike Locke in his *Essay on Human Understanding* or Kant in his *Critique of Pure Reason*), but rather prayer as an epistemological practice reflecting upon its own activity in the contemplation of God. This is *doing* or *making* theology. This is the engagement with truth, with the aim of being con-formed in, by and to that truth. It is a theological *poiesis* reflecting upon, as it participates in, *theo-poiesis*. In its creativity the prayer has a living immediacy that offers a participation in that being which is life itself, everywhere and always. The writing mediates between what Anselm called 'created life [*vita create*]' and 'creating life [*vita creatrix*]'.[58] As such it is orientated towards the vision of God, both as seeing God and seeing all things as God sees them. The recognition that the soul bears an impossible burden of longing in this task leads Anselm into the existential conditions of a double darkness, associated with the double hiddenness (divine and natural) I spoke of above, which he examines from chapter XIV to chapter XIX.

The darkness is both his own ignorance that distorts all merely human epistemologies and leads once more to confusion, grief and mourning, and the glory of God which blinds in its dazzling infinity, it ineffability, its hiddenness in light and blessedness. Once more this double darkness and double hiddenness is an expression of the negative theology that circumscribes Anselm's theological praxis, locked into the grammatical negation at the heart of his understanding of 'God' as 'that than which nothing greater can be conceived [*id quo maius cogitari non potest*]'. In this way Anselm continually delivers us back to the mystery or hiddenness of God in the world and the labour of discernment. This labour, wrought in prayer and Anselm's own writing, is related in the closing chapters of the book to the labour of God's Trinitarian love in which the truth of the Father is expressed in and as the Son and from their mutual love processes the Spirit. This is the *vita creatrix* and participating within it we arrive at the burning nub of discernment itself; for the dynamic economy of faith and understanding is bound to the intimacy of knowledge's abiding in love: 'how far they shall know thee' is inseparable from 'how much they shall love thee'.[59] In its own way, in a poetry carved in a

---

[57] Ibid., chapter IX, p.62.   [58] Ibid., chapter XXIV, p.75.
[59] Ibid., chapter XXIV, p.79.

Latin minimalist style and honed by a vision of the utter simplicity, harmony, and oneness of God, Anselm arrives at a very similar conclusion as, almost 250 years later, Dante did in his final vision of the Trinity in the last Canto of *Paradiso*: 'the love that moves the sun and the other stars'.

To associate love with knowledge is to associate epistemology with ontology and both with the somatic and affective. It is in this way that the ethical emerges in life *as* life. Read theologically, in terms of Christology, these associations will provide us with the starting point for the faith that seeks understanding in Volume II, as radical incarnation. Anselm does not develop his Christology here. His Christology was developed later in *Cur Deus Homo?* (completed in 1098) and *De Incarnatione Verbi* (completed in the winter of 1092–3). But even in the *Monologion* and *Proslogion*, although scant attention is paid to the life and work of Christ and attention is focussed much more on Christ's Trinitatrian character as the Word and expression of the Father, we can appreciate through the pedagogical practice (what in contemporary terms would be called 'active learning') and the continual return in his Trinitarian theology to truth and life that Anselm's *ratio fidei* is a *poiesis* repeating in its own way Christ's proclamation 'I am the Way, the Truth and the Life' (John 14.6). As has often been observed by Biblical scholars, the 'I am' sayings in John refer back to the revelation of God to Moses in the burning bush. Understanding this modifies Anselm's own statement in the Preface to *Monologion* where he informs his readers that the reasoning proceeds in a way 'that nothing in Scripture should be urged on the authority of Scripture itself'.[60] For *ratio fidei* does not prove anything through Scripture or argue through Scriptural exegesis, but it does nevertheless continually refer to Scripture by means of verbal echoes. The Scriptures are profoundly internalized in both treatises as that which has been inwardly digested and in this way provide the very sustenance for the dialectic of believing and understanding. It is a Scripture that has soaked itself into ecclesial practices, disciplines of reading, transcribing and meditation, and liturgies of the Word; no less central to Anselm than Hugh of St. Victor.

If Scripture gives the sustenance to the belief, then the seeking and the understanding, although aided by illumination, are guided by the newly emerging secular sciences of grammar and logic, particularly the grammarian's attention to the definition of words (like 'God'), formulations (like 'that than which nothing greater can be conceived'), and their extended explanation (like the body of the *Proslogion* as it proceeds from this formulation).[61] We need to appreciate a profound coherence in Anselm here between the

---

[60] *Monologium* in *St. Anselm: Basic Writings* (n.27), p.81.

[61] On Anselm's use of 'equipollent' arguments and the new theology informed by Aristotelian grammar and logic that emerged in the debates between Anselm teacher Lanfranc and Berengar, see R.W. Southern, *Saint Anselm and His Biographer* (n.38), pp.21–5.

necessary logic of the form of the treatise (what in Latin would be *ordo dis-serendi* from *dissero* to argue) and God as necessary being (which constituted the *ordo naturae*). We need to understand this because it is the intention of this work to follow a similar coherence; that is, the systematic order of the theological *poiesis* is an unfolding of the very principle from which order itself issues. Christ as the divine Logos is not only the Word of God, but also the eloquence of divine reasoning. As such faith seeking understanding, which is the pedagogy of discipleship and what St. Paul called the 'training in righteousness [*paideian tēn en dikaiosunē*]' (2 Tim.3.16), not only has its beginning and ending in Christ, it has its form in Christ. Reasoning, in such a theological frame, is a spiritual gift. It is not either the mechanical cognitive process of the early modern epistemologists (like Locke or even Kant) or the computational process of some contemporary cognitive scientists who model the operations of the brain on cybernetics.

The form that emerges from this Christological reasoning evolves, is organic and dynamic, governed and inspired by the Spirit of Christ. It produces rational form developed out of the system of relations between tenets of faith produced. In Greek *logos* is related to *logizomai* (to reckon, calculate on the bases of reason) found nineteen times in *Romans* alone, Paul's most developed theological argument.[62] What then is systematic in a presentation of Christian theology issues from and coheres to a theo-logic pertaining to the *theo-logos* and in this way a correspondence is maintained between the *ordo disserendi* and the *ordo naturae*. In this Anselm is in complete agreement with Gergory of Nyssa in the *Great Oration* (commented upon in Chapter 1).

I too will be drawing upon the secular sciences as therapies and tools in that examination and questioning that constitutes the intellectual aspect of the more somatic and affective longing and seeking. These secular sciences inform our contemporary cultural situation in the way grammar and logic informed Anselm's cultural situation, and their use is justified on the same basis as Anselm's use of them: the oneness and unity of the truth—though they have to be used with critical discernment just because they have not been developed and honed with theology in mind. Pertinent here is the way in which our cultural situation, informed by various secular sciences, the nature of believing and belief with respect to knowledge (and indirectly with respect to faith) is changing. As we observed with Anselm's *Proslogion*, although the early title and the Preface to the treatise refer to faith (*fides*) seeking understanding, the first chapter refines that statement in terms of a relationship between understanding and belief (from the verb *credo*—to credit, to believe). Significantly, there is no Latin substantive from the verb *credo*; the

---

[62] It is related also to *logikos* (rational) and *logismos* (reasoning), but these are less well used by Paul; the former once and the latter twice.

substantive 'belief' is *fides*. There is an adjectival form *credibilis*—worthy of belief, likely, credible. There is also a noun *creditor* that means the same as it does in English and the noun *creditum* that signifies a loan. It is entirely suitable, given Anselm's attention to logic, that *credo* is associated with *intelligam* (the subjunctive 'I may understand')—that is, with probabilities and calculations of likelihood. I noted above that the verb *credo* attends to a process of coming to believe, of coming to accredit through discernment. Furthermore, the lack of two distinct words means the faith and belief for Anselm was synonymous.[63] Even faith's relationship to financial transactions is not to be erased, because the process of accreditation is a transactional process; it avers to those communicative relations we spoke about at the beginning. We believe in someone, in something. In John's Gospel, which has much to say about believing (*pistis*), the verb form is nearly always intransitive. Believing is not a static but a continually shifting position. As such knowledge is always and only approximate, always and only provisional. And this is completely acceptable theologically to Anselm; because existing as limited, finite and fallen intelligences within God, darknesses and hiddenness can never be overcome, as we saw. But, in the advent and wake of modernity, we have come to demand much more from knowledge; we have aspired to certainty. Such an aspiration has changed the meaning and the epistemological status of both 'belief' and 'faith'.

FAITH AND BELIEF

We touched on this above, but now we need to enquire more deeply. *Fides* is both a mode of knowing *and* the content or object of that knowing, but the emergence of two separate terms from the twelfth century introduced new epistemological possibilities. The two separate words arose from the mix of languages. 'Belief' comes from the Old English term for belief or faith, *geleafa*, which in turn arose from the old Saxon word *ga-lauben*. *Ga* is a prefix intensifying the verb *lauben* meaning to desire or to love. So *ga-lauben* was to greatly desire or esteem. It was not necessarily associated with God or Christian faith. *Geleafa* was a vernacular term; *fides* was used only by those speaking Latin. From this, three semantic possibilities developed: a) belief as a mode of knowledge that might or might not relate to an acceptance of certain Christian creedal propositions; b) faith as a mode of knowledge related to an acceptance of certain Christian creedal propositions; and c) faith as the contents of the Christian faith. In the secularization of the sciences that took place in modernity, faith came to

---

[63] German is similar in this regard, with *Glauben* meaning either belief or faith.

be closely associated with religious piety. Not entirely, we still speak of having faith in someone meaning that we trust them—and such a trust goes back to a necessary requirement for the transactional relationship implied in the Latin *fides* (increasingly with respect to finance). Belief, on the other hand, could be accepted within the vocabulary of the secularized sciences, but only as epsiemologically distinct. Belief became associated with a weak form of knowledge or an unexamined opinion received through habit or custom; and knowledge became associated with the facts of the matter, established by various means from experimentation, inductive reasoning and data collection.[64]

Of course, belief as a weak form of knowledge goes back to Plato's theory of the forms. In the line–analogy, as Socrates enlarges upon it in *Republic*, we move from the visible world, the knowledge of which is governed by images and reflections (*eikasia*) and beliefs (*pistis*) to the intelligible world governed by mathematical reasoning (*dianoia*) and finally understanding (*noesis*).[65] The weakness of believing for Plato was ontological, moral, and epistemological. Further away from the Forms, believing had lesser grasp upon being, the Good beyond being and therefore true knowledge, which was knowledge of the Forms. Belief as a weak form of knowledge is not of this order in modernity.[66] To appreciate the differences, and the distance from Anselm's understanding of belief as faith, we need to explore what has been termed 'historical epistemology', which takes as its assumption that the way we conceive knowledge, the categories through which we structure an understanding of what is knowledge, change with time.[67] We have a concrete example of this in the changes we already noted to 'faith' with respect to Melanchthon and Luther.

Indicative of the modern understanding of belief as a weak form of knowledge, is the opening chapter of John Locke's *Essay Concerning Human Understanding* (1690). Here is laid out the purpose of his work: 'to inquire into the Original, Certainty, and Extent of humane Knowledge, together with the Grounds and Degrees of Belief, Opinion, and Assent'.[68] He takes up belief again in Book IV, concerning knowledge and probability. There he defines knowledge as 'nothing but the perception of the connexion of and

[64] See here Mary Poovey, *The History of the Modern Fact: Knowledge in the Sciences of Wealth and Society* (Chicago: University of Chicago Press, 1998).

[65] Plato, *Republic*, 509d–510a.

[66] For a deeper examination of *pistis* in Plato see Graham Ward, *Unbelievable: Why We Believe and Why We Don't* (London: I.B.Taurus, 2015), pp.24–9. Plato's text segues the whole of the book.

[67] The term, and the genre of investigation it inaugurated, was coined by Lorraine Daston in her work on constructivism and in the history of science. See Lorraine Daston, 'The Moral Economy of Science' in *Constructing Knowledge in the History of Science*, edited by Arnold Thackray (Chicago: Chicago University Press, 1995); and 'Baconian Facts, Academic Civility, and the Prehistory of Objectivity' in *Annals of Scholarship* 8, nos. 3–4 (1991).

[68] John Locke, *Essay Concerning Human Understanding* (Oxford: Oxford University Press 1975), p.43.

agreement, or disagreement and repugnancy of any of our ideas. In this alone it consists. Where this Perception is, there is Knowledge, and where it is not, there, though we may fancy, guess or believe, yet we always come short of Knowledge.'[69] In chapter I, section 9, where he examines two kinds of 'habitual knowledge'—truths laid up in memory and truths of which we are convinced but concerning which we have forgotten the proofs demonstrating them—Locke writes about believing the memory rather than really knowing, associates such believing with something 'between Opinion and Knowledge', and examines 'a sort of assurance that exceeds bare Belief'.[70] Until, finally, in chapter XV on probability, he defines belief:

> Being that which makes us presume things to be true, before we know them to be so. Probability is likeliness to be true, the very notation of the Word signifying such a Proposition, for which there be Arguments or Proofs to make it pass, or be received for true. The entertainment the Mind gives this sort of Proposition is called *Belief, Assent,* or *Opinion,* which is the admitting or receiving any Proposition for true, upon Arguments or Proofs that are found to perswade us to receive it as true, without certain Knowledge that it is so. And herein lies the *difference between Probability and Certainty, Faith,* and *Knowledge,* that in all the parts of Knowledge there is intuition; each immediate *Idea,* each step has its visible and certain connexion: in belief, not so. That which makes me believe, is something extraneous to the thing I believe; something not evidently joined on both sides to, and so not manifestly showing the Agreement or Disagreement of those *Ideas,* that are under consideration.[71]

Here we have set out for us all of the modern understanding about the epistemology of belief and believing. All cognitive activity takes place in the receiving and receptive mind. The world is 'out there' and the senses deliver it to us such that the mind becomes a theatre of intellectual representations of what is out there. The mind 'entertains' and sometimes its ideas connect to what is out there immediately and sometimes they don't. Either way the epistemological problem is based on the dualism of the world and the subject —a subject who is like the homunculus operators lodged in the heads of those monstrous androids in *Men in Black* (1997). Because knowledge is organized in and around this 'problem' of how does what goes on in the head hook up to what is out there in the world, then belief is related to: a) a calculation on the basis of likelihood, itself based on a series of pre-established certainties with which we are familiar; b) the reception of a persuasive argument (and therefore, implicitly, trust in the authority of the supplier of that argument); c) the absence of certain knowledge based upon the immediate relation between idea and thing; d) the absence of 'steps' that might make the 'connexion' between intuition of the thing and certainty; and e) the separation between

---

[69] Ibid., p.525.   [70] Ibid., p.528.   [71] Ibid., p.655.

the object of belief and that 'which makes me believe'. The implication of the last sentence is that with certain knowledge there is no separation between the object and my perception of it—there is no 'extraneous' persuasion.

Belief and faith, in this section of the *Essay*, are synonymous and remain distinct from knowledge. But one can see that with the association of belief with opinion, fancy, and guessing; the variety of possible degrees between probability and improbability; and the notion of there being 'bare belief' which, presumably (for Locke does not develop the idea) is an opinion, fancy, or guess which is both weakly persuasive and without any proofs or demonstration—in such a semantic field, Locke, a Christian believer, would have to distinguish between belief and faith. The language of assurance throughout Locke's treatise is telling here; for assurance is an affective counter to fear. The fear is doubt. Recall the pre-gothic horrors of John Bunyan's Doubting Castle in *The Pilgrim's Progress* (published only twelve years earlier than Locke's *Essay* and with a far-wider circulation that points to an inflamed pustule in the popular imagination). Doubting Castle is occupied by the feudal tyrant, the Giant Despair, and Pilgrim very nearly succumbs to madness during his imprisonment and torture there. The word 'doubt' haunts Book IV of Locke's *Essay on Human Understanding* and certain knowledge offers assurance (and reassurance) because it keeps doubt—and the spectre of scepticism that is always epistemology's *bête noire*—at bay.

Furthermore, 'proof', although associated with mathematics and the theory of probability is shifting historically at this time towards 'supported by evidence'; because probability is a matter of 'what counts'.[72] In Book IV, even though Locke is discussing ideas in the mind and not facts as such, there are numerous references to 'evidence' (especially the self-evidence of maxims)—though, at this point in the transmission of ideas 'evidence' plays a secondary role to rational proof and demonstration.

For example, in Book IV, chapter II on the degrees of knowledge, Locke describes in sections 3 and 4 almost a hierarchy in which proof comes first, then demonstration and finally evidence which, in certain forms of knowledge (even where that knowledge is established by proofs) 'is not altogether clear and bright'. This hierarchy is related to there being three degrees of knowledge—the intuitive, the demonstrative, and the sensitive. There is a curious slippage here in Locke's language, indicative of things to come. The slippage is from proof that is based on self-evident maxims and evidence based on empirical data used to support the truth of the demonstration made

---

[72] For a much more detailed account of the cultural shift here that began to distinguish between the evident and evidence, a shift which gives rise to experimental science in which repeatable results constitute, on the grounds of probability and evidence is found to support or disqualify a theory or hypothesis, see Peter Dear, *Discipline and Experience: The Mathematical Way in the Scientific Revolution* (Chicago: University of Chicago Press, 1995).

from the proof. We can observe the slippage best by tracing back the language of self-evident maxims, which, in medieval scholasticism were known as *principia* per se *nota*. These were the first principles that organized knowledge [*scientia*] as medieval scholasticism understood Aristotle. They did not concern the empirical and so bore no relation to evidence. The questions that followed deductively from the first principles of a science were concerned not with *that* something is the case, but *why* something is the case. Locke's language of evidence slips between the self-evidence of deductive proof on the basis of *principia* per se *nota* and an inductive demonstration on the basis of evidence.[73]

More clearly than the character of belief, the character of what is certain knowledge emerges as that which goes beyond persuasion; beyond the rhetorical process of *making* me believe. It is founded upon what Francis Bacon called 'true axioms' and the demonstrable connexion between the proposition and these axioms. The word that will become increasingly problematic here is 'proposition', for Locke is convinced truth is a matter of propositions and that there is a transparency about the language in which such propositions are couched. A century earlier the propositional understanding of truth was, as we saw in Chapter 3, a key characteristic of confessionalism. Sharing this conviction of an attainable transparency for language, Locke was one among a host of others (most famously Thomas Spratt in the early years of the Royal Society).

The conviction was carried by a difference in the style of representation: the rejection of ornament, which implied that communication could be stripped of and distinguished from rhetoric. Persuasion became a purely cerebral, rather than somatic, matter. The transparency of truth was still a stylistic effect but, as Locke practised it in his own writing, it *made* the separation between a proposition and a persuasion and, therefore, distinguished knowledge from belief. But both are understood as verbal acts, and the transparent style remains a rhetorical style regardless of what is claimed for it. That is why 'proposition' as a mode of representation, when recognized also as a mode of rhetorical persuasion, becomes problematic. What happens when we have to frost the transparency of language with the crystalline complexities of hermeneutics? As Bishop Thomas Spratt was extolling the virtues of stylistic simplicity in his *History of the Royal-Society of London, for the Improving of Natural Knowledge* (1667), a fellow founder of the Royal Society and a fellow bishop, John Wilkins, who, in 1641, had published the first detailed treatise on interpretation (*Mercury, or the Secret and Swift Messenger*) was working on

---

[73] For a moral detailed account of 'self-evident' principles and knowledge as *scientia* in Aquinas and other medieval scholastics, see Fredrick Christian Bauerschmidt, *Thomas Aquinas: Faith, Reason, and Following Christ* (Oxford: Oxford University Press, 2013), pp. 51–5.

his influential volume (published in 1668) *An Essay towards a Real Character and a Philosophical Language*. Hermeneutics was about to emerge—on the basis of enquiries into the practices of interpreting the Bible and legal pro-scriptions. With the science of interpretation, which the growing attention to the historical specificity of contexts in the eighteenth century encouraged, a proposition was understood as *made* in the same way and to the same extent as a belief is *made*. The persuasiveness of both articulations must be read and interpreted.

Furthermore, interpretation comes to be recognized not as a secondary or derivative act, but as primary. In Bishop Wilkins's startlingly original study of decoding cryptograms (in *Mercury*), there was the code and there was the breaking of the code or its interpretation. Interpretation was an act *after* the facts of the case; the facts came first just as what the senses received was sub-sequently represented in the mind such that a response or judgement might follow. But beginning with Schleiermacher's work on hermeneutics in the early nineteenth century, the sign itself was understood to be an interpreta-tion. We read the world and in reading produce and reproduce the worlds we inhabit. Interpretation goes all the way down. We are not simply dealing with reception and response any more. If we already interpret what comes to us then there is a projection or anticipation of the meaning of what we receive. So the economy of interpretation is a spiral of projection–reception–response in an endless feed-forward and feed-back loop.

I am not wishing, and have not the space, to delineate a genealogy of believ-ing; only to point to the sell-by date and shelf-life of certain key terms that we are treating here with the production and organization of knowledge. Locke's *Essay* gives us insight into an epistemological structure within which 'belief' featured in a certain historical context, which we associate with modernity. As such, 'belief' was uncoupled from 'faith', secularized as a mode of human cognition and situated within a hierarchy governed no longer, as with Plato, by an ontological, moral, and epistemological order, but governed rather by an ideal—the transparent, certainty of knowledge. That ideal has continu-ously been subject to critique from various and distinctive forms of philo-sophical scepticism—Hume, Kant, and Schopenhauer, to say nothing of the so-called 'masters of suspicion': Marx, Nietzsche, and Freud.[74]

With hermeneutics, Locke's secularized 'belief' (and therefore its coun-terpart 'knowledge') was now situated within a different semantic field: the field of the three 'I's—interpretation, ideology, and the internalization of instruction (more broadly, the sociology of knowledge). As such hermeneutics structures the organization of knowledge differently so that now 'knowl-edge'—certainly 'knowledge' as Locke conceived it—has become enfeebled

---

[74] Named and examined famously by Paul Ricoeur in *Freud and Philosophy: An Essay on Interpretation*, trans. Dennis Savage (New Haven: Yale University Press, 1970).

and recognized to be freighted with 'interests'.[75] Today, in the light of investigations into embodied cognition, neuroscience, and emotional intelligence with respect to human action and understanding, 'knowledge' is far from being certain and transparent. It is understood to be constituted as much by the body's habitation in the world as by any theatre of mental representations. On Locke's terms, then, there is more belief than knowledge. It is illustrative here that the contemporary neuroscientist, David Linden, can write: 'We all believe things we cannot prove. Those unproven ideas that are ultimately subject to falsifying experiment or observation constitute "scientific faith". Those that are not constitute religious faith . . . Our brains evolve to make us believers.'[76]

We need to appreciate the changes brought about by this shift in the semantic structure of believing because they impact upon how, today, the processes involved in faith seeking understanding might be reconceived. In appreciating the shift we can also reconnect 'belief' with 'faith', in a theological manner; but the detailed development of the theological anthropology that is required here, I will postpone until Volume II when we will undertake the dogmatic inquiry as such. This volume is only treating the approach to such an inquiry. But if, as I have been arguing, the life blood of the theological enterprise, an enterprise all Christians have to undertake, is faith seeking understand then we need to make some preliminary statements about the relationship of believing as a mode of cognition and faith as the theological orientation of such a cognition by the revelation and reception of God's grace.

---

[75] The book that summed up this modern trend and examined it was Jürgen Habermas, *Knowledge and Human Intertests*, trans. Jeremy Shapiro (Boston: Beacon Press, 1972).

[76] David Linden, *The Accidental Mind* (Cambridge, MA: Harvard University Press, 2008), p.234.

9

What Makes a Belief Believable?

The question is not mine[1] but it has haunted me since I first came across it in the writings of the French Jesuit Michel de Certeau. I will come to de Certeau below ('Two Forms of Believing: Virtuality'). But prior to encountering him I need to qualify a term I used towards the end of the last chapter with respect to believing: 'cognition'—belief as a mode of cognition. I need to qualify this because frequently 'cognition' is understood to be a purely mental activity, and that is not how we have come to understand cognition more recently. Cognition is embodied; mental activity is, at every point, infused with corporeal affect, or should be. I say 'should be' because it is the burden of Iain McGilchrist's ground-breaking volume—*The Master and His Emissary*[2]—that the purely cognitive functions of being human belong to the productions of the left hemisphere of the brain. McGilchrist, who is a British psychiatrist, informs us that the right hemisphere has awarenesses of its own, creative, intuitive, emotional, imaginative, and much of it pre-conscious. This division in the brain, a division that has evolved as we have evolved, has profoundly impacted the history of Western culture and brought about an imbalance between the two hemispheres such that the left hemisphere now dominates—with significant pathological results. But to be fully human requires we address this imbalance and recover the wealth of creative understanding produced in the right hemisphere of the brain. To continue to neglect this hemisphere will have evolutionary consequences; because the brain is so plastic those associated links within the brain which are underused will not being strengthened—so imagination weakens and likewise the capacity to be creative and to respond intuitively to the environment.

---

[1] A much more detailed answer to this question constitutes the argument of Graham Ward, *Unbelievable: Why We Believe and Why We Don't* (London: I.B.Taurus, 2015) from which some material is drawn for this chapter.

[2] I. McGilchrist, *The Master and His Emissary: The Divided Brain and the Making of the Western World* (New Haven: Yale University Press, 2009), p.170.

An extended citation from McGilchrist's book will assist here:

> Belief is not to be reduced to thinking that such-and-such might be the case. It is
> not a weaker form of thinking, laced with doubt . . . Since the left hemisphere is
> concerned with what is certain, with knowledge of the facts, its version of belief
> is that it is just absence of certainty. If the facts were certain, according to its
> view, I should be able to say 'I know that' instead. This view of belief comes from
> the left hemisphere's disposition towards the world . . . So belief is just a feeble
> form of knowing, as far as it is concerned.
>
>   But belief in terms of the right hemisphere is different, because the disposition
> towards the world is different. The right hemisphere does not 'know' anything,
> in the sense of certain knowledge. For it, belief is a matter of care: it describes
> a *relationship*, where there is a calling and an answering, the root concept of
> 'responsibility'. Thus if I say that 'I believe in you', it does not mean that I think
> that such-and-such things are the case about you, but can't be certain that I
> am right. It means that I stand in a certain sort of relation of care towards you,
> that entails me in certain kinds of ways of behaving (acting and being) towards
> you, and entails on you the responsibility of certain ways of acting and being as
> well . . . It has the characteristic right-hemisphere qualities of being a between-
> ness: a reverberative, 're-sonant', 'respons-ible' relationship in which each party
> is altered by the other and by the relationship between the two, whereas the
> relationship of the believer to the believed in the left-hemisphere sense is inert,
> unidirectional, and centres on control rather than care.[3]

McGilchrist is careful not to construct a binarism between the left and
right hemispheres (although his work helps us to understand how such bin-
arisms can be constructed and pass themselves off as true and natural).

> [T]he right hemisphere, though it is not dependent on the left hemisphere in the
> same way that the left is on the right, nonetheless needs it in order to achieve
> its full potential, in some sense to become fully itself. Meanwhile the left hemi-
> sphere is dependent upon the right hemisphere both to ground its world, at the
> 'bottom' end, and to lead it back to life, at the 'top'.[4]

So there are myriad and subtle ways in which they can and should inform
each other; although the 'controlling' character of left-hemisphere thinking
can assert an overriding command and be convinced of its autonomy. Hence,
I said above, believing should be understood as a mode of cognition, a mental
activity, imbued with the affective—summed up in McGilchrist in the term
'care' as a disposition towards the world.[5] Right hemisphere believing is more
directly in contact with the world. The right hemisphere does have cognitive

---

[3] Ibid., p.170.   [4] Ibid., p.437.
[5] Ibid., p.447. 'Cognition in the right hemisphere is not a process of something coming into
being through adding piece to piece in a sequence, but of something that is out of focus coming
into focus, as a whole.'

capacities. It apprehends, though not always in a fully conscious way, more quickly than the left hemisphere—by a full half-second according to certain neuroscientists.[6] It is, particularly, the production site for the creative imagination, whilst simultaneously related to the emotional life of the body and its autonomic responsiveness. But the articulation and analysis of belief is more a left hemisphere activity because the left hemisphere governs consciousness, language production, and the instrumental, abstractive processes of ratiocination. It also governs any notion we have of 'self'.[7]

Working together, the left and the right hemispheres of the brain, believing is a mode of cognition associated with imagination, motivation, intuition, and feeling. But the left can dominate. That's the point. And so belief as an embodied cognition is subsequently stripped of its associations with the body such that cognition now becomes cold, instrumental, forensic, and ideological in ways that are 'unnatural'. That is, out of sync with the totality of who and what we are. Belief as issuing from the right balance of the right and left hemispheres, on the other hand, captures the provisionality and elusiveness of knowing. It motivates and energizes as it issues from the swirl within embodiment itself in relation to and in response to all that is given to it. It is orientated by appetite—Spinoza would say *conatus* (the self-protective drive to live)—and desire (which is more than appetite, deeper than appetite, because it longs for what it cannot name).[8] Belief is unavoidable; it is fundamental to the way we live. It is one of the great capacities given to self-aware human beings. Animals do not believe, cannot believe, because they cannot translate the immediate intuitions of belief, rooted in unconscious and nonconscious sensory states, into higher order perceptions, thoughts, representations and experiences.[9] Because we live in the world, because the world lives in us, we relate to it and we make sense of it. Belief is key to *making* the sensed and sensory sensible. In McGilchrist's term, we care. As such *credo* is

---

[6] Ibid., p.164.

[7] See the results of certain experiments in Julian Paul Keenan, Aaron Nelson, Margaret O'Connor, and Alvaro Pascual-Leone 'Neurology: Self-Recognition and Right Hemisphere', *Nature* 409 (6818), 305 (18 January 2001). For a critical examination of these conclusions, see Alain Morin, 'Right Hemisphere Self-Awareness: A Critical Assessment in *Consciousness and Cognition* 11 (2002) 396–401.

[8] Slavjo Žižek speaks about 'the abyss of the Other's impenetrable desire' in *The Plague of Fantasies* (London: Verso, 1997), p.31.

[9] Theories of higher order perceptions, thoughts, respresentations and experiences have been developed by a number of cognitive scientists examining 'the mental state one is aware of being in and mental states one is not aware of being in' (William G. Lycan, 'The Superiority of HOP not HOT' in Rocco J. Gennaro [ed.], *Higher Order Theories of Consciousness: An Anthology* [Amsterdam: John Benjamins, 2004], p.93–113 (p.96). Those theorists wishing to emphasize experience speak of the way mental states 'feel' and affirm that there are multiple unconscious and nonconscious sensory states. Allied with dispositions like belief, hope, and desire these states can become experienced states of consciousness. See Peter Carruthers, 'HOP over FOR, HOT Theory' in *Higher Order Theories of Consciousness*, pp.115–35.

no longer linked to a calculus of probabilities, but to categories like trust, loyalty, and empathy. Drawing attention to the etymological association of truth and belief, McGilchrist writes: 'The Latin word *verum* (true) is cognate with a Sanskrit word meaning to choose or believe: the option one chooses, the situation in which one place's one's trust. Such a situation is not an absolute—it tells us not only about the chosen thing, but also about the chooser. It cannot be certain: it involves an act of faith, and it involves being faithful to one's intuitions.'[10]

At this point, when it seems that a recovery of right hemisphere believing, rather than left hemisphere certainty, delivers new possibilities for moral, social, philosophical, and aesthetic development we have to pause. It is McGilchrist's alignment of belief with choice that creates the room for this pause. For who is doing the choosing? John F. Kihlstrom, in a classic article titled 'The Cognitive Unconsciousness',[11] set out to provide a provisional taxonomy of nonconscious mental structures and processes. He identifies three forms of nonconscious activity: automatic responses, where we have learned something by practice such that it requires little conscious attention to engage with that practice; subliminal perception, where stimuli too weak to be consciously detected (exposed to us for between one and five milliseconds) impact on our impressions, judgements, and actions and engage 'preattentive processes'; and implicit memory, where events that cannot be consciously remembered have a palpable effect upon our experience, thought, and action. He lists, albeit tentatively, a fourth form of nonconscious processing related to hypnosis and amnesia, suggesting that 'posthypnotic' suggestion and 'hypnotic amnesia' both expand the domain of nonconscious activity and give some insight into nonconscious structures. But, for our purposes, we can leave that fourth investigative probing to one side. One point is salient: Freud's 'unconscious' is not nearly as amorphous as he supposed, but it nevertheless subtends all our conscious processes such that 'consciousness is not to be identified with any particular perceptual-cognitive functions such as discriminative response to stimulation, perception, memory, or the higher processes involved in judgement and problem-solving. All these functions can take place outside of phenomenal awareness.'[12]

Kihlstrom published his article back in 1987, and considerable work has been done on every aspect of the forms of 'cognitive unconscious' he exposed. For example, more recently, neuroscientists have explored that important 'time lag' in the way human beings respond to the circumstances in which they find themselves. They demonstrate and reiterate that there is a mode

---

[10] I. McGilchrist, *The Master and His Emissary* (n.2), p.151.
[11] John F. Kihlstrom, 'The Cognitive Unconscious', *Science*, vol.237, pp.1445–52.
[12] Ibid., p.1450.

of liminal processing, related to embodiment and affectivity, which 'thinks' more quickly and reacts more instinctively than our conscious rational deliberation. Beneath and prior to interpretation, and the conflicts of meaning, lie sets of remembered associations and assumptions woven tightly into the processes of how we *make* sense. These associations and assumptions have been taught and arrived at through all the adaptive and trial and error scenarios of evolution. They are not innate. They are not genetic. And they are not always articulated. These assumptions constitute what some social anthropologists (Pierre Bourdieu, for example) have called 'habitus'—encultured dispositions, socialized mindsets, and biases.[13]

It is to these dispositions and biases, emerging we know not how (yet) from the body's processing of its environment through the neural, molecular, and ionic operations in and across the brain and the nervous system that I am pointing when I speak of 'beliefs'. Analytical philosophers (left-hemisphere doyens) often wish to speak of belief as 'propositional attitudes' and, as such, speak about 'judgements'. But there is too much evidence that the operations of belief come before judgement. Beliefs are 'dispositions towards judgements' or even 'dispositional attitudes'—where 'attitudes' picks up something of the affective as it pertains to believing. Just as Kihlstrom (among others) shows that our 'cognitive unconscious' arrives at judgements and impressions prior to conscious attentiveness, so we can infer that beliefs inform perception, interpretation, experience, and action prior to rationalization. Furthermore, there is no linear route from perception, belief, and thought to experience, interpretation, and action. If actions can precede consciousness and interpretation (and they can), then we are examining not a linear process but a complex set of feedback and feed-forward loops in which believing is deeply implicated.

Of course beliefs can be cognitive, as the very ability to affirm 'I believe' demonstrates. Beliefs can have explanatory value, as the developmental biologist Lewis Wolpert[14] has recently claimed in his examination of 'causal beliefs' that arise from clarifying the nature of cause and effect. 'Causal beliefs', which Wolpert argues are at the very root of believing itself, are 'ideas about how' disciplines such as science, say, win out over religion because of their commitment to efficient causation. But if belief impacts on perception, cognition, judgement, and evaluation—even precipitating action prior to these cognitive activities—then it is not simply cognitive, and can indeed *inform* why we explain things in the ways we do. The origin of belief does not lie in the early scientific imagination, seeking out 'reasons for'. Such a view already assumes

---

[13] Pierre Bourdieu, *In Other Words: Essays Toward a Reflexive Sociology*, trans. Matthew Adamson (Stanford: Stanford University Press, 1990), p.56.

[14] Lewis Wolpert, *Six Impossible Things Before Breakfast: The Evolutionary Origins of Belief* (London: Faber and Faber, 2006).

reasoning is instrumental—and it's only partly so. Beliefs are deeper, earlier, and more primitive than 'reasons for'.

Belief as an unalienable disposition towards the world, an anthropological a priori, would not be a matter of self-conscious choice; not unless we could choose that towards which we wish to be disposed. Such choosing, such decision-taking on the basis of being 'faithful to one's intuitions' would involve left hemisphere activity. McGilchrist is certainly arguing that the left hemisphere should serve, as emissary to right hemisphere mastery. So that it is not that belief has nothing to do with choice. But we need to be clearer about the relation that pertains between them, and they cannot be the same thing (despite what etymology might indicate). The question of their relationship, theologically, is highly significant with respect to faith, as the debates we encountered in Chapter 3 on faith, will, and *affectus* among the first generation Reformers demonstrate. McGilchrist flattens any distinction between belief and faith in a way that returns us to what is troubling, or at least making a pause necessary, about choice and belief:

> Some people choose to believe in materialism; they act 'as if' such a philosophy is true. An answer to the question of whether God exists could only come from my acting 'as if' God is, and in this way being true to God, and experiencing God (or not, as the case might be) as true to me. If I am a believer I have to believe in God, and God, if he exists, has to believe in me.[15]

This is stylistically neat, with an echo of Meister Eckhart, but for a Christian believer, for theology, it actually drives a wedge between belief and faith on a couple of grounds.

First, that characterization of believing as acting 'as if' is rather condescending; for from what exalted level can one judge another person to be acting 'as if' what they believe is true—rather than acting in conviction that this is indeed true? The logic of 'as if' here introduces into belief a degree of untruth, a degree of being true that is less than the true. Of course with belief there are no certainties, but the motivating force of some beliefs (I haven't defined what might characterize such beliefs yet) would not admit that one's experience of the world was just a matter of optatives and subjunctives, hopeful wishes and might-be's.

Secondly, to what extent does anyone 'choose to believe'? I can think of one parallel to such a situation which does actually treat 'choosing to believe' 'as if' something were true. It is a scene from the Wachowski brother's film *Matrix* [1999] in which Cypher, who has betrayed Morpheus, Trinity, Neo, and the others who exist outside the simulated world created by the intelligent machines, sits in a restaurant with the agents who have been trying to track

---

15 I. McGilchrist, *The Master and His Emissary* (n.2), pp.170–1.

down the felons. He stares at the steak on his plate, lifts his knife and fork, and tells the two agents that he knows it is not real, that the matrix has engineered this simulacrum, but nevertheless he gives himself up to enjoying the illusion. But the nature of such believing has the pathological logic of sadomasochism; that is, the satisfaction of a desire knowing the true object of that desire has been substituted for an illusory one. And so pleasure is taken in what desire knows is lacking.[16] This is the logic of the 'as if . . . but nevertheless'. Agreed, there is a choice, and Cypher articulates that choosing very clearly; but it is a perverse choice and a perversion of choice, for this is the freedom to choose the form of one's bondage.

Let me take this further because we can omit the 'as if' element and still legitimately explore the question of choosing what one believes. In fact, such a liberty is the basis of rational-choice theory. I can choose to be a materialist, to take McGilchrist's example, or a Marxist. Actually it does not necessarily follow that my actions and behaviour are dictated by such a choice. There are materialist atheists like Daniel Dennett and Richard Dawkins who accept that every organism is a disposable machine for the transmission of DNA—only DNA survives; everything else is used to ensure that survival. But, really, is that how either of them see members of their family or their friends? Is that how they respond when there are reports of children who have had their throats slit and lie in a dusty street of a Syrian town? I can choose to believe that, rationally calculated, materialism best fits the facts as we have them, but this form of believing is much more akin to Locke's account of knowledge; it is believing very much in service to the probability calculus of left hemisphere thinking. It cannot be equated, as McGilchrist does, with faith. Certainly, there is a circularity about believing in God that is an important aspect of a pious pedagogy: the more one submits to faith the more one is confirmed within that faith (though still allowance has to be made for very ordinary periods of what mystics, in a more elevated sense, called the dark night of the soul). But I do not choose to believe in the same manner that I choose to vote Labour or grow rhubarb rather than radishes. In fact, choice here is far too locked into the assumption of a Cartesian, monadic ego who does the choosing. In right hemisphere activity there is self-awareness because of the concern for relation, but not the ego-controller. There are accounts, some of them Scriptural, which bear witness to an experience not of choosing God but being chosen by God. The account of communicative relations in Chapter 5 would not support faith as a choosing; despite Pascal, it is not a rational-theory option. Faith is a response to a recognition of a prior calling; the cosmic calling of Christ in whom and by whom and through whom

---

[16] See Graham Ward, 'Theology and Cultural Sadomasochism' in *Svensk Teologisk Kvartalskrift*, Årg. 78 (2001), 2–10.

all things were created and are. Such a re-cognition is based in something familiar, something half-known, known intuitively, known in the very sub-structures of our being human; that we are created, that we have a Creator. So McGilchrist's characterization of the links between believing, choosing, and the 'as if' neither does justice to the rich complexity of belief in God, nor accurately describes how one comes to such a belief.

All I have said does not invalidate McGilchrist's important observations on belief. It simply helps us to clarify the difference between belief and faith, and their relationship. On his analysis of the relation between choosing and belief he seems to slip from either right hemisphere activity or the recon-ciliation of right with left hemisphere activity, into purely left hemisphere ratiocination. It's easily done because of our modern training in various dis-ciplines. The distinction between belief and faith, though, is crucial. For there is something too reassuring about McGilchrist's more morally responsible, empathetic, and generously accepting right hemisphere activity and the cre-ative believing it engenders. To get at what most troubles me here we must recall the whole thesis of *The Master and His Emissary*: that Western his-tory and culture reveals the increasing reliance upon left hemisphere activity such that human beings are no longer being true to the whole of their nature. We need an 'unworlding' of the world made in the left hemisphere's image. The advocacy for this 'unworlding' is most keenly pursued in the penultimate chapter of McGilchrist's book, where he presents the modern and the post-modern world-view that has issued from the slide into the predominance of left-hemisphere instrumental rationalism.

The twentieth and early twenty-first century culture of the West is character-ized by 'a loss of meaning in the experienced world'[17] which inaugurates a cer-tain schizophrenia. In fact, in McGilchrist, for whom the operations of the brain not only constitute the world in its own image but that world in turn informs the operations of the brain, an analysis of the world of a schizophrenic provides us with insights into the world that we live in. In this schizophrenia while there is an increasing drive towards certainty, transparency, and the immediacy of knowing, there is also, simultaneously, a drive towards 'derealisation' in which the world is 'robbed of its substantiality'.[18] As such the world is increasingly unworlded by left hemisphere predilections because it is increasingly emptied of 'its human resonance or significance'.[19] And so we have fragmentation, alien-ation, and reductive abstractions, on the one hand, and the crass of appeal to the self-evidently material on the other. In rather telling phrases, McGilchrist writes about how 'the left hemisphere interposes a simulacrum between reality and our consciousness'[20] and the '[i]ncreasing virtuality'[21] of human experience. It is exactly with these terms 'simulacrum' and 'virtuality', and the acceleration

---

[17] I. McGilchrist, *The Master and His Emissary* (n.2), p.390.   [18] Ibid., p.398.
[19] Ibid.   [20] Ibid., p.402.   [21] Ibid., p.407.

in their production, that the changes are announced in the structures that organize our understanding of knowledge, and therefore, the nature of believing, the nature of faith, and their relationship.

TWO FORMS OF BELIEVING: FAITH

Before I give a specific example and pursue an analysis of contemporary believing, let me recap what McGilchrist's work has enabled us to recognize, because there is a question and a hope here that I wish to extract from some complexity. Three points are salient. First, believing not as a weak form of knowing but a faithful entrustment to one's intuitions that will always remain somewhat inchoate, even if resonant with meaning, is a right hemisphere cognitive and affective activity. It is a faithfulness to pursuing those intuitions, seeking to understand them; it makes faith possible. Secondly, modernity is driven by the need for true and certain knowledge discovered, measured, and evaluated through instrumental reasoning that requires faster and increasingly more efficient forms of technology, bureaucracy, and surveillance to filter out untruth and illusion. This drive expresses the betrayal of the Master (right hemisphere activity) by the emissary (left hemisphere activity). Thirdly, cutting itself off from the experiential grounding, the concern for context and time, caring and empathetic attentiveness of right hemisphere activity, modernity increasingly generates an image of itself (upon which it increasingly reflects), convinced that what it views in the mirror of its representations is the truth about all that is. Hence in the staggering over-production of simulacra and virtual realities, another form of believing emerges from this left hemisphere tyranny that is not the same as the believing that issues from right hemisphere activity.

At the conclusion of chapter twelve, McGilchrist teases out the difference between believing in point one and believing that issues on the basis of point three:

> Post-modern indeterminacy affirms not that there is a reality, towards which we must carefully, tentatively, patiently struggle; it does not posit a truth which is nonetheless real because it defies the determinacy imposed upon it by the self-conscious left-hemisphere interpreter . . . On the contrary, it affirms that there *is* no reality, no truth to interpret or determine. The contrast here is like the difference between the 'unknowing' of a believer and the 'unknowing' of an atheist. Both believer and atheist may quite coherently hold the position that any assertion about God will be untrue; but their reasons are diametrically opposed . . . One say 'I do not know', the other 'I know—that there is nothing to know'. One believes that one cannot know: the other 'knows' that one cannot believe.[22]

[22] Ibid., p.427.

My suggestion here is that McGilchrist is treating, and that contemporary Western culture is expressing, two different forms of believing. The first form of believing is conducive to faith (right hemisphere activity) and the other form of believing is what emerges when the epistemological conditions are such that there is neither truth nor reality, only simulacrum. The latter condition links into Locke's understanding of believing as a weak mode of knowledge taken to its extreme, where knowledge itself implodes and scepticism goes all the way down a hall of broken mirrors. The first form of believing is possible on the basis of truth, empathy, and belonging to a context far broader than the atomized individual. The latter form of believing is the product of fragmentation, lack of trust and over-reliance on the convictions of an isolated subject afloat upon a world where any objective truth or reality is denied. The first form is a believing *in*—there is an object, a relation, and an active commitment. The second form lacks an object, relation, or commitment. It is a passive residual state when the gods have fled and in their place is a profound distrust in what one is told to be certain. This is the condition of being profoundly lost. The hope to which I alluded above lies exactly in the possibility of the epistemological conditions of this last understanding of believing providing some basis for conversion to the first form of believing. The question, to which I also alluded above, arises from an inquiry into what makes a belief believable; for only by attempting to distinguish different forms of making a belief believable can we begin to disentangle the two forms of believing prevalent in our contemporary culture and recognize how the first (right hemisphere form) might be encouraged and educated in its self-understanding. Such an encouragement and education would mean, in McGilchrist's terms, reconnecting it with left-hemisphere activity. That connection, I would maintain, is at the very core of what it means for faith to seek understanding.

In terms of faith's relationship to belief as a dominant right hemisphere activity handed over to the emissary, the left hemisphere, so it might be better lit and articulated, three points can be made that clarify both the distinctiveness of belief from faith and the extent to which they work together.

First, religious faith is a specific commitment to belief, to the invisible that pertains to and subtends the visible. It values believing; in fact, in the reversal of the modern order in which knowledge and understanding take priority over belief. I believe in order that I may know. But, as I have been arguing throughout, this is the way things are: any knowing is always knowing *as* just as any perceiving is seeing *as*. Knowing and perceiving are always partial. They are always a dwelling 'in uncertainties, mysteries, doubts' (Keats on 'negative capability'). It is a knowing and perceiving shot through with and issuing from deeper primordial dispositions *to* believe.

Secondly, religious faith is therefore a specific orientation of the more primordial disposition to believe. It is not a different type of believing. It is the same disposition framed by and exercised within specific religious practices. This does not mean that the culturally and historically informed practices are interchangeable between religious faiths. Neither does this mean that these practices are only the symbolic clothing for a deeper ontological reality (as in the liberal theologian Paul Tillich's discussion of 'ultimate concern'). Belief is rooted in and always oriented towards the material. To use a Christian metaphor: belief incarnates and is always incarnational. The symbolic activity of higher order consciousness is not divorced from the physiological and emotional activity of believing. Each are continually informing and modifying the other. Religious faith as experienced by a Muslim and religious faith as experienced by a Jew, a Christian, a Hindu, is not the same; although each faith and experience is an orientation of the primordial disposition, and that disposition is a response to what is given in the call of divine communicative relations. How they experience the modes of that giveness cannot be the same, because what is meaningful and what becomes meaningful in the experience cannot be separated from the cultural and historical specificities that have shaped and given expression to that experience within a specific (and never culturally isolated, never homogenous) religious tradition.

Theologians from and of these various traditions might wish to develop theologies of experience, but there is never something generic that might be called just 'religious experience'. Tillich (and liberal Christian theologians of his ilk) is wrong because his account of human experience is wrong. Can we say then that each of these different theologies reveals aspects of the one God? That sounds like another, albeit more complex, take on liberal theology. And, as a statement, it too would be wrong, because all we know about 'aspects' relates to objects. I visit a cathedral and see one aspect of it from outside, and there is another aspect of it from inside. But whatever 'God' is or names, God is not an object. So we cannot speak of these theologies as different aspects of the one God. Therefore, what can we say? Only that the mystery pertaining to the invisible in the visible, the mystery of consciousness itself that cannot either understand the relationship between mind and brain or dissolve one into the other—a mystery then that constitutes the mystery of being human itself—is considerably deepened when it comes to the call of divine communicative relations and any notion of a transcendent intentionality written into our being created at all. We will return to this in Volume IV.

Thirdly, if believing is constitutive of knowing *as* and seeing *as*, then religious believing is a mode of perception. In the Gospel of St. John, chapter 12, we find the following account of Jesus praying publicly after his baptism. 'Father, glorify thy name.' Then came a voice from heaven saying, 'I have both glorified it, and will glorify it again.' The people therefore that stood by, and heard it, said that it thundered; others said, 'An angel spoke to him.' Jesus answered and said, 'This voice came not for me, but for your sakes.' It is well known that one of the major themes in John's gospel concerns believing and its relationship to seeing and hearing the gospel preached. The theme culminates in the penultimate chapter of John's gospel with the scene between Christ and doubting Thomas and the statement: 'blessed are they that have not seen and have believed' (John 20.29). The one experience is perceived in three different ways: it thundered, an angel spoke, and the voice of the Father. There is a hierarchy of interpretations of this experience, with the truth lying with Jesus's own perception of the event and why it occurred. What it points towards is that religious believing is a way of responding to the world that recognizes and valorizes the invisible operative *within* what is materially visible of that world. All knowing and seeing *as* is interpretative. We don't just know or see. So in religious believing there is an interpretative process, as there is in every other knowing and seeing *as*. This might explain why in several languages (German and Greek for example) the word for 'belief' and the word for 'faith' are the same (*Glauben* and *pistis* in the two languages cited). We live, inhabit, and continually negotiate invisibilities within the visible; knowledge and perception are always incomplete. In fact, the incompleteness is built into knowledge and perception such that we are continually haunted by a sense of what we do not know. 'The foundations of knowledge eludes us,' the neuroanatomist Rayond Tallis informs us.[23] 'Our gaze sees not only what is visible, but also that there are things or parts of things that are invisible ... The visual field is dappled with *visible invisibilities*.'[24] So if transcendence begins in the recognition that I am not *this* chair here or *that* person over there, *this* dog or *that* tree, if transcendence begins with the knowledge and perception of what is other and external, then transcendence itself begins and ends in what is hidden, concealed—the original Greek meaning of the word *mysterion*. What transcends is our being hidden with Christ in God.

We would expect, then—in the practice of faith seeking understanding, of believing in order to know—multiple forms of belief cooperating with and diverging from different modes of perception.

BUT—and this returns us to the analogical—a 'gap' remains between the human and the divine, human *scientia* and divine knowledge. We are led to that gap, that visible invisibility, between Adam's finger and God's in Michelangelo's painting in the Sistine Chapel. The gap is unbridgeable *for us*, but it opens up the greatest of all space of possibles. The space demands we point ahead of ourselves, into what is hidden in the invisibility, into the heart of believing itself—for something being given and for something for which we are groping. Encountering this space of possibles is depicted in the

---

[23] Raymond Tallis, *In Defence of Wonder and Other Philosophical Reflections* (Durham: Acumen, 2012), pp.34–5. For a more in-depth analysis see his *Aping Mankind: Neuromania, Darwinitis and the Misrepresentation of Humanity* (Durham: Acumen, 2011). Tallis self-identifies as an atheist.

[24] Ibid., p.69.

story of a father who comes to Jesus with a child who is possessed. The case is a bad one, and Jesus tells the man that a miracle is possible, for 'All things are possible for the one who believes.' The father responds: 'I believe; help my unbelief!' (Mark 9.23–4).

TWO FORMS OF BELIEVING: VIRTUALITY

There is a second form of believing indicated in McGilchrist's work, as we noted. This form is the product of the usurped mastery of the left hemisphere. It is characteristic of postmodernity, a contemporary culture based in the schizophrenic imaginary that produces and inhabits 'simulacrum' and 'virtuality'. Nominalism becomes rampant as signs and logos, image and icon are increasingly detached from material entities and take on an independent life. This is the age of the brand name. McGilchrist offers us his analysis to demonstrate the deepening human condition that issues from a neglect of right hemisphere sensitivities. His descriptions of this condition, in which the embodied and therefore the social (and political) is engulfed by the cultural, point to a significant change in the structures of believing with which theology as faith seeking understanding has to engage. In order to understand the struggle to discern that is demanded of faith today (a struggle that cannot be filtered out of that 'seeking' of understanding by and through faith), we need to be aware of the cultural transformations in the production of belief that have been taking place throughout modernity, but at a greater accelerated pace since the end of the Second World War. We enter other forests in which we are lost and, in foraging for a direction like the film crew in *The Blair Witch Project*, penetrate even further into the nightmares of disorientation.

At the beginning of Chapter 3, we saw how it has become intellectually fashionable to examine the genealogy of this nominalism as a causal force in a narrative of the decline in Christian orthodoxy; and as a key driver in secularism itself. As I pointed out, such narratives began to emerge with *nouvelle théologie*, particularly with the work of Henri de Lubac and Yves Congar. De Certeau, himself a Jesuit and student of de Lubac, in *La Fable Mystique*, explores the historical details of this narrative: the rise of nominalism in late medieval scholasticism led to the certain cultural 'opacity' which, in turn, impacted upon modernity's preoccupation with transparency and the immediate. 'Ockhamism—and this is a symbol of a larger evolution—stripped discourse of its ultimate verification.'[25] Other more recent cultural historians,

---

[25] Michel De Certeau, *La Fable Mystique*, vol. 1, XVIe-XVIIe Siècle (Paris: Editions Gallimard, 1982). Trans. *The Mystic Fable: Volume One: The Sixteen and Seventeenth Centuries*, Michael B. Smith (Chicago: The University of Chicago Press, 1992), p.29.

such as Cyril O'Regan, have examined this phenomenon in terms of a new Gnosticism infecting modernity from the seventeenth century.[26] Frequently, critics of these narratives of decline, this eclipse of sacramental realism where signs participate in their materialities they signify and God's communicative relations, argue that they are exercises in nostalgia; haunted by a theological desire to return to and re-establish the pre-Ockhamite ontology upon the basis of which theological knowledge and ethics can once more flourish. They sense a loss, a melancholy, and a mourning in these narratives. De Certeau's work, interested as it is with psychoananlysis, scrutinizes this loss.

De Certeau views the decline of Christendom as concomitant with 'the evolution of a society, its stresses and aspirations'.[27] His 'evolution' avoids even a wiff of nostalgia because he pushes the origin of Christianity's decline right back to the moment the historical body of Jesus the Christ ascends to heaven. From that point a body is lost, but that loss is concealed in a vast and distending dissemination of the Logos—a dissemination in which ecclesial corporations will wax and wane. The immediacy of the Word, what de Certeau calls '*the event* which inaugurated',[28] is from henceforth mediated through various Christian discourses that no one could or can control. Every mediation is related to the event and permitted by it, 'but none is identical to it'.[29] The event itself is irrecoverable; and because it is irrecoverable the foundations for theological and ecclesial mediations can never be grasped as such. God's Word, as other, continually goes forth and human societies are continually being transformed. The dissemination of the discursive effects of that transcendent Saying (Christ as Logos, as God's most manifest communicative relations *for us*) appeals to and yearns towards another embodiment that cannot be captured.[30] When orthodoxy, which is an attempt to police the dissemination in the name of 'fidelity' to the original event, is produced then it will always occur negatively through naming what is heterodox, heretical, and anathema. But for de Certeau that dualism of orthodoxy and heterodoxy can only hold while the institution insisting upon it is strong and culturally dominant. As Christendom develops, its power to police and enforce implodes. 'Schism' names the new territory; a new cultural condition, upon which modernity founds itself.

So, for de Certeau, pluralism is intrinsic to the event of Christ itself; an event made possible by the loss of the body of Christ. In fact, the '"truth" of

---

[26] Cyril O'Regan, *Gnostic Return in Modernity* (New York, SUNY Press, 2001).
[27] Michel de Certeau, 'Culture and Spiritual Experience', *Concilium* (1966), p.4.
[28] Michel de Certeau, 'How is Christianity Thinkable Today?' in Graham Ward (ed.), *The Postmodern God* (Oxford: Blackwell, 1998), pp.142–55, p.142.
[29] Ibid., p.144.
[30] De Certeau sketches this new embodiment lyrically and evasively in the final coda of *The Mystic Fable* (n.25).

the beginning of an event is revealed only through the possibilities which it opens up.'[31] For an 'event' only remains an 'event', can be understood as an 'event', if it propagates endless possibilities. There will always be new religious movements 'for those who testify and claim that by "new words" and present actions [they] are truly bearing witness to the work of the Holy Spirit in their day and age'.[32] De Certeau is not buying into modern ideologies of progress (or declines) because there is no human standpoint from which such progress towards (or decline from) the Promised Land is possible. Nevertheless, because all possibilities relate back to the inaugural event, an event in Christianity that promises a consummation (the return of the Word, the return of the body of Christ), then he holds to an eschatology, a work of the Holy Spirit, in which the old ways of saying things get taken up in a different way and proffer new articulations. Because the event itself is never recoupable and something other than the event itself always inhabits the new expressions of that event, then the social and cultural operations of dissemination with respect to faith are not without their crises and ruptures: sites where an intensification of an abiding tension between tradition and new articulations become most evident.

He investigates one of these sites in his book *The Possession at Loudon*: the explosion of Satanic possessions in the early seventeenth century.[33] But even these crises and ruptures are not without their continuities with what had gone before them. As the unity of the faith is shattered with the Reformation so that unity is refocused, finding an new political form in the unity of the state and nationalism. 'While religious behaviour and symbols still obtained, their functioning was changing.'[34]

Unlike the narratives of decline we examined in Chapter 3, de Certeau does not evaluate the cultural transformations that follow from the event of the loss of Christ's historical body. They are neither good nor bad. He does not prioritize as some benchmark of the faith, one historical expression of that faith. Because there is no evaluation of change, then his language of evolution is neither Hegelian nor Darwinian. While his appreciation of change is eschatological—'faith speaks prophetically of a Presence who is both immediately felt and yet still to come'[35]—it is not teleological. Because there is social movement and cultural transformation, because there is a history of the mediated effects of the inaugural event, then believing comes to the fore as an operation of 'weak' knowing or what de Certeau terms 'fable'. 'The spoken word [*parole*] in particular, so closely bound to religious traditions [because of Christ as the

---

[31] De Certeau, 'How Christianity is Thinkable Today' (n.28), p.145.

[32] De Certeau, 'Culture and Spiritual Experience' (n.27), p.4.

[33] Michel de Certeau, *The Possession at Loudon*, trans. Michael B. Smith (Chicago: Chicago University Press, 1996).

[34] De Certeau, 'Culture and Spiritual Experience' (n.27), p.19   [35] Ibid., p.11.

Word], has evolved, since the sixteenth century, into what its scientific "examiners" and "observers" have for three centuries designated as the "fable".[36] The *Aufklarung* may have rejected or downgraded such fables as fictions, but they miss the point in wanting to move too quickly towards foundational truths, transparency, and the knowledge of angels. Narrative is more primordial than causality and induction; narrative is the articulation and the practice that best articulates the operation of desire for the other, the transcendence of the Logos that is always finding new discursive accommodations. The 'accommodations', for de Certeau, are a recognition that the Messianic spoken word is the condition for the possibility of all articulations that follow, and this condition can only achieve its consummate articulation in Christ's return. 'Faith is the discovery which recognizes in everyday language that there is Someone speaking to whom one can reply. It is thus already aware that all human speech has a divine meaning.'[37] What remain, what abide, are 'fables'. But these narratives can nevertheless provide scintillas of a Presence that is 'immediately felt'. De Certeau remains faithful to an analogical relation between the divine and the human; he does not capitulate to nominalism while exploring the consequences for the proliferation of knowledges that nominalism (among several other cultural movements) fostered.

There is much here that could relate to my theology of communicative relations, but de Certeau does not enter such theological waters. Rather, he explores the spiritual cries of the mystics and the possessed in the sixteenth and seventeenth century. His historical examinations, particularly in *Possession du Loudon* and *La Fable Mystique* expose the crises of belief that are concomitant with crises of knowledge and representation. Changes then in the structures of believing become particularly prominent when we enter forests of diverse knowledges where scepticism thrives not because there is evident confusion so much as there are too many reasoned possibilities accounting for a particular object such that the object itself cannot be grasped. For de Certeau, the seventeenth century possession of the Ursuline nuns in Loudon composes a singular historical occasion that forces us to face this forest of knowledges and the condition of being lost. What his analysis of the documentation affirms is the prevalence of the fable; that knowledge is never simply 'what is out there'—it is never simply a collection of named persons, a set of actions, an accumulation of objects or a collection of facts. Knowledge is 'made to appear'; it is produced. And what certain events reveal, like the exorcisms of the nuns and the burning alive of the 'sorcerer' Urbain Grandier, are the processes of production, legitimation, and dissemination as these knowledges are 'made to appear' and interfere with each other's 'making sense'.

---

[36] Ibid., p.12.   [37] Ibid., p.11.

Production here does not condemn us to constructivism: the names of persons, the sets of actions, the accumulation of objects, and the collection of facts all have empirical existence. But rather like contemporary cosmology, where 'dark stars' first postulated by John Michell in 1793 became the 'black holes' demonstrated by Roy Kerr in 1963, this knowledge is the 'product' of numerous mediations. Kerr, like Scharzschild before him, was handling mathematical calculations. The actual observation of 'black holes' was only made possible after 1998, and even then what is 'observed' takes place through the mediation of the Hubble telescope and rests upon certain inferences drawn from photographs: of 'accretion disks' and swirling gases to which are applied Newton's laws of motion to arrive at orbital velocities. Knowledge then, whatever the empirical data, is always mediated. It requires various technologies in order 'to appear'—from the presence of the host or the monstrance which forces the devils to speak through the bodies of the nuns, through institutions (the Church with its exorcists, the scientific establishments through its doctors, the state through its lawyers, etc.) that interpret these articulations, to the written representations of these 'dialogues' and their circumstances that were greedily taken up by the publishing houses, pamphleteers, and newspapers for wider circulation. With the recognition of the production of knowledge the questions begin to proliferate, primarily: who is producing, for what reasons, with what authority, and what data is forgotten, elided, or bent in this production? And always circulating these questions are the words true, truth, truly, and truthfully. Like comets, these knowledges have tails reaching back into the past. Some have much longer traditions than others—theological and legal knowledges. Others are emerging from new approaches interpreting the world—the natural and then the social sciences. Some alliances are formed; some trenches are dug; and some enemies are identified.

DESCARTES' WOOD

It is in this way that we encounter, as I promised we would in Chapter 5, the forest of knowledges that Descartes describes in the third part of his *Discourse on Method* (*methodos*—a way of inquiring, a '*demonstratio viae* [which] pointing out the path').[38] Entry into this intellectual wood leads to his radical employment of doubt in his *Meditations* and the arrival at what he hopes is a 'way' (*odos*) to certainty. The first two parts of *Discourse* form an express confession of the 'shifting foundations' and the plethora of different

---

[38] De Certeau, *The Mystic Fable* (n.25), p.127.

opinions held by learned men.[39] In fact, in the very first part Descartes comes to the conclusion that 'there was no body of knowledge in the world such as I had been led previously to have existed'.[40] So despite his commitment to 'the plumb-line of reason'[41] and the reason's natural light, Descartes 'learned not to believe too firmly'.[42] Then, in part three, he develops four maxims for how to proceed, the second of which concerns orientation in a forest:

> My second maxim was to be as firm and resolute in my actions as I could, and to follow no less constantly [*constamment*] the most doubtful [*douteuses*] opinions, once I determined [*déterminé*] on them, than I would if they were very assured [*assurées*], imitating in this travellers, who, finding themselves astray in some forest, must not wander, turning now this way and now that, and even less stop in one place, but must walk always as straight as they can in a given direction, and not to change direction for weak reasons [*faibles raisons*], even though it was perhaps only chance in the first place [*peut-être été au commencement que le hasard*] which made them chose it; for, by this means, if they do not go exactly where they wish [*justement où ils désirent*] to go they will arrive at least somewhere in the end [*au moins à la fin quelque part*] where they will very likely [*vraisemblablement*] be better off [*mieux*] than in the middle of the forest.[43]

The French is important in understanding the dizzying structure of this passage in which knowledge founded upon reason (that belongs to the semantic field of *constamment, déterminé, assures,* and *justement*) is invaded by the more insubstantial mists of belief (that belong to the semantic field of *faibles raisons, peut-être,* and *le hazard*). The concluding clause sums up the see-sawing and vacillation. Poised between the spectrum of possibilities that separates *au moins* from *mieux*, the arrival is only at a highly indefinite *quelque part* and though the travellers may no longer be in the middle of the forest (actually to determine a forest's middle would be a major contribution to one's orientation) they are only *vraisemblablement* better off. *Vraisemblablement* translates as 'seemingly' but the verb *'sembler'* (to seem, to appear to be the case is suffixed by *'vrai'* meaning 'true' as 'that based upon fact'). The portmanteau combination creates something of an oxymoron: a 'true appearance', a 'factual possibility'. No less than Chaucer in the forest of the *Book of the Duchess* or the film crew in *The Blair Witch Project*, what is lost in this forest is twofold: the subject 'I' and a 'body of knowledge'. Both the subject and the object are missing, such that Descartes is both attempting to find himself and the foundations for a knowledge of the world in which that self is located—like a detective thrown into self-doubt and confusion because

---

[39] *Discourse on Method and The Meditations*, trans. F.E. Sutcliffe (Harmondsworth: Penguin Books, 1968), p.32. The French text, *Discours de la method*, can be found online at <http://www.gutenberg.org/files/13846/13846-h/13846-h.htm>, accessed August 2015.
[40] Ibid., p.29.   [41] Ibid., p.37.   [42] Ibid., 33.   [43] Ibid., pp.46-7.

he cannot find the body he knows must be buried somewhere in the woods. We will return to the missing 'body' in a moment.

For now it is significant that '[m]ethod appeared above all as a temporal way of proceeding from one site to another'.[44] It was not concerned with discovering universal laws, but rather with finding a way out of the labyrinth. It had the 'logic of a game'[45] that broke with the past in favour of what was most useful for the present. 'The idea of usefulness allowed for the construction of a future to replace respect for tradition.'[46] The forest, as we have seen, is a trope for total confusion, and Descartes, like Chaucer, does not emerge from such a forest with the confidence of having understood something anew. Though he does emerge, while the film crew in *The Blair Witch Project* does not. But neither Chaucer's nor Descartes' experiences—unlike Sir Gawain's and Dante's—furnishes a new wisdom. Here, as with our other two examples, the trope of the forest announces a paralysing crisis, a breakdown of sense that is both personal and cultural. In terms of contemporary neuroscience, in a forest of knowledges a subject experiences extreme cognitive dissonance because he or she is unable to 'model the world'.[47] There are too many conflicting possibilities being offered. The forest of knowledges then pictures a paradise gone wild; a paradise after the expulsion of those human beings given the responsibility of tending it. From the tree of the knowledge of good and evil, seed has fallen and been blown by the winds of time so that now a bewildering woodland of possibilities, trails and tracks, conceals a host of potential friends and enemies who announce tests, challenges, and temptations. A 'disquieting insecurity'[48] prevails in what Alexander Pope, in the early eighteen century will term 'the Sylvan war'.[49] The way out of Descartes' forest, fostered by the ontological, epistemological, and ethical crises of the seventeenth century—with the Wars of Religion throughout the first half and then the establishment of the secular state—was what became Enlightenment reason. This left hemisphere reasoning brought a new organization—a system of differentiations, taxonomies, denominations, and tables—to the forest of knowledges.

The difference between the forest Dante finds himself in and the forest from which Descartes emerges is that for Dante the entry into the forest is by way of a 'straying'. There is a right path; orthodoxy remains. And there is a way back to that orthodoxy—even though he must first circuit Hell and

---

[44] De Certeau, *The Mystic Fable* (n.25), p.127.   [45] Ibid., p.128.

[46] Ibid., p.129.

[47] For the neuropsychology of modelling the world see 'The Biology of Knowing', Part III of Antonio Damasio's *The Feeling of What Happens: Body, Emotion and the Making of Consciousness*, pp.131–276.

[48] De Certeau, *The Mystic Fable* (n.25), p.59.

[49] Alexander Pope, *Windsor Forest* in *The Poems of Alexander Pope* (London: Methuen & Co. Ltd, 1963), p.200.

Purgatory. For Descartes there is no path from which he 'strayed'. Because, post-Reformation, no orthodoxy remains, only schism, so there is no direction discernable ahead that is not questionable. In the space of the indecidable he forges a way forward, an *odos*, by mean of a technique, a *meth-odos*. He works instrumentally in a manner similar to huge machines filmed cutting through swaths of the Amazonian rainforest to create fields for the production of biocrops.[50] The foundations for knowledge, for *scientia*, are 'made'; and these foundations provide the possibility for new faiths: like the faith in the therapeutic powers of psychoanalysis, or the faith in the revolutionary power of Marxism; or the current faith in free market economics for the global redistribution of wealth. Each of these new faiths is an exercise in *Heilsgeschichte*—once the provenance of Christian eschatology. What connects Dante's forest to Descartes' is a certain continuity that remains with the tradition—though it is a tradition now transposed into other languages, which has located new sites for a different dissemination. Descartes' forest will eventually give way to the manicured and trained gardens of the eighteenth century's fabrication of a new Eden:

> Here Hills and Vales, the Woodland and the Plain,
> Here Earth and Water seem to strive again,
> Not *Chaos*-like together crush'd and bruis'd,
> But as the World, harmoniously confus'd:
> Where Order in Variety we see,
> And where, tho' all things differ, all agree.[51]

THE FOREST OF BELIEFS

What takes place in this new dissemination, following the shattering of Christendom's unifying ideology, is the manufacture of numerous sciences, ideologies or mythologies that sometimes compete for a legitimation founded upon their explanatory power (and an institutional authorization for that explanatory power) and sometimes form uneasy alliances one with another. Just as the Satanic possessions of Loudon created a conflict of interpretation

---

[50] This metaphor is not incidental. Descartes' notion of the *ego cogito* emerges with a context of colonial expansion such that Enrique Dussel has made a comparison between this ego and the ideal conquistador. On the relationship between *ego cogito* and *ego conquiro* and the movement into certainty from radical scepticism see N. Maldonado-Torres, 'On the Coloniality of Being: Contributions to the Development of a Concept,' *Cultural Studies*, 21, 2–3, 2007.

[51] De Certeau, *The Mystic Fable* (n.25), p.195. Of course this was the time when Louis XIV of France turned a waterlogged wilderness behind his father's old hunting lodge into the palace and gardens of Versailles.

(and interests) between the former doctors of the church and the doctors of a new medical science, so today, psychoanalysis will compete with psychiatry as two discourses and methods of treating pathology, and accumulative capitalism will ally itself with the triumphant march of democracy (which, in turn, will avail itself of various social Darwinian myths of progress through selection). 'Knowledge will henceforth consist of regions whose differences are insurmountable and whose methods are specific to each region,' de Certeau writes.[52]

In a forest of knowledges transgression becomes meaningless and each wandering expresses a new fable and initiates another narrative. Nevertheless, the wandering while occasionally 'mad' because it capitulates to the arbitrary, is orchestrated. Where 'uncertain frames of reference'[53] prevail there nevertheless remains, for de Certeau, not only the desire to believe, the promise of Logos yet to come, but the solicitation of belief (like those prophets maligned by Christ who come in His name and say, 'I am he'—Mark.13.6). When an old order goes into an eclipse a new order must emerge. Objects of belief will be produced; things will be 'shown' to be the case; coherences will be 'made' to appear. Demonstration of what is true is always, in the forest of knowledges, a persuasion of what is true. Such demonstrations, like the methods they either give rise to (inductively) or are based upon (deductively), provide 'clearings'. But the haunting possibility of deception or delusion, that requires a subjection to further interpretation and discernment, clings to the surface of certainties. Nothing can be the object of a pure gaze and the call for evermore transparency follows from the recognition that the system is fissured with deviant behaviours and semantic opacities. The fissuring introduces obfuscation into the processes of verification and adjudication. Acts of believing (as they may or may not evolve into practices of believing) form slowly; emerging from tenuously organized nodal points: trust, coherence (with other things believed), what can be seen, what works (in being able to produce what it says it can produce), what is reliable (over a series of encounters), what is probable (according to some calculus based upon previous experience or the acceptance of other people's experience), what is plausible (which relates to a spectrum of what might be believed and what others have believed), what can be inferred (a logical process from a matrix of experiences similar and dissimilar from which conclusions can be drawn) and what guarantees (which already indicate a certain fallibility in believing) or legitimates.

The organizational structure for believing is not static. According to many cognitive neuroscientists, while 'we are susceptible to prior beliefs and social constrains that greatly limit our ability to deal with evidence rationally',[54] and this impedes the process of changing our beliefs, nevertheless, we are continually

---

[52] Ibid., p.104.   [53] De Certeau, *The Possession at Loudon* (n.33), p.27.
[54] *Neuroscience*, January 2009, vol.10, p.52.

updating our belief systems. Trust is the key point in the organization of belief; and related to trust is a confidence which means taking a risk, moving to an elsewhere which cannot be grasped either *as* the move is made or *when* the move has been made. The ability or inability to entrust oneself opens (or forestalls) the full spectrum of belief: from weak believing (that does not translate itself into acts but remains at the level of unenquiring acceptance) to a commitment of faith (which is a commitment not just to act 'in the name of' but to practise—and thereby be formed by—what is believed). We saw in the early chapters, outlining the shift from creed to dogmatics and when examining truth, *praxis* is more profound than 'knowledge of'. *Praxis* is both the acting that issues *from* a believing and the acting that issues *in* coming to believe. *Praxes* perform more than, and frequently transgress, what is codified in any discursive knowledge. And so de Certeau can claim that 'the practise of Christians has always been, and remains today, something other than official laws and theological teaching'.[55] Its doctrine is lived.

Theologically understood, de Certeau sketches here an ecclesiology that he never develops systematically. It is an ecclesiology that relates to but remains far wider than any institutionalized church. Practised believing transgresses institutionally policed dogma and belonging. In doing so it participates in and produces new relations and therefore new, though quite liquid, communities. For the commitment of faith is also an-identification-with—it is an act of belonging that participates in what Hegel termed 'recognition' [*Anerkennung*]. This recognition comes from others and supports the act of believing.[56] In such recognition and identification a body is constituted: a body of knowledge, and a community of the faithful who seek to institutionalize and perpetuate that knowledge, and an institutional corporation promoting and patrolling access to that body of knowledge (devising and requiring professional qualifications for admittance, for example). As I explained, de Certeau always relates believing to the loss of and the seeking for a body; that finds its primary focus in the ascension of the historical body of Christ and the formation of the Church (later the body of Christ as the Eucharistic body, paraded in a monstrance and the focus of a public liturgy, *Corpus mysticum*). 'By "body",' he writes, 'I mean the historical and social existence [*être-là*] of an organised site.'[57] But, on his own logic, the body is never lost it is always being transposed. The formations of new

---

[55] De Certeau, 'How is Christianity Thinkable Today' (n.28), p.152.

[56] On the importance and nature of 'recognition', in Hegel and other social theorists such as Charles Taylor and Nancy Fraser, see Amy Gutmann, ed., *Multiculturalism and 'The Politics of Recognition'* (Princeton: Princeton University Press, 1992).

[57] 'The Weakness of Believing' in Graham Ward, *The de Certeau Reader* (Oxford: Blackwell, 1999), pp.214–43, p.215. The essays collected by Luce Giard that constitute his last book *La faiblesse de croire* (Paris: Éditions de Seuil, 1987) reveal some of de Certeau's later thought on 'weak believing'. Sometimes this 'weak believing' teeters on the edge of the mystical and sometimes on the melancholic.

bodies (of knowledge and the communities that articulate that corporality and seek to be faithful to it) are transpositions of embodiment; fundamentally, for de Certeau, a divine embodiment, a divine meaning that both haunts and galvanizes all believing. Modern and secular manifestations are modes of its cultural dissemination, the divine traces of what remains of the inaugural event's utopian character: the foraging for a foundational law, axiom, or unified theory; the correlative hope for full understanding, transparency; the grasping of what is essentially meaningful; the perfect society; a *credo in uno* etc.

Through these practices of believing, that which is divine—the other that inaugurates the event but in being withdrawn from history is at a distance from the disseminating effects of the event—moves through time, spaces, peoples, and cultures. In an essay written in 1971 de Certeau describes this as the 'movement of transcendence'.[58] But by the time he came to write his essay 'From the Body to Writing, a Christian Transit' in 1973 de Certeau was rethinking dissemination without transcendence: the other 'is no longer God'.[59] No secure site for the production of Christian believing could be found; the fable becomes a dream; the transposition becomes dissolution as the effects of difference are diffused across 'an unforeseeable plurality of systems'.[60] We will return to this in the concluding section. For the moment it is important to recognize that the fundamental organizations structuring belief remain in the transpositions of believing—even if they are facilitating the disappearance of a Christian ground. For de Certeau, the meaning of 'verification'—the proof of the truth of the inaugurating event—lies not in some dictionary definition, nor in some approved (by whom?) method in arriving at a fact of the case. Rather verification is made manifest in the ability of the event to continue this movement of transposition and transfiguration. The effects, the operations, and the works are each aspects that 'are ultimately its [Christianity's] real "verification"'.[61] The 'verification' is placed within inverted commas because it does not rely upon a seeing, a collaboration by empirical facts, an induction drawn from a series of similar results undertaken under laboratory conditions. The French for such a procedure is, tellingly, '*contrôle*'—as in the English 'a controlled experiment'. 'Verification' is the production (from the Latin *facere* and the French *faire*) of what is true (*vrai*). It is not a verification that would pass as such in contemporary science or positivist philosophy. Truth lies in the testimony of the inaugural event that produces a prolonged and continuing dissemination. The record of a tradition—in which, evidently, the more longstanding the tradition the more 'truthful' the inaugurating event—is both an indication of its truth and the

---

[58] De Certeau, 'How is Christianity Thinkable Today? (n.28), p.154.
[59] De Certeau, *La faiblesse de croire* (n.57), p.225.   [60] Ibid., p.235.
[61] De Certeau, 'How is Christianity Thinkable Today? (n.28), p.147.

gradual universalization of that truth. And so although de Certeau recognizes both Freudian psychoanalysis and Marxist socialism as truth-bearing 'events' as such, the coming of Jesus Christ (and his Ascension) is the benchmark of all believing in the West—even though that believing is detaching itself from its divine object and pursuing more immanent forms of otherness.[62]

BELIEVING NOW

De Certeau, as I said, provides a rich genealogy for McGilchrist's thesis of left hemisphere dominance. His abiding concern in doing this was the question what makes a belief believable and the articulation of what it means today to say 'Credo'. Essays written between the mid 1960s to the late 1970s in prominent theological venues such as *Concilium*, *Esprit*, and *Christus*, the most important of which were collected by Luce Giard and published in the volume *La faiblesse de croire* (1987), demonstrate as much. But we have moved elsewhere in the West since then. Guided by de Certeau, one would predict that the Christian faith *would* move elsewhere, *would* be written and newly practised in different ways and with different effects. Believing has certainly gone on a walkabout—away from the institutional structures of specific Christian sites (the Roman Catholic, Orthodox, and Protestant churches). But what we have been witnessing over the 1990s and first decade of the twenty-first century is a new visibility of religion in the public sphere and the development by certain prominent thinkers like Habermas and Derrida of depictions of a 'postsecular' condition.[63] The wave of Roman Catholic following in Latin America turned into a wave of Pentecostalism that has swept not only through that continent, but also through other continents such as Africa and Asia. In 2006 the Pew Foundation estimated almost two billion people world-wide belonged to this movement, which is now making important inroads into China. The new visibility concerns not just the Christian religion: Judaism and Islam have also gained prominence, with new messianic and millenarian sects arising, and some important political alliances being forged: between evangelical Christians and Zionism, for example. All I wish to pay attention to here is that the 'weakness of believing' that de Certeau pointed to in the 1970s and expected to spread exponentially has morphed

---

[62] There are close parallels between de Certeau's understanding of the Christian belief endless diseeminating itself in other, more secular, forms and Charles Taylor's view of the supernova of believing that follows the 'great disembedding'. See, *A Secular Age* (Cambridge, MA: The Belknap Press of Harvard University Press, 2007), pp.299–313.

[63] For an analysis of this condition see Graham Ward, *The Politics of Discipleship* (Grand Rapids, MI: Baker Academic Press, 2009), pp.117–58.

into something else. De Certeau, with hindsight, capitulated to the demise of religion being advocated by triumphalist secularists in the 1970s. I view 'weak believing' as on the increase and uncoupled now from disciplined practices of piety, Christian or otherwise, organized by concrete institutions (the mosque, the temple, the synagogue, the church, etc.). This is because we are entering another forest of knowledges like the forests of Peter Jackson's trilogies *The Lord of the Rings* [2001–2003] and *The Hobbit* [2012–2014], where while some of the trees are actual or mechanically animated the majority are virtual.

So consider then the contemporary forms of the second type of believing in the virtual and in simulacra; believing that is passive and asks nothing in the way of commitment, despite it frequent use of the imperative. Forms such as Sky TV's logo 'Believe in Better' or Sony's commercial logo 'Make. Believe' or the commercial logo for Ninetendo games, 'Believe your Eyes'. Or there's the British Olympic Team's logo for 2012, 'Genuine Belief', the title of Justin Bieber's acclaimed movie *Believe* [2013], the name of Britney Spears' own brand of perfume, 'Believe', or Apple's advertisement for the iPad 2 which opens with the statement 'This is what we believe.' Notably, all these indications of believing or calls to belief are associated with the media— that technology at the forefront of producing so much of our contemporary simulacra and virtuality. Response required for this summons to believe by the media is as negligible as it is nebulous. But it is indicative—especially so given the amount of money spent in market-research prior to the launch of any product—that believing (rather than knowing) is being given increasing cultural attention. And although there is no commitment necessary for such believing, that the believing itself is either without an object or so fluid a phenomenon that it can continually migrate between any number of proffered objects, it does not follow that there are no consequences from this weakness of believing. For the use of the word with respect to faith and religious piety transposed to iPads and perfumes liquefies believing, rendering the Christian creed just one more consumer choice in a shopping mall of possibilities. All objects for belief become commodified in this way. That does not mean that religious conviction will not win out over the frank and cheap commercialization of believing, but it does mean it will only win out after a struggle; a struggle to discern one form of believing from another. That struggle involves both an existential struggle over authenticity and illusion, and an existential commitment. This analysis does not undercut McGilchrist's comforting and optimistic presentation of right hemisphere belief, but it does make manifest that any Teddy Bear's Picnic in our contemporary culture is ringed with more sinister possibilities.

For example, consider: I download video clips of the UN intervention in the Libyan crisis. I listen to interviews and commentary on the crisis from officials in the US, France, and Britain about the possible deployment of troops, the bombing of Gaddafi's armed tanks, the maintenance of a no-fly zone, and the reassurances that this is not another Iraq or Afghanistan. I read of the rebels in Bengazi dancing on their cars in jubilation at the UN resolution, fireworks and music inflaming their resistance. I see photographs taken on mobile phones of children smiling and making victory signs, of women armed with Kalashnikovs, of young men with determined faces shouting out their defiance. I watch what I am told is Gaddafi being captured and shot. There are reports in the papers that the great tyrant whimpered and begged for his life as the rebel forces surrounded him. And what am I to make of all this? What do I know—of this situation, of the experiences of these people, of their culture or even their history? I know only, as someone who has studied Christian history, that along the coast from Alexandria to Carthage (now Tunis) a string of churches were built in cities that are no longer there or only white ruins, sand-blown and moon-washed. I see, I hear, I read, I think—and so I experience the unfolding of this violent and uncertain chain of events. There was and is and will continue to be pain, and blood, and hunger, and despair. There will be grief and joy, outrage and consolation, greed and sacrifice, friendships and enmities—experiences that will shape and scar the souls of millions for generations. But what do I know of this and why?

I don't know. I believe.

I believe history is unfolding there as the consequences of the Arab Spring unfolds, moving now to horrors in the streets of Syria while I tap the keyboard here, overlooking a garden almost ready to burst from bud to blossom as April arrives. I believe the reports of news reporters and camera crew, television and radio stations, and the clips on Youtube and Facebook. Believe in the sense that I am convinced the situation being transmitted is occurring. It is not a Hollywood production set somewhere in the Sierra Nevada with an epic cast of hirelings. It is happening but what I don't know is how to evaluate what is happening. Who is right and who is wrong, and who can say and on what basis, and with what authority? Whose interests are being served in the presentation of these different situations in the Middle East and in the action (either by rebel forces, presidents, or the UN troops) that is taken? Who desires what and why in these events? And where does religion figure (the Muslim Middle East and the Christian West with its Jewish allies); and politics (the spread of democracy and the rule of dictatorship), and economics (the oil fields, the lakes of black gold)? Believing gives way to a hazy realm of half-hatched conjectures, snuffling surmise, and nightmarish images of mutilated corpses, and the howling pain of life lost. Lost. We are back once again in Chaucer's forest, bewildered, sleepless, 'mased' with the horrors that might await us expressed in *The Blair Witch Project*.

I draw attention to this mediatization of the real and the confusion it generates in what to believe—in Christ, the saviour of the world, or the anti-ageing properties of a new cosmetic mousse—because although believing is an embodied cognitive process, an anthropological a priori, in cultures that prize high levels of self-consciousness and therefore awareness of embodied cognitive processes, believing can be manufactured, consciously so. Advertising is only one of the blatant forms of making a belief believable. Ours is an age of galloping dematerialization. Virtual realities proliferate.[64] They are not just on our desk-tops, our TV screens, our movie DVDs, and our theme-parks, demanding our interactive involvement. They populate our high streets where company logos (Starbucks, Nike, Virgin, etc.) float free of the goods they brand. They infect our banking systems where money liquidizes in electronic flows. These dematerializations generate belief and liquefy knowledge; for to know, in a world organized by science, is to have a stable evidential base. To know has ostensive power: 'This is a . . . ', 'That is a . . .' To know requires a shared reasoning about the furniture of the world. To know requires that there are certainties to which appeal can be made. But in an age of galloping dematerialization an ethos reigns which glories in the ambivalent, the polyvalent, the aporetic, the constructed, the multiplication of types of reason; power and knowledge is discursive.

Take that rejuvenating face-cream, 'proven' to be a more effective agent against ageing than any other. Who or what 'guarantees' that what is said here is a fact? Laboratories handing the testing of such creams operate only through a series of complex mediations. There are the mediations which make possible the empirical evidence: microscopes, the sublimation of chemicals, thermometers (digital and analogue), Petri dishes for the cultivation of bacterias, incubators, various modes for calibration, human and animal bodies to which the 'formulae' are applied and monitored, etc. . . There are mediations implicated in the interpretation of the 'facts' produced:[65] machines that correlate and populate certain statistics, scientists who read these statistics, etc. And finally there are mediations between the product produced and the public who the producers wish to buy it: campaigns by the pharmaceutical companies (with an interest in sales) that communicate these 'experimental trials'. Billboards all over the world trade in this socialized knowledge, trade 'facts' in advertising events; and exercise the craft of persuasion. We are caught up, then, in a world dictated by the dissemination of rhetorics and by

---

[64] If we accept, as I would, de Certeau's analysis of Mannerism, then real virtualities began to make their appearance from the sixteenth century when 'Virtuosity in what was also called "practice" was beginning to replace the humanist theory of "imitation"'—*The Mystic Fable* (n.25), p.141. With Mannerism there was an 'elaboration of language upon itself, the subtle and sumptuous effects of which illustrated indefinite capacities'. Modernity's (and postmodernity's) preoccupation with the kitsch only takes this aesthetic one step further. Linguistic and fine art virtuosity draws attention to itself as fabrication. Depths are depicted that draw attention to their superficiality—an aesthetic sublimity that masks an ethical and metaphysical void.

[65] See here Mary Poovey, *A History of the Modern Fact: Knowledge in the Sciences of Wealth and Society* (Chicago: University of Chicago Press, 1998).

the proliferation of aestheticized knowledges each soliciting our 'belief', each affirming our freedom to choose what we believe.

In such a rampaging nominalism what then does it mean to say *'Credo in unum Deo'*? And without that initial *credo* then there can be no faith seeking understanding. What does it mean to say *'Credo'* when the Church is displaced as the dominant site for the production of belief, by the media, by our mediated civil society, our mediated secular state and the mediated plethora of opinion that comes from numerous institutionalized experts? This is a time when the Gospel's injunction to 'follow me' 'has nothing which is proper to it, no concrete place and no abstract expression. It is no longer anything except the tracing of a passage—made possible by it—a relation between an arrival (birth) and a departure (death), then a return (resurrection) and a disappearance (ascension), indefinitely. Nothing but a name without a site?'[66] What does it mean to say *'Credo'* in a historical and cultural situation that follows from de Certeau's observation—a situation marked by descriptors like 'postsecular' and the 'new visibility of religion'?

Theories of secularism have been challenged but, depending upon what we mean by secularism, they still hold to some extent. Nevertheless, as I pointed out earlier, there is a proliferation of new sites for the production of belief some of which have religious affiliation, some of which draw some symbolic resonance from religious affiliations for aesthetic or rhetorical effect, and some of which have no religious associations at all and appeal to people to invent themselves, their life-styles, and their relations with other virtual people. So although Iain McGilchrist, in *The Master and His Emissary*, does not detail the rich cultural and philosophical landscape of 'simulacrum' and 'virtualities' he is spot on in recognizing this mass manufacture of illusions which necessitates believing rather than knowing despite it being the product of left hemisphere activity. Kierkegaard, from whom we derived inspiration for an account of truth in Chapter 6, presciently described our current situation: 'He who has observed the present generation can hardly deny that the discrepancy in it and the reason for its anxiety and unrest is this, that in one direction truth increases in scope and quantity, and partly also in abstract clarity, while in the opposite direction certainly constantly declines.'[67] And while a great streak of New Age paganism and ancient Gnosticism colours the contemporary Western horizon, these new sites for the production of belief and the practices they have fostered have taken the pursuit and response to transcendence elsewhere. This elsewhere is no better and no worse than what has always been. It too is 'permitted'—that is, can be

---

[66] De Certeau, 'The Weakness of Believing' (n.57), p.227.
[67] *The Concept of Irony*, trans. Howard V. Hong and Edna V. Hong (Princeton: Princeton University Press, 1992), p.139.

understood in terms of de Certeau's earlier writings as a dispensation or dissemination, eschatological in orientation, of divine Providence. I have spent a good deal of my academic career trying to assess where this 'elsewhere' is: how we might read the signs of the times. I am not alone in this task: much spin doctoring requires the same diagnosis. Only the tools used there are sociological, economic, historical, cultural, and political; tools which are unable and unwilling to examine the 'movement of transcendence' given not only their commitment to, but their dependence upon, the unquestioned acceptance that the immanent is all there is; their acceptance of and commitment to the secular.

Saying *Credo* today (whether as part of a Jewish, Christian, Islamic, or Hindu confession) is not the same as saying *Credo* in the 1970s. That is the point, and the significance of that point impacts greatly upon the mode faith seeking understanding must take today. On de Certeau's analysis of believing this new 'saying' will operate in transformed structural organizations of belief and new languages. We find the Christian *Credo*, for example, issuing in novels as different as J.K. Rowling's *Harry Potter* septet and Cormac McCarthy's *The Road*; Christian mythemes are revisited and rewritten in films as different as *Titanic* and *I am Legend*; Christian symbolism is being set to work in new sets in the visual arts, as the work of Damien Hirst's *Stations of the Cross* illustrates. It seems today Christian utterance as distinct, for de Certeau, from Christian statement[68] is being displaced across a 'plurality of systems'. It is becoming increasing heterogeneous, as de Certeau predicted, but it is not simply '[r]elegated to the private sphere and destined to lose itself in history'.[69] It is not the case, to take just Christianity, that it 'has nothing which is proper to it, no concrete place and no abstract expression'.[70] While strong expressions of Christian faith, Christian statement, remain in the public's attention, whether expressed in Vatican spectacles such as John Paul II's funeral and Benedict XVI's World Youth Day or the glass 'cathedrals' of Dallas or Seoul, then all the rewritings and discursive transformations of Christianity are benchmarked by the operations of concrete sites and sociocultural practices. There is then *something* of a nostalgia, even melancholy in de Certeau for a Roman Catholic hegemony; which, theologically read, is calling for new conceptions of what it is to be Church. That is, not the acceptance of a loss or the 'progressive collapse of the "body"',[71] but a recognition that embodiment too is being understood differently today; that there are new articulations of ecclesiology yet to be written but which *do refer* to a practice of belief continuing, and a production that is regaining its symbolic weight. Such a conclusion does not rob all of de Certeau's examination of believing

---

[68] De Certeau, 'The Weakness of Believing' (n.57), p.222. [69] Ibid., p.229.
[70] Ibid., p.227. [71] Ibid., p.226.

of its persuasive power. Quite to the contrary, his work facilitates new explorations in the question what makes a belief believable today.

CONCLUSION

Where does this leave us? The theological project as faith seeking understanding has to recognize it is part of a culture war that concerns believing itself. If we accept McGilchrist's characterization of this war, then it issues from the increasing betrayal of the master (right-hemisphere operations) by the emissary (left-hemisphere operations). As such, the cultural and the biological are working in tandem here. In this situation theology is necessarily involved in a persuasion, in making belief believable, and it is in a highly competitive market along with purveyors of ideologies, *prêt-à-porter* fabrications for self-invention, and the arts of simulation. But there should be no mistake, these other purveyors are not simply in the entertainment business; or perhaps put another way, the entertainment business is much more complex in its productions, manipulations, and effects than *Tom and Jerry* give out. Believing matters; right believing matters even more. And both the access to and the formation of that right believing for Christians is discipleship. Discipleship is inseparable, as I have said, from faith seeking understanding. In the closing pages of his wonderful novel, *Cloud Atlas*, David Mitchell, speaking through the journal entry of his nineteenth century character, Adam Ewing, writes:

> What precipitates outcomes? Vicious & virtuous acts.
> What precipitates acts? Belief.
> Belief is both the prize & battlefield, within the mind & in the mind's mirror, the world. If we *believe* humanity is a ladder of tribes, a colosseum of confrontation, exploitation & bestiality, such a humanity is surely brought into being, & history's Horroxes, Boerhaaves and Gooses shall prevail. You & I, the moneyed, the privileged, the fortunate, shall not fare so badly in this world, provided our luck holds. What of it if our consciences itch? Why undermine the dominance of our race, our gunships, our heritage & our legacy. Why fight the 'natural' (oh, weasely word!) order of things?
> Why? Because of this:—one fine day, a purely predatory world *shall* consume itself. Yes, the devil shall take the hindmost until the foremost *is* the hindmost. In an individual, selfishness uglifies the soul; the human species, selfishness is extinction.
> Is this the entropy written within our nature?
> If we *believe* that humanity may transcend tooth & claw, if we *believe* divers races & creeds can share this world as peaceably as orphans share their candle-nut tree, if we *believe* leaders much be just, violence muzzled, power accountable & the riches of the Earth & its Oceans shared equitably, such a world will come to pass. I am not deceived. It is the hardest of worlds to make real. Tortuous

advances won over generations can be lost by a single stroke of a myopic president's pen or a vainglorious general's sword.[72]

Horroxe, Boerhaave, and Goose are all villains who have added to the misery of Adam's life. Maybe at one time the worst the practice of any theology could do was to craft and administer placebos, encouraging dependencies through the cultivation of consolations. If this is true (and I'm not sure it is, although that is exactly what Freud proposed), today the practice of theology can have much more dramatic consequences, for both good and evil—because it tampers with those tendrils of believing. These are the cultural conditions of our own lostness and it is in these conditions that faith must seek its understanding; understanding not for the sake of knowledge in and of itself, but the knowledge is that afforded by a deeper and deeper acquaintance with God 'in knowledge of whom standeth our eternal life'.[73]

If theology is to be alert to its own making it has also to be alert to its context. We saw in the first three chapters how systematic theology has always wrestled with and served the histories and the cultures in which it was situated. It passed through, responded and maybe even contributed to cycles of lostness. What I have tried to demonstrate in this chapter is that in the West (widely understood) we have moved from Descartes' forest of knowledges into de Certeau's forest of beliefs. A dogmatics is needed which engages with the confusions, alienations, melancholias, bereavements, and the beauties of where we are now in a way that leads us towards salvation, *salus*, healing. Chaucer's *Book of the Duchess* points to a possibility. What the man in sable is ignorant of, and what the poet never informs or reminds him of, is the resurrection of the dead. The trees in paradise grew wild with the fruits of the tree of the knowledge of Good and Evil, until the Tree of Life raised itself above them and made it possible again for us to eat the fruits of its wisdom and truth.

---

[72] David Mitchell, *Cloud Atlas* (London: Hodder and Stoughton, 2004), p.528.
[73] The Second Collect for Morning Prayer in the *Book of Common Prayer*.

Part Three

Ethical Life

And the Lord God planted a garden in Eden, in the east; and there he put the man who he had formed. Out of the ground the Lord God made to grow every tree that is pleasant to the sight and good for food, and the tree of life also in the midst of the garden, and the tree of the knowledge of good and evil. (Genesis 2.8–9)

We will begin with an unorthodox question announcing a similarly unorthodox project. The question is this: how can we knit a living tree? The question is created out of the metaphorical act of bringing together the *craft* of knitting and the *cultivation* of a tree. There have been trees created out of wool or polyester or cotton. I have jumper with a green fir-tree pattern. But the trees that make up the pattern on my jumper are not cultivated; they were neither grown nor continue to grow. The trees are not living organisms. I want to suggest the kind of systematic theology ventured here is an exercise in knitting a living tree.

10

Sittlichkeit [Ethical Life]

Creation as a project was not entirely finished on the sixth day—it's still ongoing, evolving, adapting—from new strains of virus (ebola), to seedless grapes,
to domestic dogs, to green carnations (Prado). Welcome to the anthropocene.
Always it is emerging, like grace and in line with God's providential foresight;
although now it is not emerging from that primordial nothing—if it did then
creation would be eternal; an eternal emanation of the divine. Creation is
not eternal and there was no necessity of God to extend Himself into creation. Creation, in being maintained by the Triune, is given over to its own
furthering and freedom to love and respond to love. Every aspect of creation
affects, effects, impacts upon the furtherance of creation's project—from the
delicate ecosystems, the orbits of the planets, the birth and death of stars, and
the swirl of galaxies, to the expansion of the universe itself and the bubbling
up, possibly, of an infinite number of Big Bangs[1]: everything is in movement,
in its singularity and in its multiplicity. With this we recognize that we do
not possess ourselves or anything else, for 'Be sure that the Lord is God: he
had made us and we are not our own; we are his people, and the sheep of his
pasture' (Psalm 100.3).

In the beginning, then, is multiplicity, not the one. The multiple brings forth
multiplicity. God is multiple. God is one in being multiple. Only God can do
that, be that, and know that. The oneness is the expression of absolute and total
simplicity in being three. We imagine, in fact our philosophies have often been
dominated by, oneness. But we have no true idea of what oneness is with respect
to the simplicity of God—or anything else. We have to learn something of this
simplicity through being immersed in the multiplicity that both the created
world and our sin has brought us into: the forests of knowledges, fears, and obfus-
cations that Chaucer and Descartes, Tolkien, and the *Blair Witch Project* each
announce in their different ways. *This* multiplicity is not constituted through

---

[1] See Mary-Jane Rubenstein, *Worlds Without End: The Many Lives of the Multiverse*
(New York: Columbia University Press, 2013).

divine simplicity; it is the negative analogue of divine simplicity and divine multiplicity that sin as the usurpation of God's priority by self-prioritization both installs and proliferates. The difference is slight and total. In Greek, it is the slide from an epsilon (*theos*) to an upsilon (*thuon*—a burnt sacrifice, a slaughtering). Creation too now is fallen because human beings have come to dominate its ecosystems.[2] This is what the anthropocene announces. In that fallenness there can never be rational comprehension of God as one and multiple: our rationality deals only with imagined unities, defined fields, intelligible grids, and systems. It is a rationality that determines and is determinative in order to mask the question put by God 'Where are you?' Ours is a fallen rationality that has to be taught how to reason aright. That's why any engaged systematic theology is provisional and its discourse both rhetorical and self-critical. It has to be given over to a pedagogy and a providence not entirely within human hands. Even this theology, especially this theology as prayer, has to undergo the discipline of a Christian *paideia*. What is important is the engagement; the system is secondary and only the diffracted effect of Christ as Logos. The rhetoric facilitates that engagement, that provisionality. In provisionality lies possibility, the depth of all that is or might be possible, the creative and generative openness that is the nearest human being comes to freedom.

We will treat more of this notion of creator, creation, sin, and multiplicity in the next volume under the doctrines of creation and salvation. But from what has been outlined we can infer that life, the life of all things, is suspended in the loving grace that created us. Life then *is* ethical. That is a corollary of God's pronouncement on the sixth day, viewing all that He had made, that creation was 'very good' (Gen.1.31). As Michael Welker has reminded us, the Hebrew word for 'good' is *tov*—that is, beneficial to life.[3] Ethics is not based on values added to a basic 'bare life', in Agamben's terminology.[4] Value

---

[2] This is one reason why, in Volume II, I avoid exploring redemption in terms of 'reconciliation' and wish to understand its operation in terms of *salus*, healing. 'Reconciliation' is a key terms for redemption in Karl Barth's theology, but it is a process too tied to human relations. It details the restoration of right relations with God, and that is proper and true. But redemption is not the restoration of right relations between the human and the divine; it is the restoration of right relations between creator and creation. Human beings, as the anthropocene as a new geological era informs us, are deeply associated with all of creation and therefore the healing of the human condition will effect the healing of all things. For all things are in God. 'He is *epi pantōn kai dia pantōn kai en pansin*' (Eph.4.6).

[3] Michael Welker, *God the Revealed: Christology*, trans. Douglas W. Stott (Grand Rapids, MI: Eerdmans, 2013), p.281.

[4] Giorgio Agamben, *Homo Sacer: Sovereign Power and Bare Life*, trans. Daniel Heller-Roazen (Stanford, CA: Stanford University Press, 1998). Agamben opens his thesis with a distinction in Ancient Greek between *zōē* and *bios*. The former used to describe that which is common to all animated beings from plants to gods; the latter being more a way of life, a mode of living. Politics belongs then, classically, to *bios* not *zōē*. He cites Aristotle in *Politics* suggesting that 'there is probably some kind of good in the mere fact of living itself [*kata to*

is not epiphenomenal—an 'ought' [*Sollen*] supervening upon what 'is' [*ist*]; a question of what is right founded upon, though not necessarily intrinsically related to, a question of fact.[5] Value is already intrinsic to there being phenomena at all. But is not a value that can be extracted, traded, and possessed, like gold and diamonds. For this value, the value of life itself, is bound up in processes of emergence. The processes of emergence, though highly complex in their multiplicity and differentiation, are not just blind and random, not just chaotic or purely contingent. There are fluxes and flows but the intrinsic value of life, the 'it is very good' factor that for many (though not all) is aroused and attested in the arrival of new child, is inseparable from the order within creation. And this too is not an order immediately calculable, graspable. But then there are so very few things and perhaps none that are immediately calculable, graspable.

Nevertheless, life doesn't just pulsate; it pulsates in a direction. It is 'inclined towards', 'disposed towards', its continuation and its optimal thriving. It has a catalytic dynamism irreducible to function or genetic coding. The three basic principles for there being life at all are self-organization 'attended by some kind of autocatalytic behaviour'[6], self-replication, and self-reproduction. These principles are governed by hierarchical complexities from which properties not foreseen or identifiable emerge through processes of upward causation (emergence), downward causation (the way the new relatedness of parts within the emerging system impact upon the behaviour of those parts) and ongoing, non-linear activity from the combination

---

zēn auto monon]' (p.2), but politics is not understood as an attribute of *zōē*. Agamben's thesis about 'bare life' concerns those beyond the pale of the political, the outsider, and their status with respect to the governed. Leaving aside his interpretation of Aristotle, which I question, I am affirming that natural life is not distinct from life as a mode of being; that one is the basis for the other and intimately related to it. There is too much of a nature/nurture divide as a presupposition for Agamben's thesis that I do not accept—nor would any modern epigeneticist or neuroscientist. The contemporary view runs more along the lines of Terrence W. Deacon that there is a co-evolution as the environment is continually shaped and made more hospitable to flourishing through interactions among species, particularly by animals and human beings. See *Incomplete Nature: How Mind Emerged from Matter* (New York: W. W. Norton & Company, 2012).

[5] This is the Kantian and neo-Kantian—particularly with Heinrich Rickert (1863-1963)—moral paradigm based upon a transcendental reading of the conditions for the possibility of objective knowledge (of appearances, not things in themselves). Perception is distinct here from representation. What I am arguing for is an ontological relationship between perception and representation, our living the good life and our self-conscious reflections upon what that good life is. Body and mind (which is larger than, though contains, consciousness) are profoundly inter-associated.

[6] See Pier Luigi Luisi, *The Emergence of Life, From Chemical Origins to Synthetic Biology* (Cambridge: Cambridge University Press, 2006), p.92. See also the earlier, but still considered relevant, reflections on the physical aspect of the living cell by Erwin Schrödinger, *What Is Life?* (Cambridge: Cambridge University Press, 1967), pp.3–90.

of these causes (reciprocal causation).[7] Aquinas's secondary causation is made a great deal more complex. But this complexity means that we cannot reduce any form of life to 'single-cell components, such as DNA, proteins, sugars, vitamins, lipids, etc., or even the cellular organelles such as vesicles, ribosomes etc.'[8] Furthermore, such a reduction will not 'explain' life because all of these are inanimate substances. They all lack the 'catalytic power of enzymes' and the 'encoding power of nucleic acids'.[9] This is why it has proved impossible to date to understand how 'life' arises. There is any number of hypotheses and a vast accumulation of attempts to simulate prebiotic conditions to enable scientists to demonstrate how, from cooling larva and clay, asteroid storms and the formation of climate, organic existence arises. How the chemical produces the biological. But no one, to date, has been able to create life in a laboratory; though there are some impressive forms of synthetic biology attempting to mimick molecular evolutionary processes, and remarkable investigations into fatty acids as candidates for prebiotic membranes.[10]

And then once we have life, we have organisms; the casual complexity continues. There is no one direction that evolution will take; genes are not destiny. The two 'eyes' on a butterfly's wings may have evolved, at one time, because the back of the butterfly is most vulnerable from predators; the fake 'eyes' operated like the fake burglar-alarm boxes installed on some house fronts. This is an adaption to a certain environment. It manifests a plasticity in the relationship between pheneotypes and genes that has exposed contradictions in the theory of evolution. It has led certain biologists to propose the phenotype, as the product of environmental responses (to climate, for example), is first.[11] Epigenetics, genetic 'drift' and developmental biology study the results of this potentiality for change (blind and directed) that modifies genetic determinism. Our cells are responding to the world

---

[7] Pier Luigi Luisi, *The Emergence of Life*, (n.6), pp.119–23.

[8] Ibid., p.126.   [9] Ibid., p.59.

[10] Throughout Luisi's *The Emergence of Life* (n.6) there is a persistent mantra, 'we do not know the answer'. That doesn't mean that there isn't an answer that might be determined—that we are talking about mysterious forces here (known as 'strong emergence')—but it is not clear, to date, we have the intellectual and technological ability. For a daring attempt to create 'synthetic life' see the experimental research in synthetic genomics led by Craig Ventor in Daniel G. Gibson *et.al.*, 'Creation of a Bacterial Cell Controlled by a Chemically Synthesized Genome'. *Science* 2 July 2010: vol. 329 no. 5987 pp.52–6.

[11] For a comprehensive account of this biological phenomenon and its investigation see, Mary Jane West-Eberhard, *Developmental Plasticity and Evolution* (Oxford: Oxford University Press, 2003). For both 'phenotype fixation' and 'polyphenism' in butterflies, see, pp.532–3. See also, her explosive final chapter, pp.630–7, on sex. 'Sex transforms life' (p.630) and the cost of reproduction to females. We will be looking at this more closely, both when elaborating a doctrine of creation in Volume II and when examining gender with respect to ecclesiology in Volume III.

and purpose is irreducible to function. The life of a single cell is not the outworking of some predetermined genetic blueprint (the cell's nucleus). Its development owes perhaps much more to the relations it establishes, positive and negative, with its involvement in complex and unstable material systems, dissipative structures, intercellular signalling, and energetic environmental exchanges.

From the 1970s this fact has become the basis for another contemporary science: signal transduction.[12] Life lies in that cell's awakening and responsiveness to the given; the complex inner activity between nucleus, mitochondria (an organelle which takes in nutrients from around it, 'digesting' them and turning them into energy), the protective membrane and the cytoplasmic fluids. Life on this planet began with amino acids forming complex chemical chains into peptides, polypeptides, and then proteins. Out of this seminal and chemical soup emerge single cells (bacteria, algae, protozoans) mutating, generating proteins and anti-body proteins to protect itself from toxic invasion, and coming together to co-operatively organize themselves. It is estimated that for the first three million years of evolution the single cell was the only organism on this planet. That was before they began to join forces to intensify their potential for flourishing and develop more complex forms of life. Cells are sentient, that's the point, and this is where sensing and even *making* sense both begin. Life, pulsating purposefully, has to find its optimal thriving in the climate of ever-changing other purposeful pulsations. This is the same for the single cell as it is for a complex cluster, a butterfly or a human person (composed of approximately fifty trillion cells). Nature is composed of multiple interactions between organic and inorganic, both subject to time, change, transformation and adaptive processes: the endless surging restlessness of life. So much energy and heat is generated, distributed, and spent. Causation is never linear and all things are immersed within variegated distributions and transactions of energy and matter. Causation might be better understood as 'correlation'.

Our account of the pedagogy of the senses, so fundamental to learning the language of the faith that fashions the experience and understanding of that faith, has to begin here. We will develop this further with respect to ecclesiology in Volume III, returning 'nature' back to 'creation'.

---

[12] For an introduction to the findings of molecular biology on understanding ligands and receptors, their semiotic relationship to endocrinology, the production of emotions and moods, and effects upon behavior (mental and physical) see Candace B. Pert, *Molecules of Emotion: Why You Feel the Way You Feel* (London: Simon & Schuster, 1998). 'Amino acids are the letters. Peptides, including polypetides and proteins, are the words made from these letters. And they all come together to make up a language that composes and directs every cell, organ, and system in your body' (p.65).

SYSTEM DER SITTLICHKEIT

For now, let us dive into a rich, obscure, poetic, and suggestive passage by Hegel written in the winter 1802 to be delivered as a lecture, while he was living in Jena:

> The first level [*Potenz*] is natural ethical life [*Sittlichkeit*] as intuition [*Anschauung*]—the complete undifferentiateness of ethical life [*Differentlosigkeit derselben*], or the subsumption of concept under intuition, or nature proper [*eigentliche*].
>
> But the ethical is inherently [*an und für sich*] by its own essence a resumption of difference into itself, reconstruction; identity rises out of difference and is essentially negative; its being this presupposes the existence of what it cancels. Thus this ethical nature is also an unveiling [*Enthüllung*], an emergence [*Auftreten*] of the universal in the face of the particular, but in such a way that this emergences is itself wholly something particular—the identical, absolute quantity remains entirely hidden. This intuition, wholly immersed in the singular, is feeling [*Gefühl*], and we will call this the level [*Potenz*] of practice.[13]

Following a rather opaque Introduction and a note on absolute ethical life based in relationality, this is the opening passage of Hegel's first attempt to write a *System of Ethical Life*. It was found among Hegel's *Nachlass* and the publication of the complete text did not occur until 1913. What is remarkable to me about this opening is its prescience. There are secret conversations going on here between Hegel and Schleiermacher,[14] who's *Speeches* he had read and even commented upon in his doctoral dissertation, *The Difference between Fichte's and Schelling's System of Philosophy* (1801), and Hegel and Schiller, who's book *On the Aesthetic Education of Man* (1794) Hegel greeted as '*ein Meisterstrück*'.[15] We're going to put those conversations to one side. What is significant and prescient in these paragraphs is the emphasis upon process, the transformative dynamics of being in relation, potency [*Potenz*],[16]

---

[13] *System der Sittlichkeit. Reinschriftentwurf* in Georg Wilhelm Friedrich Hegel, *Gesammelte Werke*, Bd. 5, *Schriften und Entwürfe 1799–1808*), p.281. *System of Ethical Life and First Philosophy of Spirit*, eds. and trans. H.S. Harris and T.M. Knox (Albany: SUNY Press, 1979), p.103.

[14] The conversation, I suggest, concerns the relationship between intuition and feeling. Unlike in Fichte and Schelling, where intuition remains intellectual, Hegel, like Schleiermacher is able to develop a notion of a 'real' intuition because of the natural conditions from which it emerges: immersion in what is sensed and subsequently felt. In the later Jena lectures Hegel abandons the use of 'intuition', immediate experience cannot be immediate enough and so he employs the term *das Bekannte* (the familiar, popular, personally known) and the conversation ends.

[15] Letter to Schelling, 16 April 1795, cited in Steffen Schmidt, *Hegels* System der Sittlichkeit (Berlin: Akademie Verlag GmbH, 2007), p.25.

[16] I am not denying that this word is taken from Schelling where it has more that meaning of 'level' as the translators recognize, but given operations dominate Hegel's thinking that, later, were explicitly framed in Aristotlean terms of 'potentiality' and 'actuality', I think 'potency'

emergence and the primacy of intuition [*Anschauung*] and feeling [*Gefühl*]. Here is an account of a certain genesis, the emergence of form through the process of transformation (*umzuformen*—in Schiller's language). And the emergence begins in a sensuous immersion in the material that is 'felt'. Intuition, *Anschauung*—a verbal noun, emphasizing movement towards that which appears [*Schau*] or a seeing-towards, emerges from an unveiling [*Enthüllung*], or contemplation—issues from the immersion. Ethical life begins here, with this emergence from what is sensed [*Sinne*] in the given environment to what is felt, not just perceived [*Empfindung*] but what is experienced [*Gefühl*]. In Hegel's German, the individual disposition to what is sensed [*Sinne*] is *die Gesinnung*. Ethical life is completed only with the completion of history itself, and so what *Sittlichkeit* is at any given moment, what is ethical in any particular action, cannot be pre-judged.

There is much here philosophically that can be deepened by molecular biology, epigenetics, and an investigation into sensing itself. Sensing is not passive. It might seem so in Hegel, but since the mid 1960s and the pioneering work of the environmental psychologist James J. Gibson, we recognize the senses as aggressive, searching mechanisms.[17] Receptors on the membrane of a cell change 'shape, switching back and forth between any number of predominant configurations, all the while vibrating and swaying rhythmically to some as yet unknown melodic key'.[18] To go beyond or behind the primary sensing and the ocean of feeling in Hegel, then, we have to look forward—first, to the end of *System der Sittlichkeit* when Hegel breaks off just as he approaches the governance, the State, and absolute religion; second, to more developed notions of *Sittlichkeit* in *The Phenomenology of Spirit* (1807). For what lies ahead and just about mentioned in this treatise, absolute religion, is what lies also at the beginning: the doctrine of the Trinity.

There has been much attention drawn recently to Hegel's development of *Sittlichkeit* or ethical life from the so-called non-metaphysical interpretation of Hegel's work that began with Klaus Hartmann's 1972 essay in a collection of essays on Hegel edited by Alasdair MacIntyre.[19] Hartman is only

---

is clearly involved. *System der Sittlichkeit* is itself divided into 'levels' one and two (the first concerning nature and the second treating infinity, ideality, and form), nevertheless there is a relation operative between them. There is no dualism in Hegel's understanding of relations (*Verhältnisse*—living relations—not *Beziehungen*—formal connections). Each of the 'levels' in *System der Sittlichkeit* indicate an incomplete part which has to surrender itself to the sublation that both negates it as a part and raises it towards a greater recognition of the whole.

[17] James J. Gibson, *The Senses Considered as Perceptual Systems* (Westport, Conn.: Greenwood Press, 1966). Later he produced his more famous book *The Ecological Approach to Perception* in 1979. For an evaluation of the importance of Gibson's work see Mrs. Edward S. Reed *James J. Gibson and the Psychology of Perception* (New Haven: Yale University Press, 1989).

[18] Candace Pert, *Molecules of Emotion* (n.12), p.84.

[19] 'Hegel: A Non-Metaphysical View' in Alasdair MacIntyre (ed.), *Hegel – A Collection of Essays* (Garden City, New Jersey: Double Day Anchor, 1972), pp.101–24.

continuing a line of neo-Kantian sociological theory that wished to drop Hegel's notion of the 'absolute' spirit while retaining Hegel's commitment to social and cultural transformation. Nevertheless, for the English speaking world, volumes and essays developing this interpretation and specifically associating it with the sociality of reason,[20] or ethical rationalism,[21] appeared throughout the late 1980s and 90s. Both Charles Taylor's early book on Hegel[22] and Allen Wood's book *Hegel's Ethical Thought*[23] put the case boldest: Hegel's contributions to social, political, and ethical thinking can only be relevant today if they are severed from his metaphysical concerns. Well, I disagree, and such a disagreement is a very tall order to detail because Hegel was concerned with all the various aspects of *Sittlichkeit* throughout his writings. It would take a book, probably a thick book, to outline why I disagree and initiate a reading of Hegel that resists the non-metaphysical, pragmatic interpretation.[24] But the late Gillian Rose puts the case in her usual succinct fashion: '[T]he "absolute" is not an optional extra, as it were ... Hegel's philosophy has *no* social [and therefore ethical] import if the absolute is banished or suppressed, if the absolute cannot be thought.'[25] All I wish to advance here is that the Trinity, and its eschatological operations, are key to Hegel's understanding of *Sittlichkeit*. He provides a theology of ethical life upon which we can build.

The *System der Sittlichkeit* is a preparatory text for the study of speculative philosophy.[26] The early 1802/3 lectures were given shortly after the completion of some of his important early theological essays (like 'The Spirit of Christianity') and his doctoral dissertation. The lectures probably follow an earlier course Hegel delivered on natural law in which he announces, though does not demonstrate phenomenologically, that 'there is posited a relation of absolute ethical life which would reside entirely within individuals and be their essence, to relative ethical life which is equally real in individuals'.[27]

---

[20] Terry Pinkard, *Hegel's Phenomenology: The Sociality of Reason* (Cambridge: Cambridge University Press, 1986).

[21] Robert Pippin, *Hegel's Practical Philosophy: Rational Agency as Ethical Life* (Cambridge: Cambridge University Press, 2008).

[22] Charles Taylor, *Hegel* (Cambridge: Cambridge University Press, 1975).

[23] Allen Wood, *Hegel's Ethical Thought* (Cambridge: Cambridge University Press, 1990).

[24] See Graham Ward, 'How Hegel Became a Philosopher: Logos and the Economy of Logic', *Critical Research in Religion*, 1/3 (December 2013), 270–92.

[25] Gillian Rose, *Hegel Contra Sociology* (London: The Athlone Press, 1981), p.45.

[26] For an excellent Introduction to the text and its biographical context see, H.S. Harris, 'Hegel's System of Ethical Life: An Interpretation' in *System of Ethical Life and First Philosophy of Spirit*, pp.3–96.

[27] 'Über die wissenschaftlichen Behandlungsarten des Naturrechts' in *G.W.F. Hegel Werke: Jenaer Schriften 1801–1807* Band 2 (Frankfurt am Main: Suhrkamp, 1986), p.489. Trans. *Natural Law. The Scientific Ways of Treating Natural Law, Its Place in Moral Philosophy, and Its Relation to the Positive Sciences of Law*, T.M. Knox (Philadelphia: University of Philadelphia Press, 1975), p.99.

They were given while he was writing one of his most important essays of this period, 'Faith and Knowledge', and probably revising his essay 'On the German Constitution'. 'Faith and Knowledge' will culminate in Hegel's infamous and much debated conclusion: that what must be 're-established for philosophy [is] the Idea of absolute freedom and along with it the absolute Passion or the speculative Good Friday that was otherwise the historical [*der sonst historische*] Good Friday. Good Friday must be speculatively re-established in the whole truth and harshness of its God-forsakenness. Because the happier [*Heitere*], superficial [*Ungründlichere*], and more individual style of the dogmatic philosophies as well as the natural religions must vanish, the highest totality can and must achieve its resurrection, encompassing everything, and ascending in all its earnestness and out of its deepest ground to the happiest freedom of its form [*die höchste Totalität in ihrem ganzen Ernst und aus ihrem tiefsten Grunde, zugleich allumfassend und in die heiterste Freiheit ihrer Gestalt auferstenhen kann und muss*].'[28] Elsewhere I have advanced my own reading of this famous passage,[29] what is important for this argument is that Hegel's early approach to a *System der Sichlichkeit*, and its expansive revision in *Phenomenology*, cannot be separated from Hegel's theological (and metaphysical) ruminations on nature, law, and logic.

We can see this quite clearly in the four-fold (rather than the later triadic) structure of Hegel's system in these early Jena lectures. Karl Rosenkrantz, auditor, disciple and biographer of Hegel, in his *Hegels Leben*, refers to this:[30] First, there is Logic or the Science of the Idea—where science refers to the development of consciousness itself; secondly, the philosophy of nature in which the Idea is embodied and realizes itself; thirdly, ethical life as Spirit; and, finally, Religion as the perfection of the whole and the return to the primitive simplicity of the Idea. Religion, at this point then, is quite clearly, 'the highest synthesis of theoretical and practical cognition . . . the culmination of the whole system'.[31] Hegel had himself made the same point with explicit reference to the Trinity in *Difference*: 'the original identity must now unite both in the self-intuition of the Absolute, which is becoming object

---

[28] 'Glauben und Wissen', in *G.W.F. Hegel Werke: Jenaer Schriften 1801–1807*, Band 2 (Frankfurt: Suhrkamp Verlag, 1986), pp.432–3. My translation. The German language performs a progressive movement: from 'happier' to 'happiest', from 'superficiality' or 'the lack of grounds', through the deepest ground to resurrection. There is a translation available: *Hegel: Faith and Reason*, eds. and trans. Walter Cerf and H.S. Harris (New York: SUNY Press, 1988).

[29] Graham Ward, 'How Hegel Became a Philosopher' (n.24).

[30] Karl Rosenkrantz, *Georg Wilhelm Friedrich Hegels Leben* (Berlin, 1844 reprinted Darmstadt: Wissenschaftliche Buchgesellschaft, 1963), pp.179–93. The relevant passages from the book are translated in H.S. Harris' '*Hegel's System of Ethical Life*' (n.26), pp.254–65.

[31] H.S. Harris, 'Hegel's System of Ethical Life (n.26), p.6.

to itself in completed totality. It must unite in the intuition of God's eternal human Incarnation, the begetting of the Word from the beginning.'[32]

Now this is far from being transparent, especially to those who are not initiates of Hegel-speak. But before I start to unpack it, we need to understand a series of distinctions and I am going to explain why straightaway. Hegel's early theological essays focus on Christology. In these essays there is a distinct importance given to the Gospel of John, particularly the Prologue—we give hear the reference in the passage I just cited. There is also a concern with the 'life' that proceeds from the Logos and the Spirit of Christianity. *Sittlichkeit* is I think best translated as 'ethical life' because it is associated with social ethics, customs, traditions of common decency or *Anstand* (good manners), and in this way it is distinct from two other terms (all three are to be found in Kant): *Sittenlehre* (ethical teaching or moral philosophy) and *Moralität* (morality).[33] In other words, I want to argue that *Sittlichkeit* is the lived out ethical life announced in and as Christ the Logos and disseminated through the Holy Spirit.[34] This does not mean we can, as Christians, discard moral philosophy or morality. There is no pure ethical life available outside Christ and the Spirit. As David Kelsey has recently argued: given the complex interrelationships between Christians and the distinctive 'host cultures' which they inhabit then at the very human level 'theological ethics engages and appropriates arguments from secular ethics and information from secular analyses of morally problematic social situations'.[35] But above and beyond this engagement and these appropriations, something deeper moves: our formation in the goodness of God.

This is where, I would argue, communities of living Christian faith have much to learn from Hegel's conception and analysis of *Sittlichkeit*, even while

---

[32] *Differenz des Fichteschen und Schellingschen Systems der Philosophie*' in *G.W.F. Hegel Werke: Jenaer Schriften 1801–1807*, vol.2 (Frankfurt: Suhrkamp Verlag, 1986), p.112. *The Difference between Fichte's and Schelling's System of Philosophy*, trans. H.S. Harris and Walter Cerf (Albany: SUNY Press, 1977), p.171.

[33] Recently, the moral philosopher (of a certain Kantian persuasion) Ronald Dworkin has emphasized the unity of ethics and morals and their interdependence with respect to the overriding category of 'value'. See *Justice for Hedgehogs* (Cambridge, MA: Harvard University Press, 2011). We will be returning to Dworkin's work in Volume III.

[34] There are at least two other recent Hegel scholars who have recognized the Christo-logic behind Hegel's thinking. Martin Wendt has explored some of these issues with respect to what he calls the 'Chalcedonian' formula in *Gottmenschliche Einheit bei Hegel: Eine logische und theologische Untersuchung* (Berlin: de Gruyter, 2007), pp.2–9. Nicholas Adams: *The Eclipse of Grace*, takes up Wendt's observations: 'Hegel's project is—in my conception—an attempt to render Chalcedonian logic available once again' (p.38). But Adams rightly warns us that the logical forms that Hegel develops, especially concerning the doctrine of the Trinity, are not 'themselves doctrinal formulations' (p.10). But, for Hegel, this 'logic' is lived—whatever its doctrinal formulation.

[35] David Kelsey, *Eccentric Existence: A Theological Anthropology*, volume one (Louisville: Westminster John Knox Press, 2009), p.7.

accepting that there are certain heterodox moments in Hegel's theology. These occur, primarily, around the relation of Christology and creation. Although I certainly think there is more ambiguity in Hegel's theology than my friend Cyril O'Regan argues for in his book *The Heterodox Hegel.*[36] With ambiguity there is room for other interpretations. I am far then from announcing, like another friend, the Irish philosopher and one time President of the Hegel Society, William Desmond, in his book *Hegel's God: A Counterfeit Double?*[37], that it's time for philosophical theologians to bid him farewell.

Now, let me return to those gnomic sentences in Hegel's doctoral dissertation that point to the highest synthesis and consummation of science in the life of the Trinity. He actually ascribes them to Schelling's system, but that is a sleight of hand. He is discussing Schelling at this point in the text. By 'the original identity' Hegel means the relating of both subject and object that overcomes their dichotomy. Consciousness arises out of a necessary splitting within this original identity, where the I encounters the other. The evolution of self-consciousness, which logic both describes and performs, is a return to this original identity in the Absolute 'which is becoming object to itself in completed totality'.[38] What is important for Hegel is that the emerging self-consciousness, whose knowledge is a matter of finite contingency, is not dissolved as such in returning to the Absolute. Hegel does not understand the science of logic as prescribing a situation 'where everything finite is drowned in the infinite'.[39] That would be Fichte's position, Hegel says. Certainly it would be Spinoza's. Hegel rejects such a '[m]ystic rapture [the word used is the Pietistic *Schwärmerei*] [which] holds fast to this colourless light'.[40] Hegel rather views the science of logic as prescribing not the annihilation of the subject-object difference, which would be the eclipse of all conscious knowledge, but rather its suspension: 'In the absolute identity subject and object are suspended, but because they are within the absolute identity they both have standing too. This standing is what makes knowledge possible.'[41] That is why it is a '*self-intuition* of the Absolute, which is becoming object to itself in completed totality'. In the culminating sentence Hegel transposes the philosophical idiom into a theological one: 'It must unite in the intuition of God's eternal human Incarnation, the begetting of the Word from the beginning.'[42] The 'It' is the 'self-intuition of the Absolute' that must now be united in the Logos as 'intuition of God's eternal human Incarnation'. In this way conscious, finite knowledge is maintained for it participates in the Word of God and the Word of God is the human incarnation of God's own self-intuition.

---

[36] C. O'Regan, *The Heterodox Hegel* (Albany: SUNY Press, 1994).

[37] W. Desmond, *Hegel's God: A Counterfeit Double?* (Aldershot: Ashgate, 2003).

[38] G.W.F. Hegel, *Differenz des Fichteschen und Schellingschen Systems der Philosophie*, p.112. *The Difference between Fichte's and Schelling's System of Philosophy*, p.171, (n.32).

[39] Ibid. 95/156.   [40] Ibid.   [41] Ibid.   [42] Ibid., p.112/171.

In the words of Irenaeus: 'Our Lord Jesus Christ, the word of God . . . became what we are that he might make us what he is himself.'[43]

Just one more elucidation: the nature of that participation in the Logos. Finite consciousness participates in the Logos because the object of that consciousness, the object galvanizing the very process of that consciousness towards knowledge, is the Logos itself. As Quentin Lauer puts it, in describing the same story of consciousness in the *Phenomenology*: 'in the consistently sustained experience of the object the object reveals itself more and more as what it truly is'.[44] The Logos is, then, both the object of the consciousness's 'self-intuition of the Absolute' and the object of God's own self-intuition— that is why they can be united. The Logos as object of consciousness is appropriated through the logical development of consciousness and the experience of consciousness itself. In that way, Logos as the object of consciousness is immanent to consciousness itself. It is also the Word that is transcendently begotten of God.

Now before I go on to elaborate this Trinitarian framing for the sciences of logic, nature, and ethical life, let me point something out here: the order of the philosophical and the theological. Famously, in the closing sections of the *Phenomenology of Spirit*, Hegel reverses this order. Religious representation is 'pictorial' and this is sublated by the philosophical in a higher operation of self-consciousness in which there is self-consciousness of self-consciousness itself. This is the knowledge of Spirit returning to itself. Absolute knowledge. What is happening in these two accounts of the order of philosophy and theology, separated by six years?

In the first account, what does explicit reference to Trinitarian procession enable Hegel to do? I would suggest that it enables Hegel to maintain finite knowledge of subjective contingency within the Absolute in contrast to the dissolution of such finitude in Fichte, Spinoza, and Pietistic *Schwärmerei*. His analysis of the emergence and development of self-consciousness, the logic, is not then arbitrary but necessary for this is the nature and operation of the Logos itself: the Logos as 'God's eternal human incarnation'. I will have much more to say about that phrase in a moment. For now, let's continue with the order of philosophy and theology. To some extent the explicit reference to the Trinity in *Difference* is proof of the validity of the system as a whole; it is valid because recognized to be a necessary corollary of Trinitarian procession. What is an immanent process of an evolving consciousness coming to self-conscious understanding of itself is given a transcendent referent. Now it might appear, read this way, that the transcendent referent is only a regulative

[43] Irenaeus, *Against Heresies*, in *Ante-Nicene Fathers*, vol. 1, ed. Alexander Roberts and James Donaldson (Peabody, MA: Hendrickson Publishers, 2004), v.
[44] Quentin Lauer, *A Reading of Hegel's Phenomenology of Spirit* (New York: Fordham University Press, 1976), p.40.

rule for understanding the immanent process. But that is far too Kantian. For the statement is also claiming that Trinitarian procession is the highest conceptualization of what Houlgate will call 'the structures or fundamental determinations of thought and being'.[45] And so the transcendent is operative constitutively within the immanent. Hence, when Hegel gives his account of the development of religion and the relation of Christianity to other faiths, as with Schleiermacher, Christianity will be the consummate religion. For Hegel it is the consummate religion on two grounds: a) because of this Trinitarian conceptualization that makes a shadowy appearance in other religions but its clearest manifestation in Christianity; and b) not unrelated to a), it is revealed. Hegel always adds the adjective 'revealed' to Christianity.

There are three degrees of religious expression that inform a community's *Sittlichkeit: natürliche Religion, kunst-Religion,* and *offenbare Religion.* Thus in Hegel's *Lectures of the Philosophy of History,* he defines the 'axis on which the History of the World turns' as: 'Christ has appeared—a Man who is God—God who is Man.'[46] It is not that these other forms of religion do not bear some analogy to what is revealed in Christ as the Logos. Indeed they do, and it is the long task of Hegel in his *Lectures on the Philosophy of Religion* to detail the intimations of the consummate religion in what is translated as all other 'determinate religions' (*bestimmte Religione*). Furthermore, the evolution of self-consciousness and knowledge, when related to Trinitarian processions, that is, to the creation of all things through the Word, is not simply an exercise in epistemology. The logic it announces, the Christo-logic because it is an unfolding of the Logos, is an ontological logic—the unification of both 'thought and being'. The rational (which for Hegel is never separable for the embodied, the social, the historical, the political, and the economic) is lived, is life. Another Johannine passage, which Hegel cites in his earlier theological writings, comes to mind: 'I am the way [*odos*], the truth and the life.' So what is the reversal of order about in the *Phenomenology of Spirit*?

First point: recognition of this ontological logic is absolute knowing. This is the concluding section of the *Phenomenology.* It follows the account of Revealed Religion and opens by announcing a further step or sublation that it must now itself undergo: 'The Spirit of the Revealed Religion has not yet surmounted its consciousness as such . . . it's actual self-conscious is not the object of its consciousness.'[47] As I read this, Hegel is not announcing that

[45] Stephen Houlgate, *An Introduction to Hegel: Freedom, Truth, and History* (Oxford: Blackwell, 2nd edn. 2005), p.48.

[46] G.W.F. Hegel, *Lectures on the Philosophy of History,* trans. J. Sibree (New York: Dover Books, 1956), p.324.

[47] *Phänomenologie des Geistes* in *G.W.F. Hegel: Werke* Band 3 (Frankfurt am Main: Suhrkamp, 1986), p.575. *The Phenomenology of Spirit,* trans. A.A. Miller (Oxford: Oxford University Press, 1977), p.479.

philosophy supersedes the theological, but rather that the philosophical sublation makes clear the essence or logic of Christianity. This final sublation makes absolute knowing available. Listen then to how that section on absolute knowing concludes: 'So although this Spirit starts afresh and apparently from its own resources to bring itself to maturity, it is none the less on a higher level. The realm of the Spirit which is formed in this way in the outer world constitutes a succession in Time in which one Spirit relieved another of its charge and each took over the empire of the world from its predecessor. Their goal is the revelation of the depth of Spirit, and this is the *absolute Notion [Ihr Ziel ist die Offenbarung der Tiefe, und diese ist der absolute Begrifft].*'[48] I give you the German because it does not say the 'depth of the Spirit' but 'the depth' and for those, like Hegel's readers, steeped in Luther's translation of the Bible this language would have brought to mind two texts. The first is *Romans* 11.33: 'O the depth of the riches and the wisdom and the knowledge of God … who has known the mind of the Lord.' The second is *1 Corinthians* 2.10: 'For the spirit searches everything, even the depth of God … no one comprehends the thoughts of God except the Spirit of God.' Note Hegel's little throwaway observation that the evolution of consciousness makes these sublations in coming to absolute knowing 'apparently from its own resources'. For what it understands in 'the Spirit knowing itself as Spirit' is that the origin of its becoming lies in the 'depth'. So that what takes place in absolute knowing is 'alike the inwardizing and the Calvary [*die Erinerrung und die Schädelstätte*] of absolute Spirit, the actuality, truth, and certainty of his throne, without which he would be lifeless and alone'.[49] The German again in clearer: 'the recollection, the remembrance, and the place of the skull', which once more has echoes of Luther's translation of the Bible.

Several observations follow from this exposition. First: philosophy is not the sublation of theology or a higher way. Philosophy as a phenomenology of consciousness comes upon that which is revealed of Trinitarian truth. It does so in and through an immanent process, but as it approaches absolute knowing it recognizes that its immanent becoming was transcendently resourced. We can liken what takes place here to the movement of the *cogito* in Descartes *Meditations* where Descartes too, beginning from thought only, comes to understand the idea of God within his mind. Only, for Hegel, the detail of the process undertaken is much more finely grained, concerns not the single *cogito* but the history of human kind in all its cultural manifestations, and the God revealed is not Descartes's single and frozen deity, but Trinitarian, dynamic and life-giving. The last book Hegel was preparing for publication was on the ontological argument for the existence of God.

---

[48] Ibid., p.591/492.   [49] Ibid.

Secondly: there is both a unity and a knowledge of that unity. The unity here is only another way of phrasing what Hegel has already said in his dissertation: it is 'the objective Truth and [of] the knowing Self in an immediate unity'.[50] There is no dissolving, although Hegel through the syntax in the closing lines of the *Phenomenology* blurs the distinction between human and divine in describing this unity. In his vocabulary he will never use the German *die Einigkeit*, that is union. There is no union between the human and the divine. The word is always *die Einheit*, the being at one. If there is a knowing then there cannot be a dissolving of difference and an object must remain even in absolute knowing. Houlgate identifies this in his own interpretation: 'absolute knowing still has an object or *Gegenstand* ... Yet this object is understood not just to be an *object* and so to be fundamentally *distinct* from consciousness, but to be *identical* in form to consciousness.'[51] This is very important and challenges certain theological readings of Hegel that interpret him as advocating the absorption of all human *Geistes* into the divine *Geist*. There is a distinction and there is an identity. Houlgate does not press this in a theological direction, but to my mind what Hegel is describing here as absolute knowing is what St. Paul describes in *1 Corinthians 13.12*: 'now I know in part, but then I shall know even as also I am known'. Many commentators have observed that the *Phenomenology* orchestrates a journey into self-discovery.

Thirdly: all things come from and return to the mind of God. Hegel announces a profoundly participative account of the becoming or determinativeness of material culture as the dialectical and collective outworking of human consciousness in God. It is the nature of that *panentheism* that we need to understand.

PANENTHEISM

Let's begin with a definition and a distinction. *Panentheism* is that all things exist in God; unlike *pantheism* in which all things are God or are modifications of God. Both are committed to the immanent operations of divinity. Now there is strong New Testament backing for panentheism. It seems to define Paul's own account of participation in Christ. The question with Hegel, as a number of philosophers and theologians have read him, is whether the immanent operations of God are all there is about deity. *Letter to the Ephesians* 4.6 speaks of 'one God and Father of us all, who is above all and through all and in all'. But the three prepositions are important

---

[50] Ibid. p.598/491.   [51] Stephen Houlgate, *An Introduction to Hegel* (n.45), p.64.

here. God 'in all [*en pasin*]' but this is only because God is 'above all [*epi pantōn*]'. By being above, God does not simply indwell all things, but God acts 'through all [*dia pantōn*]'. I have already said that absolute knowing is not union, but being at one with. *Pantheism* announces union; *panentheism* does not necessarily. Of course, moving as Hegel does through a phenomenological analysis of the evolution and purification of consciousness, he is committed to articulating an immanent process: the discovery of the structure and determinations of the Logos intimately within oneself. Augustine will make a similar move in *Confessions*. But in order to understand that Hegel is not collapsing God's transcendence into a purely immanent operation we have to return in the *Phenomenology* to the point where understanding becomes reason and reason becomes Spirit. For we have to be clear here: human beings acquire spirituality, they realize the Spirit working within them—which already puts a question mark against a univocal use by Hegel of *Geist* with respect to the human and the divine. Entry into the Spirit is participation of human understanding in divine Reason. It is also participation in a Christic kenosis that surrenders itself as ego in ethical life. This life is described in *System der Sittlichkeit*, and all other accounts of ethical life in Hegel up to and including *Elements of the Philosophy of Right* (1820), first as family, then as civil society and finally as State. There is only one Spirit. Human beings have the potential, in their ability to think and understand, to become Spirit and to recognize the Spirit that dwells within them is absolute Spirit.

The Spirit, which is the very entry into *Sittlichkeit*, only appears in part six of the *Phenomenology*, following a long examination of Reason in part five, which itself follows an analysis of understanding and self-consciousness. The move towards Reason takes place when consciousness experiences its unhappiness. Why does it experience unhappiness? Because it both recognizes something about the character of Reason itself and recognizes its own alienation from it. What it recognizes about the perfection of Reason is that it is Unchangeable, whereas the dialectic within consciousness and self-consciousness is committed to the vicissitudes of change. The Spirit will drive self-consciousness towards its unity with that pure Reason, towards, that is, absolute knowing. But it is the characterization of the perfection of thought and being as the Unchangeable that is interesting and gives us a clue to the continuing transcendence of the divine in Hegel's analysis.

The word in German is the noun form of the adverb *unwandelbar*. God as unchanging and yet given to change is a core theme in Augustine's work. In *Confessions* he declares in Book I, which treats the nature of God's transcendence and immanence, God is 'unchangeable, and yet changing all things'. The Latin for unchangeable is *immutabilis*. God is immutable, while also being the God from whose depth the Spirit emerges (a more Trinitarian language would use 'proceeds'), as Hegel describes it at the end of *Phenomenology*. Now there were no German translations of Augustine's *Confessions* when Hegel was writing. There was no need because Hegel, and others interested in Augustine, read Latin fluently. But, when a German translation did appear in 1888, by Otto F. Lachmann then that phrase of Augustine's from Book 1 was translated '*unwandelbar und doch alles wandelnd*'.[52] If this is Hegel's conception of the divine, then his evident panentheism—which would issue on the same grounds as the observation by Aquinas that we never treat what God is in Godself, we can only treat the operations of God in the world—does not compromise the immutability of the divine who is 'above all things'. Participation of human thought and being in divine thought and being, absolute knowing, not only then announces a distinction between the knowing self and the object that is being known, it also announces a depth and an immutability of the divine that can never be appropriated or known. In Hegel's words: 'it will behold itself as it is' and this is '[p]ure self-recognition in absolute otherness'.[53] Only the absolute otherness of God prevents Hegel's system from collapsing into subjective idealism, which would conflate the object of consciousness with consciousness itself.

With the recognition of the Unchangeable within the changeable, the Unchangeable even within one's own mutability, then consciousness engages with Reason rather than just understands. And as I said, the engagement with what is truly rational and therefore universal is an engagement with Spirit. The *telos* of the work of Spirit is the overcoming of the alienation within consciousness that is summed up, as we have seen, with knowing even as I am myself known. Hegel: 'reciprocal recognition . . . is Absolute Spirit [*ein gegenseitiges Anerkennen, welches der absolute Geist ist*]'[54] at work in all the shapes of human self-consciousness that compose 'the shapes of the world' (*Gestalten einer Welt*).[55] That is: its laws, its cultural life (*Bildung*), and the substance of its faith (*Religion*). These spiritual outworkings of the pursuit of the Unchangeable, the pure reason, the absolute knowing is *Sittlichkeit*. In the mutual recognition it fosters lies what Hegel calls 'absolute freedom'. Hegel: 'In this absolute freedom . . . all social groups or classes which are the spiritual spheres into which the whole is articulated are abolished; the individual consciousness that belonged to any such sphere and willed and fulfilled itself in it, has put aside its limitation; its purpose is the general purpose, its language universal law, its work the universal work.'[56]

[52] Otto F. Lachmann, *Die Bekenntnisse des hl. Augustinus* (Leipzig: Reclam, 1888). It is still the German translation most widely available today.
[53] *Phänomenologie des Geistes* (n.47), p.29/14.   [54] Ibid., p.493/408.
[55] Ibid., p.326/265. For an analysis of Hegel's notion of 'shapes of the world' see Marco Haase, *Grundnorm, Gemeinwille, Geist* (Tübingen: Mohr Siebeck, 2004), pp.239–72.
[56] Ibid., p.433/357.

TRINITARIAN LIVING

Allow me now to sketch *Sittlichkeit* from within this Trinitarian, and not simply triadic, frame. Much more will be said towards the end of Volume III, but for now it is important to understand that we live the Trinity, because all our thinking is inseparable from being and all our material, cultural, and religious histories are the outpouring (*kenosis*) and consummation (*plerosis*) of eternal life. Ethics then is associated with *ethos*. The ethics governing social and cultural life are not in accord with a deontological morality of duties. This separates 'is' from the 'ought', establishing public norms many of which can be embodied in law. Law is important to Hegel, but it has to emerge from, and be an expression of, the community's *Sittlichkeit*. The is/ought distinction divides potentiality from actuality, in part because time and change have no bearing upon it. Hegel's dialectic converts potentiality into actuality or rather moves from one state of actuality to another in an unfolding of all that is potential and, for him, indeterminate within the Godhead. But in the absolute idea, as Hegel recognized, there is no distinction between thought and being. So, in the realm of becoming, all will be realized. In an individual's immersion in what is, in their rational progress towards that which is perfected in Christ as Logos, then, because God is good, we will live out that goodness. The virtues emerge from a deepening mutual recognition (being known even as I am known, in Pauline terms). For example, humility and love emerge from a dialectic of confession and forgiveness worked out within concrete social and cultural praxes.

It is in this way that a moral community is formed, sustained by an ongoing process of reconciliation and healing. Although, on the scale of world history, there is a dark, tragic side to this progress. In the *Lectures of the Philosophy of History*, as I said, the incarnation is the axis of time itself, and yet history is still described as a 'slaughter-bench at which the happiness of peoples, the wisdom of states, and the virtue of individuals has been sacrificed'.[57] Hegel was not interested in history as such; only the slow and sometimes painful unfolding and development of a divine action in which a theological understanding of eschatology is conflated with a philosophical understanding of teleology. But the theodicy that emerges is still very much open-ended.

Here I only wish to distinguish a Trinitarian *Sittlichkeit* from other forms of *Sittenlehre* and *Moralität*. In doing that we can observe that, with *Sittlichkeit*, there cannot be a distinction between fact and value because there is a moral ontology. And yet such a distinction lies behind both utilitarian and consequentialist ethics where the facts are themselves neutral

---

[57] G.W.F. Hegel, *Lectures on the Philosophy of History* (n.46), p.21.

and given values by the way we employ them *for the best*. But this separation suggests that empirical facts (about things and situations) are all that is. This is the truth about the way things are. For Hegel there is no Spirit in facts. For Hegel a 'fact' is at best an indeterminate and immediate effect: like a sense perception. A thing *is*. But this in itself is not only an empty tautology it is not the truth of what *is*. A perception is registered in consciousness, but once it becomes conscious of itself then the complex relation of what *is* and the beholder of what *is* begins to unfold. Until eventually, with the entry into Reason, there is Spirit. As and in Spirit, material facticity as such is more than sensory data because ultimately everything is a manifestation of God's Logos written into all things, governed by the universal law of Reason, and evoking the evolution of human consciousness. While then *Sittlichkeit* does become enshrined in the laws and customs governing a people, they are laws and customs that increasingly make manifest a mutual recognition that is at the heart of not only Trinitarian operations, but also the Trinity in itself.

Sittlichkeit traces and articulates this moral ontology, while duty to the law (in the Kantian sense of duty) is only *Moralität*. At best this can function as conscience, but conscience is still too ego-bound and subject to the ego's choice. The law has to be within and lived before it appears as legislation. It is in this way that we must understand what Hegel writes in the conclusion of his *Lectures of the Philosophy of History*: 'we must understand the state to be founded upon religion'[58] and the conclusion of his *Elements of a Philosophy of Right* where the *telos* of the State in the coming down of the kingdom of heaven upon earth.[59] They are analogies of the orders of creation itself, rooted in and issuing from the nature of the Creator Himself. They participate in the unfolding of the Trinity. They are not arbitrary; they are profoundly rational. They are not simply there to restrain the people. They exist to make evident to the people the justice and the goodness of the Creative Logos and the dynamic movement of the Spirit in all the concrete particularity and historical materialism of a community.

The keys to understanding the relationship between *Sittlichkeit* and divine life are: to understand the relationship between what was later called the immanent and the economic Trinity; the nature of our participation in God; and the construction of an analogical, rather than either univocal or equivocal, account of divine *Geist* and human *Geist*. In a developing examination of these keys we will be employing distinctions that Hegel either ambivalently or sometimes altogether failed to employ. For example, (and I did say I would

[58] Ibid., p.417.
[59] *Elements of a Philosophy of Right*, trans. H.B. Nisbet (Cambridge: Cambridge University Press, 1991), p.380.

return to it) let's take his description of the Logos as 'God's eternal human incarnation'. There is a Scriptural basis for such a description. *Revelation* 13.8 talks about the Lamb of God being slaughtered from before the foundations of the earth. But Hegel's phrase is awkward because it fails to make a Christological distinction. In the words of Tertullian: 'The Father is distinct from His Son [in his humanity] not from [the Son in] his divinity.'[60] It is the distinction—and we have got to proceed carefully with how far we can push such a distinction because it cannot be an ontological divide—between the eternal Logos and the historical Christ. It is a distinction founded upon the priority of one over the other. The Logos as 'God's eternal *human* incarnation' fails to make that distinction and leaves open a possible confusion, which Hegel does develop at times, between Christ and Creation that renders creation eternal. We will encounter this distinction, its importance, and its complexity again, when we look at 'nature' (*phusis*) in the Chalcedon symbolum of the hypostatic union (in Volume II).

But just to demonstrate the theological ambivalences here, let me pursue this a little further. As noted, human thinking about the Godhead can only treat what God has revealed of Godself, in Christ and in the Scriptures that bear witness to and disseminate the Christ-event—Scriptures which have been shaped and arranged by the Spirit-led reflections of the Church. For Hegel, Christ's appearing is 'revelation' (*die Offenbarung*), and that is why Christianity is the revealed religion (*die Offenbarungsreligion*). Christ's appearing is not a disclosure (either *die Enthüllung* or with Heidegger *die Erschlossenheit*) of God on what Deleuze would call a 'plane of immanence'.[61] We treat then the operations of God revealing Godself in the world; we cannot transcend the world and the finite categories we have cultivated for understanding and creating our conceptions of that world. If we attempt to peer into the nature of the Trinity beyond these operations, then we have to proceed through theological inferences made on the basis of these operations. God created us. We are as we are by God's design and desire. Though creation is not an emanation from God (and therefore necessary to God), creation must be an expression of the Godhead. Otherwise the understanding we have of God in Christ, a God who is love, does not correspond to the way we use the word God. A God for whom creation was not an expression of God's design and desire is omnipotent but not loving. This God can create but what is created has only an arbitrary relationship to such a God. That is not how Christians use and understand the word 'God'. In and through our creation God establishes a relation. Creation is a

[60] Tertullian, *Adversus Praxean*, trans. Ernest Evans (Eugene, OR: Wipf & Stock Pub; Blg Rep edition, 2011), 29.

[61] Gilles Deleuze, *Pure Immanence: Essays on a Life*, trans. Anne Boyman (New York: Urzone, 2001), p.27.

communication of Godself. Given this then there must be *in God* a relation to humanity.

My intention is not to proclaim an orthodox Hegel, but rather to challenge, through a close reading, those who are too quick to announce his heterodoxy. I have only treated his work between 1801 and 1807—the lectures on the philosophy of religion are much later when Hegel is in Berlin and faced with Schleiermacher. It has also been my intention to present a case for why Hegel still remains an important resource for an engaged systematic theology—though a resource which would need to be supplemented by the Christological and Trinitarian distinctions of the Alexandrian and the Cappodocian fathers, and Augustine. There are three reasons why he remains an important resource.

First, there is his commitment, on the basis of the incarnation, to what has come to be called cultural materialism—that is, the materializations of human thought and desires in social, political, economic, and cultural praxes. Only Augustine matches such a commitment. The Logos Christologies of the Alexandrian School, for example, are much more abstract; though the Cappodocian fathers were more attuned to the biological, physiological, and medical.

Secondly, there is the relation, on the basis of a Trinitarian theology, between the historical processes of this cultural materialism and the operations of God with respect to creation.

Thirdly, there is the relation, on the basis of a Logos Christology, between a Christo-logic and embodied human reasoning, Hegel's 'determinate being.'

The salvific implications of these three important aspects of Hegel's work are summed up astutely by Stephen Houlgate who acknowledges Hegel's critical reasoning is 'Christ-like': 'logic is thus a continuous process of conceptual revision and redefinition that demands of us the greatest willingness to be transformed and challenged by thought'.[62] Hegel's logic is therefore ontological in two senses: it is concerned with the identity of thought and being, which becoming desires to recognize; and it is itself, in its exposition of thought's development, an exercise in becoming—a participative pedagogy. Christ as the Logos, from whom and by whom and in whom all things were created is the immanent structure and economy of true thinking. Put this way Hegel's system provides both an account and a discipline for what Gregory of Nyssa would call our endless *metanoia*, what St. Anselm adjudged to be faith seeking understanding, and what Luther understood as the process of our sanctification—not just as individuals, but as individuals within social and political communities who recognize the truth of Christ in each other.

---

[62] Stephen Houlgate, *An Introduction to Hegel* (n.45), p.41.

PAN, PANEN, AND PROCESS

What I have presented so far—the biochemistry of life developed by Hegel as *Sittlichkeit* and Christ as the true life of all things—presents two concepts of 'life': biological or natural ethical life, and Christ as the one through whom we have 'eternal life'. If we employ the Greek terms we may indeed arrive at three concepts: *bios* as life as biological and cellular; *zōē* as social and ethical life; and Christ who is the way, the truth, and the life (also *zōē*). The relationship between these three forms of life is not equivocal. *Bios* is the condition for all three forms. This condition is only possible because of 'autopoiesis'. Biologically, this is defined as a self-maintaining system, 'open to the input of matter but closed with regard to the dynamics of the relations that generate it'.[63] As Pier Luigi Luisi argues, autopoiesis 'is a necessary condition, but then it takes cognition, at least at the simplest stage, to arrive at the process of life. The union of autopoiesis and the most elementary form of cognition is the minimum that is needed for life.'[64] As such *bios* extends itself in complex, hierarchically organized developments into *zōē*. Hegel relates these two forms of life, the material and the cognitive, to absolute ethical life (Trinitarian life as it is extended through an operation in and through creation) and relative ethical life (which is what individuals have in their natural condition, a condition of immediacy that is continually being dialectically sublated). They are related not united. For Hegel the intuition (*Anschauung*) has to come to a recognition (*Anerkennung*) of what is both absent and yet dynamically present in relations as such; and the recognition has to understand that it is also a misrecognition because its understanding is incomplete. This is how reasoning emerges from the immediate engagement with nature; where reasoning is governed by a Christo-logic. The absolute ethical life is not immediately available. But then neither is it a regulative idea because that would make it an 'ought'. I said above that where the waters muddy with Hegel is when he comes to define the relationship between Christ and creation. If we conflate these two uses of 'life' then the difference between God and the cosmos collapses into univocity. We end up with a form of 'process theology'. Hegel's thought (or an interpretation of Hegel's thought) is one of the philosophical and metaphysical roots of 'process theology'. If we keep the two forms of life entirely separate then the difference becomes incommensurate and equivocal. There is separation and dualism, rather than participative relation, engagement.

We don't need to settle the case for Hegel. Elsewhere I have tried to show the complexity involved here through an examination of the language Hegel

---

[63] Humberto Maturana, cited by Luisi, *The Emergence of Life* (n.6), p.158.
[64] Luisi, *The Emergence of Life* (n.6), p.171.

uses to talk about Christ with respect to the Father and Christ with respect to Creation, and how his understanding of the immanent life of the Trinity relates to the economic life of the Trinity.[65] Though the terms 'immanent' and 'economic' Trinity were a later German innovation. What is important in the argument here is that I am proposing an analogical and therefore participative relation between biological life and life in Christ, based upon a relationship between Creator and creation, and the Pauline teaching that our 'lives are hidden with Christ in God' (Colossians 3.3). The analogy does not just hold linguistically; it traces an ontological relation. Let us pursue this participative relation.

There are two key dynamics propelling all living organisms forward: the propulsion to flourish and the fight against threat. In higher order creatures these dynamics are translated into desire and wrath (or anger or fury). One is embracing and productive; the other protective and consuming. Desire is *need* in animal life below self-consciousness. Wrath is *struggle*: either fight or flee, attack or yield. In lower animals both forces are manifest in reflexive actions; in human beings they are evident in both reflexive (such as autonomic) events and conscious events (through the exercise of agency). Both dynamics have divine correlates. Culturally, much has been said in recent years about desire—philosophies of desire, theologies of desire. God loves us. God draws us to Himself. But little has been said about God's fury because it's not fashionable to be furious in a liberal democratic culture—where God becomes omnitolerant. But God's fury plays no small part in the Hebrew Bible and even surfaces in Christ dispelling the money-changers from the temple precincts. Under philosophical theologians like Marsilio Ficino (who we met in Chapter 3 in relation to Melanchthon), pneumatology was the science of understanding divine *furor*. We will have more to say about this dynamic in Volume III when I explore the Person of the Holy Spirit with respect to leading the Church into all truth, and the operations of God through the sacramental life of the Church in its relations to the world. But for now I only wish to point to the energies of fury in advancing life, and to correct a theological balance that has focused on the importance of desire.

Desire *is* important. But as any sports person has testified, and will testify, fury is more powerful than desire. Watch the wonderful documentary film of the racing-driver Aryton Senna—*Senna* (2010)—or the film about the rivalry between James Hunt and Niki Lauda—*Rush* (2013). Organic life is propelled forward by contestation and fear, as well as need/desire. Both are required. Stability and flourishing depend upon both being in balance. Pedagogy depends on both being in balance. In human physiology a different

[65] Graham Ward, 'Hegel and the Grandeur of Reason' in *The Grandeur of Reason: Religion, Tradition and Universalism*, eds. Conor Cunningham and Peter Candler (London: SCM, 2010).

hormone governs each propulsion: epinephrine or adrenalin for fury, testosterone for desire. In the endocrinal economy, epinephrine is a short term and explosive neurotransmitter whereas testosterone is long term and, when not met, intensifying. Again, the sports person knows how desire creates a rich personal life and is key to the enjoyment of playing tennis, say. It also generates a healthy ambition—to play better. But you don't enter 'the zone' or 'the flow' through desire, and the best learning curve is a steep and aggressive one. You learn more about how to play and how to play better, you achieve more in your game, by 'hating' your opponent and wanting to dominate.

We could play this behavioural, affective, and biochemical interchange out theologically through Augustinian categories—*amor dei* and *amor sui* structure the human orientation to God and to the image of God within oneself (not all *amor sui* is sinful); *libido dominandi* is like fury, the wrath that desires conquest, subjugation, even annihilation of the 'enemy'. At this point I only wish to draw attention to a Trinitarian analogue: God's love and God's wrath. Analogy, we have to recall continually, is only suggestive of a similarity; a greater dissimilarity pertains. There is a discussion and examination of 'affective' life in God with respect to God's impassibility (which occurs in Volume II), but I see no reason to label God's 'wrath' as an anthropomorphism but not God's love, or mercy, or joy. The Holy Spirit's visitation to Mary was one of love—God's love for His creation, for human beings, such that He came to be with them, heal them, re-form them. Incarnation is always an act of love and an orientation towards finding that resting place in God. The Holy Spirit's inauguration of the Church at Pentecost was in tongues of fire leading to ecstatic frenzy. The Church was born in God's fury to redeem by recreating. Though we have no Scriptural testimony, I warrant the resurrection was also an act of God's fury generated by a love stronger than death, a love that would conquer death as an enemy with respect to the origin of life in Christ (Acts 2.24).[66] The wrath of God is no less a part of God's redemptive love; His grace in fulfilling His promise of deliverance. The Holy Spirit may indeed be a Comforter, a Paraclete, but, as Tirian reminds us in C.S. Lewis's *The Last Battle*, Aslan is not a tame lion.

This is complex and difficult ground. Agonistic philosophies—where anger, *ressentiment*, fury, and endless conflict are viewed a primal, transcendental conditions—from Hobbes to Darwin, Nietzsche to Bataille, are viewed as nihilistic, endorsing a new paganism, and to be shunned by theologies orientated towards an 'ontology of peace'.[67] In his own way, Hegel's notion of *Sittlichkeit* challenged the social atomism of an 'each against all' philosophy

---

[66] 'God raised him up, having loosed the pangs of death, because it was not possible for him to be held by it [*ouk ēn dunaton krateisthai auton up' autou*].' The Greek synatical juxtaposition of *auton up' autou* connotes two subjects confronting each other in a struggle for victory.

[67] John Milbank, *Theology and Social Theory* (Oxford: Blackwell, 1999), pp.422–34.

that was the basis for the State as an imagined 'contract' (and a formal rather than real conception of freedom).[68] More has to be said, and will be said, about this fundamental antagonism—though we can recall that one of the basic cellular operations that has evolved is a co-operation that organizes cells first into clusters and then into distinct functions (the nervous system, the digestive system, the respiratory system, etc.). If fury is individualistic and competitive, desire is relational. For now what is important is to understand that life, ethical life, is governed by relation, operations, *energia* and *dunamos*, ethos and environment, but individuals remain. We are back to those opening paragraphs of Hegel's early *System der Sittlichkeit*: relations, *Potenz*, subsumption, in and for itself (*an und für*) and *Gefühl*. These pedagogical and developmental propulsions, even when brought into a Trinitarian and eschatological economy of salvation, even when brought into the economy of salvific grace, concern biology, physiology, affect, and embodied cognition. In sum: experience. Doctrine is lived. It is, in fact, a living process of faith seeking understanding. And the first doctrine to be lived is the Trinity itself.

Ultimately, the account of analogical relations, and Trinitarian life as it relates to biological life, has to focus on the work Christ, the events of the incarnation, the crucifixion, the resurrection and ascension, and the work of the Holy Spirit. Attention to Christ and the Spirit delivers us from pantheism, pandeism, and process theology. It can accommodate some form of panentheism, as long as the stress is upon the unbridgeable gulf (that analogy accepts) between the transcendent Creator and the immanent orders of creation. Recently the process theologian, Catherine Keller, has been working with what she terms 'apophatic panentheism'. I argued above with respect to Hegel that the Christian use and understanding of *theos* cannot announce a simple panentheism; so what about an 'apophatic panentheism' where the 'in' designates 'creation as incarnation'?[69]

Apophasis, along with a series of other terms with a privative prefix (like infinite and impassable), assist in clarifying what we can and what we cannot say accurately with respect to the term *theos*, and therefore what we can and what we cannot understand about God. It refers to an unsaying. Apophasis is not agnosticism. It is not a name describing the ambivalences of undecidability or indeterminancy, abyssal aporia or the gaps in knowledge that sub-atomic physics on the nature of materiality and neuroscience on the

---

[68] The coherence of Hegel's notion of *Sittlichkeit*, its relation to his politics and notion of the State is a matter of debate. We will not be venturing into the ambiguities that arise, and the changes that Hegel makes in his various lectures on the Philosophy of Right between 1821 and 1827 (on the role of the monarch, for example). But Hegel's thinking, theologically construed, is something to build on for a project examining ethical life.

[69] Catherine Keller, *Face of the Deep: A Theology of Becoming* (London: Routledge, 2002), p.219.

nature of mind cannot yet plug with explanations. Neither is it mystery in terms of some darkness within which God hides Godself. God does not hide Godself—the gift of Godself is given absolutely and eternally. So any incomprehension here lies with our inability to adequately know what we designate when we use the word 'God'. Apophasis is the result of our creaturely limitations in which the knowledge of God that we articulate self-consciously deconstructs itself. We do not employ apophatic discourse in order to safeguard God's holy distinctiveness, but rather to regulate our God-talk *for our sake*—because to claim more than can be claimed or inferred from what can be claimed, to fly off into mystical speculations, doesn't help 'save' us. At its most benign it is just escapism; at its most malign it can constitute a delusive ideology that will only perpetuate those violences I spoke of earlier. But, as an adjective qualifying panentheism, what is the object of that admission of a 'learned ignorance'? Surely, it can only be that '*en*'; that indwelling of the divine within 'all things'. So the question becomes: does the apophasis concern *how* God dwells within all things or the nature of God *in* the divine indwelling of all things or both? As one marker which describes God-with-us in a way that refutes hierarchical dualisms such as transcendence over immanence, divine grace over nature, and affirms the incarnation of the divine, then panentheism is helpful and apophatic panentheism would remind us of a restricted understanding of the nature of God in God's divine indwelling. That is, a difference between our knowledge of the immanent and eternal trinity and our attempts to grapple with the effects of the temporal operations of the economic trinity. But we do have knowledge of *how* God indwells within all things that is not apophatic. It may never be a perfect knowledge, but there is the knowledge of being called that the verse from *Ephesians* speaks of. There is knowledge of a divine election, a divine governance or providence, a process of sanctification, the kingdom that is coming, human sin and its redemption. We have knowledge above all on the basis of the incarnation of God in time and place. We have knowledge then of God's economic operations in the world that allows us to use cataphatic discourse on the basis of the life, work, and teachings of Jesus Christ as God. But, and, this is the point—and a point that returns to the question of revelation and Scriptural authority—it is a knowledge on the basis of faith; faith in the articles of the Christian faith distilled by the Church over decades of discernment from the Scriptures, and summed up in the creeds. And 'faith is the assurance of things hoped for, the conviction of things not seen' (Hebrews 11.1). It is certainly no access to certainty; it is quite definitely and necessarily open, vulnerable, and blind. Faith is a suffering in the same way that continuing to 'hope ... against hope' (Rom. 4.18) demands more from us than despair. Faith is not about making assertions; it is a courageous groping towards promises in Christ that may or may not have been understood.

So, sharpening my question even further, does the adjective 'apophatic'—when associated by Catherine Keller with panentheism—name a certain theological investigation which accepts God's indwelling of creation, and examines that indwelling in terms of evolutionary biology, quantum mechanics, mathematics, and the theory of multiplicity, while rejecting the foundation of the Christian faith that God has revealed Godself in Jesus Christ and the Christian Scriptures which participate in some very complex manner in that revelation? Does apophatic creep into the gap left when the call to and substance of the Christian faith is dissolved? If the answers to these last questions are yes, then this is a transferred, even metaphorical use of *apophasis* as it is employed and understood in the context of the Christian tradition. More pointedly: what is the role of the crucified and risen Christ in 'apophatic panentheism'?

As we have seen, the transcendent is not antithetical to the immanent, and that is revealed to us in Christ; creation is in and through God's Word. I can only speak of creation *as* incarnation because of Christ. Without the historical and scandalous particularity of Christ, creation *as* incarnation is just a mystical soup. The singularities of a faith order and organize its worship, individual and collective. In Christ, our talk of transcendence and immanence does not resort to ontological dualism; rather the transcendent Word maintains immanence of what was created in and through that Word—the immanent is suspended within divine grace such that no one can say where transcendence begins and immanence ends. If panentheism allows for the God who is above all, as well as the God who is in all and through all, then the apophasis of the 'above' presides. I will have more to say about this apophasis in Volume III when I discuss God as Father. For now I only insist, following Hegel, that ethical life issues from Trinitarian life as exhibited in creation and incarnation, creation *as* incarnation, and the economy of redemption. The details of this ethical life—its politics, its economics, its sociality—will also command attention in Volume III. As it stands, at the end of this first Volume, it may all come down to a porous membrane seven millionths of a millimetre thick. For it is this cellular membrane, that arose from who knows where, that reads the given, the environment, the world, and translates it into sense, *making* sense; modifying all behaviour.[70] This cellular membrane is the basis for all perception (and knowledge). It makes life possible. Adam and Eve

---

[70] See Bruce H. Lipton, *The Biology of Belief: Unleashing the Power of Consciousness, Matter & Miracles* (London: Hay House UK, 2008), chapter 3 for a lucid discussion of the work of receptor and effector proteins in a cell's membrane, pp.45–63. Receptor proteins operate like sensory nerves, while effector proteins are like motor nerves. For a more detailed study see Gerhard Krauss, *The Biochemistry of Signal Transduction and Regulation* (Weinheim: Wiley-VCH Verlag, 2008, 4th edition), especially pp.1–52 on the basics of cell communication, and pp.181–210 on the signalling of nuclear receptors.

may have been expelled from an Eden now guarded by Cherubim with flaming swords, but the tree of life remains planted there (Genesis 3.24). It remains also at the end of all things, according to Revelation 22.2.

THE TREE OF LIFE

The Tree of Life is an ensign for hope, healing, and redemption. It stands with mythic beauty and poetic resonance in the forests of our confused dreams (Chaucer), amidst what we most fear in being so lost (Conrad's *Heart of Darkness*, Daniel Myrick, and Eduardo Sánchez's *The Blair Witch Project*), and in the forest of signs and knowledges (Descartes). It is also symbolic of our shared phylogenetic inheritance and the evolution of all species; an ethical symbol in so far as it speaks to what is common to all living things. It links the palaeontologist to the anthropologist, the dog breeder to the Greenpeace activist. As Darwin wrote: 'the great Tree of Life . . . fills with its dead broken branches the crust of the earth, and covers the surface with its ever branching and beautiful ramifications.'[71] As the cosmic tree, the *axis mundi* linking the underworld to the heavenly, the Tree of Life is found all over the world—from the religion of the pre-Columbian Mesoamericans and the Chinese Taoists, to the paganism of the Norse. In Islam it becomes the Tree of Immortality. The tree drawings of the Sculptor Henry Moore often capture these mythic resonances in the agonistic twisting of trunks and roots, stripped branches clawing hysterically at the stark white paper, and voluptuously curved boles. In quite different ways, the icon has recently been given wonderful prominence in James Cameron's *Avatar* (2009) and Terrence Malik's *The Tree of Life* (2011).

Avatar treats the inter-connectivity of all life not under the goddess Gaia, but Eywa.[72] Action takes place on a remote moon in the Alpha Centuri star system called Pandora. On Pandora each material body is bound to all other bodies through profound communicative relations. It is a planet conceived as accepting 'the notion of the body as the centre of a "situation" and a set of possible situations', understanding 'the body's life as continuous with the intelligible input of the environment' (to employ Rowan Williams' depiction of language as a material practice).[73] Human beings, greedy for the mineral

---

[71] Charles Darwin, *On the Origin of Species by Means of Natural Selection, or the Preservation of Favoured Races in the Struggle for Life* (London: John Murray, 1859), p.130.

[72] For an account of Gaia as a description for the Earth as a self-regulating organism, see James Ephraim Lovelock, *Gaia: A New Look at Life on Earth* (Oxford: Oxford University Press, 1979).

[73] Rowan Williams, *The Edge of Words: God and the Habits of Language* (London: Bloomsbury, 2014), p.116.

resources on the planet, having despoiled and depleted the resources on Earth, seek the subjugation of Pandora's indigenous people, the Na'vi, in order to plunder them of their mineral wealth. To infiltrate this native people they create avatars, genetically engineered bodies imitating the Na'vi hominoid, but controlled by human beings in distant laboratories. In a war, the new conquistadors destroy the tree that is the life-nurturing heart of the moon (the Hometree). But guided by the Providence of Eywa, and in answer to prayers offered by Na'vi and the one remaining avatar, the eco-system fights back, and wins.

All this is swashbuckling stuff with corporate, capitalist avariciousness (dominated by men) pitched against a sacramental world in which the natural and the spiritual inform each other (and men and women share equally in its governance). But it is the closing moments of the narrative that are most startling, because most magical. For the film is made possible by the very technology that is portrayed as evil, aggressive, acquisitive, and life-threatening. Cameron conceived the plot in 1994, but the digital and computer technology needed to create it was not available at that time. He had to wait (completing his successful *Titanic* movie in the interval). There is then something of a paradoxical tension with respect to the technological. In the closing sequence the avatar is placed under the Tree of Souls, the Tree that links the eternal world with the temporal one. By his side is the broken body of the human being who controlled the avatar from a remote distance. Prayers are offered to Eywa and the soul of the human awakes within the body of what is no longer an avatar but a Na'vi. The human dies. It is a resurrection moment, a miracle, a gift, made possible through a complex set of inter-connected love relations—Eywa for Pandora and the Na'vi, the Na'vi for this one human being who has led them into victory over human exploitation and Eywa, and Jake (the human being) for Neytiri (Na'vi woman who rescued Jake). In Hegelian terms this is the 'subsumption of concept under intuition, or nature proper [*eigentliche*]'; the intuition issuing from its immersion in feeling [*Gefühl*]. In Cameron's closing shots dialectic resolves the tension of *techne* and *phusis* through resurrection.[74] Resurrection life is figured as an attunement between the physical, spiritual, and cosmic.

Cameron has acknowledged the Christian and Hindu ideas behind the film—incarnation and transmigration. He has also commented upon the politics of our lost condition; that is, the film as a critique of remote, mechanized warfare such as was seen deployed by the US in the Gulf and Iraq wars. But it is the Tree that I wish to focus upon, the healing and resurrection it symbolizes and provides. In Malik's film the Tree is explicitly Christian (and

---

[74] In Hegel's Lutheran German: *Aufhebung* is performed through *Auferstehung* (and *vice versa*).

Jewish), with montage shots of churches and Biblical echoes of Adam and
Eve, Cain and Abel. It is imaged in several different trees in the film—mature
trees bending in the wind and newly planted trees (in a suburban garden
and outside an office block in the city), trees climbed by the children, woods
walked by the mother. There is nothing sensational in the action of this film.
It is a story about grief for the death of a well-loved son and brother's guilt
set in the context of two verses from the *Book of Job* (38.4 and 7) which opens
the film: 'Where were you when I laid the foundations of the Earth? . . . When
the morning stars sang together, and all the sons of God shouted for joy?'
Long and beautiful interludes on the origins of life (from a seemingly stray
meteorite striking Earth) and the evolution of the planet from strings of
amino acids develop a theology of creation within which the O'Brien family
history is situated.[75] It is a history that sees the Christian father as a strict,
authoritarian figure often associated with gardening and nature asking his
eldest son for forgiveness for his harsh treatment; and a Christian mother
who is playful, imaginative, and nurturing.

The redemptive theme focuses on Jack, the elder brother, now a successful
architect, who, in a dream, sees his brother calling to him from a desert landscape. 'Find me,' he tells him. Images break in like memories upon his daily
life—a life sad, dull, and empty like the architecture that surrounds him and
the buildings he designs. We see him first being born—the first-born son—
and his mother (in a whispered voice-over) receiving him as a gift from God,
and giving him back to God. Later, alone as an adult, his parents and famiy
dead, he recalls, 'Always you were calling me.' We see Jack emerging into
adolescence and into sin—lust, envy, jealousy, murderous thoughts. Many of
these flashbacks come as he is riding the elevator at work. Then he has what
various critics call 'a vision'. He is asked to follow a woman who takes him
both into a wilderness and then a seascape. On the shores of the sea people
are walking towards the sun on the horizon, among them his parents and
brothers. They meet, they embrace, and for a time they walk together while
a requiem mass setting is being sung. At the end of this sequence the mother
again reiterates her prayer of giving Jack back to God. In another voice over
she prays: 'Keep us. Guard us. To the end of time.' Jack emerges into the fore-
court of the building where he works at first surprised and then finally smiling, reconciled, forgiven (having forgiven himself). The final shot is of Jack's
life, the O'Brien lives, again viewed cosmically—enfolded in a field of orange
energy, gaseous, shape-shifting, floating off into deep space.

---

[75] Malik is notorious for hiding from the public and not giving interviews. It would, though,
be interesting to understand whether one of the influences for the film was Augustine's
Confessions—where biography also gives way to a theological cosmology albeit in the form of
a commentary upon the opening verses of Genesis.

Malik's film is profoundly liturgical and doxological—engaged and engaging. The Christian story is played out against a sense of a loving God who is far greater and ineffable than the Christian religion itself (imaged in prayers at meals and blessings at church). The overpowering sense is of a God who loves us, a God whose loves protects and guides us in ways far beyond our thoughts, in complex weaves of relations, far exceeding anything we could grasp. We are led into a profound forgiveness, reconciliation, healing, and peace. But Christ doesn't figure at all, unless He *is* the Tree of Life. A providence and an eschatology govern all things and all things are hidden deep within God in whom ethical life and the Tree of Life come consumately together. For a brief moment, for one man, Hegel's *Sittlichkeit* kingdom comes down to earth.

In each film, the Tree of Life orders the relationship between *bios* and *zōē*. It organizes each film's semantic field visually and dramatically and it announces that we have not forgotten our mythic roots. Something remains, despite forests of confusion in which human beings become aggressively competitive and accumulative, fretted with anxieties and enervated by fears. As a root metaphor it is commonly owned and recognized, like one of Jung's archetypes of the unconscious. It returns to us and we are returned to it, in deep dreaming. And each of these films, like films generally, are our public dreams.

In the cathedral it's Advent: the season of darkness and the dawn of hope. A late autumn night presses against the stain glass. There's not an empty seat to be found, and the silence is the silence of five hundred people gathered beneath the vaulted ceiling, each holding a thin taper. The lights are low, flowing down the walls from the high clerestory windows, the shadows soft and deep in the aisles and transept, the candles burn, and the choir sings. They sing a carol that has a long history in the Christian tradition, surfacing frequently in writing from the second century, with memorable poems written on the theme from the fourth: *de ligno vitae*—the tree of life. This is an eighteenth-century version:

> The tree of life my soul hath seen
> Laden with fruit and always green:
> The tree of nature fruitless be
> Compared with Christ the apple tree.
> His beauty doth all things excel:
> By faith I know, but ne're can tell,
> The glory which I now can see
> In Jesus Christ the apple tree.
> For happiness I long have sought,
> And pleasure dearly have I bought:
> I miss of all: but now I see
> 'Tis found in Christ the apple tree.

I'm weary with my former toil.
Here I will sit and rest awhile:
Under the shadow I will be
Of Jesus Christ the apple tree.
This fruit doth make my soul to thrive,
It keeps my dying faith alive;
Which makes my soul in haste to be
With Jesus Christ the apple tree.[76]

This is a dark paradox of crucifixion and eternal life, death, and consummate beauty. History is variegated: some of us are on its slaughter-bench and some of us enjoy dry martinis in revolving restaurants overlooking sunset bays. And several of us are in the kitchens preparing the peanuts and pretzels. I don't know what this says about our generic human condition. This is where I am most lost; because many people don't live with meaning and that's what I'm trying to trace here. They live with need: where to find fresh water, where to find food, where to find protection, where to find whatever they have come to depend upon to give them relief from trying to find meaning: sex, drugs, entertainment, love, booze, even violence: a little relief, a little comfort, a little forgetfulness. We have to know this, not just recognize and remember it, as we theologians preach the gospel and seek understanding. Understanding for many is a luxury. Prepare to descend into hell. If we can't descend into hell then I am not sure we can ascend very far towards heaven. Fortunately, one has gone before us and in whose strength we live, depend. The hymn to the Cross as the Tree of Life points a way forward, but I don't think Jesus is an easy answer either. Nevertheless, I want to understand what I believe in being taught the language of that belief—and Jesus Christ is central to that belief. And the cross is central to that belief; for the cross reveals the beating heart of God's love. With the Tree of Life, then, there is an intimation of what is at the beginning and what will still be there at the end: a living from a Good beyond our good; a formation by that Good beyond our good; a life-long teaching by that Good beyond our good—so that our doctrine is lived in being learnt in love. It fashions our life. It is engaged in a *theo-poiesis*. It offers us another kind of normal.

---

[76] From *Divine Hymns, or Spiritual Songs: for the use of Religious Assemblies and Private Christians* compiled by Joshua Smith. It was composed in the eighteenth century by an unknown writer and modelled on Old English and medieval lyrics on a similar theme. In the West Country (England) there was a tradition of wassailing the apple trees in winter. The tune it is often sung to in Adent by choirs is by Elizabeth Poston, 1905–1987. For an earlier example of this tradition see *Early Christian Latin Poets*, ed. and trans. Carolinne White (London: Routledge, 2000), pp.136–9.

Bibliography

Abelard, *Dialectica*, ed. and trans. L.M. de Rijk (Assen: Van Gorcam, 1970, 2nd edition).

Abelard, *Historia calamitatum* in *The Letters of Abelard and Heloise*, trans. Betty Radice (Harmondsworth: Penguin, 1974).

Abelard, *Sic et Non,* trans. *Peter Abailard, Sic et Non: A Critical Edition*, eds. B.B. Boyer and R. McKeon (Chicago: University of Chicago Press, 1978).

Abelard, *Peter Abelard, Soliloquium: A Critical Edition*, trans. Charles Burnett, *Studi Medievali* 25 (1984), 857–94.

Abelard, *Theologia Summi Boni,* eds. E.M. Buytaert and C.J. Mews, *Petri Abaelardi opera theological* III, Corpus Christianorum continuatio mediaevalis 13 (Turnhout, Belgium: Brepolis, 1987).

Adams, Nicholas, *The Eclipse of Grace: Divine and Human Action in Hegel* (Blackwell: Oxford, 2013).

Agamben, Giorgio, *Homo Sacer: Sovereign Power and Bare Life*, trans. Daniel Heller-Roazen (Stanford, CA: Stanford University Press, 1998).

Agamben, Giorgio, *The Kingdom and the Glory: For a Theological Genealogy of Economy and Government*, trans. Lorenzo Chiesa (with Matteo Mandarini) (Stanford: Stanford University Press, 2011).

Agha, Asif, *Language and Social Relations* (Cambridge: Cambridge University Press, 2007).

Andrew of Saint-Victor, *Commentary on Isaiah* in Beryl Smalley, *The Study of the Bible in the Middle Ages*, (Oxford: Blackwell, 1984, 3rd edition), pp.121–3 and 378–9.

Anselm, *Monologium*, in *St. Anselm: Basic Writings*, trans. S.N. Deane (La Salle, IL: Open Court Publishing Company, 1962). Latin text (with an amended translation), *A New, Interpretive Translation of St. Anselm's* Monologion *and* Proslogion, Jasper Hopkins (ed.), (Minneapolis: A.J. Banning Press, 1986).

Aquinas, Thomas, *Summa Theologicae*, Latin/English text, ed. and trans. Thomas Gilby *et al.* (London: Eyre & Spottiswoode, 1964–1981).

Aquinas, Thomas, *De Veritate*. Latin text on line: <http://www.corpusthomisticum.org/iopera.html>. Translation: Robert W. Mulligan *et al.*, Truth, three volumes (Indianapolis: Hackett Publishing Company, 1995).

Aristotle, *Physics: Books I and II*, trans. William Charlton (Oxford: Oxford University Press, 1970).

Aristotle, *Metaphysics: Bks.1–9* (Loeb Classical Library), trans. Hugh Tredennick (Cambridge, Mass: Loeb, Harvard University Press, 1989).

Athanasius, *Oration Against the Arians,* ed. Archibald Robertson in the *Nicene and Post-Nicene Fathers*, vol.4: *Athanasius: Select Works and Letters*, eds. Philip Schaff and Henry Wace (Peabody, MA: Hendrickson Publishers, 1994).

Augustine *Sermons*, available on line at: http://www.newadvent.org/fathers/1603.htm

Augustine, *De consensu evangelistarum*, Migne. *Patrologia Latina*. 34. Available on line at: <http://www.documentacatholicaomnia.eu/03d/0354-0430,_Augustinus,_ De_Consensu_Evangelistarum_Libri_Quatuor_%5BSchaff%5D,_EN.pdf>.

Augustine, *City of God*, trans. Henry Bettenson, (Harmondsworth: Penguin, 1984).

Augustine, *Confessions*, trans. Henry Chadwick (Oxford: Oxford University Press, 1991).

Auuman, Jordan O.P., 'Appendix 2: Historical Background,' in St. Thomas Aquinas, *Summa Theologiae* vol.46: *Action and Contemplation*, Jordan Auman O.P. trans. (London: Eyre & Spottiswoode, 1966), pp.90–101.

Ayres, Lewis, *Nicaea and its Legacy: An Approach to Fourth-Century Trinitarian Theology* (Oxford: Oxford University Press, 2004).

Ayres, Lewis, 'Into the Poem of the Universe: *Exempla*, Conversion, and the Church in Augustine's *Confessiones' ZAC*, vol.13, 263–81.

Bader, Günter, *Psalterium affectum palaestra: Prolegomena zu einer Theologie des Psalters* (Tübingen: Mohr Siebeck, 1996),

Baldovin, John F., *Liturgy in Ancient Jerusalem* (Bramcote: Grove Books, 1989).

Balthasar, Hans Urs von, *Glory of the Lord*, Volume II: *Clerical Styles*, trans. Andrew Louth, *et al.* (Edinburgh: T. & T. Clark, 1986).

Balthasar, Hans Urs von, *Glory of the Lord,* Volume III: *Lay Styles*, trans. Andrew Louth, *et al.* (Edinburgh: T. & T. Clark, 1986).

Balthasar, Hans Urs, *Glory of The Lord*, Volume V: *The Realm of Metaphysics in the Modern Age*, trans. Oliver Davies *et al.* (Edinburgh: T.&T. Clark, 1991).

Balthasar, Hans Urs von, *Mysterium Paschale*, trans. Aidan Nichols O.P. (Edinburgh: T. & T. Clark, 1990).

Balthasar, Hans Urs, von, *Theo-Drama: Theological Dramatic Theory* III, trans. Graham Harrison (San Francisco: Ignatius Press, 1992); *Theodramatik: Zweiter Band* (Einsiedeln: Joahnnes Verlag, 1978).

Barker, Margaret, *King of the Jews: Temple Theology in John's Gospel* (London: SPCK, 2015).

Barnes, Timothy D., *Athanasius and Constantius: Theology and Politics in the Constantinian Empire* (Cambridge, MA: Harvard University Press, 1993).

Barnes, Timothy D., 'Christians and Pagan in the Reign of Constantius', In *Eusebius to Augustine* (Aldershot: Ashgate, 1994), pp.322–37.

Baron, Roger, 'L'Idée de liberté chez Anselme et Hugues de Saint-Victor', *Recherches de Théologie Ancienne et Médiévale*, 32 (1965), 117–21.

Barth, Karl, *Church Dogmatics* I.1, trans. G.W. Bromiley, G.T. Thomson and Harold Knight (Edinburgh: T. & T. Clark, 2010).

Barth, Karl, *Church Dogmatics* I.2, trans. G.T. Thomson and Harold Knight (Edinburgh: T. & T. Clark, 1956).

Bath, Michael, *Speaking Pictures: English Emblem Books and Renaissance Culture* (London: Longman, 1994).

Bath, Michael and Russell, Daniel, eds. *Deceitful Settings: English Renaissance Emblem and its Context* (New York: AMS Press, 1999).

Bätschmann, Oskar and Griener, Pascal, *Hans Holbein* (London: Reaktion Books, 1999).

Bauerschmidt, Fredrick Christian, *Thomas Aquinas: Faith, Reason, and Following Christ* (Oxford: Oxford University Press, 2013).

Bautier, Robert-Henri, 'Les Origines et les premiers dévolopments de l'abbaye Saint-Victor de Paris', *L'Abbaye Parisienne de Saint-Victor au Moyen Age*, ed. Jean Longère (Biblioteca Victorina, I. Turnout, 1991).

Behr, John, *The Way to Nicaea: The Formation of Christian Theology* vol. 1 (Crestwood, NY: St. Vladimir's Seminary Press, 2001).

Behr, John, *The Nicene Faith: The Formation of Christian Theology* vol. 2, Part 1 and Part 2 (Crestwood, NY: St. Vladimir's Seminary Press, 2004).

Bettelheim, Bruno, *The Uses of Enchantment: The Meaning and Importance of Fairy Tales* (London: Penguin Books, 1991).

Bisson, Thomas N., *The Crisis of the Twelfth Century: Power, Lordship, and the Origins of European Government* (Princeton: Princeton University Press, 2009).

Blondel, Maurice, *The Letter on Apologetics and History and Dogma*, trans. A. Dru and I. Trethowan (Edinburgh: T. & T. Clark, 1994).

Bogdanos, Theodore, *Pearl: Image of the Ineffable: A Study of Mediaeval Poetic Symbolism* (University Park: Pennsylvania State University Press, 1983).

Borges, Jorge Luis, 'The Circular Ruins' in *Labyrinths: Selected Stories and Other Essays*, eds. Donald A. Yates and James E. Irby (Harmondsworth: Penguin Books, 1964).

Bornkamm, Heinrich, 'Melanchthons Menschenbild', in Walter Elliger (hrsg.), *Philipp Melanchthon: Forschungsbeiträge zur vierhundertsten Wiederkehr seines Todestages dargeboten in Wittenberg, 1960* (Göttingen: Vandenhoeck & Ruprecht, 1960), pp.76–92.

Bossy, John, *Christianity in the West 1400–1700* (Oxford: Oxford University Press, 1985).

Boulnois, Olivier, 'Reading Duns Scotus: From History to Philosophy' in *Modern Theology* 21 (2005), pp.603–8.

Bourdieu, Pierre, *In Other Words: Essays Toward a Reflexive Sociology*, trans. Matthew Adamson (Stanford: Stanford University Press, 1990).

Bourdieu, Pierre, *The Field of Cultural Production*, trans. and ed. Randal Johnston (New York: Columbia University Press, 1993).

Braaten, Carl E. and Jenson, Robert W. (eds.), *Union with Christ: The New Finnish Interpretation of Luther* (Grand Rapids, MI: Eerdmans, 1998).

Braudel, Fernand, *The Mediterranean and the Mediterranean World in the Time of Philip II* in two volumes, trans. Sian Reynolds (Berkeley: University of California Press, 1995 and 1996).

Breen, Qurinus, 'The Terms "*Loci Communes*" and "*Loci*" in Melanchthon', *Church History* 16 (1947), pp.197–209.

Bringhurst, Robert, *The Tree of Meaning* (Berkeley, CA: Counterpoint, 2007).

Brito-Martins, Manuela, 'The Concept of Peregrination in St. Augustine and Its Influences' in: *Exile in the Middle Ages*, Laura Napran and Elisebeth van Houts (eds.) *International Mediaeval Research*, vol.13 (Turnhout, Belgium: Brepolis 2004), pp.83–94.

Brown, Peter, *The World of Late Antiquity* (London: Thames and Hudson, 1999).

Buckley, Michael J., *At the Origins of Modern Atheism* (New Haven: Yale University Press, 1990).

Bulgakov Sergius, *The Lamb of God*, trans. Boris Jakim (Grand Rapids, MI: Eerdmans Publishing Company, 2008).

Burdett, Michael S., *Eschatology and the Technological Future* (London: Routledge, 2015).

Burrus, Virginia, *'Begotten Not Made': Conceiving Manhood in Late Antiquity* (Stanford: Stanford University Press, 2000).

Cadden, Joan, *Meaning of Sex Difference in the Middle Ages: Medicine, Science, and Culture* (Cambridge: Cambridge University Press, 1993).

Candler, Peter M., Jr. *Theology, Rhetoric, Manduction, or Reading Scripture Together on the Path to God* (Grand Rapids, MI: William B. Eerdmans, 2006).

Carruthers, Peter, 'HOP over FOR, HOT Theory' in *Higher Order Theories of Consciousness*, in Rocco J. Gennaro, ed. *Higher Order Theories of Consciousness: An Anthology* (Amsterdam: John Benjamins, 2004), pp.115–35.

Chadwick, Henry, *Early Christian Thought and the Classical Tradition* (Oxford: Oxford University Press, 1966).

Chadwick, Henry, 'The Role of the Bishop in Ancient Society', Centre for Hermeneutical Studies, Berkeley: Colloquy 35, 1980, pp.1–22.

Chapman, Mark D., *Anglican Theology* (London: T. & T. Clark, 2012).

Châtillon, Jean, *Le Mouvement canonical au moyen âge: réforme de l'église, spiritualité et culture* (Paris: Bibliotheca Victorina 3, 1992).

Chaucer, Geoffrey, 'The Book of the Duchess' in *Dream Visions and Other Poems: Geoffrey Chaucer*, ed. Kathryn L. Lynch (New York: W.W. Norton & Company, 2007).

Chemero, Anthony, *Radical Embodied Cognitive Science* (Boston: MIT Press, 2011).

Chenu, Marie-Dominique, *La Saulchair: Une école de la théologie* (Paris: Étoiles, 1937).

Chenu, Marie-Dominque, *Man, Nature, and Society in the Twelfth Century*, trans. Lester. K. Little (Toronto: University of Toronto Press, 1997).

Clanchy, M.T., *Abelard: Medieval Life* (Oxford: Blackwell, 1997).

Clausen, M.H., ' "Peregrinatio" and "Peregrini" in Augustine's *City of God*', *Traditio* vol.46, 1991, 35–75.

Coakley, Sarah, *God, Sexuality, and the Self: An Essay 'On the Trinity'* (Cambridge: Cambridge University Press, 2013).

Constable, Giles, *The Reformation of the Twelfth Century* (Cambridge: Cambridge University Press, 1996).

Cohn, Norman, *The Pursuit of the Millennium: Revolutionary Millenarians and Mystical Anarchists of the Middle Ages* (London: Paladin Books, 1970).

Collins, Randall, *Interaction Ritual Chains* (Princeton, NJ: Princeton University Press, 2004).

Congar, Yves, 'La "réception" comme réalité ecclésiologique', *Revue des Sciences Philosophiques et Théologiques* 56 (1972): 369–403.

Coolman, Boyd Taylor, *The Theology of Hugh of St. Victor: An Interpretation* (Cambridge: Cambridge University Press, 2010).

Courtney, Francis, *Cardinal Robert Pullen: An English Theologian of the 12th Century*, *Analecta Gregoriana*, 64, 1954.

Chrétien, Jean-Louis, *Traversées de l'imminence* (Paris: Les éditions de l'Herne, 1989).

Chrétien, Jean-Louis, *La Voix nue: Phénoménologie de la promesse* (Paris: Les Éditions de Minuit, 1990).

Chrétien, Jean-Louis, 'The Wounded Word: The Phenomenology of Prayer', in *Phenomenology and the 'Theological Turn': The French Debate*, Dominique Janicaud ed., trans. B.G. Prusak (New York: Fordham University Press, 2000).

Chrétien, Jean-Louis, *The Call and the Response*, trans. Anne A. Devonport (New York: Fordham University Press, 2004).

Cunningham, Andrew and Grell, Ole Peter, *The Four Horsemen of the Apocalypse: Religion, War, Famine and Death in Reformation Europe* (Cambridge: Cambridge University Press, 2000).

Cyril of Jerusalem, *The Catechetical Lectures*, trans. Edwin Hamilton Gifford, in *Nicene and Post-Nicene Fathers*, vol.7, ed. Philip Schaff and Henry Wace (Peabody, MA: Hendrickson Publishers, 1994), p.5. The Greek text can be found in Migne. *Patrologia Graeca* vol.33.

Damasio, Antonio, *The Feeling of What Happens: Body, Emotion, and the Making of Consciousness* (London: Vintage Books, 2000).

Damasio, Antonio, *Self Comes to Mind: Constructing the Conscious Brain* (London: Vintage, 2012).

Daniélou, Jean, *Origène: Le Génie du Christianisme* (Paris: La Table Ronde, 1948).

Daniélou, Jean, *Histoire des doctrines chrétiennes avant Nicée*, 3 vols. (Paris: Desclée, Éditions du Cerf, 1958–1978).

Dante Alighieri, *Hell,* trans. Dorothy L. Sayer (Harmondsworth: Penguin, 1949).

Dante Alighieri, *Inferno*, trans. Robin Kirkpatrick (Harmondsworth: Penguin Classics, 2006).

Darwin, Charles, *On the Origin of Species by Means of Natural Selection, or the Preservation of Favoured Races in the Struggle for Life* (London: John Murray, 1859).

Daston, Lorraine, 'Baconian Facts, Academic Civility, and the Prehistory of Objectivity' in *Annals of Scholarship* 8, nos. 3–4 (1991).

Daston, Lorraine, 'The Moral Economy of Science' in *Constructing Knowledge in the History of Science*, edited by Arnold Thackray (Chicago: Chicago University Press, 1995).

Deacon, Terrence W., *The Symbolic Species: The Co-evolution of Language and the Human Brain* (London: Allen Lane, 1997).

Deacon, Terrence W., *Incomplete Nature: How Mind Emerged from Matter* (New York: W. W. Norton & Company, 2012).

Dear, Peter, *Discipline and Experience: The Mathematical Way in the Scientific Revolution* (Chicago: University of Chicago Press, 1995).

De Certeau, Michel, 'Culture and Spiritual Experience', *Concilium: International Journal for Theology* (1966), 3–16.

De Certeau, Michel, 'How is Christianity Thinkable Today?' in Graham Ward, ed. *The Postmodern God* (Oxford: Blackwell, 1998), pp.142–55.

De Certeau, Michel, *La Fable Mystique*, vol. 1, XVIe–XVIIe Siècle (Paris: Editions Gallimard, 1982). Trans. *The Mystic Fable: Volume One: The Sixteen and Seventeenth Centuries*, Michael B. Smith (Chicago: The University of Chicago Press, 1992).

De Certeau, Michel, *La Possession de Loudun* (Paris: Editions Gallimard, 1970). Trans. *The Possession at Loudon*, Michael B. Smith (Chicago: The University of Chicago Press, 1996).

De Certeau, Michel, 'Walking in the City' in Graham Ward, ed. *The Certeau Reader* (Oxford: Blackwell, 2000), pp.101–18.

De Certeau, Michel, 'The Weakness of Believing' in Graham Ward, ed. *The Certeau Reader,* (Oxford: Blackwell, 2000), pp.214–43. *La faiblesse de croire* (Paris: Éditions de Seuil, 1987).

Deleuze, Gilles, *Pure Immanence: Essays on a Life,* trans. Anne Boyman (New York: Urzone, 2001).

De Lubac, Henri, *Corpus Mysticum: Essai sur L'Eucharistie et l'Église au moyen âge,* (Paris: Aubier, 1944).

De Lubac, *Surnaturel: études historiques,* (1946). A new French edn. issued by (Paris: Desclée de Brouwer, 1991).

De Lubac, Henri, *Exégèse medieval: les quarter sens de l'écriture* (Paris: Aubier, 1959–64). *Medieval Exegesis: The Four Senses of Scripture,* trans. E.M. Macierowski (vol.3) (Grand Rapids, MI: William B. Eerdmans Publishing Company, 2009).

De Saint Aubert, Emmanuel ' "Incarnation change tout." Merleau-Ponty critiques de la "theologie explicative" ', *Archives de Philosophie,* 71.3 (2008).

Dillard, Peter S., *Foundation & Restoration in Hugh of St. Victor's* De Sacramentis (New York: Palgrave Macmillan, 2014).

Descartes, René, *Discourse on Method and The Meditations,* trans. F.E. Sutcliffe (Harmondsworth: Penguin Books, 1968).

Desmond, William, *Hegel's God: A Counterfeit Double?* (Aldershot: Ashgate, 2003).

Dostoyevsky, Fyodor, *The Idiot,* trans. David Magarshack (Harmondsworth: Penguin Books, 1955).

Doval, Alexis James, *Cyril of Jerusalem, Mystagogue: Authoriship of the Mystagogic Catecheses* (Washington: The Catholic University of America Press, 2001).

Drijvers, Jan Willem, *Cyril of Jerusalem: Bishop and City* (Leiden: Brill, 2004).

Engen, John H. Van, 'Images and Ideas: The Achievements of Gerhart Burian Ladner', *Viator* 20 (1989), 85–115.

Duffy, Eamon, *The Stripping of the Altars* (New Haven: Yale University Press, 1992).

Dunbar, Robin, *Grooming, Gossip and the Evolution of Language* (London: Faber and Faber, 1996).

Dworkin Ronald, *Justice for Hedgehogs* (Cambridge, MA: Harvard University Press, 2011).

Eichberger, Dagmar and Zika, Charles, eds. *Dürer and His Culture* (Cambridge: Cambridge University Press, 1998).

Eusebius, *Epistola Eusebii* prepared by Archibald Robertson in the *Nicene and Post-Nicene Fathers,* vol.4: *Athanasius: Select Works and Letters,* eds. Philip Schaff and Henry Wace (Peabody, MA: Hendrickson Publishers, 1994).

Eusebius, *Life of Constantine,* translated by Rev. Arthur Cushman McGriffert in the *Nicene and Post-Nicene Fathers,* vol.10: *The Church History of Eusebius,* eds. Philip Schaff and Henry Wace (Peabody, MA: Hendrickson Publishers, 1994).

Eusebius, *Life of Constantine,* trans. Averil Cameron and Stuart G. Hall (Oxford: Oxford University Press, 1999).

Evagarius Ponticus, 'On Prayer' in *Evagarius Ponticus*, ed. A.M. Cassidy (London: Routledge, 2006), pp.185–201.

Fassler, Margot, *Gothic Song: Victorine Sequences and Augustinian Reform in Twelfth-Century Paris* (Notre Dame, IN.: University of Notra Dame Press, 2nd edition 2011).

Flaubert, Gustave, *Madame Bovary*, trans. Margaret Mauldon (Oxford: Oxford University Press, 2004).

Fleming, Gerald, 'On the Origins of the Passioni Christi und Antichristi and Lucas Cranach the Elder's Contribution to Reformation Polemics in the Iconography of the Passional', *Gutenberg Jahrbuch* (1973), pp.351–68.

Foucault, Michel, *The History of Sexuality*, Part One: *An Introduction*, trans. Robert Hurley (London: Allen Lane, 1979).

Fraenkel, Peter, 'Revelation and Tradition: Notes on some Aspects of Doctrinal Continuity in the Theology of Philip Melanchthon,' *Studia Theologica – Nordic Journal of Theology* 13, Issue 1 (1959): 97–133.

Franke, John R., *The Character of Theology* (Grand Rapids: Baker Press, 2005).

Frede, Michael, 'On Galen's Epistemology' in Vivan Nutton, ed. *Galen: Problems and Prospects* (London: Wellcome Institute for the History of Medicine, 1981) pp.65–84.

Friedländer, Max J. and Rosenberg, Jakob, *The Paintings of Lucas Cranach* (New York: AbeBooks, 1978), first published in 1911.

Frijda, N.J., 'Moods, emotion episodes, and emotions' in Michael Lewis and J.M. Haviland, eds. *Handbook of Emotions* (New York: Guilford Press, 1993), pp.381–403.

Geyer, H.-G., *Von der Geburt des wahren Menschen* (Neukirchen, 1965).

Gibson, Daniel G. *et al.*, 'Creation of a Bacterial Cell Controlled by a Chemically Synthesized Genome', *Science* 2 July 2010: vol. 329 no. 5987 pp.52–6.

Gibson, James J., *The Senses Considered as Perceptual Systems* (Westport, Conn.: Greenwood Press, 1966).

Gillespie, Michael Allen, *The Theological Origins of Modernity* (Chicago: University of Chicago Press, 2008).

Godwin, Joscelyn, *The Pagan Dream of the Renaissance* (London: Thames & Hudson, 2002).

Goleman, Daniel, *Emotional Intelligence: Why It Can Matter More Than IQ* (New York: Bantam Books, 1995).

Graybill, Gregory B., *Evangelical Free Will: Philipp Melanchthon's Doctrinal Journey on the Origins of Faith* (Oxford: Oxford University Press, 2010).

Greeley, Andrew, *The Catholic Imagination* (Berkeley: University of California Press, 2000).

Greenblatt, Stephen, *Renaissance Self-Fashioning: From More to Shakespeare* (Chicago: University of Chicago Press, 1980).

Gregory of Nyssa, 'On "Not Three Gods"', in *Selected Writings and Letters of Gregory, Bishop of Nyssa*, trans. W. Moore and H. Wilson (Grand Rapids, MI: Eerdmans, 1979).

Gregory of Nyssa, 'The Great Catechism', *Oratio Catechetica* in *Gregorii Nysseni Opera Dogmatica Minora, Pars IV*, ed. Ekkehardus Mühlenberg (Leiden: E.J. Brill,

1996). Translation: William More and Henry Austen Wilson, *Nicene and Post-Nicene Fathers: Gregory of Nyssa: Dogmatic Treatises* vol.5, eds. Philip Schaff and Henry Wace (Peabody, MA: Hendrickson Publishers, 1994).

Grossberg, Lawrence, *We Gotta Get Out Of This Place: Popular Conservatism and Postmodern Culture* (New York: Routledge, 1992).

Gunton, Colin, 'An English Systematic Theology', *Scottish Journal of Theology* 46 (1993), 479–96.

Gutmann, Amy, ed. *Multiculturalism and 'The Politics of Recognition'* (Princeton: Princeton University Press, 1992).

Guyot-Bachy, Isabelle, 'Les victorins et l'histoire: des maître sans disciples?' in *Bibliotheca Victorina XXII: L'École de Saint-Victor de Paris*, actes réunis par Dominique Poirel (Turnhout, Belgium: Brepolis: 2010), pp.179–96.

Gwynn, David M., *Athanasius of Alexandria: Bishop, Theologian, Ascetic, Father* (Oxford: Oxford University Press, 2012).

Haase, Marco, *Grundnorm, Gemeinwille, Geist* (Tübingen: Mohr Siebeck, 2004).

Habermas, Jürgen, *Knowledge and Human Intertests*, trans. Jeremy Shapiro (Boston: Beacon Press, 1972).

Harries, Jill, *Law and Empire in Late Antiquity* (Cambridge: Cambridge University Press, 2001).

Hall, H. Ashby, *Philip Melanchthon and the Cappadocians* (Göttingen: Vandenhoeck & Ruprecht, 2014).

Harrison, Carol, 'Augustine and the Art of Music' in Jeremy S. Begbie and Stephen R. Guthrie, *Resonant Witness: Conversations between Music and Theology* (Grand Rapids, MI: William B. Eerdmans, 2011), pp.27–45.

Harrison, Carol, *The Art of Listening in the Early Church* (Oxford: Oxford University Press, 2013).

Hartmann, Klaus, 'Hegel: A Non-Metaphysical View' in Alasdair MacIntyre, ed. *Hegel—A Collection of Essays* (Garden City, New Jersey: Double Day Anchor, 1972), pp.101–24.

Harvey, Susan Ashbrook, *Scenting Salvation: Ancient Christianity and the Olfactory Imagination* (Oakland, CA: University of California Press, 2006).

Hegel, Georg Wilhelm Friedrich, *System der Sittlichkeit. Reinschriftentwurf* in Georg Wilhelm Friedrich Hegel, *Gesammelte Werke*, Bd. 5, *Schriften und Entwürfe 1799–1808*. *System of Ethical Life and First Philosophy of Spirit*, ed. and trans. H.S. Harris and T.M. Knox (Albany: SUNY Press, 1979).

Hegel, Georg Wilhelm Friedrich, *Enzyklopädie der philosophischen Wissenschften I, Die Wissenschaft der Logik*. Trans. *The Encyclopedia of Logic*, T.F. Geraets, W.A. Suchting, and H. Harris (Indianapolis: Hackett Publishing Company, 1991).

Hegel, Georg Wilhelm Friedrich, *The Philosophy of History*, trans. J. Sibree (New York: Dover Publications Inc., 1956). *Vorlessungen über die Philosophie der Geschichte*, Werke 12 (Frankfurt am Main: Suhrkamp, 1986).

Hegel, Georg Wilhelm Friedrich, *Elements of a Philosophy of Right*, trans. H.B. Nisbet (Cambridge: Cambridge University Press, 1991).

Hegel, Georg Wilhelm Friedrich, 'Glauben und Wissen', in *G.W.F. Hegel Werke: Jenaer Schriften 1801–1807*, Band 2 (Frankfurt: Suhrkamp Verlag, 1986), pp.432–3.

Translation: *Hegel: Faith and Reason*, eds. and trans. Walter Cerf and H.S. Harris (New York, SUNY Press, 1988).

Hegel, Georg Wilhelm Friedrich, 'Über die wissenschaftlichen Behandlungsarten des Naturrechts' in *G.W.F. Hegel Werke: Jenaer Schriften 1801-1807* Band 2 (Frankfurt am Main: Suhrkamp, 1986). Trans. *Natural Law. The Scientific Ways of Treating Natural Law, Its Place in Moral Philosophy, and Its Relation to the Positive Sciences of Law*, T.M. Knox (Philadelphia: University of Philadelphia Press, 1975).

Hegel, Georg Wilhelm Friedrich, *Differenz des Fichteschen und Schellingschen Systems der Philosophie*' in *G.W.F. Hegel Werke: Jenaer Schriften 1801-1807*, vol.2 (Frankfurt: Suhrkamp Verlag, 1986). Translation: *The Difference between Fichte's and Schelling's System of Philosophy*, trans. H.S. Harris and Walter Cerf (Albany: SUNY Press, 1977).

Hegel, Georg Wilhelm Friedrich, *Phänomenologie des Geistes* in *G.W.F. Hegel Werke: Band 3* (Frankfurt am Main: Suhrkamp, 1986). *The Phenomenology of Spirit*, trans. A.A. Miller (Oxford: Oxford University Press, 1977).

Hegel, Georg Wilhelm Friedrich, *Lectures on the Philosophy of History*, trans. J. Sibree (New York: Dover Books, 1956).

Hemming, Laurence Paul and Parsons, Susan Frank, eds. and trans. *Restoring Faith in Reason* (London, SCM Press, 2002).

Henry, Michel, *Incarnation: Une philosophie de la chair* (Paris: Éditions du Seuil, 2000).

Herms, Eilert, 'Objective Truth: Relations between Truth and Revelation in the Encyclical *Fides et ratio*' in *Restoring Faith in Reason*, eds. and trans. Laurence Paul Hemming and Susan Frank Parsons (London: SCM Press, 2002), pp.206–24.

Hildebrandt, Franz, *Melanchthon: Alien or Ally?* (Cambridge: Cambridge University Press, 1946).

Hirschfield, Jane, *Nine Gates: Entering the Mind of Poetry* (New York: Harper Perennial, 1998).

Hoff, Johannes, 'The Rise and Fall of the Kantian Paradigm of Modern Theology' in Peter Candler, ed. *The Grandeur of Reason: Religion, Tradition and Universalism* (London: SCM Press, 2010).

Hogg, David S, *Anselm of Canterbury The Beauty of Theology* (Aldershot: Ashgate Press, 2004).

Hollingworth, Miles, *The Pilgrim City: St. Augustine of Hippo and his Innovation in Political Thought* (London: T. & T. Clark, 2010).

Höß, I., 'Humanismus und Reformation', in *Geschichte Thüringens*, H. Patze and W. Schlesinger, eds. Teil III (Köln: Böhlau, 1967): 71–84.

Houlgate, Stephen, *An Introduction to Hegel: Freedom, Truth, and History* (Oxford: Blackwell, 2nd edn. 2005).

Hugh of St. Victor, *The Didascalicon of Hugh of St. Victor: A Mediaeval Guide to the Arts*, ed. and trans. with introduction and notes, Jerome Taylor (New York: Records of Western Civilization: Sources and Studies 64, 1991). Latin text available on: <http://www.thelatinlibrary.com/hugo.html>.

Hugh of St. Victor, *De Arca Noe Morali*. Migne. *Patrologia Latina*. 176. Available on line at: <http://www.documentacatholicaomnia.eu/04z/z_1096-1141__Hugo_ De_S_Victore__De_Arca_Noe_Morali_Libri_IV__MLT.pdf.html>.

HUGH OF SAINT-VICTOR: Selected Spiritual Writings, trans. and ed. Adred Squire (New York: Harper & Row, 1962).

Hugh of St. Victor, *In Salomonis Ecclesiasten Homiliae*, Migne. *Patrologia Latina*, 175. Available on line at: <http://www.documentacatholicaomnia.eu/04z/z_1096-1141__Hugo_De_S_Victore__In_Salomonis_Ecclesiasten_Homiliae_XIX__MLT.pdf.html>.

Hugh of St. Victor, *De sapientia animae Christi*, Migne. *Patrologia Latina* 176. Available on line at: <http://www.documentacatholicaomnia.eu/04z/z_1096-1141__Hugo_De_S_Victore__De_Sapientia_Animae_Christi._An_Aequalis_Cum_Divina_Fuerit__MLT.pdf.html>.

Hugh of St. Victor, *De Vanitate Mundi et Transeuntium Usu*, Migne. *Patrologia Latina* 176. Available on line at: <http://www.documentacatholicaomnia.eu/04z/z_1096-1141__Hugo_De_S_Victore__De_Vanitate_Mundi_Et_Rerum_Transeuntium_Usu_Libri_Quatuor__MLT.pdf.html>.

Translation: The Vanity of the World. HUGH OF SAINT-VICTOR: Selected Spiritual Writings, trans. and ed. Adred Squire (New York: Harper & Row, 1962).

Hugh of St. Victor, *De Sacramentis Christianae Fidei*. Migne. *Patrologia Latina*. 176. Available online at: <http://www.documentacatholicaomnia.eu/04z/z_1096-1141__Hugo_De_S_Victore__De_Sacramentis_Christianae_Fidei__MLT.pdf.html>. Trans. Roy J. Deferrari, *Hugh of St. Victor on the Sacraments of the Christian Faith* (Eugene, OR: Wipf and Stock, 2007).

Husserl, Edmund, *Ideas: General Introduction to Pure Phenomenology*, trans. W.R. Boyce Gibson (London: Allen & Unwin and Humanities Press, 1931).

Husserl, Edmund, *The Crisis of European Sciences and Transcendental Phenomenology*, trans. D. Carr (Evanston, IL: Northwestern University Press, 1970).

Husserl, Edmund, *The Idea of Phenomenology*, trans. L. Hardy (Dordrecht: Kluwer Academic, 1999).

Husserl, Edmund, *Logical Investigations*, Volume I, trans. J.N. Findlay, ed. Dermot Moran (London: Routledge, 2001).

Irenaeus, *Against Heresies* in *Ante-Nicene Fathers*, Vol. 1, ed. Alexander Roberts and James Donaldson (Peabody, MA: Hendrickson Publishers, 2004).

Irvine, Judith I. 'Shadow Conversations: The Indeterminacy of Participant Roles' in Michael Silverstein and Greg Urban, eds. *Natural History of Discourse* (Chicago: University of Chicago Press, 1996), pp.131–59.

Jacobi, Klaus, 'Logic (ii): the late twelfth century' in Peter Dronke, *A History of Twelfth-Century Western Philosophy* (Cambridge: Cambridge University Press, 1992), pp.227–51.

Jaeger, Werner, *Early Christianity and Greek Paideia* (Cambridge, MA: Harvard University Press, 1961).

Janicaud, Dominique, *Phenomenology and the 'Theological Turn'*, trans. B.G. Prusak (New York: Fordham University Press, 2000).

Janicaud, Dominique, *Phenomenology 'Wide Open': After the French Debate*, trans. Charles N. Cabral (New York: Fordham University Press, 2005).

John Climacus, *The Ladder of Divine Ascent*, trans. Colm Luibheid and Norman Russell (New York: Paulist Press, 1982).

John Damascene, *De Fidei Orthodoxa*. St. John of Damascus, *Writings: The Fount of Knowledge: The Philosophical Chapters, On Heresies, The Orthodox Faith*, trans. Frederic H. Chase Jr. (Washington: The Catholic University of America Press, 1958).

John of Salisbury, *Policraticus*, by Cary J. Nederman (Cambridge: Cambridge University Press, 1990).

John Paul II, *Faith and Reason*, in *Restoring Faith in Reason*, eds. and trans. Laurence Paul Hemming and Susan Frank Parsons (London: SCM Press, 2002).

Jones, Serene, *Trauma and Grace: Theology in a Ruptured World* (Louisville, KN: Westminster John Knox Press, 2009).

Kantorowicz, Hermann, 'Note on the Development of the Gloss in the Justinian and Canon Law' in Beryl Smalley, *The Study of the Bible in the Middle Ages*, (Oxford: Blackwell, 1984, 3rd edition), pp.52–5.

Karant-Nunn, Susan, *The Reformation of Feeling: Shaping the Religious Emotions in Early Modern Germany* (Oxford: Oxford University Press, 2010).

Keefer, Michael, 'Cornelius Agrippa's Double Presence in the Faustian Century' in James M. van der Laan and Andrew Weekes, eds. *The Faustian Century: German Literature and Culture in the Age of Luther and Faust* (Rochester, NY: Camden House, 2013).

Keen, Ralph, *A Melanchthon Reader*, trans. Ralph Keen (New York: Peter Lang, 1988).

Keller, Catherine, *Face of the Deep: a Theology of Becoming* (London: Routledge, 2002).

Kelly, J.N.D., *Early Christian Creeds* (London: Longmans, Green and Co., 1950).

Kelsey, David, *Eccentric Existence: A Theological Anthropology*, volume one (Louisville: Westminster John Knox Press, 2009).

Keenan, Julian Paul, Nelson, Aaron, O'Connor, Margaret & Pascual-Leone Alvaro, 'Neurology: Self-Recognition and Right Hemisphere', *Nature* 409 (6818), 305 (18 January 2001).

Kerr, Fergus, *Twentieth Century Catholic Theologians: From Neoscholasticism to Nuptial Mystery* (Malden, MA; Oxford: Blackwell, 2007).

Kierkegaard, Soren, *The Practice of Christianity*, ed. and trans. Howard V. Hong and Edna H. Hong (Princeton: Princeton University Press, 1991).

Kierkegaard, Soren, *The Concept of Irony*, trans. Howard V. Hong and Edna V. Hong (Princeton: Princeton University Press, 1992).

Kihlstrom, John F., 'The Cognitive Unconscious', *Science*, vol.237, (1987) pp.1445–52.

Kinzig, Wolfram, Markschies, Christoph, and Vinzent, Markus, *Trauffragen und Bekenntnis. Studien zur sogenannten* Traditio Apostolica *zu den* Interrogationes de fide *und zum Römischen Glabensbekenntnis,* Arbeiten zur Kirchengeschichte, 74 (Berlin, 1998).

Kinzig, Wolfram and Vinzent, Markus, 'Recent Research on the Origin of the Creed', *Journal of Theological Studies*, NS, vol.50, Pt. 2, October 1999, 535–59.

Kinzig, Wolfram, Markschies, Christoph, and Vinzent, Markus, *Der Ursprung des Apostolikums im Urteil der kritischen Forschung*, Forschungen zur Kirche—und Dogmengeschichte 89 (Göttingen, 2006).

Kisch, Guido, *Melanchthons Rechts—und Sozialehre* (Berlin: Walter de Gruyer & Co., 1967).

Kleinz, John P., *The Theory of Knowledge of Hugh of Saint Victor* (Washington: The Catholic University of America Press, 1944).

Knowles, David, *The Evolution of Medieval Theology* (New York: Random House, 1998).

Kolb, Robert, 'The Ordering of the *Loci Communes Theologici*: The Structuring of the Melanchthonian Dogmatic Tradition', *Concordia Journal* 23 (1997), 313–37.

Kopecek, T. A., *A History of Neo-Arianism* (Cambridge, MA: Philadelphia Patristic Foundation, 1979).

Krauss, Gerhard, *The Biochemistry of Signal Transduction and Regulation* (Weinheim: Wiley-VCH Verlag, 2008, 4th edition).

Kristeva, Julia, *Black Son: Depression and Melancholia*, trans. Leon S. Roudiez (New York: Columbia University Press, 1989).

Kusukawa, Sachiko, *The Transformation of Natural Philosophy: The Case of Philip Melanchthon* (Cambridge: Cambridge University Press, 1995).

Lachmann, Otto F., *Die Bekenntnisse des hl. Augustinus* (Leipzig: Reclam, 1888).

Ladner, Gergart H., *The Idea of Reform: Its Impact on Christian Thought and Action in the Age of the Fathers* (Cambridge, Mass: Harvard University Press, 1954).

Lakoff, George and Johnson, Mark, *The Metaphors We Live By* (Chicago: Chicago University Press, 1980).

Lamoreaux, John C., 'Episcopal Courts in Late Antiquity', *Journal of Early Christian Studies*, vol.3, no. 2 (Summer 1995).

Lane Fox, Robin, *Pagans and Christians* (Harmondsworth: Penguin Books, 1988).

Laqueur, Thomas, *Making Sex: Body and Gender from the Greeks to Freud* (Cambridge, MA: Harvard University Press, 1990).

Lash, Nicholas, *Believing Three Ways in One God: A Reading of the Apostles' Creed* (London: SCM Press, 1992).

Lash, Nicholas, *The Beginning and the End of 'Religion'* (Cambridge: Cambridge University Press, 1996).

Lash, Nicholas, '*Visio Unica et Ordinata Scientiae*' in *Restoring Faith in Reason,* eds. and trans. Laurence Paul Hemming and Susan Frank Parsons (London: SCM Press, 2002), pp.225–37.

Latour, Bruno, *We Have Never Been Modern: An Essay in Symmetical Anthropology,* trans. Catherine Porter (London: Harvester Wheatsheaf, 1993).

Latour, Bruno, *Reassembling the Social: An Introduction to Actor-Network-Theory* (Oxford: Oxford University Press, 2005).

Latour, Bruno, 'Thou Shalt Not Freeze-Frame: or How Not to Misunderstand the Science and Religion Debate' in James D. Proctor, ed. *Science, Religion and Human Experience* (New York: Oxford University Press, 2005), pp.27–48.

Latour, Bruno, *An Inquiry into Modes of Existence: An Anthropology of the Moderns,* trans. Catherine Porter (Cambridge, MA: Harvard University Press, 2013).

Lauer, Quentin, *A Reading of Hegel's Phenomenology of Spirit* (New York: Fordham University Press, 1976).

Levinas, Emmanuel, 'God and Philosophy' in *E. Levinas: Collected Philosophical Papers*, trans. Alphonso Lingis (Dordrecht: Matinus Nijhoff Publishers, 1987), pp.153–74.

Liebeschuetz, J.H.W.G., *The Decline and Fall of the Roman City* (Oxford: Oxford University Press, 2001).

Linden, David, *The Accidental Mind* (Cambridge, MA: Harvard University Press, 2008).

Lipton, Bruce H., *The Biology of Belief: Unleashing the Power of Consciousness, Matter & Miracles* (London: Hay House UK, 2008).

Locke, John, *Essay Concerning Human Understanding* (Oxford: Oxford University Press, 1975).

Lovelock, James Ephraim, *Gaia: A New Look at Life on Earth* (Oxford: Oxford University Press, 1979).

Luisi, Pier Luigi, *The Emergence of Life: From Chemical Origins to Synthetic Biology* (Cambridge: Cambridge University Press, 2006).

Luscombe, D.E., *The School of Peter Abelard* (Cambridge: Cambridge University Press, 1969).

Luther, Martin, 'Ninety-Five Theses', trans. Bertram Lee Woolf, *Reformation Writings by Martin Luther* (London: The Lutterworth Press, 1937). The Latin text is available on <http://www.luther.de/en/95th-lat.html>.

Luther, Martin, 'On the Pagan Servitude of the Church', trans. Benjamin Lee Woolf, *Reformation Writings of Martin Luther* (London: Lutterworth Press, 1952).

Luther, Martin, 'An Open Letter to the Pope (1520)', trans. Bertram Lee Woolf, *Reformation Writings by Martin Luther* (London: The Lutterworth Press, 1937).

Luther, Martin, 'Address to the German Nobility', trans. Charles M. Jacobs in *Luther's Works*, vol.44: *The Christian in Society I*, ed. James Atkinson, gen.ed. Helmut T. Lehmann (Philadelphia: Fortress Press, 1966).

Luther, Martin, *Martin Luther: Studienausgabe*, Band 2, Hans-Ulrich Delius (hrsg.) (Berlin: Evangelische Verlagsanstalt, 1982).

Lycan, William G., 'The Superiority of HOP not HOT' in Rocco J. Gennaro, ed. *Higher Order Theories of Consciousness: An Anthology* (Amsterdam: John Benjamins, 2004), pp.93–113.

Lyotard, Jean-François, *The Postmodern Condition: A Report on Knowledge*, trans. Geoff Bennington and Brian Massumi (Manchester: Manchester University Press, 1984).

MacCulloch, Diarmaid, *The Reformation* (London: Penguin Books, 2005).

Macdonald, Graham and Papineau, David, eds. *Teleosemantics: New Philosphical Essays* (Oxford: Oxford University Press, 2006).

MacIntyre, Alasdair, *Three Rival Versions of Moral Enquiry* (Notre Dame, IN: University of Notre Dame Press, 1990).

MacKinnon, Donald, 'Tillich, Frege, Kittel: Some Reflections on a Dark Theme' in *Explorations in Theology 5: Donald MacKinnon* (London: SCM Press, 1979).

Maiese, Michelle, *Embodiment, Emotion, and Cognition (New Directions in Philosophy and Cognitive Science)* (Basingstoke: Palgrave Macmillan, 2011).

Maldonado-Torres, N., 'On the Coloniality of Being: Contributions to the Development of a Concept,' *Cultural Studies*, 21, 2–3, 2007.

Mâle, Emile, *The Gothic Image: Religious Art in France in the Thirteenth Century*, trans. Dora Nussey (New York: Harper & Row, 1958).

Manning, John, *The Emblem* (London: Reaktion Books, 2002).

Manschreek, Clyde L., *Melanchthon: The Quiet Reformer* (New York: Abingdon Press, 1958).

Marion, Jean-Luc, 'The Face: An Endless Hermeneutics', *Harvard Divinity Bulletin* 28, no.2–3 (1999), 9–10.

Marion, Jean-Luc, *In Excess: Studies of Saturated Phenomena*, trans. Robyn Horner (New York: Fordham University Press, 2004).

Marenbon, John, *Later Medieval Philosophy (1150–1350)* (London: Routledge, 1987).

Marenbon, John, *The Philosophy of Peter Abelard* (Cambridge: Cambridge University Press, 1997).

Martyrdom of Polycarp 15.1–16.1 in Herbert Musurillo (ed.), *The Acts of the Christian Martyrs* (Oxford: Clarendon Press, 1972), pp.14–15.

Mauer, Wilhelm, 'Zur Komposition der Loci Melanchthons von 1521: ein Beitrage zur Frage Melanchthon und Luther', *Luther-Jahrbuch* 25 (1958), 146–80.

Maurer, Wilhelm, *Der junge Melanchthon*. Band 1 (Göttingen: Vandenhoeck & Ruprecht, 1967).

McGilchrist, Iain, *The Master and His Emissary: The Divided Brain and the Making of the Western World* (New Haven: Yale University Press, 2009).

McGinn, Bernard, 'Late Mediaeval Mystics' in Paul L. Gavrilyuk and Sarah Coakley, eds. *The Spiritual Senses: Perceiving God in Western Christianity* (Cambridge: Cambridge University Press, 2012), pp.190–209.

McLelland, Joseph C., ed. *Peter Martyr Vermigli and the Italian Reform* (Waterloo: Wilfred Laurier University Press, 1977).

Melanchthon, Philip, *Loci Communes Theologici* (1521), trans. Lowell J. Satre, revised and edited by Wilhelm Pauck for the Library of Christian Classics, *Melanchthon and Bucer* (Louisville: Westminster John Knox Press, 1969), pp.18–152. For the Latin text: Robert Stupperich, *Melanchthons Werke*, Bd.II/1, Hans Engelland (hrsg.) (Gütersloh: C. Bertelsmann Verlag, 1952).

Melanchthon, Philip, *Orations on Philosophy and Education*, ed. Sachiko Kusukawa, trans. Christine F. Salazar (Cambridge: Cambridge University Press, 1999).

Melanchthon, Philip, *Elementa Rhetorices*, ed. Volkhard Wels (Berlin: Weidler Buchverlag, 2001).

Melanchthon, Philip, *The Chief Theological Topics: Loci Praecipui Theologici, 1559*, trans. J.A.O. Preus (St. Louis: Concordia Publishing House, 2011). For the Latin text: Hans Engelland's edition in Robert Stupperich, *Melanchthons Werke*.

Merlin, Donald, *The Origins of the Modern Mind: Three Stages in the Evolution of Culture and Cognition* (Cambridge, MA: Harvard University Press, 1991).

Merleau-Ponty, Maurice, *Phenomenology of Perception*, trans. C. Smith (London: Routledge & Kegan Paul, 1962).

Merleau-Ponty, Maurice, *The Primacy of Perception*, ed. and trans. J.M. Edie (Evanston, IL: Northwestern University Press, 1964).

Merleau-Ponty, Maurice, *The Visible and the Invisible*, trans. A. Lingis, ed. C. Lefort (Evanston: Northwestern University Press, 1968).

Mews, Constant J., 'Between the Schools of Abelard and Saint-Victor in the mid Twelfth Century: the Witness of Robert of Melun' in *Bibliotheca Victorina XXII: L'École de Saint-Victor de Paris*, actes réunis par Dominique Poirel (Turnhout, Belgium: Brepolis: 2010), pp.121–38.

Midgley, Mary, *The Myths We Live By* (London: Routledge, 2004).

Milbank, John, *The Word Made Strange: Theology, Language, Culture* (Oxford: Blackwell, 1997).

Milbank, John, *Theology and Social Theory* (Oxford: Blackwell, 1999).

Milbank, John, 'The Grandeur of Reason and the Perversity of Rationalism: Radical Orthodoxy's First Decade', in Simon Oliver and John Milbank, eds. *The Radical Orthodoxy Reader* (London: Routledge, 2009), pp.367–405.

Milbank, John, *Beyond Secular Order: The Representation of Being and the Representation f the People* (Oxford: Wiley Blackwell, 2013).

Milbank, John, 'A Closer Walk on the Wild Side' in Michael Warner, Jonathan Vanantwerpen and Craig Calhoun, eds. *Varieties of Secularism in a Secular Age* (Cambridge, Mass: Harvard University Press, 2013), pp.54–82.

Miller, Madeline, *The Song of Achilles* (London: Bloomsbury, 2011).

Millikan, Ruth, *Language, Thought, and Other Biological Categories: New Foundations for Realism* (Cambridge, MA: MIT Press, 1984).

Mirandola, Pico della, *Opera Omnia* (Basle, 1557). Reprinted by G. Olms: Cornell University, 1969 and digitalized 6 November 2012.

Mitchell, David, *Cloud Atlas* (London: Hodder and Stoughton, 2004).

Morin, Alain, 'Right Hemisphere Self-Awareness: A Critical Assessment in *Consciousness and Cognition* 11 (2002) 396–401.

Mühlen, Karl-Heinz zur, 'Die Affektenlehre in Spätmittelalter und in der Reformationszeit' in Johannes Brosseder (hrsg.) *Reformatorisches Profil: Studien zum Weg Martin Luthers und der Reformation* (Göttingen, 1995), pp.101–22.

Mühlen, Karl-Heinz zur, 'Melanchthons Auffassung vom Affekt in *Loci communes* 1521' in Michael Beyer and Günther Wartenberg (hrsg.) *Humanismus und Wittenberger Reformation* (Leipzig: Evangelische Verlagsanstalt, 1996), pp.327–36.

Murdoch, Iris, *Metaphysics as a Guide to Morals* (London: Chatto and Windus, 1992).

Murphy Nancey and Brown, Warren S., *Did My Neurons Make Me Do It?: Philosophical and Neurobiological Perspectives on Moral Responsibility and Free Will* (Oxford: Oxford University Press, 2009).

Naess, Arne, 'Reflections of Gestalt Ontology', *The Trumpeter* 21, no.1 (2005), 119–28.

Nauert, Charles G., *Agrippa and the Crisis of Renaissance Thought* (Urbana, IL: University of Illinois Press, 1965).

Ngai, Sianne, *Ugly Feelings* (Cambridge, MA: Harvard University Press, 2005).

Nicholas of Cusa, 'On the Gift of the Father of Lights', trans. Jasper Hopkins in his book *Nicholas of Cusa's Metaphysic of Contraction* (Minneapolis: Arthur J. Benning Press, 1983), p.372–86.

Norderal, Øyvind, 'The Emperor Constantine and Arius: Unity in the Church and Unity in the Empire', *Studia Theologica – Nordic Journal of Theology*, Issue 1, 42 (1988), 113–50.

Nutton, Vivan, ed. *Galen: Problems and Prospects* (London: Wellcome Institute for the History of Medicine, 1981).

Oakley, Keith, *Best Laid Schemes: The Psychology of Emotions* (Cambridge: Cambridge University Press, 1992).

Oberman, Heiko A., 'Three Sixteenth-Century Attitudes to Judaism: Reuchlin, Erasmus and Luther' in *Jewish Thought in the Sixteenth Century*, ed. Bernard Dov Cooperman (Cambridge, MA: Harvard University Press, 1983).

Oberman, Heiko A., *The Reformation: Roots and Ramifications,* trans. Andrew Colin Gow (Bloomsbury: T.& T. Clark, 2004).

Oliver, Simon, *Philosophy, God and Motion* (London: Routledge, 2013).

O'Regan, Cyril, *Gnostic Return in Modernity* (New York: SUNY Press, 2001).

O'Regan, Cyril, *The Heterodox Hegel* (Albany: SUNY Press, 1994).

Ozment, Steven E., *Homo Spiritualis: A Comparative Study of the Anthropology of Johannes Tauler, Jean Gerson, and Martin Luther (1509–16) in the Context of their Theological Thought* (Leiden: E.J. Brill, 1969).

Pabst, Adrian, *Metaphysics: The Creation of Hierarchy* (Grand Rapids, MI: Eerdmann, 2012).

Panovsky, Erwin, *The Life and Art of Albrecht Dürer* (Princeton, NJ: University of Princeton Press, 1971, rev. edn.).

Pannenberg, Wolfgang, *Systematic Theology*, vol. 1, trans. Geoffrey W. Bromiley (Edinburgh: T. & T. Clark, 1991).

Pauck, William, 'Editor's Preface' to Melanchthon's *Loci communes theologici, Melanchthon and Bucer* in *The Library of Christian Classics* (Louisville: Westminster John Knox Press, 1969).

Pelikan, Jaroslav, *The Christian Tradition: A History of the Development of Doctrine*, vol. 1: *The Emergence of the Catholic Tradition (100–600)*, J.N.D. Kelly's *Early Christian Doctrines* (London: A. & C. Black, 1977).

Pert, Candace B., *Molecules of Emotion: Why You Feel the Way You Feel* (London: Simon & Schuster, 1998).

Pettegree, Andrew, '"The Law and the Gospel": The Evolution of an Evangelical Pictorial Theme in the Bibles of the Reformation', in Orlaith O'Sullivan, ed. *The Bible as Book: The Reformation* (London, 2000), pp.123–35.

Pettegree, Andrew, *Reformation and the Culture of Persuasion* (Cambridge: Cambridge University Press, 2005).

Pinkard, Terry, *Hegel's Phenomenology: The Sociality of Reason* (Cambridge: Cambridge University Press, 1986).

Pinker, Steven, *The Language Instinct: How the Mind Creates Language* (New York: William Murrow, 1994).

Pippin, Robert, *Hegel's Practical Philosophy: Rational Agency as Ethical Life* (Cambridge: Cambridge University Press, 2008).

Plato, *Republic*, trans. Desmond Less (Harmondsworth: Penguin Books, 1955).

Poel, Marc van der, *Cornelius Agrippa: The Humanist Theologian and His Declamations* (Leiden: Brill, 1997).

Poirel, Dominique, *Livre de la nature et débat trinitaire au XIIe siècle: le 'De tribus diebus' de Hugues de Saint-Victor* (Paris: Bibliotheca Victorina 14, Turnhout, 2002).

Poovey, Mary, *The History of the Modern Fact: Knowledge in the Sciences of Wealth and Society* (Chicago: University of Chicago Press, 1998).

Pope, Alexander, *Windsor Forest* in *The Poems of Alexander Pope* (London: Methuen & Co. Ltd, 1963).

Przywara, Erich, *Analogia Entis: Metaphysics: Original Structure and Universal Rhythm*, trans. John R. Betz and David Bentley Hart (Grand Rapids, MI: W.B. Eerdmans, 2014).

Pyke, J.B., *Frivolities of Courtiers and the Footprints of Philosophers* (Minneapolis: University of Minnesota Press, 1938).

Rahner, Karl, *Foundations of the Christian Faith*, trans. William V. Dych (London: Darton Longman & Todd, 1978).

Reed, Mrs. Edward S., *James J. Gibson and the Psychology of Perception* (New Haven: Yale University Press, 1989).

Rees, Martin, *Our Final Century: Will the Human Race Survive the Twenty-first Century?* (London: Arrow, new edition 2004).

Reuchlin, Johannes, *De verbo mirifico*, see Widu-Wolfgang Ehlers (hrgs.) *Johannes Reuchlin: Sämtliche Werke* Band I,1, *De verbo mirifico/Das wundertätige Wort* (Stuttgart: Bad Cannstatt, 1996) for a superb new German edition of the Latin text with a German translation.

Ricoeur, Paul, *Freud and Philosophy: An Essay on Interpretation*, trans. Dennis Savage (New Haven: Yale University Press, 1970).

Ricoeur, Paul, *Du texte à l'action: Essais d'hermeneutique, II* (Paris: Editions du Seuil, 1986), translated into English by Kathleen Blamey and John Thompson, *From Text to Action* (Evanston: Northwestern University Press, 1991).

Riley, Hugh M., *Christian Initiation: A Comparative Study of the Interpretation of the Baptismal Liturgy in the Mystagogical Writings of Cyril of Jerusalem, John Chrysostom, Theodore of Mopsuestia and Ambrose of Milan* (Washington, DC: Catholic University of America Press, 1974).

Riis, Ole and Woodhead, Linda. *The Sociology of Religious Emotion* (Oxford: Oxford University Press, 2010).

Rocca, Gregory P., *Speaking the Incomprehensible God: Thomas Aquinas and the Interplay of Positive and Negative Theology* (Washington: Catholic University of America Press, 2004).

Rogers, Eugene, *Aquinas and the Supreme Court: Race, Gender, and the Failure of Natural Law in Thomas's Biblical Commentaries* (Oxford: Wiley-Blackwell, 2013).

Root, Michael, 'Necessity and Unfittingness in Anselm's *Cur Deus Homo*'. *Scottish Journal of Theology* vol.40, 211–30.

Rorem, Paul, *Hugh of St. Victor* (Oxford: Oxford University Press, 2009).

Rose, Gillian, *Hegel Contra Sociology* (London: The Athlone Press, 1981).

Rosemann, Philipp W., *Peter Lombard* (Oxford: Oxford University Press, 2004).

Rosemann, Philipp W., *The Story of the Great Mediaeval Book: Peter Lombard's 'Sentences'* (Peterborough: Broadview Press, 2007).

Rosenkrantz, Karl, *Georg Wilhelm Friedrich Hegels Leben* (Berlin, 1844 reprinted Darmstadt: Wissenschaftliche Buchgesellschaft, 1963).

Rosenwein, Barbara H., *Emotional Communities in the Early Middle Ages* (Ithaca: Cornell University Press, 2006).

Ross, Maggie, *Silence: A User's Guide* (London: Darton, Longman and Todd, 2014).

Rousselle, Aline, *Porneia: On Desire and the Body in Antiquity*, trans. Felicia Pheasant (Oxford: Blackwell, 1993).

Rowlands, John, *Holbein: The Paintings of Hans Holbein the Younger* (New York: Phaidon, 1985).

Rubenstein, Mary-Jane, *Worlds Without End: The Many Lives of the Multiverse* (New York: Columbia University Press, 2013).

Rupp, Gordon, 'Luther against "The Turk, the Pope and the Devil"' in Peter Newman Brooks, ed. *Seven-Headed Luther* (Oxford: Oxford University Press, 1983), pp.255–73.

Ruse, Michael, *The Philosophy of Human Evolution* (Cambridge: Cambridge University Press, 2012).

Ryan, Fáinche, *Formation in Holiness: Thomas Aquinas on* Sacra doctrina (Leuven: Peeters, 2007).

Saarinen, Risto, *Gottes Wirken auf uns: Die transcendentale Deutung des Gegenwart-Christi-Motivs in der Lutherforschung* (Stuttgart: Steiner Verlag, 1989).

Saarinen, Risto, *The Weakness of the Will in Renaissance and Reformation Thought* (Oxford: Oxford University Press, 2011).

Sacc, U. Columbo, *John Paul II and World Politics: Twenty Years of Search for A New Approach 1978–1998* (Leuven: Peeters, 1999).

Saxl, Fritz, 'Holbein and the Reformation', in *Lectures* (London: Warburg Institute, University of London, 1957), vol.1: 277–85.

Schäfer, Rolf, *Christologie und Sittlichkeit in Melanchthons frühen Loci* (J.C.B. Mohre: Tübingen, 1961).

Schillebeeckx, Edward, *Jesus in our Western Culture: Mysticism, Ethics and Politics*, trans. John Bowden, (London: SCM Press, 1986).

Schmidt, Steffen, *Hegels* System der Sittlichkeit (Berlin: Akademie Verlag GmbH, 2007).

Schmitt, Carl, *Political Theology: Four Chapters on the Concept of Sovereignty*, trans. George Swarb (Cambridge, MA: MIT Press, 1985).

Schmitt, Carl, *Dictatorship*, trans. Michael Hoelzl and Graham Ward (Cambridge: Polity Press, 2012, 2013).

Schneider, John R., *Philip Melanchthon's Rhetorical Construction of Biblical Authority* (Lampeter: Edwin Mellen Press, 1990).

Schrödinger, Erwin, *What Is Life?* (Cambridge: Cambridge University Press, 1967).

Schuchardt, Günter, *Gesetze und Genade: Cranach, Luther und die Bilder* (Torgau: Wartburg Stiftung Eisenach, 1994).

Schumacher, Lydia, *Divine Illumination: The History and Future of Augustine's Theory of Knowledge* (Oxford: Wiley-Blackwell, 2011).

Schumltz, Jacob, 'La Doctrine médiévale des causes et la théologie de la nature pure (XIIIe–XVIIe siècles)', *Revue Thomiste, Surnaturel:Une controverse* au coeur du thomisme au xxE siècle (Janvier–Juin. 2001), 217–64.

Schmultz, Jacob, 'Mediaeval Philosophy After the Middle Ages' in John Marenbon, ed. *The Oxford Handbook of Mediaeval Philosophy* (Oxford: Oxford University Press, 2013), pp.245–66.

Scribner, R.W., *For the Sake of Simple Folk: Popular Propaganda for the German Reformation* (Cambridge: Cambridge University Press, 1981).

Sellers, R.V., *The Council of Chalcedon: A Historical and Doctrinal Survey* (London: SPCK, 1953)

Serres, Michel, *Genesis*, trans. Geneviève James and James Nelson (Ann Arbor: University of Michigan Press, 1995).

Shapiro, Lawrence, *Embodied Cognition* (New York: Routledge, 2010).

Silverstein, Michael and Urban, Greg, eds. *Natural Histories of Discourse* (Chicago: University of Chicago Press, 1996).

Simonds, Peggy Muñoz, 'The Aesthetics of Magic' in Michael Bath and Daniel Russell, eds. *Deceitful Settings: English Renaissance Emblem and its Context* (New York: AMS Press, 1999).

Smalley, Beryl, *The Study of the Bible in the Middle Ages* (Oxford: Blackwell, 1984, 3rd. edn.).

Smith, Timothy L., ed. *Faith and Reason* (Chicago: St. Augustine's Press, 2001).

Soskice, Janet Martin, *Metaphor and Religious Language* (Oxford: Oxford University Press, 1985).

Soskice, Oliver, 'Painting and the Absence of Grace', *Modern Painters: A Quarterly Journal of Fine Arts*, issue 4 1991, 63–5.

Southern, R. W., *Saint Anselm and His Biographer* (Cambridge: Cambridge University Press, 1963).

Southern, R.W., ed. Eadmer's *The Life of St. Anselm, Archbishop of Canterbury* (London: Thomas Nelson and Sons Ltd., 1966).

Southern, R.W., *Scholastic Humanism and the Unification of Europe* (Oxford: Blackwell, 1997).

Steinmetz, D.C., *Luther and Staupitz: An Essay in the Intellectual Origins of the Protestant Reformation* (Durham, NC: Duke University Press, 1980).

Strahle, Jutta, *Cranach im Detail: Buchschmuck Lucas Cranachs des Ältens und seiner Werkstatt* (Wittenberg: Drei Kastanien 1994).

Stevenson, James (ed.), *Creeds, Councils and Controversies: Documents Illustrating the History of the Church ad 337–461*, revised version (London: SPCK, 1989).

Swanson, R. N., *The Twelfth Century Renaissance* (Manchester and New York: Manchester University Press: 1999).

Tallis, Raymond, *Aping Mankind: Neuromania, Darwinitis and the Misrepresentation of Humanity* (Durham: Acumen, 2011).

Tallis, Raymond, *In Defence of Wonder and Other Philosophical Reflections* (Durham: Acumen, 2012).

Taylor, Charles, 'Self-Interpreting Animals' in his *Philosophical Papers: Volume I, Human Agency and Langauge* (Cambridge: Cambridge University Press, 1985).

Taylor, Charles, *Hegel* (Cambridge: Cambridge University Press, 1975).

Taylor, Charles, *A Secular Age* (Cambridge, MA: The Belknap Press of Harvard University Press, 2007).

Taylor, Mark C., *The Moment of Complexity: Emerging Network Culture* (Chicago: Chicago University Press, 2001).

Terpstra, Nicholas, *Lay Confraternities and Civic Religion in Renaissance Bologna* (Cambridge: Cambridge University Press, 1995).

Tertullian, *Against Praxeas*, trans. Ernest Evans (Eugene, OR: Wipf & Stock Pub; Blg Rep edition, 2011).

Testa, Lizzi, 'The Bishop *vir venerabilis*: fiscal privileges and status definition in late antiquity', *Studia patristica* XXXIV (2001), pp.125–44.

Torrance, Thomas, 'The Hermeneutics of John Reuchlin, 1455–1522' in *Church, Word, and Spirit: Historical and Theological Essays in Honor of Geoffrey W. Bromiley*, eds. James E. Bradley and Richard A. Muller (Grand Rapids: Eerdmans, 1987).

Tweedale, Martin M, 'Logic (i): from the late eleventh century to the time of Abelard' and in Peter Dronke, *A History of Twelfth-Century Western Philosophy* (Cambridge: Cambridge University Press, 1992), pp.196–226.

Vernard, Olivier-Thomas, *Thomas d'Aquin poète théologien Vol.1: Littéature et thélogie: une saison en enfer* (Genève: Ad Solem, 2002); *Thomas d'Aquin poète théologien Vol.2: La langue de l'ineffable: essai sur le fondement théologique de la metaphysique* (Genève: Ad Solem, 2004); and *Thomas d'Aquin poète théolo-gien Vol.3: Pagina sacra: le passage de l'Écriture sainte à l'écriture thélogique* (Genève: Ad Solem, 2004).

Wainwright, Geoffrey, *Doxology: The Praise of God in Worship, Doctrine, and Life: A Systematic Theology* (Oxford: Oxford University Press, 1980),

Walker, P.W.L., *Holy City, Holy Places? Christian Attitudes to Jerusalem and the Holy Land in the Fourth Century* (Oxford: Oxford University Press, 1990).

Wallmann, J., 'Luthers letztes Wort in Bauernkrieg' in *Der Wirklichkeitsanspruch von Theologie und Religion*, D. Henke *et al.* eds. (Tübingen, 1976): pp.57–75.

Wolpert, Lewis, *Six Impossible Things Before Breakfast: The Evolutionary Origins of Belief* (London: Faber and Faber, 2006).

Wannenwetsch, Bernd, 'Affekt and Gebot: Zur ethischen Bedeutung der Leidenschaften im Licht der Theologie Luthers und Melanchthons' in *Passion, Affekt und Leidenschat in der Frühen Neuzeit*, Bd. 1, Johann Anselm Steiger (hrsg.) (Wiesbaden: Harrassowitz Verlag, 2005), pp.203–15.

Ward, Graham, 'To be a Reader: Bunyan and the Language of Scripture', *Literature and Theology* (vol.4), March 1990, pp.29–49.

Ward, Graham, *The de Certeau Reader* (Oxford: Blackwell, 1999).

Ward, Graham, *Cities of God* (London: Routledge, 2000).

Ward, Graham, 'Theology and Cultural Sadomasochism' in *Svensk Teologisk Kvartalskrift*, Årg. 78 (2001), pp.2–10.

Ward, Graham, *À Cultural Transformations and Religious Practice* (Cambridge: Cambridge University Press, 2004).

Ward, Graham, 'The Body of the Church and its Erotic Politics', *Christ and Culture* (Oxford: Blackwell, 2005), pp.92–109.

Ward, Graham, 'The *Logos*, the Body and the World: On the Phenomenological Border' in Kevin Vanhoozer and Martin Warner, eds., *Transcending the Boundaries in Philosophy and Theology: Reason, Meaning and Experience* (Aldershot: Ashgate Publishing Company, 2007), pp.105–26.

Ward, Graham, 'Hegel and the Grandeur of Reason' in *The Grandeur of Reason: Religion, Tradition and Universalism*, eds. Conor Cunningham and Peter Candler (London: SCM, 2010).

Ward, Graham, *Politics of Discipleship: Becoming Postmaterial Citizens* (Grand Rapids, Michigan: Baker Academic, 2009).

Ward, Graham, 'How Literature Resists Secularity', *Literature and Theology*, vol.21, no. 1 (2010), pp.73–88.

Ward, Graham, 'The Making of Modern Theology and the Metropolis' in Nicholas Adams, George Pattison, and Graham Ward, eds. *The Oxford Handbook of Theology and Modern European Thought* (Oxford: Oxford University Press, 2012), pp.61–82.

Ward, Graham, '*Kenosis, Poiesis* and *Genesis:* Or the Theological Aesthetics of Suffering' in Adrian Pabst and Christoph Schneider, eds. *Encounter Between Eastern Orthodoxy and Radical Orthodoxy* (Aldershot: Ashgate, 2009), pp.165–75.

Ward, Graham, *The Politics of Discipleship* (Grand Rapids, MI: Baker Academic Press, 2009).

Ward, Graham, 'How Hegel Became a Philosopher: Logos and the Economy of Logic', *Critical Research in Religion*, 1/3 (December 2013), pp.270–92.

Ward, Graham, 'The Myth of Secularism', *Telos* (vol. 167), Summer 2014, pp.162–79.

Ward, Graham, *Unbelievable: Why We Believe and Why We Don't* (London: I.B.Taurus, 2015).

Warnke, Martin, *Cranachs Luther: Entwürfe für ein Image* (Frankfurt: Fischer Taschenbuch Verlag, 1984).

Webb, Jeremy, ed. *Nothing: From Absolute Zero to Cosmic Oblivion—Amazing Insights into Nothingness* (London: Profile Books, 2013).

Weber, A., 'The "surplus of meaning". Biosemantic aspects of Francisco J. Varela's philosophy of cognition' in *Cybernetics & Human Knowing*, 9, Issue 2, 2002, 11–29.

Webster, John, *The Domain of the Word: Scripture and Theological Reason* (London: Bloomsbury, 2013).

Welker, Michael, *God the Revealed: Christology*, trans. Douglas W. Stott (Grand Rapids, MI: Eerdmans, 2013).

Wendt, Martin, *Gottmenschliche Einheit bei Hegel: Eine logische und theologische Untersuchung* (Berlin: de Gruyter, 2007).

Wengert, Timothy J., *Human Freedom, Christian Righteousness: Philip Melanchthon's Exegetical Dispute With Erasmus of Rotterdam* (New York: Oxford University Press, 1998).

Wengert, Timothy J., 'Philip Melanchthon and the Origins of the "Three Causes" (1533–1535): An Examination of the Roots of the Controversey over the Freedom of the Will' in Irene Dingel, Robert Kolb, Nicole Kuropka, and Timothy J. Wengert, *Philip Melanchthon: Theologian in Classroom, Confession, and Controversy* (Göttingen: Vandenhoeck & Ruprecht, 2012), pp.183–208.

West-Eberhard, Mary Jane, *Developmental Plasticity and Evolution* (Oxford: Oxford University Press, 2003).

White, Carolinne, ed. and trans. *Early Christian Latin Poets* (London: Routledge, 2000).

Williams, Forrest W., Appendix 1: 'Merleau-Ponty's Early Project Concerning Perception' in Maurice Merleau-Ponty in *Texts and Dialogues: On Philosophy, Politics and Cultures*, eds. Hugh J. Silverman and James Barry, Jr. (Atlantic Highlands, NJ: Humanities Press International, 1992).

Williams, Rowan, *Arius: Heresy and Tradition* (London: Darton, Longman & Todd, 1987).

Williams, Rowan, ed. *The Making of Orthodoxy: Essays in Honour of Henry Chadwick* (Cambridge: Cambridge University Press, 1989).

Williams, Rowan, *The Edge of Words: God and the Habits of Language* (London: Bloomsbury, 2014).

Wittgenstein, Ludwig, *On Certainty*, trans. Denis Paul and G.E.M. Anscombe (Oxford: Blackwell, 1974).

Wood, Allen, *Hegel's Ethical Thought* (Cambridge: Cambridge University Press, 1990).

Wright, N. T., *The Resurrection of the Son of God* (London: SPCK, 2003).

Wüstenberg, Ralf K., *Bonhoeffer and Beyond: Promoting a Dialogue between Religion and Politics* (Frankfurt am Main: Peter Lang, 2008).

Yanneras, Christos, *Orthodoxy and the West: Hellenic Self-Identity in the Modern Age* (Brookline, MA: Holy Cross Orthodox Press, 2006).

Yanneras, Christos and Russell, Norman, *Against Religion: The Alienation of the Ecclesial Event* (Brookline, MA: Holy Cross Orthodox Press, 2013).

Yarnold, Edward, *The Awe-Inspiring Rites of Initiation: Baptismal Homilies of the Fourth Century* (Slough: St. Paul Publications, 1971).

Yarnold, Edward, *Cyril of Jerusalem* (London: Routledge, 2000).

Yates, Frances, *The Occult Philosophy of the Elizabethan Age* (London: Ark Paperbacks, 1983).

Young, Francis, *The Making of the Creeds* (London: SCM Press, 1991).

Young, Frances, *From Nicaea to Chalcedon* (London: S.C.M., 1983).

Zachhuber, Johannes, *Theology as Science in Nineteenth-Century Germany: From F.C. Baur to Ernst Troelsch* (Oxford: Oxford University Press, 2013).

Zahl, Simeon, 'The Bondage of the Affections: Willing, Feeling, and Desiring in Luther's Theology, 1513–25' in Dale Coulter and Amos Yong, eds. *The Spirit, the Affections, and the Christian Tradition* (Notre Dame, IL: University of Notre Dame Press, forthcoming).

Zambelli, Paola, 'Magic and Radical Reformation in Agrippa of Nettesheim', *Journal Of the Warburg and Courtauld Institutes*, vol. XXXIX (1976), 69–103.

Zika, Charles, 'Reuchlin's *De Verbo Mirifico* and the Magic Debate of the Late Fifteenth Century', *Journal Of the Warburg and Courtauld Institutes*, vol. XXXIX (1976), 104–38.

Zika, Charles, *Exorcising Our Demons: Magic, Witchcraft, and Visiual Culture in Early Modern Europe* (Leiden: Brill, 2003).

Zinn, Grover, '*Historia fundamentum est*: The Role of History in the Contemplative Life According to Hugh of St. Victor' in *Contemporary Reflections on the Medieval Christian Tradition: Essays in Honor of Roy C. Petry*, ed. George H. Shiver (Durham, NC: Duke University Press, 1974), pp.135–58.

Žižek, Slavjo, *The Plague of Fantasies* (London: Verso, 1997).

Index

HOW THE LIGHT GETS IN